The Book of Jasher

With Lessons and Commentary

Edited by Joseph Lumpkin

Joseph B. Lumpkin

THE BOOK OF JASHER

With Lessons and Commentary

Copyright © 2010 Joseph B. Lumpkin.

All rights reserved.

Printed in the United States of America. No part of this book may be used or reproduced in any manner whatsoever without written permission except in the case of brief quotations embodied in critical articles and reviews.

First time or interested authors, contact Fifth Estate Publishers, Post Office Box 116, Blountsville, AL 35031.

First Printing February, 2010

Cover Design by An Quigley

Printed on acid-free paper

Library of Congress Control No: 2010921384

ISBN: 9781933580890

Fifth Estate 2010

Joseph B. Lumpkin

Special thanks go out to Leigh Smith, a scholar and friend in South Africa, who provided wonderful insights. His lessons on the Book of Jasher are printed herein with his written consent.

Table of Contents

Preface	7
The History Of The Book Of Jasher	9
The Book of Jasher	14

Lessons and Commentary

Water	362
Comfortably Numb	369
Racial Offenses	374
North, South, East, and West	378
Tongues	386
Ephriam	393
Husband of Blood	400
Watch What You Say	408
Noah's Ark	413
Abel's Prayer	421
Three Doors	434
You are Gods	446
Noah's Prayer	457
Accuser	463
Once, Twice, Thrice	477
Min Dae	488
Nimrod's Death	493
Millenary	498
Jochebed	511
Third Reference	520
Jannes and Jambres	527
Notes From Latter-Day Saints	554

Joseph B. Lumpkin

Preface
Jasher and The Church of Jesus Christ of Latter day Saints.

The Book of Jasher is a secular history covering a period from the creation to the period of the Judges in Israel. The book is referenced in the Holy Bible twice by two different authors. Three purported versions of the Jasher have been translated, but only this one is looked upon as authentic. The Prophet Joseph Smith quoted from it in Times and Seasons. Soon after, certain members of The Church of Jesus Christ of Latter-day Saints secured the copyright and republished the work in 1887 in Salt Lake City.

The Book of Jasher is almost certainly authentic, as it contains many specific details which are in agreement with modern revelation, such as "The Book of Moses," which was published before the Book of Jasher became available on the American continent. However, it seems to contain modifications from its original form. When studying it, the Lord's advice in Doctrine and Covenants 91 still stands and should be followed.

"Verily, thus saith the Lord unto you concerning the Apocrypha — There are many things contained therein that are true, and it is mostly translated correctly; There are many things contained therein that are not true, which are interpolations by the hands of men. Verily, I say unto you, that it is not needful that the Apocrypha should be translated. Therefore, whoso readeth it, let him understand, for the Spirit manifesteth truth; And whoso is enlightened by the Spirit shall obtain benefit And whoso receiveth not by the Spirit, cannot be benefited. Therefore it is not needful that it should be translated. Amen." D&C 91:1-6
From www.mormonwiki.com

Doctrine and Covenants address the status of the Book of Jasher as compared to DC.

DC 84:14 Melchizedek...received it through the lineage of his fathers...

Ancient Jewish traditions and the apocryphal work, The Book of Jasher, suggest that Melchizedek is none other than Shem, the favored son of Noah. Probably based on The Book of Jasher, John Taylor, proposed the same thing in Times and Seasons 5:746, dated Dec. 15, 1844. Over the years, this has led to the tradition that Shem and Melchizedek are the same individual. A careful reading of D&C 84:14 refutes this claim. If Melchizedek was Shem, the verse would read, "Which Abraham received the priesthood from

Melchizedek; and Melchizedek received it under the hand of his father Noah." Instead, the text indicates that there are multiple generations between Melchizedek and Noah, for Melchizedek "received it through the lineage of his fathers, even till Noah." Certainly, we should believe the Doctrine and Covenants as the supreme doctrinal treatise over apocryphal works and Jewish traditions.

The History Of The Book Of Jasher

The Book Of Jasher, or Sefer Ha Yashar, is referred to in the books of Joshua and Second Samuel of the Holy Bible.

"Behold it is written in the Book of Jasher."--II Samuel, i. 18

"Is not this written in the Book of Jasher?"--Joshua, x. 13.

Jasher (Yashar) is a Hebrew word meaning "upright". Jasher is not the name of the author or any prophet or judge of Israel, as scholars had previously thought. The name refers to the fact that the record, facts, and history are upright, correct, and thus, trustworthy.

The value of The Book of Jasher is seen in the large quantity of additional detail revealed in the period between divine creation and the time of Joshua's leadership over Israel when the Israelites enter into the land of Canaan.

The Book of Jasher includes details about the antediluvian patriarchs, angels, watchers, the flood, the tower of Babel, and many other events mentioned in the Bible. The tales are expanded and infused with detail not previously available.

This means we receive insight into the lives of Abraham, Noah, Enoch, Joseph, and many other biblical figures. We come to understand how they became great and why they acted as they did. We are also given hitherto unknown knowledge of historical events. We are shown how God's hand shaped history through his love and anger. We see how his disappointment with men and angels ended in earth's near total destruction.

We learn how the power of Nimrod, the great hunter, arose. We are told how all animals were guided to the ark of Noah, and why the tower of Babel was attacked by God and angels. Such detailed accounts bring the Old Testament into an understandable focus.

According to the Encyclopedia Judaica, Volume 14, p. 1099, Jasher was "probably written in the 13th century A.D." However, some scholars have proposed various dates between the 9th century and 16th century A.D.

There are three separate and different books named Jasher, however the Church of Jesus Christ of Latter-day Saints (The Mormon Church) considers this rendition of Jasher to be the book referenced in the Old Testament. The belief of the church leadership is bolstered by the preface in the 1625 version, which claims its original source came from the ruins of Jerusalem in 70 A.D.

Jasher is held in high repute by many Mormons but is not officially endorsed by the Mormon Church. The official stance of the Mormon Church falls short of making Jasher part of their Holy Scriptures but does endorse the book as being valid and authentic.

The Mormon Church places the book of Jasher on the same level as other apocryphal writings and states in the church magazine, The Ensign, After reviewing the standard scholarly analysis of how the book appears to have been composed of old Jewish legends, the book of Jasher is considered to be of great benefit to the reader. The article concluded with an injunction to treat it according to the Lord's advice on how to study the Apocrypha. The article goes on to quote the church stance on the Apocrypha. This stance has been previously quoted but bears repeating.

"Verily, thus saith the Lord unto you concerning the Apocrypha — There are many things contained therein that are true, and it is mostly translated correctly; There are many things contained therein that are not true, which are interpolations by the hands of men. Verily, I say unto you, that it is not needful that the Apocrypha should be translated. Therefore, whoso readeth it, let him understand, for the Spirit manifesteth truth; And whoso is enlightened by the Spirit shall obtain benefit And whoso receiveth not by the Spirit, cannot be benefitted. Therefore it is not needful that it should be translated. Amen." (D.&C. 91:1-6)

In the early 1800s, Moses Samuel of Liverpool, England, was given a copy of the 1625 A.D. Hebrew work. Jasher, he found, was written in a theological or Rabbinical type of Hebrew, which is a more classical Hebrew. Samuel translated the text into English and in 1839 sold it to Mordecai Manuel Noah, a Jewish New York publisher, who published it in 1840.

Copyright of the translation was obtained by J. H. Parry & Company in Salt Lake City, who published it in 1887.

Samuel's translation was written in "Elizabethan or King James" English and contained archaic words, phrases, and idioms.

The translation offered here is taken from the J. H. Parry translation with all archaic language and idioms edited and restated in modern English.

According to Bernard Wasserstein, in the Transactions of the Jewish Historical Society of England Vol. XXXV, Samuel translated into English the pseudo-biblical Book of Jasher, a supposedly ancient Hebrew text which Samuel convinced himself was authentic. After failing to persuade the Royal Asiatic Society to publish it, he sold his translation for £150 in 1839 to the American Jewish newspaper-owner and philanthropist Mordecai M. Noah. It appeared in New York the following year but with Noah's name and not Samuel's on the title page. "I did not put my name to it as my Patron and myself differed about its authenticity", Samuel later explained. This was odd since Noah seems to have had a lower opinion of the work's authenticity than Samuel. The translation was accepted as accurate, but the publication provoked criticism by scholars who rejected the claims made on behalf of the text. It won acceptance, however, by the Mormon prophet Joseph Smith. (p. 2)

The prophet, Joseph Smith's attraction to the book was due in part to the history contained in the preface of the book.

According to the history documented in the preface of the Book of Jasher, Titus destroyed Jerusalem in 70 A.D. but the book was miraculously rescued at that time. During the destruction of the Jewish temple a Roman officer named Sidrus discovered a Hebrew scholar hiding in a library. The officer took the scholar and all the books safely back to his estates in Seville, Spain. The manuscript was transferred to the Jewish college in Cordova, Spain. The book was kept there until its printings in Venice in 1625.

There is some evidence to substantiate these claims, and there is nothing to conclusively dismiss the claims. Proof of the authenticity of Jasher will be further discussed.

As with any ancient text, there were likely various authors and additions. Part of the confusion arises from the fact that Jasher seems to be a compilation of several stories gathered by priests over many generations. Most of the stories and history contain reliable, authentic Jewish terms and traditions. It is the weight of these correct facts and references that lend credence to the authenticity of the seed literature that formed Jasher.

Scholars view Jasher with much skepticism due to the absence of any evidence or mention of the book prior to 1625. The basis of the stories contained in Jasher are mythically old, but the book itself has not been found in its present form prior to the printing in the 1600s. However, it is the opinion of the editor that Jasher is authentic and will offer some insight into the murky and sometimes sparse historical landscape of Genesis. At the least, we may state that the book reflects what the priestly scholars who wrote the book believed.

One major stumbling block in Book of Jasher research has been the lack of evidence that this Book of Jasher is the real and truly ancient. There has been no hard evidence to prove that this Book of Jasher existed prior to 1625, but there has been proof. It may have been staring us in the face all along.

In the Masoretic Text and Septuagint of Gen. 5:18 it is written: "And Jared lived one hundred and sixty two years". But the Book of Jasher 2:37 has "And Jared lived sixty two years". This agrees with the Samaritan Pentateuch of Gen. 5:18.

The Book of Jasher and the Samaritan Pentateuch share the same scribal error, or it shares the same source materials, which allowed the error to be copied. If the Book of Jasher were a late compilation made in the Middle Ages, it would have copied from the available Masoretic Text. The Samaritan Pentateuch would not have been used as it was not available. This is evidence for the ancient origin of the Book of Jasher.

There is also a similar scribal error in Jasher 5:13 where Methuselah begets Lamech at eighty seven. In the Masoretic Text this number is given as one hundred and eighty seven. In the Septuagint it is given as one hundred and sixty seven, and in the Samaritan Pentateuch as sixty seven.

Here the reading agrees with the Samaritan Pentateuch in the omission of "one hundred" but it agrees with the Masoretic Text in reading "eighty seven." This error is more evidence that The Book of Jasher is part of the ancient Samaritan textual tradition and does not reference the more readily available Masoretic Text.

The texts presented here represents an accurate version of the Book of Jasher rendered in modern English. Although the book was translated in the 1800s, the translator chose to use the more stilted and less accessible Elizabethan or King James style of English in order to add weight and religious authority to the text. This made the book less than pleasant to read for the modern audience. In the translation before you archaic words and expressions were replaced with their modern counterparts. A word for word replacement was not attempted. When an archaic word needed to be replaced with a phrase for the purpose of clarity this technique was embraced so as to render the text readily understandable. It is our sincere hope our goal was accomplished and the reader will find this version interesting and easy to read.

Notes, commentary, and lessons are to be found in the section of this book following The Book of Jasher. Lessons are sourced from Leigh Smith, The Book of Moses, The Book of Abraham, The Holy Bible, Doctrine and Covenants, and various L.D.S. sources.

The Book of Jasher

THIS IS THE BOOK OF THE GENERATIONS OF MAN WHOM GOD CREATED ON THE EARTH ON THE DAY WHEN THE LORD GOD MADE HEAVEN AND EARTH.

CHAPTER 1

1 God said, Let us make man in our image, in our likeness, and God created man in his own image.

2 God formed man from the dirt, and he blew into his nostrils the breath of life, and man became a living soul with the capacity of speech.

3 And the Lord said, It is not good for man to be alone; I will make him a helper and a mate.

4 The Lord caused a deep sleep to come on Adam, and he slept. God took away one of his ribs, and he fashioned flesh on it, and formed it and brought it to Adam. Adam awoke from his sleep, and saw a woman was standing in front of him.

5 He said, This is bone of my bones and it shall be called woman, because it has been taken from man. Adam named her Eve, because she was the mother of all living (mankind).

6 God blessed them and on the day he created them he called their names Adam and Eve. The Lord God said, Be prolific and reproduce and fill the earth.

7 The Lord God took Adam and his wife, and he placed them in the garden of Eden to farm it and to keep it. He commanded them and said, "You may eat from every tree of the garden, but you may never eat from the tree of the knowledge of good and evil. On the day that you eat thereof you will certainly die.

8 When God had blessed and commanded them, he departed from them. Adam and his wife lived in the garden according to the command which the Lord had commanded them.

9 The serpent, which God had created with them in the earth, came to them to incite them to go contrary to the command of God which he had

commanded them.

10 And the serpent enticed and persuaded the woman to eat from the tree of knowledge, and the woman listened to the voice of the serpent, and she went contrary to the word of God, and took from the tree of the knowledge of good and evil, and she ate, and she took from it and gave also to her husband and he ate.

11 And Adam and his wife went contrary to the command of God which he commanded them, and God knew it, and his anger was set ablaze against them and he cursed them.

12 And the Lord God drove them that day from the garden of Eden, to till the ground from which they were taken, and they went and lived at the east of the garden of Eden; and Adam had sex with his wife Eve and she bore two sons and three daughters.

13 She called the name of the first born Cain, saying, I have obtained a man from the Lord, and the name of the other she called Abel, for she said, Empty we came into the earth, and empty we shall be taken from it.

14 And the boys grew up and their father gave them a possession in the land; and Cain was a farmer of the ground, and Abel a keeper of sheep.

15 And it was at the expiration of a few years, that they brought a first-fruit offering to the Lord, and Cain brought from the fruit of the ground, and Abel brought from the firstlings of his flock from the fat thereof, and God turned and inclined to Abel and his offering, and a fire came down from the Lord from heaven and consumed it.

16 And to Cain and his offering the Lord did not turn, and he did not incline to it, for he had brought from the inferior fruit of the ground before the Lord, and Cain was jealous against his brother Abel on account of this, and he sought an opportunity to kill him.

17 Some time after, Cain and Abel his brother went one day into the field to do their work; and they were both in the field, Cain farming and plowing his ground, and Abel feeding his flock; and the flock passed that part which Cain had plowed in the ground, and it sorely grieved Cain on this account.

18 And Cain approached his brother Abel in anger, and he said to him, What gives you the right to come and live here and bring your flock to feed in my land?

19 And Abel answered his brother Cain and said to him, What gives you the right to eat the flesh of my flock and clothe yourself with their wool?

20 Take off the wool of my sheep with which you have clothed yourself,

and pay me for their resources you have used and flesh which you have eaten, and when you shall have done this, I will then go from your land as you have said.

21 Cain said to his brother Abel, Certainly if I kill you this day, who will require your blood from me?

22 And Abel answered Cain, saying, Certainly God who has made us in the earth, he will avenge my cause, and he will require my blood from you should you kill me, for the Lord is the judge and arbiter, and it is he who will repay man according to his evil, and the wicked man according to the wickedness that he may do on earth.

23 And now, if you should kill me here, certainly God knows your secret views, and will judge you for the evil which you did declare to do to me this day.

24 When Cain heard the words which Abel his brother had spoken, the anger of Cain was set ablaze against his brother Abel for declaring this thing.

25 Cain hurried and rose up, and took the iron part of his plowing instrument, with which he suddenly struck his brother and he killed him, and Cain spilt the blood of his brother Abel on the earth, and the blood of Abel streamed on the earth before the flock.

26 And after this Cain repented having slain his brother, and he was sadly grieved, and he wept over him and it troubled him greatly.

27 Cain rose up and dug a hole in the field, wherein he put his brother's body, and he turned the dust over it.

28 And the Lord knew what Cain had done to his brother, and the Lord appeared to Cain and said to him, Where is Abel your brother that was with you?

29 And Cain lied, and said, I do not know. Am I my brother's keeper? And the Lord said to him, What have you done? The voice of your brother's blood cries to me from the ground where you have slain him.

30 For you have slain your brother and have lied before me, and imagined in your heart that I saw you not, nor knew all your actions.

31 But you did this thing and did kill your brother for naught and because he spoke rightly to you, and now, therefore, cursed be you from the ground which opened its mouth to receive your brother's blood from your hand, and wherein you did bury him.

32 It shall be when you shall till it, the land will no longer give you its

strength as in the beginning, for thorns and thistles shall the ground produce, and you shall be moving and wandering in the earth until the day of your death.

33 And at that time Cain went out from the presence of the Lord, from the place where he was, and he went moving and wandering in the land toward the east of Eden, he and all those belonging to him.

34 Cain had sex with his wife in those days, and she conceived and gave birth to a son, and he called his name Enoch, saying, In that time the Lord began to give him rest and quiet in the earth.

35 At that time Cain also began to build a city: and he built the city and he called the name of the city Enoch, according to the name of his son; for in those days the Lord had given him rest on the earth, and he did not move about and wander as in the beginning.

36 And Irad was born to Enoch, and Irad had Mechuyael and Mechuyael had Methusael.

CHAPTER 2

1 It was in the hundred and thirtieth year of the life of Adam on the earth, that he again had sex with Eve his wife, and she conceived and gave birth to a son and he looked like Adam, and she called his name Seth, saying, Because God has appointed me another offspring in the place of Abel, for Cain has slain him.

2 And Seth lived one hundred and five years, and he had a son; and Seth called the name of his son Enosh, saying, Because in that time the sons of men began to reproduce, and to afflict their souls and hearts by disobeying and rebelling against God.

3 It was in the days of Enosh that the sons of men continued to rebel and go contrary to God, to increase the anger of the Lord against the sons of men.

4 And the sons of men went and they served other gods, and they forgot the Lord who had created them in the earth: and in those days the sons of men made images of brass and iron, wood and stone, and they bowed down and served them.

5 Every man made his god and they bowed down to them, and the sons of men turned away from the Lord all the days of Enosh and his children;

and the anger of the Lord was set ablaze on account of their works and abominations which they did in the earth.

6 The Lord caused the waters of the river Gihon to overwhelm them, and he destroyed and consumed them, and he destroyed the third part of the earth. Notwithstanding this, the sons of men did not turn from their evil ways, and their hands were yet extended to do evil in the sight of the Lord.

7 In those days there was neither sowing nor reaping in the earth; and there was no food for the sons of men and the famine was very great in those days.

8 And the seed which they sowed in those days in the ground became thorns, thistles and briers; for from the days of Adam was this declaration concerning the earth, of the curse of God, which he cursed the earth, on account of the sin which Adam sinned before the Lord.

9 And it was when men continued to rebel and go contrary to God, and to corrupt their ways, that the earth also became corrupt.

10 And Enosh lived ninety years and he had Cainan.

11 Cainan grew up and he was forty years old, and he became wise and had knowledge and skill in all wisdom, and he reigned over all the sons of men, and he led the sons of men to wisdom and knowledge; for Cainan was a very wise man and had understanding in all wisdom, and with his wisdom he ruled over spirits and demons.

12 Cainan knew by his wisdom that God would destroy the sons of men for having sinned on earth, and that the Lord would in the latter days bring on them the waters of the flood.

13 And in those days Cainan wrote on tablets of stone what was to take place in time to come, and he put them in his treasure troves.

14 Cainan reigned over the whole earth, and he turned some of the sons of men to the service of God.

15 When Cainan was seventy years old, he had three sons and two daughters.

16 These are the names of the children of Cainan; the name of the first born was Mahlallel, the second was Enan, and the third was Mered, and their sisters were Adah and Zillah; these are the five children of Cainan that were born to him.

17 Lamech, the son of Methusael, became related to Cainan by marriage, and he took his two daughters for his wives, and Adah conceived and

gave birth to a son to Lamech, and she called his name Jabal.

18 And she again conceived and gave birth to a son, and called his name Jubal; and Zillah, her sister, was unable to conceive in those days and had no offspring.

19 For in those days the sons of men began to trespass against God, and to go contrary to the commandments which he had given Adam, to be prolific and reproduce in the earth.

20 Some of the sons of men caused their wives to drink a mixture that would render them unable to conceive, in order that they might retain their figures and their beautiful appearance might not fade.

21 And when the sons of men caused some of their wives to drink, Zillah drank with them.

22 The child-bearing women appeared abominable in the sight of their husbands and they treated them as widows, while their husbands lived with those unable to conceive and to those women they were attached.

23 And in the end of days and years, when Zillah became old, the Lord opened her womb.

24 She conceived and gave birth to a son and she called his name Tubal Cain, saying, After I had withered away have I obtained him from the Almighty God.

25 And she conceived again and gave birth to a daughter, and she called her name Naamah, for she said, After I had withered away have I obtained pleasure and delight.

26 Lamech was old and advanced in years, and his eyes were dim that he could not see, and Tubal Cain, his son, was leading him and it was one day that Lamech went into the field and Tubal Cain his son was with him, and while they were walking in the field, Cain the son of Adam advanced towards them; for Lamech was very old and could not see much, and Tubal Cain his son was very young.

27 Tubal Cain told his father to draw his bow, and with the arrows he struck Cain, who was yet far off, and he killed him, because he appeared be an animal to them.

28 And the arrows entered Cain's body although he was at a distance from them, and he fell to the ground and died.

29 The Lord rewarded Cain's evil according to his wickedness, which he had done to his brother Abel, according to the word of the Lord which he had spoken.

30 And it came to pass when Cain had died, that Lamech and Tubal went to see the animal which they had slain, and they saw, and behold Cain their grandfather was fallen dead on the earth.

31 Lamech was very much grieved at having done this, and in clapping his hands together (in grief) he struck his son and caused his death.

32 And the wives of Lamech heard what Lamech had done, and they sought to kill him.

33 The wives of Lamech hated him from that day, because he killed Cain and Tubal Cain, and the wives of Lamech separated from him, and would not listen to him in those days.

34 And Lamech came to his wives, and he begged them to listen to him about this matter.

35 He said to his wives Adah and Zillah, Hear my voice O wives of Lamech, attend to my words, for now you have imagined and said that I killed a man with my wounds, and a child with my stripes for they did no violence, but certainly know that I am old and grey-headed, and that my eyes are heavy through age, and I did this thing unknowingly.

36 And the wives of Lamech listened to him in this matter, and they returned to him with the advice of their father Adam, but they bore no children to him from that time, knowing that God's anger was increasing in those days against the sons of men, to destroy them with the waters of the flood for their evil acts.

37 Mahlallel the son of Cainan lived sixty-five years and he had Jared; and Jared lived sixty-two years and he had Enoch.

CHAPTER 3

1 Enoch lived sixty-five years and he had Methuselah; and Enoch walked with God after having a son, Methuselah, and he served the Lord, and despised the evil ways of men.

2 And the soul of Enoch was wrapped up in the instruction of the Lord, in knowledge and in understanding; and he wisely retired from the sons of men, and cloistered himself from them for many days.

3 It was at the expiration of many years, while he was serving the Lord, and praying before him in his house, that an angel of the Lord called to

him from Heaven, and he said, Here am I.

4 And he said, Rise, go forth from your house and from the place where you hide yourself, and appear to the sons of men, in order that you may teach them the way in which they should go and the work which they must accomplish in order to enter into the ways of God.

5 Enoch rose up according to the word of the Lord, and went forth from his house, from his place and from the chamber in which he was concealed; and he went to the sons of men and taught them the ways of the Lord, and at that time assembled the sons of men and acquainted them with the instruction of the Lord.

6 He ordered it to be proclaimed in all places where the sons of men lived, saying, Where is the man who wishes to know the ways of the Lord and good works? Let him come to Enoch.

7 And all the sons of men then assembled to him, for all who desired this thing went to Enoch, and Enoch reigned over the sons of men according to the word of the Lord, and they came and bowed to him and they heard his word.

8 The spirit of God was on Enoch, and he taught all his men the wisdom of God and his ways, and the sons of men served the Lord all the days of Enoch, and they came to hear his wisdom.

9 And all the kings of the sons of men, both greatest and least, together with their princes and judges, came to Enoch when they heard of his wisdom, and they bowed down to him, and they also required of Enoch to reign over them, to which he consented.

10 They assembled in all, one hundred and thirty kings and princes, and they made Enoch king over them and they were all under his power and command.

11 And Enoch taught them wisdom, knowledge, and the ways of the Lord; and he made peace among them, and peace was throughout the earth during the life of Enoch.

12 Enoch reigned over the sons of men two hundred and forty-three years, and he did justice and righteousness with all his people, and he led them in the ways of the Lord.

13 These are the generations of Enoch, Methuselah, Elisha, and Elimelech, three sons; and their sisters were Melca and Nahmah, and Methuselah lived eighty-seven years and he had Lamech.

14 It was in the fifty-sixth year of the life of Lamech when Adam died. Nine hundred and thirty years old was he at his death. His two sons, with

Enoch and Methuselah his son, buried him with great grandeur, as at the burial of kings, in the cave which God had told him.

15 And in that place all the sons of men mourned and wept greatly on account of Adam; it has therefore become a custom among the sons of men to this day.

16 Adam died because he ate of the tree of knowledge; he and his children after him, as the Lord God had spoken.

17 And it was in the year of Adam's death which was the two hundred and forty-third year of the reign of Enoch, in that time Enoch resolved to separate himself from the sons of men and to cloister himself as at first in order to serve the Lord.

18 Enoch did so, but did not entirely cloister himself from them, but kept away from the sons of men three days and then went to them for one day.

19 During the three days that he was in his chamber, he prayed to, and praised the Lord his God, and the day on which he went and appeared to his subjects he taught them the ways of the Lord, and all they asked him about the Lord he told them.

20 And he did in this manner for many years, and he afterward concealed himself for six days, and appeared to his people one day in seven; and after that once in a month, and then once in a year, until all the kings, princes and sons of men sought for him, and desired again to see the face of Enoch, and to hear his word; but they could not, as all the sons of men were greatly afraid of Enoch, and they feared to approach him on account of the Godlike awe that was seated on his countenance; therefore no man could look at him, fearing he might be punished and die.

21 All the kings and princes resolved to assemble the sons of men, and to come to Enoch, thinking that they might all speak to him at the time when he should come forth among them, and they did so.

22 The day came when Enoch went forth and they all assembled and came to him, and Enoch spoke to them the words of the Lord and he taught them wisdom and knowledge, and they bowed down before him and they said, May the king live! May the king live!

23 Some time after, when the kings and princes and the sons of men were speaking to Enoch, and Enoch was teaching them the ways of God, an angel of the Lord then called to Enoch from heaven, and wished to bring him up to heaven to make him reign there over the sons of God, as he had reigned over the sons of men on earth.

24 When at that time Enoch heard this he went and assembled all the

inhabitants of the earth, and taught them wisdom and knowledge and gave them divine instructions, and he said to them, I have been required to ascend into heaven; but I do not know the day of my going.

25 And now therefore I will teach you wisdom and knowledge and will give you instruction before I leave you, how to act on earth so that you may live (as you should); and he did so.

26 He taught them wisdom and knowledge, and gave them instruction, and he rebuked them, and he placed before them statutes and judgments to do on earth, and he made peace among them, and he taught them everlasting life, and lived with them some time teaching them all these things.

27 At that time the sons of men were with Enoch, and Enoch was speaking to them, and they lifted up their eyes and the likeness of a great horse descended from heaven, and the horse paced in the air.

28 And they told Enoch what they had seen, and Enoch said to them, On my account does this horse descend on earth; the time is come when I must go from you and I shall no more be seen by you.

29 The horse descended at that time and stood before Enoch, and all the sons of men that were with Enoch saw him.

30 Enoch then again ordered a voice to be proclaimed, saying, Where is the man who delights to know the ways of the Lord his God, let him come this day to Enoch before he is taken from us.

31 All the sons of men assembled and came to Enoch that day; and all the kings of the earth with their princes and counselors remained with him that day; and Enoch then taught the sons of men wisdom and knowledge, and gave them divine instruction; and he bade them serve the Lord and walk in his ways all the days of their lives, and he continued to make peace among them.

32 It was after this that he rose up and rode on the horse; and he went forth and all the sons of men went after him, about eight hundred thousand men; and they went with him one day's journey.

33 And the second day he said to them, Return home to your tents, why will you go? Perhaps you may die; and some of them went from him, and those that remained went with him six day's journey; and Enoch said to them every day, Return to your tents, that you may die; but they were not willing to return, and they went with him.

34 And on the sixth day some of the men remained and clung to him, and they said to him, We will go with you to the place where you go; as the Lord lives, only death shall separate us.

35 They urged so much to go with him that he ceased speaking to them; and they went after him and would not return.

36 When the kings returned they caused a census to be taken, in order to know the number of remaining men that went with Enoch; and it was on the seventh day that Enoch ascended into heaven in a whirlwind, with horses and chariots of fire.

37 And on the eighth day all the kings that had been with Enoch sent to bring back the number of men that were with Enoch, in that place from which he ascended into heaven.

38 All those kings went to the place and they found the earth there filled with snow, and on the snow were large stones of snow, and one said to the other, Come, let us break through the snow and see, perhaps the men that remained with Enoch are dead, and are now under the stones of snow, and they searched but could not find Enoch, for he had ascended into heaven.

CHAPTER 4

1 All the days that Enoch lived on earth, were three hundred and sixty-five years.

2 And when Enoch had ascended into heaven, all the kings of the earth rose and took Methuselah his son and anointed him, and they caused him to reign over them in the place of his father.

3 Methuselah acted uprightly in the sight of God, as his father Enoch had taught him, and he likewise during the whole of his life taught the sons of men wisdom, knowledge and the fear of God, and he did not turn from the good way either to the right or to the left.

4 But in the latter days of Methuselah, the sons of men turned from the Lord; they corrupted the earth, they robbed and plundered each other, and they rebelled against God; they went contrary to, they corrupted their ways, and would not listen to the voice of Methuselah, but rebelled against him.

5 And the Lord was greatly wroth against them, and the Lord continued to destroy the offspring in those days, so that there was neither sowing nor reaping in the earth.

6 For when they sowed the ground in order that they might obtain food for their support, behold, thorns and thistles were produced which they did not sow.

7 And still the sons of men did not turn from their evil ways, and their hands were still extended to do evil in the sight of God, and they provoked the Lord with their evil ways, and the Lord was very wroth, and repented that he had made man.

8 He thought to destroy and annihilate them and he did so.

9 In those days when Lamech the son of Methuselah was one hundred and sixty years old, Seth the son of Adam died.

10 And all the days that Seth lived were nine hundred and twelve years, and he died.

11 Lamech was one hundred and eighty years old when he took Ashmua, the daughter of Elishaa the son of Enoch his uncle, and she conceived.

12 And at that time the sons of men sowed the ground, and a little food was produced, yet the sons of men did not turn from their evil ways, and they trespassed and rebelled against God.

13 The wife of Lamech conceived and gave birth to a son at that time, at the revolution of the year.

14 And Methuselah called his name Noah, saying, The earth was in his days at rest and free from corruption, and Lamech his father called his name Menachem, saying, This one shall comfort us in our works and miserable toil in the earth, which God had cursed.

15 The child grew up and was weaned, and he went in the ways of his father Methuselah, perfect and upright with God.

16 And all the sons of men departed from the ways of the Lord in those days as they multiplied on the face of the earth with sons and daughters, and they taught one another their evil practices and they continued sinning against the Lord.

17 Every man made to himself a god, and they robbed and plundered every man his neighbor as well as his relative, and they corrupted the earth, and the earth was filled with violence.

18 And their judges and rulers went to the daughters of men and took their wives by force from their husbands according to their choice, and the sons of men in those days took from the cattle of the earth, the beasts of the field and the fowls of the air, and taught the mixture of animals of one species with the other, in order therewith to provoke the Lord; and God saw the whole earth and it was corrupt, for all flesh had corrupted its

ways on earth, all men and all animals.

19 And the Lord said, I will blot out man that I created from the face of the earth, yea from man to the birds of the air together with cattle and beasts that are in the field, for I repent that I made them.

20 All men who walked in the ways of the Lord died in those days, before the Lord brought the evil on man which he had declared, for this was from the Lord that they should not see the evil which the Lord spoke of concerning the sons of men.

21 And Noah found grace in the sight of the Lord, and the Lord chose him and his children to raise up offspring on the face of the whole earth.

CHAPTER 5

1 It was in the eighty-fourth year of the life of Noah that Enoch the son of Seth died; he was nine hundred and five years old at his death.

2 In the one hundred and seventy ninth year of the life of Noah, Cainan the son of Enosh died, and the age of Cainan was nine hundred and ten years, and he died.

3 And in the two hundred and thirty fourth year of the life of Noah, Mahlallel the son of Cainan died, and the days of Mahlallel were eight hundred and ninety-five years, and he died.

4 Jared the son of Mahlallel died in those days, in the three hundred and thirty-sixth year of the life of Noah; and all the days of Jared were nine hundred and sixty-two years, and he died.

5 And all who followed the Lord died in those days, before they saw the evil which God declared to do on earth.

6 After the lapse of many years, in the four hundred and eightieth year of the life of Noah, when all those men who followed the Lord had died away from among the sons of men, and only Methuselah was then left, God said to Noah and Methuselah,

7 Speak ye, and proclaim to the sons of men, saying, Thus says the Lord, return from your evil ways and turn away from your works, and the Lord will repent of the evil that he declared to do to you, so that it shall not come to pass.

8 For thus says the Lord, Behold I give you a period of one hundred and twenty years; if you will turn to me and turn away from your evil ways, then will I also turn away from the evil which I told you, and it shall not exist, says the Lord.

9 And Noah and Methuselah spoke all the words of the Lord to the sons of men, day after day, constantly speaking to them.

10 But the sons of men would not listen to them, nor incline their ears to their words, and they were stubborn.

11 And the Lord granted them a period of one hundred and twenty years, saying, If they will return, then will God repent of the evil, so as not to destroy the earth.

12 Noah the son of Lamech refrained from taking a wife in those days to beget children, for he said, Certainly now God will destroy the earth, wherefore then shall I beget children?

13 Noah was a just man, he was perfect in his generation, and the Lord chose him to raise up offspring from his offspring on the face of the earth.

14 And the Lord said to Noah, Take to you a wife, and beget children, for I have seen you righteous before me in this generation.

15 You shall raise up offspring, and your children with you, in the midst of the earth; and Noah went and took a wife, and he chose Naamah the daughter of Enoch, and she was five hundred and eighty years old.

16 And Noah was four hundred and ninety-eight years old, when he took Naamah for a wife.

17 Naamah conceived and gave birth to a son, and he called his name Japheth, saying, God has enlarged me in the earth; and she conceived again and gave birth to a son, and he called his name Shem, saying, God has made me a remnant, to raise up descendants the midst of the earth.

18 And Noah was five hundred and two years old when Naamah gave birth to Shem, and the boys grew up and went in the ways of the Lord, in all that Methuselah and Noah their father taught them.

19 Lamech the father of Noah, died in those days; yet verily he did not go with all his heart in the ways of his father, and he died in the hundred and ninety-fifth year of the life of Noah.

20 And all the days of Lamech were seven hundred and seventy years, and he died.

21 All the sons of men who knew the Lord, died in that year before the Lord brought evil on them; for the Lord willed them to die, so as not to

behold the evil that God would bring on their brothers and relatives, as he had so declared to do.

22 In that time, the Lord said to Noah and Methuselah, Stand forth and proclaim to the sons of men all the words that I spoke to you in those days, perchance they may turn from their evil ways, and I will then repent of the evil and will not bring it.

23 And Noah and Methuselah stood forth, and said in the ears of the sons of men, all that God had spoken concerning them.

24 But the sons of men would not listen, neither would they incline their ears to all their declarations.

25 It was after this that the Lord said to Noah, The end of all flesh is come before me on account of their evil deeds, and behold I will destroy the earth.

26 And take with you gopher wood, and go to a certain place and make a large ark, and place it in that spot.

27 Thus shall you make it; three hundred cubits in length, fifty cubits broad and thirty cubits high.

28 And you shall make a door, open at its side, and to a cubit you shall finish above, and cover it within and without with pitch.

29 And behold I will bring the flood of waters on the earth, and all flesh will be destroyed; from under the heavens all that is on earth shall perish.

30 You and your household shall go and gather two couple of all living things, male and female, and shall bring them to the ark, to raise up offspring from them on earth.

31 Gather to you all food that is eaten by all the animals, that there may be food for you and for them.

32 You shall choose for your sons three maidens from the daughters of men, and they shall be wives to your sons.

33 And Noah rose up, and he made the ark, in the place where God had commanded him, and Noah did as God had ordered him.

34 In his five hundred and ninety-fifth year Noah commenced to make the ark, and he made the ark in five years, as the Lord had commanded.

35 Then Noah took the three daughters of Eliakim, son of Methuselah, for wives for his sons, as the Lord had commanded Noah.

36 It was at that time Methuselah the son of Enoch died; he was nine

hundred and sixty years old at his death.

CHAPTER 6

1 At that time, after the death of Methuselah, the Lord said to Noah, Go with your household into the ark; behold I will gather to you all the animals of the earth, the beasts of the field and the fowls of the air, and they shall all come and surround the ark.

2 You shall go and seat yourself by the doors of the ark, and all the beasts, the animals, and the fowls, shall assemble and place themselves before you, and such of them as will come and crouch before you, you shall take and deliver into the hands of your sons, who will bring them to the ark, and all that will stand before you you shall leave.

3 And the Lord brought this about on the next day, and animals, beasts and fowls came in great multitudes and surrounded the ark.

4 Noah went and seated himself by the door of the ark, and of all flesh that crouched before him he brought into the ark, and all that stood before him he left on earth.

5 A lioness came with her two whelps, male and female, and the three crouched before Noah; the two whelps rose up against the lioness and struck her, and made her flee from her place, and she went away, and they returned to their places and crouched on the earth before Noah.

6 And the lioness ran away, and stood in the place of the lions.

7 And Noah saw this and wondered greatly, and he rose and took the two whelps and brought them into the ark.

8 Noah brought into the ark from all living creatures that were on earth, so that there was none left but those which Noah brought into the ark.

9 Two and two came to Noah into the ark, but from the clean animals and clean fowls, he brought seven couples as God had commanded him.

10 And all the animals, and beasts, and fowls were still there, and they surrounded the ark at every place, and the rain had not descended till seven days after.

11 On that day the Lord caused the whole earth to shake, and the sun darkened, and the foundations of the world raged, and the whole earth was moved violently, and the lightning flashed, and the thunder roared, and all the fountains in the earth were broken up, such as was not known to the inhabitants before; and God did this mighty act in order to terrify the sons of men, that there might be no more evil on earth.

12 And still the sons of men would not return from their evil ways, and they increased the anger of the Lord at that time, and did not even direct their hearts to all this.

13 At the end of seven days, in the six hundredth year of the life of Noah, the waters of the flood were on the earth.

14 All the fountains of the deep were broken up, and the windows of heaven were opened, and the rain was on the earth forty days and forty nights.

15 And Noah and his household, and all the living creatures that were with him, came into the ark on account of the waters of the flood, and the Lord shut him in.

16 All the sons of men that were left on the earth became exhausted through evil on account of the rain, for the waters were coming more violently on the earth, and the animals and beasts were still surrounding the ark.

17 And the sons of men assembled together, about seven hundred thousand men and women, and they came to Noah to the ark.

18 They called to Noah, saying, Open for us that we may come to you in the ark--and wherefore shall we die?

19 And Noah, with a loud voice answered them from the ark, saying, Have you not all rebelled against the Lord, and said that he does not exist? Therefore the Lord brought on you this evil, to destroy and cut you off from the face of the earth.

20 Is not this the thing that I spoke to you of one hundred and twenty years back, and you would not listen to the voice of the Lord, and now do you desire to live on earth?

21 They said to Noah, We are ready to return to the Lord; only open for us that we may live and not die.

22 And Noah answered them, saying, Behold now that you see the trouble of your souls, you wish to return to the Lord; why did you not return during these hundred and twenty years, which the Lord granted

you as the determined period?

23 But now you come and tell me this on account of the troubles of your souls, now also the Lord will not listen to you, neither will he give ear to you on this day, so that you will not now succeed in your wishes.

24 The sons of men approached in order to break into the ark, to come in on account of the rain, for they could not bear the rain on them.

25 And the Lord sent all the beasts and animals that stood around the ark. And the beasts overpowered them and drove them from that place, and every man went his way and they again scattered themselves on the face of the earth.

26 The rain was still descending on the earth, and it descended forty days and forty nights, and the waters prevailed greatly on the earth; all flesh that was on the earth or in the waters died, whether men, animals, beasts, creeping things or birds of the air, and there only remained Noah and those that were with him in the ark.

27 The waters prevailed and they greatly increased on the earth, and they lifted up the ark and it was raised from the earth.

28 And the ark floated on the face of the waters; it was tossed on the waters so that all the living creatures within were turned about like pottage in a cauldron.

29 Great anxiety seized all the living creatures that were in the ark, and the ark was like to be broken.

30 And all the living creatures that were in the ark were terrified: the lions roared, and the oxen lowed, and the wolves howled, and every living creature in the ark spoke and lamented in its own language, so that their voices reached to a great distance, and Noah and his sons cried and wept in their troubles; they were greatly afraid that they had reached the gates of death.

31 And Noah prayed to the Lord, and cried to him on account of this, and he said, O Lord help us, for we have no strength to bear this evil that has encompassed us, for the waves of the waters have surrounded us, mischievous torrents have terrified us, the snares of death have come before us; answer us, O Lord, answer us, light up your countenance toward us and be gracious to us, redeem us and deliver us.

32 The Lord listened to the voice of Noah, and the Lord remembered him.

33 And a wind passed over the earth; the waters were still and the ark rested.

34 The fountains of the deep and the windows of heaven were stopped, and the rain from heaven was restrained.

35 And the waters decreased in those days, and the ark rested on the mountains of Ararat.

36 Noah then opened the windows of the ark, and Noah still called out to the Lord at that time and he said, O Lord, who did form the earth and the heavens and all that are therein, bring forth our souls from this confinement, and from the prison wherein you have placed us, for I am much wearied with sighing.

37 And the Lord listened to the voice of Noah, and said to him, When you have completed a full year you shall then go forth.

38 And at the revolution of the year, when a full year was completed to Noah's dwelling in the ark, the waters were dried from off the earth, and Noah put off the covering of the ark.

39 At that time, on the twenty-seventh day of the second month, the earth was dry, but Noah and his sons and those that were with him did not go out from the ark until the Lord told them.

40 And the day came that the Lord told them to go out, and they all went out from the ark.

41 They went and returned every one to his way and to his place, and Noah and his sons lived in the land that God had told them; they served the Lord all their days, and the Lord blessed Noah and his sons on their going out from the ark.

42 And he said to them, Be prolific and fill all the earth; become strong and increase abundantly in the earth and reproduce therein.

CHAPTER 7

1 And these are the names of the sons of Noah: Japheth, Ham and Shem; and children were born to them after the flood, for they had taken wives before the flood.

2 These are the sons of Japheth: Gomer, Magog, Madai, Javan, Tubal, Meshech, and Tiras, seven sons.

3 And the sons of Gomer were Askinaz, Rephath and Tegarmah.

4 And the sons of Magog were Elichanaf and Lubal.

5 And the children of Madai were Achon, Zeelo, Chazoni and Lot.

6 And the sons of Javan were Elisha, Tarshish, Chittim and Dudonim.

7 And the sons of Tubal were Ariphi, Kesed and Taari.

8 And the sons of Meshech were Dedon, Zaron and Shebashni.

9 And the sons of Tiras were Benib, Gera, Lupirion and Gilak; these are the sons of Japheth according to their families, and their numbers in those days were about four hundred and sixty men.

10 And these are the sons of Ham: Cush, Mitzraim, Phut and Canaan, four sons; and the sons of Cush were Seba, Havilah, Sabta, Raama and Satecha, and the sons of Raama were Sheba and Dedan.

11 And the sons of Mitzraim were Lud, Anom and Pathros, Chasloth and Chaphtor.

12 And the sons of Phut were Gebul, Hadan, Benah and Adan.

13 And the sons of Canaan were Zidon, Heth, Amori, Gergashi, Hivi, Arkee, Seni, Arodi, Zimodi and Chamothi.

14 These are the sons of Ham, according to their families, and their numbers in those days were about seven hundred and thirty men.

15 And these are the sons of Shem: Elam, Ashur, Arpachshad, Lud and Aram, five sons; and the sons of Elam were Shushan, Machul and Harmon.

16 And the sons of Ashar were Mirus and Mokil, and the sons of Arpachshad were Shelach, Anar and Ashcol.

17 And the sons of Lud were Pethor and Bizayon, and the sons of Aram were Uz, Chul, Gather and Mash.

18 These are the sons of Shem, according to their families; and their numbers in those days were about three hundred men.

19 These are the generations of Shem: Shem had Arpachshad and Arpachshad had Shelach, and Shelach had Eber and to Eber were born two children, the name of one was Peleg, for in his days the sons of men were divided, and in the latter days the earth was divided.

20 And the name of the second was Yoktan, meaning that in his day the lives of the sons of men were diminished and lessened.

21 These are the sons of Yoktan: Almodad, Shelaf, Chazarmoveth, Yerach, Hadurom, Ozel, Diklah, Obal, Abimael, Sheba, Ophir, Havilah and Jobab;

all these are the sons of Yoktan.

22 And Peleg his brother had Yen, and Yen had Serug, and Serug had Nahor and Nahor had Terah, and Terah was thirty-eight years old, and he had Haran and Nahor.

23 And Cush the son of Ham, the son of Noah, took a wife in those days in his old age, and she gave birth to a son, and they called his name Nimrod, saying, At that time the sons of men again began to rebel and go contrary to God; the child grew up, and his father loved him greatly, for he was the son of his old age.

24 The garments of skin which God made for Adam and his wife, when they went out of the garden, were given to Cush.

25 For after the death of Adam and his wife, the garments were given to Enoch, the son of Jared, and when Enoch was taken up to God, he gave them to Methuselah, his son.

26 At the death of Methuselah, Noah took them and brought them to the ark, and they were with him until he went out of the ark.

27 And in their going out, Ham stole those garments from Noah his father; he took them and hid them from his brothers.

28 When Ham had his first born Cush, he gave him the garments in secret, and they were with Cush many days.

29 Cush also concealed them from his sons and brothers, and when Cush had begotten Nimrod, he gave him those garments through his love for him, and Nimrod grew up, and when he was twenty years old he put on those garments.

30 Nimrod became strong when he put on the garments, and God gave him might and strength, and he was a mighty hunter in the earth. He was a mighty hunter in the field, and he hunted the animals and he built altars, and he offered on them the animals before the Lord.

31 Nimrod strengthened himself, and he rose up from among his brothers, and he fought the battles of his brothers against all their enemies round about.

32 The Lord delivered all the enemies of his brothers in his hands, and God prospered him from time to time in his battles, and he reigned on earth.

33 Therefore it became current in those days, when a man ushered forth those that he had trained up for battle, he would say to them, like God did to Nimrod who was a mighty hunter in the earth and who succeeded in

the battles that prevailed against his brothers, that he delivered them from the hands of their enemies: so may God strengthen us and deliver us this day.

34 And when Nimrod was forty years old, there was a war between his brothers and the children of Japheth, so that they were in the power of their enemies.

35 Nimrod went forth at that time, and he assembled all the sons of Cush and their families, about four hundred and sixty men; he hired also from some of his friends and acquaintances about eighty men, and he gave them their hire; he went with them to battle, and when he was on the road, Nimrod strengthened the hearts of the people that went with him.

36 And he said to them, Do not fear, neither be alarmed, for all our enemies will be delivered into our hands, and you may do with them as you please.

37 All the men that went were about five hundred, and they fought against their enemies; they destroyed them, and subdued them, and Nimrod placed standing officers over them in their respective places.

38 He took some of their children as security, and they were all servants to Nimrod and to his brothers, and Nimrod and all the people that were with him turned homeward.

39 When Nimrod had joyfully returned from battle, after having conquered his enemies, all his brothers, together with those who knew him before, assembled to make him king over them and they placed the regal crown on his head.

40 He set over his subjects and people, princes, judges, and rulers, as is the custom among kings.

41 He placed Terah the son of Nahor the prince of his host, and he dignified him and elevated him above all his princes.

42 And while he was reigning according to his heart's desire, after having conquered all his enemies around, he advised with his counselors to build a city for his palace, and they did so.

43 They found a large valley opposite to the east, and they built him a large and extensive city, and Nimrod called the name of the city that he built Shinar, for the Lord had vehemently shaken his enemies and destroyed them.

44 Nimrod lived in Shinar, and he reigned securely, and he fought with his enemies and he subdued them; he prospered in all his battles, and his kingdom became very great.

45 All nations and tongues heard of his fame, and they gathered themselves to him, and they bowed down to the earth; they brought him offerings, and he became their lord and king, and they all lived with him in the city at Shinar; Nimrod reigned in the earth over all the sons of Noah, and they were all under his power and counsel.

46 And all the earth was of one tongue and words of union, but Nimrod did not go in the ways of the Lord; he was more wicked than all the men that were before him, from the days of the flood until those days.

47 He made gods of wood and stone, he bowed down to them, he rebelled against the Lord, and taught all his subjects and the people of the earth his wicked ways; Mardon his son was more wicked than his father.

48 And every one that heard of the acts of Mardon the son of Nimrod would say, concerning him, From the wicked goes forth wickedness. Therefore it became a proverb in the whole earth, saying, From the wicked goes forth wickedness, and it was current in the words of men from that time to this.

49 Terah the son of Nahor, prince of Nimrod's host, was in those days very great in the sight of the king and his subjects, and the king and princes loved him, and they elevated him very high.

50 And Terah took a wife and her name was Amthelo the daughter of Cornebo; the wife of Terah conceived and gave birth to a son in those days.

51 Terah was seventy years old when he had him, and Terah called the name of his son Abram, because the king had raised him in those days, and dignified him above all his princes that were with him.

CHAPTER 8

1 It was in the night that Abram was born, that all the servants of Terah, and all the wise men of Nimrod and his conjurors came and ate and drank in the house of Terah, and they rejoiced with him on that night.

2 When all the wise men and conjurors went out from the house of Terah, they lifted up their eyes toward heaven that night to look at the stars; they saw, and behold, one very large star came from the east and ran in the heavens; he swallowed up the four stars from the four sides of the heavens.

3 And all the wise men of the king and his conjurors were astonished at the sight, and the sages understood this matter, and they knew its import.

4 They said to each other, This only betokens the child that has been born to Terah this night, who will grow up and be prolific, and reproduce, and possess all the earth, he and his children for ever, and he and his descendants will kill great kings, and inherit their lands.

5 The wise men and conjurors went home that night; in the morning all these wise men and conjurors rose up early, and assembled in an appointed house.

6 And they spoke and said to each other, Behold the sight that we saw last night is hidden from the king; it has not been made known to him.

7 And should this thing get known to the king in the latter days, he will say to us, Why have you concealed this matter from me, and then we shall all suffer death; therefore, now let us go and tell the king the sight which we saw, and the interpretation thereof, and we shall then remain clear.

8 And they did so; they all went to the king and bowed down to him to the ground, and they said, May the king live, may the king live.

9 We heard that a son was born to Terah the son of Nahor, the prince of your host, and we last night came to his house, and we ate and drank and rejoiced with him that night.

10 And when your servants went out from the house of Terah, to go to our respective homes to abide there for the night, we lifted up our eyes to heaven and we saw a great star coming from the east, and the same star ran with great speed and swallowed up four great stars, from the four sides of the heavens.

11 And your servants were astonished at the sight which we saw, and were greatly terrified; we made our judgment on the sight and knew by our wisdom the proper interpretation thereof, that this thing applies to the child that is born to Terah, who will grow up and reproduce greatly, and become powerful and kill all the kings of the earth, and inherit all their lands, he and his offspring forever.

12 Now our lord and king, behold we have truly acquainted you with what we have seen concerning this child.

13 If it seems good to the king to give his father value for this child, we will kill him before he shall grow up and increase in the land, and his evil increase against us, that we and our children perish through his evil.

14 And the king heard their words and they seemed good in his sight, and he sent and called for Terah, and Terah came before the king.

15 And the king said to Terah, I have been told that a son was last night born to you, and after this manner was observed in the heavens at his birth.

16 And now therefore give me the child, that we may kill him before his evil springs up against us, and I will give you for his value, your house full of silver and gold.

17 Terah answered the king and said to him: My Lord and king, I have heard your words, and your servant shall do all that his king desires.

18 But my lord and king, I will tell you what happened to me last night, that I may see what advice the king will give his servant, and then I will answer the king on what he has just spoken. The king said, Speak.

19 And Terah said to the king, Ayon, son of Mored, came to me last night, saying,

20 Give to me the great and beautiful horse that the king gave you, and I will give you silver and gold, and straw and provender for its value; and I said to him, Wait till I see the king concerning your words, and behold whatever the king says, that will I do.

21 And now my lord and king, behold I have made this thing known to you, and the advice which my king will give to his servant, that will I follow.

22 The king heard the words of Terah, and his anger was set ablaze and he considered him in the light of a fool.

23 And the king answered Terah and said to him, Are you so silly, ignorant, or deficient in understanding to do this thing, to give your beautiful horse for silver and gold or even for straw and provender?

24 Are you so short of silver and gold that you should do this thing, because you cannot obtain straw and provender to feed your horse? And what is silver and gold to you, or straw and provender, that you should give away that fine horse which I gave you, like which there is none to be had on the whole earth?

25 The king left off speaking, and Terah answered the king, saying, Like to this has the king spoken to his servant;

26 I beseech you, my lord and king, what is this which you did say to me, Give your son that we may kill him, and I will give you silver and gold for his value; what shall I do with silver and gold after the death of my son? Who shall inherit me? Certainly then at my death, the silver and gold will return to my king who gave it.

27 And when the king heard the words of Terah, and the parable which he brought concerning the king, it grieved him greatly and he was troubled at this thing, and his anger burned within him.

28 And Terah saw that the anger of the king was set ablaze against him, and he answered the king, saying, All that I have is in the king's power; whatever the king desires to do to his servant, that let him do, yea, even my son, he is in the king's power, without value in exchange, he and his two brothers that are older than he.

29 And the king said to Terah, No, but I will purchase your younger son for a price.

30 Terah answered the king, saying, I beseech you my lord and king to let your servant speak a word before you, and let the king hear the word of his servant, and Terah said, Let my king give me three days' time till I consider this matter within myself, and consult with my family concerning the words of my king; and he pressed the king greatly to agree to this.

31 The king listened to Terah, and he did so and he gave him three days' time. Terah went out from the king's presence, and he came home to his family and spoke to them all the words of the king; and the people were greatly afraid.

32 And it was in the third day that the king sent to Terah, saying, Send me your son for a price as I spoke to you; and should you not do this, I will send and kill all you have in your house, so that you shall not even have a dog remaining.

33 And Terah hurried (as the thing was urgent from the king), and he took a child from one of his servants, which his handmaid had born to him that day, and Terah brought the child to the king and received value for him.

34 And the Lord was with Terah in this matter, that Nimrod might not cause Abram's death. The king took the child from Terah and with all his might dashed his head to the ground, for he thought it had been Abram; this was concealed from him from that day, and it was forgotten by the king, as it was the will of Providence not to suffer Abram's death.

35 And Terah took Abram his son secretly, together with his mother and nurse, and he concealed them in a cave, and he brought them their provisions monthly.

36 The Lord was with Abram in the cave and he grew up, and Abram was in the cave ten years, and the king and his princes, soothsayers and sages, thought that the king had killed Abram.

CHAPTER 9

1 And Haran, the son of Terah, Abram's oldest brother, took a wife in those days.

2 Haran was thirty-nine years old when he took her; and the wife of Haran conceived and gave birth to a son, and he called his name Lot.

3 She conceived again and gave birth to a daughter, and called her name Milca; and she again conceived and gave birth to a daughter and called her name Sarai.

4 Haran was forty-two years old when he had Sarai, which was in the tenth year of the life of Abram; and in those days Abram and his mother and nurse went out from the cave, as the king and his subjects had forgotten the affair of Abram.

5 When Abram came out from the cave, he went to Noah and his son Shem, and he remained with them to learn the instruction of the Lord and his ways; no man knew where Abram was, and Abram served Noah and Shem his son for a long time.

6 Abram was in Noah's house thirty-nine years, and Abram knew the Lord from three years old; he went in the ways of the Lord until the day of his death, as Noah and his son Shem had taught him, and all the sons of the earth in those days greatly went contrary to the Lord, and they rebelled against him and they served other gods. They forgot the Lord who had created them in the earth; and the inhabitants of the earth made to themselves, at that time, every man his god; gods of wood and stone which could neither speak, hear, nor deliver, and the sons of men served them and they became their gods.

7 The king and all his servants, and Terah with all his household were then the first of those that served gods of wood and stone.

8 And Terah had twelve gods of large size, made of wood and stone, after the twelve months of the year, and he served each one monthly, and every month Terah would bring his meat offering and drink offering to his gods; thus did Terah all the days.

9 All that generation were wicked in the sight of the Lord, and they thus made every man his god, but they turned away from the Lord who had created them.

10 And there was not a man found in those days in the whole earth who

knew the Lord (for they served each man his own god) except Noah and his household; and all those who were under his counsel knew the Lord in those days.

11 Abram the son of Terah was becoming great in those days in the house of Noah, and no man knew it, and the Lord was with him.

12 The Lord gave Abram an understanding heart, and he knew all the works of that generation were vain, and that all their gods were vain and were of no avail.

13 And Abram saw the sun shining on the earth, and Abram said to himself, Certainly now this sun that shines on the earth is God, and him will I serve.

14 And Abram served the sun in that day and he prayed to him, and when evening came the sun set as usual, and Abram said within himself, Certainly this cannot be God?

15 And Abram still continued to speak within himself, Who is he who made the heavens and the earth? Who created on earth? Where is he?

16 And night darkened over him; he lifted up his eyes toward the west, north, south, and east, and he saw that the sun had vanished from the earth, and the day became dark.

17 And Abram saw the stars and moon before him, and he said, Certainly this is the God who created the whole earth as well as man, and behold these his servants are gods around him: and Abram served the moon and prayed to it all that night.

18 And in the morning when it was light and the sun shone on the earth as usual, Abram saw all the things that the Lord God had made on earth.

19 And Abram said to himself, Certainly these are not gods that made the earth and all mankind, but these are the servants of God. And Abram remained in the house of Noah and there knew the Lord and his ways. He served the Lord all the days of his life, and all that generation forgot the Lord, and served other gods of wood and stone, and rebelled all their days.

20 And king Nimrod reigned securely, and all the earth was under his control, and all the earth was of one tongue and words of union.

21 And all the princes of Nimrod and his great men took counsel together: Phut, Mitzraim, Cush and Canaan with their families, and they said to each other, Come let us build ourselves a city and in it a strong tower and its top reaching heaven, and we will make ourselves famed so that we may reign on the whole world, in order that the evil of our

enemies may cease from us; that we may reign mightily over them, and that we may not become scattered over the earth on account of their wars.

22 They all went before the king, and they told the king these words, and the king agreed with them in this affair, and he did so.

23 All the families assembled consisting of about six hundred thousand men, and they went to seek an extensive piece of ground to build the city and the tower, and they sought in the whole earth and they found none like one valley at the east of the land of Shinar, about two days' walk, and they journeyed there and they lived there.

24 And they began to make bricks and burn fires to build the city and the tower that they had imagined to complete.

25 And the building of the tower was to them a transgression and a sin, and they began to build it While they were building against the Lord God of heaven, they imagined in their hearts to war against him and to ascend into heaven.

26 And all these people and all the families divided themselves in three parts; the first said, We will ascend into heaven and fight against him; the second said, We will ascend to heaven and place our own gods there and serve them; and the third part said, We will ascend to heaven and strike him with bows and spears. And God knew all their works and all their evil thoughts, and he saw the city and the tower which they were building.

27 They built themselves a great city and a very high and strong tower; on account of its height, the mortar and bricks did not reach the builders in their ascent to it until those who went up had completed a full year, and after that, they reached the builders and gave them the mortar and the bricks; thus was it done daily.

28 And behold these ascended and others descended the whole day; and if a brick should fall from their hands and get broken, they would all weep over it; if a man fell and died, none of them would look at him.

29 The Lord knew their thoughts, and it came to pass when they were building they cast the arrows toward the heavens, and all the arrows fell on them filled with blood; when they saw them they said to each other, Certainly we have slain all those that are in heaven.

30 For this was from the Lord in order to cause them to err, and in order to destroy them from off the face of the ground.

31 They built the tower and the city, and they did this thing daily until many days and years were elapsed.

32 And God said to the seventy angels who stood foremost before him, to those who were near to him, saying, Come let us descend and confuse their tongues, that one man shall not understand the language of his neighbor, and they did so to them.

33 From that day following, they forgot each man his neighbor's tongue, and they could not understand to speak in one tongue; when the builder took from the hands of his neighbor lime or stone which he did not order, the builder would cast it away and throw it on his neighbor, that he would die.

34 And they did so many days, and they killed many of them in this manner.

35 The Lord struck the three divisions that were there, and he punished them according to their works and designs; those who said, We will ascend to heaven and serve our gods, became like apes and elephants; those who said, We will strike the heaven with arrows, the Lord killed them, one man through the hand of his neighbor; and the third division of those who said, We will ascend to heaven and fight against him, the Lord scattered them throughout the earth.

36 Those who were left among them, when they knew and understood the evil which was coming on them, turned away from the building, and they also became scattered on the face of the whole earth.

37 And they ceased building the city and the tower; therefore he called that place Babel, for there the Lord confounded the Language of the whole earth; behold it was at the east of the land of Shinar.

38 As to the tower which the sons of men built, the earth opened its mouth and swallowed up one third part thereof, and a fire also descended from heaven and burned another third, and the other third is left to this day; it is of that part which was aloft, and its circumference is three days' walk.

39 Many of the sons of men died in that tower, a people without number.

CHAPTER 10

1 Peleg the son of Eber died in those days, in the forty-eighth year of the life of Abram son of Terah, and all the days of Peleg were two hundred and thirty-nine years.

2 When the Lord had scattered the sons of men on account of their sin at the tower, behold they spread forth into many divisions, and all the sons

of men were dispersed into the four corners of the earth.

3 And all the families became each according to its language, its land, or its city.

4 And the sons of men built many cities according to their families, in all the places where they went, and throughout the earth where the Lord had scattered them.

5 Some of them built cities in places from which they later abandoned, and they called these cities after their own names, or the names of their children, or after their particular occurrences.

6 The sons of Japheth, the son of Noah went and built themselves cities in the places where they were scattered; they called all their cities after their names, and the sons of Japheth were divided on the face of the earth into many divisions and languages.

7 And these are the sons of Japheth according to their families: Gomer, Magog, Medai, Javan, Tubal, Meshech and Tiras; these are the children of Japheth according to their generations.

8 Tthe children of Gomer, according to their cities, were the Francum, who dwell in the land of Franza, by the river Franza, by the river Senah.

9 And the children of Rephath are the Bartonim, who dwell in the land of Bartonia by the river Ledah, which empties its waters in the great sea Gihon, that is, Oceanus.

10 The children of Tugarma are ten families, and these are their names: Buzar, Parzunac, Balgar, Elicanum, Ragbib, Tarki, Bid, Zebuc, Ongal and Tilmaz; all these spread and rested in the north and built themselves cities.

11 And they called their cities after their own names; those are they who abide by the rivers Hithlah and Italac to this day.

12 But the families of Angoli, Balgar and Parzunac, they dwelll by the great river Dubnee; and the names of their cities are also according to their own names.

13 The children of Javan are the Javanim who dwell in the land of Makdonia, and the children of Medaiare are the Orelum that dwell in the land of Curson, and the children of Tubal are those that dwell in the land of Tuskanah by the river Pashiah.

14 The children of Meshech are the Shibashni and the children of Tiras are Rushash, Cushni, and Ongolis; all these went and built themselves cities; those are the cities that are situated by the sea Jabus by the river Cura, which empties itself into the river Tragan.

15 And the children of Elishah are the Almanim, and they also went and built themselves cities; those are the cities situated between the mountains of Job and Shibathmo; and of them were the people of Lumbardi who dwell opposite the mountains of Job and Shibathmo, and they conquered the land of Italia and remained there to this day.

16 The children of Chittim are the Romim who dwell in the valley of Canopia by the river Tibreu.

17 The children of Dudonim are those who dwell in the cities of the sea Gihon, in the land of Bordna.

18 These are the families of the children of Japheth according to their cities and languages when they were scattered after the tower; they called their cities after their names and occurrences; and these are the names of all their cities according to their families which they built in those days after the tower.

19 And the children of Ham were Cush, Mitzraim, Phut and Canaan according to their generation and cities.

20 All these went and built themselves cities as they found fit places for them, and they called their cities after the names of their fathers Cush, Mitzraim, Phut and Canaan.

21 The children of Mitzraim are the Ludim, Anamim, Lehabim, Naphtuchim, Pathrusim, Casluchim and Caphturim, seven families.

22 All these dwell by the river Sihor, that is the brook of Egypt, and they built themselves cities and called them after their own names.

23 The children of Pathros and Casloch intermarried together, and from them went forth the Pelishtim, the Azathim, and the Gerarim, the Githim and the Ekronim, in all five families; these also built themselves cities, and they called their cities after the names of their fathers to this day.

24 The children of Canaan also built themselves cities, and they called their cities after their names, eleven cities and others without number.

25 Four men from the family of Ham went to the land of the plain; these are the names of the four men: Sodom, Gomorrah, Admah and Zeboyim.

26 And these men built themselves four cities in the land of the plain, and they called the names of their cities after their own names.

27 They and their children and all belonging to them lived in those cities, and they were prolific and multiplied greatly and lived peaceably.

28 Seir the son of Hur, son of Hivi, son of Canaan, went and found a valley opposite to Mount Paran, and he built a city there; he and his seven

sons and his household lived there, and he called the city which he built Seir, according to his name; that is the land of Seir to this day.

29 These are the families of the children of Ham, according to their languages and cities, when they were scattered to their countries after the tower.

30 Some of the children of Shem, son of Noah, father of all the children of Eber, also went and built themselves cities in the places wherein they were scattered, and they called their cities after their names.

31 The sons of Shem were Elam, Ashur, Arpachshad, Lud and Aram, and they built themselves cities and called the names of all their cities after their names.

32 Ashur, son of Shem, and his children and household went forth at that time, a very large body of them, and they went to a distant land that they found; they met with a very extensive valley in the land that they went to, and they built themselves four cities, and they called them after their own names and occurrences.

33 And these are the names of the cities which the children of Ashur built: Ninevah, Resen, Calach and Rehobother; the children of Ashur dwell there to this day.

34 The children of Aram also went and built themselves a city, and they called the name of the city Uz after their eldest brother; they dwell therein. That is the land of Uz to this day.

35 And in the second year after the tower a man from the house of Ashur, whose name was Bela, went from the land of Ninevah to sojourn with his household wherever he could find a place; they came until opposite the cities of the plain against Sodom, and they lived there.

36 And the man rose up and built there a small city, and called its name Bela, after his name; that is the land of Zoar to this day.

37 These are the families of the children of Shem according to their language and cities, after they were scattered on the earth after the tower.

38 And every kingdom, city, and family of the families of the children of Noah built themselves many cities after this.

39 And they established governments in all their cities in order to be regulated by their orders; so did all the families of the children of Noah forever.

CHAPTER 11

1 Nimrod son of Cush was still in the land of Shinar, and he reigned over it and lived there, and he built cities in the land of Shinar.

2 These are the names of the four cities which he built, and he called their names after the occurrences that happened to them in the building of the tower:

3 He called the first Babel, saying, Because the Lord there confounded the language of the whole earth. The name of the second he called Erech, because from there God dispersed them.

4 And the third he called Eched, saying there was a great battle at that place; the fourth he called Calnah, because his princes and mighty men were consumed there, and they troubled the Lord; they rebelled and went contrary to him.

5 When Nimrod had built these cities in the land of Shinar, he placed in them the remainder of his people, his princes and his mighty men that were left in his kingdom.

6 Nimrod lived in Babel, and there he renewed his reign over the rest of his subjects, and he reigned securely, and the subjects and princes of Nimrod called his name Amraphel, saying that at the tower his princes and men fell through his means.

7 Notwithstanding this, Nimrod did not return to the Lord, and he continued in wickedness and teaching wickedness to the sons of men; and Mardon, his son, was worse than his father and continued to add to the abominations of his father.

8 And he caused the sons of men to sin; therefore it is said, From the wicked goes forth wickedness.

9 At that time there was war between the families of the children of Ham, as they were dwelling in the cities which they had built.

10 And Chedorlaomer, king of Elam, went away from the families of the children of Ham; he fought with them and he subdued them, and he went to the five cities of the plain; he fought against them and he subdued them, and they were under his control.

11 And they served him twelve years and gave him a yearly tax.

12 At that time Nahor, son of Serug died, in the forty-ninth year of the life of Abram, son of Terah.

13 In the fiftieth year of the life of Abram, son of Terah, Abram came forth from the house of Noah, and went to his father's house.

14 And Abram knew the Lord, and he followed in his ways and instructions, and the Lord his God was with him.

15 Terah his father was in those days still captain of the host of king Nimrod, and he still followed strange gods.

16 And Abram came to his father's house and saw twelve gods standing there in their temples, and the anger of Abram was set ablaze when he saw these images in his father's house.

17 And Abram said, As the Lord lives these images shall not remain in my father's house; so shall the Lord who created me do to me if in three days' time I do not break them all.

18 Abram went from them, and his anger burned within him. And Abram hurried and went from the chamber to his father's outer court, and he found his father sitting in the court, and all his servants with him, and Abram came and sat before him.

19 Abram asked his father, saying, Father, tell me where is God who created heaven and earth, and all the sons of men on earth, and who created you and me. And Terah answered his son Abram and said, Behold those who created us are all with us in the house.

20 And Abram said to his father, My lord, show them to me I pray you. And Terah brought Abram into the chamber of the inner court, and Abram saw, and behold the whole room was full of gods of wood and stone, twelve great images and others less than they without number.

21 And Terah said to his son, Behold these are they which made all you see on earth, and which created me and you, and all mankind.

22 Terah bowed down to his gods, and he then went away from them, and Abram, his son, went away with him.

23 When Abram had gone from them he went to his mother and sat before her, and he said to his mother, Behold, my father has shown me those who made heaven and earth, and all the sons of men.

24 Now, therefore, hurry and fetch a kid from the flock, and make of it savory meat, that I may bring it to my father's gods as an offering for them to eat; perhaps I may thereby become acceptable to them.

25 And his mother did so; she fetched a kid, and made savory meat thereof, and brought it to Abram, and Abram took the savory meat from his mother and brought it before his father's gods, and he drew nigh to

them that they might eat; and Terah his father, did not know of it.

26 Abram saw on the day when he was sitting among them, that they had no voice, no hearing, no motion, and not one of them could stretch forth his hand to eat.

27 And Abram mocked them, and said, Certainly the savory meat that I prepared has not pleased them, or perhaps it was too little for them, and for that reason they would not eat; therefore tomorrow I will prepare fresh savory meat, better and more plentiful than this, in order that I may see the result.

28 It was on the next day that Abram directed his mother concerning the savory meat, and his mother rose and fetched three fine kids from the flock; she made of them some excellent savory meat, such as her son was fond of, and she gave it to her son Abram, and Terah his father did not know of it.

29 Abram took the savory meat from his mother and brought it before his father's gods into the chamber; he came nigh to them that they might eat, and he placed it before them, and Abram sat before them all day thinking perhaps they might eat.

30 Abram viewed them, and behold they had neither voice nor hearing, nor did one of them stretch forth his hand to the meat to eat.

31 And in the evening of that day in that house Abram was clothed with the spirit of God.

32 He called out and said, Woe to my father and this wicked generation, whose hearts are all inclined to vanity, who serve these idols of wood and stone which can neither eat, smell, hear nor speak, who have mouths without speech, eyes without sight, ears without hearing, hands without feeling, and legs which cannot move; like them are those that made them and that trust in them.

33 When Abram saw all these things his anger was set ablaze against his father, and he hurried and took a hatchet in his hand, and came to the chamber of the gods; he broke all his father's gods.

34 And when he was done breaking the images, he placed the hatchet in the hand of the great god which was there before them, and he went out; and Terah his father came home, for he had heard at the door the sound of the striking of the hatchet; so Terah came into the house to know what this was about.

35 Terah, having heard the noise of the hatchet in the room of images, ran to the room to the images, and he met Abram going out.

36 And Terah entered the room and found all the idols fallen down and broken, and the hatchet in the hand of the largest, which was not broken, and the savory meat which Abram his son had made was still before them.

37 When Terah saw this his anger was greatly set ablaze, and he hurried and went from the room to Abram.

38 And he found Abram his son still sitting in the house; and he said to him, What is this work you have done to my gods?

39 Abram answered Terah his father and he said, Not so my lord, for I brought savory meat before them, and when I came near to them with the meat that they might eat, they all at once stretched forth their hands to eat before the great one had put forth his hand to eat.

40 And the large one saw their works that they did before him, and his anger was violently set ablaze against them, and he went and took the hatchet that was in the house and came to them and broke them all, and behold the hatchet is yet in his hand as you see.

41 And Terah's anger was set ablaze against his son Abram, when he spoke this; and Terah said to Abram his son in his anger, What is this tale that you have told? You speak lies to me.

42 Is there in these gods spirit, soul or power to do all you have told me? Are they not wood and stone, and have I not myself made them, and can you speak such lies, saying that the large god that was with them struck them? It is you that did place the hatchet in his hands, and then said he struck them all.

43 Abram answered his father and said to him, And how can you then serve these idols in whom there is no power to do any thing? Can those idols in which you trust deliver you? Can they hear your prayers when you call on them? Can they deliver you from the hands of your enemies, or will they fight your battles for you against your enemies, that you should serve wood and stone which can neither speak nor hear?

44 And now certainly it is not good for you nor for the sons of men that are connected with you, to do these things; are you so silly, so foolish or so short of understanding that you will serve wood and stone, and do after this manner?

45 And forget the Lord God who made heaven and earth, and who created you in the earth, and thereby bring a great evil on your souls in this matter by serving stone and wood?

46 Did not our fathers in days of old sin in this manner, and the Lord God of the universe brought the waters of the flood on them and destroyed the

whole earth?

47 And how can you continue to do this and serve gods of wood and stone, who cannot hear, or speak, or deliver you from oppression, thereby bringing down the anger of the God of the universe on you?

48 Now therefore my father refrain from this, and bring not evil on your soul and the souls of your household.

49 And Abram hurried and sprang from before his father, and took the hatchet from his father's largest idol, with which Abram broke it and ran away.

50 Terah, seeing all that Abram had done, hurried to go from his house; he went to the king and he came before Nimrod and stood before him, and he bowed down to the king and the king said, What do you want?

51 And he said, I beseech you my lord, to hear me--Now fifty years back a child was born to me, and thus has he done to my gods and thus has he spoken; and now therefore, my lord and king, send for him that he may come before you, and judge him according to the law, that we may be delivered from his evil.

52 The king sent three men of his servants, and they went and brought Abram before the king. And Nimrod and all his princes and servants were that day sitting before him, and Terah also sat before them.

53 And the king said to Abram, What is this that you have done to your father and to his gods? And Abram answered the king in the words that he spoke to his father, and he said, The large god that was with them in the house did to them what you have heard.

54 And the king said to Abram, Had they power to speak and eat and do as you have said? And Abram answered the king, saying, And if there be no power in them why do you serve them and cause the sons of men to err through your follies?

55 Do you imagine that they can deliver you or do anything small or great, that you should serve them? And why will you not sense the God of the whole universe, who created you and in whose power it is to kill and keep alive?

56 0 foolish, simple, and ignorant king, woe to you forever.

57 I thought you would teach your servants the upright way, but you have not done this; you have filled the whole earth with your sins and the sins of your people who have followed your ways.

58 Do you not know, or have you not heard, that this evil which you do, our ancestors sinned therein in days of old, and the eternal God brought

the waters of the flood on them and destroyed them all, and also destroyed the whole earth on their account? And will you and your people rise up now and do like this work, in order to bring down the anger of the Lord God of the universe, and to bring evil on you and the whole earth?

59 Now therefore put away this evil deed which you did, and serve the God of the universe, as your soul is in his hands, and then it will be well with you.

60 And if your wicked heart will not listen to my words to cause you to turn away from your evil ways, and to serve the eternal God, then you will die in shame in the latter days, you, your people and all who are connected with you, hearing your words or walking in your evil ways.

61 When Abram had ceased speaking before the king and princes, Abram lifted up his eyes to the heavens, and he said, The Lord sees all the wicked, and he will judge them.

CHAPTER 12

1 When the king heard the words of Abram he ordered him to be put into prison; and Abram was ten days in prison.

2 At the end of those days the king ordered that all the kings, princes and governors of different provinces and the sages should come before him, and they sat before him, and Abram was still in the house of confinement.

3 The king said to the princes and sages, Have you heard what Abram, the son of Terah, has done to his father? Thus has he done to him, and I ordered him to be brought before me, and thus has he spoken; his heart did not misgive him, neither did he stir in my presence, and behold now he is confined in the prison.

4 Therefore decide what judgment is due to this man who reviled the king; who spoke and did all the things that you heard.

5 And they all answered the king saying, The man who reviles the king should be hanged on a tree; but having done all the things that he said and having despised our gods, he must therefore be burned to death, for this is the law in this matter.

6 If it pleases the king to do this, let him order his servants to kindle a fire both night and day in your brick furnace, and then we will cast this man

into it. And the king did so, and he commanded his servants that they should prepare a fire for three days and three nights in the king's furnace, that is in Casdim; and the king ordered them to take Abram from prison and bring him out to be burned.

7 And all the king's servants, princes, lords, governors, and judges, and all the inhabitants of the land, about nine hundred thousand men, stood opposite the furnace to see Abram.

8 And all the women and little ones crowded on the roofs and towers to see what was going on with Abram, and they all stood together at a distance; and there was not a man left that did not come that day to behold the scene.

9 When Abram was come, the conjurors of the king and the sages saw Abram, and they cried out to the king, saying, Our sovereign lord, certainly this is the man whom we know to have been the child at whose birth the great star swallowed the four stars, which we declared to the king fifty years ago.

10 And behold now his father has also gone contrary to your commands, and mocked you by bringing you another child, which you did kill.

11 And when the king heard their words, he was greatly angered, and he ordered Terah to be brought before him.

12 And the king said, Have you heard what the conjurors have spoken? Now tell me truly, how did you? If you shall speak truth you shall be acquitted.

13 Seeing that the king's anger was so much set ablaze, Terah said to the king, My lord and king, you have heard the truth, and what the sages have spoken is right. And the king said, How could you do this thing, to go contrary to my orders and to give me a child that you did not beget, and to take value for him?

14 Terah answered the king, Because my tender feelings were excited for my son, at that time, I took a son of my handmaid, and I brought him to the king.

15 And the king said, Who advised you to do this? Tell me, do not hide anything from me, and then you shall not die.

16 And Terah was greatly terrified in the king's presence, and he said to the king, It was Haran my eldest son who advised me to do this. Haran was in those days that Abram was born, two and thirty years old.

17 But Haran did not advise his father to do anything, for Terah said this to the king in order to deliver his soul from the king, for he feared greatly.

The king said to Terah, Haran your son who advised you to do this shall die through fire with Abram; for the sentence of death is on him for having rebelled against the king's desire in doing this thing.

18 Haran at that time felt inclined to follow the ways of Abram, but he kept it within himself.

19 And Haran said in his heart, Behold now the king has seized Abram on account of these things which Abram did, and it shall come to pass, that if Abram prevail over the king I will follow him, but if the king prevail I will go after the king.

20 When Terah had spoken this to the king concerning Haran his son, the king ordered Haran to be seized with Abram.

21 And they brought them both, Abram and Haran his brother, to cast them into the fire; and all the inhabitants of the land and the king's servants and princes and all the women and little ones were there standing over them that day.

22 And the king's servants took Abram and his brother, and they stripped them of all their clothes excepting their lower garments which were on them.

23 And they bound their hands and feet with linen cords, and the servants of the king lifted them up and cast them both into the furnace.

24 The Lord loved Abram and he had compassion over him, and the Lord came down and delivered Abram from the fire and he was not burned.

25 But all the cords with which they bound him were burned, while Abram remained and walked about in the fire.

26 Haran died when they had cast him into the fire, and he was burned to ashes, for his heart was not perfect with the Lord; and those men who cast him into the fire, the flame of the fire spread over them, and they were burned, and twelve of them died.

27 Abram walked in the midst of the fire three days and three nights, and all the servants of the king saw him walking in the fire, and they came and told the king, saying, Behold we have seen Abram walking about in the midst of the fire, and even the lower garments which are on him are not burned, but the cord with which he was bound is burned.

28 When the king heard their words his heart fainted and he would not believe them; so he sent other faithful princes to see this matter, and they went and saw it and told it to the king. And the king rose to go and see it, and he saw Abram walking to and fro in the midst of the fire, and he saw

Haran's body burned, and the king wondered greatly.

29 The king ordered Abram to be taken out from the fire; and his servants approached to take him out and they could not, for the fire was round about and the flame ascending toward them from the furnace.

30 The king's servants fled from it, and the king rebuked them, saying, Make haste and bring Abram out of the fire that you shall not die.

31 The servants of the king again approached to bring Abram out, and the flames came on them and burned their faces so that eight of them died.

32 When the king saw that his servants could not approach the fire that would burn them,, the king called to Abram, O servant of the God who is in heaven, go forth from amidst the fire and come here before me. And Abram listened to the voice of the king, and he went forth from the fire and came and stood before the king.

33 When Abram came out, the king and all his servants saw Abram coming before the king with his lower garments on him that were not burned, but the cord with which he was bound was burned.

34 And the king said to Abram, How is it that you were not burned in the fire?

35 Abram said to the king, The God of heaven and earth in whom I trust and who has all in his power, he delivered me from the fire into which you did cast me.

36 Haran the brother of Abram was burned to ashes, and they sought for his body; they found it consumed.

37 Haran was eighty-two years old when he died in the fire of Casdim. And the king, princes, and inhabitants of the land, seeing that Abram was delivered from the fire, came and bowed down to Abram.

38 And Abram said to them, Do not bow down to me, but bow down to the God of the world who made you, and serve him, and go in his ways for it is he who delivered me from out of this fire; it is he who created the souls and spirits of all men, and formed man in his mother's womb, and brought him forth into the world; it is he who will deliver those who trust in him from all pain.

39 This thing seemed very wonderful in the eyes of the king and princes, that Abram was saved from the fire and that Haran was burned. And the king gave Abram many presents and he gave him his two head servants from the king's house; the name of one was Oni and the name of the other was Eliezer.

40 All the kings, princes and servants gave Abram many gifts of silver

and gold and pearl, and the king and his princes sent him away, and he went in peace.

41 Abram went forth from the king in peace, and many of the king's servants followed him, and about three hundred men joined him.

42 And Abram returned on that day and went to his father's house, he and the men that followed him, and Abram served the Lord his God all the days of his life; he walked in his ways and followed his law.

43 From that day forward Abram inclined the hearts of the sons of men to serve the Lord.

44 At that time Nahor and Abram took to themselves wives, the daughters of their brother Haran; the wife of Nahor was Milca and the name of Abram's wife was Sarai. And Sarai, wife of Abram, was unable to conceive; she had no children in those days.

45 At the expiration of two years from Abram's going out of the fire, that is in the fifty-second year of his life, behold king Nimrod sat in Babel on the throne, and the king fell asleep and dreamed that he was standing with his troops and hosts in a valley opposite the king's furnace.

46 And he lifted up his eyes and saw a man in the likeness of Abram coming forth from the furnace; he came and stood before the king with his drawn sword, and then sprang to the king with his sword, when the king fled from the man, for he was afraid; while he was running, the man threw an egg on the king's head, and the egg became a great river.

47 And the king dreamed that all his troops sank in that river and died, and the king took flight with three men who were before him and he escaped.

48 The king looked at these men and they were clothed in princely dresses as the garments of kings, and had the appearance and majesty of kings.

49 And while they were running, the river again turned to an egg before the king; there came forth from the egg a young bird which came before the king, and flew at his head and plucked out the king's eye.

50 The king was grieved at the sight, and he awoke out of his sleep and his spirit was agitated; he felt a great terror.

51 In the morning the king rose from his couch in fear, and he ordered all the wise men and magicians to come before him, when the king related his dream to them.

52 And a wise servant of the king, whose name was Anuki, answered the

king, saying, This is nothing else but the evil of Abram and his offspring which will spring up against my Lord and king in the latter days.

53 And behold the day will come when Abram and his offspring and the children of his household will war with my king, and they will strike all the king's hosts and his troops.

54 And as to what you have said concerning three men which you did see like yourself, and which did escape, this means that only you will escape with three kings from the kings of the earth who will be with you in battle.

55 And that which you saw of the river which turned to an egg as at first, and the young bird plucking out your eye, this means nothing else but the offspring of Abram which will kill the king in latter days.

56 This is my king's dream, and this is its interpretation, and the dream is true, and the interpretation which your servant has given you is right.

57 Now therefore my king, certainly you know that it is now fifty-two years since your sages saw this at the birth of Abram, and if my king will suffer Abram to live in the earth it will be to the injury of my lord and king, for all the days that Abram lives neither you nor your kingdom will be established, for this was known formerly at his birth; and why will not my king kill him, that his evil may be kept from you in latter days?

58 And Nimrod listened to the voice of Anuki; he sent some of his servants in secret to go and seize Abram and bring him before the king to suffer death.

59 Eliezer, Abram's servant whom the king had given him, was at that time in the presence of the king, and he heard what Anuki had advised the king, and what the king had said to cause Abram's death.

60 Eliezer said to Abram, Hasten, rise up and save your soul, that you may not die through the hands of the king, for thus did he see in a dream concerning you, and thus did Anuki interpret it, and thus also did Anuki advise the king concerning you.

61 Abram listened to the voice of Eliezer, and Abram hurried and ran for safety to the house of Noah and his son Shem, and he concealed himself there and found a place of safety; and the king's servants came to Abram's house to seek him, but they could not find him, and they searched throughout the country and he was not to be found; they went and searched in every direction and he was not to be met with.

62 And when the king's servants could not find Abram they returned to the king, but the king's anger against Abram was stilled, as they did not find him, and the king drove from his mind this matter concerning Abram.

63 Abram was concealed in Noah's house for one month, until the king had forgotten this matter, but Abram was still afraid of the king; and Terah came to see Abram his son secretly in the house of Noah, and Terah was very great in the eyes of the king.

64 Abram said to his father, Do you not know that the king thinks to kill me, and to annihilate my name from the earth by the advice of his wicked counselors?

65 Now whom have you here and what have you in this land? Arise, let us go together to the land of Canaan, that we may be delivered from his hand, that you not perish also through him in the latter days.

66 Do you not know or have you not heard, that it is not through love that Nimrod gives you all this honor, but it is only for his benefit that he bestows all this good on you?

67 And if he does to you greater good than this, certainly these are only vanities of the world, for wealth and riches cannot avail in the day of wrath and anger.

68 Now therefore listen to my voice, and let us arise and go to the land of Canaan, out of the reach of injury from Nimrod; and serve the Lord who created you in the earth and it will be well with you; and cast away all the vain things which you pursue.

69 And Abram ceased to speak when Noah and his son Shem answered Terah, saying, True is the word which Abram hath said to you.

70 And Terah listened to the voice of his son Abram, and Terah did all that Abram said, for this was from the Lord that the king should not cause Abram's death.

CHAPTER 13

1 Terah took his son Abram and his grandson Lot, the son of Haran, and Sarai his daughter-in-law, the wife of his son Abram, and all the souls of his household and went with them from Ur Casdim to go to the land of Canaan. And when they came as far as the land of Haran they remained there, for it was very good land for pasture, and of sufficient territory for those who accompanied them.

2 And the people of the land of Haran saw that Abram was good and

upright with God and men, and that the Lord his God was with him. Some of the people of the land of Haran came and joined Abram, and he taught them the instruction of the Lord and his ways; these men remained with Abram in his house and they adhered to him.

3 Abram remained in the land three years, and at the expiration of three years the Lord appeared to Abram and said to him; I am the Lord who brought you forth from Ur Casdim, and delivered you from the hands of all your enemies.

4 Now therefore if you will listen to my voice and keep my commandments, my statutes and my laws, I will cause your enemies to fall before you. I will reproduce your descendants like the stars of heaven, and I will send my blessing on all the works of your hands, and you shall lack nothing.

5 Arise now, take your wife and all belonging to you and go to the land of Canaan and remain there. And I, God, will be there for you and I will bless you. And Abram rose and took his wife and all belonging to him, and he went to the land of Canaan as the Lord had told him; and Abram was fifty years old when he went from Haran.

6 Abram came to the land of Canaan and lived in the midst of the city, and there he pitched his tent among the children of Canaan, inhabitants of the land.

7 The Lord appeared to Abram when he came to the land of Canaan, and said to him, This is the land which I gave to you and to your descendants after you forever, and I will make them like the stars of heaven, and I will give to your descendants all the lands which you see for an inheritance.

8 And Abram built an altar in the place where God had spoken to him, and there Abram called on the name of the Lord.

9 At that time, at the end of three years of Abram's dwelling in the land of Canaan, in that year Noah died, which was the fifty-eighth year of the life of Abram; all the days that Noah lived were nine hundred and fifty years and he died.

10 Abram lived in the land of Canaan, he, his wife, and all belonging to him, and all those that accompanied him, together with those that joined him from the people of the land; but Nahor, Abram's brother, and Terah his father, and Lot the son of Haran and all belonging to them lived in Haran.

11 In the fifth year of Abram's dwelling in the land of Canaan the people of Sodom and Gomorrah and all the cities of the plain revolted from the power of Chedorlaomer, king of Elam; for all the kings of the cities of the

plain had served Chedorlaomer for twelve years, and given him a yearly tax, but in those days in the thirteenth year, they rebelled against him.

12 In the tenth year of Abram's dwelling in the land of Canaan there was war between Nimrod king of Shinar and Chedorlaomer king of Elam, and Nimrod came to fight with Chedorlaomer and to subdue him.

13 For Chedorlaomer was at that time one of the princes of the hosts of Nimrod, and when all the people at the tower were dispersed and those that remained were also scattered on the face of the earth, Chedorlaomer went to the land of Elam and reigned over it and rebelled against his lord.

14 In those days when Nimrod saw that the cities of the plain had rebelled, he came with pride and anger to war with Chedorlaomer, and Nimrod assembled all his princes and subjects, about seven hundred thousand men, and went against Chedorlaomer, and Chedorlaomer went out to meet him with five thousand men, and they prepared for battle in the valley of Babel which is between Elam and Shinar.

15 All those kings fought there, and Nimrod and his people were smitten before the people of Chedorlaomer, and there fell from Nimrod's men about six hundred thousand, and Mardon the king's son fell among them.

16 And Nimrod fled and returned in shame and disgrace to his land, and he was under subjection to Chedorlaomer for a long time, and Chedorlaomer returned to his land and sent princes of his host to the kings that lived around him, to Arioch king of Elasar, and to Tidal king of Goyim, and made a covenant with them, and they were all obedient to his commands.

17 It was in the fifteenth year of Abram's dwelling in the land of Canaan, which is the seventieth year of the life of Abram, the Lord appeared to Abram in that year and said to him, I am the Lord who brought you out from Ur Casdim to give you this land for an inheritance.

18 Now therefore walk before me and be perfect and keep my commands, for to you and to your descendants I will give this land for an inheritance, from the river Mitzraim to the great river Euphrates.

19 And you shall come to your fathers in peace and in good age, and the fourth generation shall return here in this land and shall inherit it forever. And Abram built an altar, and he called on the name of the Lord who appeared to him, and he brought up sacrifices on the altar to the Lord.

20 At that time Abram returned and went to Haran to see his father and mother, and his father's household, and Abram and his wife and all belonging to him returned to Haran; Abram lived in Haran five years.

21 And many of the people of Haran, about seventy-two men, followed Abram and Abram taught them the instruction of the Lord and his ways, and he taught them to know the Lord.

22 In those days the Lord appeared to Abram in Haran, and he said to him, Behold, I spoke to you twenty years ago saying,

23 Go forth from your land, from your birth-place and from your father's house, to the land which I have shown you to give it to you and to your children, for there in that land I will bless you, and make you a great nation, and make your name great, and in you shall the families of the earth be blessed.

24 Now therefore arise, go forth from this place, you, your wife, and all belonging to you, also every one born in your house and all the souls you have made in Haran, and bring them out with you from here, and rise to return to the land of Canaan.

25 And Abram arose and took his wife Sarai and all belonging to him and all that were born to him in his house and the souls which they had made in Haran, and they came out to go to the land of Canaan.

26 Abram went and returned to the land of Canaan, according to the word of the Lord. And Lot the son of his brother Haran went with him; Abram was seventy-five years old when he went forth from Haran to return to the land of Canaan.

27 And he came to the land of Canaan according to the word of the Lord to Abram, and he pitched his tent and he lived in the plain of Mamre, and with him was Lot his brother's son, and all belonging to him.

28 And the Lord again appeared to Abram and said, To your offspring I will give this land; there he built an altar to the Lord who appeared to him, which is still to this day in the plains of Mamre.

CHAPTER 14

1 In those days there was in the land of Shinar a wise man who had understanding in all wisdom, and of a beautiful appearance, but he was poor and indigent; his name was Rikayon and he was hard set to support himself.

2 And he resolved to go to Egypt, to Oswiris the son of Anom king of Egypt, to show the king his wisdom; for perhaps he might find grace in his

sight, to raise him up and give him maintenance; and Rikayon did so.

3 When Rikayon came to Egypt he asked the inhabitants of Egypt concerning the king, and the inhabitants of Egypt told him the custom of the king of Egypt, for it was then the custom of the king of Egypt that he went from his royal palace and was seen abroad only one day in the year, and after that the king would return to his palace to remain there.

4 On the day when the king went forth he passed judgment in the land, and every one having a suit came before the king that day to obtain his request.

5 When Rikayon heard of the custom in Egypt and that he could not come into the presence of the king, he grieved greatly and was very sorrowful.

6 In the evening Rikayon went out and found a house in ruins, formerly a bake house in Egypt, and he abode there all night in bitterness of soul and pinched with hunger, and sleep was removed from his eyes.

7 And Rikayon considered within himself what he should do in the town until the king made his appearance, and how he might maintain himself there.

8 And he rose in the morning and walked about, and met in his way those who sold vegetables and various sorts of offspring with which they supplied the inhabitants.

9 Rikayon wished to do the same in order to get a maintenance in the city, but he was unacquainted with the custom of the people, and he was like a blind man among them.

10 And he went and obtained vegetables to sell for his support, and the crowd assembled about him and ridiculed him, and took his vegetables from him and left him nothing.

11 He rose up from there in bitterness of soul, and went sighing to the bake house in which he had remained all the night before, and he slept there the second night.

12 On that night again he reasoned within himself how he could save himself from starvation, and he devised a scheme how to act.

13 And he rose up in the morning and acted ingeniously, and went and hired thirty strong men of the crowd, carrying their war instruments in their hands, and he led them to the top of the Egyptian sepulchre, and he placed them there.

14 He commanded them, saying, Thus says the king, Strengthen yourselves and be valiant men, and let no man be buried here until two

hundred pieces of silver be given, and then he may be buried; and those men did according to the order of Rikayon to the people of Egypt the whole of that year.

15 In eight months time Rikayon and his men gathered great riches of silver and gold, and Rikayon took a great quantity of horses and other animals, and he hired more men, and he gave them horses and they remained with him.

16 When the year came round, at the time the king went forth into the town, all the inhabitants of Egypt assembled together to speak to him concerning the work of Rikayon and his men.

17 The king went forth on the appointed day, and all the Egyptians came before him and cried to him, saying,

18 May the king live forever. What is this thing you do in the town to your servants, not to allow a dead body buried until so much silver and gold be given? Was there ever the like to this done in the whole earth, from the days of former kings, yes even from the days of Adam, to this day, that the dead should be buried only for a set price?

19 We know it to be the custom of kings to take a yearly tax from the living, but you do not only do this, but from the dead also you exact a tax day by day.

20 Now, O king, we can no more bear this, for the whole city is ruined on this account, and do you not know it?

21 When the king heard all that they had spoken he was very angry, and his anger burned within him at this affair, for he had known nothing of it.

22 And the king said, Who and where is he that dares to do this wicked thing in my land without my command? Certainly you will tell me.

23 They told him all the works of Rikayon and his men, and the king's anger was aroused, and he ordered Rikayon and his men to be brought before him.

24 And Rikayon took about a thousand children, sons and daughters, and clothed them in silk and embroidery, and he set them on horses and sent them to the king by means of his men, and he also took a great quantity of silver and gold and precious stones, and a strong and beautiful horse, as a present for the king, with which he came before the king and bowed down to the earth before him; the king, his servants and all the inhabitants of Egypt wondered at the work of Rikayon; they saw his riches and the presents that he had brought to the king.

25 It greatly pleased the king and he wondered at it; and when Rikayon

sat before him the king asked him concerning all his works, and Rikayon spoke all his words wisely before the king, his servants and all the inhabitants of Egypt.

26 When the king heard the words of Rikayon and his wisdom, Rikayon found grace in his sight, and he met with grace and kindness from all the servants of the king and from all the inhabitants of Egypt, on account of his wisdom and excellent speeches, and from that time they loved him greatly.

27 And the king answered and said to Rikayon, Thy name shall no more be called Rikayon but Pharaoh shall be your name, since you did exact a tax from the dead; and he called his name Pharaoh.

28 The king and his subjects loved Rikayon for his wisdom, and they consulted with all the inhabitants of Egypt to make him prefect under the king.

29 All the inhabitants of Egypt and its wise men did so, and it was made a law in Egypt.

30 They made Rikayon Pharaoh prefect under Oswiris king of Egypt, and Rikayon Pharaoh governed over Egypt, daily administering justice to the whole city, but Oswiris the king would judge the people of the land one day in the year, when he went out to make his appearance.

31 And Rikayon Pharaoh cunningly usurped the government of Egypt, and he exacted a tax from all the inhabitants of Egypt.

32 And all the inhabitants of Egypt greatly loved Rikayon Pharaoh, and they made a decree to call every king that should reign over them and their descendants in Egypt, Pharaoh.

33 Therefore all the kings that reigned in Egypt from that time forward were called Pharaoh to this day.

CHAPTER 15

1 In that year there was a heavy famine throughout the land of Canaan, and the inhabitants of the land could not remain on account of the famine for it was very severe.

2 Abram and all belonging to him rose and went down to Egypt on account of the famine, and when they were at the brook Mitzraim they

remained there some time to rest from the fatigue of the road.

3 Abram and Sarai were walking at the border of the brook Mitzraim, and Abram beheld his wife Sarai that she was very beautiful.

4 And Abram said to his wife Sarai, Since God has created you with such a beautiful countenance, I am afraid of the Egyptians that they will kill me and take you away, for the fear of God is not in these places.

5 Certainly then you shall do this, Say you are my sister to all that may ask you, in order that it may be well with me, and that we may live and not be put to death.

6 And Abram commanded the same to all those that came with him to Egypt on account of the famine; also his nephew Lot he commanded, saying, If the Egyptians ask you concerning Sarai say she is the sister of Abram.

7 And yet with all these orders Abram did not put confidence in them, but he took Sarai and placed her in a chest and concealed it among their vessels, for Abram was greatly concerned about Sarai on account of the wickedness of the Egyptians.

8 Abram and all belonging to him rose up from the brook Mitzraim and came to Egypt; and they had scarcely entered the gates of the city when the guards stood up to them saying, Give tithe to the king from what you have, and then you may come into the town; Abram and those that were with him did so.

9 Abram and the people that were with him came to Egypt and they brought the chest in which Sarai was concealed, and the Egyptians saw the chest.

10 And the king's servants approached Abram, saying, What have you here in this chest which we have not seen? Now open the chest and give tithe to the king of all that it contains.

11 Abram said, This chest I will not open, but all you demand on it I will give. And Pharaoh's officers answered Abram, saying, It is a chest of precious stones, give us the tenth of its value.

12 Abram said, All that you desire I will give, but you must not open the chest.

13 And the king's officers pressed Abram; they reached the chest and opened it with force, and they saw a beautiful woman was in the chest.

14 When the officers of the king saw Sarai they were struck with admiration at her beauty, and all the princes and servants of Pharaoh assembled to see Sarai, for she was very beautiful. The king's officers ran

and told Pharaoh all that they had seen, and they praised Sarai to the king; Pharaoh ordered her to be brought, and the woman came before the king.

15 Pharaoh observed Sarai and she pleased him greatly, and he was struck with her beauty; the king rejoiced greatly on her account, and made presents to those who brought him the news concerning her.

16 The woman was then brought to Pharaoh's house, and Abram grieved on account of his wife; he prayed to the Lord to deliver her from the hands of Pharaoh.

17 And Sarai also prayed at that time and said, O Lord God you did tell my Lord Abram to go from his land and from his father's house to the land of Canaan, and you did promise to do well with him if he would perform your commands; now behold we have done that which you commanded us; we left our land and our families, and we went to a strange land and to a people whom we have not known before.

18 We came to this land to avoid the famine, and this evil accident has befallen me; now therefore, O Lord God, deliver us and save us from the hand of this oppressor, and do well with me for the sake of your mercy.

19 The Lord listened to the voice of Sarai, and the Lord sent an angel to deliver Sarai from the power of Pharaoh.

20 The king came and sat before Sarai and behold an angel of the Lord was standing over them, and he appeared to Sarai and said to her, Do not fear, for the Lord has heard your prayer.

21 The king approached Sarai and said to her, What is that man to you who brought you here? and she said, He is my brother.

22 The king said, It is incumbent on us to make him great, to elevate him and to do to him all the good which you shall command us. At that time the king sent to Abram silver and gold and precious stones in abundance, together with cattle, men servants and maid servants; and the king ordered Abram to be brought and he sat in the court of the king's house, and the king greatly exalted Abram on that night.

23 The king approached to speak to Sarai and he reached out his hand to touch her when the angel struck him heavily; he was terrified and he refrained from reaching to her.

24 And when the king came near to Sarai, the angel struck him to the ground, and acted thus to him the whole night, and the king was terrified.

25 The angel on that night struck heavily all the servants of the king, and his whole household, on account of Sarai, and there was a great

lamentation that night among the people of Pharaoh's house.

26 And Pharaoh, seeing the evil that befell him, said, Certainly on account of this woman has this thing happened to me, and he removed himself at some distance from her and spoke pleasing words to her.

27 The king said to Sarai, Tell me I pray you concerning the man with whom you came here; and Sarai said, This man is my husband, and I said to you that he was my brother for I was afraid that you would put him to death through wickedness.

28 And the king kept away from Sarai, and the plagues of the angel of the Lord ceased from him and his household; Pharaoh knew that he was smitten on account of Sarai, and the king was greatly astonished at this.

29 In the morning the king called for Abram and said to him, What is this you have done to me? Why did you say, She is my sister, since I wanted to take her as a wife, and this heavy plague has therefore come on me and my household.

30 Now therefore here is your wife, take her and go from our land so we don't all die on her account. And Pharaoh took more cattle, men servants and maid servants, and silver and gold, to give to Abram, and he returned to him Sarai his wife.

31 And the king took a maiden whom he had by his concubines, and he gave her to Sarai for a handmaid.

32 The king said to his daughter, It is better for you my daughter to be a handmaid in this man's house than to be mistress in my house, after we have seen the evil that came upon us on account of this woman.

33 Abram arose, and he and all belonging to him went away from Egypt; and Pharaoh ordered some of his men to accompany him and all that went with him.

34 And Abram returned to the land of Canaan, to the place where he had made the altar, where he at first had pitched his tent.

35 Lot the son of Haran, Abram's brother, had a heavy stock of cattle, flocks and herds and tents, for the Lord was bountiful to them on account of Abram.

36 When Abram was dwelling in the land the herdsmen of Lot quarrelled with the herdsmen of Abram, for their property was too great for them to remain together in the land, and the land could not bear them on account of their cattle.

37 When Abram's herdsmen went to feed their flock they would not go into the fields of the people of the land, but the cattle of Lot's herdsmen

did otherwise, for they were allowed to feed in the fields of the people of the land.

38 And the people of the land saw this occurrence daily, and they came to Abram and quarrelled with him on account of Lot's herdsmen.

39 And Abram said to Lot, What is this you are doing to me, to make me despicable to the inhabitants of the land, that you ordered your herdsman to feed your cattle in the fields of other people? Do you not know that I am a stranger in this land among the children of Canaan, and why will you do this to me?

40 Abram quarrelled daily with Lot on account of this, but Lot would not listen to Abram; he continued to do the same and the inhabitants of the land came and told Abram.

41 And Abram said to Lot, How long will you be to me a stumbling block with the inhabitants of the land? Now I petition you let there be no more quarrelling between us, for we are kinsmen.

42 I request you to separate from me, go and choose a place where you may dwell with your cattle and all belonging to you, but keep yourself at a distance from me, you and your household.

43 And don't be afraid in going from me, for if any one does an injury to you, let me know and I will avenge your cause from him, only remove from me.

44 When Abram had spoken all these words to Lot, then Lot arose and lifted up his eyes toward the plain of Jordan.

45 And he saw that all of this place was well watered, and good for man as well as affording pasture for the cattle.

46 Lot went from Abram to that place, and he there pitched his tent and he lived in Sodom, and they were separated from each other.

47 And Abram lived in the plain of Mamre, which is in Hebron, and he pitched his tent there, and Abram remained in that place many years.

CHAPTER 16

1 At that time Chedorlaomer king of Elam sent to all the neighboring kings, to Nimrod, king of Shinar who was then under his power, and to

Tidal, king of Goyim, and to Arioch, king of Elasar, with whom he made a covenant, saying, Come up to me and assist me, that we may strike all the towns of Sodom and its inhabitants, for they have rebelled against me these thirteen years.

2 These four kings went up with all their camps, about eight hundred thousand men, and they went as they were, and struck every man they found in their road.

3 And the five kings of Sodom and Gomorrah, Shinab king of Admah, Shemeber king of Zeboyim, Bera king of Sodom, Bersha king of Gomorrah, and Bela king of Zoar, went out to meet them, and they all joined together in the valley of Siddim.

4 These nine kings made war in the valley of Siddim; and the kings of Sodom and Gomorrah were smitten before the kings of Elam.

5 The valley of Siddim was full of lime pits and the kings of Elam pursued the kings of Sodom, and the kings of Sodom with their camps fled and fell into the lime pits; all that remained went to the mountain for safety. The five kings of Elam came after them and pursued them to the gates of Sodom, and they took all that there was in Sodom.

6 They plundered all the cities of Sodom and Gomorrah, and they also took Lot, Abram's brother's son, and his property; they seized all the goods of the cities of Sodom, and they went away. Unic, Abram's servant, who was in the battle, saw this, and told Abram all that the kings had done to the cities of Sodom, and that Lot was taken captive by them.

7 Abram heard this, and he rose up with about three hundred and eighteen men that were with him, and that night he pursued these kings and struck them; they all fell before Abram and his men, and there was none remaining but the four kings who fled, and they each went his own road.

8 Abram recovered all the property of Sodom, and he also recovered Lot and his property, his wives and little ones and all belonging to him, so that Lot lacked nothing.

9 And when he returned from smiting these kings, he and his men passed the valley of Siddim where the kings had made war together.

10 Bera king of Sodom, and the rest of his men that were with him, went out from the lime pits into which they had fallen, to meet Abram and his men.

11 And Adonizedek king of Jerusalem, the same was Shem, went out with his men to meet Abram and his people, with bread and wine, and they remained together in the valley of Melech.

12 Adonizedek blessed Abram, and Abram gave him a tenth from all that he had brought from the spoil of his enemies, for Adonizedek was a priest before God.

13 And all the kings of Sodom and Gomorrah who were there, with their servants, approached Abram and begged him to return their servants whom he had made captive, and to take to himself all the property.

14 Abram answered the kings of Sodom, saying, As the Lord lives who created heaven and earth, and who redeemed my soul from all affliction, and who delivered me this day from my enemies and gave them into my hand, I will not take anything belonging to you, that you may not boast tomorrow, saying, Abram became rich from our property that he saved.

15 For the Lord my God in whom I trust said to me, You shall lack nothing, for I will bless you in all the works of your hands.

16 Now here is all belonging to you, take it and go; as the Lord lives I will not take from a living soul down to a shoetie or thread, excepting the expense of the food of those who went out with me to battle, as also the portions of the men who went with me, Anar, Ashcol, and Mamre, they and their men, as well as those also who had remained to watch the baggage, they shall take their portion of the spoil.

17 And the kings of Sodom gave Abram according to all that he had said; they pressed him to take of whatever he chose, but he would not.

18 He sent away the kings of Sodom and the remainder of their men, and he gave them orders about Lot, and they went to their respective places.

19 And Lot, his brother's son, he also sent away with his property, and he went with them, and Lot returned to his home, to Sodom, and Abram and his people returned to their home to the plains of Mamre, which is in Hebron.

20 At that time the Lord again appeared to Abram in Hebron, and he said to him, Do not fear, your reward is very great before me, for I will not leave you until I shall have multiplied you and blessed you and made your offspring like the stars in heaven, which cannot be measured nor numbered.

21 And I will give to your descendants all these lands that you see with your eyes, I will give them for an inheritance forever, only be strong and do not fear, walk before me and be perfect.

22 In the seventy-eighth year of the life of Abram, in that year Reu died, the son of Peleg, and all the days of Reu were two hundred and thirty-nine years, and he died.

23 And Sarai, the daughter of Haran, Abram's wife, was still unable to conceive in those days; she did not bear to Abram either son or daughter.

24 When she saw that she gave birth to no children she took her handmaid Hagar, whom Pharaoh had given her, and she gave her to Abram her husband for a wife.

25 For Hagar learned all the ways of Sarai as Sarai taught her; she was not in any way deficient in following her good ways.

26 Sarai said to Abram, Behold here is my handmaid Hagar, go to her that she may bring forth on my knees, that I may also obtain children through her.

27 At the end of ten years of Abram's dwelling in the land of Canaan, which is the eighty-fifth year of Abram's life, Sarai gave Hagar to him.

28 And Abram listened to the voice of his wife Sarai; he took his handmaid Hagar and Abram came to her and she conceived.

29 When Hagar saw that she had conceived she rejoiced greatly, and her mistress was despised in her eyes; she said within herself, This can only be that I am better before God than Sarai my mistress, for all the days that my mistress has been with my lord, she did not conceive, but me the Lord has caused in so short a time to conceive by him.

30 And when Sarai saw that Hagar had conceived by Abram, Sarai was jealous of her handmaid, and Sarai said within herself, This is certainly nothing else but that she must be better than I am.

31 Sarai said to Abram, My wrong be on you, for at the time when you prayed before the Lord for children why did you not pray on my account, that the Lord should give me offspring from you?

32 When I speak to Hagar in your presence she hates my word because she has conceived so you will say nothing to her; may the Lord judge between me and you for what you have done to me.

33 And Abram said to Sarai, Behold your handmaid is in your hand, do to her as it may seem good in your eyes; and Sarai afflicted her, and Hagar fled from her to the wilderness.

34 An angel of the Lord found her in the place where she had fled, by a well, and he said to her, Do not fear, for I will reproduce your offspring, for you shall bear a son and you shall call his name Ishmael; now then return to Sarai your mistress, and submit yourself under her hands.

35 And Hagar called the place of that well Beer-lahai-roi; it is between Kadesh and the wilderness of Bered.

36 And Hagar at that time returned to her master's house, and at the end of days Hagar gave birth to a son to Abram, and Abram called his name Ishmael; and Abram was eighty-six years old when he had him.

CHAPTER 17

1 In those days, in the ninety-first year of the life of Abram, the children of Chittim made war with the children of Tubal, for when the Lord had scattered the sons of men on the face of the earth, the children of Chittim went and settled in the plain of Canopia, and they built themselves cities there and lived by the river Tibreu.

2 The children of Tubal lived in Tuscanah, and their boundaries reached the river Tibreu, and the children of Tubal built a city in Tuscanan, and they called the name Sabinah, after the name of Sabinah son of Tubal their father, and they lived there to this day.

3 It was at that time the children of Chittim made war with the children of Tubal, and the children of Tubal were smitten before the children of Chittim; the children of Chittim caused three hundred and seventy men to fall from the children of Tubal.

4 At that time the children of Tubal swore to the children of Chittim, saying, You shall not intermarry among us, and no man shall give his daughter to any of the sons of Chittim.

5 For all the daughters of Tubal were in those days fair, for no women were then found in the whole earth so fair as the daughters of Tubal.

6 And all who delighted in the beauty of women went to the daughters of Tubal and took wives from them, and the sons of men, kings and princes, who greatly delighted in the beauty of women, took wives in those days from the daughters of Tubal.

7 At the end of three years after the children of Tubal had sworn to the children of Chittim not to give them their daughters for wives, about twenty men of the children of Chittim went to take some of the daughters of Tubal, but they found none.

8 For the children of Tubal kept their oaths not to intermarry with them, and they would not break their oaths.

9 In the days of harvest the children of Tubal went into their fields to get in their harvest, when the young men of Chittim assembled and went to the city of Sabinah, and each man took a young woman from the

daughters of Tubal, and they came to their cities.

10 And the children of Tubal heard of it and they went to make war with them; they could not prevail over them, for the mountain was very high; when they saw they could not prevail over them they returned to their land.

11 And at the revolution of the year the children of Tubal went and hired about ten thousand men from those cities that were near them, and they went to war with the children of Chittim.

12 And the children of Tubal went to war with the children of Chittim, to destroy their land and to distress them. In this engagement the children of Tubal prevailed over the children of Chittim, and the children of Chittim, seeing that they were greatly distressed, lifted up the children which they had had by the daughters of Tubal, on the wall which had been built, to be before the eyes of the children of Tubal.

13 And the children of Chittim said to them, Have you come to make war with your own sons and daughters, and have we not been considered your flesh and bones from that time till now?

14 When the children of Tubal heard this they ceased to make war with the children of Chittim, and they went away.

15 They returned to their cities and the children of Chittim at that time assembled and built two cities by the sea; they called one Purtu and the other Ariza.

16 And Abram the son of Terah was then ninety-nine years old.

17 At that time the Lord appeared to him and said, I will make my covenant between me and you, and I will greatly reproduce your offspring, and this is the covenant which I make between me and you, that every male child be circumcised, you and your descendants after you.

18 At eight days old shall it be circumcised, and this covenant shall be in your flesh for an everlasting covenant.

19 And now therefore your name shall no more be called Abram but Abraham, and your wife shall no more be called Sarai but Sarah.

20 For I will bless you both, and I will reproduce your descendants, that you shall become a great nation, and kings shall come forth from you.

CHAPTER 18

1 Abraham rose and did all that God had ordered him; he took the men of his household and those bought with his money, and he circumcised them as the Lord had commanded him.

2 There was not one left whom he did not circumcise, and Abraham and his son Ishmael were circumcised in the flesh of their foreskin; Ishmael was thirteen years old when he was circumcised in the flesh of his foreskin.

3 And in the third day Abraham went out of his tent and sat at the door to enjoy the heat of the sun, during the pain of his flesh.

4 The Lord appeared to him in the plain of Mamre and sent three of his ministering angels to visit him, and he was sitting at the door of the tent. He lifted his eyes and saw three men were coming from a distance; he rose up and ran to meet them, and he bowed down to them and brought them into his house.

5 And he said to them, If now I have found favor in your sight, turn in and eat a morsel of bread. He urged them, they turned in and he gave them water and they washed their feet, and he placed them under a tree at the door of the tent.

6 Abraham ran and took a calf, tender and good, and he hurried to kill it, and gave it to his servant Eliezer to dress.

7 And Abraham came to Sarah into the tent, and said to her, Make ready quickly three measures of fine meal, knead it and make cakes to cover the pot containing the meat, and she did so.

8 Abraham hurried and brought before them butter and milk, beef and mutton, and put it before them to eat, before the flesh of the calf was sufficiently done, and they ate.

9 When they were done eating one of them said to him, I will return to you according to the time of life, and Sarah your wife shall have a son.

10 And the men afterward departed and went their ways, to the places to which they were sent.

11 In those days all the people of Sodom and Gomorrah, and of the whole five cities, were greatly wicked and sinful against the Lord. They provoked the Lord with their abominations, and they grew worse as they aged abominably and scornfully before the Lord, and their wickedness and crimes were in those days great before the Lord.

12 They had in their land a very extensive valley, about half a day's walk,

and in it there were fountains of water and a great deal of herbage surrounding the water.

13 All the people of Sodom and Gomorrah went there four times a year, with their wives and children and all belonging to them, and they rejoiced there with timbrels and dances.

14 In the time of rejoicing they would all rise and lay hold of their neighbor's wives, and some, the virgin daughters of their neighbors, and they enjoyed them; each man saw his wife and daughter in the hands of his neighbor and did not say a word.

15 And they did so from morning to night; afterward they returned home each man to his house and each woman to her tent; so they always did four times in the year.

16 Also when a stranger came into their cities and brought goods which he had purchased with a view to dispose of there, the people of these cities would assemble, men, women and children, young and old, and go to the man and take his goods by force, giving a little to each man until there was an end to all the goods of the owner which he had brought into the land.

17 And if the owner of the goods quarreled with them, saying, What is this work which you have done to me, then they would approach him one by one, and each would show him the little which he took and taunt him, saying, I only took that little which you did give me; when he heard this from them all, he would arise and go from them in sorrow and bitterness of soul. Then they would all arise and go after him, and drive him out of the city with great noise and tumult.

18 There was a man from the country of Elam who was leisurely going on the road, seated on his ass, which carried a fine mantle of varied colors, and the mantle was bound with a cord on the ass.

19 The man was on his journey passing through the street of Sodom when the sun set in the evening; he remained there in order to abide during the night, but no one would let him into his house. At that time there was in Sodom a wicked and mischievous man, one skillful to do evil, and his name was Hedad.

20 And he lifted up his eyes and saw the traveler in the street of the city, and he came to him and said, Whence come you and where do you go?

21 The man said to him, I am traveling from Hebron to Elam where I belong, and as I passed the sun set and no one would invite me to enter his house; you have bread and water and also straw and feed for my ass, and I am short of nothing.

22 And Hedad answered and said to him, All that you shall want shall be

supplied by me, but in the street you shall not abide all night.

23 Hedad brought him to his house, and he took off the mantle from the ass with the cord, and brought them to his house. He gave the ass straw and feed while the traveler ate and drank in Hedad's house, and he abode there that night.

24 And in the morning the traveler rose up early to continue his journey, when Hedad said to him, Wait, comfort your heart with a morsel of bread and then go, and the man did so; and he remained with him, and they both ate and drank together during the day, then the man rose up to go.

25 And Hedad said to him, Behold now the day is declining, you had better remain all night that your heart may be comforted; and he pressed him so that he tarried there all night, and on the second day he rose up early to go away, when Hedad pressed him, saying, Comfort your heart with a morsel of bread and then go, and he remained and ate with him also the second day. Then the man rose up to continue his journey.

26 And Hedad said to him, Behold now the day is declining, remain with me to comfort your heart and in the morning rise up early and go your way.

27 The man would not remain, but rose and saddled his ass, and while he was saddling his ass the wife of Hedad said to her husband, Behold this man has remained with us for two days eating and drinking and he has given us nothing, and now shall he go away from us without giving anything? Hedad said to her, Be silent.

28 And the man saddled his ass to go, and he asked Hedad to give him the cord and mantle to tie it on the ass.

29 And Hedad said to him, What do you say? And he said to him, That you my lord shall give me the cord and the mantle made with varied colors which you concealed in your house to take care of it.

30 And Hedad answered the man, saying, This is the interpretation of your dream, the cord which you did see means that your life will be lengthened out like a cord, and having seen the mantle colored with all sorts of colors, means that you shall have a vineyard in which you will plant trees of all fruits.

31 And the traveler answered, saying, Not so my lord, for I was awake when I gave you the cord and also a mantle woven with different colors, which you took off the ass to put by for me; and Hedad answered and said, Certainly I have told you the interpretation of your dream and it is a good dream, and this is the interpretation of it.

32 Now the sons of men give me four pieces of silver, which is my charge for interpreting dreams, and of you only I require three pieces of silver.

33 And the man was provoked at the words of Hedad, and he cried bitterly, and he brought Hedad to Serak judge of Sodom.

34 And the man laid his cause before Serak the judge, when Hedad replied, saying, It is not so, but thus the matter stands. And the judge said to the traveler, This man Hedad tells you truth, for he is famed in the cities for the accurate interpretation of dreams.

35 And the man cried at the word of the judge, and he said, Not so my Lord, for it was in the day that I gave him the cord and mantle which was on the ass, in order to put them by in his house; they both disputed before the judge, the one saying, Thus the matter was, and the other declaring otherwise.

36 Hedad said to the man, Give me four pieces of silver that I charge for my interpretations of dreams; I will not make any allowance; give me the expense of the four meals that you ate in my house.

37 And the man said to Hedad, Truly I will pay you for what I ate in your house, only give me the cord and mantle which you did conceal in your house.

38 Hedad replied before the judge and said to the man, Did I not tell you the interpretation of your dream? The cord means that your days shall be prolonged like a cord, and the mantle, that you will have a vineyard in which you will plant all kinds of fruit trees.

39 This is the proper interpretation of your dream, now give me the four pieces of silver that I require as a compensation, for I will make you no allowance.

40 And the man cried at the words of Hedad and they both quarreled before the judge; the judge gave orders to his servants, who drove them rashly from the house.

41 And they went away quarreling from the judge. When the people of Sodom heard them, they gathered about them and spoke harshly against the stranger, and they drove him rashly from the city.

42 And the man continued his journey on his ass with bitterness of soul, lamenting and weeping.

43 And while he was on his way he wept at what had happened to him in the corrupt city of Sodom.

CHAPTER 19

1 The cities of Sodom had four judges to four cities, and these were their names, Serak in the city of Sodom, Sharkad in Gomorrah, Zabnac in Admah, and Menon in Zeboyim.

2 Eliezer Abraham's servant applied to them different names, and he converted Serak to Shakra, Sharkad to Shakrura, Zebnac to Kezobim, and Menon to Matzlodin.

3 By desire of their four judges the people of Sodom and Gomorrah had beds erected in the streets of the cities and if a man came to these places, they laid hold of him and brought him to one of their beds and by force made him to lie in them.

4 As he lay down, three men would stand at his head and three at his feet, and measure him by the length of the bed; if the man was less than the bed, these six men would stretch him at each end, and when he cried out to them they would not answer him.

5 If he was longer than the bed, they would draw together the two sides of the bed at each end, until the man had reached the gates of death.

6 And if he continued to cry out to them, they would answer him, saying, Thus it shall be done to a man that comes into our land.

7 When men heard all these things that the people of the cities of Sodom did, they refrained from coming there.

8 And when a poor man came to their land they would give him silver and gold, and cause a proclamation in the whole city not to give him a morsel of bread to eat. If the stranger should remain there some days and die from hunger, not having been able to obtain a morsel of bread, then at his death all the people of the city would come and take their silver and gold which they had given to him.

9 Those that could recognize the silver or gold which they had given him took it back, and at his death they also stripped him of his garments, and they would fight about them; he that prevailed over his neighbor took them.

10 After that they would carry him and bury him under some of the shrubs in the desert; so they did all the days to any one that came to them and died in their land.

11 And in the course of time Sarah sent Eliezer to Sodom, to see Lot and inquire after his welfare.

12 Eliezer went to Sodom, and he met a man of Sodom fighting with a stranger, and the man of Sodom stripped the poor man of all his clothes and went away.

13 And this poor man cried to Eliezer and begged his favor on account of what the man of Sodom had done to him.

14 He said to him, Why do you act thus to the poor man who came to your land?

15 The man of Sodom answered Eliezer, saying, Is this man your brother, or have the people of Sodom made you a judge this day, that you speak about this man?

16 Eliezer strove with the man of Sodom on account of the poor man, and when Eliezer approached to recover the poor man's clothes from the man of Sodom, he hurried and with a stone struck Eliezer in the forehead.

17 The blood flowed copiously from Eliezer's forehead, and when the man saw the blood he caught hold of Eliezer, saying, Give me my wage for having rid you of this bad blood that was in your forehead, for such is the custom and the law in our land.

18 And Eliezer said to him, You have wounded me and require me to pay you your wage? Eliezer would not listen to the words of the man of Sodom.

19 And the man laid hold of Eliezer and brought him to Shakra the judge of Sodom for judgment.

20 The man spoke to the judge, saying, I beseech you my lord, thus has this man done, for I struck him with a stone that the blood flowed from his forehead, and he is unwilling to give me my wage.

21 And the judge said to Eliezer, This man speaks truth to you, give him his wage, for this is the custom in our land. Eliezer heard the words of the judge, and he lifted up a stone and struck the judge; the stone struck on his forehead, and the blood flowed copiously from the forehead of the judge, and Eliezer said, If this then is the custom in your land give to this man what I should have given him, for this has been your decision; you did decree it.

22 And Eliezer left the man of Sodom with the judge, and he went away.

23 When the kings of Elam had made war with the kings of Sodom, the kings of Elam captured all the property of Sodom and they took Lot captive with his property, and when it was told to Abraham he went and

made war with the kings of Elam. He recovered from their hands all the property of Lot as well as the property of Sodom.

24 At that time the wife of Lot gave birth to a daughter, and he called her name Paltith, saying, Because God had delivered him and his whole household from the kings of Elam. Paltith daughter of Lot grew up, and one of the men of Sodom took her for a wife.

25 And a poor man came into the city to seek a maintenance, and he remained in the city some days, and all the people of Sodom caused a proclamation of their custom not to give this man a morsel of bread to eat until he dropped dead on the earth, and they did so.

26 And Paltith the daughter of Lot saw this man lying in the streets starved with hunger and no one would give him any thing to keep him alive; he was just on the point of death.

27 And her soul was filled with pity on account of the man and she fed him secretly with bread for many days, and the soul of this man was revived.

28 For when she went forth to fetch water she would put the bread in the water pitcher, and when she came to the place where the poor man was, she took the bread from the pitcher and gave it him to eat; so she did many days.

29 And all the people of Sodom and Gomorrah wondered how this man could bear starvation for so many days.

30 And they said to each other, This can only be because he eats and drinks, for no man can bear starvation for so many days or live as this man has, without even his countenance changing. Three men concealed themselves in a place where the poor man was stationed to know who it was that brought him bread to eat.

31 Paltith daughter of Lot went forth that day to fetch water and she put bread into her pitcher of water; she went to draw water by the poor man's place and took out the bread from the pitcher and gave it to the poor man and he ate it.

32 And the three men saw what Paltith did to the poor man, and they said to her, It is you then who have supported him, and therefore he has not starved, nor changed in appearance nor died like the rest.

33 The three men went out of the place in which they were concealed, and they seized Paltith and the bread which was in the poor man's hand.

34 They took Paltith and brought her before their judges, and they said to

them, Thus did she do, and it is she who supplied the poor man with bread, therefore he did not die all this time; now therefore declare to us the punishment due to this woman for having gone contrary to our law.

35 And the people of Sodom and Gomorrah assembled and set ablaze a fire in the street of the city, and they took the woman and cast her into the fire and she was burned to ashes.

36 In the city of Admah there was a woman to whom they did the same.

37 For a traveler came into the city of Admah to stay there all night, with the intention of going home in the morning. He sat opposite the door of the house of the young woman's father, to remain there, as the sun had set when he had reached that place; the young woman saw him sitting by the door of the house.

38 He asked her for a drink of water and she said to him, Who art you? And he said to her, I was this day going on the road, and reached here when the sun set, so I will stay here all night, and in the morning I will arise early and continue my journey.

39 And the young woman went into the house and fetched the man bread and water to eat and drink.

40 This affair became known to the people of Admah, and they assembled and brought the young woman before the judges, that they should judge her for this act.

41 And the judge said, The judgment of death must pass on this woman because she went contrary to our law, and this therefore is the decision concerning her.

42 The people of those cities assembled and brought out the young woman, and anointed her with honey from head to foot, as the judge had decreed, and they placed her before a swarm of bees which were then in their hives, and the bees flew on her and stung her that her whole body was swelled.

43 The young woman cried out on account of the bees, but no one took notice of her or pitied her, and her cries ascended to heaven.

44 And the Lord was provoked at this and at all the works of the cities of Sodom, for they had abundance of food, and had tranquility among them, and still would not sustain the poor and the needy. In those days their evil doings and sins became great before the Lord.

45 The Lord sent for two of the angels that had come to Abraham's house, to destroy Sodom and its cities.

46 And the angels rose up from the door of Abraham's tent, after they had

eaten and drunk, and they reached Sodom in the evening, and Lot was then sitting in the gate of Sodom. When he saw them he rose to meet them, and he bowed down to the ground.

47 He welcomed them greatly and brought them into his house, and he gave them food which they ate, and they stayed all night in his house.

48 And the angels said to Lot, Arise, go forth from this place, you and all belonging to you, that you not be consumed in the iniquity of this city, for the Lord will destroy this place.

49 The angels laid hold on the hand of Lot and on the hand of his wife, and on the hands of his children, and all belonging to him, and they brought him forth and set him outside of the cities.

50 And they said to Lot, Escape for your life. He fled and all belonging to him.

51 Then the Lord rained on Sodom and on Gomorrah and on all these cities brimstone and fire from the Lord out of heaven.

52 And he overthrew these cities, all the plain and all the inhabitants of the cities, and that which grew on the ground; Ado the wife of Lot looked back to see the destruction of the cities, for her compassion was moved on account of her daughters who remained in Sodom, for they did not go with her.

53 And when she looked back she became a pillar of salt, and it is yet in that place to this day.

54 The oxen which stood in that place daily licked up the salt to the extremities of their feet, and in the morning it would spring forth afresh, and they again licked it up to this day.

55 Lot and two of his daughters that remained with him fled and escaped to the cave of Adullam, and they remained there for some time.

56 And Abraham rose up early in the morning to see what had been done to the cities of Sodom; and he looked and beheld the smoke of the cities going up like the smoke of a furnace.

57 Lot and his two daughters remained in the cave, and they made their father drink wine, and they lay with him, for they said there was no man on earth that could produce descendants from them, for they thought that the whole earth was destroyed.

58 They both lay with their father and conceived and gave birth to sons. The first born called the name of her son Moab, saying, From my father did I conceive him; he is the father of the Moabites to this day.

59 And the younger also called her son Benami; he is the father of the children of Ammon to this day.

60 After this Lot and his two daughters went away from there, and he lived on the other side of the Jordan with his two daughters and their sons, and the sons of Lot grew up, and they went and took themselves wives from the land of Canaan, and they had children and they were prolific and multiplied.

CHAPTER 20

1 At that time Abraham journeyed from the plain of Mamre and he went to the land of the Philistines, and he lived in Gerar; it was in the twenty-fifth year of Abraham's being in the land of Canaan, and the hundredth year of the life of Abraham, that he came to Gerar in the land of the Philistines.

2 And when they entered the land he said to Sarah his wife, Say you are my sister, to any one that shall ask you, in order that we may escape the evil of the inhabitants of the land.

3 As Abraham was dwelling in the land of the Philistines, the servants of Abimelech, king of the Philistines, saw that Sarah was greatly beautiful, and they asked Abraham concerning her, and he said, She is my sister.

4 And the servants of Abimelech went to Abimelech, saying, A man from the land of Canaan is come to dwell in the land, and he has a sister that is exceeding fair.

5 Abimelech heard the words of his servants who praised Sarah to him, and Abimelech sent his officers, and they brought Sarah to the king.

6 And Sarah came to the house of Abimelech; the king saw that Sarah was beautiful, and she pleased him greatly.

7 And he approached her and said to her, What is that man to you with whom you did come to our land? And Sarah answered and said, He is my brother, and we came from the land of Canaan to dwell wherever we could find a place.

8 Abimelech said to Sarah, Behold my land is before you, place your brother in any part of this land that pleases you, and it will be our duty to exalt and elevate him above all the people of the land since he is your

brother.

9 And Abimelech sent for Abraham, and Abraham came to Abimelech.

10 Abimelech said to Abraham, Behold I have given orders that you shall be honored as you desire on account of your sister Sarah.

11 And Abraham went forth from the king, and the king's present followed him.

12 As at evening time, before men laid down to rest, the king was sitting on his throne, and a deep sleep fell on him, and he lay on the throne and slept till morning.

13 He dreamed that an angel of the Lord came to him with a drawn sword in his hand, and the angel stood over Abimelech and wished to kill him with the sword; the king was terrified in his dream and said to the angel, In what have I sinned against you that you come to kill me with your sword?

14 And the angel answered and said to Abimelech, Behold you die on account of the woman which last night you brought to your house, for she is a married woman, the wife of Abraham who came to your house; now therefore return that man his wife, for she is his wife; should you not return her, know that you will certainly die, you and all belonging to you.

15 On that night there was a great outcry in the land of the Philistines, and the inhabitants of the land saw the figure of a man standing with a drawn sword in his hand, and he struck the inhabitants of the land with the sword, yes, he continued to strike them.

16 And the angel of the Lord struck the whole land of the Philistines on that night, and there was a great confusion on that night and on the following morning.

17 Every womb was closed, and all their issues, and the hand of the Lord was on them on account of Sarah, wife of Abraham, whom Abimelech had taken.

18 And in the morning Abimelech rose with terror and confusion and with a great dread; he sent and had his servants called in; he related his dream to them, and the people were greatly afraid.

19 One man standing among the servants of the king answered the king, saying, O sovereign king, restore this woman to her husband, for he is her husband, for the same happened to the king of Egypt when this man came to Egypt.

20 He said concerning his wife, She is my sister, for such is his manner of

doing when he comes to dwell in the land in which he is a stranger.

21 Pharaoh sent and took this woman for a wife and the Lord brought on him grievous plagues until he returned the woman to her husband.

22 Now therefore, O sovereign king, know what happened last night to the whole land, for there was a very great consternation and great pain and lamentation, and we know that it was on account of the woman which you did take.

23 Now, therefore, restore this woman to her husband, that it should not happen to us as it did to Pharaoh king of Egypt and his subjects, and that we may not die. Abimelech hurried and had Sarah called for, and she came before him, and he had Abraham called for, and he came before him.

24 Abimelech said to them, What is this work you have been doing in saying you are brother and sister, and I took this woman for a wife?

25 And Abraham said, Because I thought I would suffer death on account of my wife; and Abimelech took flocks and herds, and men servants and maid servants, and a thousand pieces of silver, and he gave them to Abraham, and he returned Sarah to him.

26 Abimelech said to Abraham, Behold the whole land is before you, dwell in it wherever you shall choose.

27 And Abraham and Sarah, his wife, went forth from the king's presence with honor and respect, and they lived in the land, even in Gerar.

28 All the inhabitants of the land of the Philistines and the king's servants were still in pain through the plague which the angel had inflicted on them the whole night on account of Sarah.

29 Abimelech sent for Abraham, saying, Pray now for your servants to the Lord your God, that he may put away this mortality from among us.

30 And Abraham prayed on account of Abimelech and his subjects, and the Lord heard the prayer of Abraham, and he healed Abimelech and all his subjects.

CHAPTER 21

1 It was at that time the end of a year and four months of Abraham's dwelling in the land of the Philistines in Gerar, that God visited Sarah, and the Lord remembered her and she conceived and gave birth to a son to

Abraham.

2 Abraham called the name of the son which Sarah gave birth to him, Isaac.

3 And Abraham circumcised his son Isaac at eight days old, as God had commanded Abraham to do to his descendants after him; Abraham was one hundred and Sarah ninety years old when Isaac was born to them.

4 The child grew up and was weaned, and Abraham made a great feast on the day that Isaac was weaned.

5 Shem and Eber and all the great people of the land, and Abimelech king of the Philistines and his servants, and Phicol, the captain of his host, came to eat and drink and rejoice at the feast which Abraham made on the day of his son Isaac's being weaned.

6 Also Terah, the father of Abraham, and Nahor his brother, came from Haran, they and all belonging to them, for they greatly rejoiced on hearing that a son had been born to Sarah.

7 They came to Abraham, and they ate and drank at the feast which Abraham made on the day of Isaac's being weaned.

8 Terah and Nahor rejoiced with Abraham, and they remained with him many days in the land of the Philistines.

9 At that time Serug the son of Reu died, in the first year of the birth of Isaac son of Abraham.

10 And all the days of Serug were two hundred and thirty-nine years, and he died.

11 Ishmael the son of Abraham was grown up in those days; he was fourteen years old when Sarah gave birth to Isaac to Abraham.

12 And God was with Ishmael the son of Abraham, and he grew up, and he learned to use the bow and became an archer.

13 When Isaac was five years old he was sitting with Ishmael at the door of the tent.

14 Ishmael came to Isaac and seated himself opposite to him, and he took the bow and drew it and put the arrow in it, and intended to kill Isaac.

15 Sarah saw the act which Ishmael desired to do to her son Isaac, and it grieved her greatly on account of her son; she sent for Abraham, and said to him, Cast out this bondwoman and her son, for her son shall not be heir with my son, for thus did he seek to do to him this day.

16 Abraham listened to the voice of Sarah, and he rose up early in the morning. He took twelve loaves and a bottle of water which he gave to Hagar, and sent her away with her son, and Hagar went with her son to the wilderness. They lived in the wilderness of Paran with the inhabitants of the wilderness; Ishmael was an archer, and he lived in the wilderness a long time.

17 He and his mother afterward went to the land of Egypt, and they lived there; Hagar took a wife for her son from Egypt, and her name was Meribah.

18 And the wife of Ishmael conceived and gave birth to four sons and two daughters. Ishmael and his mother and his wife and children afterward went and returned to the wilderness.

19 They made themselves tents in the wilderness, in which they lived, and they continued to travel and then to rest monthly and yearly.

20 And God gave Ishmael flocks and herds and tents on account of Abraham his father, and the man increased in cattle.

21 Ishmael lived in deserts and in tents, traveling and resting for a long time, and he did not see the face of his father.

22 Some time later, Abraham said to Sarah his wife, I will go and see my son Ishmael, for I have a desire to see him, for I have not seen him for a long time.

23 Abraham rode on one of his camels to the wilderness to seek his son Ishmael, for he heard that he was dwelling in a tent in the wilderness with all belonging to him.

24 Abraham went to the wilderness and reached the tent of Ishmael about noon, and he asked after Ishmael; he found the wife of Ishmael sitting in the tent with her children, and Ishmael her husband and his mother were not with them.

25 Abraham asked the wife of Ishmael, saying, Where has Ishmael gone? And she said, He has gone to the field to hunt. Abraham was still mounted on the camel, for he would not get off to the ground as he had sworn to his wife Sarah that he would not get off from the camel.

26 And Abraham said to Ishmael's wife, My daughter, give me a little water that I may drink, for I am fatigued from the journey.

27 And Ishmael's wife answered and said to Abraham, We have neither water nor bread. She continued sitting in the tent and did not notice Abraham, neither did she ask him who he was.

28 But she was beating her children in the tent, and she was cursing them,

and she also cursed her husband Ishmael and reproached him. Abraham heard the words of Ishmael's wife to her children, and he was very angry and displeased.

29 Abraham called to the woman to come out to him from the tent, and the woman came and stood opposite to Abraham, for Abraham was still mounted on the camel.

30 And Abraham said to Ishmael's wife, When your husband Ishmael returns home say these words to him,

31 A very old man from the land of the Philistines came here to seek you, and thus was his appearance and figure; I did not ask him who he was, and seeing you were not here he spoke to me and said, When Ishmael your husband returns tell him thus did this man say, When you come home put away this nail of the tent which you have placed here, and place another nail in its stead.

32 Abraham finished his instructions to the woman, and he turned and went off on the camel homeward.

33 After that Ishmael came from the hunt by him and his mother, and returned to the tent, and his wife spoke these words to him,

34 A very old man from the land of the Philistines came to seek you, and thus was his appearance and figure; I did not ask him who he was, and seeing you were not at home he said to me, When your husband comes home tell him, thus says the old man, Put away the nail of the tent which you have placed here and place another nail in its stead.

35 Ishmael heard the words of his wife, and he knew that it was his father, and that his wife did not honor him.

36 And Ishmael understood his father's words that he had spoken to his wife, and Ishmael listened to the voice of his father; Ishmael cast off that woman and she went away.

37 Ishmael afterward went to the land of Canaan, and he took another wife and he brought her to his tent to the place where he then lived.

38 And at the end of three years Abraham said, I will go again and see Ishmael my son, for I have not seen him for a long time.

39 He rode on his camel and went to the wilderness, and he reached the tent of Ishmael about noon.

40 He asked after Ishmael, and his wife came out of the tent and said, He is not here my lord, for he has gone to hunt in the fields, and to feed the camels. And the woman said to Abraham, Turn in my lord into the tent,

and eat a morsel of bread, for your soul must be wearied on account of the journey.

41 And Abraham said to her, I will not stop for I am in haste to continue my journey, but give me a little water to drink, for I have thirst; the woman hurried and ran into the tent and she brought out water and bread to Abraham, which she placed before him and she urged him to eat; he ate and drank and his heart was comforted and he blessed his son Ishmael.

42 He finished his meal and he blessed the Lord, and he said to Ishmael's wife, When Ishmael comes home say these words to him,

43 A very old man from the land of the Philistines came here and asked after you, and you were not here; and I brought out bread and water and he ate and drank and his heart was comforted.

44 And he spoke these words to me: When Ishmael your husband comes home, say to him, The nail of the tent which you have is very good, do not put it away from the tent.

45 Abraham finished commanding the woman, and he rode off to his home to the land of the Philistines; and when Ishmael came to his tent his wife went forth to meet him with joy and a cheerful heart.

46 And she said to him, An old man came here from the land of the Philistines and thus was his appearance, and he asked after you and you were not here, so I brought out bread and water, and he ate and drank and his heart was comforted.

47 And he spoke these words to me, When Ishmael your husband comes home say to him, The nail of the tent which you have is very good, do not put it away from the tent.

48 Ishmael knew that it was his father, and that his wife had honored him, and the Lord blessed Ishmael.

CHAPTER 22

1 Ishmael then rose up and took his wife and his children and his cattle and all belonging to him, and he journeyed from there and he went to his father in the land of the Philistines.

2 Abraham related to Ishmael his son the transaction with the first wife that Ishmael took, according to what she did.

3 Ishmael and his children lived with Abraham many days in that land, and Abraham lived in the land of the Philistines a long time.

4 And the days increased and reached twenty six years; after that Abraham with his servants and all belonging to him went from the land of the Philistines and removed to a great distance, and they came near to Hebron and remained there. The servants of Abraham dug wells of water, and Abraham and all belonging to him lived by the water. The servants of Abimelech king of the Philistines heard the report that Abraham's servants had dug wells of water in borders of the land.

5 They came and quarreled with the servants of Abraham and robbed them of the great well which they had dug.

6 Abimelech king of the Philistines heard of this affair; he with Phicol the captain of his host and twenty of his men came to Abraham, and Abimelech spoke to Abraham concerning his servants; Abraham rebuked Abimelech concerning the well of which his servants had robbed him.

7 Abimelech said to Abraham, As the Lord lives who created the whole earth, I did not hear of the act which my servants did to your servants until this day.

8 And Abraham took seven ewe lambs and gave them to Abimelech, saying, Take these, I pray you, from my hands that it may be a testimony for me that I dug this well.

9 Abimelech took the seven ewe lambs which Abraham had given to him, for he had also given him cattle and herds in abundance; Abimelech swore to Abraham concerning the well, therefore he called that well Beersheba, for there they both swore concerning it.

10 And they both made a covenant in Beersheba, and Abimelech rose up with Phicol the captain of his host and all his men; they returned to the land of the Philistines, and Abraham and all belonging to him lived in Beersheba and he was in that land a long time.

11 Abraham planted a large grove in Beersheba, and he made to it four gates facing the four sides of the earth; he planted a vineyard in it, so that if a traveler came to Abraham he entered any gate which was in his road, and remained there and ate and drank and satisfied himself and then departed.

12 For the house of Abraham was always open to the sons of men that passed and returned, who came daily to eat and drink in the house of Abraham.

13 Any man who had hunger and came to Abraham's house, Abraham

would give him bread that he might eat and drink and be satisfied; any one that came naked to his house he would clothe with garments as he might choose and give him silver and gold, and make known to him the Lord who had created him in the earth; this did Abraham all his life.

14 Abraham and his children and all belonging to him lived in Beersheba, and he pitched his tent as far as Hebron.

15 And Abraham's brother Nahor and his father and all belonging to them lived in Haran, for they did not come with Abraham to the land of Canaan.

16 And children were born to Nahor which Milca the daughter of Haran, and sister to Sarah, Abraham's wife, gave birth to, to him.

17 These are the names of those that were born to him: Uz, Buz, Kemuel, Kesed, Chazo, Pildash, Tidlaf, and Bethuel, being eight sons; these are the children of Milca which she gave birth to, to Nahor, Abraham's brother.

18 And Nahor had a concubine and her name was Reumah, and she also gave birth to, to Nahor: Zebach, Gachash, Tachash and Maacha, being four sons.

19 The children that were born to Nahor were twelve sons besides his daughters, and they also had children born to them in Haran.

20 And the children of Uz the first born of Nahor were Abi, Cheref, Gadin, Melus, and Deborah their sister.

21 And the sons of Buz were Berachel, Naamath, Sheva, and Madonu.

22 And the sons of Kemuel were Aram and Rechob.

23 And the sons of Kesed were Anamlech, Meshai, Benon and Yifi; the sons of Chazo were Pildash, Mechi and Opher.

24 And the sons of Pildash were Arud, Chamum, Mered and Moloch.

25 And the sons of Tidlaf were Mushan, Cushan and Mutzi.

26 And the children of Bethuel were Sechar, Laban and their sister Rebecca.

27 These are the families of the children of Nahor, that were born to them in Haran; and Aram the son of Kemuel and Rechob his brother went away from Haran, and they found a valley in the land by the river Euphrates.

28 And they built a city there, and they called the name of the city after the name of Pethor the son of Aram, that is Aram Naherayim to this day.

29 The children of Kesed also went to dwell where they could find a place, and they found a valley opposite to the land of Shinar, and they

lived there.

30 There they built themselves a city, and they called the name of the city Kesed after the name of their father; that is the land Kasdim to this day, and the Kasdim lived in that land and they were prolific and multiplied greatly.

31 Terah, father of Nahor and Abraham, went and took another wife in his old age, and her name was Pelilah, and she conceived and gave birth to him a son and he called his name Zoba.

32 Terah lived twenty-five years after he had Zoba.

33 And Terah died in that year, that is in the thirty-fifth year of the birth of Isaac son of Abraham.

34 The days of Terah were two hundred and five years, and he was buried in Haran.

35 Zoba the son of Terah lived thirty years and he had Aram, Achlis and Merik.

36 Aram, son of Zoba son of Terah, had three wives and he had twelve sons and three daughters; the Lord gave to Aram the son of Zoba, riches and possessions, and abundance of cattle, and flocks and herds, and the man increased greatly.

37 Aram the son of Zoba and his brother and all his household journeyed from Haran, and they went to dwell where they should find a place, for their property was too great to remain in Haran; for they could not stop in Haran together with their brothers the children of Nahor.

38 Aram the son of Zoba went with his brothers, and they found a valley at a distance toward the eastern country and they lived there.

39 They also built a city there, and they called the name thereof Aram, after the name of their eldest brother; that is Aram Zoba to this day.

40 Isaac the son of Abraham was growing up in those days, and Abraham his father taught him the way of the Lord to know the Lord, and the Lord was with him.

41 When Isaac was thirty-seven years old, Ishmael his brother was going about with him in the tent.

42 And Ishmael boasted of himself to Isaac, saying, I was thirteen years old when the Lord spoke to my father to circumcise us, and I did according to the word of the Lord which he spoke to my father, and I gave my soul to the Lord, and I did not go contrary to his word which he

commanded my father.

43 Isaac answered Ishmael, saying, Why do you boast to me about this, about a little bit of your flesh which you did take from your body, concerning which the Lord commanded you?

44 As the Lord lives, the God of my father Abraham, if the Lord should say to my father, Take now your son Isaac and bring him up an offering before me, I would not refrain but I would joyfully accede to it.

45 And the Lord heard the word that Isaac spoke to Ishmael, and it seemed good in the sight of the Lord, and he thought to try Abraham in this matter.

46 The day arrived when the sons of God came and placed themselves before the Lord, and Satan also came with the sons of God before the Lord.

47 And the Lord said to Satan, Wherefore do you come? Satan answered the Lord and said, From going to and fro in the earth, and from walking up and down in it.

48 And the Lord said to Satan, What is your word to me concerning all the children of the earth? Satan answered the Lord and said, I have seen all the children of the earth who serve you and remember you when they require anything from you.

49 When you give them the thing which they require from you, they sit at their ease and turn away from you, and they remember you no more.

50 Have you seen Abraham the son of Terah, who at first had no children? He served you and erected altars to you wherever he came, and he brought up offerings on them, and he proclaimed your name continually to all the children of the earth.

51 And now that his son Isaac is born to him, he has forsaken you, he has made a great feast for all the inhabitants of the land, and the Lord he has forgotten.

52 For amidst all that he has done he brought you no offering; neither burnt offering nor peace offering, neither ox, lamb nor goat of all that he killed on the day that his son was weaned.

53 Even from the time of his son's birth till now, being thirty-seven years, he built no altar before you, nor brought any offering to you, for he saw that you did give what he requested before you, and he therefore turned away from you.

54 And the Lord said to Satan, Have you thus considered my servant Abraham? for there is none like him on earth, a perfect and an upright man before me, one that fears God and avoids evil; as I live, were I to say

to him, Bring up Isaac your son before me, he would not withhold him from me, much more if I told him to bring up a burnt offering before me from his flock or herds.

55 Satan answered the Lord and said, Speak then now to Abraham as you have said, and you will see whether he will not this day go contrary to and cast aside your words.

CHAPTER 23

1 At that time the word of the Lord came to Abraham, and said to him, Abraham. And Abraham said, Here I am.

2 He said to him, Take now your son, your only son whom you love, even Isaac, and go to the land of Moriah, and offer him there for a burnt offering on one of the mountains which shall be shown to you, for there you will see a cloud and the glory of the Lord.

3 And Abraham said within himself, How shall I separate my son Isaac from Sarah his mother, in order to bring him up for a burnt offering before the Lord?

4 Abraham came into the tent, and he sat before Sarah his wife, and he spoke these words to her,

5 My son Isaac is grown up and he has not for some time studied the service of his God; tomorrow I will go and bring him to Shem, and Eber his son, and there he will learn the ways of the Lord. For they will teach him to know the Lord as well as to know that when he prays continually before the Lord, he will answer him; there he will know the way of serving the Lord his God.

6 And Sarah said, You have spoken well, go my lord and do to him as you have said, but remove him not at a great distance from me, neither let him remain there too long, for my soul is bound within his soul.

7 Abraham said to Sarah, My daughter, let us pray to the Lord our God that he may do good with us.

8 And Sarah took her son Isaac and he abode all that night with her, and she kissed and embraced him, and gave him instructions till morning.

9 She said to him, O my son, how can my soul separate itself from you? And she still kissed him and embraced him, and she gave Abraham

instructions concerning him.

10 Sarah said to Abraham, O my lord, I pray you take care of your son, and watch over him, for I have no other son or daughter but him.

11 Turn not away from him. If he is hungry give him bread, and if he is thirsty give him water to drink; do not let him go on foot, neither let him sit in the sun.

12 Neither let him go by himself in the road, neither force him from whatever he may desire, but do to him as he may say to you.

13 Sarah wept bitterly the whole night on account of Isaac, and she gave him instructions till morning.

14 In the morning Sarah selected a very fine and beautiful garment from those garments which she had in the house, that Abimelech had given to her.

15 She dressed Isaac her son with them, and she put a turban on his head; she enclosed a precious stone in the top of the turban, and gave them provision for the road. They went forth, and Isaac went with his father Abraham, and some of their servants accompanied them to see them on their way.

16 Sarah went out with them, and she accompanied them on the road to see them off; they said to her, Return to the tent.

17 When Sarah heard the words of her son Isaac she wept bitterly, and Abraham her husband wept with her, and their son wept with them a great weeping; also those who went with them wept greatly.

18 And Sarah caught hold of her son Isaac, and she held him in her arms, and she embraced him and continued to weep with him. And Sarah said, Who knows if after this day I shall ever see you again?

19 They still wept together, Abraham, Sarah and Isaac, and all those that accompanied them on the road wept with them, and Sarah afterward turned away from her son, weeping bitterly; then all her men servants and maid servants returned with her to the tent.

20 And Abraham went with Isaac his son to bring him up as an offering before the Lord, as He had commanded him.

21 Abraham took two of his young men with him, Ishmael the son of Hagar and Eliezer his servant, and they went together with them. While they were walking in the road the young men spoke these words to themselves,

22 Ishmael said to Eliezer, Now my father Abraham is going with Isaac to

bring him up for a burnt offering to the Lord, as He commanded him.

23 When he returns he will give to me all he possesses, to inherit after him, for I am his firstborn.

24 And Eliezer answered Ishmael and said, Certainly Abraham did cast you away with your mother, and swear that you should not inherit any thing of all he possesses. To whom will he give all that he has, with all his treasures, but to me his servant, who has been faithful in his house, who has served him night and day, and has done all he desired me? To me he will bequeath at his death all he possesses.

25 While Abraham was proceeding with his son Isaac along the road, Satan came and appeared to Abraham in the figure of a very aged man, humble and of contrite spirit; he approached Abraham and said to him, Are you silly or brutish, that you go to do this thing today to your only son?

26 For God gave you a son in your latter days, in your old age, and will you go and slaughter him today because he committed no violence, and will you cause the soul of your only son to perish from the earth?

27 Do you not know and understand that this thing cannot be from the Lord? For the Lord cannot do to man such evil on earth to say to him, Go slaughter your child.

28 Abraham heard this and knew that it was the word of Satan who endeavored to draw him aside from the way of the Lord, but Abraham would not listen to the voice of Satan, and Abraham rebuked him so that he went away.

29 Satan returned and came to Isaac; he appeared to Isaac in the figure of a young man comely and well favored.

30 He approached Isaac and said to him, Do you not know and understand that your old silly father brings you to the slaughter today for nothing?

31 Now therefore, my son, do not listen or attend to him, for he is a silly old man; let not your precious soul and beautiful figure be lost from the earth.

32 And Isaac heard this, and said to Abraham, Have you heard, my father, that which this man has spoken? Even thus has he spoken.

33 And Abraham answered his son Isaac and said to him, Take heed of him and do not listen to his words, nor attend to him, for he is Satan, endeavoring to draw us aside this day from the commands of God.

34 Abraham still rebuked Satan, and Satan went from them; seeing he could not prevail over them he hid himself from them, and he went and passed before them in the road; he transformed himself to a large brook of water in the road. Abraham and Isaac and his two young men reached that place, and they saw a brook large and powerful as the mighty waters.

35 They entered the brook and passed through it, and the waters at first reached their legs.

36 And they went deeper in the brook and the waters reached up to their necks. They were all terrified on account of the water and while they were going over the brook Abraham recognized that place, and he knew that there was no water there before.

37 Abraham said to his son Isaac, I know this place in which there was no brook or water, now therefore it is Satan who does all this to us, to draw us aside on this day from the commands of God.

38 And Abraham rebuked him and said to him, The Lord rebuke you, O Satan, begone from us for we go by the commands of God.

39 And Satan was terrified at the voice of Abraham, and he went away from them; the place again became dry land as it was at first.

40 Abraham went with Isaac toward the place that God had told him.

41 And on the third day Abraham lifted up his eyes and saw the place at a distance which God had told him of.

42 A pillar of fire appeared to him that reached from the earth to heaven, and a cloud of glory on the mountain, and the glory of the Lord was seen in the cloud.

43 And Abraham said to Isaac, My son, do you see in that mountain, which we perceive at a distance, that which I see on it?

44 And Isaac answered and said to his father, I see and there is a pillar of fire and a cloud, and the glory of the Lord is seen on the cloud.

45 And Abraham knew that his son Isaac was accepted before the Lord for a burnt offering.

46 Abraham said to Eliezer and to Ishmael his son, Do you also see that which we see on the mountain which is at a distance?

47 And they answered and said, We see nothing more than like the other mountains of the earth. Abraham knew that they were not accepted before the Lord to go with them, and Abraham said to them, Stay here with the ass while I and Isaac my son will go to yonder mount and worship there before the Lord and then return to you.

48 Eliezer and Ishmael remained in that place, as Abraham had commanded.

49 And Abraham took wood for a burnt offering and placed it on his son Isaac, and he took the fire and the knife, and they both went to that place.

50 When they were on the way Isaac said to his father, Behold, I see here the fire and wood, and where then is the lamb that is to be the burnt offering before the Lord?

51 And Abraham answered his son Isaac, saying, The Lord has made choice of you my son, to be a perfect burnt offering instead of the lamb.

52 And Isaac said to his father, I will do all that the Lord spoke to you with joy and cheerfulness of heart.

53 Abraham again said to Isaac his son, Is there in your heart any thought or counsel concerning this, which is not proper? Tell me my son, I pray you, O my son conceal it not from me.

54 And Isaac answered his father Abraham and said to him, O my father, as the Lord lives and as your soul lives, there is nothing in my heart to cause me to deviate either to the right or to the left from the word that he has spoken to you.

55 Neither limb nor muscle has moved or stirred at this, nor is there in my heart any thought or evil counsel concerning this.

56 But I am of joyful and cheerful heart in this matter, and I say, Blessed is the Lord who has this day chosen me to be a burnt offering before Him.

57 Abraham greatly rejoiced at the words of Isaac, and they went on and came together to that place that the Lord had spoken of.

58 Abraham approached to build the altar in that place, and Abraham was weeping. Isaac took stones and mortar until they had finished building the altar.

59 And Abraham took the wood and placed it in order on the altar which he had built.

60 He took his son Isaac and bound him in order to place him on the wood which was on the altar, to kill him for a burnt offering before the Lord.

61 Isaac said to his father, Bind me securely and then place me on the altar that I should not turn and move, and break loose from the force of the knife on my flesh and thereof profane the burnt offering; and Abraham did so.

62 Isaac still said to his father, O my father, when you have slain me and burnt me for an offering, take with you that which remains of my ashes to bring to Sarah my mother, and say to her, This is the sweet smelling savor of Isaac. But do not tell her this if she should sit near a well or on any high place, that she would cast her soul after me and die.

63 And Abraham heard the words of Isaac, and he lifted up his voice and wept when Isaac spake these words. Abraham's tears gushed down on Isaac his son, and Isaac wept bitterly; he said to his father, Hasten, O my father, and do with me the will of the Lord our God as He has commanded you.

64 The hearts of Abraham and Isaac rejoiced at this thing which the Lord had commanded them; but the eye wept bitterly while the heart rejoiced.

65 And Abraham bound his son Isaac and placed him on the altar on the wood, and Isaac stretched forth his neck on the altar before his father. Abraham stretched forth his hand to take the knife to kill his son as a burnt offering before the Lord.

66 At that time the angels of mercy came before the Lord and spoke to him concerning Isaac, saying,

67 0 Lord, you are a merciful and compassionate King over all that you have created in heaven and in earth, and you support them all; give therefore ransom and redemption instead of your servant Isaac, and pity and have compassion on Abraham and Isaac his son who are this day performing your commands.

68 Have you seen, O Lord, how Isaac the son of Abraham your servant is bound down to the slaughter like an animal? Now therefore let your pity be roused for them, O Lord.

69 At that time the Lord appeared to Abraham and called to him from heaven, and said to him, Lay not your hand on the lad, neither do anything to him, for now I know that you fear God in performing this act, and in not withholding your son, your only son, from me.

70 And Abraham lifted up his eyes and looked, and behold, a ram was caught in a thicket by his horns; that was the ram which the Lord God had created in the earth in the day that he made earth and heaven.

71 For the Lord had prepared this ram from that day, to be a burnt offering instead of Isaac.

72 This ram was advancing to Abraham when Satan caught hold of him and entangled his horns in the thicket, so that he might not advance to Abraham, in order that Abraham might kill his son.

73 And Abraham, seeing the ram advancing to him and Satan withholding him, fetched him and brought him before the altar; he loosened his son Isaac from his binding, and he put the ram in his stead. Abraham killed the ram on the altar, and brought it up as an offering in the place of his son Isaac.

74 Abraham sprinkled some of the blood of the ram on the altar, and he exclaimed and said, This is in the place of my son, and may it be considered this day as the blood of my son before the Lord.

75 And all that Abraham did on this occasion by the altar, he would exclaim and say, This is in place of my son, and may it this day be considered before the Lord in the place of my son; and Abraham finished the whole service by the altar, and the service was accepted before the Lord, and was accounted as if it had been Isaac; and the Lord blessed Abraham and his descendants on that day.

76 Satan went to Sarah, and he appeared to her in the figure of an old man very humble and meek, and Abraham was yet engaged in the burnt offering before the Lord.

77 And he said to her, Do you not know all the work that Abraham has made with your only son this day? For he took Isaac and built an altar, and killed him, and brought him up as a sacrifice on the altar; Isaac cried and wept before his father, but he looked not at him, neither did he have compassion over him.

78 Satan repeated these words, and he went away from her. Sarah heard all the words of Satan, and she imagined him to be an old man from among the sons of men who had been with her son, and had come and told her these things.

79 And Sarah lifted up her voice and wept and cried out bitterly on account of her son; she threw herself on the ground and she cast dust on her head, and she said, O my son, Isaac my son, O that I had this day died instead of you. And she continued to weep and said, It grieves me for you, O my son, my son Isaac, O that I had died this day in your stead.

80 She still continued to weep, and said, It grieves me for you after I have reared you and have brought you up; now my joy is turned into mourning over you; I who had a longing for you, and cried and prayed to God till I gave birth to you at ninety years old. And now you have served this day for the knife and the fire, to be made an offering.

81 But I console myself with you, my son, in its being the word of the Lord, for you did perform the command of your God. Who can go contrary to the word of our God, in whose hands is the soul of every living

creature?

82 You are just, O Lord our God, for all your works are good and righteous; for I also am rejoiced with your word which you did command; while my eye weeps bitterly my heart rejoices.

83 Sarah laid her head on the bosom of one of her handmaids, and she became as still as a stone.

84 Afterward she rose up and went about making inquiries till she came to Hebron; she inquired of all those whom she met walking in the road and no one could tell her what had happened to her son.

85 She came with her maid servants and men servants to Kireath-arba, which is Hebron, and she asked concerning her son; she remained there while she sent some of her servants to seek where Abraham had gone with Isaac. They went to seek him in the house of Shem and Eber, and they could not find him, and they sought throughout the land and he was not there.

86 And then Satan came to Sarah in the shape of an old man; he came and stood before her, and said to her, I spoke falsely to you, for Abraham did not kill his son and he is not dead. When she heard the word her joy was so greatly violent on account of her son, that her soul went out through joy; she died and was gathered to her people.

87 When Abraham had finished his service he returned with his son Isaac to his young men, and they rose up and went together to Beersheba, and they came home.

88 And Abraham sought for Sarah, and could not find her, and he made inquiries concerning her. They said to him, She went as far as Hebron to seek you both where you had gone, for thus was she informed.

89 Abraham and Isaac went to her to Hebron, and when they found that she was dead they lifted up their voices and wept bitterly over her; Isaac fell on his mother's face and wept over her, and he said, O my mother, my mother, how have you left me, and where have you gone? O how, how have you left me!

90 And Abraham and Isaac wept greatly and all their servants wept with them on account of Sarah, and they mourned over her a great and heavy mourning.

CHAPTER 24

1 The life of Sarah was one hundred and twenty-seven years, and Sarah died; and Abraham rose up from before his dead to seek a burial place to bury his wife Sarah. He went and spoke to the children of Heth, the inhabitants of the land, saying,

2 I am a stranger and a sojourner with you in your land; give me possession of a burial place in your land, that I may bury my dead from before me.

3 And the children of Heth said to Abraham, Behold the land is before you, in the choice of our sepulchers bury your dead, for no man shall withhold you from burying your dead.

4 Abraham said to them, If you are agreeable to this, go and entreat Ephron the son of Zochar for me, requesting that he may give me the cave of Machpelah which is in the end of his field, and I will purchase it of him for whatever he desires for it.

5 And Ephron lived among the children of Heth, and they went and called for him, and he came before Abraham. Ephron said to Abraham, Behold all you require your servant will do; Abraham said, No, but I will buy the cave and the field which you have for value, in order that it may be for possession of a burial place forever.

6 And Ephron answered and said, Behold the field and the cave are before you, give whatever you desire. Abraham said, Only at full value will I buy it from your hand, and from the hands of those that go in at the gate of your city, and from the hand of your descendants forever.

7 Ephron and all his brothers heard this, and Abraham weighed to Ephron four hundred shekels of silver in the hands of Ephron and in the hands of all his brothers. Abraham wrote this transaction; he wrote it and testified it with four witnesses.

8 And these are the names of the witnesses: Amigal son of Abishna the Hittite, Adichorom son of Ashunach the Hivite, Abdon son of Achiram the Gomerite, Bakdil the son of Abudish the Zidonite.

9 Abraham took the book of the purchase and placed it in his treasures, and these are the words that Abraham wrote in the book, namely:

10 That the cave and the field Abraham bought from Ephron the Hittite and from his descendants, and from those that go out of his city, and from their descendants forever, are to be a purchase to Abraham and to his

descendants and to those that go forth from his loins, for a possession of a burial place forever. And he put a signet to it and testified it with witnesses.

11 The field and the cave that was in it and all that place were made sure to belong to Abraham and to his descendants after him, from the children of Heth; behold it is before Mamre in Hebron which is in the land of Canaan.

12 After this Abraham buried his wife Sarah there, and that place and all its boundary became to Abraham and to his descendants for a possession of a burial place.

13 And Abraham buried Sarah with pomp as observed at the interment of kings, and she was buried in very fine and beautiful garments.

14 At her bier was Shem, his sons Eber and Abimelech, together with Anar, Ashcol and Mamre, and all the grandees of the land followed her bier.

15 The days of Sarah were one hundred and twenty-seven years and she died, and Abraham made a great and heavy mourning, and he performed the rites of mourning for seven days.

16 And all the inhabitants of the land comforted Abraham and Isaac his son on account of Sarah.

17 When the days of their mourning passed by Abraham sent away his son Isaac. He went to the house of Shem and Eber, to learn the ways of the Lord and his instructions, and Abraham remained there three years.

18 At that time Abraham rose up with all his servants, and they went and returned homeward to Beersheba, and Abraham and all his servants remained in Beersheba.

19 At the revolution of the year Abimelech king of the Philistines died in that year; he was one hundred and ninety-three years old at his death. Abraham went with his people to the land of the Philistines, and they comforted the whole household and all his servants, and then he turned and went home.

20 It was after the death of Abimelech that the people of Gerar took Benmalich his son, and he was only twelve years old, and they made him lay the place of his father.

21 And they called his name Abimelech after the name of his father, for thus it was their custom to do in Gerar. Abimelech reigned instead of Abimelech his father, and he sat on his throne.

22 And Lot the son of Haran also died in those days, in the thirty-ninth

year of the life of Isaac; all the days that Lot lived were one hundred and forty years and he died.

23 And these are the children of Lot, that were born to him by his daughters; the name of the first born was Moab, and the name of the second was Benami.

24 The two sons of Lot went and took themselves wives from the land of Canaan, and they gave birth to children to them. The children of Moab were Ed, Mayon, Tarsus, and Kanvil, four sons; these are fathers to the children of Moab to this day.

25 And all the families of the children of Lot went to dwell wherever they should light on, for they were prolific and increased abundantly.

26 And they went and built themselves cities in the land where they lived, and they called the names of the cities which they built after their own names.

27 Nahor the son of Terah, brother to Abraham, died in those days in the fortieth year of the life of Isaac. All the days of Nahor were one hundred and seventy-two years; he died and was buried in Haran.

28 And when Abraham heard that his brother was dead he grieved sadly, and he mourned over his brother many days.

29 Abraham called for Eliezer his head servant to give him orders concerning his house, and he came and stood before him.

30 And Abraham said to him, Behold I am old, I do not know the day of my death; for I am advanced in days; now therefore rise up, go forth and do not take a wife for my son from this place and from this land, from the daughters of the Canaanites among whom we dwell.

31 But go to my land and to my birthplace, and take from there a wife for my son. The Lord God of Heaven and earth who took me from my father's house and brought me to this place, and said to me, To your offspring will I give this land for an inheritance forever, he will send his angel before you and prosper your way, that you may obtain a wife for my son from my family and from my father's house.

32 The servant answered his master Abraham and said, Behold I go to your birthplace and to your father's house, and take a wife for your son from there; but if the woman be not willing to follow me to this land, shall I take your son back to the land of your birthplace?

33 And Abraham said to him, See that you do not bring my son here again, for the Lord before whom I have walked will send his angel before

you and prosper your way.

34 Eliezer did as Abraham ordered him, and Eliezer swore to Abraham his master on this matter; and Eliezer rose up and took ten camels of the camels of his master, and ten men from his master's servants with him, and they rose up and went to Haran, the city of Abraham and Nahor, in order to fetch a wife for Isaac the son of Abraham. While they were gone Abraham sent to the house of Shem and Eber, and they brought from there his son Isaac.

35 Isaac came home to his father's house to Beersheba, while Eliezer and his men came to Haran; and they stopped in the city by the watering place, and he made his camels to kneel down by the water and they remained there.

36 Eliezer, Abraham's servant, prayed and said, O God of Abraham my master; send me I pray you good speed this day and show kindness to my master, that you shall appoint this day a wife for my master's son from his family.

37 And the Lord listened to the voice of Eliezer, for the sake of his servant Abraham, and he happened to meet with the daughter of Bethuel, the son of Milcah, the wife of Nahor, brother to Abraham, and Eliezer came to her house.

38 Eliezer related to them all his concerns, and that he was Abraham's servant; they greatly rejoiced at him.

39 And they all blessed the Lord who brought this thing about; they gave him Rebecca, the daughter of Bethuel, for a wife for Isaac.

40 The young woman was of a beautiful appearance; she was a virgin, and Rebecca was ten years old in those days.

41 And Bethuel and Laban and his children made a feast on that night, and Eliezer and his men came and ate and drank and rejoiced there on that night.

42 Eliezer rose up in the morning, he and the men that were with him, and he called to the whole household of Bethuel, saying, Send me away that I may go to my master; they rose up and sent away Rebecca and her nurse Deborah, the daughter of Uz, and they gave her silver and gold, men servants and maid servants, and they blessed her.

43 And they sent Eliezer away with his men and the servants took Rebecca; he went and returned to his master to the land of Canaan.

44 Isaac took Rebecca and she became his wife, and he brought her into the tent.

45 And Isaac was forty years old when he took Rebecca, the daughter of his uncle Bethuel, for a wife.

CHAPTER 25

1 It was at that time that Abraham again took a wife in his old age, and her name was Keturah, from the land of Canaan.

2 She gave birth to, to him: Zimran, Jokshan, Medan, Midian, Ishbak and Shuach, being six sons. And the children of Zimran were Abihen, Molich and Narim.

3 The sons of Jokshan were Sheba and Dedan, and the sons of Medan were Amida, Joab, Gochi, Elisha and Nothach; and the sons of Midian were Ephah, Epher, Chanoch, Abida and Eldaah.

4 The sons of Ishbak were Makiro, Beyodua and Tator.

5 The sons of Shuach were Bildad, Mamdad, Munan and Meban; all these are the families of the children of Keturah the Canaanitish woman which she gave birth to, to Abraham the Hebrew.

6 And Abraham sent all these away, and he gave them gifts; they went away from his son Isaac to dwell wherever they would find a place.

7 And all these went to the mountain at the east, and they built themselves six cities in which they lived to this day.

8 But the children of Sheba and Dedan, children of Jokshan, with their children, did not dwell with their brothers in their cities; they journeyed and encamped in the countries and wildernesses to this day.

9 And the children of Midian, son of Abraham, went to the east of the land of Cush. There they found a large valley in the eastern country, and remained there and built a city. They lived therein; that is the land of Midian to this day.

10 Midian lived in the city which he built, he and his five sons and all belonging to him.

11 And these are the names of the sons of Midian according to their names in their cities: Ephah, Epher, Chanoch, Abida and Eldaah.

12 And the sons of Ephah were Methach, Meshar, Avi and Tzanua, and the sons of Epher were Ephron, Zur, Alirun and Medin; the sons of

Chanoch were Reuel, Rekem, Azi, Alyoshub and Alad.

13 The sons of Abida were Chur, Melud, Kerury, Molchi; and the sons of Eldaah were Miker, and Reba, and Malchiyah and Gabol. These are the names of the Midianites according to their families, and afterward the families of Midian spread throughout the land of Midian.

14 These are the generations of Ishmael the son of Abraham, whom Hagar, Sarah's handmaid, gave birth to, to Abraham.

15 And Ishmael took a wife from the land of Egypt, and her name was Ribah, the same is Meribah.

16 And Ribah gave birth to, to Ishmael: Nebayoth, Kedar, Adbeel, Mibsam and their sister Bosmath.

17 And Ishmael cast away his wife Ribah, and she went from him and returned to Egypt to the house of her father. She lived there, for she had been very bad in the sight of Ishmael, and in the sight of his father Abraham.

18 And Ishmael afterward took a wife from the land of Canaan, and her name was Malchuth, and she gave birth to, to him: Nishma, Dumah, Masa, Chadad, Tema, Yetur, Naphish and Kedma.

19 These are the sons of Ishmael, and these are their names, being twelve princes according to their nations. And the families of Ishmael afterward spread forth, and Ishmael took his children and all the property that he had gained, together with the souls of his household and all belonging to him, and they went to dwell where they should find a place.

20 They went and lived near the wilderness of Paran, and their dwelling was from Havilah to Shur, that is before Egypt as you come toward Assyria.

21 Ishmael and his sons lived in the land, and they had children born to them, and they were prolific and increased abundantly.

22 These are the names of the sons of Nebayoth the first born of Ishmael: Mend, Send, Mayon; and the sons of Kedar were Alyon, Kezem, Chamad and Eli.

23 The sons of Adbeel were Chamad and Jabin; and the sons of Mibsam were Obadiah, Ebedmelech and Yeush; these are the families of the children of Ribah the wife of Ishmael.

24 The sons of Mishma the son of Ishmael were Shamua, Zecaryon and Obed; and the sons of Dumah were Kezed, Eli, Machmad and Amed.

25 The sons of Masa were Melon, Mula and Ebidadon; and the sons of

Chadad were Azur, Minzar and Ebedmelech; and the sons of Tema were Seir, Sadon and Yakol.

26 The sons of Yetur were Merith, Yaish, Alyo, and Pachoth; and the sons of Naphish were Ebed-Tamed, Abiyasaph and Mir; and the sons of Kedma were Calip, Tachti, and Omir; these were the children of Malchuth the wife of Ishmael according to their families.

27 All these are the families of Ishmael according to their generations, and they lived in those lands wherein they had built themselves cities to this day.

28 Rebecca the daughter of Bethuel, the wife of Abraham's son Isaac, was unable to conceive in those days, she had no children. Isaac lived with his father in the land of Canaan, and the Lord was with Isaac. Arpachshad the son of Shem the son of Noah died in those days, in the forty-eighth year of the life of Isaac, and all the days that Arpachshad lived were four hundred and thirty-eight years, and he died.

CHAPTER 26

1 In the fifty-ninth year of the life of Isaac the son of Abraham, Rebecca his wife was still unable to conceive in those days.

2 And Rebecca said to Isaac, Truly I have heard, my lord, that your mother Sarah was unable to conceive in her days until my Lord Abraham, your father, prayed for her and she conceived by him.

3 Now therefore stand up, you also pray to God and he will hear your prayer and remember us through his mercies.

4 And Isaac answered his wife Rebecca, saying, Abraham has already prayed for me to God to reproduce his descendants, now therefore this barrenness must proceed to us from you.

5 And Rebecca said to him, But arise now you also and pray, that the Lord may hear your prayer and grant me children. Isaac listened to the words of his wife, and Isaac and his wife rose up and went to the land of

Moriah to pray there and to seek the Lord, and when they had reached that place Isaac stood up and prayed to the Lord on account of his wife because she was unable to conceive.

6 And Isaac said, O Lord God of heaven and earth, whose goodness and mercies fill the earth, you who did take my father from his father's house and from his birthplace, and brought him to this land, and did say to him, To your descendants I will give the land, and you did promise him and did declare to him, I will reproduce your descendants as the stars of heaven and as the sand of the sea, now may your words be verified which you did speak to my father.

7 For you are the Lord our God, our eyes are toward you to give us descendants of men, as you did promise us, for you are the Lord our God and our eyes are directed toward you only.

8 And the Lord heard the prayer of Isaac the son of Abraham; the Lord was entreated of him and Rebecca his wife conceived.

9 And in about seven months after the children struggled together within her, it pained her greatly and she was wearied on account of them. She said to all the women who were then in the land, Did such a thing happen to you as it has to me? And they said to her, No.

10 And she said to them, Why am I alone in this among all the women that were on earth? And she went to the land of Moriah to seek the Lord on account of this; she went to Shem and Eber his son to make inquiries of them in this matter, that they should seek the Lord in this thing respecting her.

11 She also asked Abraham to seek and inquire of the Lord about all that had befallen her.

12 They all inquired of the Lord concerning this matter, and they brought her word from the Lord and told her, Two children are in your womb, and two nations shall rise from them; one nation shall be stronger than the other, and the greater shall serve the younger.

13 When her days to be delivered were completed, she knelt down, and behold there were twins in her womb, as the Lord had spoken to her.

14 The first came out red all over like a hairy garment, and all the people of the land called his name Esau, saying, This one was made complete from the womb.

15 And after that came his brother, and his hand took hold of Esau's heel, therefore they called his name Jacob.

16 Isaac, the son of Abraham, was sixty years old when he had them.

17 The boys grew up to their fifteenth year, and they came among the society of men. Esau was a designing and deceitful man, and an expert hunter in the field; Jacob was a man perfect and wise, dwelling in tents, feeding flocks and learning the instructions of the Lord and the commands of his father and mother.

18 Isaac and the children of his household lived with his father Abraham in the land of Canaan, as God had commanded them.

19 Ishmael the son of Abraham went with his children and all belonging to them; they returned there to the land of Havilah, and they lived there.

20 And all the children of Abraham's concubines went to dwell in the land of the east, for Abraham had sent them away from his son and had given them presents, and they went away.

21 Abraham gave all that he had to his son Isaac, and he also gave him all his treasures.

22 And he commanded him saying, Do you not know and understand the Lord is God in heaven and in earth, and there is no other beside him?

23 It was he who took me from my father's house, and from my birthplace, and gave me all the delights on earth; who delivered me from the counsel of the wicked, for in him I did trust.

24 He brought me to this place, and delivered me from Ur Casdim, and said to me, To your descendants I will give all these land and they shall inherit them when they keep my commandments, my statutes and my judgments that I have commanded you, and which I shall command them.

25 Now therefore my son, listen to my voice, and keep the commandments of the Lord your God, which I commanded you. Do not turn from the right way either to the right or to the left, in order that it may be well with you and your children after you forever.

26 And remember the wonderful works of the Lord and his kindness that he has shown toward us, in having delivered us from the hands of our enemies; the Lord our God caused them to fall into our hands; now therefore keep all that I have commanded you and turn not away from the commandments of your God; serve none beside him, in order that it may be well with you and your descendants after you.

27 Teach your children and your descendants the instructions of the Lord and his commandments, and teach them the upright way in which they should go, in order that it may be well with them forever.

28 Isaac answered his father and said to him, That which my Lord has

commanded thatI will do, and I will not depart from the commands of the Lord my God; I will keep all that he commanded me. And Abraham blessed his son Isaac, and also his children, and Abraham taught Jacob the instruction of the Lord and his ways.

29 It was at that time that Abraham died, in the fifteenth year of the life of Jacob and Esau, the sons of Isaac, and all the days of Abraham were one hundred and seventy-five years. He died and was gathered to his people in good old age, old and satisfied with days, and Isaac and Ishmael his sons buried him.

30 When the inhabitants of Canaan heard that Abraham was dead, they all came with their kings and princes and all their men to bury Abraham.

31 All the inhabitants of the land of Haran, all the families of the house of Abraham, all the princes and grandees, and the sons of Abraham by the concubines, all came when they heard of Abraham's death. They rewarded Abraham's kindness, and comforted Isaac his son, and they buried Abraham in the cave which he bought from Ephron the Hittite and his children, for the possession of a burial place.

32 All the inhabitants of Canaan, and all those who had known Abraham, wept for Abraham a whole year; men and women mourned over him.

33 AlII the little children, and all the inhabitants of the land wept on account of Abraham, for Abraham had been good to them all, because he had been upright with God and men.

34 There arose not a man who feared God like Abraham, for he had feared his God from his youth, and had served the Lord, and had gone in all his ways during his life from his childhood to the day of his death.

35 And the Lord was with him and delivered him from the counsel of Nimrod and his people; when he made war with the four kings of Elam he conquered them.

36 He brought all the children of the earth to the service of God and he taught them the ways of the Lord, and caused them to know the Lord.

37 He formed a grove and planted a vineyard therein, and he had always prepared in his tent meat and drink to those that passed through the land, that they might satisfy themselves in his house.

38 The Lord God delivered the whole earth on account of Abraham.

39 It was after the death of Abraham that God blessed his son Isaac and his children, and the Lord was with Isaac as he had been with his father Abraham, for Isaac kept all the commandments of the Lord as Abraham his father had commanded him; he did not turn to the right or to the left

from the right path which his father had commanded him.

CHAPTER 27

1 Esau at that time, after the death of Abraham, frequently went in the field to hunt.

2 Nimrod king of Babel, the same was Amraphel, also frequently went with his mighty men to hunt in the field, and to walk about with his men in the cool of the day.

3 Nimrod was observing Esau all those days, for jealousy was formed in the heart of Nimrod against Esau.

4 On a certain day Esau went in the field to hunt, and he found Nimrod walking in the wilderness with his two men.

5 All his mighty men and his people were with him in the wilderness, but they kept at a distance; they went from him in different directions to hunt, and Esau concealed himself from Nimrod, and he lurked for him in the wilderness.

6 And Nimrod and his men that were with him did not know him. Nimrod and his men frequently walked about in the field at the cool of the day, and to know where his men were hunting in the field.

7 Nimrod and two of his men that were with him came to the place where they were, when Esau appeared suddenly from his lurking place, drew his sword, and hurriedly ran to Nimrod and cut off his head.

8 Esau fought a desperate fight with the two men that were with Nimrod, and when they called out to him, Esau turned to them and struck them to death with his sword.

9 All the mighty men of Nimrod, who had left him to go to the wilderness, heard the cry at a distance, and they knew the voices of those two men; they ran to know the cause of it and they found their king and the two men that were with him lying dead in the wilderness.

10 When Esau saw the mighty men of Nimrod coming at a distance, he fled, and thereby escaped. Esau took the valuable garments of Nimrod

which Nimrod's father had bequeathed to Nimrod, with which Nimrod prevailed over the whole land; he ran and concealed them in his house.

11 Esau took those garments and ran into the city on account of Nimrod's men, and he came to his father's house wearied and exhausted from fight, and he was ready to die through grief when he approached his brother Jacob and sat before him.

12 And he said to his brother Jacob, Behold I shall die this day; wherefore then do I want the birthright? And Jacob acted wisely with Esau in this matter, and Esau sold his birthright to Jacob, for it was so brought about by the Lord.

13 Esau's portion in the cave of the field of Machpelah, which Abraham had bought from the children of Heth for the possession of a burial ground, Esau also sold to Jacob, and Jacob bought all this from his brother Esau for value given.

14 Jacob wrote all of this in a book and he testified the same with witnesses, and sealed it, and the book remained in the hands of Jacob.

15 When Nimrod the son of Cush died, his men lifted him up and brought him in consternation, and buried him in his city, and all the days that Nimrod lived were two hundred and fifteen years and he died.

16 The days that Nimrod reigned on the people of the land were one hundred and eighty-five years; and Nimrod died by the sword of Esau in shame and contempt, and the descendants of Abraham caused his death as he had seen in his dream.

17 At the death of Nimrod his kingdom became divided into many divisions, and all those parts that Nimrod reigned over were restored to the respective kings of the land, who recovered them after the death of Nimrod. All the people of the house of Nimrod were for a long time enslaved to all the other kings of the land.

CHAPTER 28

1 In those days, after the death of Abraham, in that year the Lord brought a heavy famine in the land. While the famine was raging in the land of Canaan, Isaac rose up to go down to Egypt on account of the famine, as his father Abraham had done.

2 And the Lord appeared that night to Isaac and said to him, Do not go down to Egypt but rise and go to Gerar, to Abimelech king of the Philistines, and remain there till the famine shall cease.

3 Isaac rose up and went to Gerar, as the Lord commanded him, and he remained there a full year.

4 And when Isaac came to Gerar, the people of the land saw that Rebecca his wife was of a beautiful appearance, and the people of Gerar asked Isaac concerning his wife, and he said, She is my sister, for he was afraid to say she was his wife that the people of the land should kill him on account of her.

5 The princes of Abimelech went and praised the woman to the king, but he answered them not, neither did he give attention to their words.

6 But he heard them say that Isaac declared her to be his sister, so the king reserved this within himself.

7 And when Isaac had remained three months in the land, Abimelech looked out the window, and he saw Isaac was sporting with Rebecca his wife, for Isaac lived in the outer house belonging to the king, so that the house of Isaac was opposite the house of the king.

8 And the king said to Isaac, What is this you have done to us in saying of your wife, She is my sister? How easily might one of the great men of the people have lain with her, and you would then have brought guilt on us.

9 And Isaac said to Abimelech, Because I was afraid that I die on account of my wife, therefore I said, She is my sister.

10 At that time Abimelech gave orders to all his princes and great men, and they took Isaac and Rebecca his wife and brought them before the king.

11 The king commanded that they should dress them in princely garments, and make them ride through the streets of the city, and proclaim before them throughout the land, saying, This is the man and this is his wife; whoever touches this man or his wife shall certainly die. And Isaac returned with his wife to the king's house, and the Lord was with Isaac and he continued to become great and lacked nothing.

12 And the Lord caused Isaac to find favor in the sight of Abimelech, and in the sight of all his subjects, and Abimelech acted well with Isaac, for Abimelech remembered the oath and the covenant that existed between his father and Abraham.

13 Abimelech said to Isaac, Behold the whole earth is before you; dwell wherever it may seem good in your sight until you shall return to your land. Abimelech gave Isaac fields and vineyards and the best part of the land of Gerar, to sow and reap and eat the fruits of the ground until the days of the famine would have passed by.

14 And Isaac sowed in that land, and received a hundred-fold in the same year, and the Lord blessed him.

15 The man became great, and he had possession of flocks and possession of herds and a great store of servants.

16 When the days of the famine had passed away the Lord appeared to Isaac and said to him, Rise up, go forth from this place and return to your land, to the land of Canaan; Isaac rose up and returned to Hebron which is in the land of Canaan, he and all belonging to him as the Lord commanded him.

17 Ater this Shelach the son at Arpachshad died in that year, which is the eighteenth year of the lives of Jacob and Esau; all the days that Shelach lived were four hundred and thirty-three years and he died.

18 At that time Isaac sent his younger son Jacob to the house of Shem and Eber, and he learned the instructions of the Lord; Jacob remained in the house of Shem and Eber for thirty-two years; Esau his brother did not go for he was not willing to go, and he remained in his father's house in the land of Canaan.

19 Esau was continually hunting in the fields to bring home what he could get, so did Esau all the days.

20 Esau was a designing and deceitful man, one who hunted after the hearts of men and inveigled them, and Esau was a valiant man in the field; in the course of time he went as usual to hunt and came as far as the field of Seir, the same is Edom.

21 And he remained in the land of Seir hunting in the field a year and four months.

22 Esau there saw in the land of Seir the daughter of a man of Canaan, and her name was Jehudith, the daughter of Beeri, son of Epher, from the families of Heth the son of Canaan.

23 Esau took her for a wife, and he came to her; forty years old was Esau when he took her, and he brought her to Hebron, the land of his father's dwelling place, and he lived there.

24 It came to pass in those days, in the hundred and tenth year of the life of Isaac, that is in the fiftieth year of the life of Jacob, in that year Shem the son of Noah died; Shem was six hundred years old at his death.

25 And when Shem died Jacob returned to his father to Hebron which is in the land of Canaan.

26 And in the fifty-sixth year of the life of Jacob, people came from Haran, and Rebecca was told concerning her brother Laban the son of Bethuel.

27 The wife of Laban was unable to conceive in those days, and gave birth to no children, and also all his handmaids gave birth to none, to him.

28 And the Lord afterward remembered Adinah the wife of Laban, and she conceived and gave birth to twin daughters, and Laban named his daughters: the name of the elder Leah, and the name of the younger Rachel.

29 And those people came and told these things to Rebecca, and Rebecca rejoiced greatly that the Lord had visited her brother and that he had gotten children.

CHAPTER 29

1 Isaac the son of Abraham became old and advanced in days, and his eyes became heavy through age; they were dim and could not see.

2 At that time Isaac called to Esau his son, saying, Get I pray you your weapons, your quiver and your bow; rise up and go forth into the field and get me some venison, make me savory meat and bring it to me that I may eat in order that I may bless you before my death, as I have now become old and gray-headed.

3 And Esau did so; he took his weapon and went forth into the field to hunt for venison, as usual, to bring to his father as he had ordered him, so that he might bless him.

4 And Rebecca heard all the words that Isaac had spoken to Esau, and she hurried and called her son Jacob, saying, Thus did your father speak to your brother Esau, and thus did I hear, now therefore hurry and make that which I shall tell you.

5 Rise up and go, I pray you, to the flock and fetch me two fine kids of the goats; I will get the savory meat for your father and you shall bring the savory meat that he may eat before your brother will have come from the hunt, in order that your father may bless you.

6 And Jacob hurried and did as his mother had commanded him, and he made the savory meat and brought it before his father before Esau had come from his hunt.

7 And Isaac said to Jacob, Who are you, my son? And he said, I am your first born Esau. I have done as you did order me, now therefore rise up I

pray you and eat of my hunt, in order that your soul may bless me as you did speak to me.

8 And Isaac rose up and he ate and drank, and his heart was comforted; he blessed Jacob and Jacob went away from his father. As soon as Isaac had blessed Jacob and had gone away from him, behold Esau came from his hunt in the field, and he also made savory meat and brought it to his father to eat thereof and to bless him.

9 And Isaac said to Esau, And who was he that has taken venison and brought it me before you came and whom I did bless? And Esau knew that his brother Jacob had done this, and the anger of Esau was set ablaze against his brother Jacob that he had acted thus toward him.

10 And Esau said, Is he not rightly called Jacob? For he has supplanted me twice, he took away my birthright and now he has taken away my blessing. And Esau wept greatly. When Isaac heard the voice of his son Esau weeping, Isaac said to Esau, What can I do, my son, your brother came with subtlety and took away your blessing? Esau hated his brother Jacob on account of the blessing that his father had given him, and his anger was greatly roused against him.

11 And Jacob was very much afraid of his brother Esau; he rose up and fled to the house of Eber the son of Shem, and he concealed himself there on account of his brother. Jacob was sixty-three years old when he went forth from the land of Canaan from Hebron, and Jacob was concealed in Eber's house fourteen years on account of his brother Esau, and he continued there to learn the ways of the Lord and his commandments.

12 When Esau saw that Jacob had fled and escaped from him, and that Jacob had cunningly obtained the blessing, then Esau grieved greatly. He was also troubled at his father and mother; he rose up and took his wife and went away from his father and mother to the land of Seir, and he lived there. Esau saw there a woman from among the daughters of Heth whose name was Bosmath, the daughter of Elon the Hittite, and he took her for a wife in addition to his first wife, and Esau called her name Adah, saying the blessing had in that time passed from him.

13 And Esau lived in the land of Seir six months without seeing his father and mother, and afterward Esau took his wives and rose up and returned to the land of Canaan. And Esau placed his two wives in his father's house in Hebron.

14 The wives of Esau troubled and provoked Isaac and Rebecca with their works, for they walked not in the ways of the Lord, but served their father's gods of wood and stone as their father had taught them; they were more wicked than their father.

15 They went according to the evil desires of their hearts, and they sacrificed and burnt incense to the Baalim, and Isaac and Rebecca became weary of them.

16 And Rebecca said, I am weary of my life because of the daughters of Heth; if Jacob took a wife of the daughters of Heth, such as these which are of the daughters of the land, what good then is life to me?

17 In those days Adah the wife of Esau conceived and gave birth to him a son, and Esau called the name of the son that was born to him Eliphaz, and Esau was sixty-five years old when she gave birth to him.

18 Ishmael the son of Abraham died in those days, in the sixty-fourth year of the life of Jacob, and all the days that Ishmael lived were one hundred and thirty-seven years and he died.

19 And when Isaac heard that Ishmael was dead he mourned for him, and Isaac lamented over him many days.

20 At the end of fourteen years of Jacob's residing in the house of Eber, Jacob desired to see his father and mother, and Jacob came to the house of his father and mother to Hebron, and Esau had in those days forgotten what Jacob had done to him in having taken the blessing from him.

21 And when Esau saw Jacob coming to his father and mother he remembered what Jacob had done to him, and he was greatly incensed against him and he sought to kill him.

22 And Isaac the son of Abraham was old and advanced in days, and Esau said, Now my father's time is drawing nigh that he must die, and when he shall die I will kill my brother Jacob.

23 This was told to Rebecca, and she hurried and sent and called for Jacob her son, and she said to him, Arise, go and flee to Haran to my brother Laban and remain there for some time, until your brother's anger be turned from you and then shall you come back.

24 And Isaac called to Jacob and said to him, Take not a wife from the daughters of Canaan, for thus did our father Abraham command us according to the word of the Lord which he had commanded him, saying, Unto your offspring will I give this land; if your children keep my covenant that I have made with you, then I will also perform to your children that which I have spoken to you and I will not turn away from them.

25 Now therefore my son listen to my voice, to all that I shall command you, and refrain from taking a wife from among the daughters of Canaan; arise, go to Haran to the house of Bethuel your mother's father, and take to

you a wife from there from the daughters of Laban your mother's brother.

26 Therefore be careful that you should not forget the Lord your God and all his ways in the land to which you go, and should get connected with the people of the land and pursue vanity and turn away from the Lord your God.

27 But when you come to the land there serve the Lord, do not turn to the right or to the left from the way which I commanded you and which you did learn.

28 And may the Almighty God grant you favor in the sight of the people of the earth, that you may take there a wife according to your choice; one who is good and upright in the ways of the Lord.

29 May God give to you and your descendants the blessing of your father Abraham, and make you prolific and reproduce, and may you become a multitude of people in the land where you go; may God cause you to return to this land, the land of your father's dwelling, with children and with great riches, with joy and with pleasure.

30 And Isaac finished commanding Jacob and blessing him, and he gave him many gifts, together with silver and gold, and he sent him away. Jacob listened to his father and mother; he kissed them and arose and went to Padan-aram, and Jacob was seventy-seven years old when he went out from the land of Canaan from Beersheba.

31 When Jacob went away to go to Haran Esau called to his son Eliphaz, and secretly spoke to him, saying, Now hurry, take your sword in your hand and pursue Jacob and pass before him in the road, and lurk for him; kill him with your sword in one of the mountains, and take all belonging to him and come back.

32 Eliphaz the son of Esau was an active man and expert with the bow as his father had taught him, and he was a noted hunter in the field and a valiant man.

33 Eliphaz did as his father had commanded him, and Eliphaz was at that time thirteen years old; Eliphaz rose up and went and took ten of his mother's brothers with him and pursued Jacob.

34 He closely followed Jacob, and he lurked for him in the border of the land of Canaan opposite to the city of Shechem.

35 And Jacob saw Eliphaz and his men pursuing him; Jacob stood still in the place in which he was going, in order to know what this was, for he did not know the thing. Eliphaz drew his sword and he went on advancing, he and his men, toward Jacob. And Jacob said to them, Why have you come here, and what does it mean that you pursue with your

swords?

36 And Eliphaz came near to Jacob and he answered and said to him, Thus did my father command me, and now therefore I will not deviate from the orders which my father gave me. When Jacob saw that Esau had spoken to Eliphaz to employ force, Jacob then approached and supplicated Eliphaz and his men, saying to him,

37 Behold all that I have and which my father and mother gave to me, that you should take and go from me, and do not kill me; may this thing be accounted to you a righteousness.

38 And the Lord caused Jacob to find favor in the sight of Eliphaz the son of Esau, and his men, and they listened to the voice of Jacob, and they did not put him to death; Eliphaz and his men took all belonging to Jacob together with the silver and gold that he had brought with him from Beersheba; they left him nothing.

39 Eliphaz and his men went away from him and they returned to Esau to Beersheba, and they told him all that had occurred to them with Jacob, and they gave him all that they had taken from Jacob.

40 Esau was indignant at Eliphaz his son, and at his men that were with him, because they had not put Jacob to death.

41 And they answered and said to Esau, Because Jacob supplicated us in this matter not to kill him, our pity was increased toward him, and we took all belonging to him and brought it to you. Esau took all the silver and gold which Eliphaz had taken from Jacob and he put them by in his house.

42 At that time when Esau saw that Isaac had blessed Jacob, and had commanded him, saying, You shall not take a wife from among the daughters of Canaan, and that the daughters of Canaan were bad in the sight of Isaac and Rebecca,

43 Then he went to the house of Ishmael his uncle, and in addition to his older wives he took Machlath the daughter of Ishmael, the sister of Nebayoth, for a wife.

CHAPTER 30

1 Jacob went forth continuing his road to Haran, and he came as far as mount Moriah, and he stayed there all night near the city of Luz. The Lord appeared there to Jacob on that night and said to him, I am the Lord God of Abraham and the God of Isaac your father; the land on which you dwell I will give to you and your descendants.

2 Behold I am with you and will keep you wherever you go, and I will reproduce your descendants as the stars of Heaven, and I will cause all your enemies to fall before you; when they make war with you they shall not prevail over you, and I will bring you again to this land with joy, with children, and with great riches.

3 Jacob awoke from his sleep and he rejoiced greatly at the vision which he had seen, and he called the name of that place Bethel.

4 Jacob rose up from that place quite jubilant, and when he walked his feet felt light to him for joy, and he went from there to the land of the children of the East, and returned to Haran and sat by the shepherd's well.

5 There he found some men going from Haran to feed their flocks, and Jacob made inquiries of them, and they said, We are from Haran.

6 And he said to them, Do you know Laban, the son of Nahor? And they said, We know him and look, his daughter Rachel is coming along to feed her father's flock.

7 While he was yet speaking with them, Rachel the daughter of Laban came to feed her father's sheep, for she was a shepherdess.

8 When Jacob saw Rachel, the daughter of Laban, his mother's brother, he ran and kissed her and lifted up his voice and wept.

9 Jacob told Rachel that he was the son of Rebecca, her father's sister, and Rachel ran and told her father; Jacob continued to cry because he had nothing with him to bring to the house of Laban.

10 When Laban heard that his sister's son Jacob had come, he ran, kissed him and embraced him, brought him into the house and gave him bread, and he ate.

11 And Jacob related to Laban what his brother Esau had done to him, and what his son Eliphaz had done to him in the road.

12 Jacob resided in Laban's house for one month, and Jacob ate and drank in the house of Laban, and afterward Laban said to Jacob, Tell me what shall be your wages, for how can you serve me for nothing?

13 Laban had no sons but only daughters; his other wives and handmaids were still unable to conceive in those days. These are the names of Laban's daughters which his wife Adinah had borne to him: the name of the elder was Leah and the name of the younger was Rachel. Leah was tender-eyed, but Rachel was beautiful and well favored, and Jacob loved her.

14 And Jacob said to Laban, I will serve you seven years for Rachel your younger daughter; and Laban consented to this and Jacob served Laban seven years for his daughter Rachel.

15 In the second year of Jacob's dwelling in Haran, that is in the seventy ninth year of the life of Jacob, Eber the son of Shem died; he was four hundred and sixty-four years old at his death.

16 And when Jacob heard that Eber was dead he grieved greatly; he lamented and mourned over him many days.

17 In the third year of Jacob's dwelling in Haran, Bosmath, the daughter of Ishmael, the wife of Esau, gave birth to him a son, and Esau called his name Reuel.

18 And in the fourth year of Jacob's residence in the house of Laban, the Lord visited Laban and remembered him on account of Jacob, and sons were born to him: his first born was Beor, his second was Alib, and the third was Chorash.

19 The Lord gave Laban riches and honor, sons and daughters, and the man increased greatly on account of Jacob.

20 In those days Jacob served Laban in all manner of work, in the house and in the field, and the blessing of the Lord was in all that belonged to Laban in the house and in the field.

21 In the fifth year Jehudith died, the daughter of Beeri, the wife of Esau, in the land of Canaan, and she had no sons but daughters only.

22 These are the names of her daughters which she gave birth to, to Esau: the name of the elder was Marzith, and the name of the younger was Puith.

23 And when Jehudith died, Esau rose up and went to Seir to hunt in the field, as usual, and Esau lived in the land of Seir for a long time.

24 In the sixth year Esau took for a wife, in addition to his other wives, Ahlibamah, the daughter of Zebeon the Hivite, and Esau brought her to the land of Canaan.

25 And Ahlibamah conceived and gave birth to, to Esau, three sons: Yeush, Yaalan, and Korah.

26 In those days, in the land of Canaan, there was a quarrel between the herdsmen of Esau and the herdsmen of the inhabitants of the land of Canaan, for Esau's cattle and goods were too abundant for him to remain in the land of Canaan, in his father's house; the land of Canaan could not bear him on account of his cattle.

27 And when Esau saw that his quarreling increased with the inhabitants of the land of Canaan, he rose up and took his wives and his sons and his daughters, and all belonging to him, and the cattle which he possessed, and all his property that he had acquired in the land of Canaan; he went away from the inhabitants of the land to the land of Seir, and Esau and all belonging to him lived in the land of Seir.

28 But from time to time Esau would go and see his father and mother in the land of Canaan, and Esau intermarried with the Horites, and he gave his daughters to the sons of Seir, the Horite.

29 He gave his elder daughter Marzith to Anah, the son of Zebeon, his wife's brother, and Puith he gave to Azar, the son of Bilhan the Horite; Esau lived in the mountain, he and his children, and they were prolific and multiplied.

CHAPTER 31

1 In the seventh year, Jacob's service to Laban was completed, and Jacob said to Laban, Give me my wife, for the days of my service are fulfilled; Laban did so, and Laban and Jacob assembled all the people of that place and they made a feast.

2 In the evening Laban came to the house, and afterward Jacob came there with the people of the feast, and Laban extinguished all the lights that were there in the house.

3 Jacob said to Laban, Why do you do this thing to us? And Laban answered, Such is our custom to act in this land.

4 Afterward Laban took his daughter Leah, and he brought her to Jacob, and he came to her and Jacob did not know that she was Leah.

5 And Laban gave his daughter Leah his maid Zilpah for a handmaid.

6 All the people at the feast knew what Laban had done to Jacob, but they didn't tell a thing to Jacob.

7 All the neighbors came that night to Jacob's house, and they ate and

drank and rejoiced, and played before Leah on timbrels, and with dances, and they responded before Jacob, Heleah, Heleah.

8 Jacob heard their words but did not understand their meaning, but he thought such might be their custom in this land.

9 And the neighbors spoke these words before Jacob during the night, and all the lights that were in the house Laban had that night been extinguished.

10 In the morning, when daylight appeared, Jacob turned to his wife and he saw it was Leah that had been lying in his bosom, and Jacob said, So now I know what the neighbors said last night, Heleah, they said, and I knew it not.

11 Jacob called to Laban, and said to him, What is this that you did to me? Certainly I served you for Rachel; why did you deceive me and give me Leah?

12 Laban answered Jacob, saying, Not so is it done in our place to give the younger before the elder; therefore if you desire to take her sister likewise, take her to you for the service which you will serve me for another seven years.

13 Jacob did so, and he also took Rachel for a wife; he served Laban seven years more, and Jacob also came to Rachel, and he loved Rachel more than Leah; Laban gave her his maid Bilhah for a handmaid.

14 When the Lord saw that Leah was hated, the Lord opened her womb and she conceived and gave birth to Jacob four sons in those days.

15 And these are their names: Reuben, Simeon, Levi, and Judah, and afterward she ceased bearing.

16 At that time Rachel was unable to conceive and had no children, and Rachel envied her sister Leah. When Rachel saw that she gave birth to no children to Jacob, she took her handmaid Bilhah, and she gave birth to Jacob two sons, Dan and Naphtali.

17 When Leah saw that she had ceased bearing, she also took her handmaid Zilpah, and she gave her to Jacob for a wife. Jacob also came to Zilpah, and she gave birth to Jacob two sons, Gad and Asher.

18 Leah again conceived and gave birth to Jacob in those days two sons and one daughter, and these are their names: Issachar, Zebulon, and their sister Dinah.

19 Rachel was still unable to conceive in those days and Rachel prayed to the Lord at that time, and she said, O Lord God remember me and visit

me, I beg you, for now my husband will cast me off, for I have borne him no children.

20 Now O Lord God, hear my supplication before you, and see my affliction, and give me children like one of the handmaids, that I may no more bear my reproach.

21 God heard her and opened her womb, and Rachel conceived and gave birth to a son, and she said, The Lord has taken away my reproach. She called his name Joseph, saying, May the Lord add to me another son; Jacob was ninety-one years old when she gave birth to him.

22 At that time Jacob's mother, Rebecca, sent her nurse Deborah the daughter of Uz, and two of Isaac's servants to Jacob.

23 They came to Jacob to Haran and said to him, Rebecca has sent us to you that you shall return to your father's house to the land of Canaan; Jacob listened to them of this which his mother had spoken.

24 At that time, the other seven years which Jacob served Laban for Rachel were completed, and it was at the end of fourteen years that he had lived in Haran, Jacob said to Laban, Give me my wives and send me away that I may go to my land, for behold my mother did send to me from the land at Canaan that I should return to my father's house.

25 And Laban said to him, Not so I pray you; if I have found favor in your sight do not leave me; tell me your wages and I will give them, and remain with me.

26 Jacob said to him, This is what you shall give me for wages, that I shall this day pass through all your flock and take away from them every lamb that is speckled and spotted and such as are brown among the sheep, and among the goats, and if you will do this thing for me I will return and feed your flock and keep them as at first.

27 Laban did so, and Laban removed from his flock all that Jacob had said and gave them to him.

28 And Jacob placed all that he had removed from Laban's flock in the hands of his sons, and Jacob was feeding the remainder of Laban's flock.

29 When the servants of Isaac which he had sent to Jacob saw that Jacob would not return with them to the land of Canaan to his father, they went away from him and returned home to the land of Canaan.

30 And Deborah remained with Jacob in Haran; she did not return with the servants of Isaac to the land of Canaan, and Deborah resided with Jacob's wives and children in Haran.

31 Jacob served Laban six years longer, and when the sheep brought

forth, Jacob removed from them such as were speckled and spotted, as he had determined with Laban; Jacob did so at Laban's for six years, and the man increased abundantly. He had cattle and maid servants and men servants, camels, and asses.

32 Jacob had two hundred drove of cattle, and his cattle were of large size and of beautiful appearance and were very productive; all the families of the sons of men desired to get some of the cattle of Jacob, for they were greatly prosperous.

33 Many of the sons of men came to procure some of Jacob's flock, and Jacob gave them a sheep for a man servant or a maid servant or for an ass or a camel, or whatever Jacob desired from them they gave him.

34 Jacob obtained riches and honor and possessions by means of these transactions with the sons of men, and the children of Laban envied him of this honor.

35 In the course of time he heard the words of Laban's sons, saying, Jacob has taken away all that was our father's, and of that which was our father's has he acquired all this glory.

36 And Jacob observed the countenance of Laban and of his children, and it was not toward him in those days as it had been before.

37 The Lord appeared to Jacob at the expiration of the six years, and said to him, Arise, go forth out of this land, and return to the land of your birthplace and I will be with you.

38 And Jacob rose up at that time and he mounted his children and wives and all belonging to him on camels, and he went forth to go to the land of Canaan to his father Isaac.

39 Laban did not know that Jacob had gone from him, for Laban had been sheep-shearing that day.

40 Rachel stole her father's images, and she took them and concealed them on the camel on which she sat, and she went on.

41 And this is the manner of the images: in taking a man who is the firstborn and slaying him and taking the hair off his head; taking salt and salting the head and anointing it in oil, then taking a small tablet of copper or a tablet of gold and writing the name on it and placing the tablet under his tongue; taking the head with the tablet under the tongue and putting it in the house and lighting up lights before it and bowing down to it.

42 And at the time when they bow down to it, it speaks to them in all matters that they ask of it, through the power of the name which is written

in it.

43 And some make them in the figures of men, of gold and silver, and go to them in times known to them, and the figures receive the influence of the stars, and tell them future things; in this manner were the images which Rachel stole from her father.

44 Rachel stole these images which were her father's in order that Laban might not know through them where Jacob had gone.

45 Laban came home and he asked concerning Jacob and his household, and he was not to be found; Laban sought his images to know where Jacob had gone, and could not find them. He went to some other images, and he inquired of them and they told him that Jacob had fled from him to his father's, to the land of Canaan.

46 Laban then rose up and took his brothers and all his servants, and he went forth and pursued Jacob, and he overtook him in mount Gilead.

47 And Laban said to Jacob, What is this you have done to me to flee and deceive me, and lead my daughters and their children as captives taken by the sword?

48 You did not suffer me to kiss them and send them away with joy, and you did steal my gods and did go away.

49 And Jacob answered Laban, saying, Because I was afraid that you would take your daughters by force from me; and now with whomsoever you find your gods he shall die.

50 And Laban searched for the images and he examined in all Jacob's tents and furniture, but could not find them.

51 And Laban said to Jacob, We will make a covenant together and it shall be a testimony between me and you; if you shall afflict my daughters, or shall take other wives besides my daughters, even God shall be a witness between me and you in this matter.

52 And they took stones and made a heap, and Laban said, This heap is a witness between me and you. He called the name thereof Gilead.

53 Jacob and Laban offered sacrifice on the mount, and they ate there by the heap, and they stayed in the mount all night. Laban rose up early in the morning; he wept with his daughters and he kissed them, and he returned to his place.

54 He hurried and sent off his son Beor, who was seventeen years old, with Abichorof the son of Uz, the son of Nahor, and with them were ten men.

55 They hurried and went and passed on the road before Jacob, and they came by another road to the land of Seir.

56 They came to Esau and said to him, Thus says your brother and relative, your mother's brother Laban, the son of Bethuel, saying,

57 Have you heard what Jacob your brother has done to me, who first came to me naked and gave birth to? I went to meet him and brought him to my house with honor; I made him great, and I gave him my two daughters for wives and also two of my maids.

58 And God blessed him on my account; he increased abundantly, and had sons, daughters and maid servants.

59 He has also an immense stock of flocks and herds, camels and asses, also silver and gold in abundance; when he saw that his wealth increased, he left me while I went to shear my sheep, and he rose up and fled in secrecy.

60 He lifted his wives and children on camels, and he led away all his cattle and property which he acquired in my land, and he lifted up his countenance to go to his father Isaac, to the land of Canaan.

61 He did not let me kiss my daughters and their children; he led my daughters as captives taken by the sword, and he also stole my gods and he fled.

62 And now I have left him in the mountain of the brook of Jabuk, him and all belonging to him; he lacks nothing.

63 If it be your wish to go to him, go then and there you will find him, and you can do to him as your soul desires; and Laban's messengers came and told Esau all these things.

64 Esau heard all the words of Laban's messengers, and his anger was greatly set ablaze against Jacob, and he remembered his hatred, and his anger burned within him.

65 Esau hurried and took his children and servants and the souls of his household, being sixty men; he went and assembled all the children of Seir the Horite and their people, being three hundred and forty men. He took all this number of four hundred men with drawn swords, and he went to Jacob to strike him.

66 Esau divided this number into several parts, and he took the sixty men of his children and servants and the souls of his household as one head, and gave them in care of Eliphaz his eldest son.

67 The remaining heads he gave to the care of the six sons of Seir the

Horite, and he placed every man over his generations and children.

68 The whole of this camp went as it was, and Esau went among them toward Jacob, and he conducted them with speed.

69 And Laban's messengers departed from Esau and went to the land of Canaan, and they came to the house of Rebecca the mother of Jacob and Esau.

70 They told her saying, Behold your son Esau has gone against his brother Jacob with four hundred men, for he heard that he was coming, and he is gone to make war with him, and to strike him and to take all that he has.

71 Rebecca hurried and sent seventy two men from the servants of Isaac to meet Jacob on the road; for she said, Perhaps Esau may make war in the road when he meets him.

72 These messengers went on the road to meet Jacob, and they met him in the road of the brook on the opposite side of the brook Jabuk. Jacob said when he saw them, This camp is destined to me from God. And Jacob called the name of that place Machnayim.

73 And Jacob knew all his father's people, and he kissed them and embraced them and came with them. Jacob asked them concerning his father and mother, and they said, They were well.

74 These messengers said to Jacob, Rebecca your mother has sent us to you, saying, I have heard, my son, that your brother Esau has gone forth against you on the road with men from the children of Seir the Horite.

75 Therefore, my son, listen to my voice and see with your counsel what you will do; when he comes up to you, supplicate him, and do not speak rashly to him, and give him a present from what you possess, and from what God has favored you with.

76 And when he asks you concerning your affairs, conceal nothing from him, perhaps he may turn from his anger against you and you will thereby save your soul, you and all belonging to you, for it is your duty to honor him, for he is your elder brother.

77 When Jacob heard the words of his mother which the messengers had spoken to him, Jacob lifted up his voice and wept bitterly, and did as his mother then commanded him.

CHAPTER 32

1 At that time Jacob sent messengers to his brother Esau toward the land of Seir, and he spoke to him words of supplication.

2 He commanded them, saying, Thus shall you say to my lord, to Esau, Thus says your servant Jacob, Let not my lord imagine that my father's blessing with which he did bless me has proved beneficial to me.

3 For I have been these twenty years with Laban, and he deceived me and changed my wages ten times, as it has all been already told to my lord.

4 And I served him in his house very laboriously, and God afterward saw my affliction, my labor and the work of my hands, and he caused me to find grace and favor in his sight.

5 And afterward through God's great mercy and kindness I acquired oxen and asses and cattle, and men servants and maid servants.

6 And now I am coming to my land and my home to my father and mother, who are in the land of Canaan; I have sent to let my lord know all this in order to find favor in the sight of my lord, so that he may not imagine that I have of myself obtained wealth, or that the blessing with which my father blessed me has benefited me.

7 Those messengers went to Esau, and found him on the borders of the land of Edom going toward Jacob, and four hundred men of the children of Seir the Horite were standing with drawn swords.

8 And the messengers of Jacob told Esau all the words that Jacob had spoken to them concerning Esau.

9 Esau answered them with pride and contempt and said to them, Certainly I have heard and truly it has been told to me what Jacob has done to Laban, who exalted him in his house and gave him his daughters for wives, and he had sons and daughters, and abundantly increased in wealth and riches in Laban's house through his means.

10 When he saw that his wealth was abundant and his riches great he fled with all belonging to him, from Laban's house, and he led Laban's daughters away from the face of their father, as captives taken by the sword without telling him of it.

11 And not only to Laban has Jacob done thus but also to me has he done so and has twice supplanted me, and shall I be silent?

12 Now therefore I have this day come with my camps to meet him, and I will do to him according to the desire of my heart.

13 And the messengers returned and came to Jacob and said to him, We came to your brother, to Esau, and we told him all your words, and thus has he answered us; behold he comes to meet you with four hundred men.

14 Now then know and see what you shall do, and pray before God to deliver you from him.

15 And when he heard the words of his brother which he had spoken to the messengers of Jacob, Jacob was greatly afraid and he was distressed.

16 And Jacob prayed to the Lord his God, and he said, O Lord God of my fathers, Abraham and Isaac, you did say to me when I went away from my father's house, saying,

17 I am the Lord God of your father Abraham and the God of Isaac, to you do I give this land and your descendants after you, and I will make your descendants as the stars of heaven, and you shall spread forth to the four sides of heaven, and in you and in your offspring shall all the families of the earth be blessed.

18 You did establish your words, and did give to me riches and children and cattle, as the utmost wishes of my heart did you give to your servant; you gave to me all that I asked from you, so that I lacked nothing.

19 Afterward you said to me, Return to your parents and to your birth place and I will still do well with you.

20 And now that I have come, and you did deliver me from Laban, I shall fall in the hands of Esau who will kill me, yea, together with the mothers of my children.

21 Now therefore, O Lord God, deliver me, I pray you, also from the hands of my brother Esau, for I am greatly afraid of him.

22 And if there is no righteousness in me, do it for the sake of Abraham and my father Isaac.

23 For I know that through kindness and mercy I have acquired this wealth; now therefore I beseech you to deliver me this day with your kindness and to answer me.

24 And Jacob ceased praying to the Lord; he divided the people that were with him with the flocks and cattle into two camps, and he gave the half to the care of Damesek, the son of Eliezer, Abraham's servant, for a camp, with his children; the other half he gave to the care of his brother Elianus the son of Eliezer, to be for a camp with his children.

25 And he commanded them, saying, Keep yourselves at a distance with your camps, and do not come too near each other, and if Esau comes to one camp and kills it, the other camp at a distance from it will escape him.

26 Jacob tarried there that night, and during the whole night he gave his servants instructions concerning the forces and his children.

27 The Lord heard the prayer of Jacob on that day, and the Lord then delivered Jacob from the hands of his brother Esau.

28 The Lord sent three angels of the angels of heaven, and they went before Esau and came to him.

29 And these angels appeared to Esau and his people as two thousand men, riding on horses furnished with all sorts of war instruments, and they appeared in the sight of Esau and all his men to be divided into four camps, with four chiefs to them.

30 And one camp went on and they found Esau coming with four hundred men toward his brother Jacob, and this camp ran toward Esau and his people and terrified them. Esau fell off the horse in alarm, and all his men separated from him in that place, for they were greatly afraid.

31 And the whole camp shouted after them when they fled from Esau, and all the warlike men answered, saying,

32 Certainly we are the servants of Jacob, who is the servant of God, and who then can stand against us? And Esau said to them, O then, my lord and brother Jacob is your lord, whom I have not seen for these twenty years, and now that I have this day come to see him, do you treat me in this manner?

33 And the angels answered him saying, As the Lord lives, were not Jacob of whom you speak your brother, we would not let one remain from you and your people, but only on account of Jacob we will do nothing to them.

34 And this camp passed from Esau and his men and it went away, and Esau and his men had gone from them about a league when the second camp came toward him with all sorts of weapons, and they also did to Esau and his men as the first camp had done to them.

35 And when they had left it to go on, behold the third camp came toward him and they were all terrified, and Esau fell off the horse, and the whole camp cried out, and said, Certainly we are the servants of Jacob, who is the servant of God, and who can stand against us?

36 Esau again answered them saying, O then, Jacob my lord and your lord is my brother, and for twenty years I have not seen his countenance and hearing this day that he was coming, I went this day to meet him, and do you treat me in this manner?

37 They answered him, and said to him, As the Lord lives, were not Jacob

your brother as you did say, we would not leave a remnant from you and your men, but on account of Jacob of whom you speak being your brother, we will not meddle with you or your men.

38 And the third camp also passed from them, and he still continued his road with his men toward Jacob, when the fourth camp came toward him, and they also did to him and his men as the others had done.

39 When Esau beheld the evil which the four angels had done to him and to his men, he became greatly afraid of his brother Jacob, and he went to meet him in peace.

40 And Esau concealed his hatred against Jacob, because he was afraid for his life on account of his brother Jacob, and because he imagined that the four camps that he had lighted on were Jacob's servants.

41 And Jacob tarried that night with his servants in their camps, and he resolved with his servants to give to Esau a present from all that he had with him, and from all his property; Jacob rose up in the morning, he and his men, and they chose from among the cattle a present for Esau.

42 And this is the amount of the present which Jacob chose from his flock to give to his brother Esau: he selected two hundred and forty head from the flocks, and he selected from the camels and asses thirty each, and of the herds he chose fifty kine.

43 He put them all in ten droves, and he placed each sort by itself; he delivered them into the hands of ten of his servants, each drove by itself.

44 He commanded them, and said to them, Keep yourselves at a distance from each other, and put a space between the droves, and when Esau and those who are with him shall meet you and ask you, saying, Whose are you, and where do you go, and to whom belongs all this before you, you shall say to them, We are the servants of Jacob, and we come to meet Esau in peace, and behold Jacob comes behind us.

45 And that which is before us is a present sent from Jacob to his brother Esau.

46 And if they shall say to you, Why does he delay behind you, from coming to meet his brother and to see his face, then you shall say to them, Certainly he comes joyfully behind us to meet his brother, for he said, I will appease him with the present that goes to him, and after this I will see his face; per chance he will accept me.

47 So the whole present passed on in the hands of his servants, and went before him on that day, and he lodged that night with his camps by the border of the brook of Jabuk. He rose up in the middle of the night and took his wives and his maid servants and all belonging to him, and that

night he passed them over the ford Jabuk.

48 When he passed all belonging to him over the brook, Jacob was left by himself; a man met him, and he wrestled with him that night until the breaking of the day, and the hollow of Jacob's thigh was out of joint through wrestling with him.

49 At the break of day the man left Jacob there, and he blessed him and went away; Jacob passed the brook at the break of day, and he rested on his thigh.

50 And the sun rose on him when he had passed the brook, and he came up to the place of his cattle and children.

51 They went on till midday, and while they were going the present was passing on before them.

52 And Jacob lifted up his eyes and looked, and behold Esau was at a distance, coming along with many men, about four hundred, and Jacob was greatly afraid of his brother.

53 Jacob hurried and divided his children to his wives and his handmaids, and his daughter Dinah he put in a chest, and delivered her into the hands of his servants.

54 He passed before his children and wives to meet his brother, and he bowed down to the ground, yes, he bowed down seven times until he approached his brother. And God caused Jacob to find grace and favor in the sight of Esau and his men, for God had heard the prayer of Jacob.

55 The fear of Jacob and his terror fell on his brother Esau, for Esau was greatly afraid of Jacob for what the angels of God had done to Esau, and Esau's anger against Jacob was turned into kindness.

56 And when Esau saw Jacob running toward him, he also ran toward him and he embraced him, and he fell on his neck, and they kissed and they wept.

57 And God put fear and kindness toward Jacob in the hearts of the men that came with Esau, and they also kissed Jacob and embraced him.

58 Also Eliphaz, the son of Esau, with his four brothers, sons of Esau, wept with Jacob, and they kissed him and embraced him, for the fear of Jacob had fallen on them all.

59 And Esau lifted up his eyes and saw the women with their children, the children of Jacob, walking behind Jacob and bowing along the road to Esau.

60 And Esau said to Jacob, Who are these with you, my brother? Are they your children or your servants? And Jacob answered Esau and said, They are my children which God hath graciously given to your servant.

61 While Jacob was speaking to Esau and his men, Esau beheld the whole camp, and he said to Jacob, How did you get the whole camp that I met last night? And Jacob said, To find favor in the sight of my lord, it is that which God graciously gave to your servant.

62 The present came before Esau, and Jacob pressed Esau, saying, Take I pray you the present that I have brought to my lord. And Esau said, Why should I? Keep that which you have to yourself.

63 And Jacob said, It is incumbent on me to give all this, since I have seen your face, that you still live in peace.

64 Esau refused to take the present, and Jacob said to him, I beseech you my lord, if now I have found favor in your sight, then receive my present at my hand, for I have therefore seen your face, as you I had seen a god-like face, because you were pleased with me.

65 And Esau took the present, and Jacob also gave to Esau silver and gold and bdellium, for he pressed him so much that he took them.

66 Esau divided the cattle that were in the camp, and he gave half to the men who had come with him, for they had come on hire, and the other half he delivered to the hands of his children.

67 The silver and gold and bdellium he gave in the hands of Eliphaz his eldest son, and Esau said to Jacob, Let us remain with you, and we will go slowly along with you until you come to my place with me, that we may dwell there together.

68 And Jacob answered his brother and said, I would do as my lord speaks to me, but my lord knows that the children are tender, and the flocks and herds with their young who are with me go but slowly, for if they went swiftly they would all die, for you know their burdens and their fatigue.

69 Therefore let my lord pass on before his servant, and I will go on slowly for the sake of the children and the flock until I come to my lord's place to Seir.

70 And Esau said to Jacob, I will place with you some of the people that are with me to take care of you in the road, and to bear your fatigue and burden, and he said, I will do so, my lord, if I may find grace in your sight?

71 Behold I will come to you to Seir to dwell there together as you have

spoken, go then with your people for I will follow you.

72 Jacob said this to Esau in order to remove Esau and his men from him, so that Jacob might afterward go to his father's house to the land of Canaan.

73 Esau listened to the voice of Jacob, and Esau returned with the four hundred men that were with him on their road to Seir, and Jacob and all belonging to him went that day as far as the extremity of the land of Canaan in its borders, and he remained there some time.

CHAPTER 33

1 Some time after Jacob went away from the borders of the land, he came to the land of Shalem, that is the city of Shechem, which is in the land of Canaan, and he rested in front of the city.

2 And he bought a parcel of the field which was there from the children of Hamor, the people of the land, for five shekels.

3 Jacob there built himself a house and pitched his tent there, and he made booths for his cattle; therefore he called the name of that place Succoth.

4 And Jacob remained in Succoth a year and six months.

5 At that time some of the women of the inhabitants of the land went to the city of Shechem to dance and rejoice with the daughters of the people of the city, and when they went forth then Rachel and Leah the wives of Jacob with their families also went to behold the rejoicing of the daughters of the city.

6 And Dinah the daughter of Jacob also went along with them and saw the daughters of the city, and they remained there before these daughters

while all the people of the city were standing by them to behold their rejoicings, and all the great people of the city were there.

7 Shechem the son of Hamor, the prince of the land was also standing there to see them.

8 Shechem saw Dinah the daughter of Jacob sitting with her mother before the daughters of the city, and the damsel pleased him greatly, and he asked his friends and his people, saying, Whose daughter is that sitting among the women whom I do not know in this city?

9 And they said to him, Certainly this is the daughter of Jacob the son of Isaac the Hebrew, who has lived in this city for some time, and when it was reported that the daughters of the land were going forth to rejoice she went with her mother and maid servants to sit among them as you see.

10 Shechem saw Dinah the daughter of Jacob, and when he looked at her his soul became fixed on Dinah.

11 And he sent and had her taken by force, and Dinah came to the house of Shechem; he seized her forcibly and lay with her and humbled her, and he loved her greatly and placed her in his house.

12 And they came and told the thing to Jacob, and when Jacob heard that Shechem had defiled his daughter Dinah, Jacob sent twelve of his servants to fetch Dinah from the house of Shechem, and they went and came to the house of Shechem to take away Dinah from there.

13 When they came Shechem went out to them with his men and drove them from his house, and he would not let them come before Dinah, but Shechem was sitting with Dinah kissing and embracing her before their eyes.

14 The servants of Jacob came back and told him, saying, When we came, he and his men drove us away, and thus did Shechem do to Dinah before our eyes.

15 Jacob knew moreover that Shechem had defiled his daughter, but he said nothing; his sons were feeding his cattle in the field, and Jacob remained silent till their return.

16 Before his sons came home Jacob sent two maidens from his servants' daughters to take care of Dinah in the house of Shechem, and to remain with her, and Shechem sent three of his friends to his father Hamor the son of Chiddekem, the son of Pered, saying, Get me this damsel for a wife.

17 Hamor the son of Chiddekem the Hivite came to the house of Shechem his son, and he sat before him, and Hamor said to his son, Shechem, Is there not a woman among the daughters of your people, that you will

take an Hebrew woman who is not of your people?

18 And Shechem said to him, Her only must you get for me, for she is delightful in my sight. Hamor did according to the word of his son, for he was greatly beloved by him.

19 And Hamor went forth to Jacob to commune with him concerning this matter, and when he had gone from the house of his son Shechem, before he came to Jacob to speak to him, the sons of Jacob had come from the field as soon as they heard the thing that Shechem the son of Hamor had done.

20 And the men were very much grieved concerning their sister, and they all came home fired with anger, before the time of gathering in their cattle.

21 They came and sat before their father and they spoke to him set ablaze with wrath, saying, Certainly death is due to this man and to his household, because the Lord God of the whole earth commanded Noah and his children that man shall never rob, nor commit adultery; now behold Shechem has both ravaged and committed fornication with our sister, and not one of all the people of the city spoke a word to him.

22 Certainly you know and understand that the judgment of death is due to Shechem, and to his father, and to the whole city on account of the thing which he has done.

23 And while they were speaking before their father in this matter, Hamor the father of Shechem came to speak to Jacob the words of his son concerning Dinah, and he sat before Jacob and before his sons.

24 And Hamor spoke to them, saying, The soul of my son Shechem longs for your daughter; I pray you give her to him for a wife and intermarry with us; give us your daughters and we will give you our daughters, and you shall dwell with us in our land and we will be as one people in the land.

25 For our land is very extensive, so dwell and trade therein and get possessions in it, and do therein as you desire, and no one shall prevent you by saying a word to you.

26 And Hamor ceased speaking to Jacob and his sons, and behold Shechem his son had come after him, and he sat before them.

27 And Shechem spoke before Jacob and his sons, saying, May I find favor in your sight that you will give me your daughter, and whatever you say to me that will I do for her.

28 Ask me for abundance of dowry and gift, and I will give it, and

whatever you say to me that will I do, and whoever he be that will rebel against your orders, he shall die; only give me the damsel for a wife.

29 And Simeon and Levi answered Hamor and Shechem his son deceitfully, saying, All you have spoken to us we will do for you.

30 And behold our sister is in your house, but keep away from her until we send to our father Isaac concerning this matter, for we can do nothing without his consent.

31 For he knows the ways of our father Abraham, and whatever he says to us we will tell you; we will conceal nothing from you.

32 And Simeon and Levi spoke this to Shechem and his father in order to find a pretext, and to seek counsel what was to be done to Shechem and to his city in this matter.

33 And when Shechem and his father heard the words of Simeon and Levi, it seemed good in their sight, and Shechem and his father rose to go home.

34 And when they had gone, the sons of Jacob said to their father, Behold, we know that death is due to these wicked ones and to their city, because they went contrary to that which God had commanded to Noah and his children and his descendants after them.

35 And also because Shechem did this thing to our sister Dinah in defiling her, for such vileness shall never be done among us.

36 Now therefore know and see what you will do, and seek counsel and pretext what is to be done to them, in order to kill all the inhabitants of this city.

37 Simeon said to them, Here is a proper advice for you: tell them to circumcise every male among them as we are circumcised, and if they do not wish to do this, we shall take our daughter from them and go away.

38 And if they consent to do this and will do it, then when they are sunk down with pain, we will attack them with our swords, as on one who is quiet and peaceable, and we will kill every male person among them.

39 Simeon's advice pleased them, and Simeon and Levi resolved to do to them as it was proposed.

40 And on the next morning Shechem and Hamor his father came again to Jacob and his sons, to speak concerning Dinah, and to hear what answer the sons of Jacob would give to their words.

41 And the sons of Jacob spoke deceitfully to them, saying, We told our father Isaac all your words, and your words pleased him.

42 But he spoke to us, saying, Thus did Abraham his father command him from God the Lord of the whole earth, that any man who is not of his descendants that should wish to take one of his daughters, shall cause every male belonging to him to be circumcised, as we are circumcised, and then we may give him our daughter for a wife.

43 Now we have made known to you all our ways that our father spoke to us, for we cannot do this of which you spoke to us, to give our daughter to an uncircumcised man, for it is a disgrace to us.

44 But herein we will consent to you, to give you our daughter, and we will also take to ourselves your daughters, and will dwell among you and be one people as you have spoken, if you will listen to us and consent to be like us, to circumcise every male belonging to you as we are circumcised.

45 And if you will not listen to us, to have every male circumcised as we are circumcised, as we have commanded, then we will come to you, and take our daughter from you and go away.

46 Shechem and his father Hamor heard the words of the sons of Jacob, and the thing pleased them greatly, and Shechem and his father Hamor hurried to do the wishes of the sons of Jacob, for Shechem was very fond of Dinah, and his soul was riveted to her.

47 Shechem and his father Hamor hurried to the gate of the city, and they assembled all the men of their city and spoke to them the words of the sons of Jacob, saying,

48 We came to these men, the sons of Jacob, and we spoke to them concerning their daughter, and these men will consent to do according to our wishes, and behold our land is of great extent for them, and they will dwell in it, and trade in it, and we shall be one people; we will take their daughters, and our daughters we will give to them for wives.

49 But only on this condition will these men consent to do this thing, that every male among us be circumcised as they are circumcised, as their God commanded them, and when we shall have done according to their instructions to be circumcised, then they will dwell among us, together with their cattle and possessions, and we shall be as one people with them.

50 When all the men of the city heard the words of Shechem and his father Hamor, then all the men of their city were agreeable to this proposal, and they obeyed to be circumcised; for Shechem and his father Hamor were greatly esteemed by them, being the princes of the land.

51 On the next day, Shechem and Hamor his father rose up early in the

morning, and they assembled all the men of their city into the middle of the city, and they called for the sons of Jacob, who circumcised every male belonging to them on that day and the next.

52 And they circumcised Shechem and Hamor his father, and the five brothers of Shechem, and then every one rose up and went home; for this thing was from the Lord against the city of Shechem, and from the Lord was Simeon's counsel in this matter, in order that the Lord might deliver the city of Shechem into the hands of Jacob's two sons.

CHAPTER 34

1 The number of all the males that were circumcised were six hundred and forty-five men, and two hundred and forty-six children.

2 But Chiddekem, son of Pered, the father of Hamor, and his six brothers, would not listen to Shechem and his father Hamor; they would not be circumcised, for the proposal of the sons of Jacob was loathsome in their sight, and their anger was greatly roused at this, that the people of the city had not listened to them.

3 In the evening of the second day, they found eight small children who had not been circumcised, for their mothers had concealed them from Shechem and his father Hamor, and from the men of the city.

4 And Shechem and his father Hamor sent to have them brought before them to be circumcised, when Chiddekem and his six brothers sprang at them with their swords, and sought to kill them.

5 And they sought to kill also Shechem and his father Hamor and they sought to kill Dinah with them on account of this matter.

6 They said to them, What is this thing that you have done? Are there no women among the daughters of your brothers the Canaanites, that you wish to take to yourselves daughters of the Hebrews, whom ye knew not before, and will do this act which your fathers never commanded you?

7 Do you imagine that you will succeed through this act which you have done? And what will you answer in this affair to your brothers the Canaanites who will come tomorrow and ask you concerning this thing?

8 If your act shall not appear just and good in their sight, what will you do for your lives, and me for our lives, in your not having listened to our voices?

9 And if the inhabitants of the land and all your brothers the children of Ham, shall hear of your act, saying,

10 On account of a Hebrew woman did Shechem and Hamor his father, and all the inhabitants of their city, do that with which they had been unacquainted and which their ancestors never commanded them, where then will you fly or where conceal your shame all your days before your brothers, the inhabitants of the land of Canaan?

11 Now therefore we cannot bear up against this thing which you have done, neither can we be burdened with this yoke on us which our ancestors did not command us.

12 Behold tomorrow we will go and assemble all our brothers, the Canaanitish brothers who dwell in the land, and we will all come and strike you and all those who trust in you, that there shall not be a remnant left from you or them.

13 And when Hamor and his son Shechem and all the people of the city heard the words of Chiddekem and his brothers, they were terribly afraid of their lives at their words, and they repented of what they had done.

14 And Shechem and his father Hamor answered their father Chiddekem and his brothers, and they said to them, All the words which you spoke to us are true.

15 Now do not say, nor imagine in your hearts that on account of the love of the Hebrews we did this thing that our ancestors did not command us.

16 But because we saw that it was not their intention and desire to accede to our wishes concerning their daughter as to our taking her, except on this condition, so we listened to their voices and did this act which you saw in order to obtain our desire from them.

17 And when we shall have obtained our request from them, we will then return to them and do to them that which you say to us.

18 We petition you then to wait and tarry until our flesh will be healed and we again become strong, and we will then go together against them, and do to them that which is in your hearts and in ours.

19 And Dinah the daughter of Jacob heard all these words which Chiddekem and his brothers had spoken, and what Hamor and his son Shechem and the people of their city had answered them.

20 She hurried and sent one of her maidens, that her father had sent to take care of her in the house of Shechem, to Jacob her father and to her brothers, saying:

21 Thus did Chiddekem and his brothers advise concerning you, and thus did Hamor and Shechem and the people of the city answer them.

22 And when Jacob heard these words he was filled with wrath, and he was indignant at them, and his anger was set ablaze against them.

23 And Simeon and Levi swore and said, As the Lord lives, the God of the whole earth, by this time tomorrow, there shall not be a remnant left in the whole city.

24 Twenty young men had concealed themselves who were not circumcised, and these young men fought against Simeon and Levi, and Simeon and Levi killed eighteen of them, and two fled from them and escaped to some lime pits that were in the city, and Simeon and Levi sought for them, but could not find them.

25 And Simeon and Levi continued to go about in the city, and they killed all the people of the city at the edge of the sword, and they left none remaining.

26 There was a great consternation in the midst of the city, and the cry of the people of the city ascended to heaven, and all the women and children cried aloud.

27 And Simeon and Levi killed all the city; they left not a male remaining in the whole city.

28 And they killed Hamor and Shechem his son at the edge of the sword, and they brought away Dinah from the house of Shechem and they went from there.

29 The sons of Jacob went and returned, and came on the slain, and spoiled all their property which was in the city and the field.

30 And while they were taking the spoil, three hundred men stood up and threw dust at them and struck them with stones. Then Simeon turned to them and he killed them all with the edge of the sword, and Simeon turned before Levi and came into the city.

31 They took away their sheep and their oxen and their cattle, and also the remainder of the women and little ones, and they led all these away; they opened a gate and went out and came to their father Jacob with vigor.

32 When Jacob saw all that they had done to the city, and saw the spoil that they took from them, Jacob was very angry at them, and Jacob said to them, What is this that you have done to me? I had obtained rest among the Canaanitish inhabitants of the land; none of them meddled with me.

33 And now you have done this to make me obnoxious to the inhabitants of the land, among the Canaanites and the Perizzites, and I am but of a

small number; they will all assemble against me and kill me when they hear of your work with their brothers, and I and my household will be destroyed.

34 Simeon and Levi and all their brothers with them answered their father Jacob and said to him, Behold we live in the land, and shall Shechem do this to our sister? Why are you silent at all that Shechem has done? And shall he deal with our sister as with a harlot in the streets?

35 The number of women whom Simeon and Levi took captives from the city of Shechem, whom they did not kill, was eighty-five who had not known man.

36 And among them was a young damsel of beautiful appearance and well favored, whose name was Bunah, and Simeon took her for a wife, and the number of the males which they took captives and did not kill was forty-seven men, and the rest they killed.

37 All the young men and women that Simeon and Levi had taken captives from the city of Shechem were servants to the sons of Jacob and to their children after them, until the day of the sons of Jacob going forth from the land of Egypt.

38 And when Simeon and Levi had gone forth from the city, the two young men that were left, who had concealed themselves in the city and did not die among the people of the city, rose up; these young men went into the city and walked about in it, and found the city desolate without man, and only women weeping, and these young men cried out and said, Behold, this is the evil which the sons of Jacob the Hebrew did to this city in their having this day destroyed one of the Canaanitish cities, and were not afraid of their lives of all the land of Canaan.

39 These men left the city and went to the city of Tapnach, and they came there and told the inhabitants of Tapnach all that had befallen them, and all that the sons of Jacob had done to the city of Shechem.

40 The information reached Jashub king of Tapnach, and he sent men to the city of Shechem to see those young men, for the king did not believe them in this account, saying, How could two men lay waste such a large town as Shechem?

41 The messengers of Jashub came back and told him, saying, We came to the city, and it is destroyed, there is not a man there; only weeping women; neither is any flock or cattle there, for all that was in the city the sons of Jacob took away.

42 Jashub wondered at this, saying, How could two men do this thing to

destroy so large a city, and not one man able to stand against them?

43 For the like has not been from the days of Nimrod, and not even from the remotest time, has the like taken place; and Jashub, king of Tapnach, said to his people, Be courageous and we will go and fight against these Hebrews, and do to them as they did to the city; we will avenge the cause of the people of the city.

44 Jashub, king of Tapnach, consulted with his counselors about this matter, and his advisers said to him, Alone you will not prevail over the Hebrews, for they must be powerful to do this work to the whole city.

45 If two of them laid waste the whole city, and no one stood against them, certainly if you will go against them, they will all rise against us and destroy us likewise.

46 But if you will send to all the kings that surround us, and let them come together, then we will go with them and fight against the sons of Jacob; then you will prevail against them.

47 Jashub heard the words of his counselors, and their words pleased him and his people, and he did so; Jashub king of Tapnach sent to all the kings of the Amorites that surrounded Shechem and Tapnach, saying,

48 Go up with me and assist me, and we will strike Jacob the Hebrew and all his sons, and destroy them from the earth, for thus did he do to the city of Shechem, and do you not know of it?

49 And all the kings of the Amorites heard the evil that the sons of Jacob had done to the city of Shechem, and they were greatly astonished at them.

50 The seven kings of the Amorites assembled with all their armies about ten thousand men with drawn swords, and they came to fight against the sons of Jacob; Jacob heard that the kings of the Amorites had assembled to fight against his sons, and Jacob was greatly afraid; it distressed him.

51 And Jacob exclaimed against Simeon and Levi, saying, What is this act that you did? Why have you injured me, to bring against me all the children of Canaan to destroy me and my household? For I was at rest, even I and my household, and you have done this thing to me and provoked the inhabitants of the land against me by your proceedings.

52 Judah answered his father, saying, Was it for naught my brothers Simeon and Levi killed all the inhabitants of Shechem? Certainly it was because Shechem had humbled our sister, and went contrary to the command of our God to Noah and his children, for Shechem took our sister away by force, and committed fornication with her.

53 Shechem did all this evil and not one of the inhabitants of his city interfered with him, to say, Why will you do this? Certainly for this my brothers went and struck the city, and the Lord delivered it into their hands, because its inhabitants had gone contrary to the commands of our God. Is it then for naught that they have done all this?

54 Now why are you afraid or distressed, and why are you displeased at my brothers, and why is your anger set ablaze against them?

55 Certainly our God who delivered into their hand the city of Shechem and its people, he will also deliver into our hands all the Canaanitish kings who are coming against us, and we will do to them as my brothers did to Shechem.

56 Now be tranquil about them and cast away your fears, but trust in the Lord our God, and pray to him to assist us and deliver us, and deliver our enemies into our hands.

57 Judah called to one of his father's servants, Go now and see where those kings who are coming against us are situated with their armies.

58 And the servant went and looked far off, and went up opposite Mount Sihon, and saw all the camps of the kings standing in the fields, and he returned to Judah and said, Behold the kings are situated in the field with all their camps, a people greatly numerous like the sand on the seashore.

59 And Judah said to Simeon and Levi, and to all his brothers, Strengthen yourselves and be sons of valor, for the Lord our God is with us, do not fear them.

60 Stand forth each man, equipped with his weapons of war, his bow and his sword, and we will go and fight against these uncircumcised men; the Lord is our God, He will save us.

61 They rose up, and each put on his weapons of war, great and small, eleven sons of Jacob, and all the servants of Jacob with them.

62 All the servants of Isaac who were with Isaac in Hebron, all came to them equipped in all sorts of war instruments, and the sons of Jacob and their servants, being one hundred and twelve men, went towards these kings, and Jacob also went with them.

63 And the sons of Jacob sent to their father Isaac the son of Abraham to Hebron, the same is Kireath-arba, saying,

64 Pray we beseech you for us to the Lord our God, to protect us from the hands of the Canaanites who are coming against us, and to deliver them into our hands.

65 Isaac the son of Abraham prayed to the Lord for his sons, and he said, O Lord God, you did promise my father, saying, I will reproduce your descendants as the stars of heaven, and you did also promise me, and establish you your word, now that the kings of Canaan are coming together, to make war with my children because they committed no violence.

66 Now therefore, O Lord God, God of the whole earth, pervert, I pray you, the counsel of these kings that they may not fight against my sons.

67 And impress the hearts of these kings and their people with the terror of my sons and bring down their pride, that they may turn away from my sons.

68 With your strong hand and outstretched arm deliver my sons and their servants from them, for power and might are in your hands to do all this.

69 And the sons of Jacob and their servants went toward these kings, and they trusted in the Lord their God, and while they were going, Jacob their father also prayed to the Lord and said, O Lord God, powerful and exalted God, who has reigned from days of old, from thence till now and forever;

70 You are He who stirs up wars and causes them to cease, in your hand are power and might to exalt and to bring down; O may my prayer be acceptable before you that you may turn to me with your mercies, to impress the hearts of these kings and their people with the terror of my sons, and terrify them and their camps, and with your great kindness deliver all those that trust in you, for it is you who can bring people under us and reduce nations under our power.

CHAPTER 35

1 All the kings of the Amorites came and took their stand in the field to consult with their counselors what was to be done with the sons of Jacob, for they were still afraid of them, saying, Take notice that two of them killed the whole city of Shechem.

2 And the Lord heard the prayers of Isaac and Jacob, and he filled the hearts of all these kings' advisers with great fear and terror that they unanimously exclaimed,

3 Are you silly or is there no understanding in you, that you will fight with the Hebrews; why will you take delight in your own destruction this day?

4 See, two of them came to the city of Shechem without fear or terror, and they killed all the inhabitants of the city, that no man stood up against them, and how will you be able to fight with them all?

5 Certainly you know that their God is greatly fond of them and has done mighty things for them, such as have not been done from days of old and among all the gods of nations; there is none can do like his mighty deeds.

6 Certainly he delivered their father Abraham, the Hebrew, from the hand of Nimrod, and from the hand of all his people who had many times sought to kill him.

7 He delivered him also from the fire in which king Nimrod had cast him, and his God delivered him from it.

8 And who else can do like this? Certainly it was Abraham who killed the five kings of Elam when they had touched his brother's son who in those days lived in Sodom.

9 And took his servant that was faithful in his house and a few of his men, and they pursued the kings of Elam in one night and killed them; then restored to his brother's son all his property which they had taken from him.

10 Certainly you know the God of these Hebrews is much delighted with them, and they are also delighted with him, for they know that he delivered them from all their enemies.

11 And consider this, through his love toward his God, Abraham took his only and precious son and intended to bring him up as a burnt offering to his God; had it not been for God who prevented him from doing this, he would then have done it through his love to his God.

12 God saw all his works and swore to him, and promised him that he would deliver his sons and all his descendants from every trouble that would befall them, because he had done this thing and through his love to his God stifled his compassion for his child.

13 And have you not heard what their God did to Pharaoh king of Egypt and to Abimelech king of Gerar through taking Abraham's wife, who said of her, She is my sister; that they might kill him on account of her and think of taking her for a wife? And God did to them and their people all that you heard of.

14 And then, we ourselves saw with our own eyes that Esau, the brother of Jacob, came to him with four hundred men with the intention of slaying him, for he remembered that he had taken away from him his father's blessing.

15 And he went to meet him when he came from Syria to strike the mother with the children, and who delivered him from his hands but his God in whom he trusted? He delivered him from the hand of his brother and also from the hands of his enemies, and certainly he again will protect them.

16 Who does not know that it was their God who inspired them with strength to do to the town of Shechem the evil which you heard of?

17 Could it then be with their own strength that two men could destroy such a large city as Shechem had it not been for their God in whom they trusted? He spoke and did to them all this to kill the inhabitants of the city in their city.

18 And can you then prevail over them who have come forth together from your city to fight with all of them, even if a thousand times as many more should come to your assistance?

19 Certainly you know and understand that you do not come to fight with them, but you come to war with their God who chose them, and you have therefore all come this day to be destroyed.

20 So refrain from this evil which you are endeavoring to bring on yourselves, and it will be better for you not to go to battle with them, although they are but few in numbers, because their God is with them.

21 When the kings of the Amorites heard all the words of their advisers, their hearts were filled with terror; they were afraid of the sons of Jacob and would not fight against them.

22 They inclined to believe the words of their advisers and they listened to all their words. The words of the counselors greatly pleased the kings, and they did so.

23 And the kings turned and refrained from the sons of Jacob, for they dared not approach them to make war with them; they were greatly afraid of them, and their hearts melted within them from their fear.

24 For this proceeded from the Lord to them; he heard the prayers of his servants Isaac and Jacob, for they trusted in him. And all these kings returned with their camps on that day, each to his own city, and they did not at that time fight with the sons of Jacob.

25 The sons of Jacob kept their station that day till evening opposite mount Sihon, and seeing that these kings did not come to fight against them, the sons of Jacob returned home.

CHAPTER 36

1 At that time the Lord appeared to Jacob saying, Arise, go to Bethel and remain there; make there an altar to the Lord who appears to you, who delivered you and your sons from affliction.

2 And Jacob rose up with his sons and all belonging to him; they went and came to Bethel according to the word of the Lord.

3 Jacob was ninety-nine years old when he went up to Bethel, and Jacob and his sons and all the people that were with him remained in Bethel in Luz; he built an altar there to the Lord who appeared to him, and Jacob and his sons remained in Bethel six months.

4 At that time Deborah the daughter of Uz, the nurse of Rebecca, who had been with Jacob died and Jacob buried her beneath Bethel under an oak that was there.

5 And Rebecca the daughter of Bethuel, the mother of Jacob, also died at that time in Hebron, the same is Kireath-arba. She was buried in the cave of Machpelah which Abraham had bought from the children of Heth.

6 And the life of Rebecca was one hundred and thirty-three years, and she died. When Jacob heard that his mother Rebecca was dead he wept bitterly for his mother, and made a great mourning for her and for Deborah her nurse beneath the oak. He called the name of that place Allon-bachuth.

7 Laban the Syrian died in those days, for God struck him because he went contrary to the covenant that existed between him and Jacob.

8 Jacob was a hundred years old when the Lord appeared to him and blessed him and called his name Israel, and Rachel the wife of Jacob conceived in those days.

9 At that time Jacob and all belonging to him journeyed from Bethel to go to his father's house, to Hebron.

10 And while they were going on the road, and there was yet but a little way to come to Ephrath, Rachel gave birth to a son; she had hard labor and died.

11 Jacob buried her on the way to Ephrath, which is Bethlehem, and he set a pillar on her grave which is there to this day; the days of Rachel were forty-five years when she died.

12 Jacob called the name of his son that was born to him, which Rachel gave birth to, Benjamin, for he was born to him in the land on the right hand.

13 It was after the death of Rachel that Jacob pitched his tent in the tent of her handmaid Bilhah.

14 And Reuben was jealous for his mother Leah on account of this; he was filled with anger, and he rose up in his anger and went and entered the tent of Bilhah and then removed his father's bed.

15 At that time the portion of birthright, together with the kingly and priestly offices, was removed from the sons of Reuben for he had profaned his father's bed; the birthright was given to Joseph, the kingly office to Judah, and the priesthood to Levi, because Reuben had defiled his father's bed.

16 These are the generations of Jacob who were born to him in Padan-aram, and the sons of Jacob were twelve:

17 The sons of Leah were Reuben the first born, and Simeon, Levi, Judah, Issachar, Zebulun, and their sister Dinah; and the sons of Rachel were Joseph and Benjamin.

18 The sons of Zilpah, Leah's handmaid, were Gad and Asher, and the sons of Bilhah, Rachel's handmaid, were Dan and Naphtali; these are the sons of Jacob which were born to him in Padan-aram.

19 Jacob and his sons and all belonging to him journeyed and came to Mamre, which is Kireath-arba, that is in Hebron, where Abraham and Isaac sojourned; Jacob with his sons and all belonging to him lived with his father in Hebron.

20 His brother Esau, his sons and all belonging to him went to the land of Seir and lived there and had possessions in the land of Seir, and the children of Esau were prolific and multiplied greatly in the land of Seir.

21 These are the generations of Esau that were born to him in the land of Canaan, and the sons of Esau were five:

22 And Adah gave birth to, to Esau, his first born Eliphaz, and she also gave birth to, to him, Reuel, and Ahlibamah gave birth to, to him, Jeush, Yaalam and Korah.

23 These are the children of Esau who were born to him in the land of Canaan; the sons of Eliphaz the son of Esau were: Teman, Omar, Zepho, Gatam, Kenaz and Amalex; the sons of Reuel were Nachath, Zerach, Shamah and Mizzah.

24 The sons of Jeush were Timnah, Alvah, Jetheth; the sons of Yaalam

were Alah, Phinor and Kenaz.

25 And the sons of Korah were Teman, Mibzar, Magdiel and Eram; these are the families of the sons of Esau according to their territories in the land of Seir.

26 These are the names of the sons of Seir the Horite, inhabitants of the land of Seir: Lotan, Shobal, Zibeon, Anah, Dishan, Ezer and Dishon, being seven sons.

27 The children of Lotan were Hori, Heman and their sister Timna, that is Timna who came to Jacob and his sons; they would not give ear to her and she became a concubine to Eliphaz the son of Esau; she gave birth to, to him, Amalek.

28 And the sons of Shobal were Alvan, Manahath, Ebal, Shepho, and Onam, and the sons of Zibeon were Ajah, and Anah; this was that Anah who found the Yemim in the wilderness when he fed the asses of Zibeon his father.

29 And while he was feeding his father's asses he led them to the wilderness at different times to feed them.

30 There was a day that he brought them to one of the deserts on the seashore, opposite the wilderness of the people, and while he was feeding them, suddenly a very heavy storm came from the other side of the sea and rested on the asses that were feeding there, and they all stood still.

31 Afterward about one hundred and twenty great and terrible animals came out from the wilderness at the other side of the sea; they all came to the place where the asses were, and they placed themselves there.

32 And those animals, from their middle downward, were in the shape of the children of men; from their middle upward, some had the likeness of bears, and some the likeness of the keephas, with tails behind them from between their shoulders reaching down to the earth, like the tails of the ducheephath. These animals came and mounted and rode on these asses, and led them away, and they went away to this day.

33 One of these animals approached Anah, struck him with his tail, and then fled from that place.

34 And when he saw this work he was greatly afraid of his life, and he fled and escaped to the city.

35 He related to his sons and brothers all that had happened to him, and many men went to seek the asses but could not find them. Anah and his brothers went no more to that place from that day on for they were greatly

afraid for their lives.

36 The children of Anah the son of Seir, were Dishon and his sister Ahlibamah; the children of Dishon were Hemdan, Eshban, Ithran and Cheran; the children of Ezer were Bilhan, Zaavan and Akan, and the children of Dishon were Uz and Aran.

37 These are the families of the children of Seir the Horite, according to their dukedoms in the land of Seir.

38 Esau and his children lived in the land of Seir the Horite, the inhabitant of the land, and they had possessions in it and were prolific and multiplied greatly. Jacob and his children and all belonging to them lived with their father Isaac in the land of Canaan, as the Lord had commanded Abraham their father.

CHAPTER 37

1 In the one hundred and fifth year of the life of Jacob, that is the ninth year of Jacob's dwelling with his children in the land of Canaan, he came from Padan-aram.

2 And in those days Jacob journeyed with his children from Hebron; they went and returned to the city of Shechem, they and all belonging to them and they lived there, for the children of Jacob obtained good and fattening pasture land for their cattle in the city of Shechem, the city of Shechem having then been rebuilt; there were in it about three hundred men and women.

3 Jacob and his children and all belonging to him lived in the part of the field which Jacob had bought from Hamor the father of Shechem, when he came from Padan-aram before Simeon and Levi had smitten the city.

4 And all those kings of the Canaanites and Amorites that surrounded the city of Shechem heard that the sons of Jacob had again come to Shechem and lived there.

5 They said, Shall the sons of Jacob the Hebrew again come to the city and dwell therein, after that they have smitten its inhabitants and driven them out? Shall they now return and also drive out those who are dwelling in the city or kill them?

6 And all the kings of Canaan again assembled, and they came together to make war with Jacob and his sons.

7 Jashub king of Tapnach sent also to all his neighboring kings, to Elan king of Gaash, and to Ihuri king of Shiloh, and to Parathon king of Chazar, and to Susi king of Sarton, and to Laban king of Bethchoran, and to Shabir king of Othnay-mah, saying,

8 Come up to me and assist me, and let us strike Jacob the Hebrew and his sons and all belonging to him, for they are again come to Shechem to possess it and to kill its inhabitants as before.

9 And all these kings assembled together and came with all their camps, a people greatly plentiful like the sand on the seashore, and they were all opposite to Tapnach.

10 Jashub king of Tapnach went forth to them with all his army, and he encamped with them opposite to Tapnach outside the city; all these kings they divided into seven divisions, being seven camps against the sons of Jacob.

11 And they sent a declaration to Jacob and his son, saying, All of you come forth to us that we may have an interview together in the plain, and revenge the cause of the men of Shechem whom you killed in their city; you will now again return to the city of Shechem and dwell therein, and kill its inhabitants as before.

12 The sons of Jacob heard this and their anger was set ablaze greatly at the words of the kings of Canaan, and ten of the sons of Jacob hurried and rose up, and each of them put on his weapons of war; and there were one hundred and two of their servants with them equipped in battle array.

13 And all these men, the sons of Jacob with their servants, went toward these kings and Jacob their father was with them; they all stood on the heap of Shechem.

14 Jacob prayed to the Lord for his sons, and he spread forth his hands to the Lord, and said, O God, you are an Almighty God, you are our father; you did form us and we are the works of your hands; I pray you deliver my sons through your mercy from the hand of their enemies who are this day coming to fight with them and save them from their hand, for in your hand is power and might to save the few from the many.

15 And give to my sons, your servants, strength of heart and might to fight with their enemies, to subdue them, and to make their enemies fall before them. Let not my sons and their servants die through the hands of the children of Canaan.

16 But if it seems good in your eyes to take away the lives of my sons and their servants, take them in your great mercy through the hands of your

ministers, that they may not perish this day by the hands of the kings of the Amorites.

17 When Jacob ceased praying to the Lord the earth shook from its place, and the sun darkened, and all these kings were terrified and a great consternation seized them.

18 The Lord listened to the prayer of Jacob, and the Lord impressed the hearts of all the kings and their hosts with the terror and awe of the sons of Jacob.

19 For the Lord caused them to hear the voice of chariots, and the voice of mighty horses from the sons of Jacob, and the voice of a great army accompanying them.

20 And these kings were seized with great terror at the sons of Jacob; while they were standing in their quarters, behold the sons of Jacob advanced on them with one hundred and twelve men, with a great and tremendous shouting.

21 And when the kings saw the sons of Jacob advancing toward them, they were still more panic stricken; they were inclined to retreat from before the sons of Jacob as at first and not to fight with them.

22 But they did not retreat, saying, It would be a disgrace to us to retreat twice from before the Hebrews.

23 The sons of Jacob came near and advanced against all these kings and their armies, and what they saw was a very mighty people, numerous as the sand of the sea.

24 And the sons of Jacob called to the Lord and said, Help us O Lord, help us and answer us, for we trust in you, and let us not die by the hands of these uncircumcised men who this day have come against us.

25 The sons of Jacob put on their weapons of war and they took in their hands each man his shield and his javelin, and they approached to do battle.

26 And Judah, the son of Jacob, ran first before his brothers and ten of his servants with him, and he went toward these kings.

27 Jashub, king of Tapnach, also came forth first with his army before Judah, and Judah saw Jashub and his army coming toward him, and Judah's wrath was set ablaze; his anger burned within him, and he approached to the fight in which Judah ventured his life.

28 Jashub and all his army were advancing toward Judah and he was riding on a very strong and powerful horse; Jashub was a very valiant man, and covered with iron and brass from head to foot.

29 And while he was on the horse, he shot arrows with both hands from before and behind, as was his manner in all his battles; he never missed the place to which he aimed his arrows.

30 When Jashub came to fight with Judah and was darting many arrows against Judah, the Lord bound the hand of Jashub and all the arrows that he shot rebounded on his own men.

31 And in spite of this Jashub kept advancing toward Judah, to challenge him with the arrows, but the distance between them was about thirty cubits. When Judah saw Jashub darting forth his arrows against him, he ran to him with his wrath-excited strength.

32 Judah took up a large stone from the ground, its weight was sixty shekels, and Judah ran toward Jashub and with the stone struck him on his shield, so that Jashub was stunned with the blow and fell off his horse to the ground.

33 The shield burst asunder out of the hand of Jashub, and through the force of the blow sprang to the distance of about fifteen cubits, and the shield fell before the second camp.

34 The kings that came with Jashub saw at a distance the strength of Judah, the son of Jacob, and what he had done to Jashub; they were terribly afraid of Judah.

35 And they assembled near Jashub's camp, seeing his confusion, and Judah drew his sword and struck forty-two men of the camp of Jashub, and the whole of Jashub's camp fled before Judah. No man stood against him and they left Jashub and fled from him, and Jashub was still prostrate on the ground.

36 Jashub, seeing that all the men of his camp had fled from him, hurried and rose up with terror against Judah and stood on his legs opposite Judah.

37 And Jashub had a single combat with Judah, placing shield toward shield, and Jashub's men all fled for they were greatly afraid of Judah.

38 Jashub took his spear in his hand to strike Judah on his head, but Judah had quickly placed his shield to his head against Jashub's spear so that the shield of Judah received the blow from Jashub's spear, and the shield was split in two.

39 And when Judah saw that his shield was split, he hastily drew his sword and struck Jashub at his ankles and cut off his feet, so that Jashub fell on the ground and the spear fell from his hand.

40 Judah hastily picked up Jashub's spear with which he severed his head and cast it next to his feet.

41 When the sons of Jacob saw what Judah had done to Jashub, they all ran into the ranks of the other kings and the sons of Jacob fought with the army of Jashub and the armies of all the kings that were there.

42 The sons of Jacob caused fifteen thousand of their men to fall, and they struck them as if smiting at gourds, and the rest fled for their lives.

43 Judah was still standing by the body of Jashub and stripped Jashub of his coat of mail.

44 Judah also took off the iron and brass that were around Jashub, and then nine men of the captains of Jashub came along to fight against Judah.

45 Judah hurried and took up a stone from the ground, and with it struck one of them on the head; his skull was fractured and the body also fell from the horse to the ground.

46 And the eight captains that remained, seeing the strength of Judah, were greatly afraid and they fled; Judah with his ten men pursued them and they overtook them and killed them.

47 The sons of Jacob were still smiting the armies of the kings, and they killed many of them, but those kings daringly kept their stand with their captains and did not retreat from their places; they shouted against those of their armies that fled from before the sons of Jacob, but none would listen to them, for they were afraid for their lives that they should die.

48 And all the sons of Jacob, after having smitten the armies of the kings, returned and came before Judah; Judah was still slaying the eight captains of Jashub and stripping off their garments.

49 And Levi saw Elon, king of Gaash, advancing toward him with his fourteen captains to strike him, but Levi did not know it for certain.

50 Elon with his captains approached nearer, and Levi looked back and saw that battle was coming to him from the rear. Levi ran with twelve of his servants, and they went and killed Elon and his captains with the edge of the sword.

CHAPTER 38

1 Ihuri king of Shiloh came up to assist Elon and he approached Jacob,

when Jacob drew his bow that was in his hand and with an arrow struck Ihuri, which caused his death.

2 And when Ihuri king of Shiloh was dead, the four remaining kings fled from their station with the rest of the captains; they endeavored to retreat, saying, We have no more strength with the Hebrews after their having killed the three kings and their captains who were more powerful than we are.

3 When the sons of Jacob saw that the remaining kings had left their station, they pursued them and Jacob also came from the heap of Shechem from the place where he was standing; they went after the kings and they approached them with their servants.

4 And the kings and the captains with the rest of their armies, seeing that the sons of Jacob approached them, were afraid for their lives and fled till they reached the city of Chazar.

5 The sons of Jacob pursued them to the gate of the city of Chazar, and they struck a great smiting among the kings and their armies, about four thousand men. While they were smiting the army of the kings, Jacob was occupied with his bow, confining himself to smiting the kings and killed them all.

6 And he killed Parathon king of Chazar at the gate of the city of Chazar and afterward struck Susi king of Sarton, and Laban king of Bethchorin, and Shabir king of Machnaymah; he killed them all with arrows, an arrow to each of them, and they died.

7 The sons of Jacob, seeing that all the kings were dead and that they were broken up and retreating, continued to carry on the battle with the armies of the kings opposite the gate of Chazar, and they still struck about four hundred of their men.

8 Three men of the servants of Jacob fell in that battle and when Judah saw that three of his servants had died, it grieved him greatly and his anger burned within him against the Amorites.

9 And all the men that remained of the armies of the kings were greatly afraid for their lives, and they ran and broke the gate of the walls of the city of Chazar; they all entered the city for safety.

10 They concealed themselves in the midst of the city of Chazar, for the city of Chazar was very large and extensive, and when all these armies had entered the city, the sons of Jacob ran after them to the city.

11 Four mighty men, experienced in battle, went forth from the city and stood against the entrance of the city with drawn swords and spears in

their hands; they placed themselves opposite the sons of Jacob and would not let them enter the city.

12 Naphtali ran and came between them and with his sword struck two of them, and cut off their heads at one stroke.

13 He turned to the other two and saw that they had fled; he pursued them, overtook them, struck them and killed them.

14 When the sons of Jacob came to the city and saw there was another wall to the city, they sought for the gate of the wall and could not find it; Judah sprang on the top of the wall and Simeon and Levi followed him, and they all three descended from the wall into the city.

15 Simeon and Levi killed all the men who ran for safety into the city and also the inhabitants of the city with their wives and little ones they killed with the edge of the sword, and the cries of the city ascended up to heaven.

16 And Dan and Naphtali sprang on the wall to see what caused the noise of the wailing, for the sons of Jacob felt anxious about their brothers; they heard the inhabitants of the city speaking with weeping and pleas, saying, Take all that we possess in the city and go away, only do not put us to death.

17 When Judah, Simeon, and Levi had ceased smiting the inhabitants of the city, they ascended the wall and called to Dan and Naphtali, who were on the wall, and to the rest of their brothers; Simeon and Levi informed them of the entrance into the city, and all the sons of Jacob came to gather the spoil.

18 And the sons of Jacob took the spoil of the city of Chazar, the flocks and herds, and the property, and they took all that could be captured, and went away that day from the city.

19 On the next day the sons of Jacob went to Sarton, for they heard that the men of Sarton who had remained in the city were assembling to fight with them for having slain their king. Sarton was a very high and fortified city, and it had a deep rampart surrounding the city.

20 And the pillar of the rampart was about fifty cubits and its breadth forty cubits; there was no place for a man to enter the city on account of the rampart. The sons of Jacob saw the rampart of the city, and they sought an entrance in it but could not find it.

21 For the entrance to the city was at the rear, and every man that wished to come into the city came by that road and went around the whole city, and afterwards entered the city.

22 The sons of Jacob seeing they could not find the way into the city, their anger was set ablaze greatly, and the inhabitants of the city seeing that the sons of Jacob were coming to them were greatly afraid of them, for they had heard of their strength and what they had done to Chazar.

23 And the inhabitants of the city of Sarton could not go out toward the sons of Jacob after having assembled in the city to fight against them, that they might thereby not get into the city. But when they saw that they were coming toward them, they were greatly afraid of them, for they had heard of their strength and what they had done to Chazar.

24 So the inhabitants of Sarton speedily took away the bridge of the road of the city from its place, before the sons of Jacob came, and they brought it into the city.

25 The sons of Jacob came and sought the way into the city, and could not find it and the inhabitants of the city went up to the top of the wall, and saw that the sons of Jacob were seeking an entrance into the city.

26 The inhabitants of the city reproached the sons of Jacob from the top of the wall and they cursed them, and the sons of Jacob heard the reproaches and they were greatly incensed; their anger burned within them.

27 The sons of Jacob were provoked at them, and they all rose and sprang over the rampart with the force of their strength, and through their might passed the forty cubits' breadth of the rampart.

28 And when they had passed the rampart they stood under the wall of the city, and they found all the gates of the city enclosed with iron doors.

29 The sons of Jacob came near to break open the doors of the gates of the city, and the inhabitants did not let them, for from the top of the wall they were casting stones and arrows on them.

30 And the number of the people that were on the wall was about four hundred men, and when the sons of Jacob saw that the men of the city would not let them open the gates of the city, they sprang and ascended the top of the wall, and Judah went up first to the east part of the city.

31 And Gad and Asher went up after him to the west corner of the city, and Simeon and Levi to the north, and Dan and Reuben to the south.

32 The men who were on the top of the wall, the inhabitants of the city, seeing that the sons of Jacob were coming up to them, all fled from the wall, descended into the city and concealed themselves in the middle of the city.

33 Issachar and Naphtali that remained under the wall approached and

broke the gates of the city, and set ablaze a fire at the gates of the city that the iron melted, and all the sons of Jacob came into the city, they and all their men; they fought with the inhabitants of the city of Sarton and struck them with the edge of the sword, and no man stood up before them.

34 About two hundred men fled from the city and they all went and hid themselves in a certain tower in the city; Judah pursued them to the tower and broke down the tower which fell on the men, and they all died.

35 The sons of Jacob went up the road of the roof of that tower, and they looked and there was another strong and high tower at a distance in the city, and the top of it reached to heaven. The sons of Jacob hurried and descended and went with all their men to that tower, and found it filled with about three hundred men, women and little ones.

36 The sons of Jacob struck a great smiting among those men in the tower and they ran away and fled from them.

37 And Simeon and Levi pursued them when twelve mighty and valiant men came out to them from the place where they had concealed themselves.

38 And those twelve men maintained a strong battle against Simeon and Levi, and Simeon and Levi could not prevail over them; those valiant men broke the shields of Simeon and Levi, and one of them struck at Levi's head with his sword when Levi hastily placed his hand to his head, for he was afraid of the sword. The sword struck Levi's hand, and the hand of Levi was nearly cut off.

39 Levi seized the sword of the valiant man in his hand and took it forcibly from the man; with it he struck at the head of the powerful man and he severed his head.

40 Eleven men approached to fight with Levi, for they saw that one of them was killed; the sons of Jacob fought but the sons of Jacob could not defeat them, for those men were very powerful.

41 And the sons of Jacob seeing that they could not win over them, Simeon gave a loud and tremendous shriek, and the eleven powerful men were stunned at the voice of Simeon's shrieking.

42 Judah at a distance knew the voice of Simeon's shouting, and Naphtali and Judah ran with their shields to Simeon and Levi and found them fighting with those powerful men, unable to defeat them as their shields were broken.

43 Naphtali saw that the shields of Simeon and Levi were broken and he took two shields from his servants and brought them to Simeon and Levi.

44 And Simeon, Levi and Judah on that day fought all three against the eleven mighty men until the time of sunset, but they could not win over them.

45 This was told to Jacob, and he was very grieved; he prayed to the Lord, and he and Naphtali his son went against these mighty men.

46 Jacob approached, drew his bow, and came near to the mighty men, and killed three of their men with the bow; the remaining eight turned back and then the war waged against them in the front and rear. They were greatly afraid for their lives and could not stand before the sons of Jacob, and they fled from before them.

47 In their flight they met Dan and Asher coming toward them, and they suddenly fell on them and fought with them, and killed two of them; Judah and his brothers pursued them and struck the remainder of them, and killed them.

48 All the sons of Jacob returned and walked through the city searching if they could find any men; they found about twenty young men in a cave in the city; Gad and Asher struck them all and Dan and Naphtali lighted on the rest of the men who had fled and escaped from the second tower, and they struck them all.

49 The sons of Jacob struck all the inhabitants of the city of Sarton, but the women and little ones they left in the city and did not kill them.

50 And all the inhabitants of the city of Sarton were powerful men; one of them would pursue a thousand, and two of them would not flee from ten thousand of the rest of men.

51 The sons of Jacob killed all the inhabitants of the city of Sarton with the edge of the sword; no man stood up against them, and they left the women in the city.

52 The sons of Jacob took all the spoil of the city and captured what they desired, and they took flocks and herds and property from the city; the sons of Jacob did to Sarton and its inhabitants as they had done to Chazar and its inhabitants, and they turned and went away.

CHAPTER 39

1 When the sons of Jacob went from the city of Sarton, they had gone about two hundred cubits when they met the inhabitants of Tapnach coming toward them, for they went out to fight with them because they had smitten the king of Tapnach and all his men.

2 So all that remained in the city of Tapnach came out to fight with the sons of Jacob and they thought to retake from them the booty and the spoil which they had captured from Chazar and Sarton.

3 The rest of the men of Tapnach fought with the sons of Jacob in that place, and the sons of Jacob struck them and they fled before them. They pursued them to the city of Arbelan and they all fell before the sons of Jacob.

4 The sons of Jacob returned and came to Tapnach to take away the spoil of Tapnach; when they came to Tapnach they heard that the people of Arbelan had gone out to meet them to save the spoil of their brothers. The sons of Jacob left ten of their men in Tapnach to plunder the city, and they went out toward the people of Arbelan.

5 The men of Arbelan went out with their wives to fight with the sons of Jacob, for their wives were experienced in battle; they went out, about four hundred men and women.

6 And all the sons of Jacob shouted with a loud voice; they all ran toward the inhabitants of Arbelan with a great and tremendous voice.

7 The inhabitants of Arbelan heard the noise of the shouting of the sons of Jacob and their roaring like the noise of lions and like the roaring of the sea and its waves.

8 And fear and terror possessed their hearts on account of the sons of Jacob; they were terribly afraid of them and they retreated and fled before them into the city. The sons of Jacob pursued them to the gate of the city and they came on them in the city.

9 The sons of Jacob fought with them in the city, and all their women were engaged in slinging against the sons of Jacob; the combat was very severe among them all of that day till evening.

10 And the sons of Jacob could not prevail over them; the sons of Jacob had almost perished in that battle. The sons of Jacob cried to the Lord and greatly gained strength toward evening; the sons of Jacob struck all the inhabitants of Arbelan by the edge of the sword, men, women and little ones.

11 Also the remainder of the people who had fled from Sarton, the sons of

Jacob struck them in Arbelan, and the sons of Jacob did to Arbelan and Tapnach as they had done to Chazar and Sarton. When the women saw that all the men were dead, they went on the roofs of the city and struck the sons of Jacob by showering down stones like rain.

12 And the sons of Jacob hurried and came into the city and seized all the women and struck them with the edge of the sword. The sons of Jacob captured all the spoil and booty, flocks and herds and cattle.

13 The sons of Jacob did to Machnaymah as they had done to Tapnach, to Chazar and to Shiloh, and they turned from there and went away.

14 On the fifth day the sons of Jacob heard that the people of Gaash had gathered against them to battle, because they had slain their king and their captains, for there had been fourteen captains in the city of Gaash, and the sons of Jacob had slain them all in the first battle.

15 And the sons of Jacob that day put on their weapons of war, and they marched to battle against the inhabitants of Gaash. In Gaash there was a strong and mighty people of the people of the Amorites; Gaash was the strongest and best fortified city of all the cities of the Amorites, and it had three walls.

16 The sons of Jacob came to Gaash and they found the gates of the city locked and about five hundred men standing at the top of the outer-most wall; a people numerous as the sand on the sea shore were in ambush for the sons of Jacob from outside the city at the rear.

17 And the sons of Jacob approached to open the gates of the city, and while they were drawing near to it, those who were in ambush at the rear of the city came forth from their places and surrounded the sons of Jacob.

18 The sons of Jacob were enclosed between the people of Gaash, and the battle was both to their front and rear; all the men that were on the wall were casting from the wall on them, arrows and stones.

19 And Judah, seeing that the men of Gaash were getting too strong for them, gave a most piercing and tremendous shriek and all the men of Gaash were terrified at the voice of Judah's cry; men fell from the wall at his powerful shriek and all those that were from without and within the city were greatly afraid of their lives.

20 And the sons of Jacob still came closer to break the doors of the city when the men of Gaash threw stones and arrows on them from the top of the wall, and made them flee from the gate.

21 The sons of Jacob returned against the men of Gaash who were with them from outside the city and they struck them terribly, as striking

against gourds, and they could not stand against the sons of Jacob for fright and terror had seized them at the shriek of Judah.

22 The sons of Jacob killed all those men who were outside the city, and the sons of Jacob still drew nearer to make an entrance into the city and to fight under the city walls, but they could not for all the inhabitants of Gaash who remained in the city had surrounded the walls of Gaash in every direction; the sons of Jacob were unable to approach the city to fight with them.

23 The sons of Jacob came near to one corner to fight under the wall; the inhabitants of Gaash threw arrows and stones on them like showers of rain, and they fled from under the wall.

24 And the people of Gaash who were on the wall, seeing that the sons of Jacob could not prevail over them from under the wall, reproached the sons of Jacob in these words, saying,

25 What is the matter with you in the battle that you cannot prevail? Can you then do to the mighty city of Gaash and its inhabitants as you did to the cities of the Amorites that were not so powerful? Certainly to those weak ones among us you did those things and killed them in the entrance of the city, for they had no strength when they were terrified at the sound of your shouting.

26 And will you now then be able to fight in this place? Certainly here you will all die, and we will avenge the cause of those cities that you have laid waste.

27 And the inhabitants of Gaash greatly reproached the sons of Jacob and reviled them with their gods, and continued to cast arrows and stones on them from the wall.

28 Judah and his brothers heard the words of the inhabitants of Gaash and their anger was greatly roused, and Judah was zealous of his God in this matter, and he called out and said, O Lord, help, send help to us and our brothers.

29 And he ran at a distance with all his might with his drawn sword in his hand, and he sprang from the earth and by dint of his strength mounted the wall, and his sword fell from his hand.

30 And Judah shouted on the wall, and all the men that were on the wall were terrified; some of them fell from the wall into the city and died, and those who were yet on the wall, when they saw Judah's strength were greatly afraid and fled for their lives into the city for safety.

31 And some were emboldened to fight with Judah on the wall; they came close to kill him when they saw there was no sword in Judah's hand

and they thought of casting him from the wall to his brothers; twenty men of the city came up to assist them, they surrounded Judah and all shouted over him, and approached him with drawn swords; they terrified Judah, and Judah cried out to his brothers from the wall.

32 And Jacob and his sons drew the bow from under the wall, and struck three of the men that were on the top of the wall, and Judah continued to cry and he exclaimed, O Lord help us, O Lord deliver us, and he cried out with a loud voice on the wall, and the cry was heard at a great distance.

33 After this cry he again repeated a shout, and all the men who surrounded Judah on the top of the wall were terrified; they each threw his sword from his hand at the sound of Judah's shouting and his tremor and fled.

34 Judah took the swords which had fallen from their hands and he fought with them and killed twenty of their men on the wall.

35 About eighty men and women still ascended the wall from the city and they all surrounded Judah, and the Lord impressed the fear of Judah in their hearts so that they were unable to approach him.

36 And Jacob and all who were with him drew the bow from under the wall, and they killed ten men on the wall; they fell below the wall in front of Jacob and his sons.

37 And the people on the wall seeing that twenty of their men had fallen still ran toward Judah with drawn swords, but they could not approach him for they were greatly terrified at Judah's strength.

38 And one of their mighty men whose name was Arud approached to strike Judah on the head with his sword, when Judah hastily put his shield to his head; the sword hit the shield and it was split in two.

39 This mighty man after he had struck Judah ran for his life at the fear of Judah, and his feet slipped on the wall and he fell among the sons of Jacob who were below the wall, and the sons of Jacob struck him and killed him.

40 And Judah's head pained him from the blow of the powerful man; Judah had nearly died from it.

41 And Judah cried out on the wall owing to the pain produced by the blow, when Dan heard him, and his anger burned within him; he also rose up and went a distance and ran and sprang from the earth and mounted the wall with his wrath-excited strength.

42 And when Dan came on the wall near to Judah, all the men on the wall fled who had stood against Judah; they went up to the second wall and

they threw arrows and stones on Dan and Judah from the second wall and endeavored to drive them from the wall.

43 And the arrows and stones struck Dan and Judah and they had nearly been killed on the wall; wherever Dan and Judah fled from the wall they were attacked with arrows and stones from the second wall.

44 Jacob and his sons were still at the entrance of the city below the first wall, and they were not able to draw their bow against the inhabitants of the city as they could not be seen by them, being on the second wall.

45 Dan and Judah, when they could no longer bear the stones and arrows that fell on them from the second wall, both sprang onto the second wall near the people of the city; when the people of the city who were on the second wall saw that Dan and Judah had come to them on the second wall, they all cried out and descended below between the walls.

46 Jacob and his sons heard the noise of the shouting from the people of the city and they were still at the entrance of the city; they were anxious about Dan and Judah who were not seen by them, they being on the second wall.

47 Naphtali went up with his wrath-excited might and sprang on the first wall to see what caused the noise of shouting which they had heard in the city; Issachar and Zebulun came near to break the doors of the city, and they opened the gates of the city and came into the city.

48 Naphtali leaped from the first wall to the second and came to assist his brothers; the inhabitants of Gaash who were on the wall, seeing that Naphtali was the third who had come up to assist his brothers, all fled and descended into the city, and Jacob and all his sons and all their young men came into the city to them.

49 Judah and Dan and Naphtali descended from the wall into the city and pursued the inhabitants of the city, and Simeon and Levi were from outside the city and didn't know that the gate was opened; they went up from there to the wall and came down to their brothers into the city.

50 The inhabitants of the city had all descended into the city and the sons of Jacob came to them from different directions; the battle waged against them from the front and the rear, and the sons of Jacob struck them terribly and killed about twenty thousand of them men and women; not one of them could stand up against the sons of Jacob.

51 And the blood flowed plentifully in the city, and it was like a brook of water; the blood flowed like a brook to the outer part of the city, and reached the desert of Bethchorin.

52 And the people of Bethchorin saw at a distance the blood flowing from

the city of Gaash and about seventy men from among them ran to see the blood, and they came to the place where the blood was.

53 They followed the track of the blood and came to the wall of the city of Gaash, and they saw the blood issue from the city. They heard the voice of crying from the inhabitants of Gaash, for it ascended to heaven, and the blood was continuing to flow abundantly like a brook of water.

54 And all the sons of Jacob were still smiting the inhabitants of Gaash, and were engaged in slaying them till evening, about twenty thousand men and women. And the people of Chorin said, Certainly this is the work of the Hebrews, for they are still carrying on war in all the cities of the Amorites.

55 And those people hurried and ran to Bethchorin, and each took his weapons of war; they cried out to all the inhabitants of Bethchorin, who also put on their weapons of war to go and fight with the sons of Jacob.

56 When the sons of Jacob had done smiting the inhabitants of Gaash, they walked about the city to strip all the slain. Coming into the innermost part of the city and farther on they met three very powerful men, and there was no sword in their hand.

57 The sons of Jacob came up to the place where they were and the powerful men ran away; one of them had taken Zebulun, who he saw was a young lad and of short stature, and with his might dashed him to the ground.

58 And Jacob ran to him with his sword and Jacob struck him below his loins with the sword and cut him in two, and the body fell on Zebulun.

59 The second one approached and seized Jacob to fell him to the ground; Jacob turned to him and shouted to him, while Simeon and Levi ran and struck him on the hips with the sword and felled him to the ground.

60 And the powerful man rose up from the ground with wrath-excited might; Judah came to him before he had gained his footing and struck him on the head with the sword, and his head was split and he died.

61 The third powerful man, seeing that his companions were killed, ran from before the sons of Jacob and the sons of Jacob pursued him into the city; while the powerful man was fleeing he found one of the swords of the inhabitants of the city, he picked it up and turned to the sons of Jacob and fought them with that sword.

62 The powerful man ran to Judah to strike him on the head with the sword, and there was no shield in the hand of Judah; while he was aiming to strike him, Naphtali hastily took his shield and put it to Judah's head

and the sword of the powerful man hit the shield of Naphtali, and Judah escaped the sword.

63 Simeon and Levi ran onto the powerful man with their swords and struck at him forcibly with their swords, and the two swords entered the body of the powerful man and divided it in two, length-wise.

64 And the sons of Jacob struck the three mighty men at that time, together with all the inhabitants of Gaash, and the day was about to decline.

65 And the sons of Jacob walked about Gaash and took all the spoil of the city, even the little ones and women they did not allow to live, and the sons of Jacob did to Gaash as they had done to Sarton and Shiloh.

CHAPTER 40

1 And the sons of Jacob led away all the spoil of Gaash, and went out of the city by night.

2 They were going out marching toward the castle of Bethchorin, and the inhabitants of Bethchorin were going to the castle to meet them; on that night the sons of Jacob fought with the inhabitants of Bethchorin, in the castle of Bethchorin.

3 And all the inhabitants of Bethchorin were mighty men; one of them would not flee from before a thousand men, and they fought on that night on the castle; their shouts were heard on that night from afar and the earth quaked at their shouting.

4 And all the sons of Jacob were afraid of those men as they were not accustomed to fight in the dark, and they were greatly perplexed. The sons of Jacob cried to the Lord, saying, Give help to us O Lord, deliver us that we may not die by the hands of these uncircumcised men.

5 And the Lord listened to the voice of the sons of Jacob, and the Lord caused great terror and confusion to seize the people of Bethchorin; they fought among themselves with one another in the darkness of night, and struck each other in great numbers.

6 The sons of Jacob, knowing that the Lord had brought a spirit of perverseness among those men, and that they fought each man with his neighbor, went forth from among the bands of the people of Bethchorin and went as far as the descent of the castle of Bethchorin, and farther.

They stayed there securely with their young men on that night.

7 And the people of Bethchorin fought the whole night, one man with his brother, and the other with his neighbor; they cried out in every direction on the castle and their cry was heard at a distance, and the whole earth shook at their voice for they were powerful above all the people of the earth.

8 And all the inhabitants of the cities of the Canaanites, the Hittites, the Amorites, the Hivites and all the kings of Canaan, and also those who were on the other side of the Jordan heard the noise of the shouting that night.

9 They said, Certainly these are the battles of the Hebrews who are fighting against the seven cities, who came near to them; who can stand against those Hebrews?

10 All the inhabitants of the cities of the Canaanites and all those who were on the other side of the Jordan were greatly afraid of the sons of Jacob, for they said, Behold the same will be done to us as was done to those cities, for who can stand against their mighty strength?

11 And the cries of the Chorinites were very great on that night and continued to increase; they struck each other till morning, and numbers of them were killed.

12 And the morning appeared; all the sons of Jacob rose up at daybreak and went up to the castle, and they struck those who remained of the Chorinites in a terrible manner and they were all killed in the castle.

13 And the sixth day appeared, and all the inhabitants of Canaan saw at a distance all the people of Bethchorin lying dead in the castle of Bethchorin, and scattered about as the carcasses of lambs and goats.

14 And the sons of Jacob led all the spoil which they had captured from Gaash and went to Bethchorin; they found the city full of people like the sand of the sea, and they fought with them, and the sons of Jacob struck them there till evening time.

15 And the sons of Jacob did to Bethchorin as they had done to Gaash and Tapnach, and as they had done to Chazar, to Sarton and to Shiloh.

16 The sons of Jacob took with them the spoil of Bethchorin and all the spoil of the cities, and on that day they went home to Shechem.

17 And the sons of Jacob came home to the city of Shechem and they remained outside the city, and then rested there from the war, and stayed there all night.

18 And all their servants together with all the spoil that they had taken from the cities, were left outside the city, and they did not enter the city, for they said, Perhaps there may yet be more fighting against us, and they may come to besiege us in Shechem.

19 Jacob and his sons and their servants remained that night and the next day in the portion of the field which Jacob had purchased from Hamor for five shekels, and all that they had captured was with them.

20 All the booty which the sons of Jacob had captured was in the portion of the field, immense as the sand on the seashore.

21 The inhabitants of the land observed them from afar, and they all were afraid of the sons of Jacob who had done this thing, for no king from the days of old had ever done the like.

22 The seven kings of the Canaanites resolved to make peace with the sons of Jacob, for they were greatly afraid for their lives on account of the sons of Jacob.

23 And on that day, being the seventh day, Japhia king of Hebron sent secretly to the king of Ai, and to the king of Gibeon, and to the king of Shalem, and to the king of Adulam, and to the king of Lachish, and to the king of Chazar, and to all the Canaanitish kings who were under their subjection, saying,

24 Go up with me, and come to me that we may go to the sons of Jacob, and I will make peace with them and form a treaty with them, that all your lands not be destroyed by the swords of the sons of Jacob as they did to Shechem and the cities around it, as you have heard and seen.

25 And when you come to me, do not come with many men, but let every king bring his three head captains and every captain bring three of his officers.

26 And come all of you to Hebron; we will go together to the sons of Jacob and request them to form a treaty of peace with us.

27 And all those kings did as the king of Hebron had sent to them, for they were all under his counsel and command, and all the kings of Canaan assembled to go to the sons of Jacob to make peace with them; the sons of Jacob returned and went to the portion of the field that was in Shechem, for they did not put confidence in the kings of the land.

28 And the sons of Jacob returned and remained in the portion of the field ten days, and no one came to make war with them.

29 When the sons of Jacob saw that there was no appearance of war, they all assembled and went to the city of Shechem, and the sons of Jacob

remained in Shechem.

30 And at the expiration of forty days, all the kings of the Amorites assembled from all their places and came to Hebron, to Japhia, king of Hebron.

31 The number of kings that came to Hebron to make peace with the sons of Jacob was twenty-one kings, and the number of captains that came with them was sixty-nine, and their men were one hundred and eighty-nine; all these kings and their men rested by Mount Hebron.

32 And the king of Hebron went out with his three captains and nine men, and these kings resolved to go to the sons of Jacob to make peace.

33 They said to the king of Hebron, Go before us with your men, speak for us to the sons of Jacob, and we will come after you and confirm your words, and the king of Hebron did so.

34 The sons of Jacob heard that all the kings of Canaan had gathered together and rested in Hebron, and the sons of Jacob sent four of their servants as spies, saying, Go and spy these kings, and search and examine their men whether they are few or many, and if they are but few in number, count them all and come back.

35 And the servants of Jacob went secretly to these kings, and did as the sons of Jacob had commanded them. On that day they came back to the sons of Jacob, and said to them, We came to those kings, and they are few in number; we counted them all, and surely there were two hundred and eighty-eight, kings and men.

36 The sons of Jacob said, They are but few in number, therefore we will not all go out to them. In the morning the sons of Jacob rose up and chose sixty-two of their men, and ten of the sons of Jacob went with them; and they put on their weapons of war, for they said, They are coming to make war with us. For they didn't know that they were coming to make peace with them.

37 And the sons of Jacob went with their servants to the gate of Shechem, toward those kings, and their father Jacob was with them.

38 And when they had come forth, there the king of Hebron and his three captains and nine men with him were coming along the road toward the sons of Jacob; the sons of Jacob lifted up their eyes, and saw at a distance Japhia, king of Hebron, with his captains, coming toward them, And the sons of Jacob took their stand at the place of the gate of Shechem, and did not proceed.

39 The king of Hebron continued to advance, he and his captains, until he

came near to the sons of Jacob; he and his captains bowed down to them to the ground, and the king of Hebron sat with his captains in front of Jacob and his sons.

40 The sons of Jacob said to him, What has happened to you, O king of Hebron? Why have you come to us this day? What do you require from us? And the king of Hebron said to Jacob, I petition you my lord, all the kings of the Canaanites have this day come to make peace with you.

41 And the sons of Jacob heard the words of the king of Hebron; they would not consent to his proposals; the sons of Jacob had no faith in him, for they imagined that the king of Hebron had spoken deceitfully to them.

42 The king of Hebron knew from the words of the sons of Jacob that they did not believe his words, and the king of Hebron approached nearer to Jacob, and said to him, I beg you, my lord, to be assured that all these kings have come to you on peaceable terms, for they have not come with all their men, neither did they bring their weapons of war with them, for they have come to seek peace from my lord and his sons.

43 The sons of Jacob answered the king of Hebron, saying, Go to all these kings and if you speak truth to us, let them each come singly before us; if they come to us unarmed, we shall then know that they seek peace from us.

44 And Japhia, king of Hebron, sent one of his men to the kings and they all came before the sons of Jacob, and bowed down to them to the ground; these kings sat before Jacob and his sons and spoke to them, saying,

45 We have heard all that you did to the kings of the Amorites with your sword and greatly mighty arm, so that no man could stand up before you; we were afraid of you for the sake of our lives, that it would happen to us as it did to them.

46 So we have come to you to form a treaty of peace between us, and now therefore contract with us a covenant of peace and truth, that you will not meddle with us, inasmuch as we have not meddled with you.

47 And the sons of Jacob knew that they had really come to seek peace from them. And the sons of Jacob listened to them, and formed a covenant with them.

48 The sons of Jacob swore to them that they would not meddle with them, and all the kings of the Canaanites swore also to them, and the sons of Jacob made them pay tribute from that day forward.

49 And after this all the captains of these kings came with their men before Jacob, with presents in their hands for Jacob and his sons, and they bowed down to him to the ground.

50 These kings then urged the sons of Jacob and begged of them to return all the spoil they had captured from the seven cities of the Amorites, and the sons of Jacob did so; they returned all that they had captured, the women, the little ones, the cattle and all the spoil which they had taken, and they sent them off; they went away each to his city.

51 And all these kings again bowed down to the sons of Jacob, and they sent or brought them many gifts in those days; the sons of Jacob sent off these kings and their men, and they went peaceably away from them to their cities, and the sons of Jacob also returned to their home, to Shechem.

52 And there was peace from that day forward between the sons of Jacob and the kings of the Canaanites, until the children of Israel came to inherit the land of Canaan.

CHAPTER 41

1 At the revolution of the year the sons of Jacob journeyed from Shechem, and they came to Hebron, to their father Isaac; they lived there, but their flocks and herds they fed daily in Shechem, for there was there in those days good and fattening pasture. Jacob and his sons and all their household lived in the valley of Hebron.

2 It was in those days, in that year, being the hundred and sixth year of the life of Jacob, in the tenth year of Jacob's coming from Padan-aram, that Leah the wife of Jacob died; she was fifty-one years old when she died in Hebron.

3 Jacob and his sons buried her in the cave of the field of Machpelah, which is in Hebron, which Abraham had bought from the children of Heth for the possession of a burial place.

4 The sons of Jacob lived with their father in the valley of Hebron; all the inhabitants of the land knew their strength and their fame went throughout the land.

5 Joseph the son of Jacob and his brother Benjamin, the sons of Rachel, the wife of Jacob, were yet young in those days, and did not go out with their brothers during their battles in all the cities of the Amorites.

6 And when Joseph saw the strength of his brothers and their greatness, he praised them and extolled them, but he ranked himself greater than them and extolled himself above them; Jacob, his father, also loved him more than any of his sons for he was a son of his old age, and through his love toward him he made him a coat of many colors.

7 And when Joseph saw that his father loved him more than his brothers, he continued to elevate himself above his brothers, and he brought to his father evil reports concerning them.

8 The sons of Jacob seeing all of Joseph's conduct toward them, and that their father loved him more than any of them, hated him and could not ever speak peaceably to him.

9 Joseph was seventeen years old, and he was still magnifying himself above his brothers, and thought of raising himself above them.

10 At that time he dreamed a dream, and he came to his brothers and told them his dream, and he said to them, I dreamed a dream, and behold we were all binding sheaves in the field, and my sheaf rose and placed itself on the ground and your sheaves surrounded it and bowed down to it.

11 And his brothers answered him and said to him, What means this dream that you did dream? Do you imagine in your heart to reign or rule over us?

12 And he still came and told the thing to his father Jacob, and Jacob kissed Joseph when he heard these words from his mouth, and Jacob blessed Joseph.

13 When the sons of Jacob saw that their father had blessed Joseph and had kissed him, and that he loved him greatly, they became jealous of him and hated him all the more.

14 After this Joseph dreamed another dream and related the dream to his father in the presence of his brothers, and Joseph said to his father and brothers, Behold I have again dreamed a dream, and behold the sun and the moon and the eleven stars bowed down to me.

15 And his father heard the words of Joseph and his dream, and seeing that his brothers hated Joseph on account of this matter, Jacob therefore rebuked Joseph before his brothers on account of this thing, saying, What does this dream mean which you have dreamed, and this magnifying yourself before your brothers who are older than you are?

16 Do you imagine in your heart that I and your mother and your eleven brothers will come and bow down to you, that you speak these things?

17 And his brothers were jealous of him on account of his words and

dreams; they continued to hate him, and Jacob reserved the dreams in his heart.

18 The sons of Jacob went one day to feed their father's flock in Shechem, for they were still herdsmen in those days; while the sons of Jacob were that day feeding in Shechem they delayed, and the time of gathering in the cattle was passed, and they had not arrived.

19 And Jacob saw that his sons were delayed in Shechem, and Jacob said within himself, Perhhaps the people of Shechem have risen up to fight against them, therefore they have delayed coming today.

20 And Jacob called Joseph his son and commanded him, saying, Behold your brothers are feeding in Shechem this day and look, they have not yet come back; therefore go and see where they are, and bring back word to me concerning the welfare of your brothers and the welfare of the flock.

21 And Jacob sent his son Joseph to the valley of Hebron; Joseph came for his brothers to Shechem, and could not find them, and Joseph went toward the field which was near Shechem to see where his brothers had turned. But he missed his road in the wilderness and didn't know which way he should go.

22 And an angel of the Lord found him wandering in the road toward the field, and Joseph said to the angel of the Lord, I seek my brothers; have you not heard where they are feeding? And the angel of the Lord said to Joseph, I saw your brothers feeding here, and I heard them say they would go to feed in Dothan.

23 Joseph listened to the voice of the angel of the Lord, and he went to his brothers in Dothan and he found them in Dothan feeding the flock.

24 Joseph advanced to his brothers but before he had come near them, they had resolved to kill him.

25 Simeon said to his brothers, Behold the man of dreams is coming to us this day, so now come and let us kill him and cast him into one of the pits that are in the wilderness; when his father shall seek him from us, we will say an evil beast has devoured him.

26 Reuben heard the words of his brothers concerning Joseph and said to them, You should not do this thing, for how can we look up to our father Jacob? Cast him into this pit to die there, but do not put forth a hand on him to spill his blood. Reuben said this in order to deliver him from their hand, to bring him back to his father.

27 When Joseph came to his brothers he sat before them, and they rose upon him and seized him and struck him to the earth, and stripped the

coat of many colors which he had on.

28 They took him and cast him into a pit and in the pit there was no water, but serpents and scorpions. And Joseph was afraid of the serpents and scorpions that were in the pit. Joseph cried out with a loud voice and the Lord hid the serpents and scorpions in the sides of the pit, and they did no harm to Joseph.

29 And Joseph called out from the pit to his brothers, and said to them, What have I done to you, and in what have I sinned? Why do you not fear the Lord concerning me? Am I not of your bones and flesh, and is not Jacob your father, my father? Why do you do this thing to me this day, and how will you be able to look up to our father Jacob?

30 And he continued to cry out and call to his brothers from the pit, and he said, O Judah, Simeon, and Levi, my brothers, lift me up from the place of darkness in which you have placed me, and come this day to have compassion on me, you children of the Lord and sons of Jacob my father. And if I have sinned to you, are you not the sons of Abraham, Isaac, and Jacob? If they saw an orphan they had compassion over him, or one that was hungry, they gave him bread to eat, or one that was thirsty, they gave him water to drink, or one that was naked, they covered him with garments!

31 And how then can you withhold your pity from your brother, for I am of your flesh and bones, and if I have sinned to you, certainly you will do this on account of my father!

32 Joseph spoke these words from the pit, and his brothers could not listen to him, nor incline their ears to the words of Joseph, and Joseph was crying and weeping in the pit.

33 And Joseph said, O that my father knew this day, the act which my brothers have done to me and the words which they have this day spoken to me.

34 All his brothers heard his cries and weeping in the pit, and his brothers went and removed themselves from the pit, so that they might not hear the cries of Joseph and his weeping in the pit.

CHAPTER 42

1 They went and sat on the opposite side, about the distance of a bow-shot, and they sat there to eat bread; while they were eating they held

counsel together what was to be done with him, whether to kill him or to bring him back to his father.

2 They were holding the counsel when they lifted up their eyes, and saw at once there was a company of Ishmaelites coming at a distance by the road of Gilead, going down to Egypt.

3 And Judah said to them, What gain will it be to us if we kill our brother? Perhaps God will require him from us; this then is the counsel proposed concerning him, which you shall do to him: Look at this company of Ishmaelites going down to Egypt,

4 So now let us dispose of him to them and let not our hand be on him; they will lead him along with them and he will be lost among the people of the land and we will not put him to death with our own hands. And the proposal pleased his brothers and they did according to the word of Judah.

5 While they were discussing this matter and before the company of Ishmaelites had come up to them, seven trading men of Midian passed by them; as they passed they were thirsty and they lifted up their eyes and saw the same pit in which Joseph was held, and they looked and saw every species of bird was on him.

6 These Midianites ran to the pit to drink water for they thought that it contained water, and on coming to the pit they heard the voice of Joseph crying and weeping in there, and they looked down into the pit, and they saw there was a youth of good-looking appearance and well-favored.

7 They called to him and said, Who are you and who brought you here, and who placed you in this pit in the wilderness? And they all assisted to raise up Joseph and they drew him out and brought him up from the pit, and took him and went away on their journey and passed by his brothers.

8 And these said to them, Why do you do this, to take our servant from us and to go away? Certainly we placed this youth in the pit because he rebelled against us, and you come and bring him up and lead him away; now then give us back our servant.

9 And the Midianites answered and said to the sons of Jacob, Is this your servant, or does this man attend you? Perhaps you are all his servants, for he is more handsome and well-favored than any of you, and why do you all speak falsely to us?

10 So we will not listen to your words nor give you our attention, for we found the youth in the pit in the wilderness and we took him; we will therefore go on.

11 And all the sons of Jacob approached them and rose up to them and said to them, Give us back our servant, and why will you all die by the edge of the sword? And the Midianites cried out against them and they drew their swords and approached to fight with the sons of Jacob.

12 Then Simeon rose up from his seat against them, and sprang on the ground and drew his sword and approached the Midianites and he gave a terrible shout before them, so that his shouting was heard at a distance, and the earth shook at Simeon's shouting.

13 The Midianites were terrified on account of Simeon and the noise of his shouting, and they fell on their faces and were excessively alarmed.

14 Simeon said to them, Surely I am Simeon, the son of Jacob the Hebrew, who have only with my brothers destroyed the city of Shechem and the cities of the Amorites; so shall God moreover do to me if all your brothers, the people of Midian, and also the kings of Canaan, were to come with you; they could not fight against me.

15 Now therefore give us back the youth whom you have taken, or I'll give your flesh to the birds of the skies and the beasts of the earth.

16 The Midianites were more afraid of Simeon, and they approached the sons of Jacob with terror and fright, and with pathetic words, saying,

17 Certainly you have said that the young man is your servant and that he rebelled against you, and therefore you placed him in the pit; what then will you do with a servant who rebels against his master? So now sell him to us, and we will give you all that you require for him. The Lord was pleased to do this in order that the sons of Jacob should not kill their brother.

18 And the Midianites saw that Joseph was of a good-looking appearance and well-favored; they desired him in their hearts and were urgent to purchase him from his brothers.

19 The sons of Jacob listened to the Midianites and they sold their brother Joseph to them for twenty pieces of silver. Reuben their brother was not with them, and the Midianites took Joseph and continued their journey to Gilead.

20 They were going along the road, and the Midianites repented of what they had done, in having purchased the young man, and one said to the other, What is this thing that we have done, in taking this youth from the Hebrews who is of good-looking appearance and well-favored?

21 Perhaps this youth is stolen from the land of the Hebrews, and why then have we done this thing? If he should be sought for and found in our hands we shall die through him.

22 Now certainly hardy and powerful men have sold him to us, the strength of one of whom you saw this day; perhaps they stole him from his land with their might and with their powerful arm, and have therefore sold him to us for the small value which we gave to them.

23 While they were thus discussing together, they looked and saw the company of Ishmaelites which was coming at first, and which the sons of Jacob saw, was advancing toward the Midianites; the Midianites said to each other, Come let us sell this youth to the company of Ishmaelites who are coming toward us. We will take for him the little that we gave for him, and we will be delivered from his evil.

24 And they did so, and they reached the Ishmaelites, and the Midianites sold Joseph to the Ishmaelites for twenty pieces of silver which they had given for him to his brothers.

25 And the Midianites went on their road to Gilead, and the Ishmaelites took Joseph and they let him ride on one of the camels, and they were leading him to Egypt.

26 When Joseph heard that the Ishmaelites were proceeding to Egypt, Joseph lamented and wept at this thing that he was to be so far removed from the land of Canaan, from his father, and he wept bitterly while he was riding on the camel. One of their men observed him, and made him go down from the camel and walk on foot, and still Joseph continued to cry and weep, and he said, O my father, my father.

27 One of the Ishmaelites rose up and struck Joseph on the cheek, and still he continued to weep; and Joseph was fatigued in the road, and was unable to proceed on account of the bitterness of his soul; they all struck him and afflicted him in the road, and they terrified him in order that he might cease from weeping.

28 And the Lord saw the condition of Joseph and his trouble, and the Lord brought down on those men darkness and confusion, and the hand of everyone that struck him became withered.

29 And they said to each other, What is this thing that God has done to us in the road? And they knew not that this befell them on account of Joseph. And the men proceeded on the road, and they passed along the road of Ephrath where Rachel was buried.

30 Joseph reached his mother's grave, and Joseph hurried and ran to his mother's grave, and fell on the grave and wept.

31 Joseph cried aloud on his mother's grave and said, O my mother, my mother, O you who did give me birth, awake now, and rise and see your

son, how he has been sold for a slave, and no one to pity him.

32 O rise and see your son, weep with me on account of my troubles, and see the heart of my brothers.

33 Arouse my mother, arouse, awake from your sleep for me, and direct your battles against my brothers. O how have they stripped me of my coat and sold me already twice for a slave, and separated me from my father, and there is no one to pity me.

34 Arouse and lay your cause against them before God, and see whom God will justify in the judgment, and whom he will condemn.

35 Rise, O my mother, rise, awake from your sleep and see my father how his soul is with me this day, and comfort him and ease his heart.

36 And Joseph continued to speak these words, and Joseph cried aloud and wept bitterly on his mother's grave; and he ceased speaking, and from bitterness of heart he became still as a stone on the grave.

37 And Joseph heard a voice speaking to him from beneath the ground, which answered him with bitterness of heart, and with a voice of weeping and praying in these words:

38 My son, my son Joseph, I have heard the voice of your weeping and the voice of your lamentation; I have seen your tears; I know your troubles, my son, and it grieves me for your sake, and abundant grief is added to my grief.

39 Now therefore my son, Joseph my son, hope in the Lord, and wait for him and do not fear, for the Lord is with you, he will deliver you from all trouble.

40 Rise my son, go down to Egypt with your masters and do not fear, for the Lord is with you, my son. And she continued to speak like these words to Joseph, and she was still.

41 And Joseph heard this, and he wondered greatly at this, and he continued to weep. After this one of the Ishmaelites observed him crying and weeping on the grave, and his anger was set ablaze against him, and he drove him from there, and he struck him and cursed him.

42 And Joseph said to the men, May I find grace in your sight to take me back to my father's house, and he will give you abundance of riches.

43 And they answered him, saying, Are you not a slave, and where is your father? And if you had a father you would not already twice have been sold for a slave for so little value; their anger was still roused against him, and they continued to strike him and to chastise him, and Joseph wept bitterly.

44 The Lord saw Joseph's affliction, and the Lord again struck these men, and chastised them, and the Lord caused darkness to envelope them on the earth, and the lightning flashed and the thunder roared, and the earth shook at the voice of the thunder and of the mighty wind; the men were terrified and knew not where they should go.

45 The beasts and camels stood still, and they led them, but they would not go, they struck them, and they crouched on the ground; the men said to each other, What is this that God has done to us? What are our transgressions and what are our sins that this thing has thus befallen us?

46 One of them answered and said to them, Perhaps on account of the sin of afflicting this slave has this thing happened this day to us; now we should implore him strongly to forgive us and then we shall know on whose account this evil befalls us; if God willl have compassion over us, then we shall know that all this comes to us on account of the sin of afflicting this slave.

47 And the men did so, and they supplicated Joseph and pressed him to forgive them; and they said, We have sinned to the Lord and to you, now therefore vouchsafe to request of your God that he shall put away this death from among us, for we have sinned to him.

48 Joseph did according to their words and the Lord listened to Joseph, and the Lord put away the plague which he had inflicted on those men on account of Joseph; the beasts rose up from the ground and they conducted them, and they went on; the raging storm abated and the earth became tranquilized and the men proceeded on their journey to go down to Egypt. The men knew that this evil had befallen them on account of Joseph.

49 And they said to each other, We now know that it was on account of his affliction that this evil befell us; now why shall we bring this death on our souls? Let us hold counsel what to do to this slave.

50 And one answered and said, Certainly he told us to bring him back to his father; so come, let us take him back and we will go to the place that he will tell us, and take from his family the price that we gave for him and we will then go away.

51 One answered again and said, Behold this counsel is very good, but we cannot do so for the way is very far from us, and we cannot leave our road.

52 One more answered and said to them, This is the counsel to be adopted, we will not swerve from it; behold we are this day going to Egypt and when we shall have come to Egypt, we will sell him there at a high price, and we will be delivered from his evil.

53 And this thing pleased the men and they did so; they continued their journey to Egypt with Joseph.

CHAPTER 43

1 When the sons of Jacob had sold their brother Joseph to the Midianites, their hearts were smitten on account of him and they repented of their acts, and they sought for him to bring him back but could not find him.

2 Reuben returned to the pit in which Joseph had been put in order to lift him out and restore him to his father; Reuben stood by the pit and heard not a word. He called out Joseph! Joseph! and no one answered or uttered a word.

3 And Reuben said, Joseph has died through fright, or some serpent has caused his death. Reuben descended into the pit, searched for Joseph and could not find him in the pit, and he came out again.

4 And Reuben tore his garments and he said, The child is not there, and how shall I reconcile my father about him if he is dead? He went to his brothers and found them grieving on account of Joseph, and counseling together how to appease their father about him. Reuben said to his brothers, I came to the pit and behold Joseph was not there, what then shall we say to our father, for my father will only seek the lad from me.

5 His brothers answered him saying, Thus and thus we did, and our hearts afterward struck us on account of this act, and we now sit to seek a pretext how we shall appease our father to it.

6 And Reuben said to them, What is this you have done to bring down the grey hairs of our father in sorrow to the grave? This thing is not good that you have done.

7 And Reuben sat with them, and they all rose up and swore to each other not to tell this thing to Jacob. They all said, The man who will tell this to our father or his household, or who will report this to any of the children of the land, we will all rise up against him and kill him with the sword.

8 And the sons of Jacob feared each other in this matter, from the youngest to the oldest; no one spoke a word, and they concealed the thing in their hearts.

9 Afterward they sat down to determine and invent something to say to their father Jacob concerning all these things.

10 Issachar said to them, Here is advice for you if it seems good in your eyes to do this thing. Take the coat which belongs to Joseph and tear it, and kill a kid of the goats and dip it in its blood.

11 And send it to our father and when he sees it he will say an evil beast has devoured him, therefore tear his coat and behold his blood will be on his coat, and by your doing this we shall be free of our father's murmurings.

12 Issachar's advice pleased them and they listened to him, and they did according to the word of Issachar which he had counselled them.

13 They hurried and took Joseph's coat and tore it, and they killed a kid of the goats and dipped the coat in the blood of the kid, and then trampled it into the dust. They sent the coat to their father Jacob by the hand of Naphtali, and they commanded him to say these words:

14 We had gathered in the cattle and had come as far as the road to Shechem and farther, when we found this coat on the road in the wilderness dipped in blood and in dust; now therefore know whether it is your son's coat or not.

15 And Naphtali went and he came to his father and he gave him the coat, and he spoke to him all the words which his brothers had commanded him.

16 Jacob saw Joseph's coat and he knew it and he fell on his face to the ground, and became as still as a stone Afterward he rose up and cried out with a loud and weeping voice and said, It is the coat of my son Joseph!

17 Jacob hurried and sent one of his servants to his sons, who went to them and found them coming along the road with the flock.

18 The sons of Jacob came to their father about evening, and behold their garments were torn and dust was on their heads, and they found their father crying out and weeping with a loud voice.

19 Jacob said to his sons, Tell me truly what evil have you this day suddenly brought on me? They answered their father Jacob, saying, We were coming along this day after the flock had been gathered in, and we came as far as the city of Shechem by the road in the wilderness; we found this coat filled with blood on the ground, and we knew it and we sent it to you so you could know it.

20 Jacob heard the words of his sons and he cried out with a loud voice,

and he said, It is the coat of my son; an evil beast has devoured him. Joseph is rent in pieces, for I sent him this day to see whether it was well with you and well with the flocks and to bring me word again from you; he went as I commanded him, and this has happened to him today while I thought my son was with you.

21 And the sons of Jacob answered and said, He did not come to us, neither have we seen him from the time of our going out from you until now.

22 When Jacob heard their words he again cried out aloud, and he rose up and tore his garments; he put sackcloth on his loins and he wept bitterly; he mourned and lifted up his voice in weeping and exclaimed and said these words,

23 Joseph my son, O my son Joseph, I sent you this day after the welfare of your brothers, and behold you have been torn in pieces; through my hand has this happened to my son.

24 It grieves me for you Joseph my son, it grieves me for you; how sweet you were to me during life, and now how greatly bitter is your death to me.

25 0 that I had died in your stead Joseph my son, for it grieves me sadly for you my son, O my son, my son. Joseph my son, where are you, and where have you been drawn? Arouse, arouse from your place, and come and see my grief for you, O my son Joseph.

26 Come now and number the tears gushing from my eyes down my cheeks, and bring them up before the Lord, that his anger may turn from me.

27 0 Joseph my son, how did you fall, by the hand of one by whom no one had fallen from the beginning of the world to this day; for you have been put to death by the smiting of an enemy, inflicted with cruelty, but certainly I know that this has happened to you on account of the multitude of my sins.

28 Arise now and see how bitter is my trouble for you my son, although I did not rear you nor fashion you nor give you breath and soul, but it was God who formed you and built your bones and covered them with flesh and breathed in your nostrils the breath of life, and then he gave you to me.

29 Now truly God who gave you to me, he has taken you from me; such then has happened to you.

30 And Jacob continued to speak like these words concerning Joseph, and he wept bitterly; he fell to the ground and became still.

Joseph B. Lumpkin

31 All the sons of Jacob seeing their father's trouble repented of what they had done, and they also wept bitterly.

32 And Judah rose up and lifted his father's head from the ground, and placed it on his lap; he wiped his father's tears from his cheeks, and Judah wept a very great weeping while his father's head was reclining on his lap, still as a stone.

33 The sons of Jacob saw their father's trouble, and they lifted up their voices and continued to weep; Jacob was yet lying on the ground still as a stone.

34 And all his sons and his servants and his servant's children rose up and stood round him to comfort him, and he refused to be comforted.

35 The whole household of Jacob rose up and mourned a great mourning on account of Joseph and their father's trouble, and the sad news reached Isaac, the son of Abraham, the father of Jacob, and he wept bitterly on account of Joseph, he and all his household. He went from the place where he lived in Hebron, and his men with him, and he comforted Jacob his son but he refused to be comforted.

36 And after this, Jacob rose up from the ground, and his tears were running down his cheeks, and he said to his sons, Rise up and take your swords and your bows, and go forth into the field, and seek whether you can find my son's body and bring it to me that I may bury it.

37 Seek also, I pray you, among the beasts and hunt them, and that which shall come the first before you seize and bring it to me; perhaps the Lord will this day pity my affliction, and prepare before you that which tore my son in pieces; bring it to me, and I will avenge the cause of my son.

38 And his sons did as their father had commanded them, and they rose up early in the morning, and each took his sword and his bow in his hand, and they went forth into the field to hunt the beasts.

39 And Jacob was still crying aloud and weeping and walking to and fro in the house, and smiting his hands together, saying, Joseph my son, Joseph my son.

40 The sons of Jacob went into the wilderness to seize the beasts, and there a wolf came toward them; they seized him and brought him to their father and said to him, This is the first we have found, and we have brought him to you as you did command us, and your son's body we could not find.

41 And Jacob took the beast from the hands of his sons, and he cried out with a loud and weeping voice, holding the beast in his hand, and he

spoke with a bitter heart to the beast, Why did you devour my son Joseph, and how did you have no fear of the God of the earth, or of my trouble for my son Joseph?

42 You did devour my son for nothing. He committed no violence. I was responsible for him. God will require him that is persecuted.

43 And the Lord opened the mouth of the beast in order to comfort Jacob with its words, and it answered Jacob and spoke these words to him,

44 As God lives who created us in the earth, and as your soul lives, my lord, I did not see your son, neither did I tear him to pieces, but from a distant land I also came to seek my son who went from me this day, and I know not whether he is living or dead.

45 And I came this day into the field to seek my son, and your sons found me, and seized me and increased my grief, and have this day brought me before you, and I have now spoken all my words to you.

46 Now therefore, O son of man, I am in your hands, and do to me this day as it may seem good in your sight, but by the life of God who created me, I did not see your son nor did I tear him to pieces, neither has the flesh of man entered my mouth all the days of my life.

47 When Jacob heard the words of the beast he was greatly astonished, and sent forth the beast from his hand, and she went her way.

48 And Jacob was still crying aloud and weeping for Joseph day after day, and he mourned for his son many days.

CHAPTER 44

1 The sons of Ishmael who had bought Joseph from the Midianites, who had bought him from his brothers, went to Egypt with Joseph. They came on the borders of Egypt and when they came near to Egypt, they met four men of the sons of Medan the son of Abraham, who had gone forth from the land of Egypt on their journey.

2 The Ishmaelites said to them, Do you desire to purchase this slave from us? And they said, Deliver him over to us, and they delivered Joseph over to them; they observed him that he was a very good-looking youth and they purchased him for twenty shekels.

3 The Ishmaelites continued their journey to Egypt and the Medanim also returned that day to Egypt. The Medanim said to each other, Look, we

have heard that Potiphar, an officer of Pharaoh, captain of the guard, seeks a good servant who willl stand before him to attend him, and to make him overseer over his house and all belonging to him.

4 So let us sell him for what we may desire, if he is able to give us that which we shall require for him.

5 And these Medanim came to the house of Potiphar, and said to him, We have heard that you seek a good servant to attend you; here we have a servant that will please you, if you can give to us that which we may desire and we will sell him to you.

6 And Potiphar said, Bring him before me, and I will see him; if he please me I will give to you that which you may require for him.

7 And the Medanim went and brought Joseph and placed him before Potiphar, and he observed him, and he pleased him greatly and Potiphar said to them, Tell me what you require for this youth.

8 And they said, Four hundred pieces of silver we desire for him. Potiphar said, I will give it if you bring me the record of his sale to you and will tell me his history for perhaps he may be stolen, for this youth is neither a slave nor the son of a slave, but I observe in him the appearance of a goodly and handsome person.

9 And the Medanim went and brought to him the Ishmaelites who had sold him to them, and they told him, saying, He is a slave and we sold him to them.

10 And Potiphar heard the words of the Ishmaelites in his giving the silver to the Medanim, and the Medanim took the silver and went on their journey; the Ishmaelites also returned home.

11 Potiphar took Joseph and brought him to his house that he might serve him, and Joseph found favor in the sight of Potiphar; he placed confidence in him and made him overseer over his house, and all that belonged to him he delivered over into his hand.

12 And the Lord was with Joseph and he became a prosperous man; the Lord blessed the house of Potiphar for the sake of Joseph.

13 And Potiphar left all that he had in the hands of Joseph; Joseph was one that caused things to come in and go out, and everything was regulated by his wish in the house of Potiphar.

14 And Joseph was eighteen years old, a youth with beautiful eyes and of very good appearance, and no one was like him in all the land of Egypt.

15 At that time while he was in his master's house, going in and out of the

house and attending his master, Zelicah, his master's wife lifted up her eyes toward Joseph and she looked at him, and behold he was a youth handsome and well-favored.

16 And she coveted his beauty in her heart, and her soul was fixed on Joseph, and she enticed him day after day, and Zelicah persuaded Joseph daily, but Joseph did not lift up his eyes to give attention to his master's wife.

17 And Zelicah said to him, How goodly are your appearance and form, truly I have looked at all the slaves and have not seen so beautiful a slave as you are. Joseph said to her, Certainly he who created me in my mother's womb created all mankind.

18 She said to him, How beautiful are your eyes, with which you have dazzled all the inhabitants of Egypt, men and women. He said to her, How beautiful they are while we are alive, but should you behold them in the grave, certainly you would move away from them.

19 And she said to him, How beautiful and pleasing are all your words; take now, I pray you, the harp which is in the house, and play with your hands and let us hear your words.

20 And he said to her, How beautiful and pleasing are my words when I speak the praise of my God and his glory. She said to him, How very beautiful is the hair of your head, find the golden comb which is in the house, take it I pray you, and curl the hair of your head.

21 And he said to her, How long will you speak these words? Stop uttering these words to me, and rise and attend to your domestic affairs.

22 And she said to him, There is no one in my house, and there is nothing to attend to but to your words and to your wish. Yet in spite of all this, she could not bring Joseph to her, neither did he place his eyes on her, but directed his eyes below to the ground.

23 Zelicah desired Joseph in her heart that he should lie with her; at the time that Joseph was sitting in the house doing his work, Zelicah came and sat before him, and she enticed him daily with her discourse to lie with her, or even to look at her, but Joseph would not listen to her.

24 And she said to him, If you will not do according to my words, I will treat you with the punishment of death, and put an iron yoke on you.

25 And Joseph said to her, Certainly God who created man loosens the fetters of prisoners, and it is he who will deliver me from your prison and from your judgment.

26 When she could not persuade him and her soul being still fixed on

him, her desire threw her into a grave sickness.

27 All the women of Egypt came to visit her and said to her, Why are you in this declining state? You lack nothing; certainly your husband is a great and esteemed prince in the sight of the king, should you lack anything of what your heart desires?

28 Zelicah answered them, saying, This day it shall be made known to you from where this disorder comes which you see in me, and she commanded her maid servants to prepare food for all the women; she made a banquet for them, and all the women ate in the house of Zelicah.

29 And she gave them knives to peel the citrons to eat them, and she commanded that they should dress Joseph in costly garments, that he should appear before them, and Joseph came before their eyes and all the women looked on Joseph and could not take their eyes from off him; they all cut their hands with the knives that they had in their hands, and all the citrons that were in their hands were filled with blood.

30 And they knew not what they had done but they continued to look at the beauty of Joseph, and did not turn their eyelids from him.

31 Zelicah saw what they had done, and she said to them, What is this work that you have done? Look, I gave you citrons to eat and you have all cut your hands.

32 And all the women saw their hands, and truly they were full of blood, and their blood flowed down on their garments. They said to her, This slave in your house has overcome us, and we could not turn our eyelids from him on account of his beauty.

33 She said to them, Certainly this happened to you in the moment that you looked at him, and you could not contain yourselves from him; how then can I refrain when he is constantly in my house, and I see him day after day going in and out of my house? How then can I keep from declining or even from perishing on account of this?

34 And they said to her, The words are true, for who can see this beautiful form in the house and refrain from him, and is he not your slave and attendant in your house, and why do you not tell him that which is in your heart, but allow your soul to perish through this matter?

35 And she said to them, I am daily endeavoring to persuade him, and he will not consent to my wishes; I promised him everything that is good, and yet I could meet with no return from him; I am therefore in a declining state as you see.

36 Zelicah became very ill on account of her desire toward Joseph, and

she was desperately lovesick on account of him; but all the people of the house of Zelicah and her husband knew nothing of this matter, that Zelicah was ill on account of her love to Joseph.

37 All the people of her house asked her, saying, Why are you ill and declining, and lack nothing? And she said to them, I know not this thing which daily is increasing on me.

38 All the women and her friends came daily to see her, and they spoke with her, and she said to them, This can only be through the love of Joseph. They said to her, Entice him and seize him secretly; perhaps he may listen to you and put off this death from you.

39 And Zelicah became worse from her love to Joseph, and she continued to decline, till she scarcely had strength to stand.

40 On a certain day Joseph was doing his master's work in the house, and Zelicah came secretly and fell suddenly on him; Joseph rose up against her, he was more powerful than she, and he brought her down to the ground.

41 And Zelicah wept on account of the desire of her heart toward him, and she begged him with weeping, and her tears flowed down her cheeks; she spoke to him in a voice of pleading and in bitterness of soul, saying,

42 Have you ever heard, seen or known of so beautiful a woman as I am, or better than myself, who speaks daily to you, falls into a decline through love for you, confers all this honor on you, and still you will not listen to my voice?

43 If it be through fear of your master that he punish you, as the king lives no harm shall come to you from your master through this thing; now, therefore do listen to me, and consent for the sake of the honor which I have conferred on you, and put off this death from me, for why should I die for your sake? And she ceased to speak.

44 And Joseph answered her, saying, Keep away from me, and leave this matter to my master; behold my master knows not what there is with me in the house, for all that belongs to him he has delivered into my hands, and how shall I do these things in my master's house?

45 For he has also greatly honored me in his house, and he has also made me overseer over his house, and he has exalted me, and there is no one greater in this house than I am, and my master has refrained nothing from me, excepting you who are his wife. How then can you speak these words to me, and how can I do this great evil and sin to God and to your husband?

46 Now therefore keep away from me, and speak no more such words as

these, for I will not listen to your words. But Zelicah would not listen to Joseph when he spoke these words to her; she daily enticed him to listen to her.

47 It was after this that the brook of Egypt was filled above all its sides, and all the inhabitants of Egypt went forth, and also the king and princes went forth with timbrels and dances, for it was a great rejoicing in Egypt and a holiday at the time of the overflow of the sea Sihor, and they went there to rejoice all the day.

48 And when the Egyptians went out to the river to rejoice, as was their custom, all the people of the house of Potiphar went with them. But Zelicah would not go with them for she said, I am unable to. She remained alone in the house, and no other person was with her in the house.

49 And she rose up and ascended to her temple in the house, and dressed herself in princely garments, and she placed on her head precious stones of onyx stones, inlaid with silver and gold, and she beautified her face and skin with all sorts of women's purifying liquids, and she perfumed the temple and the house with cassia and frankincense, and she spread myrrh and aloes. Afterward she sat in the entrance of the temple, in the passage of the house, through which Joseph passed to do his work, and then Joseph came from the field and entered the house to do his master's work.

50 He came to the place through which he had to pass and saw all the work of Zelicah, and he turned back.

51 Zelicah saw Joseph turning back from her; she called out to him, saying What ails you Joseph? Come to your work, and look, I will make room for you until you will have passed to your seat.

52 And Joseph returned and came to the house, and passed from there to the place of his seat, and he sat down to do his master's work as usual and behold Zelicah came to him and stood before him in princely garments, and the scent from her clothes was spread some distance.

53 She hurried and caught hold of Joseph and his garments, and said to him, As the king lives if you will not perform my request you shall die this day. And she hurried and stretched forth her other hand and drew a sword from beneath her garments, and she placed it on Joseph's neck; she said, Rise and perform my request, and if not you will die this day.

54 Joseph was afraid of her doing this thing, and he rose up to flee from her; she seized the front of his garments, and in the terror of his flight the garment which Zelicah seized was torn; Joseph left the garment in the hand of Zelicah and he fled and got out, for he was afraid.

55 When Zelicah saw that Joseph's garment was torn and that he had left it in her hand, and had fled, she was afraid for her life, that the report should spread concerning her. She rose up and acted with cunning and put off the garments in which she was dressed, and she put on her other garments.

56 She took Joseph's garment and laid it beside her, and she went and seated herself in the place where she had sat in her illness, before the people of her house had gone out to the river. She called a young lad who was then in the house, and she ordered him to call the people of the house to her.

57 And when she saw them she said to them with a loud voice and lamentation, See what a Hebrew your master has brought to me in the house, for he came this day to lie with me.

58 For when you had gone out he came to the house, and seeing that there was no person in the house, he came to me and caught hold of me with intent to lie with me.

59 And I seized his garments and tore them and called out against him with a loud voice, and when I had lifted up my voice he was afraid for his life and left his garment before me, and fled.

60 The people of her house spoke nothing, but their wrath was very much set ablaze against Joseph, and they went to his master and told him the words of his wife.

61 Potiphar came home enraged, and his wife cried out to him, saying, What is this thing that you have done to me in bringing a Hebrew servant into my house, for he came to me this day to sport with me; thus did he do to me this day.

62 Potiphar heard the words of his wife and ordered Joseph to be punished with severe stripes, and they did so to him.

63 While they were smiting him, Joseph called out with a loud voice, and he lifted up his eyes to heaven, and he said, O Lord God, you know that I am innocent of all these things, and why shall I die this day through falsehood, by the hand of these uncircumcised wicked men whom you know?

64 And while Potiphar's men were beating Joseph, he continued to cry out and weep, and there was a child there eleven months old, and the Lord opened the mouth of the child, and he spake these words before Potiphar's men, who were smiting Joseph, saying,

65 What do you want of this man, and why do you do this evil to him? My mother speaks falsely and utters lies; thus was the transaction.

66 And the child told them accurately all that happened, and all the words of Zelicah to Joseph day after day did he relate to them.

67 And all the men heard the words of the child and they wondered greatly at the child's words, and the child ceased to speak and became still.

68 Potiphar was very much ashamed at the words of his son, and he commanded his men not to beat Joseph anymore, and the men ceased beating Joseph.

69 Potiphar took Joseph and ordered him to be brought to justice before the priests, who were judges belonging to the king, in order to judge him concerning this affair.

70 Potiphar and Joseph came before the priests who were the king's judges, and he said to them, Decide I beg you, what judgment is due to a servant, for thus has he done.

71 And the priests said to Joseph, Why did you do this thing to your master? and Joseph answered them, saying, Not so my lords, thus was the matter; and Potiphar said to Joseph, Certainly I entrusted in your hands all that belonged to me, and I withheld nothing from you but my wife, and how could you do this evil?

72 And Joseph answered saying, Not so my lord, as the Lord lives, and as your soul lives, my lord, the word which you did hear from your wife is untrue, for thus was the affair this day.

73 A year has elapsed to me since I have come to your house; have you seen any iniquity in me, or any thing which might cause you to demand my life?

74 The priests said to Potiphar, Send, we pray you, and let them bring before us Joseph's torn garment, and let us see the tear in it, and if it shall be that the tear is in front of the garment, then his face must have been opposite to her and she must have caught hold of him to come to her, and with deceit did your wife do all that she has spoken.

75 They brought Joseph's garment before the priests who were judges, and they saw and behold the tear was in front of Joseph, and all the judging priests knew that she had pressed him, and they said, The judgment of death is not due to this slave for he has done nothing, but his judgment is that he be placed in the prison house on account of the report, which through him has gone forth against your wife.

76 Potiphar heard their words and he placed him in the prison house, the place where the king's prisoners are confined, and Joseph was in the house of confinement twelve years.

77 And in spite of this, his master's wife did not turn from him, and she did not cease from speaking to him day after day to listen to her, and at the end of three months Zelicah continued going to Joseph to the house of confinement day by day, and she enticed him to listen to her, and Zelicah said to Joseph, How long will you remain in this house? But listen now to my voice, and I will bring you out of this house.

78 And Joseph answered her, saying, It is better for me to remain in this house than to listen to your words, to sin against God; she said to him, If you will not perform my wish, I will pluck out your eyes, add fetters to your feet, and will deliver you into the hands of them whom you did not know before.

79 Joseph answered her and said, Behold the God of the whole earth is able to deliver me from all that you can do to me, for he opens the eyes of the blind, and loosens those that are bound, and preserves all strangers who are unacquainted with the land.

80 And when Zelicah was unable to persuade Joseph to listen to her, she ceased going to entice him; Joseph was still confined in the house of confinement. And Jacob the father of Joseph, and all his brothers who were in the land of Canaan still mourned and wept in those days on account of Joseph, for Jacob refused to be comforted for his son Joseph, and Jacob cried aloud and wept and mourned all those days.

CHAPTER 45

1 It was in that year, which is the year of Joseph's going down to Egypt after his brothers had sold him, that Reuben the son of Jacob went to Timnah and took a wife Eliuram, the daughter of Avi the Canaanite, and he came to her.

2 And Eliuram the wife of Reuben conceived and gave birth, to him: Hanoch, Palu, Chetzron and Carmi, four sons; and Simeon his brother took his sister Dinah for a wife, and she gave birth to, to him: Memuel, Yamin, Ohad, Jachin and Zochar, five sons.

3 Afterward he came to Bunah the Canaanitish woman, the same is Bunah whom Simeon took captive from the city of Shechem, and Bunah was before Dinah and attended to her; Simeon came to her, and she gave birth to him, Saul.

4 And Judah went at that time to Adulam, and he came to a man of Adulam, and his name was Hirah; Judah saw there the daughter of a man from Canaan, and her name was Aliyath, the daughter of Shua. He took her and came to her, and Aliyath gave birth to, to Judah: Er, Onan and Shiloh, three sons.

5 Levi and Issachar went to the land of the east, and they took to themselves for wives the daughters of Jobab the son of Yoktan, the son of Eber; Jobab the son of Yoktan had two daughters; the name of the elder was Adinah, and the name of the younger was Aridah.

6 And Levi took Adinah, and Issachar took Aridah, and they came to the land of Canaan, to their father's house; Adinah gave birth to, to Levi: Gershon, Kehath and Merari, three sons.

7 And Aridah gave birth to, to Issachar: Tola, Puvah, Job and Shomron, four sons; Dan went to the land of Moab and took for a wife Aphlaleth, the daughter of Chamudan the Moabite, and he brought her to the land of Canaan.

8 Aphlaleth was unable to conceive, she had no children, and God afterward remembered Aphlaleth the wife of Dan, and she conceived and gave birth to a son; she called his name Chushim.

9 And Gad and Naphtali went to Haran and took from there the daughters of Amuram the son of Uz, the son of Nahor, for wives.

10 And these are the names of the daughters of Amuram: the name of the elder was Merimah, and the name of the younger Uzith; Naphtali took Merimah, and Gad took Uzith and brought them to the land of Canaan, to their father's house.

11 And Merimah gave birth to, to Naphtali: Yachzeel, Guni, Jazer and Shalem, four sons; and Uzith gave birth to, to Gad: Zephion, Chagi, Shuni, Ezbon, Eri, Arodi and Arali, seven sons.

12 Asher went forth and took Adon the daughter of Aphlal, the son of Hadad, the son of Ishmael, for a wife and he brought her to the land of Canaan.

13 And Adon the wife of Asher died in those days, she had no children; it was after the death of Adon that Asher went to the other side of the river and took for a wife Hadurah the daughter of Abimael, the son of Eber, the son of Shem.

14 The young woman was of a beautiful appearance and a woman of sense, and she had been the wife of Malkiel the son of Elam, the son of Shem.

15 Hadurah gave birth to a daughter to Malkiel, and he called her name Serach, and Malkiel died after this and Hadurah went and remained in her father's house.

16 After the death of the wife at Asher he went and took Hadurah for a wife, and brought her to the land of Canaan, and Serach her daughter he also brought with them; she was three years old and the child was brought up in Jacob's house.

17 And the girl was of a beautiful appearance and she went in the holy ways of the children of Jacob; she lacked nothing, and the Lord gave her wisdom and understanding.

18 Hadurah the wife of Asher conceived and gave birth to, to him: Yimnah, Yishvah, Yishvi and Beriah, four sons.

19 Zebulun went to Midian and took for a wife Merishah the daughter of Molad, the son of Abida, the son of Midian, and brought her to the land of Canaan.

20 And Merushah gave birth to, to Zebulun: Sered, Elon and Yachleel, three sons.

21 Jacob sent to Aram, the son of Zoba, the son of Terah, and he took for his son Benjamin Mechalia the daughter of Aram, and she came to the land of Canaan to the house of Jacob; Benjamin was ten years old when he took Mechalia the daughter of Aram for a wife.

22 And Mechalia conceived and gave birth to, to Benjamin: Bela, Becher, Ashbel, Gera and Naaman, five sons; Benjamin afterward went and took for a wife Aribath, the daughter of Shomron, the son of Abraham, in addition to his first wife, and he was eighteen years old; Aribath gave birth to, to Benjamin: Achi, Vosh, Mupim, Chupim, and Ord, five sons.

23 In those days Judah went to the house of Shem and took Tamar the daughter of Elam, the son of Shem, for a wife for his first born Er.

24 And Er came to his wife Tamar, and she became his wife; when he came to her he outwardly destroyed his offspring, and his work was evil in the sight of the Lord, and the Lord killed him.

25 It was after the death of Er, Judah's first born, that Judah said to Onan, Go to your brother's wife and marry her as the next of kin and raise up children to your brother.

26 And Onan took Tamar for a wife and he came to her; Onan also did like the work of his brother, and his work was evil in the sight of the Lord, and he killed him also.

27 When Onan died, Judah said to Tamar, Remain in your father's house

until my son Shiloh will have grown up; Judah had no more delight in Tamar, to give her to Shiloh, for he said, Perhaps he will also die like his brothers.

28 And Tamar rose up and went and remained in her father's house, and Tamar was in her father's house for some time.

29 At the revolution of the year, Aliyath the wife of Judah died; Judah was comforted for his wife, and after the death of Aliyath, Judah went up with his friend Hirah to Timnah to shear their sheep.

30 Tamar heard that Judah had gone up to Timnah to shear the sheep, and that Shiloh was grown up, and Judah did not delight in her.

31 And Tamar rose up and put off the garments of her widowhood; she put on a veil and entirely covered herself; she went and sat in the public thoroughfare which is on the road to Timnah.

32 Judah passed and saw her and took her and he came to her, and she conceived by him; at the time of being delivered there were twins in her womb, and he called the name of the first Perez and the name of the second Zarah.

CHAPTER 46

1 In those days Joseph was still confined in the prison house in the land of Egypt.

2 At that time the attendants of Pharaoh were standing before him, the chief of the butlers and the chief of the bakers which belonged to the king of Egypt.

3 And the butler took wine and placed it before the king to drink, and the baker placed bread before the king to eat, and the king drank of the wine and ate of the bread; he and his servants and ministers that ate at the king's table.

4 And while they were eating and drinking, the butler and the baker remained there, and Pharaoh's ministers found many flies in the wine which the butler had brought, and stones of nitre were found in the baker's bread.

5 And the captain of the guard placed Joseph as an attendant on Pharaoh's officers, and Pharaoh's officers were in confinement one year.

6 At the end of the year, they both dreamed dreams in one night, in the place of confinement where they were, and in the morning Joseph came to them to attend on them as usual. He saw them and their countenances were dejected and sad.

7 And Joseph asked them, Why are your countenances sad? They said, we dreamed a dream and there was no one here to interpret it. Joseph said to them, Relate, I pray you, your dream to me, and God shall give you an answer of peace as you desire.

8 The butler related his dream to Joseph and said, I saw in my dream there was a large vine before me and on that vine I saw three branches; the vine speedily blossomed and reached a great height, and its clusters were ripened and became grapes.

9 And I took the grapes and pressed them in a cup, and placed it in Pharaoh's hand and he drank; and Joseph said to him, The three branches that were on the vine are three days.

10 Yet within three days, the king will order you to be brought out and he will restore you to your office; you shall give the king his wine to drink as at first when you were his butler; but let me find favor in your sight, so that you shall remember me to Pharaoh when it will be well with you; do this kindness to me and get me brought forth from this prison, for I was stolen away from the land of Canaan and was sold for a slave in this place.

11 Also that which was told you concerning my master's wife is false, for they placed me in this dungeon for nothing. The butler answered Joseph, saying, If the king deals well with me as at first, as you last interpreted to me, I will do all that you desire and get you brought out of this dungeon.

12 And the baker, seeing that Joseph had accurately interpreted the butler's dream, also approached and related the whole of his dream to Joseph.

13 He said to him, In my dream I looked and there were three white baskets on my head; I looked again and then there were in the upper-most basket all manner of baked meats for Pharaoh; there the birds were eating them from off my head.

14 And Joseph said to him, The three baskets which you saw are three days, yet within three days Pharaoh will take off your head and hang you on a tree, and the birds will eat your flesh from off you, as you saw in your dream.

15 In those days the queen was about to be delivered, and on that day she gave birth to a son to the king of Egypt; they announced that the king had gotten his firstborn son and all the people of Egypt together with the

officers and servants of Pharaoh rejoiced greatly.

16 On the third day of his birth Pharaoh made a feast for his officers and servants, for the hosts of the land of Zoar and of the land of Egypt.

17 And all the people of Egypt and the servants of Pharaoh came to eat and drink with the king at the feast of his son, and to rejoice at the king's rejoicing.

18 All the officers of the king and his servants were rejoicing at that time for eight days at the feast, and they made merry with all sorts of musical instruments, with timbrels and with dances in the king's house for eight days.

19 And the butler, to whom Joseph had interpreted his dream, forgot Joseph and did not mention him to the king as he had promised, for this thing was from the Lord in order to punish Joseph because he had trusted in man.

20 And Joseph remained after this in the prison house two years, until he had completed twelve years.

CHAPTER 47

1 Isaac the son of Abraham was still living in those days in the land of Canaan; he was very aged, one hundred and eighty years old, and Esau his son, the brother of Jacob, was in the land of Edom; he and his sons had possessions in it among the children of Seir.

2 And Esau heard that his father's time was drawing near to die, and he and his sons and household came to the land of Canaan to his father's house. Jacob and his sons went forth from the place where they lived in Hebron and they all came to their father Isaac, and they found Esau and his sons in the tent.

3 And Jacob and his sons sat before his father Isaac, and Jacob was still mourning for his son Joseph.

4 And Isaac said to Jacob, Bring your sons here to me and I will bless them; and Jacob brought his eleven children before his father Isaac.

5 And Isaac placed his hands on all the sons of Jacob, and he took hold of them and embraced them, and kissed them one by one. Isaac blessed them on that day and he said to them, May the God of your fathers bless you

and increase your offspring like the stars of heaven for number.

6 Isaac also blessed the sons of Esau, saying, May God cause you to be a dread and a terror to all that will behold you, and to all your enemies.

7 Isaac called Jacob and his sons and they all came and sat before Isaac, and Isaac said to Jacob, The Lord God of the whole earth said to me, Unto your offspring I will give this land for an inheritance if your children keep my statutes and my ways, and I will perform to them the oath which I swore to your father Abraham.

8 Now therefore my son, teach your children and your children's children to fear the Lord, and to go in the good way which will please the Lord your God, for if you keep the ways of the Lord and his statutes the Lord will also keep to you his covenant with Abraham, and will do well with you and your descendants always.

9 When Isaac had finished commanding Jacob and his children, he gave up the ghost and died, and was gathered to his people.

10 And Jacob and Esau fell on the face of their father Isaac, and they wept, and Isaac was one hundred and eighty years old when he died in the land of Canaan, in Hebron. His sons carried him to the cave of Machpelah, which Abraham had bought from the children of Heth for a possession of a burial place.

11 And all the kings of the land of Canaan went with Jacob and Esau to bury Isaac, and all the kings of Canaan showed Isaac great honor at his death.

12 The sons of Jacob and the sons of Esau went barefooted round about, walking and lamenting until they reached Kireath-arba.

13 And Jacob and Esau buried their father Isaac in the cave of Machpelah, which is in Kireath-arba in Hebron; they buried him with very great honor, as at the funeral of kings.

14 Jacob and his sons, and Esau and his sons, and all the kings of Canaan made a great and heavy mourning, and they buried him and mourned for him many days.

15 At the death of Isaac, he left his cattle and his possessions and all belonging to him to his sons; and Esau said to Jacob, Behold I pray you, all that our father has left we will divide into two parts, and I will have the choice; Jacob said, We will do so.

16 Jacob took all that Isaac had left in the land of Canaan, the cattle and the property, and he placed them in two parts before Esau and his sons, and he said to Esau, Behold all this is before you, choose to yourself the

half which you will take.

17 And Jacob said to Esau, Hear I pray you what I will speak to you, saying, The Lord God of heaven and earth spoke to our fathers Abraham and Isaac, saying, Unto your descendants will I give this land for an inheritance forever.

18 Now therefore all that our father has left is before you, and behold all the land is before you; choose from them what you desire.

19 If you desire the whole land take it for you and your children forever, and I will take these riches, and if you desire the riches take them with you, and I will take this land for me and for my children to inherit forever.

20 Nebayoth, the son of Ishmael, was then in the land with his children, and Esau went on that day and consulted with him, saying,

21 Thus has Jacob spoken to me; thus has he answered me, now give your advice and we will listen.

22 And Nebayoth said, What is this that Jacob hath spoken to you? Behold all the children of Canaan are dwelling securely in their land, and Jacob says he will inherit it with his descendants all the days.

23 Go now therefore and take all your father's riches and leave Jacob your brother in the land, as he has spoken.

24 And Esau rose up and returned to Jacob, and did all that Nebayoth the son of Ishmael had advised; and Esau took all the riches that Isaac had left, the souls, the beasts, the cattle and the property, and all the riches; he gave nothing to his brother Jacob, and Jacob took all the land of Canaan, from the brook of Egypt to the river Euphrates, and he took it for an everlasting possession, and for his children and for his descendants after him forever.

25 Jacob also took from his brother Esau the cave of Machpelah, which is in Hebron, which Abraham had bought from Ephron for a possession of a burial place for him and his descendants forever.

26 And Jacob wrote all these things in the book of purchase, and he signed it, and testified all this with four faithful witnesses.

27 These are the words which Jacob wrote in the book, saying: The land of Canaan and all the cities of the Hittites, the Hivites, the Jebusites, the Amorites, the Perizzites, and the Gergashites, all the seven nations from the river of Egypt to the river Euphrates.

28 And the city of Hebron Kireath-arba, and the cave which is in it, the whole did Jacob buy from his brother Esau for value, for a possession and

for an inheritance for his descendants after him forever.

29 And Jacob took the book of purchase and the signature, the command and the statutes and the revealed book, and he placed them in an earthen vessel in order that they should remain for a long time, and he delivered them into the hands of his children.

30 Esau took all that his father had left him after his death from his brother Jacob, and he took all the property, from man and beast, camel and ass, ox and lamb, silver and gold, stones and bdellium, and all the riches which had belonged to Isaac the son of Abraham; there was nothing left which Esau did not take to himself from all that Isaac had left after his death.

31 Esau took all this and he and his children went home to the land of Seir the Horite, away from his brother Jacob and his children.

32 And Esau had possessions among the children of Seir, and Esau returned not to the land of Canaan from that day forward.

33 The whole land of Canaan became an inheritance to the children of Israel for an everlasting inheritance, and Esau with all his children inherited the mountain of Seir.

CHAPTER 48

1 In those days, after the death of Isaac, the Lord commanded and caused a famine on the whole earth.

2 At that time Pharaoh, king of Egypt, was sitting on his throne in the land of Egypt; he lay in his bed and dreamed dreams and Pharaoh saw in his dream that he was standing by the side of the river of Egypt.

3 While he was standing he saw seven fat fleshed and well favored cattle come up out of the river.

4 And seven other cattle, lean fleshed and ill favored, came up after them, and the seven ill favored ones swallowed up the well favored ones, and still their appearance was ill as at first.

5 And he awoke; he slept again and he dreamed a second time, and he saw seven ears of corn come up on one stalk, full and good, and seven thin ears blasted with the east wind sprang up after them, and the thin ears swallowed up the full ones, then Pharaoh awoke out of his dream.

6 In the morning the king remembered his dreams and his spirit was sadly troubled on account of his dreams, and the king hurried, sent and called for all the magicians of Egypt and the wise men, and they came and stood before Pharaoh.

7 And the king said to them, I have dreamed dreams, and there is none to interpret them; they said to the king, relate your dreams to your servants and let us hear them.

8 And the king related his dreams to them, and they all answered and said with one voice to the king, May the king live forever; this is the interpretation of your dreams.

9 The seven good cattle which you saw denotes seven daughters that will be born to you in the latter days, and the seven cattle which you saw come up after them and swallowed them up, are for a sign that the daughters which will be born to you will all die in the lifetime of the king.

10 And that which you saw in the second dream of seven full good ears of corn coming up on one stalk, this is their interpretation: that you will build to yourself in the latter days seven cities throughout the land of Egypt; that which you saw of the seven poor ears of corn springing up after them and swallowing them up while you saw them with your eyes, is for a sign that the cities which you will build will all be destroyed in the latter days, in the lifetime of the king.

11 And when they spoken these words the king did not incline his ear to their words, neither did he fix his heart on them, for the king knew in his wisdom that they did not give a proper interpretation of the dreams; when they had finished speaking before the king, he answered them, saying, What is this thing that you have spoken to me? Certainly you have uttered falsely and spoken lies; therefore now give the proper interpretation of my dreams, that you may not die.

12 The king commanded after this, and he sent and called again for other wise men, and they came and stood before the king. The king related his dreams to them, and they all answered him according to the first interpretation; the king's anger was set ablaze and he was very upset. A nd the king said to them, Certainly you speak lies and utter falsehood in what you have said.

13 The king commanded that a proclamation should be issued throughout the land of Egypt, saying, It is determined by the king and his great men, that any wise man who knows and understands the interpretation of dreams, and will not come this day before the king, shall die.

14 The man that will declare to the king the proper interpretation of his dreams, there shall be given to him all that he will require from the king. And all the wise men of the land of Egypt came before the king, together with all the magicians and sorcerers that were in Egypt and in Goshen, in Rameses, in Tachpanches, in Zoar, and in all the places on the borders of Egypt; they all stood before the king.

15 And all the nobles and the princes, and the attendants belonging to the king, came together from all the cities of Egypt and they all sat before the king, and the king related his dreams before the wise men and the princes; all that sat before the king were astonished at the vision.

16 And all the wise men who were before the king were greatly divided in their interpretation of his dreams; some of them interpreted them to the king, saying, The seven good cattle are seven kings, who from the king's lineage will be raised over Egypt.

17 And the seven bad cattle are seven princes who will stand up against them in the latter days and destroy them; the seven ears of corn are the seven great princes belonging to Egypt, who will fall in the hands of the seven less powerful princes of their enemies, in the wars of our lord the king.

18 And some of them interpreted to the king in this manner, saying, The seven good cattle are the strong cities of Egypt, and the seven bad cattle are the seven nations of the land of Canaan, who will come against the seven cities of Egypt in the latter days and destroy them.

19 And that which you saw in the second dream, of seven good and bad ears of corn, is a sign that the government of Egypt will again return to your descendants as at first.

20 And in this reign the people of the cities of Egypt will turn against the seven cities of Canaan who are stronger than they are and will destroy them, and the government of Egypt will return to your descendants.

21 Some of them said to the king, This is the interpretation of your dreams; the seven good cattle are seven queens, whom you will take for wives in the latter days, and the seven bad cattle denote that those women will all die in the lifetime of the king.

22 And the seven good and bad ears of corn which you did see in the second dream are fourteen children, and it will be in the latter days that they will stand up and fight among themselves, and seven of them will strike the seven that are more powerful.

23 Some of them said these words to the king, The seven good cattle denote that seven children will be born to you, and they will kill seven of

your children's children in the latter days; and the seven good ears of corn which you saw in the second dream are those princes against whom seven other less powerful princes will fight and destroy them in the latter days, and avenge your children's cause, and the government will again return to your offspring.

24 The king heard all the words of the wise men of Egypt and their interpretation of his dreams, and none of them pleased the king.

25 And the king knew in his wisdom that they did not altogether speak correctly in all these words, for this was from the Lord to frustrate the words of the wise men of Egypt in order that Joseph might go forth from the house of confinement, and in order that he should become great in Egypt.

26 The king saw that none among all the wise men and magicians of Egypt spoke correctly to him, and the king's wrath was set ablaze, and his anger burned within him.

27 And the king commanded that all the wise men and magicians should go out from before him, and they all went out from before the king with shame and disgrace.

28 Then the king commanded that a proclamation be sent throughout Egypt to kill all the magicians that were in Egypt, and not one of them should be allowed to live.

29 And the captains of the guards belonging to the king rose up, and each man drew his sword; they began to strike the magicians of Egypt and the wise men.

30 After this Merod, chief butler to the king, came and bowed down before the king and sat before him.

31 The butler said to the king, May the king live forever, and his government be honored in the land.

32 You were angry with your servant in those days now two years past and did place me in the ward, and I was for some time in the ward, I and the chief of the bakers.

33 And there was with us a Hebrew servant belonging to the captain of the guard, his name was Joseph, for his master had been angry with him and placed him in the house of confinement, and he attended us there.

34 Some time after when we were in the ward, we dreamed dreams in one night, I and the chief of the bakers; we dreamed, each man according to the interpretation of his dream.

35 And we came in the morning and told them to that servant, and he interpreted to us our dreams, to each man according to his dream he correctly interpreted.

36 And it came to pass as he interpreted to us, so was the event; there fell not to the ground any of his words.

37 Now therefore my lord and king do not kill the people of Egypt for nothing; consider that the slave is still confined in the house by the captain of the guard his master, in the house of confinement.

38 If it pleases the king let him send for him that he may come before you and he will make known to you the correct interpretation of the dream which you did dream.

39 The king heard the words of the chief butler, and the king ordered that the wise men of Egypt should not be slain.

40 And the king ordered his servants to bring Joseph before him, and the king said to them, Go to him and do not terrify him that he be confused and will not know to speak properly.

41 The servants of the king went to Joseph, and they brought him hastily out of the dungeon; the king's servants shaved him, and he changed his prison garment and came before the king.

42 The king was sitting on his royal throne in a princely dress surrounded with a golden ephod, and the fine gold which was on it sparkled, and the gem and the ruby and the emerald, together with all the precious stones that were on the king's head dazzled the eye, and Joseph wondered greatly at the king.

43 And the throne on which the king sat was covered with gold and silver and with onyx stones, and it had seventy steps.

44 It was their custom throughout the land of Egypt that every man who came to speak to the king, if he was a prince or one that was respected in the sight of the king, he ascended to the king's throne as far as the thirty-first step, and the king would descend to the thirty-sixth step and speak with him.

45 If he was one of the common people, he ascended to the third step, and the king would descend to the fourth and speak to him, as their custom was. Also any man who understood to speak in all the seventy languages, he ascended the seventy steps, and went up and spoke till he reached the king.

46 And any man who could not complete the seventy, he ascended as many steps as the languages which he knew to speak in.

47 It was customary in those days in Egypt that no one should reign over them, but one who understood to speak in the seventy languages.

48 When Joseph came before the king he bowed down to the ground before the king, and he ascended to the third step, and the king sat on the fourth step and spoke with Joseph.

49 The king said to Joseph, I dreamed a dream, and there is no interpreter to interpret it properly, and I commanded that all the magicians of Egypt and the wise men thereof should come before me; I related my dreams to them, and no one has properly interpreted them to me.

50 After this I heard about you, that you are a wise man, and can correctly interpret every dream that you hear.

51 And Joseph answered Pharaoh, saying, Let Pharaoh relate his dreams that he dreamed; certainly the interpretations belong to God. And Pharaoh related his dreams to Joseph, the dream of the cattle, and the dream of the ears of corn, and the king ceased speaking.

52 Joseph was then clothed with the spirit of God before the king, and he knew all the things that would befall the king from that day forward; he knew the proper interpretation of the king's dream, and he spoke before the king.

53 Joseph found favor in the sight of the king, and the king listened carefully and with his heart, and he heard all the words of Joseph. And Joseph said to the king, Do not imagine that they are two dreams, for it is only one dream, for that which God has chosen to do throughout the land he has shown to the king in his dream, and this is the proper interpretation of your dream:

54 The seven good cattle and ears of corn are seven years, and the seven bad cattle and ears of corn are also seven years; it is one dream.

55 Know this, the seven years that are coming there will be a great plenty throughout the land, and after that the seven years of famine will follow them, a very severe famine; all the plenty will be forgotten from the land, and the famine will consume the inhabitants of the land.

56 The king dreamed one dream, and the dream was therefore repeated to Pharaoh because the thing is established by God, and God will shortly bring it to pass.

57 Now therefore I will give you counsel and deliver your soul and the souls of the inhabitants of the land from the evil of the famine, that you search throughout your kingdom for a man very discreet and wise, who knows all the affairs of government, and appoint him to superintend over

the land of Egypt.

58 And let the man whom you place over Egypt appoint officers under him, that they gather in all the food of the good years that are coming, and let them lay up corn and deposit it in your appointed stores.

59 And let them keep that food for the seven years of famine, that it may be available for you and your people and your whole land, and that you and your land be not cut off by the famine.

60 Let all the inhabitants of the land also be ordered that they gather in, every man the produce of his field, of all sorts of food, during the seven good years, and that they place it in their stores; that it may be available for them in the days of the famine and that they may live on it.

61 This is the proper interpretation of your dream, and this is the counsel given to save your soul and the souls of all your subjects.

62 The king answered and said to Joseph, Who says and who knows that your words are correct? And he said to the king, This shall be a sign for you respecting all my words, that they are true and that my advice is good for you.

63 Behold your wife sits this day on the stool of delivery, and she will bear you a son and you will rejoice with him; when your child shall have gone forth from his mother's womb, your firstborn son that has been born two years ago shall die, and you will be comforted in the child that will be born to you this day.

64 Joseph finished speaking these words to the king, and he bowed down to the king and he went out, and when Joseph had gone out from the king's presence, those signs which Joseph had spoken to the king came to pass on that day.

65 The queen gave birth to a son on that day and the king heard the glad tidings about his son, and he rejoiced, and when the reporter had gone forth from the king's presence, the king's servants found the firstborn son of the king fallen dead on the ground.

66 There was great lamentation and noise in the king's house, and the king heard it and said, What is the noise and lamentation that I have heard in the house? They told the king that his firstborn son had died, then the king knew that all Joseph's words that he had spoken were correct; the king was consoled for his son by the child that was born to him on that day as Joseph had said.

CHAPTER 49

1 After these things the king sent and assembled all his officers and servants, and all the princes and nobles belonging to the king, and they all came before the king.

2 And the king said to them, Behold you have seen and heard all the words of this Hebrew man, and all the signs which he declared would come to pass, and not any of his words have fallen to the ground.

3 You know that he has given a proper interpretation of the dream, and it will certainly come to pass; now therefore take counsel, and know what you will do and how the land will be delivered from the famine.

4 Search now and see whether the likes of him can be found, in whose heart there is wisdom and knowledge, and I will appoint him over the land.

5 For you have heard what the Hebrew man has advised concerning this to save the land from the famine, and I know that the land will not be delivered from the famine but with the advice of the Hebrew man, him that advised me.

6 And they all answered the king and said, The counsel which the Hebrew has given concerning this is good; now therefore, our lord and king, behold the whole land is in your hand, do that which seems good in your sight.

7 Him whom you choose, and whom you in your wisdom know to be wise and capable of delivering the land with his wisdom, him shall the king appoint to be under him over the land.

8 And the king said to all the officers: I have thought that since God has made known to the Hebrew man all that he has spoken, there is none so discreet and wise in the whole land as he is; if it seems good in your sight I will place him over the land, for he will save the land with his wisdom.

9 All the officers answered the king and said, But certainly it is written in the laws of Egypt, and it should not be violated, that no man shall reign over Egypt, nor be the second to the king, but one who has knowledge in all the languages of the sons of men.

10 Now therefore our lord and king, behold this Hebrew man can only speak the Hebrew language; how then can he be over us as the second under government, a man who not even knows our language?

11 Now we pray you send for him, and let him come before you, and

prove him in all things, and do as you see fit.

12 And the king said, It shall be done tomorrow, and the thing that you have spoken is good. All the officers came on that day before the king.

13 But that night the Lord sent one of his ministering angels and he came into the land of Egypt to Joseph, and the angel of the Lord stood over Joseph; there Joseph was lying in the bed at night in his master's house in the dungeon, for his master had put him back into the dungeon on account of his wife.

14 The angel roused him from his sleep, and Joseph rose up and stood on his legs, and there the angel of the Lord was standing opposite to him; the angel of the Lord spoke with Joseph and he taught him all the languages of man in that night, and he called his name Jehoseph.

15 The angel of the Lord went from him and Joseph returned and lay on his bed, and Joseph was astonished at the vision which he saw.

16 It came to pass in the morning that the king sent for all his officers and servants and they all came and sat before the king, and the king ordered Joseph to be brought; the king's servants went and brought Joseph before Pharaoh.

17 And the king came forth and ascended the steps of the throne and Joseph spoke to the king in all languages; Joseph went up to him and spoke to the king until he arrived before the king in the seventieth step, and he sat before the king.

18 And the king greatly rejoiced on account of Joseph, and all the king's officers rejoiced greatly with the king when they heard all the words of Joseph.

19 That thing seemed good in the sight of the king and the officers, to appoint Joseph to be second to the king over the whole land of Egypt, and the king spoke to Joseph, saying,

20 Now you did give me counsel to appoint a wise man over the land of Egypt, in order with his wisdom to save the land from the famine. Now therefore, since God has made all this known to you, and all the words which you have spoken, there is not throughout the land a discreet and wise man like to you.

21 And your name no more shall be called Joseph, but Zaphnath Paaneah shall be your name; you shall be second to me, and according to your word shall be all the affairs of my government; at your word shall my people go out and come in.

22 Also from under your hand shall my servants and officers receive their

salary which is given to them monthly, and to you shall all the people of the land bow down; only in my throne will I be greater than you.

23 And the king took off his ring from his hand and put it on the hand of Joseph, and the king dressed Joseph in a princely garment; he put a golden crown on his head, and he put a golden chain on his neck.

24 The king commanded his servants and they made him ride in the second chariot belonging to the king, that went opposite to the king's chariot. He caused him to ride on a great and strong horse from the king's horses, and to be conducted through the streets of the land of Egypt.

25 And the king commanded that all those that played on timbrels, harps and other musical instruments should go forth with Joseph; one thousand timbrels, one thousand mecholoth, and one thousand nebalim went after him.

26 And five thousand men, with drawn swords glittering in their hands, went marching and playing before Joseph; twenty thousand of the great men of the king, with girdles of skin covered with gold, marched at the right hand of Joseph, and twenty thousand at his left. All the women and girls went on the roofs or stood in the streets playing and rejoicing at Joseph, and gazed at the appearance of Joseph and at his beauty.

27 And the king's people went before him and behind him, perfuming the road with frankincense and with cassia and with all sorts of fine perfume, and scattered myrrh and aloes along the road. Twenty men proclaimed these words before him throughout the land in a loud voice:

28 Do you see this man whom the king has chosen to be his second? All the affairs of government shall be regulated by him, and he that disobeys his orders, or that does not bow down before him to the ground, shall die, for he would be rebelling against the king and his second person in command.

29 And when the heralds had ceased announcing, all the people of Egypt bowed down to the ground before Joseph and said, May the king live, also may his second one live; all the inhabitants of Egypt bowed down along the road, and when the heralds approached them, they bowed down; they rejoiced with all sorts of timbrels, pipes and harps before Joseph.

30 And Joseph on his horse lifted up his eyes to heaven, and called out and said, He raises the poor man from the dust. He lifts up the needy from the dunghill. O Lord of Hosts, happy is the man who trusts in you.

31 And Joseph passed throughout the land of Egypt with Pharaoh's servants and officers, and they showed him the whole land of Egypt and

all the king's treasures.

32 Joseph returned and came that day before Pharaoh, and the king gave to Joseph a possession in the land of Egypt, a possession of fields and vineyards. And the king gave to Joseph three thousand talents of silver and one thousand talents of gold, and onyx stones and bdellium and many gifts.

33 On the next day the king commanded all the people of Egypt to bring to Joseph offerings and gifts, and said that he that violated the command of the king should die; they made a high place in the street of the city and spread out garments there, and whoever brought anything to Joseph put it into the high place.

34 And all the people of Egypt cast something into the high place, one man a golden earring, and the other rings and earrings, and different vessels of gold and silver work, and onyx stones and bdellium he put on the high place; every one gave something of what he possessed.

35 And Joseph took all these and placed them in his treasuries, and all the officers and nobles belonging to the king exalted Joseph. They gave him many gifts, seeing that the king had chosen him to be his second in leadership.

36 The king sent to Potiphera, the son of Ahiram priest of On, and he took his young daughter Osnath and gave her to Joseph for a wife.

37 And the girl was very beautiful, a virgin, one whom man had not known, and Joseph took her for a wife; the king said to Joseph, I am Pharaoh, and beside you none shall dare to lift up his hand or his foot to regulate my people throughout the land of Egypt.

38 Joseph was thirty years old when he stood before Pharaoh, and Joseph went out from before the king and became the king's second in command in Egypt.

39 The king gave Joseph a hundred servants to attend him in his house, and Joseph also sent and purchased many servants and they remained in the house of Joseph.

40 Joseph then built for himself a very magnificent house like to the houses of kings, before the court of the king's palace, and he made in the house a large temple, very elegant in appearance and convenient for his residence; three years Joseph spent in erecting his house.

41 And Joseph made for himself a very elegant throne of an abundance of gold and silver, and he covered it with onyx stones and bdellium; he made on it the likeness of the whole land of Egypt, and the likeness of the river of Egypt that waters the whole land of Egypt. Joseph sat securely on his

throne in his house and the Lord increased Joseph's wisdom.

42 And all the inhabitants of Egypt and Pharaoh's servants and his princes loved Joseph greatly, for this thing was from the Lord to Joseph.

43 And Joseph had an army that made war, going out in hosts and troops to the number of forty thousand six hundred men, capable of bearing arms to assist the king and Joseph against the enemy, besides the king's officers and his servants and inhabitants of Egypt without number.

44 And Joseph gave to his mighty men, and to all his army, shields and javelins, and caps and coats of mail and stones for slinging.

CHAPTER 50

1 At that time the children of Tarshish came against the sons of Ishmael, and made war with them, and the children of Tarshish fought the Ishmaelites for a long time.

2 The children of Ishmael were small in number in those days, and they could not succeed over the children of Tarshish, and they were extremely oppressed.

3 And the old men of the Ishmaelites sent a record to the king of Egypt, saying, Send I pray you to your servants: officers and army to help us to fight against the children of Tarshish, for we have been diminishing away for a long time.

4 And Pharaoh sent Joseph with the mighty men and army which were with him, and also his mighty men from the king's house.

5 They went to the land of Havilah to the children of Ishmael to assist them against the children of Tarshish, and the children of Ishmael fought with the children of Tarshish. Joseph struck the Tarshishites and he subdued all their land, and the children of Ishmael lived there to this day.

6 And when the land of Tarshish was subdued, all the Tarshishites ran away, and came to the border of their brothers the children of Javan; Joseph with all his mighty men and army returned to Egypt, not one man of them missing.

7 At the revolution of the year, in the second year of Joseph's reigning over Egypt, the Lord gave great plenty throughout the land for seven years as Joseph had spoken, for the Lord blessed all the produce of the

earth in those days for seven years; they ate and were greatly satisfied.

8 And Joseph at that time had officers under him, and they collected all the food of the good years, and heaped corn year by year, and they placed it in the treasuries of Joseph.

9 At any time when they gathered the food, Joseph commanded that they should bring the corn in the ears, and also bring with it some of the soil of the field, so that it would not spoil.

10 And Joseph did according to this year by year, and he heaped up corn like the sand of the sea for abundance, for his stores were immense and could not be numbered for abundance.

11 Also all the inhabitants of Egypt gathered all sorts of food in their stores in great abundance during the seven good years, but they did not do to it as Joseph did.

12 All the food which Joseph and the Egyptians had gathered during the seven years of plenty was secured for the land in stores for the seven years of famine, for the support of the whole land.

13 And the inhabitants of Egypt filled each man his store and his concealed place with corn, to be for support during the famine.

14 And Joseph placed all the food that he had gathered in all the cities of Egypt, and he closed all the stores and placed sentinels over them.

15 Joseph's wife Osnath the daughter of Potiphera gave birth to him two sons, Manasseh and Ephraim, and Joseph was thirty-four years old when he had them.

16 And the lads grew up and they followed in his ways and in his instructions; they did not deviate from the way which their father taught them, either to the right or left.

17 And the Lord was with the lads, and they grew up and had understanding and skill in all wisdom and in all the affairs of government. All the king's officers and his great men of the inhabitants of Egypt honored the lads, and they were brought up among the king's children.

18 The seven years of plenty that were throughout the land were at an end; the seven years of famine came after them as Joseph had spoken, and the famine spread throughout the land.

19 All the people of Egypt saw that the famine had begun in the land of Egypt, and all the people of Egypt opened their stores of corn for the famine hung over them.

20 And they found all the food that was in their stores full of vermin and

not fit to eat, and the famine stayed throughout the land; all the inhabitants of Egypt came and cried before Pharaoh, for the famine was heavy on them.

21 And they said to Pharaoh, Give food to your servants; why shall we die through hunger before your eyes, even we and our little ones?

22 And Pharaoh answered them, saying, And why do you cry to me? Did not Joseph command that the corn should be laid up during the seven years of plenty for the years of famine? Why did you not listen to his voice?

23 And the people of Egypt answered the king, saying, As your soul lives, our lord, your servants have done all that Joseph ordered, for your servants also gathered in all the produce of their fields during the seven years of plenty and laid it in the stores to this day.

24 And when the famine prevailed over your servants we opened our stores, and behold all our produce was filled with vermin and was not fit for food.

25 When the king heard all that had befallen the inhabitants of Egypt, the king was greatly afraid on account of the famine, and he was much terrified; the king answered the people of Egypt, saying, Since all this has happened to you, go to Joseph, do whatever he shall say to you; do not go contrary to his commands.

26 And all the people of Egypt went forth and came to Joseph, and said to him, Give to us food, for why shall we die before you through hunger? We gathered in our produce during the seven years as you did command, and we put it in store, and thus has it happened to us.

27 And when Joseph heard all the words of the people of Egypt and what had happened to them, Joseph opened all his stores of the produce and he sold it to the people of Egypt.

28 And the famine stayed throughout the land, and the famine was in all countries, but in the land of Egypt there was produce for sale.

29 All the inhabitants of Egypt came to Joseph to buy corn, for the famine hung over them, and all their corn was spoiled, and Joseph daily sold it to all the people of Egypt.

30 And all the inhabitants of the land of Canaan and the Philistines, and those beyond the Jordan, and the children of the east and all the cities of the lands far and near heard that there was corn in Egypt, and they all came to Egypt to buy corn, for the famine hung over them.

31 Joseph opened the stores of corn and placed officers over them, and they daily stood and sold to all that came.

32 Joseph knew that his brothers also would come to Egypt to buy corn, for the famine spread throughout the earth. And Joseph commanded all his people that they should cause it to be announced throughout the land of Egypt, saying,

33 It is the pleasure of the king, of his second and of their great men, that any person who wishes to buy corn in Egypt shall not send his servants to Egypt to purchase, but his sons; also any Egyptian or Canaanite who shall come from any of the stores from buying corn in Egypt, if he goes and sells it throughout the land, he shall die, for no one shall buy but for the support of his household.

34 And any man leading two or three beasts shall die, for a man shall only lead his own beast.

35 Joseph placed sentinels at the gates of Egypt, and commanded them, saying, Any person who may come to buy corn, permit him not to enter until his name and the name of his father, and the name of his father's father be written down; whatever is written by day, send their names to me in the evening that I may know their names.

36 And Joseph placed officers throughout the land of Egypt; he commanded them to do all these things.

37 Joseph did all these things, and made these standards in order that he might know when his brothers would come to Egypt to buy corn; Joseph's people caused it daily to be announced in Egypt according to these words and standards which Joseph had commanded.

38 And all the inhabitants of the east and west country, and of all the earth, heard of the rules and regulations which Joseph had enacted in Egypt, and the inhabitants of the extreme parts of the earth came and they bought corn in Egypt day after day, and then went away.

39 All the officers of Egypt did as Joseph had commanded, and all that came to Egypt to buy corn, the gate keepers would write their names, and their fathers' names, and daily bring them in the evening to Joseph.

CHAPTER 51

1 Jacob afterward heard that there was corn in Egypt, and he called to his

sons to go to Egypt to buy corn, for on them also did the famine occur, and he called to his sons, saying,

2 Behold I hear that there is corn in Egypt, and all the people of the earth go there to purchase; now therefore why will you show yourselves (pretend to be) satisfied before the whole earth? You go also down to Egypt and buy us a little corn among those that come there, that we may not die.

3 And the sons of Jacob listened to the voice of their father, and they rose up to go down to Egypt in order to buy corn among the rest that came there.

4 And Jacob their father commanded them, saying, When you come into the city do not enter together in one gate, on account of the inhabitants of the land.

5 And the sons of Jacob went forth and they went to Egypt, and the sons of Jacob did all as their father had commanded them; Jacob did not send Benjamin, for he said, Lest an accident might happen to him on the road like his brother. Ten of Jacob's sons went forth.

6 While the sons of Jacob were going on the road, they repented of what they had done to Joseph, and they spoke to each other, saying, We know that our brother Joseph went down to Egypt, and now we will seek him where we go, and if we find him we will take him from his master for a ransom, and if not, by force, and we will die for him.

7 And the sons of Jacob agreed to this thing and strengthened themselves on account of Joseph, to deliver him from the hand of his master, and the sons of Jacob went to Egypt; when they came near to Egypt they separated from each other, and they came through ten gates of Egypt, and the gate keepers wrote their names that day, and brought them to Joseph in the evening.

8 And Joseph read the names from the hand of the gatekeepers of the city, and he found that his brothers had entered at the ten gates of the city, and Joseph at once commanded that it should be proclaimed throughout the land of Egypt, saying,

9 Go forth all you store guards, close all the corn stores and let only one remain open, that those who come may purchase from it.

10 And all the officers of Joseph did so at that time, and they closed all the stores and left only one open.

11 Joseph gave the written names of his brothers to him that was set over the open store, and he said to him, Whosoever shall come to you to buy

corn, ask his name, and when men of these names shall come before you, seize them and send them, and they did so.

12 And when the sons of Jacob came into the city, they joined together in the city to search for Joseph before they bought themselves corn.

13 And they went to the walls of the harlots and they sought Joseph there for three days, for they thought that Joseph would come in the walls of the harlots, for Joseph was very handsome and well favored; the sons of Jacob sought Joseph for three days and they could not find him.

14 The man who was set over the open store sought for those names which Joseph had given him, and he did not find them.

15 And he sent to Joseph, saying, These three days have passed, and those men whose names you gave to me have not come, so Joseph sent servants to search for the men in all Egypt, and to bring them before Joseph.

16 Joseph's servants went and came into Egypt and could not find them, and went to Goshen and they were not there, and then went to the city of Rameses and could not find them.

17 Joseph continued to send sixteen servants to seek his brothers, and they went and spread themselves in the four corners of the city; four of the servants went into the house of the harlots, and they found the ten men there searching for their brother.

18 Those four men took them and brought them before Joseph, and they bowed down to him to the ground. Joseph was sitting on his throne in his temple, clothed with princely garments, and on his head was a large crown of gold, and all the mighty men were sitting around him.

19 And the sons of Jacob saw Joseph, and his figure and good-looks and dignity of countenance seemed wonderful in their eyes, and they again bowed down to him to the ground.

20 Joseph saw his brothers and he knew them, but they knew him not, for Joseph was very great in their eyes, therefore they knew him not.

21 And Joseph spoke to them, saying, From where did you come? And they all answered and said, Thy servants have come from the land of Canaan to buy corn, for the famine prevails throughout the earth, and your servants heard that there was corn in Egypt, so they have come among the other comers to buy corn for their support.

22 And Joseph answered them, saying, If you have come to purchase as you say, why do you come through ten gates of the city? It can only be that you have come to spy through the land.

23 And they all together answered Joseph, and said, Not so my lord, we

are right, your servants are not spies, but we have come to buy corn, for your servants are all brothers, the sons of one man in the land of Canaan, and our father commanded us, saying, When you come to the city do not enter together at one gate on account of the inhabitants of the land.

24 And Joseph again answered them and said, That is the thing which I spoke to you, you have come to spy through the land, therefore you all came through ten gates of the city; you have come to see how barren the land has become.

25 Certainly every one that comes to buy corn goes his way, and you are already three days in the land; what do you do in the walls of harlots in which you have been for these three days? Certainly spies do these things.

26 And they said to Joseph, Far be it from our lord to speak thus, for we are twelve brothers, the sons of our father Jacob, in the land of Canaan, the son of Isaac, the son of Abraham, the Hebrew; behold the youngest is with our father this day in the land of Canaan, and one is not, for he was lost from us, and we thought perhaps he might be in this land, so we are seeking him throughout the land, and have come even to the houses of harlots to seek him there.

27 And Joseph said to them, And have you then sought him throughout the earth, that there only remained Egypt for you to seek him in? And what also should your brother do in the houses of harlots, if he were in Egypt? Have you not said, that you are from the sons of Isaac, the son of Abraham, and what shall the sons of Jacob do then in the houses of harlots?

28 And they said to him, Because we heard that Ishmaelites stole him from us, and it was told to us that they sold him in Egypt, and your servant, our brother, is very handsome and well favored, so we thought he would certainly be in the houses of harlots, therefore your servants went there to seek him and give ransom for him.

29 Joseph still answered them, saying, Certainly you speak falsely and utter lies, to say of yourselves that you are the sons of Abraham; as Pharaoh lives you are spies, therefore you have come to the houses of harlots that you should not be known.

30 Joseph said to them, And now if you find him, and his master requires of you a great price, will you give it for him? And they said, It shall be given.

31 And he said to them, And if his master will not consent to part with him for a great price, what will you do to him on his account? And they answered him, saying, If he will not give him to us we will kill him, and

take our brother and go away.

32 And Joseph said to them, That is the thing which I have spoken to you; you are spies, for you are come to kill the inhabitants of the land, for we heard that two of your brothers struck all the inhabitants of Shechem, in the land of Canaan, on account of your sister, and you now come to do the same in Egypt on account of your brother.

33 Only hereby shall I know that you are true men; if you will send home one from among you to fetch your youngest brother from your father, and bring him here to me, and by doing this thing I will know that you are right.

34 And Joseph called to seventy of his mighty men, and he said to them, Take these men and bring them into the ward.

35 And the mighty men took the ten men, they laid hold of them and put them into the ward, and they were in the ward three days.

36 And on the third day Joseph had them brought out of the ward, and he said to them, Do this for yourselves if you be true men, so that you may live: one of your brothers shall be confined in the ward while you go and take home the corn for your household to the land of Canaan, and get your youngest brother, and bring him here to me, that I may know that you are true men when you do this thing.

37 And Joseph went out from them and came into the chamber, and wept a great weeping, for his pity was enlarged for them; he washed his face, and returned to them again, and he took Simeon from them and ordered him to be bound, but Simeon was not willing to be done so, for he was a very powerful man and they could not bind him.

38 And Joseph called to his mighty men and seventy valiant men came before him with drawn swords in their hands, and the sons of Jacob were terrified at them.

39 Joseph said to them, Seize this man and confine him in prison until his brothers come to him, and Joseph's valiant men hurried and they all laid hold of Simeon to bind him, and Simeon gave a loud and terrible shriek and the cry was heard at a distance.

40 All the valiant men of Joseph were so terrified at the sound of the shriek that they fell on their faces, and they were greatly afraid and fled.

41 And all the men that were with Joseph fled, for they were greatly afraid for their lives, and only Joseph and Manasseh his son remained there; Manassah the son of Joseph saw the strength of Simeon, and he was greatly angered.

42 And Manassah the son of Joseph rose up to Simeon, and Manassah struck Simeon a heavy blow with his fist against the back of his neck, and Simeon was stilled of his rage.

43 Manassah laid hold of Simeon and he seized him violently and he bound him and brought him into the house of confinement, and all the sons of Jacob were astonished at the act of the youth.

44 And Simeon said to his brothers, None of you must say that this is the smiting of an Egyptian, but it is the smiting of the house of my father.

45 After this Joseph ordered him to be called who was in charge of the storehouse, to fill their sacks with corn as much as they could carry, and to restore every man's money into his sack, and to give them provision for the road, and thus he did to them.

46 And Joseph commanded them, saying, Take care that you not go contrary to my orders to bring your brother as I have told you, and it shall be when you bring your brother here to me, then will I know that you are true men, and you shall traffic in the land, and I will restore to you your brother, and you shall return in peace to your father.

47 And they all answered and said, According as our lord speaks so will we do, and they bowed down to him to the ground.

48 Every man lifted his corn on his ass, and they went out to go to the land of Canaan to their father; and they came to the inn and Levi spread his sack to give feed to his ass, when he saw and there his money in full weight was still in his sack.

49 And the man was greatly afraid, and he said to his brothers, My money is returned, and look, it is even in my sack; the men were greatly afraid, and they said, What is this that God has done to us?

50 And they all said, And where is the Lord's kindness with our fathers, with Abraham, Isaac, and Jacob, that the Lord has this day delivered us into the hands of the king of Egypt to contrive against us?

51 Judah said to them, Certainly we are guilty sinners before the Lord our God in having sold our brother, our own flesh, and wherefore do you say, Where is the Lord's kindness with our fathers?

52 Reuben said to them, Said I not to you, do not sin against the lad, and you would not listen to me? Now God requires him from us, and how dare you say, Where is the Lord's kindness with our fathers, while you have sinned to the Lord?

53 They stayed overnight in that place, and they rose up early in the

morning and loaded their asses with their corn; they led them and went on and came to their father's house in the land of Canaan.

54 And Jacob and his household went out to meet his sons, and Jacob saw and behold their brother Simeon was not with them; Jacob said to his sons, Where is your brother Simeon, whom I do not see? And his sons told him all that had befallen them in Egypt.

CHAPTER 52

1 They entered their house, and every man opened his sack and they looked and there every man's bundle of money was there, at which they and their father were greatly terrified.

2 And Jacob said to them, What is this that you have done to me? I sent your brother Joseph to inquire after your welfare and you said to me: A wild beast did devour him.

3 And Simeon went with you to buy food and you say the king of Egypt hath confined him in prison, and you wish to take Benjamin to cause his death also, and bring down my grey hairs with sorrow to the grave on account of Benjamin and his brother Joseph.

4 Now therefore my son shall not go down with you, for his brother is dead and he is left alone, and mischief may befall him by the way in which you go, as it befell his brother.

5 Reuben said to his father, You shall kill my two sons if I do not bring your son and place him before you. Jacob said to his sons, Abide ye here and do not go down to Egypt, for my son shall not go down with you to Egypt, nor die like his brother.

6 And Judah said to them, Refrain from him until the corn is finished, and he will then say, Take down your brother, when he finds his own life and the life of his household in danger from the famine.

7 In those days the famine was severe throughout the land, and all the people of the earth went and came to Egypt to buy food, for the famine continued greatly among them, and the sons of Jacob remained in Canaan a year and two months until their corn was finished.

8 And it came to pass after their corn was finished, the whole household of Jacob was pinched with hunger, and all the infants of the sons of Jacob came together and they approached Jacob; they all surrounded him, and

said to him, Give to us bread, for why shall we all perish through hunger in your presence?

9 Jacob heard the words of his son's children, and he wept a great weeping, and his pity was roused for them. Jacob called to his sons and they all came and sat before him.

10 And Jacob said to them, Have you not seen how your children have been weeping over me this day, saying, Give to us bread, and there is none? Now therefore return and buy for us a little food.

11 And Judah answered and said to his father, If you will send our brother with us we will go down and buy corn for you, and if you will not send him then we will not go down, for certainly the king of Egypt particularly requested us, saying, You shall not see my face unless your brother is with you. The king of Egypt is a strong and mighty king, and behold if we shall go to him without our brother we shall all be put to death.

12 Do you not know and have you not heard that this king is very powerful and wise, and there is no one like him in all the earth? Behold we have seen all the kings of the earth and we have not seen one like that king, the king of Egypt; certainly among all the kings of the earth there is none greater than Abimelech king of the Philistines, yet the king of Egypt is greater and mightier than he, and Abimelech can only be compared to one of his officers.

13 Father, you have not seen his palace and his throne, and all his servants standing before him; you have not seen that king on his throne in his pomp and royal appearance, dressed in his kingly robes with a large golden crown on his head; you have not seen the honor and glory which God has given to him, for there is no one like him in all the earth.

14 Father, you have not seen the wisdom, the understanding and the knowledge which God has given in his heart, nor heard his sweet voice when he spoke to us.

15 We know not, father, who made him acquainted with our names and all that happened to us, yet he asked also after you, saying, Is your father still living, and is it well with him?

16 You have not seen the affairs of the government of Egypt regulated by him, without inquiring of Pharaoh his lord; you have not seen the awe and fear which he impressed on all the Egyptians.

17 And also when we went from him, we were threatened of doing to Egypt like to the rest of the cities of the Amorites, and we were greatly

angered against all his words which he spoke concerning us as spies; now when we shall again come before him his terror will fall on us all, and not one of us will be able to speak to him either a little or a great thing.

18 Now therefore father, send we pray you the lad with us, and we will go down and buy you food for our support, and not die through hunger. And Jacob said, Why have you dealt so ill with me to tell the king you had a brother? What is this thing that you have done to me?

19 And Judah said to Jacob his father, Give the lad into my care and we will rise up and go down to Egypt and buy corn, and then return, and it shall be when we return if the lad is not with us, then let me bear your blame forever.

20 Have you seen all our infants weeping over you through hunger and there is no power in your hand to satisfy them? Now let your pity be roused for them and send our brother with us and we will go.

21 For how will the Lord's kindness to our ancestors be manifested to you when you say that the king of Egypt will take away your son? As the Lord lives I will not leave him until I bring him and place him before you; but pray for us to the Lord, that he may deal kindly with us, to cause us to be received favorably and kindly before the king of Egypt and his men, for had we not delayed certainly by now we had returned a second time with your son.

22 And Jacob said to his sons, I trust in the Lord God that he may deliver you and give you favor in the sight of the king of Egypt, and in the sight of all his men.

23 Now therefore rise up and go to the man, and take for him in your hands a present from what can be obtained in the land and bring it before him, and may the Almighty God give you mercy before him that he may send Benjamin and Simeon your brothers with you.

24 And all the men rose up, and they took their brother Benjamin, and they took in their hands a large present of the best of the land, and they also took a double portion of silver.

25 And Jacob strictly commanded his sons concerning Benjamin, saying, Take care of him in the way in which you are going, and do not separate yourselves from him in the road, neither in Egypt.

26 And Jacob rose up from his sons and spread forth his hands and he prayed to the Lord on account of his sons, saying, O Lord God of heaven and earth, remember your covenant with our father Abraham, remember it with my father Isaac and deal kindly with my sons and deliver them not into the hands of the king of Egypt; do it I pray you O God for the sake of

your mercies and redeem all my children and rescue them from Egyptian power, and send them their two brothers.

27 And all the wives of the sons of Jacob and their children lifted up their eyes to heaven and they all wept before the Lord, and cried to him to deliver their fathers from the hand of the king of Egypt.

28 Jacob wrote a record to the king of Egypt and gave it into the hand of Judah and into the hands of his sons for the king of Egypt, saying,

29 From your servant Jacob, son of Isaac, son of Abraham the Hebrew, the prince of God, to the powerful and wise king, the revealer of secrets, king of Egypt, greeting.

30 Be it known to my lord the king of Egypt, the famine was heavy on us in the land of Canaan, and I sent my sons to you to buy us a little food from you for our support.

31 For my sons surrounded me and I being very old cannot see with my eyes, for my eyes have become very dim through age, as well as with daily weeping for my son, for Joseph who was lost from before me; I commanded my sons that they should not enter the gates of the city when they came to Egypt, on account of the inhabitants of the land.

32 And I also commanded them to go about Egypt to seek for my son Joseph, perhaps they might find him there, and they did so, and you did consider them as spies of the land.

33 Have we not heard concerning you that you did interpret Pharaoh's dream and did speak truly to him? How then do you not know in your wisdom whether my sons are spies or not?

34 Now therefore, my lord and king, behold I have sent my son before you, as you did speak to my sons; I beg you to put your eyes on him until he is returned to me in peace with his brothers.

35 For do you not know, or have you not heard that which our God did to Pharaoh when he took my mother Sarah, and what he did to Abimelech king of the Philistines on account of her, and also what our father Abraham did to the nine kings of Elam, how he struck them all with a few men that were with him?

36 And also what my two sons Simeon and Levi did to the eight cities of the Amorites, how they destroyed them on account of their sister Dinah?

37 And also on account of their brother Benjamin they consoled themselves for the loss of his brother Joseph; what will they then do for him when they see the hand of any people prevailing over them, for his

sake?

38 Do you not know, O king of Egypt, that the power of God is with us, and that also God ever hears our prayers and forsakes us not all the days?

39 And when my sons told me of your dealings with them, I called not to the Lord on account of you, for then you would have perished with your men before my son Benjamin came before you, but I thought that as Simeon my son was in your house, perhaps you might deal kindly with him, therefore I did not do this thing to you.

40 Now therefore behold Benjamin my son comes to you with my sons, take care of him and put your eyes on him, and then will God place his eyes over you and throughout your kingdom.

41 Now I have told you all that is in my heart, and behold my sons are coming to you with their brother; examine the face of the whole earth for their sake and send them back in peace with their brothers.

42 And Jacob gave the record to his sons into the care of Judah to give it to the king of Egypt.

CHAPTER 53

1 The sons of Jacob rose up and took Benjamin and all of the presents; they went and came to Egypt and they stood before Joseph.

2 And Joseph beheld his brother Benjamin with them and he saluted them, and these men came to Joseph's house.

3 Joseph commanded the superintendent of his house to give food to his brothers to eat, and he did so to them.

4 At noon time Joseph sent for the men to come before him with Benjamin, and the men told the superintendent of Joseph's house concerning the silver that was returned in their sacks; he said to them, It will be well with you, fear not. And he brought their brother Simeon to them.

5 And Simeon said to his brothers, The lord of the Egyptians has acted very kindly to me; he did not keep me bound, as you saw with your eyes, for when you went out from the city he let me free and dealt kindly with me in his house.

6 And Judah took Benjamin by the hand, and they came before Joseph,

and they bowed down to him to the ground.

7 The men gave the present to Joseph and they all sat before him, and Joseph said to them, Is it well with you, is it well with your children, is it well with your aged father? And they said, It is well. And Judah took the record which Jacob had sent and gave it into the hand of Joseph.

8 Joseph read the letter and knew his father's writing, and he wished to weep; he went into an inner room and he wept a great weeping, and he came out.

9 He lifted up his eyes and observed his brother Benjamin and said, Is this your brother of whom you spoke to me? Benjamin approached Joseph, and Joseph placed his hand on his head and he said to him, May God be gracious to you my son.

10 And when Joseph saw his brother, the son of his mother, he again wished to weep, and he entered the chamber, and he wept there; he washed his face and came out and refrained from weeping; he said, Prepare food.

11 Joseph had a cup from which he drank; it was of silver beautifully inlaid with onyx stones and bdellium, and Joseph struck the cup in the sight of his brothers while they were sitting to eat with him.

12 Joseph said to the men, I know by this cup that Reuben the first born, Simeon and Levi and Judah, Issachar and Zebulun are children from one mother; seat yourselves to eat according to your births.

13 He also placed the others according to their births and said, I know that this your youngest brother has no brother; I, like him, have no brother; he shall therefore sit down to eat with me.

14 Benjamin went up before Joseph and sat on the throne and the men beheld the acts of Joseph, and they were astonished at them; the men ate and drank at that time with Joseph, and he then gave presents to them. Joseph gave one gift to Benjamin, and Manasseh and Ephraim saw the acts of their father, and they also gave presents to him, and Osnath gave him one present, and there were five presents in the hands of Benjamin.

15 Joseph brought out wine to drink, and they would not drink; they said, From the day in which Joseph was lost we have not drunk wine, nor eaten any delicacies.

16 And Joseph swore to them, and he pressed them hard; they drank plentifully with him on that day, and Joseph afterward turned to his brother Benjamin to speak with him, and Benjamin was still sitting on the throne before Joseph.

17 Joseph said to him, Have you had any children? And he said, Your servant has ten sons, and these are their names: Bela, Becher, Ashbal, Gera, Naaman, Achi, Rosh, Mupim, Chupim, and Ord, and I called their names after my brother whom I have not seen.

18 He ordered them to bring before him his map of the stars, whereby Joseph knew all the times, and Joseph said to Benjamin, I have heard that the Hebrews are acquainted with all wisdom, do you know anything of this?

19 And Benjamin said, Thy servant knows all the wisdom which my father taught me. Joseph said to Benjamin, Look now at this instrument and understand where your brother Joseph is in Egypt, who you said went down to Egypt.

20 And Benjamin observed that instrument with the map of the stars of heaven, and he was wise and looked therein to know where his brother was. Benjamin divided the whole land of Egypt into four divisions, and he found that he who was sitting on the throne before him was his brother Joseph; Benjamin wondered greatly, and when Joseph saw that his brother Benjamin was so much astonished, he said to Benjamin, What have you seen, and why are you astonished?

21 Benjamin said to Joseph, I can see by this that Joseph my brother sits here with me on the throne, and Joseph said to him, I am Joseph your brother; reveal not this thing to your brothers. I will send you with them when they go away and I will command them to be brought back again into the city, and I will take you away from them.

22 And if they risk their lives and fight for you, then shall I know that they have repented of what they did to me; I will make myself known to them and if they turn away from you when I take you, then shall you remain with me, and I will fight with them, and they shall go away. I will not become known to them.

23 At that time Joseph commanded his officer to fill their sacks with food and to put each man's money into his sack, and to put the cup in the sack of Benjamin and give them provision for the road, and they did so to them.

24 On the next day the men rose up early in the morning and loaded their asses with their corn; they went forth with Benjamin, and went to the land of Canaan with their brother Benjamin.

25 They had not gone far from Egypt when Joseph commanded him that was set over his house, saying, Rise, pursue these men before they get too far from Egypt, and say to them, Why have you stolen my master's cup?

26 Joseph's officer rose up and he reached them, and he spoke to them all

the words of Joseph; when they heard this thing they became greatly angry, and they said, He with whom your master's cup shall be found shall die, and we will also become slaves.

27 They hurried and each man brought down his sack from his ass, and they looked in their bags and the cup was found in Benjamin's bag; they all tore their garments and they returned to the city, and they struck Benjamin in the road, continually smiting him until he came into the city, and they stood before Joseph.

28 Judah's anger was set ablaze, and he said, This man has only brought me back to destroy Egypt this day.

29 The men came to Joseph's house, and they found Joseph sitting on his throne, and all the mighty men standing at his right and left.

30 And Joseph said to them, What is this act that you have done, that you took away my silver cup and went away? But I know that you took my cup in order to know thereby in what part of the land your brother was.

31 Judah said, What shall we say to our lord, what shall we speak and how shall we justify ourselves; God has this day found the iniquity of all your servants, therefore has he done this thing to us this day.

32 Joseph rose up and caught hold of Benjamin and took him from his brothers with violence, and he came to the house and locked the door at them; Joseph commanded him that was set over his house that he should say to them, Thus says the king, Go in peace to your father, behold I have taken the man in whose hand my cup was found.

CHAPTER 54

1 When Judah saw the dealings of Joseph with them, Judah approached him and broke open the door, and came with his brothers before Joseph.

2 And Judah said to Joseph, Let it not seem bothersome in the sight of my lord, may your servant I pray you speak a word before you? And Joseph said to him, Speak.

3 Judah spoke before Joseph and his brothers were there standing before them; Judah said to Joseph, Certainly when we first came to our lord to buy food, you did consider us as spies of the land, and we brought Benjamin before you, and you still make sport of us this day.

4 Now therefore let the king hear my words and send I pray you our brother that he may go along with us to our father, that your son not perish this day with all the souls of the inhabitants of Egypt.

5 Do you not know what two of my brothers, Simeon and Levi, did to the city of Shechem and to seven cities of the Amorites on account of our sister Dinah, and also what they would do for the sake of their brother Benjamin?

6 I with my strength, who am greater and mightier than both of them, come this day on you and your land if you are unwilling to send our brother.

7 Have you not heard what our God who made choice of us did to Pharaoh on account of Sarah our mother, whom he took away from our father, that he struck him and his household with heavy plagues; even to this day the Egyptians relate this wonder to each other? So will our God do to you on account of Benjamin whom you have this day taken from his father, and on account of the evils which you this day heap over us in your land; for our God will remember his covenant with our father Abraham and bring evil on you because you have grieved the soul of our father this day.

8 Now hear my words that I have this day spoken to you, and send our brother that he may go away that you and the people of your land not die by the sword, for you cannot all prevail over me.

9 Joseph answered Judah, saying, Why have you opened wide your mouth and why do you boast over us, saying, Strength is with you? As Pharaoh lives, if I command all my valiant men to fight with you, certainly you and these your brothers would sink into the mud.

10 Judah said to Joseph, Certainly it becomes you and your people to fear me; as the Lord lives if I once draw my sword I shall not sheathe it again until I shall this day have slain all Egypt, and I will begin with you and finish with Pharaoh your master.

11 And Joseph answered and said to him, Certainly strength belongs not alone to you; I am stronger and mightier than you; certainly if you draw your sword I will put it to your neck and the necks of all your brothers.

12 Judah said to him, Certainly if I this day open my mouth against you I would swallow you up that you be destroyed from off the earth and perish this day from your kingdom. And Joseph said, Certainly if you open your mouth I have power and might to close your mouth with a stone until you shall not be able to utter a word; see how many stones are before us, truly I can take a stone and force it into your mouth and break your jaws.

13 And Judah said, God is witness between us, that we have not hereto desired to battle with you, only give us our brother and we will go from you. Joseph answered and said, As Pharaoh lives, if all the kings of Canaan came together with you, you should not take him from my hand.

14 Now therefore go your way to your father, and your brother shall be to me a slave, for he has robbed the king's house. And Judah said, What is it to you or to the character of the king, certainly the king sends forth from his house, throughout the land, silver and gold either in gifts or expenses, and you still talk about your cup which you did place in our brother's bag and say that he has stolen it from you?

15 God forbid that our brother Benjamin or any of the offspring of Abraham should do this thing to steal from you, or from any one else, whether king, prince, or any man.

16 Now therefore cease this accusation that the whole earth not hear your words, saying, For a little silver the king of Egypt argued with the men, and he accused them and took their brother for a slave.

17 And Joseph answered and said, Take this cup and go from me and leave your brother for a slave, for it is the judgment of a thief to be a slave.

18 And Judah said, Why are you not ashamed of your words, to leave our brother and to take your cup? Certainly if you give us your cup, or a thousand times as much, we will not leave our brother for the silver which is found in the hand of any man, that we will not die over him.

19 Joseph answered, And why did you turn away from your brother and sell him for twenty pieces of silver to this day; why then will you not do the same to this your brother?

20 And Judah said, The Lord is witness between me and you that we desire not your battles; now therefore give us our brother and we will go from you without quarreling.

21 And Joseph answered and said, If all the kings of the land should assemble they will not be able to take your brother from my hand. Judah said, What shall we say to our father, when he sees that our brother comes not with us, and will grieve over him?

22 Joseph answered and said, This is the thing which you shall tell to your father, saying, The rope has gone after the bucket.

23 Judah said, Certainly you are a king, and why speak you these things, giving a false judgment? Woe to the king who is like you.

24 Joseph answered and said, There is no false judgment in the word that

I spoke on account of your brother Joseph, for all of you sold him to the Midianites for twenty pieces of silver. And you all denied it to your father and said to him, An evil beast has devoured him; Joseph has been torn to pieces.

25 And Judah said, Behold the fire of Shem burns in my heart, now I will burn all your land with fire; Joseph answered and said, Certainly your sister-in-law Tamar, who killed your sons, extinguished the fire of Shechem.

26 Judah said, If I pluck out a single hair from my flesh, I will fill all Egypt with its blood.

27 Joseph answered and said, Such is your custom to do as you did to your brother whom you sold, and you dipped his coat in blood and brought it to your father in order that he might say an evil beast devoured him and here is his blood.

28 When Judah heard this thing he was greatly enraged and his anger burned within him, and there was before him in that place a stone, the weight of which was about four hundred shekels; Judah's anger was set ablaze and he took the stone in one hand and cast it to the heavens and caught it with his left hand.

29 He placed it afterward under his legs, and he sat on it with all his strength and the stone was turned into dust from the force of Judah.

30 Joseph saw the act of Judah and he was very much afraid, but he commanded Manassah his son and he also did with another stone like to the act of Judah, and Judah said to his brothers, Let not any of you say this man is an Egyptian, but by his doing this thing he is of our father's family.

31 And Joseph said, Not to you only is strength given, for we are also powerful men, and why will you boast over us all? Judah said to Joseph, Send I pray you our brother and ruin not your country this day.

32 And Joseph answered and said to them, Go and tell your father an evil beast has devoured him as you said concerning your brother Joseph.

33 Judah spoke to his brother Naphtali, and said to him, Hurry, go now and number all the streets of Egypt and come and tell me; Simeon said to him, Let not this thing be a trouble to you; now I will go to the mount and take up one large stone from the mount and level it at every one in Egypt, and kill all that are in it.

34 Joseph heard all these words that his brothers spoke before him, and they did not know that Joseph understood them for they imagined that he knew not to speak Hebrew.

35 Joseph was greatly afraid at the words of his brothers that they should destroy Egypt, and he commanded his son Manasseh, saying, Go now, hurry and gather to me all the inhabitants of Egypt, and all the valiant men together, and let them come to me now on horseback and on foot and with all sorts of musical instruments, and Manasseh went and did so.

36 Naphtali went as Judah had commanded him, for Naphtali was lightfooted as one of the swift stags, and he could walk on the ears of corn and they would not break under him.

37 He went and numbered all the streets of Egypt and found them to be twelve, and he came quickly and told Judah, and Judah said to his brothers, Hurry and put on every man his sword on his loins and we will come over Egypt and strike them all, and let not a remnant remain.

38 Judah said, Behold, I will destroy three of the streets with my strength, and you shall each destroy one street; when Judah was speaking this thing, then the inhabitants of Egypt and all the mighty men came toward them with all sorts of musical instruments and with loud shouting.

39 And their number was five hundred cavalry and ten thousand infantry, and four hundred men who could fight without sword or spear, only with their hands and strength.

40 And all the mighty men came with great storming and shouting, and they all surrounded the sons of Jacob and terrified them, and the ground quaked at the sound of their shouting.

41 When the sons of Jacob saw these troops they were greatly afraid of their lives, and Joseph did so in order to terrify the sons of Jacob to become tranquilized.

42 Judah, seeing some of his brothers terrified, said to them, Why are you afraid while the grace of God is with us? Judah saw all the people of Egypt surrounding them at the command of Joseph to terrify them, only Joseph commanded them, saying, Do not touch any of them.

43 Then Judah hurried and drew his sword and uttered a loud and bitter scream, and he struck with his sword, and he stomped on the ground and he still continued to shout against all the people.

44 When he did this thing the Lord caused the terror of Judah and his brothers to fall on the valiant men and all the people that surrounded them.

45 They all fled at the sound of the shouting, and they were terrified and fell one on the other, and many of them died as they fell, and they all fled from before Judah and his brothers and from before Joseph.

46 While they were fleeing, Judah and his brothers pursued them to the house of Pharaoh and they all escaped; Judah again sat before Joseph and roared at him like a lion, and gave a great and tremendous shriek at him.

47 The shriek was heard at a distance, and all the inhabitants of Succoth heard it, and all Egypt quaked at the sound of the shriek; also the walls of Egypt and of the land of Goshen fell in from the shaking of the earth, and Pharaoh also fell from his throne on the ground; also all the pregnant women of Egypt and Goshen miscarried when they heard the noise of the shaking, for they were terribly afraid.

48 And Pharaoh sent word, saying, What is this thing that has this day happened in the land of Egypt? They came and told him all the things from beginning to end, and Pharaoh was alarmed and he wondered and was greatly afraid.

49 His fright increased when he heard all these things, and he sent to Joseph, saying, You have brought to me the Hebrews to destroy all Egypt; what will you do with that thievish slave? Send him away and let him go with his brothers, and let us not perish through their evil, even we, you and all Egypt.

50 And if you desire not to do this thing, cast off from you all my valuable things, and go with them to their land if you delightest in it, for they will this day destroy my whole country and kill all my people; even all the women of Egypt have miscarried through their scream. See what they have done merely by their shouting and speaking? And if they fight with the sword, they will destroy the land; now therefore choose that which you desire, whether me or the Hebrews, whether Egypt or the land of the Hebrews.

51 They came and told Joseph all the words of Pharaoh that he had said concerning him, and Joseph was greatly afraid at the words of Pharaoh and Judah and his brothers were still standing before Joseph indignant and enraged, and all the sons of Jacob roared at Joseph, like the roaring of the sea and its waves.

52 Joseph was greatly afraid of his brothers and on account of Pharaoh, and Joseph sought a way to make himself known to his brothers, that they should not destroy all Egypt.

53 Joseph commanded his son Manasseh, and Manasseh went and approached Judah and placed his hand on his shoulder, and the anger of Judah was stilled.

54 And Judah said to his brothers, Let no one of you say that this is the act of an Egyptian youth for this is the work of my father's house.

55 Joseph seeing and knowing that Judah's anger was stilled, he approached to speak to Judah in the language of mildness.

56 And Joseph said to Judah, Certainly you speak truth and have this day verified your assertions concerning your strength, and may your God who delights in you, increase your welfare; but tell me truly why from among all your brothers do you argue with me on account of the lad, as none of them have spoken one word to me concerning him.

57 And Judah answered Joseph, saying, Certainly you must know that I was security for the lad to his father, saying, If I brought him not to him I should bear his blame forever.

58 So I have approached you from among all my brothers, for I saw that you were unwilling to allow him to go from you; now therefore may I find grace in your sight that you shall send him to go with us and then I will remain as a substitute for him, to serve you in whatever you desire, for whereever you shall send me I will go to serve you with great energy.

59 Send me now to a mighty king who has rebelled against you, and you shall know what I will do to him and to his land; although he may have cavalry and infantry or an exceeding mighty people, I will kill them all and bring the king's head before you.

60 Do you not know or have you not heard that our father Abraham with his servant Eliezer struck all the kings of Elam with their hosts in one night, they left not one remaining? And ever since that day our father's strength was given to us for an inheritance, for us and our descendants forever.

61 Joseph answered and said, You speak truth, and falsehood is not in your mouth, for it was also told to us that the Hebrews have power and that the Lord their God delights much in them, and who then can stand before them?

62 However, on this condition will I send your brother, if you will bring before me his brother the son of his mother, of whom you said that he had gone from you down to Egypt; it shall come to pass when you bring to me his brother I will take him in his stead, because not one of you was security for him to your father. When he shall come to me, I will then send with you his brother for whom you have been security.

63 And Judah's anger was set ablaze against Joseph when he spoke this thing, and his eyes dropped blood with anger, and he said to his brothers, How does this man this day seek his own destruction and that of all Egypt!

64 And Simeon answered Joseph, saying, Did we not tell you at first that we knew not the particular spot to which he went, and whether he be dead or alive, and why does my lord speak these things?

65 Joseph, observing the countenance of Judah discerned that his anger began to kindle when he spoke to him, saying, Bring to me your other brother instead of this brother.

66 And Joseph said to his brothers, Certainly you said that your brother was either dead or lost, now if I should call him this day and he should come before you, would you give him to me instead of his brother?

67 And Joseph began to speak and call out, Joseph, Joseph, come this day before me, and appear to your brothers and sit before them.

68 When Joseph spoke this thing before them, they looked each a different way to see from where Joseph would come before them.

69 And Joseph observed all their acts, and said to them, Why do you look here and there? I am Joseph whom you sold to Egypt, now therefore let it not grieve you that you sold me, for as a support during the famine did God send me from you.

70 And his brothers were terrified at him when they heard the words of Joseph, and Judah was greatly terrified at him.

71 When Benjamin heard the words of Joseph he was before them in the inner part of the house, and Benjamin ran to Joseph his brother and embraced him and fell on his neck, and they wept.

72 When Joseph's brothers saw that Benjamin had fallen on his brother's neck and wept with him, they also fell on Joseph and embraced him, and they wept a great weeping with Joseph.

73 And the voice was heard in the house of Joseph that they were Joseph's brothers, and it pleased Pharaoh greatly, for he was afraid of them that they should destroy Egypt.

74 Pharaoh sent his servants to Joseph to congratulate him concerning his brothers who had come to him, and all the captains of the armies and troops that were in Egypt came to rejoice with Joseph, and all Egypt rejoiced greatly about Joseph's brothers.

75 And Pharaoh sent his servants to Joseph, saying, Tell your brothers to fetch all belonging to them and let them come to me, and I will place them in the best part of the land of Egypt, and they did so.

76 Joseph commanded him that was set over his house to bring out to his brothers gifts and garments, and he brought out to them many garments being robes of royalty and many gifts, and Joseph divided them among his

brothers.

77 And he gave to each of his brothers a change of garments of gold and silver, and three hundred pieces of silver, and Joseph commanded them all to be dressed in these garments, and to be brought before Pharaoh.

78 And Pharaoh, seeing that all Joseph's brothers were valiant men, and of beautiful appearance, greatly rejoiced.

79 And afterward they went out from the presence of Pharaoh to go to the land of Canaan, to their father, and their brother Benjamin was with them.

80 Joseph rose up and gave to them eleven chariots from Pharaoh, and Joseph gave to them his chariot on which he rode on the day of his being crowned in Egypt, to fetch his father to Egypt; Joseph sent to all his brothers' children, garments according to their numbers, and a hundred pieces of silver to each of them, and he also sent garments to the wives of his brothers from the garments of the king's wives, and he sent them.

81 He gave to each of his brothers ten men to go with them to the land of Canaan to serve them, to serve their children and all belonging to them in coming to Egypt.

82 Joseph sent by the hand of his brother Benjamin ten suits of garments for his ten sons, a portion above the rest of the children of the sons of Jacob.

83 And he sent to each fifty pieces of silver, and ten chariots on the account of Pharaoh; he sent to his father ten asses laden with all the luxuries of Egypt, and ten female asses laden with corn and bread and nourishment for his father and to all that were with him as provisions for the road.

84 And he sent to his sister Dinah garments of silver and gold, and frankincense and myrrh, and aloes and women's ornaments in great plenty; he sent the same from the wives of Pharaoh to the wives of Benjamin.

85 He gave to all his brothers, also to their wives, all sorts of onyx stones and bdellium, and from all the valuable things among the great people of Egypt, nothing of all the costly things was left but what Joseph sent of to his father's household.

86 He sent his brothers away, and they went, and he sent his brother Benjamin with them.

87 And Joseph went out with them to accompany them on the road to the borders of Egypt, and he commanded them concerning his father and his

household to come to Egypt.

88 And he said to them, Do not quarrel on the road, for this thing was from the Lord to keep a great people from starvation, for there will be yet five years of famine in the land.

89 And he commanded them, saying, When you come to the land of Canaan, do not come suddenly before my father about this affair, but act in your wisdom.

90 And Joseph ceased to command them, and he turned and went back to Egypt, and the sons of Jacob went to the land of Canaan with joy and cheerfulness to their father Jacob.

91 Tthey came to the borders of the land, and they said to each other, What shall we do in this matter before our father, for if we come suddenly to him and tell him the matter, he will be greatly alarmed at our words and will not believe us.

92 They went along until they came near to their houses and they found Serach, the daughter of Asher, going forth to meet them; the damsel was very good and subtle, and knew how to play on the harp.

93 They called to her and she came before them and kissed them, and they took her and gave her a harp, saying, Go now before our father and sit before him; strike on the harp and speak these words.

94 And they commanded her to go to their house, and she took the harp and hurried before them, and she came and sat near Jacob.

95 She played well and sang, and uttered in the sweetness of her words: Joseph my uncle is living and he rules throughout the land of Egypt, and is not dead.

96 She continued to repeat and utter these words, and Jacob heard her words and they were agreeable to him.

97 He listened while she repeated them twice and three times, and joy entered the heart of Jacob at the sweetness of her words, and the spirit of God was on him and he knew all her words to be true.

98 Jacob blessed Serach when she spoke these words before him, and he said to her, My daughter, may death never prevail over you, for you have revived my spirit; only speak again before me as you have spoken, for you have uplifted me with all your words.

99 And she continued to sing these words and Jacob listened and it pleased him, and he rejoiced, and the spirit of God was on him.

100 While he was yet speaking with her, he saw his sons come to him

with horses and chariots and royal garments and servants running before them.

101 Jacob rose up to meet them and saw his sons dressed in royal garments and he saw all the treasures that Joseph had sent to them.

102 They said to him, Be informed that our brother Joseph is living, and it is he who rules throughout the land of Egypt, and it is he who spoke to us as we told you.

103 Jacob heard all the words of his sons, and his heart palpitated at their words, for he could not believe them until he saw all that Joseph had given them and what he had sent him, and all the signs which Joseph had spoken to them.

104 They opened all before him, and showed him all that Joseph had sent; they gave to each what Joseph had sent him and he knew that they had spoken the truth, and he rejoiced greatly an account of his son.

105 Jacob said, It is enough for me that my son Joseph is still living; I will go and see him before I die.

106 And his sons told him all that had happened to them, and Jacob said, I will go down to Egypt to see my son and his children.

107 Jacob rose up and put on the garments which Joseph had sent him, and after he had washed and shaved his hair, he put on his head the turban which Joseph had sent him.

108 All the people of Jacob's house and their wives put on the garments which Joseph had sent to them, and they greatly rejoiced at Joseph that he was still living and that he was ruling in Egypt.

109 And all the inhabitants of Canaan heard of this thing, and they came and rejoiced much with Jacob that he was still living.

110 Jacob made a feast for them for three days, and all the kings of Canaan and nobles of the land ate and drank and rejoiced in the house of Jacob.

CHAPTER 55

1 It came to pass after this that Jacob said, I will go and see my son in Egypt and then come back to the land of Canaan of which God had

spoken to Abraham, for I cannot leave the land of my birth-place.

2 Then the word of the Lord came to him, saying, Go down to Egypt with all your household and remain there; fear not to go down to Egypt for I will there make you a great nation.

3 Jacob said within himself, I will go and see my son whether the fear of his God is yet in his heart among all the inhabitants of Egypt.

4 And the Lord said to Jacob, Fear not about Joseph, for he still retains his integrity to serve me, as will seem good in your sight. Jacob rejoiced greatly concerning his son.

5 At that time Jacob commanded his sons and household to go to Egypt according to the word of the Lord to him, and Jacob rose up with his sons and all his household, and he went out from the land of Canaan from Beersheba with joy and gladness of heart; they went to the land of Egypt.

6 It came to pass when they came near Egypt, Jacob sent Judah before him to Joseph that he might show him a situation in Egypt, and Judah did according to the word of his father; he hurried and ran and came to Joseph and they assigned for them a place in the land of Goshen for all his household, and Judah returned and came along the road to his father.

7 Joseph harnessed the chariot and assembled all his mighty men and his servants and all the officers of Egypt in order to go and meet his father Jacob, and Joseph's mandate was proclaimed in Egypt, saying, All that do not go to meet Jacob shall die.

8 On the next day Joseph went forth with all Egypt a great and mighty host, all dressed in garments of fine linen and purple and with instruments of silver and gold and with their instruments of war with them.

9 And they all went to meet Jacob with all sorts of musical instruments, with drums and timbrels, strewing myrrh and aloes all along the road; they all went after this fashion and the earth shook at their shouting.

10 All the women of Egypt went on the roofs of Egypt and on the walls to meet Jacob, and on the head of Joseph was Pharaoh's regal crown, for Pharaoh had sent it to him to put on at the time of his going to meet his father.

11 When Joseph came within fifty cubits of his father, he alighted from the chariot and he walked toward his father; when all the officers of Egypt and her nobles saw that Joseph had gone on foot toward his father, they also alighted and walked on foot toward Jacob.

12 And when Jacob approached the camp of Joseph, Jacob observed the

camp that was coming toward him with Joseph and it gratified him, and Jacob was astonished at it.

13 Jacob said to Judah, Who is that man whom I see in the camp of Egypt dressed in kingly robes with a very red garment on him and a royal crown on his head, who has alighted from his chariot and is coming toward us? And Judah answered his father, saying, He is your son Joseph the king; and Jacob rejoiced in seeing the glory of his son.

14 Joseph came near to his father and he bowed to his father, and all the men of the camp bowed to the ground with him before Jacob.

15 And behold Jacob ran and hurried to his son Joseph and fell on his neck and kissed him, and they wept; Joseph also embraced his father and kissed him and they wept, and all the people of Egypt wept with them.

16 Jacob said to Joseph, Now I will die cheerfully after I have seen your face, that you are still living and with glory.

17 The sons of Jacob and their wives and their children and their servants, and all the household of Jacob wept greatly with Joseph and they kissed him and wept greatly with him.

18 Joseph and all his people returned home afterward to Egypt, and Jacob and his sons and all the children of his household came with Joseph to Egypt; Joseph placed them in the best part of Egypt, in the land of Goshen.

19 Joseph said to his father and his brothers, I will go up and tell Pharaoh, saying, My brothers and my father's household and all belonging to them have come to me, and now they are in the land of Goshen.

20 And Joseph did so and took from his brothers Reuben, Issachar, Zebulun and his brother Benjamin and he placed them before Pharaoh.

21 And Joseph spoke to Pharaoh, saying, My brothers and my father's household and all belonging to them, together with their flocks and cattle have come to me from the land of Canaan, to sojourn in Egypt; for the famine was severely on them.

22 And Pharaoh said to Joseph, Place your father and brothers in the best part of the land; withhold not from them all that is good, and cause them to eat of the best of the land.

23 And Joseph answered, saying, Yes, I have stationed them in the land of Goshen for they are shepherds, therefore let them remain in Goshen to feed their flocks, apart from the Egyptians.

24 And Pharaoh said to Joseph, Do with your brothers all that they shall say to you. And the sons of Jacob bowed down to Pharaoh, and they went

forth from him in peace, and Joseph afterward brought his father before Pharaoh.

25 And Jacob came and bowed down to Pharaoh, and Jacob blessed Pharaoh, and he then went out; Jacob and all his sons and all his household lived in the land of Goshen.

26 In the second year, that is in the hundred and thirtieth year of the life of Jacob, Joseph maintained his father and his brothers and all his father's household with bread according to their little ones; all the days of the famine they lacked nothing.

27 And Joseph gave to them the best part of the whole land; the best of Egypt they had, all the days of Joseph, and Joseph also gave to them and to all his father's household, clothes and garments year by year; the sons of Jacob remained securely in Egypt all the days of their brother.

28 And Jacob always ate at Joseph's table, Jacob and his sons did not leave Joseph's table day or night, besides what Jacob's children consumed in their houses.

29 And all Egypt ate bread during the days of the famine from the house of Joseph, for all the Egyptians sold all belonging to them on account of the famine.

30 Joseph purchased all the lands and fields of Egypt for bread on the account of Pharaoh, and Joseph supplied all Egypt with bread all the days of the famine; Joseph collected all the silver and gold that came to him for the corn which they bought throughout the land, and he accumulated much gold and silver, besides an immense quantity of onyx stones, bdellium and valuable garments which they brought to Joseph from every part of the land when their money was gone.

31 And Joseph took all the silver and gold that came into his hand, about seventy two talents of gold and silver, and also onyx stones and bdellium in great abundance, and Joseph went and concealed them in four parts; he concealed one part in the wilderness near the Red sea, and one part by the river Perath, and the third and fourth parts he concealed in the desert opposite to the wilderness of Persia and Media.

32 He took part of the gold and silver that was left and gave it to all his brothers, to all his father's household, and to all the women of his father's household; the rest he brought to the house of Pharaoh, about twenty talents of gold and silver.

33 Joseph gave all the gold and silver that was left to Pharaoh, and Pharaoh placed it in the treasury, and the days of the famine ceased after that in the land. They sowed and reaped in the whole land, and they

obtained their usual quantity year by year; they lacked nothing.

34 And Joseph lived securely in Egypt and the whole land was under his advice, and his father and all his brothers lived in the land of Goshen and took possession of it.

35 Joseph was very aged, advanced in days, and his two sons Ephraim and Manasseh remained constantly in the house of Jacob, together with the children of the sons of Jacob their brothers, to learn the ways of the Lord and his law.

36 And Jacob and his sons lived in the land of Egypt in the land of Goshen, and they took possession of it, and they were prolific and multiplied in it.

CHAPTER 56

1 Jacob lived in the land of Egypt seventeen years, and the days of Jacob, and the years of his life were a hundred and forty seven years.

2 At that time Jacob was attacked with that illness of which he died and he sent and called for his son Joseph from Egypt, and Joseph his son came from Egypt and came to his father.

3 Jacob said to Joseph and to his sons, Behold I die, and the God of your ancestors will visit you and bring you back to the land which the Lord swore to give to you and to your children after you; now therefore when I am dead, bury me in the cave which is in Machpelah in Hebron in the land of Canaan, near my ancestors.

4 Jacob made his sons swear to bury him in Machpelah, in Hebron, and his sons swore to him concerning this thing.

5 And he commanded them, saying, Serve the Lord your God, for he who delivered your fathers will also deliver you from all trouble.

6 And Jacob said, Call all your children to me, and all the children of Jacob's sons came and sat before him, and Jacob blessed them, and he said to them, The Lord God of your fathers shall grant you a thousand times as much and bless you, and may he give you the blessing of your father Abraham. And all the children of Jacob's sons went forth on that day after he had blessed them.

7 On the next day Jacob again called for his sons and they all assembled

and came to him and sat before him, and Jacob on that day blessed his sons before his death; each man did he bless according to his blessing. So it is written in the book of the law of the Lord pertaining to Israel.

8 And Jacob said to Judah, I know my son that you are a mighty man for your brothers; reign over them, and your sons shall reign over their sons forever.

9 Only teach your sons the bow and all the weapons of war, in order that they may fight the battles of their brother who will rule over his enemies.

10 And Jacob again commanded his sons on that day, saying, Behold I shall this day be gathered to my people; carry me up from Egypt and bury me in the cave of Machpelah as I have commanded you.

11 But take care I pray you that none of your sons carry me, only yourselves, and this is the manner you shall do to me, when you carry my body to go with it to the land of Canaan to bury me:

12 Judah, Issachar and Zebulun shall carry my bier at the eastern side; Reuben, Simeon and Gad at the south; Ephraim, Manasseh and Benjamin at the west; Dan, Asher and Naphtali at the north.

13 Let not Levi carry with you, for he and his sons will carry the ark of the covenant of the Lord with the Israelites in the camp, neither let Joseph my son carry, for as a king so let his glory be; but Ephraim and Manasseh shall be in their stead.

14 Thus shall you do to me when you carry me away; do not neglect anything of all that I command you and it shall come to pass when you do this to me, that the Lord will remember you favorably and your children after you forever.

15 And you my sons, honor each his brother and his relative, and command your children and your children's children after you to serve the Lord God of your ancestors always,

16 In order that you may prolong your days in the land, you and your children and your children's children forever, when you do what is good and upright in the sight of the Lord your God, to follow in all his ways.

17 And you, Joseph my son, forgive I pray you the prongs of your brothers and all their wrongdoings in the injury that they heaped on you, for God intended it for you and your children's benefit.

18 And O my son leave not your brothers to the inhabitants of Egypt, neither hurt their feelings, for behold I consign them to the hand of God and in your hand to guard them from the Egyptians; the sons of Jacob answered their father saying, O, our father, all that you have commanded

us, so will we do; may God only be with us.

19 Jacob said to his sons, So may God be with you when you keep all his ways; turn not from his ways either to the right or the left in performing what is good and upright in his sight.

20 For I know that many and severe troubles will befall you in the latter days in the land, yes, your children and children's children; only serve the Lord and he will save you from all trouble.

21 It shall come to pass when you shall go after God to serve him and will teach your children after you, and your children's children, to know the Lord, then will the Lord raise up to you and your children a servant from among your children; the Lord will deliver you through his hand from all affliction, and bring you out of Egypt and bring you back to the land of your fathers to inherit it securely.

22 Jacob ceased commanding his sons, and he drew his feet into the bed. He died and was gathered to his people.

23 And Joseph fell on his father and he cried out and wept over him and he kissed him, and he called out in a bitter voice, and he said, O my father, my father.

24 His son's wives and all his household came and fell on Jacob, and they wept over him and cried in a very loud voice concerning Jacob.

25 All the sons of Jacob rose up together, and they tore their garments, and they all put sackcloth on their loins; they fell on their faces, and they cast dust on their heads toward the heavens.

26 And the thing was told to Osnath Joseph's wife; she rose up and put on a sack and she with all the Egyptian women came and mourned and wept for Jacob.

27 Also all the people of Egypt who knew Jacob came all on that day when they heard this thing, and all Egypt wept for many days.

28 Also from the land of Canaan the women came to Egypt when they heard that Jacob was dead, and they wept for him in Egypt for seventy days.

29 It came to pass after this that Joseph commanded his servants the doctors to embalm his father with myrrh and frankincense and all manner of incense and perfume, and the doctors embalmed Jacob as Joseph had commanded them.

30 And all the people of Egypt and the elders and all the inhabitants of the land of Goshen wept and mourned over Jacob, and all his sons and the

children of his household lamented and mourned over their father Jacob many days.

31 After the days of his weeping had passed away, at the end of seventy days, Joseph said to Pharaoh, I will go up and bury my father in the land of Canaan as he made me swear, and then I will return.

32 Pharaoh sent Joseph, saying, Go up and bury your father as he said, and as he made you swear; Joseph rose up with all his brothers to go to the land of Canaan to bury their father Jacob as he had commanded them.

33 And Pharaoh commanded that it should be announced throughout Egypt, saying, Whoever goes not up with Joseph and his brothers to the land of Canaan to bury Jacob, shall die.

34 And all Egypt heard of Pharaoh's proclamation, and they all rose up together, and all the servants of Pharaoh, and the elders of his house, and all the elders of the land of Egypt went up with Joseph, and all the officers and nobles of Pharaoh went up as the servants of Joseph; they went to bury Jacob in the land of Canaan.

35 And the sons of Jacob carried the bier on which he lay; according to all that their father commanded them, so did his sons to him.

36 The bier was of pure gold, and it was inlaid round about with onyx stones and bdellium; and the covering of the bier was gold woven work, joined with threads, and over them were hooks of onyx stones and bdellium.

37 And Joseph placed on the head of his father Jacob a large golden crown, and he put a golden rod in his hand, and they surrounded the bier as was the custom of kings during their lives.

38 And all the troops of Egypt went before him in this array; at first all the mighty men of Pharaoh and the mighty men of Joseph, and after them the rest of the inhabitants of Egypt; they were all girded with swords and equipped with coats of mail, and the trappings of war were on them.

39 All the weepers and mourners went at a distance opposite to the bier, going and weeping and lamenting, and the rest of the people went after the bier.

40 Joseph and his household went together near the bier barefooted and weeping, and the rest of Joseph's servants went around him; each man had his ornaments on him and they were all armed with their weapons of war.

41 Fifty of Jacob's servants went in front of the bier and they scattered along the road myrrh and aloes, and all manner of perfume, and all the sons of Jacob that carried the bier walked on the perfumery; the servants

of Jacob went before them spreading the perfume along the road.

42 And Joseph went up with a heavy camp, and they did after this manner every day until they reached the land of Canaan. They came to the threshing floor of Atad, which was on the other side of Jordan, and they mourned an extremely great and heavy mourning in that place.

43 And all the kings of Canaan heard of this thing and they all went forth, each man from his house, thirty-one kings of Canaan; they all came with their men to mourn and weep over Jacob.

44 All these kings observed Jacob's bier, and there Joseph's crown was on it; they also put their crowns on the bier and encircled it with crowns.

45 All these kings made in that place a great and heavy mourning with the sons of Jacob and Egypt over Jacob, for all the kings of Canaan knew the valor of Jacob and his sons.

46 And the report reached Esau, saying, Jacob died in Egypt, and his sons and all Egypt are conveying him to the land of Canaan to bury him.

47 Esau heard this thing, and he was dwelling in mount Seir; he rose up with his sons and all his people and all his household, a people greatly great, and they came to mourn and weep over Jacob.

48 And it came to pass, when Esau came he mourned for his brother Jacob, and all Egypt and all Canaan again rose up and mourned a great mourning with Esau over Jacob in that place

49 Joseph and his brothers brought their father Jacob from that place, and they went to Hebron to bury Jacob in the cave by his fathers.

50 They came to Kireath-arba, to the cave, and as they came Esau stood with his sons against Joseph and his brothers as a hindrance in the cave, saying, Jacob shall not be buried in here, for it belongs to us and to our father.

51 Joseph and his brothers heard the words of Esau's sons, and they were greatly angered, and Joseph approached Esau, saying, What is this thing which they have spoken? Certainly my father Jacob bought it from you for great riches after the death of Isaac, now five and twenty years ago, and also all the land of Canaan he bought from you and from your sons, and your descendants after you.

52 Jacob bought it for his sons and his descendants after him for an inheritance for ever, and why do you speak these things this day?

53 And Esau answered, saying, You speak falsely and utter lies, for I sold not anything belonging to me in all this land, as you say, neither did my

brother Jacob buy what belonged to me in this land.

54 Esau spoke these things in order to deceive Joseph with his words, for Esau knew that Joseph was not present in those days when Esau sold all belonging to him in the land of Canaan to Jacob.

55 Joseph said to Esau, Certainly my father inserted these things with you in the record of purchase, and testified the record with witnesses, and behold it is with us in Egypt.

56 Esau answered, saying to him, Bring the record; all that you will find in the record, so we will do.

57 Joseph called to Naphtali his brother and said, Hurry quickly, stay not, and run I pray you to Egypt and bring all the records; the record of the purchase, the sealed record and the open record, and also all the first records in which all the transactions of the birthright are written, bring with you.

58 You shall bring them to us here, that we may know from them all the words of Esau and his sons which they spoke this day.

59 And Naphtali listened to the voice of Joseph and he hurried and ran to go down to Egypt, and Naphtali was lighter on foot than any of the stags that were on the wilderness, for he could go on ears of corn without crushing them.

60 When Esau saw that Naphtali had gone to fetch the records, he and his sons increased their resistance against the cave, and Esau and all his people rose up against Joseph and his brothers to battle.

61 All the sons of Jacob and the people of Egypt fought with Esau and his men, and the sons of Esau and his people were smitten before the sons of Jacob, and the sons of Jacob killed of Esau's people forty men.

62 Chushim the son of Dan, the son of Jacob, was at that time with Jacob's sons, but he was about a hundred cubits distant from the place of battle, for he remained with the children of Jacob's sons by Jacob's bier to guard it.

63 And Chushim was dumb and deaf, still he understood the voice of consternation among men.

64 And he asked, saying, Why do you not bury the dead, and what is this great consternation? They answered him the words of Esau and his sons and he ran to Esau in the midst of the battle; he killed Esau with a sword; he cut off his head and it sprang to a distance, and Esau fell among the people of the battle.

65 When Chushim did this thing the sons of Jacob prevailed over the sons

of Esau, and the sons of Jacob buried their father Jacob by force in the cave, and the sons of Esau watched it.

66 Jacob was buried in Hebron, in the cave of Machpelah which Abraham had bought from the sons of Heth for the possession of a burial place, and he was buried in very costly garments.

67 No king had such honor paid him as Joseph paid to his father at his death, for he buried him with great honor like the burial of kings.

68 And Joseph and his brothers made a mourning of seven days for their father.

CHAPTER 57

1 It was after this that the sons of Esau waged war with the sons of Jacob, and the sons of Esau fought with the sons of Jacob in Hebron, and Esau was still lying dead and not buried.

2 The battle was heavy between them, and the sons of Esau were smitten before the sons of Jacob, and the sons of Jacob killed of the sons of Esau eighty men, and not one died of the people of the sons of Jacob; the hand of Joseph prevailed over all the people of the sons of Esau, and he took Zepho, the son of Eliphaz, the son of Esau, and fifty of his men captive; he bound them with chains of iron, and gave them into the hands of his servants to bring them to Egypt.

3 It came to pass when the sons of Jacob had taken Zepho and his people captive, all those that remained were greatly afraid for their lives from the house of Esau, that they should also be taken captive; they all fled with Eliphaz the son of Esau and his people, with Esau's body, and they went on their road to Mount Seir.

4 They came to Mount Seir and they buried Esau in Seir, but they had not brought his head with them to Seir, for it was buried in that place where the battle had been in Hebron.

5 And it came to pass when the sons of Esau had fled from before the sons of Jacob, the sons of Jacob pursued them to the borders of Seir, but they did not kill a single man from among them when they pursued them, for Esau's body which they carried with them increased their confusion. So they fled and the sons of Jacob turned back from them and came up to the place where their brothers were in Hebron, and they remained there

on that day, and on the next day until they rested from the battle.

6 It came to pass on the third day they assembled all the sons of Seir the Horite, and they assembled all the children of the east, a multitude of people like the sand of the sea, and they went and came down to Egypt to fight with Joseph and his brothers in order to deliver their brothers.

7 Joseph and all the sons of Jacob heard that the sons of Esau and the children of the east had come on them to do battle in order to deliver their brothers.

8 Joseph and his brothers and the strong men of Egypt went forth and fought in the city of Rameses, and Joseph and his brothers dealt out a tremendous blow among the sons of Esau and the children of the east.

9 They killed of them six hundred thousand men, and they killed among them all the mighty men of the children of Seir the Horite; there were only a few of them left, and they killed also a great many of the children of the east, and of the children of Esau; Eliphaz the son of Esau, and the children of the east all fled before Joseph and his brothers.

10 Joseph and his brothers pursued them until they came to Succoth, and they yet killed of them in Succoth thirty men, and the rest escaped and they fled each to his city.

11 And Joseph and his brothers and the mighty men of Egypt turned back from them with joy and cheerfulness of heart, for they had smitten all their enemies.

12 Zepho the son of Eliphaz and his men were still slaves in Egypt to the sons of Jacob, and their pains increased.

13 When the sons of Esau and the sons of Seir returned to their land, the sons of Seir saw that they had all fallen into the hands of the sons of Jacob and the people of Egypt, on account of the battle of the sons of Esau.

14 And the sons of Seir said to the sons of Esau, You have seen and therefore you know that this camp was on your account, and not one mighty man or an adept one in war remaineth.

15 So now go forth from our land, go from us to the land of Canaan to the land of the dwelling of your fathers; wherefore shall your children inherit the effects of our children in latter days?

16 And the children of Esau would not listen to the children of Seir, and the children of Seir considered to make war with them.

17 The children of Esau sent secretly to Angeas king of Africa, the same is Dinhabah, saying,

18 Send to us some of your men and let them come to us, and we will fight together with the children of Seir the Horite, for they have resolved to fight with us to drive us away from the land.

19 And Angeas king of Dinhabah did so, for he was in those days friendly to the children of Esau, and Angeas sent five hundred valiant infantry to the children of Esau, and eight hundred cavalry.

20 The children of Seir sent to the children of the east and to the children of Midian, saying, You have seen what the children of Esau have done to us, on whose account we are almost all destroyed in their battle with the sons of Jacob.

21 So now come to us and assist us, and we will fight them together; we will drive them from the land and be avenged of the cause of our brothers who died for their sakes in their battle with their brothers the sons of Jacob.

22 And all the children of the east listened to the children of Seir, and they came to them about eight hundred men with drawn swords, and the children of Esau fought with the children of Seir at that time in the wilderness of Paran.

23 The children of Seir won over the sons of Esau, and the children of Seir killed on that day of the children of Esau in that battle about two hundred men of the people of Angeas king of Dinhabah.

24 And on the second day the children of Esau came again to fight a second time with the children of Seir, and the battle was severe on the children of Esau this second time, and it troubled them greatly on account of the children of Seir.

25 And when the children of Esau saw that the children of Seir were more powerful than they were, some men of the children of Esau turned and assisted the children of Seir their enemies.

26 And there fell yet of the people of the children of Esau in the second battle fifty-eight men of the people at Angeas king of Dinhabah.

27 And on the third day the children of Esau heard that some of their brothers had turned from them to fight against them in the second battle; and the children of Esau mourned when they heard this thing.

28 They said, What shall we do to our brothers who turned from us to assist the children of Seir our enemies? And the children of Esau again sent to Angeas king of Dinhabah, saying,

29 Send to us again other men that with them we may fight with the

children of Seir, for they have already twice been stronger than we were.

30 And Angeas again sent to the children of Esau about six hundred valiant men, and they came to assist the children of Esau.

31 In ten days' time the children of Esau again waged war with the children of Seir in the wilderness of Paran, and the battle was very severe on the children of Seir; the children of Esau won this time over the children of Seir, and the children of Seir were smitten before the children of Esau; the children of Esau killed from them about two thousand men.

32 And all the mighty men of the children of Seir died in this battle, and there only remained their young children that were left in their cities.

33 All Midian and the children of the east went themselves in flight from the battle, and they left the children of Seir and fled when they saw that the battle was severe on them; the children of Esau pursued all the children of the east until they reached their land.

34 And the children of Esau killed yet of them about two hundred and fifty men and from the people of the children of Esau there fell in that battle about thirty men, but this evil came on them through their brothers turning from them to assist the children of Seir the Horite; the children of Esau again heard of the evil doings of their brothers, and they again mourned on account of this thing.

35 It came to pass after the battle, the children of Esau turned back and came home to Seir, and the children of Esau killed those who had remained in the land of the children of Seir; they killed also their wives and little ones, they left not a soul alive except fifty young boys and girls whom they allowed to live; the children of Esau did not put them to death, and the boys became their slaves, and the girls they took for wives.

36 The children of Esau lived in Seir in the place of the children of Seir, and they inherited their land and took possession of it.

37 And the children of Esau took all belonging in the land to the children of Seir, also their flocks, their bullocks and their goods, and all belonging to the children of Seir did the children of Esau take. And the children of Esau lived in Seir in the place of the children of Seir to this day, and the children of Esau divided the land into divisions to the five sons of Esau, according to their families.

38 It came to pass in those days that the children of Esau resolved to crown a king over them in the land of which they possessed. And they said to each other, Not so, for he shall reign over us in our land; we shall be under his counsel and he shall fight our battles against our enemies, and they did so.

39 And all the children of Esau swore, saying, that none of their brothers should ever reign over them, but a strange man who is not of their brothers; for the souls of all the children of Esau were embittered every man against his son, brother and friend, on account of the evil they sustained from their brothers when they fought with the children of Seir.

40 So then the sons of Esau swore, saying, from that day forward they would not choose a king from their brothers, but one from a strange land to this day.

41 There was a man there from the people of Angeas king of Dinhabah; his name was Bela the son of Beor, who was a very valiant man, beautiful and admired and wise in all wisdom, and a man of sense and counsel; and there was none of the people of Angeas like him.

42 And all the children of Esau took him and anointed him and they crowned him for a king; they bowed down to him, and said, May the king live, may the king live.

43 They spread out the sheet, and they brought him each man earrings of gold and silver or rings or bracelets, and they made him very rich in silver and in gold, in onyx stones and bdellium, and they made him a royal throne; they placed a regal crown on his head and they built a palace for him and he lived therein, and he became king over all the children of Esau.

44 And the people of Angeas took their wages for their battle from the children of Esau, and they went and returned at that time to their master in Dinhabah.

45 And Bela reigned over the children of Esau thirty years, and the children of Esau lived in the land instead of the children of Seir, and they lived securely in their stead to this day.

CHAPTER 58

1 It came to pass in the thirty-second year of the Israelites going down to Egypt, that is in the seventy-first year of the life of Joseph, in that year died Pharaoh king of Egypt, and Magron his son reigned in his stead.

2 And Pharaoh commanded Joseph before his death to be a father to his son, Magron, and that Magron should be under the care of Joseph and under his counsel.

3 All Egypt consented to this thing that Joseph should be king over them, for all the Egyptians loved Joseph as before, only Magron the son of Pharaoh sat on his father's throne, and he became king in those days in his father's stead.

4 Magron was forty-one years old when he began to reign, and forty years he reigned in Egypt, and all Egypt called his name Pharaoh after the name of his father, as it was their custom to do in Egypt to every king that reigned over them.

5 And it came to pass when Pharaoh reigned in his father's stead, he placed the laws of Egypt and all the affairs of government in the hand of Joseph, as his father had commanded him.

6 Joseph became king over Egypt, for he superintended over all Egypt, and all Egypt was under his care and under his counsel, for all Egypt inclined to Joseph after the death of Pharaoh; they loved him greatly to reign over them.

7 But there were some people among them who did not like him, saying, No stranger shall reign over us. Still the whole government of Egypt was passed in those days onto Joseph, after the death of Pharaoh, he being the regulator, doing as he liked throughout the land without anyone interfering.

8 And all Egypt was under the care of Joseph, and Joseph made war with all his surrounding enemies, and he subdued them; also all the land and all the Philistines, to the borders of Canaan, did Joseph subdue; they were all under his power and they gave a yearly tax to Joseph.

9 Pharaoh king of Egypt sat on his throne in his father's stead, but he was under the control and counsel of Joseph, as he was at first under the control of his father.

10 Neither did he reign but in the land of Egypt only, under the counsel of Joseph, but Joseph reigned over the whole country at that time, from Egypt to the great river Perath.

11 And Joseph was successful in all his ways and the Lord was with him, and the Lord gave Joseph additional wisdom, and honor, and glory, and love toward him in the hearts of the Egyptians and throughout the land; Joseph reigned over the whole country forty years.

12 And all the countries of the Philistines and Canaan and Zidon, and on the other side of Jordan, brought presents to Joseph all his days, and the whole country was in the hands of Joseph, and they brought to him a yearly tribute as it was regulated, for Joseph had fought against all his surrounding enemies and subdued them; the whole country was in the

hands of Joseph, and Joseph sat securely on his throne in Egypt.

13 Also all his brothers the sons of Jacob lived securely in the land, all the days of Joseph, and they were prolific and multiplied greatly in the land; they served the Lord all their days as their father Jacob had commanded them.

14 It came to pass at the end of many days and years, when the children of Esau were dwelling quietly in their land with Bela their king, that the children of Esau were prolific and multiplied in the land; they resolved to go and fight with the sons of Jacob and all Egypt, and to deliver their brother Zepho, the son of Eliphaz, and his men, for they were yet in those days slaves to Joseph.

15 The children of Esau sent to all the children of the east and they made peace with them, and all the children of the east came to them to go with the children of Esau to Egypt to battle.

16 There came also to them of the people of Angeas, king of Dinhabah; they also sent to the children of Ishmael and they also came to them.

17 And all this people assembled and came to Seir to assist the children of Esau in their battle, and this camp was very large and strong with people, numerous as the sand of the sea, about eight hundred thousand men, infantry and cavalry, and all these troops went down to Egypt to fight with the sons of Jacob; they encamped by Rameses.

18 And Joseph went forth with his brothers with the mighty men of Egypt, about six hundred men, and they fought with them in the land of Rameses; the sons of Jacob at that time again fought with the children of Esau, in the fiftieth year of the sons of Jacob going down to Egypt, that is the thirtieth year of the reign of Bela over the children of Esau in Seir.

19 And the Lord gave all the mighty men of Esau and the children of the east into the hand of Joseph and his brothers, and the people of the children of Esau and the children of the east were smitten before Joseph.

20 Of the people of Esau and the children of the east that were slain, there fell before the sons of Jacob about two hundred thousand men, and their king Bela the son of Beor fell with them in the battle. When the children of Esau saw that their king had fallen in battle and was dead, their hands became weak in the combat.

21 Joseph and his brothers and all Egypt were still smiting the people of the house of Esau, and all Esau's people were afraid of the sons of Jacob and fled from before them.

22 Joseph and his brothers and all Egypt pursued them a day's journey,

and they killed yet from them about three hundred men, continuing to strike them in the road; they afterward turned back from them.

23 Joseph and all his brothers returned to Egypt, not one man was missing from them, but of the Egyptians there fell twelve men.

24 And when Joseph returned to Egypt he ordered Zepho and his men to be additionally bound, and they bound them in irons and they increased their grief.

25 All the people of the children of Esau, and the children of the east, returned in shame each to his city, for all the mighty men that were with them had fallen in battle.

26 When the children of Esau saw that their king had died in battle they hurried and took a man from the people of the children of the east; his name was Jobab the son of Zarach, from the land of Botzrah, and they caused him to reign over them instead of Bela their king.

27 Jobab sat on the throne of Bela as king in his stead, and Jobab reigned in Edom over all the children of Esau ten years; the children of Esau went no more to fight with the sons of Jacob from that day forward, for the sons of Esau knew the courage of the sons of Jacob, and they were greatly afraid of them.

28 But from that day forward the children of Esau hated the sons of Jacob, and the hatred and enmity were very strong between them all the days, to this day.

29 And it came to pass after this, at the end of ten years, Jobab, the son of Zarach, from Botzrah, died, and the children of Esau took a man whose name was Chusham, from the land of Teman, and they made him king over them instead of Jobab; Chusham reigned in Edom over all the children of Esau for twenty years.

30 And Joseph, king of Egypt, and his brothers, and all the children of Israel lived securely in Egypt in those days, together with all the children of Joseph and his brothers, having no hindrance or evil accident and the land of Egypt was at that time at rest from war in the days of Joseph and his brothers.

CHAPTER 59

1 These are the names of the sons of Israel who lived in Egypt, who had

come with Jacob; all the sons of Jacob came to Egypt, every man with his household.

2 The children of Leah were Reuben, Simeon, Levi, Judah, Issachar and Zebulun, and their sister Dinah.

3 And the sons of Rachel were Joseph and Benjamin.

4 And the sons of Zilpah, the handmaid of Leah, were Gad and Asher.

5 And the sons of Bilhah, the handmaid of Rachel, were Dan and Naphtali.

6 And these were their descendants that were born to them in the land of Canaan, before they came to Egypt with their father Jacob:

7 The sons of Reuben were Chanoch, Pallu, Chetzron and Carmi.

8 And the sons of Simeon were Jemuel, Jamin, Ohad, Jachin, Zochar and Saul, the son of the Canaanitish woman.

9 And the children of Levi were Gershon, Kehath and Merari, and their sister Jochebed, who was born to them in their going down to Egypt.

10 And the sons of Judah were Er, Onan, Shelah, Perez and Zarach.

11 And Er and Onan died in the land of Canaan; and the sons of Perez were Chezron and Chamul.

12 And the sons of Issachar were Tola, Puvah, Job and Shomron.

13 And the sons of Zebulun were Sered, Elon and Jachleel, and the son of Dan was Chushim.

14 And the sons of Naphtali were Jachzeel, Guni, Jetzer and Shilam.

15 And the sons of Gad were Ziphion, Chaggi, Shuni, Ezbon, Eri, Arodi and Areli.

16 And the children of Asher were Jimnah, Jishvah, Jishvi, Beriah and their sister Serach; and the sons of Beriah were Cheber and Malchiel.

17 And the sons of Benjamin were Bela, Becher, Ashbel, Gera, Naaman, Achi, Rosh, Mupim, Chupim and Ord.

18 And the sons of Joseph that were born to him in Egypt were Manasseh and Ephraim.

19 All the souls that went forth from the loins of Jacob were seventy souls; these are they who came with Jacob their father to Egypt to dwell there: and Joseph and all his brothers lived securely in Egypt, and they ate of the best of Egypt all the days of the life of Joseph.

20 And Joseph lived in the land of Egypt ninety-three years, and Joseph reigned over all Egypt eighty years.

21 When the days of Joseph drew near that he should die, he sent and called for his brothers and all his father's household, and they all came together and sat before him.

22 Joseph said to his brothers and all of his father's household, Behold I die, and God will certainly visit you and bring you up from this land to the land which he swore to your fathers to give to them.

23 And it shall be when God shall visit you to bring you up from here to the land of your fathers, then bring up my bones with you from here.

24 Joseph made the sons of Israel to swear for their descendants after them, saying, God will certainly visit you and you shall bring up my bones with you from here.

25 And it came to pass after this that Joseph died in that year, the seventy-first year of the Israelites going down to Egypt.

26 And Joseph was one hundred and ten years old when he died in the land of Egypt, and all his brothers and all his servants rose up and they embalmed Joseph, as was their custom, and his brothers and all Egypt mourned over him for seventy days.

27 And they put Joseph in a coffin filled with spices and all sorts of perfume; they buried him by the side of the river, that is Sihor, and his sons and all his brothers, and the whole of his father's household made a seven day's mourning for him.

28 It came to pass after the death of Joseph, all the Egyptians began in those days to rule over the children of Israel; Pharaoh, king of Egypt, who reigned in his father's stead, took all the laws of Egypt and conducted the whole government of Egypt under his counsel, and he reigned securely over his people.

CHAPTER 60

1 And when the year came round, being the seventy-second year from the Israelites going down to Egypt, after the death of Joseph, Zepho the son of Eliphaz, the son of Esau, fled from Egypt, he and his men, and they went away.

2 And he came to Africa, which is Dinhabah, to Angeas king of Africa;

Angeas received them with great honor, and he made Zepho the captain of his host.

3 And Zepho found favor in the sight of Angeas and in the sight of his people, and Zepho was captain of the host to Angeas king of Africa for many days.

4 Zepho enticed Angeas king of Africa to collect all his army to go and fight with the Egyptians, and with the sons of Jacob, and to avenge of them the cause of his brothers.

5 But Angeas would not listen to Zepho to do this thing, for Angeas knew the strength of the sons of Jacob, and what they had done to his army in their warfare with the children of Esau.

6 And Zepho was in those days very great in the sight of Angeas and in the sight of all his people, and he continually enticed them to make war against Egypt, but they would not.

7 It came to pass in those days there was in the land of Chittim a man in the city of Puzimna, whose name was Uzu, and he became degenerately deified by the children of Chittim; the man died and had no son, only one daughter whose name was Jania.

8 And the girl was greatly beautiful, admired and intelligent, there was none seen like her for beauty and wisdom throughout the land.

9 And the people of Angeas king of Africa saw her and they came and praised her to him; Angeas sent to the children of Chittim, and he requested to take her to himself for a wife, and the people of Chittim consented to give her to him for a wife.

10 When the messengers of Angeas were going forth from the land of Chittim to take their journey, behold the messengers of Turnus king of Bibentu came to Chittim, for Turnus king of Bibentu also sent his messengers to request Jania for him, to take to himself for a wife, for all his men had also praised her to him, therefore he sent all his servants to her.

11 The servants of Turnus came to Chittim, and they asked for Jania, to be taken to Turnus their king for a wife.

12 The people of Chittim said to them, We cannot give her, because Angeas king of Africa desired her to take her to him for a wife before you came, and that we should give her to him; now therefore we cannot do this thing to deprive Angeas of the girl in order to give her to Turnus.

13 For we are greatly afraid of Angeas that he come in battle against us and destroy us, and Turnus your master will not be able to deliver us from

his hands.

14 When the messengers of Turnus heard all the words of the children of Chittim, they turned back to their master and told him all the words of the children of Chittim.

15 And the children of Chittim sent a memorial to Angeas, saying, Behold Turnus has sent for Jania to take her to him for a wife, and thus have we answered him; we heard that he has collected his whole army to go to war against you, and he intends to pass by the road of Sardunia to fight against your brother Lucus, and after that he will come to fight against you.

16 Angeas heard the words of the children of Chittim which they sent to him in the record, and his anger was set ablaze and he rose up and assembled his whole army and came through the islands of the sea, the road to Sardunia, to his brother Lucus king of Sardunia.

17 Niblos, the son of Lucus, heard that his uncle Angeas was coming, and he went out to meet him with a heavy army, and he kissed him and embraced him, and Niblos said to Angeas, When you ask my father after his welfare, when I shall go with you to fight with Turnus, ask of him to make me captain of his host. Angeas did so, and he came to his brother and his brother came to meet him, and he asked him after his welfare.

18 And Angeas asked his brother Lucus after his welfare, and to make his son Niblos captain of his host, and Lucus did so; Angeas and his brother Lucus rose up and they went toward Turnus to battle, and there was with them a great army and a strong people.

19 And he came in ships, and they came into the province of Ashtorash, and behold Turnus came toward them, for he went forth to Sardunia, and intended to destroy it and afterward to pass on from there to Angeas to fight with him.

20 Angeas and Lucus his brother met Turnus in the valley of Canopia, and the battle was strong and mighty between them in that place.

21 And the battle was severe on Lucus king of Sardunia, and all his army fell, and Niblos his son fell also in that battle.

22 And his uncle Angeas commanded his servants and they made a golden coffin for Niblos and they put him into it, and Angeas again waged battle toward Turnus; Angeas was stronger than he, and he killed him, and he struck all his people with the edge of the sword, and Angeas avenged the cause of Niblos his brother's son and the cause of the army of his brother Lucus.

23 And when Turnus died, the hands of those that survived the battle became weak, and they fled from before Angeas and Lucus his brother.

24 Angeas and his brother Lucus pursued them to the highroad, which is between Alphanu and Romah, and they killed the whole army of Turnus with the edge of the sword.

25 Lucus king of Sardunia commanded his servants that they should make a coffin of brass, and that they should place therein the body of his son Niblos, and they buried him in that place.

26 And they built on it a high tower there on the highroad, and they called its name after the name of Niblos to this day; they also buried Turnus king of Bibentu there in that place with Niblos.

27 And so on the highroad between Alphanu and Romah the grave of Niblos is on one side and the grave of Turnus on the other, and a pavement is between them to this day.

28 When Niblos was buried, Lucus his father returned with his army to his land Sardunia, and Angeas his brother king of Africa went with his people to the city of Bibentu, that is the city of Turnus.

29 And the inhabitants of Bibentu heard of his fame and they were greatly afraid of him; they went forth to meet him with weeping and supplication, and the inhabitants of Bibentu entreated of Angeas not to kill them nor destroy their city; he did so, for Bibentu was in those days reckoned as one of the cities of the children of Chittim; so he did not destroy the city.

30 But from that day forward the troops of the king of Africa would go to Chittim to wreck and rob it, and whenever they went, Zepho the captain of the host of Angeas would go with them.

31 It was after this that Angeas turned with his army and they came to the city of Puzimna, and Angeas then took Jania the daughter of Uzu for a wife and brought her to his city to Africa.

CHAPTER 61

1 It came to pass at that time Pharaoh king of Egypt commanded all his people to make for him a strong palace in Egypt.

2 And he also commanded the sons of Jacob to assist the Egyptians in the

building, and the Egyptians made a beautiful and elegant palace for a royal habitation; he lived there and he renewed his government and he reigned securely.

3 And Zebulun the son of Jacob died in that year, that is the seventy-second year of the going down of the Israelites to Egypt; Zebulun died a hundred and fourteen years old and was put into a coffin and given into the hands of his children.

4 And in the seventy-fifth year his brother Simeon died; he was a hundred and twenty years old at his death, and he was also put into a coffin and given into the hands of his children.

5 Zepho the son of Eliphaz the son of Esau, captain of the host to Angeas king of Dinhabah, was still daily enticing Angeas to prepare for battle to fight with the sons of Jacob in Egypt; Angeas was unwilling to do this thing, for his servants had related to him all the might of the sons of Jacob, what they had done to them in their battle with the children of Esau.

6 And Zepho was in those days daily enticing Angeas to fight with the sons of Jacob.

7 After some time Angeas listened to the words of Zepho and consented to him to fight with the sons of Jacob in Egypt, and Angeas got all his people in order, a people numerous as the sand which is on the seashore, and he formed his resolution to go to Egypt to battle.

8 Among the servants of Angeas was a youth fifteen years old, Balaam the son of Beor was his name and the youth was very wise and understood the art of witchcraft.

9 And Angeas said to Balaam, Summon for us, I pray you, with the witchcraft, that we may know who will succeed in this battle to which we are now proceeding.

10 And Balaam ordered that they should bring him wax, and he made thereof the likeness of chariots and horsemen representing the army of Angeas and the army of Egypt; he put them in the cunningly prepared waters that he had for that purpose, and he took in his hand the boughs of myrtle trees, and he exercised his cunning; he joined them over the water, and there appeared to him in the water the resembling images of the hosts of Angeas falling before the resembling images of the Egyptians and the sons of Jacob.

11 Balaam told this thing to Angeas, and Angeas despaired and did not arm himself to go down to Egypt to battle, and he remained in his city.

12 And when Zepho the son of Eliphaz saw that Angeas despaired of going forth to battle with the Egyptians, Zepho fled from Angeas from

Africa, and he went and came to Chittim.

13 And all the people of Chittim received him with great honor, and they hired him to fight their battles all the days; Zepho became greatly rich in those days, and the troops of the king of Africa still spread themselves in those days; the children of Chittim assembled and went to Mount Cuptizia on account of the troops of Angeas king of Africa who were advancing on them.

14 It was one day that Zepho lost a young heifer and he went to seek it, and he heard it lowing round about the mountain.

15 Zepho went and he saw that there was a large cave at the bottom of the mountain, and there was a great stone there at the entrance of the cave; Zepho split the stone and he came into the cave and he looked and there a large animal was devouring the ox; from the middle upward it resembled a man, and from the middle downward it resembled an animal, and Zepho rose up against the animal and killed it with his swords.

16 The inhabitants of Chittim heard of this thing, and they rejoiced greatly, and said, What shall we do to this man who has slain this animal that devoured our cattle?

17 And they all assembled to consecrate one day in the year to him, and they called the name thereof Zepho after his name; they brought to him drink offerings year after year on that day, and they brought to him gifts.

18 At that time Jania the daughter of Uzu wife of king Angeas became ill, and her illness was heavily felt by Angeas and his officers, and Angeas said to his wise men, What shall I do to Jania and how shall I heal her from her illness? And his wise men said to him, Because the air of our country is not like the air of the land of Chittim, and our water is not like their water, therefore from this has the queen become ill.

19 For through the change of air and water she became ill, and also because in her country she drank only the water which came from Purmah, which her ancestors had brought up with bridges.

20 And Angeas commanded his servants, and they brought to him in vessels of the waters of Purmah belonging to Chittim, and they weighed those waters with all the waters of the land of Africa, and they found those waters lighter than the waters of Africa.

21 Angeas saw this thing, and he commanded all his officers to assemble the hewers of stone in thousands and tens of thousands, and they hewed stone without number; the builders came and they built a greatly strong bridge and they conveyed the spring of water from the land of Chittim to

Africa, and those waters were for Jania the queen and for all her concerns, to drink from and to bake, wash and bathe with, and also to water all offspring from which food can be obtained, and all fruit of the ground.

22 And the king commanded that they should bring of the soil of Chittim in large ships, and they also brought stones to build there; the builders built palaces for Jania the queen, and the queen became healed of her illness.

23 And at the revolution of the year the troops of Africa continued coming to the land of Chittim to rob as usual, and Zepho son of Eliphaz heard their report; he gave orders concerning them and he fought with them and they fled before him, and he delivered the land of Chittim from them.

24 And the children of Chittim saw the bravery of Zepho, and the children of Chittim resolved and made Zepho king over them; he became king over them and while he reigned they went to subdue the children of Tubal, and all the surrounding islands.

25 Their king Zepho led them and they made war with Tubal and the islands, and they subdued them; when they returned from the battle they renewed his government for him, and they built for him a very large palace for his royal habitation and seat, and they made a large throne for him; Zepho reigned over the whole land of Chittim and over the land of Italia fifty years.

CHAPTER 62

1 In that year, being the seventy-ninth year of the Israelites going down to Egypt, Reuben the son of Jacob died, in the land of Egypt; Reuben was a hundred and twenty-five years old when he died and they put him into a coffin, and he was given into the hands of his children.

2 In the eightieth year his brother Dan died; he was a hundred and twenty years at his death, and he was also put into a coffin and given into the hands of his children.

3 In that year Chusham king of Edom died, and after him reigned Hadad the son of Bedad, for thirty-five years; in the eighty-first year Issachar the son of Jacob died in Egypt, and Issachar was a hundred and twenty-two years old at his death; he was put into a coffin in Egypt, and given into the hands of his children.

4 In the eighty-second year Asher his brother died, he was a hundred and twenty-three years old at his death, and he was placed in a coffin in Egypt and given into the hands of his children.

5 In the eighty-third year Gad died; he was a hundred and twenty-five years old at his death, and he was put into a coffin in Egypt and given into the hands of his children.

6 And it came to pass in the eighty-fourth year, that is the fiftieth year of the reign of Hadad, son of Bedad, king of Edom, that Hadad assembled all the children of Esau; he got his whole army in readiness, about four hundred thousand men, and he directed his way to the land of Moab; he went to fight with Moab and to make them subordinate to him.

7 The children of Moab heard this thing, and they were very much afraid; they sent to the children of Midian to assist them in fighting with Hadad, son of Bedad, king of Edom.

8 And Hadad came to the land of Moab, and Moab and the children of Midian went out to meet him; they placed themselves in battle array against him in the field of Moab.

9 Hadad fought with Moab, and there fell of the children of Moab and the children of Midian many slain ones, about two hundred thousand men.

10 The battle was very severe on Moab, and when the children of Moab saw that the battle was so severe, they weakened their hands and turned their backs, and left the children of Midian to carry on the battle.

11 And the children of Midian knew not the intentions of Moab, but they strengthened themselves in battle and fought with Hadad and all his army, and all Midian fell before him.

12 Hadad struck all Midian with a heavy smiting, and he killed them with the edge of the sword, he left none remaining of those who came to assist Moab.

13 When all the children of Midian had perished in battle, and the children at Moab had escaped, Hadad made all Moab at that time subservient to him, and they became under his hand; they gave a yearly tax as it was ordered, and Hadad turned and went back to his land.

14 At the revolution of the year, when the rest of the people of Midian that were in the land heard that all their brothers had fallen in battle with Hadad for the sake of Moab, because the children of Moab had turned their backs in battle and left Midian to fight, then five of the princes of Midian resolved with the rest of their brothers who remained in their land to fight with Moab to avenge the cause of their brothers.

15 The children of Midian sent to all their brothers the children of the east, and all their brothers, all the children of Keturah came to assist Midian to fight with Moab.

16 The children of Moab heard this thing, and they were greatly afraid that all the children of the east had assembled together against them for battle, and they the children of Moab sent a memorial to the land of Edom to Hadad the son of Bedad, saying,

17 Come now to us and assist us and we will strike Midian, for they all assembled together and have come against us with all their brothers the children of the east to battle, to avenge the cause of Midian that fell in battle.

18 Hadad, son of Bedad, king of Edom, went forth with his whole army and went to the land of Moab to fight with Midian, and Midian and the children of the east fought with Moab in the field of Moab, and the battle was very fierce between them.

19 Hadad struck all the children of Midian and the children of the east with the edge of the sword, and Hadad at that time delivered Moab from the hand of Midian; those that remained of Midian and of the children of the east fled before Hadad and his army, and Hadad pursued them to their land and struck them with a very heavy slaughter, and the slain fell in the road.

20 Hadad delivered Moab from the hand of Midian, for all the children of Midian had fallen by the edge of the sword, and Hadad turned and went back to his land.

21 And from that day forth, the children of Midian hated the children of Moab because they had fallen in battle for their sake, and there was a great and mighty enmity between them all the days.

22 And all that were found of Midian in the road of the land of Moab perished by the sword of Moab, and all that were found of Moab in the road of the land of Midian, perished by the sword of Midian; thus did Midian to Moab and Moab to Midian for many days.

23 It came to pass at that time that Judah the son of Jacob died in Egypt, in the eighty-sixth year of Jacob's going down to Egypt, and Judah was a hundred and twenty-nine years old at his death, and they embalmed him and put him into a coffin, and he was given into the hands of his children.

24 And in the eighty-ninth year Naphtali died; he was a hundred and thirty-two years old, and he was put into a coffin and given into the hands of his children.

25 It came to pass in the ninety-first year of the Israelites going down to

Egypt, that is in the thirtieth year of the reign of Zepho the son of Eliphaz, the son of Esau, over the children of Chittim, the children of Africa came upon the children of Chittim to rob them as usual, but they had not come on them for these thirteen years.

26 They came to them in that year, and Zepho the son of Eliphaz went out to them with some of his men and struck them desperately, and the troops of Africa fled from before Zepho and the slain fell before him, and Zepho and his men pursued them, going on and smiting them until they were near to Africa.

27 And Angeas king of Africa heard the thing which Zepho had done, and it troubled him greatly, and Angeas was afraid of Zepho all the days.

CHAPTER 63

1 In the ninety-third year Levi, the son of Jacob, died in Egypt, and Levi was a hundred and thirty-seven years old when he died; they put him into a coffin and he was given into the hands of his children.

2 It came to pass after the death of Levi, when all Egypt saw that the sons of Jacob the brothers of Joseph were dead, all the Egyptians began to afflict the children of Jacob, and to embitter their lives from that day to the day of their going forth from Egypt. They took from their hands all the vineyards and fields which Joseph had given to them, and all the elegant houses in which the people of Israel lived, and all the valuables of Egypt, the Egyptians took all from the sons of Jacob in those days.

3 And the hand of all Egypt became more heavy in those days against the children of Israel, and the Egyptians injured the Israelites until the children of Israel were wearied of their lives on account of the Egyptians.

4 It came to pass in those days, in the hundred and second year of Israel's going down to Egypt, that Pharaoh king of Egypt died, and Melol his son reigned in his stead; all the mighty men of Egypt and all that generation which knew Joseph and his brothers died in those days.

5 And another generation rose up in their stead, which had not known the sons of Jacob and all the good which they had done to them, and all their might in Egypt.

6 And so all Egypt began from that day on to embitter the lives of the sons of Jacob, and to afflict them with all manner of hard labor, because

they had not known their ancestors who had delivered them in the days of the famine.

7 This was also from the Lord for the children of Israel, to benefit them in their latter days in order that all the children of Israel might know the Lord their God.

8 And in order to know the signs and mighty wonders which the Lord would do in Egypt on account of his people Israel, in order that the children of Israel might fear the Lord God of their ancestors, and walk in all his ways, they and their descendants after them all the days.

9 Melol was twenty years old when he began to reign, and he reigned ninety-four years, and all Egypt called his name Pharaoh after the name of his father, as it was their custom to do to every king who reigned over them in Egypt.

10 At that time all the troops of Angeas king of Africa went forth to scatter along the land of Chittim as usual for robbery.

11 Zepho the son of Eliphaz the son of Esau heard their report, and he went forth to meet them with his army, and he fought them there in the road.

12 Zepho struck the troops of the king of Africa with the edge of the sword, and left none remaining of them, and not even one returned to his master in Africa.

13 Angeas heard of this which Zepho the son of Eliphaz had done to all his troops, that he had destroyed them, and Angeas assembled all his troops, all the men of the land of Africa, a people numerous like the sand by the seashore.

14 And Angeas sent to Lucus his brother, saying, Come to me with all your men and help me to strike Zepho and all the children of Chittim who have destroyed my men; Lucus came with his whole army, a very great force, to assist Angeas his brother to fight with Zepho and the children of Chittim.

15 Zepho and the children of Chittim heard this thing, and they were greatly afraid and a great terror fell on their hearts.

16 Zepho also sent a letter to the land of Edom to Hadad the son of Bedad king of Edom and to all the children of Esau, saying,

17 I have heard that Angeas king of Africa is coming to us with his brother for battle against us, and we are greatly afraid of him, for his army is very great, particularly as he comes against us with his brother and his army likewise.

18 Now therefore come up also with me and help me, and we will fight together against Angeas and his brother Lucus, and you will save us out of their hands, but if not, know that we shall all die.

19 And the children of Esau sent a letter to the children of Chittim and to Zepho their king, saying, We cannot fight against Angeas and his people for a covenant of peace has been between us these many years, from the days of Bela the first king, and from the days of Joseph the son of Jacob king of Egypt with whom we fought on the other side of Jordan when he buried his father.

20 When Zepho heard the words of his brothers the children of Esau, he refrained from them, and Zepho was greatly afraid of Angeas.

21 And Angeas and Lucus his brother arrayed all their forces, about eight hundred thousand men, against the children of Chittim.

22 And all the children of Chittim said to Zepho, Pray for us to the God of your ancestors, perhaps he may deliver us from the hand of Angeas and his army, for we have heard that he is a great God and that he delivers all who trust in him.

23 Zepho heard their words, and Zepho sought the Lord and he said,

24 0 Lord God of Abraham and Isaac my ancestors, this day I know that you are a true God, and all the gods of the nations are vain and useless.

25 Remember now this day to me your covenant with Abraham our father, which our ancestors related to us, and do graciously with me this day for the sake of Abraham and Isaac our fathers; save me and the children of Chittim from the hand of the king of Africa who comes against us for battle.

26 And the Lord listened to the voice of Zepho, and he had regard for him on account of Abraham and Isaac, and the Lord delivered Zepho and the children of Chittim from the hand of Angeas and his people.

27 Zepho fought Angeas king of Africa and all his people on that day, and the Lord gave all the people of Angeas into the hands of the children of Chittim.

28 The battle was severe on Angeas, and Zepho struck all the men of Angeas and Lucus his brother with the edge of the sword, and there fell from them to the evening of that day about four hundred thousand men.

29 When Angeas saw that all his men perished, he sent a letter to all the inhabitants of Africa to come to him, to assist him in the battle, and he wrote in the letter, saying, All who are found in Africa let them come to

me from ten years old and upward; let them all come to me, and behold if he comes not he shall die; all that he has, with his whole household, the king will take.

30 All the rest of the inhabitants of Africa were terrified at the words of Angeas, and there went out of the city about three hundred thousand men and boys, from ten years upward, and they came to Angeas.

31 And at the end of ten days Angeas renewed the battle against Zepho and the children of Chittim, and the battle was very great and strong between them.

32 And from the army of Angeas and Lucus, Zepho sent many of the wounded to him about two thousand men, and Sosiphtar the captain of the host of Angeas fell in that battle.

33 And when Sosiphtar had fallen, the African troops turned their backs to flee; they fled, and Angeas and Lucus his brother were with them.

34 Zepho and the children of Chittim pursued them, and they struck them still heavily on the road, about two hundred men; they pursued Azdrubal the son of Angeas who had fled with his father, and they struck twenty of his men in the road, and Azdrubal escaped from the children of Chittim, and they did not kill him.

35 Angeas and Lucus his brother fled with the rest of their men, and they escaped and came into Africa with terror and consternation, and Angeas feared all the days that Zepho the son of Eliphaz would go to war with him.

CHAPTER 64

1 Balaam the son of Beor was at that time with Angeas in the battle, and when he saw that Zepho conquered over Angeas, he fled from there and came to Chittim.

2 And Zepho and the children of Chittim received him with great honor, for Zepho knew Balaam's wisdom, and Zepho gave to Balaam many gifts and he remained with him.

3 When Zepho had returned from the war, he commanded all the children of Chittim to be numbered who had gone into battle with him, and there not one was missing.

4 Zepho rejoiced at this thing, and he renewed his kingdom, and he

made a feast to all his subjects.

5 But Zepho remembered not the Lord and considered not that the Lord had helped him in battle, and that he had delivered him and his people from the hand of the king of Africa; he still walked in the ways of the children of Chittim and the wicked children of Esau to serve other gods which his brothers the children of Esau had taught him; it is therefore said, From the wicked goes forth wickedness.

6 Zepho reigned over all the children of Chittim securely, but knew not the Lord who had delivered him and all his people from the hand of the king of Africa; the troops of Africa came no more to Chittim to rob as usual, for they knew the power of Zepho who had smitten them all at the edge of the sword, so Angeas was afraid of Zepho the son of Eliphaz and the children of Chittim all the days.

7 At that time when Zepho had returned from the war, and when Zepho had seen how he conquered over all the people of Africa and had smitten them in battle at the edge of the sword, then Zepho advised with the children of Chittim to go to Egypt to fight with the sons of Jacob and with Pharaoh king of Egypt.

8 For Zepho heard that the mighty men of Egypt were dead and that Joseph and his brothers the sons of Jacob were dead, and that all their children, the children of Israel, remained in Egypt.

9 Zepho considered to go to fight against them and all Egypt to avenge the cause of his brothers the children of Esau, whom Joseph with his brothers and all Egypt had smitten in the land of Canaan, when they went up to bury Jacob in Hebron.

10 And Zepho sent messengers to Hadad, son of Bedad, king of Edom, and to all his brothers the children of Esau, saying,

11 Did you say that you would not fight against the king of Africa for he is a member of your covenant? Consider that I fought with him and struck him and all his people.

12 Now therefore I have resolved to fight against Egypt and the children of Jacob who are there, and I will be revenged of them for what Joseph, his brothers and ancestors did to us in the land of Canaan when they went up to bury their father in Hebron.

13 Now then if you are willing to come to me to assist me in fighting against them and Egypt, we shall avenge the cause of our brothers.

14 And the children of Esau listened to the words of Zepho, and the children of Esau gathered themselves together, a very great people; they

went to assist Zepho and the children of Chittim in battle.

15 Zepho sent to all the children of the east and to all the children of Ishmael with words like these, and they gathered themselves and came to the assistance of Zepho and the children of Chittim in the war on Egypt.

16 And all these kings, the king of Edom and the children of the east, and all the children of Ishmael, and Zepho the king of Chittim went forth and arrayed all their hosts in Hebron.

17 The camp was very large, extending in length a distance of three days' journey, a people numerous as the sand on the seashore which cannot be counted.

18 And all these kings and their hosts went down and came against all Egypt in battle, and encamped together in the valley of Pathros.

19 All Egypt heard their report and they also gathered themselves together, all the people of the land of Egypt, and of all the cities belonging to Egypt about three hundred thousand men.

20 The men of Egypt sent also to the children of Israel who were in those days in the land of Goshen, to come to them in order to go and fight with these kings.

21 The men of Israel assembled and were about one hundred and fifty men, and they went into battle to assist the Egyptians.

22 The men of Israel and of Egypt went forth, about three hundred thousand men and one hundred and fifty men, and they went toward these kings to battle; they placed themselves outside the land of Goshen opposite Pathros.

23 The Egyptians believed not in Israel to go with them in their camps together for battle, for all the Egyptians said, Perhaps the children of Israel will deliver us into the hand of the children of Esau and Ishmael, for they are their brothers.

24 And all the Egyptians said to the children of Israel, Remain here together in your stand and we will go and fight against the children of Esau and Ishmael; if these kings should gain over us, then you all come together on them and assist us, and the children of Israel did so.

25 Zepho the son of Eliphaz the son of Esau king of Chittim and Hadad the son of Bedad king of Edom and all their camps, and all the children of the east, and children of Ishmael, a people numerous as sand, encamped together in the valley of Pathros opposite Tachpanches.

26 Balaam the son of Beor the Syrian was there in the camp of Zepho, for he came with the children of Chittim to the battle, and Balaam was a man

highly honored in the eyes of Zepho and his men.

27 Zepho said to Balaam, Try by divination for us that we may know who will win the battle, we or the Egyptians.

28 And Balaam rose up and tried the art of divination, and he was skillful in the knowledge of it, but he was confused and the work was destroyed in his hand.

29 And he tried it again but it did not succeed; Balaam despaired of it and left it and did not complete it, for this was from the Lord in order to cause Zepho and his people to fall into the hand of the children of Israel, who had trusted in the Lord, the God of their ancestors, in their war.

30 Zepho and Hadad put their forces in battle array, and all the Egyptians went alone against them, about three hundred thousand men, and not one man of Israel was with them.

31 All the Egyptians fought with these kings opposite Pathros and Tachpanches, and the battle was severe against the Egyptians.

32 The kings were stronger than the Egyptians in that battle, and about one hundred and eighty men of Egypt fell on that day, and about thirty men of the forces of the kings, and all the men of Egypt fled from before the king; so the children of Esau and Ishmael pursued the Egyptians, continuing to strike them to the place where the camp of the children of Israel was.

33 And all the Egyptians cried to the children of Israel, saying, Hurry to us and assist us and save us from the hand of Esau, Ishmael and the children of Chittim.

34 The hundred and fifty men of the children of Israel ran from their station to the camps of these kings, and the children of Israel cried to the Lord their God to deliver them.

35 And the Lord listened to Israel, and the Lord gave all the men of the kings into their hands, and the children of Israel fought against these kings; the children of Israel struck about four thousand of the kings' men.

36 The Lord threw a great consternation into the camp of the kings, so that the fear of the children of Israel fell on them.

37 And all the hosts of the kings fled from before the children of Israel and the children of Israel pursued them continuing to strike them to the borders of the land of Cush.

38 The children of Israel killed of them in the road two thousand men, and of the children of Israel not one fell.

39 When the Egyptians saw that the children of Israel had fought with such few men with the kings, and that the battle was so very severe against them,

40 All the Egyptians were greatly afraid of their lives on account of the strong battle, and all Egypt fled, every man hiding himself from the arrayed forces; they hid themselves in the road, and they left the Israelites to fight alone.

41 And the children of Israel inflicted a terrible blow on the kings' men, and they returned from them after they had driven them to the border of the land of Cush.

42 All Israel knew the thing which the men of Egypt had done to them, that they had fled from them in battle, and had left them to fight alone.

43 So the children of Israel also acted with cunning, and as the children of Israel returned from battle, they found some of the Egyptians in the road and struck them there.

44 And while they killed them, they said to them these words:

45 Why did you go from us and leave us, being a few people to fight against these kings who had many people to strike us, that you might thereby save your own souls?

46 And of some which the Israelites met on the road, the children of Israel spoke to each other, saying, Smite, strike, for he is an Ishmaelite, or an Edomite, or from the children of Chittim; they stood over him and killed him, and they knew that he was an Egyptian.

47 The children of Israel did these things cunningly against the Egyptians because they had deserted in battle and had fled from them.

48 And the children of Israel killed of the men of Egypt in the road in this manner about two hundred men.

49 All the men of Egypt saw the evil which the children of Israel had done to them, so all Egypt feared greatly the children of Israel, for they had seen their great power and that not one man of them had fallen.

50 So all the children of Israel returned with joy on their road to Goshen, and the rest of Egypt returned each man to his place.

CHAPTER 65

1 It came to pass after these things that all the counselors of Pharaoh, king of Egypt, and all the elders of Egypt assembled and came before the king and bowed down to the ground, and they sat before him.

2 And the counselors and elders of Egypt spoke to the king, saying,

3 Behold the people of the children of Israel is greater and mightier than we are, and you know all the evil which they did to us in the road when we returned from battle.

4 And you have also seen their strong power, for this power is to them from their fathers, for only a few men stood up against a people numerous as the sand, and struck them at the edge of the sword; of themselves not one has fallen, so that if they had been numerous they would then have utterly destroyed them.

5 Now therefore give us counsel what to do with them, until we gradually destroy them from among us so they don't become too numerous for us in the land.

6 For if the children of Israel should increase in the land, they will become an obstacle to us; if any war should happen to take place, they with their great strength will join our enemy against us, and fight against us, destroy us from the land and go away from it.

7 So the king answered the elders of Egypt and said to them, This is the plan advised against Israel, from which we will not depart,

8 Consider in the land are Pithom and Rameses, cities unfortified against battle; it's best for you and us to build them, and to fortify them.

9 Now go also and act cunningly toward them, and proclaim a voice in Egypt and in Goshen at the command of the king, saying,

10 All ye men of Egypt, Goshen, Pathros and all their inhabitants! The king has commanded us to build Pithom and Rameses and to fortify them for battle; those among you of all Egypt, of the children of Israel and of all the inhabitants of the cities who are willing to build with us, you shall each have his wages given to him daily at the king's order. So go first and do cunningly and gather yourselves to come to Pithom and Rameses to build.

11 And while you are building, cause an announcement of this kind to be made throughout Egypt every day at the command of the king.

12 When some of the children of Israel shall come to build with you, you shall give them their wages daily for a few days.

13 And after they have built with you for their daily hire, drag yourselves

away from them daily one by one in secret, and then you shall rise up and become their taskmasters and officers; you shall leave them afterward to build without wages; should they refuse, then force them with all your might to build.

14 And if you do this it will be well with us to strengthen our land against the children of Israel, for on account of the fatigue of the building and the work, the children of Israel will decrease, because you will deprive them of their wives day by day.

15 And all the elders of Egypt heard the counsel of the king, and the counsel seemed good in their eyes and in the eyes of the servants of Pharaoh, and in the eyes of all Egypt; they did according to the word of the king.

16 And all the servants went away from the king; they caused an announcement to be made in all Egypt, in Tachpanches and in Goshen, and in all the cities which surrounded Egypt, saying,

17 You have seen what the children of Esau and Ishmael did to us, who came to war against us and wished to destroy us.

18 Now therefore the king commanded us to fortify the land, to build the cities Pithom and Rameses, and to fortify them for battle, if they should again come against us.

19 Whoever of you from all Egypt and from the children of Israel will come to build with us, he shall have his daily wages given by the king, as his command is to us.

20 And when Egypt and all the children of Israel heard all that the servants of Pharaoh had spoken, there came persons from the Egyptians and the children of Israel to build with the servants of Pharaoh, Pithom and Rameses, but none of the children of Levi came with their brothers to build.

21 All the servants of Pharaoh and his princes came at first with deceit to build with all Israel as daily hired laborers, and they gave to Israel their daily hire at the beginning.

22 And the servants of Pharaoh built with all Israel, and were employed in that work with Israel for a month.

23 And at the end of the month, all the servants of Pharaoh began to withdraw secretly from the people of Israel daily.

24 And Israel went on with the work at that time, but they then received their daily wage, because some of the men of Egypt were yet carrying on the work with Israel at that time; therefore the Egyptians gave Israel their

wage in those days in order that they, the Egyptians their fellow-workmen, might also take the pay for their labor.

25 At the end of a year and four months all the Egyptians had withdrawn from the children of Israel, so that the children of Israel were left alone engaged in the work.

26 And after all the Egyptians had withdrawn from the children of Israel they returned and became oppressors and officers over them, and some of them stood over the children of Israel as task masters, to receive from them all that they gave them for the pay of their labor.

27 And the Egyptians did in this manner to the children of Israel day by day, in order to afflict them in their work.

28 And all the children of Israel were alone engaged in the labor, and the Egyptians refrained from giving any pay to the children of Israel from that time forward.

29 When some of the men of Israel refused to work on account of the wages not being given to them, the exactors and the servants of Pharaoh oppressed them and struck them with heavy blows, and made them return by force to labor with their brothers; thus did all the Egyptians to the children of Israel all the days.

30 And all the children of Israel were greatly afraid of the Egyptians in this matter, and all the children of Israel returned and worked alone without pay.

31 The children of Israel built Pithom and Rameses; all the children of Israel did the work, some making bricks, and some building, and the children of Israel built and fortified all the land of Egypt and its walls. The children of Israel were engaged in work for many years, until the time came when the Lord remembered them and brought them out of Egypt.

32 But the children of Levi were not employed in the work with their brothers of Israel from the beginning to the day of their going forth from Egypt.

33 For all the children of Levi knew that the Egyptians had spoken all these words with deceit to the Israelites, therefore the children of Levi refrained from approaching the work with their brothers.

34 The Egyptians did not direct their attention to make the children of Levi work afterward, since they had not been with their brothers at the beginning, therefore the Egyptians left them alone.

35 And the hands of the men of Egypt were directed with continued

severity against the children of Israel in that work, and the Egyptians made the children of Israel work with rigor.

36 The Egyptians embittered the lives of the children of Israel with hard work in mortar and bricks, and also in all manner of work in the field.

37 The children of Israel called Melol the king of Egypt "Meror, king of Egypt," because in his days the Egyptians had embittered their lives with all manner of work.

38 And all the work wherein the Egyptians made the children of Israel labor, they exacted with rigor, in order to afflict the children of Israel. But the more they afflicted them, the more they increased and grew, and the Egyptians were grieved because of the children of Israel.

CHAPTER 66

1 At that time Hadad the son of Bedad king of Edom died; Samlah from Mesrekah, from the country of the children of the east, reigned in his place.

2 In the thirteenth year of the reign of Pharaoh king of Egypt, which was the hundred and twenty-fifth year of the Israelites going down into Egypt, Samlah had reigned over Edom eighteen years.

3 And when he reigned, he brought forth his army to go and fight against Zepho the son of Eliphaz and the children of Chittim, because they had made war against Angeas king of Africa, and they destroyed his whole army.

4 But he did not engage with him, for the children of Esau prevented him, saying, he was their brother; so Samlah listened to the voice of the children of Esau and turned back with all his forces to the land of Edom, and did not proceed to fight against Zepho the son of Eliphaz.

5 And Pharaoh king of Egypt heard this thing, saying, Samlah king of Edom has resolved to fight the children of Chittim, and afterward he will come to fight against Egypt.

6 When the Egyptians heard this matter, they increased the labor on the children of Israel, that the Israelites should do to them as they did to them in their war with the children of Esau in the days of Hadad.

7 So the Egyptians said to the children of Israel, Hurry and do your work, and finish your task, and strengthen the land, should the children of Esau

your brothers come to fight against us, for on your account will they come against us.

8 And the children of Israel did the work of the men of Egypt day by day, and the Egyptians afflicted the children of Israel in order to lessen them in the land.

9 But as the Egyptians increased the labor on the children of Israel, so did the children of Israel increase and reproduce, and all Egypt was filled with the children of Israel.

10 And in the hundred and twenty-fifth year of Israel's going down into Egypt, all the Egyptians saw that their counsel did not succeed against Israel, but that they increased and grew and the land of Egypt and the land of Goshen were filled with the children of Israel.

11 So all the elders of Egypt and its wise men came before the king and bowed down to him and sat before him.

12 And all the elders of Egypt and the wise men there said to the king, May the king live forever; you did counsel us the counsel against the children of Israel, and we did to them according to the word of the king.

13 But in proportion to the increase of the labor so do they increase and grow in the land, and look the whole country is filled with them.

14 So now our lord and king, the eyes of all Egypt are on you to give them advice with your wisdom, by which they may rule over Israel to destroy them, or to diminish them from the land; the king answered them saying, Give your counsel in this matter that we may know what to do to them.

15 And an officer, one of the king's counselors, whose name was Job, from Mesopotamia, in the land of Uz, answered the king, saying,

16 If it please the king, let him hear the counsel of his servant; the king said to him, Speak.

17 And Job spoke before the king, the princes, and before all the elders of Egypt, saying,

18 Behold the counsel of the king which he advised formerly respecting the labor of the children of Israel is very good, and you must not remove from them that labor forever.

19 But this is the advice counselled by which you may lessen them, if it seems good to the king to afflict them.

20 Behold we have feared war for a long time, and we said, When Israel

becomes prolific in the land, they will drive us from the land if a war would take place.

21 If it please the king, let a royal decree go forth, and let it be written in the laws of Egypt which shall not be revoked, that every male child born to the Israelites, his blood shall be spilled on the ground.

22 And by your doing this, when all the male children of Israel will have died, the evil of their wars will cease; let the king do so and send for all the Hebrew midwives and order them in this matter to execute it. So the thing pleased the king and the prince; the king did according to the word of Job.

23 The king sent for the Hebrew midwives to be called, of which the name of one was Shephrah, and the name of the other Puah.

24 And the midwives came before the king, and stood in his presence.

25 the king said to them, When you do the office of a midwife to the Hebrew women, and see them on the stools, if it be a son then you shall kill him, but if it be a daughter then she shall live.

26 But if you will not do this thing, then will I burn you up and all your houses with fire.

27 But the midwives feared God and did not listen to the king of Egypt nor to his words; when the Hebrew women brought forth to the midwife son or daughter, then did the midwife do all that was necessary to the child and let it live; thus did the midwives all the days.

28 And this thing was told to the king, and he sent and called for the midwives and he said to them, Why have you done this thing and have saved the children alive?

29 And the midwives answered and spoke together before the king, saying,

30 Let not the king think that the Hebrew women are as the Egyptian women, for all the children of Israel are vigorous, and before the midwife comes to them they are delivered, and as for us your handmaids, for many days no Hebrew woman has brought forth on us, for all the Hebrew women are their own midwives, because they are vigorous.

31 And Pharaoh heard their words and believed them in this matter, and the midwives went away from the king, and God dealt well with them; the people multiplied and increased greatly.

CHAPTER 67

1 There was a man in the land of Egypt of the children of Levi, whose name was Amram, the son of Kehath, the son of Levi, the son of Israel.

2 And this man went and took a wife, namely Jochebed the daughter of Levi his father's sister, and she was one hundred and twenty-six years old, and he came to her.

3 And the woman conceived and gave birth to a daughter, and she called her name Miriam, because in those days the Egyptians had embittered the lives of the children of Israel.

4 She conceived again and gave birth to a son and she called his name Aaron, for in the days of her conception, Pharaoh began to spill the blood of the male children of Israel.

5 In those days Zepho died, the son of Eliphaz, son of Esau, king of Chittim; Janeas reigned in his stead.

6 And the time that Zepho reigned over the children of Chittim was fifty years, and he died and was buried in the city of Nabna in the land of Chittim.

7 And Janeas, one of the mighty men of the children of Chittim, reigned after him for fifty years.

8 It was after the death of the king of Chittim that Balaam the son of Beor fled from the land of Chittim, and he went and came to Egypt to Pharaoh king of Egypt.

9 Pharaoh received him with great honor for he had heard of his wisdom, and he gave him presents and made him a counsellor and praised him.

10 Balaam lived in Egypt, in honor with all the nobles of the king, and the nobles exalted him, because they all coveted to learn his wisdom.

11 And in the hundred and thirtieth year of Israel's going down to Egypt, Pharaoh dreamed that he was sitting on his kingly throne, and lifted up his eyes and saw an old man standing before him; there were scales in the hands of the old man, such scales as are used by merchants.

12 And the old man took the scales and hung them before Pharaoh.

13 And the old man took all the elders of Egypt and all its nobles and

great men, and he tied them together and put them in one scale.

14 And he took a milk kid and put it into the other scale, and the kid's weight surpassed all.

15 And Pharaoh was astonished at this dreadful vision, why the kid should surpass all, and Pharaoh awoke and behold it was a dream.

16 Pharaoh rose up early in the morning and called all his servants and related to them the dream, and the men were greatly afraid.

17 And the king said to all his wise men, Interpret I pray you the dream which I dreamed, that I may know it.

18 Balaam the son of Beor answered the king and said to him, This means nothing else but a great evil that will spring up against Egypt in the latter days.

19 For a son will be born to Israel who will destroy all Egypt and its inhabitants, and bring forth the Israelites from Egypt with a mighty hand.

20 Now therefore, O king, take counsel on this matter, that you may destroy the hope of the children of Israel and their expectation, before this evil arises against Egypt.

21 And the king said to Balaam, And what shall we do to Israel? Certainly after a certain manner did we at first counsel against them and could not succeed over them.

22 So now you also give advice against them by which we may succeed over them.

23 Balaam answered the king, saying, Send now and call your two counselors, and we will see what their advice is on this matter and afterward your servant will speak.

24 And the king sent and called his two counselors Reuel the Midianite and Job the Uzite, and they came and sat before the king.

25 And the king said to them, Behold you have both heard the dream which I have dreamed, and the interpretation thereof; so now give counsel and know and see what is to be done to the children of Israel, whereby we may succeed over them, before their evil will spring up against us.

26 And Reuel the Midianite answered the king and said, May the king live, may the king live forever.

27 If it seems good to the king, let him desist from the Hebrews and leave them, and let him not stretch forth his hand against them.

28 For these are they whom the Lord chose in days of old, and took as the

lot of his inheritance from among all the nations of the earth and the kings of the earth; and who is there that stretched his hand against them with punishment, of whom their God was not avenged?

29 Certainly you know that when Abraham went down to Egypt, Pharaoh, the former king of Egypt, saw Sarah his wife, and took her for a wife, because Abraham said, She is my sister, for he was afraid that the men of Egypt should kill him on account of his wife.

30 And when the king of Egypt had taken Sarah then God struck him and his household with heavy plagues, until he restored to Abraham his wife Sarah, then was he healed.

31 And Abimelech the Gerarite, king of the Philistines, God punished on account of Sarah wife of Abraham, in stopping up every womb from man to beast.

32 When their God came to Abimelech in the dream of night and terrified him in order that he might restore to Abraham Sarah whom he had taken, afterward all the people of Gerar were punished on account of Sarah, and Abraham prayed to his God for them, and he was entreated of him, and he healed them.

33 And Abimelech feared all this evil that came on him and his people, and he returned to Abraham his wife Sarah, and gave him many gifts with her.

34 He did so also to Isaac when he had driven him from Gerar, and God had done wonderful things to him, that all the water courses of Gerar were dried up and their productive trees did not bring forth.

35 Until Abimelech of Gerar, and Ahuzzath one of his friends, and Pichol the captain of his host, went to him and they bent and bowed down before him to the ground.

36 They requested of him to petition for them, and he prayed to the Lord for them, and the Lord was entreated of him and he healed them.

37 Jacob also, the plain man, was delivered through his integrity from the hand of his brother Esau, and the hand of Laban the Syrian his mother's brother, who had sought his life; likewise from the hand of all the kings of Canaan who had come together against him and his children to destroy them, the Lord delivered them out of their hands, that they turned on them and struck them, for who had ever stretched forth his hand against them without penalty?

38 Certainly Pharaoh the former, your father's father, raised Joseph the son of Jacob above all the princes of the land of Egypt when he saw his

wisdom, for through his wisdom he rescued all the inhabitants of the land from the famine.

39 After which he ordered Jacob and his children to come down to Egypt in order that through their virtue, the land of Egypt and the land of Goshen might be delivered from the famine.

40 So now if it seems good in your eyes, cease from destroying the children of Israel, but if it be not your will that they shall dwell in Egypt, send them forth from here that they may go to the land of Canaan, the land where their ancestors sojourned.

41 And when Pharaoh heard the words of Jethro he was very angry with him, so that he rose with shame from the king's presence and went to Midian, his land, and took Joseph's stick with him.

42 And the king said to Job the Uzite, What do you say Job, and what is your advice respecting the Hebrews?

43 So Job said to the king, Behold all the inhabitants of the land are in your power, let the king do as it seems good in his eyes.

44 And the king said to Balaam, What do you say, Balaam? Speak your word that we may hear it.

45 And Balaam said to the king, Of all that the king has counselled against the Hebrews will they be delivered, and the king will not be able to prevail over them with any counsel.

46 For if you think to lessen them by the flaming fire, you cannot prevail over them, for certainly their God delivered Abraham their father from Ur of the Chaldeans; if you think to destroy them with a sword, certainly Isaac their father was delivered from it and a ram was placed in his stead.

47 And if with hard and rigorous labor you think to lessen them, you will not prevail even in this, for their father Jacob served Laban in all manner of hard work and prospered.

48 Now therefore, O King, hear my words, for this is the counsel which is counselled against them, by which you will prevail over them, and from which you should not depart:

49 If it please the king let him order all their children which shall be born from this day forward to be thrown into the water, for by this can you wipe away their name, for none of them nor of their fathers were tried in this manner.

50 And the king heard the words of Balaam, and the thing pleased the king and the princes, and the king did according to the word of Balaam.

51 The king ordered an announcement to be issued and a law to be made throughout the land of Egypt, saying, Every male child born to the Hebrews from this day forward shall be thrown into the water.

52 Pharaoh called to all his servants, saying, Go now and search throughout the land of Goshen where the children of Israel are, and see that every son born to the Hebrews will be cast into the river, but every daughter you shall let live.

53 And when the children of Israel heard this thing which Pharaoh had commanded, to cast their male children into the river, some of the people separated from their wives and others adhered to them.

54 And from that day forward, when the time of delivery arrived to those women of Israel who had remained with their husbands, they went to the field to bring forth there, and they brought forth in the field and left their children on the field and returned home.

55 And the Lord who had sworn to their ancestors to reproduce them sent one of his ministering angels which are in heaven to wash each child in water, to anoint and swathe it and to put into its hands two smooth stones from one of which it sucked milk and from the other honey, and he caused its hair to grow to its knees, by which it might cover itself; to comfort it and to cleave to it through his compassion for it.

56 And when God had compassion over them and had desired to reproduce them on the face of the land, he ordered his earth to receive them to be preserved therein till the time of their growing up, after which the earth opened its mouth and vomited them forth and they sprouted forth from the city like the herb of the earth, and the grass of the forest, and they returned each to his family and to his father's house, and they remained with them.

57 And the babes of the children of Israel were on the earth like the herb of the field, through God's grace to them.

58 And when all the Egyptians saw this thing, they went forth, each to his field with his yoke of oxen and his ploughshare, and they plowed it up as one ploughs the earth at offspring time.

59 And when they plowed they were unable to hurt the infants of the children of Israel, so the people increased and thrived greatly.

60 And Pharaoh ordered his officers daily to go to Goshen to seek for the babes of the children of Israel.

61 And when they had sought and found one, they took it from its mother's bosom by force, and threw it into the river, but the female child

they left with its mother; thus did the Egyptians do to the Israelites all the days.

CHAPTER 68

1 It was at that time the spirit of God was on Miriam the daughter of Amram the sister of Aaron, and she went forth and prophesied about the house, saying, Behold a son will be born to us from my father and mother this time, and he will save Israel from the hands of Egypt.

2 And when Amram heard the words of his daughter, he went and took his wife back to the house, after he had driven her away at the time when Pharaoh ordered every male child of the house of Jacob to be thrown into the water.

3 So Amram took Jochebed his wife, three years after he had driven her away, and he came to her and she conceived.

4 At the end of seven months from her conception she brought forth a son, and the whole house was filled with great light as of the light of the sun and moon at the time of their shining.

5 And when the woman saw the child that it was good and pleasing to the sight, she hid him for three months in an inner room.

6 In those days the Egyptians conspired to destroy all the Hebrews there.

7 And the Egyptian women went to Goshen where the children of Israel were, and they carried their young ones on their shoulders, their babes who could not yet speak.

8 And in those days, when the women of the children of Israel brought forth, each woman had hidden her son from the Egyptians, that the Egyptians might not know of their bringing forth, and might not destroy them from the land.

9 And the Egyptian women came to Goshen and their children who could not speak were on their shoulders, and when an Egyptian woman came into the house of a Hebrew woman her babe began to cry.

10 And when it cried the child that was in the inner room answered it, so the Egyptian women went and told it at the house of Pharaoh.

11 And Pharaoh sent his officers to take the children and kill them; thus did the Egyptians to the Hebrew women all the days.

12 And it was at that time, about three months from Jochebed's concealment of her son, that the thing was known in Pharaoh's house.

13 And the woman hurried to take away her son before the officers came, and she took for him an ark of bulrushes, and daubed it with slime and with pitch and put the child therein, and she laid it in the flags by the river's brink.

14 And his sister Miriam stood afar off to learn what would be done to him, and what would become of her words.

15 And God sent forth at that time a terrible heat in the land of Egypt, which burned up the flesh of man like the sun in his circuit, and it greatly oppressed the Egyptians.

16 And all the Egyptians went down to bathe in the river on account of the consuming heat which burned up their flesh.

17 And Bathia, the daughter of Pharaoh, went also to bathe in the river, owing to the consuming heat; her maidens walked at the riverside, and all the women of Egypt as well.

18 Bathia lifted up her eyes to the river and she saw the ark on the water, and sent her maid to

fetch it.

19 She opened it and saw the child, and then the babe wept, and she had compassion on him and said, This is one of the Hebrew children.

20 And all the women of Egypt walking on the riverside desired to give him suck, but he would not suck, for this thing was from the Lord in order to restore him to his mother's breast.

21 And Miriam his sister was at that time among the Egyptian women at the riverside, and she saw this thing and said to Pharaoh's daughter, Shall I go and fetch a nurse of the Hebrew women, that she may nurse the child for you?

22 And Pharaoh's daughter said to her, Go, and the young woman went and called the child's mother.

23 And Pharaoh's daughter said to Jochebed, Take this child away and suckle it for me, and I will pay you your wages, two bits of silver daily; and the woman took the child and nursed it.

24 At the end of two years, when the child grew up, she brought him to the daughter of Pharaoh, and he was to her as a son; she called his name Moses, for she said, Because I drew him out of the water.

25 And Amram his father called his name Chabar, for he said, It was for him that he associated with his wife whom he had turned away.

26 And Jochebed his mother called his name Jekuthiel, Because, she said, I have hoped for him to the Almighty, and God restored him to me.

27 And Miriam his sister called him Jered, for she descended after him to the river to learn what would happen to him.

28 And Aaron his brother called his name Abi Zanuch, saying, My father left my mother and returned to her on his account.

29 And Kehath the father of Amram called his name Abigdor, because on his account did God repair the breach of the house of Jacob, that they could no longer throw their male children into the water.

30 And their nurse called him Abi Socho, saying, In his tabernacle was he hidden for three months, on account of the children of Ham.

31 And all Israel called his name Shemaiah, son of Nethanel, for they said, In his days has God heard their cries and rescued them from their oppressors.

32 And Moses was in Pharaoh's house and was to Bathia, Pharaoh's daughter, as a son, and Moses grew up among the king's children.

CHAPTER 69

1 The king of Edom died in those days, in the eighteenth year of his reign, and was buried in his temple which he had built for himself as his royal residence in the land of Edom.

2 The children of Esau sent to Pethor, which is on the river, and they fetched from there a young man of beautiful eyes and handsome, whose name was Saul; they made him king over them in the place of Samlah.

3 And Saul reigned over all the children of Esau in the land of Edom for forty years.

4 When Pharaoh king of Egypt saw that the counsel which Balaam had advised respecting the children of Israel did not succeed, but that still they were prolific, multiplied and increased throughout the land of Egypt,

5 Then Pharaoh commanded in those days that a proclamation should be issued throughout Egypt to the children of Israel, saying, No man shall lessen anything of his daily labor.

6 And the man who shall be found deficient in his labor which he performs daily, whether in mortar or in bricks, then his youngest son shall be put in their place.

7 And the labor of Egypt strengthened on the children of Israel in those days, and if one brick was deficient in any man's daily labor, the Egyptians took his youngest boy by force from his mother and put him into the building in the place of the brick which his father had left wanting.

8 And the men of Egypt did so to all the children of Israel day by day, all the days for a long period.

9 But the tribe of Levi did not at that time work with the Israelites their brothers from the beginning, for the children of Levi knew the cunning of the Egyptians which they exercised at first toward the Israelites.

CHAPTER 70

1 In the third year from the birth of Moses, Pharaoh was sitting at a banquet when Alparanith the queen was sitting at his right and Bathia at his left, and the lad Moses was lying on her bosom, and Balaam the son of Beor with his two sons, and all the princes of the kingdom were sitting at table in the king's presence.

2 And the lad stretched forth his hand on the king's head, and took the crown from the king's head and placed it on his own head.

3 When the king and princes saw the work which the boy had done, the king and princes were terrified, and one man to his neighbor expressed astonishment.

4 And the king said to the princes who were before him at table, What speak you and what say you, O ye princes, in this matter, and what is to be the judgment against the boy on account of this act?

5 And Balaam the son of Beor the magician answered before the king and princes and said, Remember now, O my lord and king, the dream which you did dream many days ago, and that which your servant interpreted to you.

6 Now therefore this is a child from the Hebrew children in whom is the spirit of God, and let not my lord the king imagine that this youngster did this thing without knowledge.

7 For he is a Hebrew boy, and wisdom and understanding are with him, although he is yet a child; with wisdom has he done this and chosen to himself the kingdom of Egypt.

8 For this is the manner of all the Hebrews to deceive kings and their nobles, to do all these things cunningly, in order to make the kings of the earth and their men tremble.

9 Certainly you know that Abraham their father acted thus, who deceived the army of Nimrod king of Babel and Abimelech king of Gerar, and that he possessed himself of the land of the children of Heth and all the kingdoms of Canaan.

10 And that he descended into Egypt and said of Sarah his wife, she is my sister, in order to mislead Egypt and her king.

11 His son Isaac also did so when he went to Gerar and lived there, and his strength prevailed over the army of Abimelech king of the Philistines.

12 He also thought of making the kingdom of the Philistines stumble, in saying that Rebecca his wife was his sister.

13 Jacob also dealt treacherously with his brother and took from his hand his birthright and his blessing.

14 He went then to Padan-aram to the house of Laban his mother's brother, and cunningly obtained from him his daughter, his cattle and all belonging to him, and fled away and returned to the land of Canaan to his father.

15 His sons sold their brother Joseph, who went down into Egypt and became a slave, and was placed in the prison house for twelve years.

16 Until the former Pharaoh dreamed dreams and withdrew him from the prison house, and magnified him above all the princes in Egypt on account of his interpreting his dreams to him.

17 And when God caused a famine throughout the land he sent for and brought his father and all his brothers, and all of his father's household, and supported them without price or reward, and bought the Egyptians for slaves.

18 Now therefore my lord king behold this child has risen up in their stead in Egypt, to do according to their deeds and to trifle with every king, prince and judge.

19 If it please the king, let us now spill his blood on the ground, that he shall not grow up and take away the government from your hand, and then the hope of Egypt perish after he shall have reigned.

20 And Balaam said to the king, Let us moreover call for all the judges of Egypt and the wise men thereof, and let us know if the judgment of death is due to this boy as you did say; then we will kill him.

21 Pharaoh sent and called for all the wise men of Egypt and they came before the king; an angel of the Lord came among them, and he was like one of the wise men of Egypt.

22 And the king said to the wise men, Certainly you have heard what this Hebrew boy who is in the house has done, and thus has Balaam judged in the matter.

23 Now you judge also and see what is due to the boy for the act he has committed.

24 And the angel, who seemed like one of the wise men of Pharaoh, answered and said as follows, before all the wise men of Egypt and before the king and the princes:

25 If it please the king let the king send for men who shall bring before him an onyx stone and a coal of fire, and place them before the child; if the child shall stretch forth his hand and take the onyx stone, then shall we know that with wisdom has the youth done all that he has done, and we must kill him.

26 But if he stretches forth his hand on the coal, then shall we know that it was not with knowledge that he did this thing, and he shall live.

27 The thing seemed good in the eyes of the king and the princes, so the king did according to the word of the angel of the Lord.

28 The king ordered the onyx stone and coal to be brought and placed before Moses.

29 They placed the boy before them, and the lad endeavored to stretch forth his hand to the onyx stone, but the angel of the Lord took his hand and placed it on the coal, and the coal became extinguished in his hand; he lifted it up and put it into his mouth, and burned part of his lips and part of his tongue, and he became swollen in mouth and tongue.

30 And when the king and princes saw this, they knew that Moses had not acted with wisdom in taking off the crown from the king's head.

31 So the king and princes refrained from slaying the child. Moses remained in Pharaoh's house, growing up, and the Lord was with him.

32 And while the boy was in the king's house, he was robed in purple and he grew among the children of the king.

33 And when Moses grew up in the king's house, Bathia the daughter of Pharaoh considered him as a son, and all the household of Pharaoh honored him, and all the men of Egypt were afraid of him.

34 And he daily went forth and came into the land of Goshen where his brothers the children of Israel were, and Moses saw them daily in shortness of breath and hard labor.

35 And Moses asked them, saying, How is this labor assigned to you day by day?

36 And they told him all that had befallen them, and all the injunctions which Pharaoh had put on them before his birth.

37 And they told him all the counsels which Balaam the son of Beor had counselled against them, and what he had also counselled against him in order to kill him when he had taken the king's crown from off his head.

38 And when Moses heard these things his anger was set ablaze against Balaam, and he sought to kill him, and he was in ambush for him day by day.

39 Balaam was afraid of Moses, and he and his two sons rose up and went forth from Egypt, and they fled and delivered their souls and took themselves to the land of Cush to Kikianus, king of Cush.

40 And Moses was in the king's house going out and coming in; the Lord gave him favor in the eyes of Pharaoh and in the eyes of all his servants, and in the eyes of all the people of Egypt, and they loved Moses greatly.

41 The day arrived when Moses went to Goshen to see his brothers that he saw the children of Israel in their burdens and hard labor, and Moses was grieved on their account.

42 And Moses returned to Egypt and came to the house of Pharaoh, and came before the king, and Moses bowed down before the king.

43 And Moses said to Pharaoh, I pray you my lord, I have come to seek a small request from you, turn not away my face empty; and Pharaoh said to him, Speak.

44 And Moses said to Pharaoh, Let there be given to your servants the children of Israel who are in Goshen, one day to rest therein from their labor.

45 And the king answered Moses and said, Behold I have lifted up your face in this thing to grant your request.

46 And Pharaoh ordered an announcement to be issued throughout Egypt and Goshen, saying,

47 To you, all the children of Israel, thus says the king, for six days you shall do your work and labor, but on the seventh day you shall rest and shall not preform any work, thus shall you do all the days as the king and Moses the son of Bathia have commanded.

48 And Moses rejoiced at this thing which the king had granted to him, and all the children of Israel did as Moses ordered them.

49 For this thing was from the Lord to the children of Israel, for the Lord had begun to remember the children of Israel to save them for the sake of their fathers.

50 And the Lord was with Moses and his fame went throughout Egypt.

51 And Moses became great in the eyes of all the Egyptians, and in the eyes of all the children of Israel, seeking good for his people Israel and speaking words of peace regarding them to the king.

CHAPTER 71

1 When Moses was eighteen years old he desired to see his father and mother and he went to them at Goshen, and when Moses had come near Goshen he came to the place where the children of Israel were engaged in work, and he observed their burdens, and he saw an Egyptian smiting one of his Hebrew brothers.

2 When the man who was beaten saw Moses he ran to him for help, for the man Moses was greatly respected in the house of Pharaoh, and he said to him, My lord attend to me; this Egyptian came to my house in the night, bound me, and came to my wife in my presence, and now he seeks to take my life away.

3 And when Moses heard this wicked thing, his anger was set ablaze against the Egyptian, and he turned this way and the other, and when he saw there was no man there he struck the Egyptian and hid him in the sand, and delivered the Hebrew from the hand of him that struck him.

4 And the Hebrew went to his house, and Moses returned to his home, and went forth and came back to the king's house.

5 And when the man had returned home, he thought of leaving his wife, for it was not right in the house of Jacob for any man to come to his wife after she had been defiled.

6 The woman went and told her brothers, and the woman's brothers sought to kill him, and he fled to his house and escaped.

7 On the second day Moses went forth to his brothers, and looked and saw two men were quarreling; he said to the wicked one, Why do you strike your neighbor?

8 And he answered him and said to him, Who has set you for a prince and judge over us? Do you think to kill me as you did kill the Egyptian? And Moses was afraid and said, Certainly the thing is known?

9 And Pharaoh heard of this affair, and he ordered Moses to be slain, so God sent his angel and he appeared to Pharaoh in the likeness of a captain of the guard.

10 And the angel of the Lord took the sword from the hand of the captain of the guard, and took his head off with it, for the likeness of the captain of the guard was turned into the likeness of Moses.

11 And the angel of the Lord took hold of the right hand of Moses, and brought him forth from Egypt, and placed him outside the borders of Egypt, a distance of forty days' journey.

12 And Aaron his brother alone remained in the land of Egypt, and he prophesied to the children of Israel, saying,

13 Thus says the Lord God of your ancestors, Throw away, each man, the abominations of his eyes, and do not defile yourselves with the idols of Egypt.

14 And the children of Israel rebelled and would not listen to Aaron at that time.

15 And the Lord thought to destroy them, were it not that the Lord remembered the covenant which he had made with Abraham, Isaac and Jacob.

16 In those days the hand of Pharaoh continued to be severe against the children of Israel, and he crushed and oppressed them until the time when God sent forth his word and took notice of them.

CHAPTER 72

1 It was in those days that there was a great war between the children of Cush and the children of the east and Aram, and they rebelled against the king of Cush in whose hands they were.

2 So Kikianus king of Cush went forth with all the children of Cush, a people numerous as the sand, and he went to fight against Aram and the children of the east, to bring them under subjection.

3 When Kikianus went out, he left Balaam the magician with his two sons, to guard the city and the lowest sort of the people of the land.

4 So Kikianus went forth to Aram and the children of the east, and he fought against them and struck them; they all fell down wounded before Kikianus and his people.

5 He took many of them captives and he brought them under subjection as at first, and he encamped on their land to take tax from them as usual.

6 Balaam the son of Beor, when the king of Cush had left him to guard the city and the poor of the city, rose up and advised with the people of the land to rebel against king Kikianus, not to let him enter the city when he would come home.

7 And the people of the land listened to him and they swore to him and made him king over them, and his two sons for captains of the army.

8 So they rose up and raised the walls of the city at the two corners, and they built an exceedingly strong building.

9 At the third corner they dug ditches without number, between the city and the river which surrounded the whole land of Cush, and they made the waters of the river burst forth there.

10 At the fourth corner they collected numerous serpents by their incantations and enchantments, and they fortified the city and lived therein; no one went out or in before them.

11 Kikianus fought against Aram and the children of the east and he subdued them as before; they gave him their usual tax and he went and returned to his land.

12 When Kikianus the king of Cush approached his city and all the captains of the forces with him, they lifted up their eyes and saw that the walls of the city were built up and greatly elevated, so the men were astonished at this.

13 They said one to the other, It is because they saw that we were delayed, in battle, and were greatly afraid of us; therefore have they done this thing and raised the city walls and fortified them so that the kings of

Canaan might not come in battle against them.

14 So the king and the troops approached the city door and they looked up and behold, all the gates of the city were closed; they called out to the sentinels, saying, Open to us, that we may enter the city.

15 But the sentinels refused to open to them by the order of Balaam the magician, their king; they did not allow them enter their city.

16 So they raised a battle with them opposite the city gate, and one hundred and thirty men of the army at Kikianus fell on that day.

17 On the next day they continued to fight and they fought at the side of the river; they endeavored to pass but were not able, so some of them sank in the pits and died.

18 The king ordered them to cut down trees to make rafts, on which they might pass to them, and they did so.

19 When they came to the place of the ditches, the waters revolved by mills, and two hundred men on ten rafts were drowned.

20 On the third day they came to fight at the side where the serpents were, but they could not approach there, for the serpents killed of them one hundred and seventy men; then they ceased fighting against Cush, and they besieged Cush for nine years; no person came out or in.

21 At the time that the war and the siege were against Cush, Moses fled from Egypt from Pharaoh who sought to kill him for having slain the Egyptian.

22 Moses was eighteen years old when he fled from Egypt from the presence of Pharaoh, and he fled and escaped to the camp of Kikianus, which at that time was besieging Cush.

23 Moses was nine years in the camp of Kikianus king of Cush, all the time that they were besieging Cush, and Moses went out and came in with them.

24 And the king and princes and all the fighting men loved Moses, for he was great and worthy, his stature was like a noble lion, his face was like the sun and his strength was like that of a lion, and he was counsellor to the king.

25 And at the end of nine years, Kikianus was seized with a mortal disease, and his illness consumed him, and he died on the seventh day.

26 So his servants embalmed him, carried him and buried him opposite the city gate to the north of the land of Egypt.

27 They built over him an elegant strong and high building, and they

placed great stones below.

28 And the king's scribes engraved on those stones all the might of their king Kikianus, and all his battles which he had fought; they are written there at this day.

29 After the death of Kikianus king of Cush it grieved his men and troops greatly on account of the war.

30 So they said one to the other, Give us counsel what we are to do at this time, as we have resided in the wilderness nine years away from our homes.

31 If we say we will fight against the city many of us will fall wounded or killed, and if we remain here in the siege we shall also die.

32 For now all the kings of Aram and of the children of the east will hear that our king is dead, and they will attack us suddenly in a hostile manner; they will fight against us and leave no remnant of us.

33 So now let us go and make a king over us, and let us remain in the siege until the city is delivered up to us.

34 And they wished to choose on that day a man for king from the army of Kikianus, and they found no person of their choice like Moses to reign over them.

35 They hurried and stripped off each man his garments and cast them on the ground, and they made a great heap and placed Moses thereon.

36 And they rose up and blew with trumpets and called out before him, and said, May the king live, may the king live!

37 And all the people and nobles swore to him to give him for a wife Adoniah the queen, the Cushite, wife of Kikianus, and they made Moses king over them on that day.

38 And all the people of Cush issued an announcement on that day, saying, Every man must give something to Moses of what is in his possession.

39 They spread out a sheet on the heap, and every man cast into it something of what he had, one a gold earring and the other a coin.

40 Also of onyx stones, bdellium, pearls and marble did the children of Cush cast to Moses on the heap, also silver and gold in great abundance.

41 And Moses took all the silver and gold, all the vessels, and the bdellium and onyx stones, which all the children of Cush had given to him, and he placed them among his treasures.

42 And Moses reigned over the children of Cush on that day, in the place of Kikianus king of Cush.

CHAPTER 73

1 In the fifty-fifth year of the reign of Pharaoh king of Egypt, that is in the hundred and fifty-seventh year of the Israelites going down into Egypt, Moses reigned in Cush.

2 Moses was twenty-seven years old when he began to reign over Cush, and forty years he did reign.

3 And the Lord granted Moses favor and grace in the eyes of all the children of Cush; the children of Cush loved him greatly, so Moses was favored by the Lord and by men.

4 In the seventh day of his reign, all the children of Cush assembled and came before Moses and bowed down to him to the ground.

5 And all the children spoke together in the presence of the king, saying, Give us counsel that we may see what is to be done to this city.

6 For it is now nine years that we have been besieging round about the city and have not seen our children and our wives.

7 So the king answered them, saying, If you will listen to my voice in all that I shall command you, then the Lord will give the city into our hands and we shall subdue it.

8 For if we fight with them as in the former battle which we had with them before the death of Kikianus, many of us will fall down wounded as before.

9 Now therefore hear this counsel for you in this matter; if you will listen to my voice, then will the city be delivered into our hands.

10 So all the forces answered the king, saying, All that our lord shall command that we will do.

11 And Moses said to them, Pass through and proclaim a voice in the whole camp to all the people, saying,

12 Thus says the king, Go into the forest and bring with you of the young ones of the stork, each man a young one in his hand.

13 And any person disobeying the word of the king, who shall not bring

his young one, shall die and the king will take all belonging to him.

14 And when you bring them they shall be in your keeping; you shall rear them until they grow up, and you shall teach them to strike their prey, as is the way of the young ones of the hawk.

15 So all the children of Cush heard the words of Moses, and they rose up and caused announcement to be issued throughout the camp, saying,

16 To you, all the children of Cush, the king's order is that you all go together to the forest and catch there the young stork; each man his young one in his hand and you shall bring them home.

17 Any person violating the order of the king shall die and the king will take all that belongs to him.

18 And all the people did so, and they went out to the wood and they climbed the fir trees and each man caught a young one in his hand, all the young of the storks; they brought them into the desert and reared them by order of the king; they taught them to strike similar to the young hawks.

19 And after the young storks were reared, the king ordered them to be hungry for three days, and all the people did so.

20 On the third day the king said to them, Strengthen yourselves and become courageous men; put on each man his armor and gird on his sword, and each man ride his horse and each take his young stork in his hand.

21 And we will rise up and fight against the city at the place where the serpents are, and all the people did as the king had ordered.

22 And each man took his young one in his hand and they went away; when they came to the place of the serpents the king said to them, Send forth each man his young stork on the serpents.

23 And they sent forth each man his young stork at the king's order, and the young storks ran on the serpents and they devoured them all and destroyed them out of that place.

24 When the king and people had seen that all the serpents were destroyed in that place, all the people sent up a great shout.

25 And they approached and fought against the city and took and subdued it, and they entered the city.

26 There died on that day one thousand and one hundred men of the people of the city, all that inhabited the city, but of the people besieging not one died.

27 So all the children of Cush each went to his home, to his wife and children and to all belonging to him.

28 And Balaam the magician, when he saw that the city was taken, opened the gate and he and his two sons and eight brothers fled and returned to Egyp,to Pharaoh king of Egypt.

29 They are the sorcerers and magicians who are mentioned in the book of the law, standing against Moses when the Lord brought the plagues on Egypt.

30 So Moses took the city by his wisdom, and the children of Cush placed him on the throne instead of Kikianus king of Cush.

31 They placed the royal crown on his head and they gave him a wife Adoniah the Cushite queen, wife of Kikianus.

32 Moses feared the Lord God of his fathers so that he came not to her, nor did he turn his eyes to her.

33 For Moses remembered how Abraham had made his servant Eliezer swear, saying to him, You shall not take a woman from the daughters of Canaan for my son Isaac.

34 Also what Isaac did when Jacob had fled from his brother, when he commanded him saying, You shall not take a wife from the daughters of Canaan, nor make alliance with any of the children of Ham.

35 For the Lord our God gave Ham the son of Noah, and his children and all his descendants as slaves to the children of Shem and to the children of Japheth, and to their descendants after them for slaves forever.

36 Therefore Moses turned not his heart nor his eyes to the wife of Kikianus all the days that he reigned over Cush.

37 Moses feared the Lord his God all his life, and Moses walked before the Lord in truth with all his heart and soul; he turned not from the right way all the days of his life; he declined not from the way either to the right or to the left, in which Abraham, Isaac and Jacob had walked.

38 Moses strengthened himself in the kingdom of the children of Cush; he guided the children of Cush with his usual wisdom, and Moses prospered in his kingdom.

39 At that time Aram and the children of the east heard that Kikianus king of Cush had died, so Aram and the children of the east rebelled against Cush in those days.

40 Moses gathered all the children of Cush, a people very mighty, about thirty thousand men and he went forth to fight with Aram and the

children of the east.

41 They went at first to the children of the east and when the children of the east heard their report, they went to meet them, and engaged in battle with them.

42 And the war was severe against the children of the east, so the Lord gave all the children of the east into the hand of Moses; about three hundred men fell down slain.

43 All the children of the east turned back and retreated, so Moses and the children of Cush followed them and subdued them, and put a tax on them as was their custom.

44 So Moses and all the people with him passed from there to the land of Aram for battle.

45 And the people of Aram also went to meet them; they fought against them and the Lord delivered them into the hand of Moses, and many of the men of Aram fell down wounded.

46 Aram also was subdued by Moses and the people of Cush, and also gave their usual tax.

47 And Moses brought Aram and the children of the east under subjection to the children of Cush; Moses and all the people who were with him turned to the land of Cush.

48 Moses strengthened himself in the kingdom of the children of Cush and the Lord was with him, and all the children of Cush were afraid of him.

CHAPTER 74

1 In the end of years Saul king of Edom died, and Baal Chanan the son of Achbor reigned in his place.

2 In the sixteenth year of the reign of Moses over Cush, Baal Chanan the son of Achbor reigned in the land of Edom over all the children of Edom for thirty-eight years.

3 In his days Moab rebelled against the power of Edom, having been under Edom since the days of Hadad the son of Bedad, who struck them and Midian, and brought Moab under subjection to Edom.

4 And when Baal Chanan the son of Achbor reigned over Edom, all the children of Moab withdrew their allegiance from Edom.

5 Angeas king of Africa died in those days, and Azdrubal his son reigned in his stead.

6 And in those days Janeas king of the children of Chittim died, and they buried him in his temple which he had built for himself in the plain of Canopia for a residence; Latinus reigned in his stead.

7 In the twenty-second year of the reign of Moses over the children of Cush, Latinus reigned over the children of Chittim forty-five years.

8 And he also built for himself a great and mighty tower; he built therein an elegant temple for his residence, to conduct his government as was the custom.

9 In the third year of his reign he caused an announcement to be made to all his skilful men who made many ships for him.

10 And Latinus assembled all his forces, and they came in ships, and went there to fight with Azdrubal son of Angeas king of Africa; they came to Africa and engaged in battle with Azdrubal and his army.

11 And Latinus won over Azdrubal, and Latinus took from Azdrubal the aqueduct which his father had brought from the children of Chittim, when he took Janiah the daughter of Uzi for a wife; so Latinus overthrew the bridge of the aqueduct and struck the whole army of Azdrubal a severe blow.

12 The remaining strong men of Azdrubal strengthened themselves, and their hearts were filled with envy; they courted death, and again engaged in battle with Latinus king of Chittim.

13 The battle was severe on all the men of Africa and they all fell wounded before Latinus and his people, and Azdrubal the king also fell in that battle.

14 The king Azdrubal had a very beautiful daughter whose name was Ushpezena, and all the men of Africa embroidered her likeness on their garment on account of her great beauty and attractive appearance.

15 The men of Latinus saw Ushpezena, the daughter of Azdrubal, and praised her to Latinus their king.

16 And Latinus ordered her to be brought to him; Latinus took Ushpezena for a wife and he turned back on his way to Chittim.

17 It was after the death of Azdrubal son of Angeas, when Latinus had turned back to his land from the battle, that all the inhabitants of Africa

rose up and took Anibal the son of Angeas, the younger brother of Azdrubal, and made him king instead of his brother over the whole land at Africa.

18 And when he reigned he resolved to go to Chittim to fight with the children of Chittim, to avenge the cause of Azdrubal his brother and the cause of the inhabitants of Africa, and he did so.

19 He made many ships and he came there with his whole army, and he went to Chittim.

20 So Anibal fought with the children of Chittim, and the children of Chittim fell wounded before Anibal and his army, and Anibal avenged his brother's cause.

21 And Anibal continued the war for eighteen years with the children of Chittim, and Anibal lived in the land of Chittim and encamped there for a long time.

22 Anibal struck the children of Chittim very severely and he killed their great men and princes, and of the rest of the people he struck about eighty thousand men.

23 And at the end of days and years, Anibal returned to his land of Africa, and he reigned securely in the place of Azdrubal his brother.

CHAPTER 75

1 At that time in the hundred and eightieth year of the Israelites going down into Egypt, there went forth from Egypt courageous men, thirty thousand on foot, from the children of Israel who were all of the tribe of Joseph, of the children of Ephraim the son of Joseph.

2 For they said the period was completed which the Lord had appointed to the children of Israel in the times of old, which he had spoken to Abraham.

3 And these men prepared themselves, and each man put his sword at his side, and every man his armor on him, and they trusted to their strength; they went out together from Egypt with a mighty hand.

4 But they brought no provision for the road, only silver and gold, not even did they bring bread for that day in their hands, for they thought of getting their provision for pay from the Philistines; if not they would take

it by force.

5 These men were very mighty and bold men; one man could pursue a thousand and two could rout ten thousand, so they trusted their strength and went together as they were.

6 They directed their course toward the land of Gath, and they went down and found the shepherds of Gath feeding the cattle of the children of Gath.

7 They said to the shepherds, Give us some of the sheep for pay that we may eat, for we are hungry; we have eaten no bread this day.

8 And the shepherds said, Are they our sheep or cattle that we should give them to you even for pay? So the children of Ephraim approached to take them by force.

9 And the shepherds of Gath shouted over them so their cry was heard at a distance; all the children of Gath went out to them.

10 When the children of Gath saw the evil doings of the children of Ephraim, they returned and assembled the men of Gath; they put on each man his armor and came forth to the children of Ephraim for battle.

11 And they engaged with them in the valley of Gath, and the battle was severe; they struck from each other a great many on that day.

12 And on the second day the children of Gath sent to all the cities of the Philistines that they should come to their help, saying,

13 Come up to us and help us, that we may strike the children of Ephraim who have come forth from Egypt to take our cattle, and to fight against us without cause.

14 And the souls of the children of Ephraim were exhausted with hunger and thirst, for they had eaten no bread for three days. Forty thousand men went out from the cities of the Philistines to the assistance of the men of Gath.

15 These men were engaged in battle with the children of Ephraim, and the Lord delivered the children of Ephraim into the hands of the Philistines.

16 They struck all the children of Ephraim, all who had gone forth from Egypt, none were remaining but ten men who had run away from the engagement.

17 This evil was from the Lord against the children of Ephraim for they went contrary to the word of the Lord in going forth from Egypt, before the period had arrived which the Lord in the days of old had appointed to

Israel.

18 And of the Philistines also there fell a great many, about twenty thousand men, and their brothers carried them and buried them in their cities.

19 And the slain of the children of Ephraim remained forsaken in the valley of Gath for many days and years and were not brought to burial, and the valley was filled with men's bones.

20 The men who had escaped from the battle came to Egypt and told all the children of Israel all that had happened to them.

21 Their father Ephraim mourned over them for many days, and his brothers came to console him.

22 And he came to his wife and she gave birth to a son, and he called his name Beriah, for she was unfortunate in his house.

CHAPTER 76

1 Moses the son of Amram was still king in the land of Cush in those days, and he prospered in his kingdom; he conducted the government of the children of Cush in justice, in righteousness and integrity.

2 And all the children of Cush loved Moses all the days that he reigned over them, and all the inhabitants of the land of Cush were greatly afraid of him.

3 In the fortieth year of the reign of Moses over Cush, Moses was sitting on the royal throne while Adoniah the queen was before him, and all the nobles were sitting around him.

4 And Adoniah the queen said before the king and the princes, What is this thing which you, the children of Cush, have done for this long time?

5 Certainly you know that for forty years that this man has reigned over Cush he has not approached me, nor has he served the gods of the children of Cush.

6 Now therefore hear, O ye children of Cush, and let this man no more reign over you as he is not of our people.

7 Behold Menacrus my son is grown up, let him reign over you for it is better for you to serve the son of your lord than to serve a stranger, slave of the king of Egypt.

8 And all the people and nobles of the children of Cush heard the words which Adoniah the queen had spoken in their ears.

9 All the people were preparing until the evening, and in the morning they rose up early and made Menacrus, son of Kikianus, king over them.

10 All the children of Cush were afraid to stretch forth their hand against Moses, for the Lord was with Moses, and the children of Cush remembered the oath which they swore to Moses, therefore they did no harm to him.

11 But the children of Cush gave many presents to Moses, and sent him from them with great honor.

12 So Moses went forth from the land of Cush and went home and ceased to reign over Cush; Moses was sixty-six years old when he went out of the land of Cush, for the thing was from the Lord. For the period had arrived which he had appointed in the days of old, to bring forth Israel from the affliction of the children of Ham.

13 So Moses went to Midian, for he was afraid to return to Egypt on account of Pharaoh, and he went and sat at a well of water in Midian.

14 And the seven daughters of Reuel the Midianite went out to feed their father's flock.

15 And they came to the well and drew water to water their father's flock.

16 But the shepherds of Midian came and drove them away, and Moses rose up and helped them and watered the flock.

17 And they came home to their father Reuel, and told him what Moses did for them.

18 They said, An Egyptian man has delivered us from the hands of the shepherds; he drew up water for us and watered the flock.

19 And Reuel said to his daughters, And where is he? Why have you left the man?

20 And Reuel sent for him and fetched him and brought him home, and he ate bread with him.

21 And Moses related to Reuel that he had fled from Egypt and that he reigned forty years over Cush, and that they afterward had taken the government from him and had sent him away in peace with honor and with presents.

22 And when Reuel had heard the words of Moses, Reuel said within himself, I will put this man into the prison house, whereby I shall win over the children of Cush, for he has fled from them.

23 They took and put him into the prison house, and Moses was in prison ten years; while Moses was in the prison house, Zipporah the daughter of Reuel took pity on him, and supported him with bread and water all the time.

24 All the children of Israel were yet in the land of Egypt serving the Egyptians in all manner of hard work, and the hand of Egypt continued in severity over the children of Israel in those days.

25 At that time the Lord struck Pharaoh king of Egypt, and he was afflicted with the plague of leprosy from the sole of his foot to the crown of his head; owing to the cruel treatment of the children of Israel this plague at that time was from the Lord on Pharaoh king of Egypt.

26 For the Lord had listened to the prayer of his people the children of Israel, and their cry reached him on account of their hard work.

27 Still his anger did not turn from them, and the hand of Pharaoh was still stretched out against the children of Israel. Pharaoh hardened his neck before the Lord, he increased his yoke over the children of Israel, and embittered their lives with all manner of hard work.

28 When the Lord had inflicted the plague on Pharaoh king of Egypt, he asked his wise men and sorcerers to cure him.

29 And his wise men and sorcerers said to him that if the blood of little children were put into the wounds he would be healed.

30 Pharaoh listened to them, and sent his ministers to Goshen to the children of Israel to take their little children.

31 And Pharaoh's ministers went and took the infants of the children of Israel from the bosoms of their mothers by force, and they brought them to Pharaoh daily, a child each day, and the physicians killed them and applied them to the plague; thus they did all the days.

32 And the number of the children which Pharaoh killed was three hundred and seventy-five.

33 But the Lord listened not to the physicians of the king of Egypt, and the plague went on increasing mightily.

34 Pharaoh was ten years afflicted with that plague, still the heart of Pharaoh was more hardened against the children of Israel.

35 At the end of ten years the Lord continued to afflict Pharaoh with destructive plagues.

36 And the Lord struck him with a bad tumor and sickness in the stomach, and that plague turned to a severe boil.

37 At that time the two ministers of Pharaoh came from the land of Goshen where all the children of Israel were, and went to the house of Pharaoh and said to him, We have seen the children of Israel slacken in their work and negligent in their labor.

38 And when Pharaoh heard the words of his ministers, his anger was set ablaze against the children of Israel greatly, for he was greatly grieved at his bodily pain.

39 And he answered and said, Now that the children of Israel know that I am ill, they turn and scoff at us. Now therefore harness my chariot for me, and I will take myself to Goshen and will see the scoff of the children of Israel with which they are deriding me. So his servants harnessed the chariot for him.

40 And they took and made him ride on a horse, for he was not able to ride of himself.

41 He took with him ten horsemen and ten footmen, and went to the children of Israel to Goshen.

42 When they had come to the border of Egypt, the king's horse passed into a narrow place, elevated in the hollow part of the vineyard, fenced on both sides, the low plain country being on the other side.

43 The horses ran rapidly in that place and pressed each other, and the other horses pressed the king's horse.

44 And the king's horse fell into the low plain while the king was riding on it; he fell and the chariot turned over the king's face and the horse lay on the king, and the king cried out for his flesh was very sore.

45 And the flesh of the king was torn from him, and his bones were broken and he could not ride; this thing was from the Lord to him, for the Lord had heard the cries of his people the children of Israel and their affliction.

46 And his servants carried him on their shoulders, slowly and carefully, and they brought him back to Egypt, and the horsemen who were with him also came back to Egypt.

47 They placed him in his bed and the king knew that his end was come to die, so Aparanith the queen his wife came and cried before the king, and the king wept a great weeping with her.

48 And all his nobles and servants came on that day and saw the king in that affliction, and wept a great weeping with him.

49 The princes of the king and all his counselors advised the king to cause one to reign in his stead in the land, whomever he would choose from his sons.

50 The king had three sons and two daughters which Aparanith the queen his wife had borne to him, besides the king's children of concubines.

51 And these were their names: the firstborn Othri, the second Adikam, and the third Morion, and their sisters: the name of the elder Bathia and of the other Acuzi.

52 Othri the first born of the king was an idiot, impetuous and hurried in his words.

53 But Adikam was a cunning and wise man and knowing in all the wisdom of Egypt, but of unseemly appearance, thick in flesh and very short in stature; his height was one cubit.

54 And when the king saw Adikam his son intelligent and wise in all things, the king resolved that he should be king in his stead after his death.

55 He took for him a wife Gedudah daughter of Abilot, and he was ten years old; she gave birth to, to him, four sons.

56 And afterward he went and took three wives and had eight sons and three daughters.

57 And the disorder greatly consumed the king, and his flesh stank like the flesh of a carcass cast on the field in summer time, during the heat of the sun.

58 And when the king saw that his sickness had greatly strengthened itself over him, he ordered his son Adikam to be brought to him, and they made him king over the land in his place.

59 At the end of three years the king died, in shame, disgrace, and disgust, and his servants carried him and buried him in the sepulcher of the kings of Egypt in Zoan Mizraim.

60 But they embalmed him not as was usual with kings, for his flesh was putrid, and they could not approach to embalm him on account of the stench, so they buried him in haste.

61 For this evil was from the Lord to him, for the Lord had rewarded him evil for the evil which in his days he had done to Israel.

62 And he died with terror and with shame, and his son Adikam reigned in his place.

CHAPTER 77

1 Adikam was twenty years old when he reigned over Egypt, he reigned four years.

2 In the two hundred and sixth year of Israel's going down to Egypt did Adikam reign over Egypt, but he continued not so long in his reign over Egypt as his fathers had continued their reigns.

3 For Melol his father reigned ninety-four years in Egypt, but he was sick ten years and died, for he had been wicked before the Lord.

4 And all the Egyptians called the name of Adikam Pharaoh like the name of his fathers, as was their custom to do in Egypt.

5 And all the wise men of Pharaoh called the name of Adikam Ahuz, for short it's called Ahuz in the Egyptian language.

6 Adikam was greatly ugly, and he was a cubit and a span and he had a great beard which reached to the soles of his feet.

7 And Pharaoh sat on his father's throne to reign over Egypt, and he conducted the government of Egypt in his wisdom.

8 While he reigned he exceeded his father and all the preceding kings in wickedness, and he increased his yoke over the children of Israel.

9 He went with his servants to Goshen to the children of Israel, and he strengthened the labor over them and he said to them, Complete your work, each day's task, and let not your hands slacken from our work from this day forward as you did in the days of my father.

10 He placed officers over them from among the children of Israel, and over these officers he placed taskmasters from among his servants.

11 And he placed over them a measure of bricks for them to do according to that number, day by day, and he turned back and went to Egypt.

12 At that time the taskmasters of Pharaoh ordered the officers of the children of Israel according to the command of Pharaoh, saying,

13 Thus says Pharaoh, Do your work each day, and finish your task, and observe the daily measure of bricks; diminish not anything.

14 And it shall come to pass that if you are deficient in your daily bricks, I will put your young children in their stead.

15 And the taskmasters of Egypt did so in those days as Pharaoh had ordered them.

16 And whenever any deficiency was found in the children of Israel's measure of their daily bricks, the taskmasters of Pharaoh would go to the wives of the children of Israel and take infants of the children of Israel to the number of bricks deficient, they would take them by force from their mother's laps, and put them in the building instead of the bricks;

17 While their fathers and mothers were crying over them and weeping when they heard the weeping voices of their infants in the wall of the building.

18 And the taskmasters prevailed over Israel, that the Israelites should place their children in the building, so that a man placed his son in the wall and put mortar over him, while his eyes wept over him, and his tears ran down on his child.

19 And the taskmasters of Egypt did so to the babes of Israel for many days, and no one pitied or had compassion over the babes of the children of Israel.

20 And the number of all the children killed in the building was two hundred and seventy, some whom they had built on instead of the bricks which had been left deficient by their fathers, and some whom they had drawn out dead from the building.

21 And the labor imposed on the children of Israel in the days of Adikam exceeded in hardship that which they performed in the days of his father.

22 The children of Israel sighed every day on account of their heavy work, for they had said to themselves, Certainly when Pharaoh dies, his son will rise up and lighten our work!

23 But they increased the latter work more than the former, and the children of Israel sighed at this and their cry ascended to God on account of their labor.

24 God heard the voice of the children of Israel and their cry in those days, and God remembered to them his covenant which he had made with Abraham, Isaac and Jacob.

25 And God saw the burden of the children of Israel and their heavy work in those days, and he determined to deliver them.

26 Moses the son of Amram was still confined in the dungeon in those

days, in the house of Reuel the Midianite, and Zipporah the daughter of Reuel supported him with food secretly day by day.

27 Moses was confined in the dungeon in the house of Reuel for ten years.

28 And at the end of ten years which was the first year of the reign of Pharaoh over Egypt, in the place of his father,

29 Zipporah said to her father Reuel, No person inquires or seeks after the Hebrew man, whom you bound in prison now ten years.

30 So therefore, if it seems good in your sight, let us send and see whether he is living or dead. But her father knew not that she had supported him.

31 And Reuel her father answered and said to her, Has ever such a thing happened that a man would be shut up in a prison without food for ten years, and that he should live?

32 And Zipporah answered her father, saying, Certainly you have heard that the God of the Hebrews is great and mighty, and does wonders for them at all times.

33 He it was who delivered Abraham from the Chaldeans, and Isaac from the sword of his father, and Jacob from the angel of the Lord who wrestled with him at the ford of Jabbuk.

34 Also with this man he has done many things; he delivered him from the river in Egypt and from the sword of Pharaoh, and from the children of Cush, so also he can deliver him from famine and make him live.

35 And the thing seemed good in the sight of Reuel, and he did according to the word of his daughter, and sent to the dungeon to ascertain what became of Moses.

36 He saw, and behold the man Moses was living in the dungeon, standing on his feet, praising and praying to the God of his ancestors.

37 And Reuel commanded Moses to be brought out of the dungeon, so they shaved him and he changed his prison garments and ate bread.

38 And afterward Moses went into the garden of Reuel which was behind the house, and he there prayed to the Lord his God, who had done mighty wonders for him.

39 It was while he prayed he looked opposite to him, and there a sapphire stick was placed in the ground, which was planted in the midst of the garden.

40 He approached the stick and looked, and saw the name of the Lord God of hosts was engraved on it, written and developed on the stick.

41 And he read it and stretched forth his hand and he plucked it like a forest tree from the thicket, and the stick was in his hand.

42 This is the stick with which all the works of our God were performed, after he had created heaven and earth and all the host of them, seas, rivers and all their fish.

43 And when God had driven Adam from the garden of Eden, he took the stick in his hand and went and tilled the ground from which he was taken.

44 The stick came down to Noah and was given to Shem and his descendants, until it came into the hand of Abraham the Hebrew.

45 And when Abraham had given all he had to his son Isaac, he also gave to him this stick.

46 When Jacob had fled to Padan-aram, he took it into his hand, and when he returned to his father he had not left it behind him.

47 Also when he went down to Egypt he took it into his hand and gave it to Joseph, one portion above his brothers, for Jacob had taken it by force from his brother Esau.

48 After the death of Joseph, the nobles of Egypt came into the house of Joseph, and the stick came into the hand of Reuel the Midianite; when he went out of Egypt, he took it in his hand and planted it in his garden.

49 And all the mighty men of the Kinites tried to pluck it when they endeavored to get Zipporah his daughter, but they were unsuccessful.

50 That stick remained planted in the garden of Reuel until he who had a right to it came and took it.

51 And when Reuel saw the stick in the hand of Moses, he wondered at it, and he gave him his daughter Zipporah for a wife.

CHAPTER 78

1 At that time Baal Channan son of Achbor, king of Edom, died and was buried in his house in the land of Edom.

2 After his death the children of Esau sent to the land of Edom, and took from there a man who was in Edom, whose name was Hadad, and they made him king over them in the place of Baal Channan, their king.

3 And Hadad reigned over the children of Edom forty-eight years.

4 When he reigned he resolved to fight against the children of Moab to bring them under the power of the children of Esau as they were before, but he was not able to because the children of Moab heard this thing, and they rose up and hurried to elect a king over them from among their brothers.

5 Afterward they gathered together a large crowd, and sent them to the children of Ammon their brothers for help to fight against Hadad king of Edom.

6 And Hadad heard the thing which the children of Moab had done, and was greatly afraid of them, and refrained from fighting against them.

7 In those days Moses, the son of Amram, in Midian, took Zipporah, the daughter of Reuel the Midianite, for a wife.

8 And Zipporah walked in the ways of the daughters of Jacob, she was nothing short of the righteousness of Sarah, Rebecca, Rachel and Leah.

9 And Zipporah conceived and gave birth to a son and he called his name Gershom, for he said, I was a stranger in a foreign land; but he circumcised not his foreskin, at the command of Reuel his father-in-law.

10 And she conceived again and gave birth to a son, but circumcised his foreskin, and called his name Eliezer, for Moses said, Because the God of my fathers was my help and delivered me from the sword of Pharaoh.

11 And Pharaoh king of Egypt greatly increased the labor of the children of Israel in those days, and continued to make his yoke heavier on the children of Israel.

12 And he ordered an announcement to be made in Egypt, saying, Give no more straw to the people to make bricks with, let them go and gather themselves straw as they can find it.

13 Also the number of bricks which they shall make let them give each day, and diminish nothing from them, for they are idle in their work.

14 And the children of Israel heard this, and they mourned and sighed, and they cried to the Lord on account of the bitterness of their souls.

15 And the Lord heard the cries of the children of Israel, and saw the oppression with which the Egyptians oppressed them.

16 And the Lord was zealous for his people and his inheritance, and heard their voice, and he resolved to take them out of the affliction of Egypt, to give them the land of Canaan for a possession.

CHAPTER 79

1 Iin those days Moses was feeding the flock of Reuel the Midianite his father-in-law, beyond the wilderness of Sin, and the stick which he took from his father-in-law was in his hand.

2 And it came to pass one day that a kid of goats strayed from the flock, and Moses pursued it and it came to the mountain of God to Horeb.

3 When he came to Horeb the Lord appeared there to him in the bush, and he found the bush burning with fire, but the fire had no power over the bush to consume it.

4 Moses was greatly astonished at this sight because the bush was not consumed, and he approached to see this mighty thing; the Lord called to Moses out of the fire and commanded him to go down to Egypt to Pharaoh king of Egypt, to send the children of Israel from his service.

5 And the Lord said to Moses, Go, return to Egypt for all those men who sought your life are dead, and you shall speak to Pharaoh to send forth the children of Israel from his land.

6 The Lord showed him to do signs and wonders in Egypt before the eyes of Pharaoh and the eyes of his subjects, in order that they might believe that the Lord had sent him.

7 Moses listened to all that the Lord had commanded him, and he returned to his father-in-law and told him these things, and Reuel said to him, Go in peace.

8 Moses rose up to go to Egypt and took his wife and sons with him; he was at an inn in the road, and an angel of God came down, and sought an occasion against him.

9 He wished to kill him on account of his firstborn son because he had not circumcised him and had gone contrary to the covenant which the Lord had made with Abraham.

10 For Moses had listened to the words of his father-in-law which he had spoken to him, not to circumcise his first born son, so he did not circumcise him.

11 Zipporah saw the angel of the Lord seeking an occasion against Moses, and she knew that this thing was because of his not having circumcised her son Gershom.

12 Zipporah hurried and took some of the sharp rock stones that were

there, and circumcised her son, and delivered her husband and her son from the hand of the angel of the Lord.

13 Aaron the son of Amram, the brother of Moses, was in Egypt walking at the river side on that day.

14 And the Lord appeared to him in that place; he said to him, Go now toward Moses in the wilderness. And he went and met him in the mountain of God, and he kissed him.

15 Aaron lifted up his eyes and saw Zipporah the wife of Moses and her children, and he said to Moses, Who are these to you?

16 And Moses said to him, They are my wife and sons which God gave to me in Midian; the thing grieved Aaron on account of the woman and her children.

17 Aaron said to Moses, Send away the woman and her children that they may go to her father's house, and Moses listened to the words of Aaron, and did so.

18 Zipporah returned with her children and they went to the house of Reuel, and remained there until the time arrived when the Lord had visited his people and brought them forth from Egypt from the hand at Pharaoh.

19 Moses and Aaron came to Egypt to the community of the children of Israel and spoke to them all the words of the Lord, and the people rejoiced a very great rejoicing.

20 Moses and Aaron rose up early the next day and went to the house of Pharaoh, and they took in their hands the stick of God.

21 When they came to the king's gate, two young lions were confined there with iron instruments; no person went out or came in from before them, unless those whom the king ordered to come, when the conjurors came and withdrew the lions by their incantations, and this brought them to the king.

22 Moses hurried and lifted up the stick on the lions and loosed them, and Moses and Aaron came into the king's house.

23 The lions also came with them in joy, and they followed them and rejoiced as a dog rejoices over his master when he comes from the field.

24 When Pharaoh saw this thing he was astonished at it and was greatly terrified at the report, for their appearance was like the appearance of the children of God.

25 And Pharaoh said to Moses, What do you require? And they answered

him saying, The Lord God of the Hebrews has sent us to you, to say, Send forth my people that they may serve me.

26 When Pharaoh heard their words he was greatly terrified before them, and he said to them, Go today and come back to me tomorrow. And they did according to the word of the king.

27 When they had gone Pharaoh sent for Balaam the magician and to Jannes and Jambres his sons and to all the magicians and conjurors and counselors which belonged to the king; they all came and sat before the king.

28 And the king told them all the words which Moses and his brother Aaron had spoken to him; the magicians said to the king, But how could the men come to you, on account of the lions which were confined at the gate?

29 The king said, Because they lifted up their rod against the lions and loosed them, and came to me, and the lions also rejoiced at them as a dog rejoices to meet his master.

30 Balaam the son of Beor the magician answered the king saying, These are none other than magicians like ourselves.

31 So now send for them and let them come and we will try them, and the king did so.

32 In the morning Pharaoh sent for Moses and Aaron to come before the king, and they took the rod of God and came to the king and spoke to him saying,

33 Thus said the Lord God of the Hebrews, Send away my people that they may serve me.

34 And the king said to them, But who will believe you that you are the messengers of God and that you come to me by his order?

35 Now therefore give a wonder or sign in this matter, and then the words which you speak will be believed.

36 Aaron hurried and threw the rod out of his hand before Pharaoh and before his servants, and the rod turned into a serpent.

37 The sorcerers saw this and each man cast his rod on the ground and they became serpents.

38 The serpent of Aaron's rod lifted up its head and opened its mouth to swallow the rods of the magicians.

39 Balaam the magician answered and said, This thing has been from the

days of old that a serpent should swallow its fellow, and that living things devour each other.

40 So now restore it to a rod as it was at first and we will also restore our rods as they were at first; if your rod shall swallow our rods we will know that the spirit of God is in you, and if not, you are only a magician like ourselves.

41 Aaron hurried and stretched forth his hand and caught hold of the serpent's tail and it became a rod in his hand; the sorcerers did the same with their rod and got hold each man of the tail of his serpent, and they became rods as at first.

42 When they were restored to rods, the rod of Aaron swallowed up their rods.

43 And when the king saw this thing, he ordered the book of records that related to the kings of Egypt to be brought; they brought the book of records, the chronicles of the kings of Egypt in which all the idols of Egypt were inscribed, for they thought they would find there the name of Jehovah, but they found it not.

44 And Pharaoh said to Moses and Aaron, Behold I have not found the name of your God written in this book, and his name I do not know.

45 The counselors and wise men answered the king, We have heard that the God of the Hebrews is a son of the wise, the son of ancient kings.

46 Pharaoh turned to Moses and Aaron and said to them, I know not the Lord whom you have declared, neither will I send his people away.

47 And they answered and said to the king, The Lord God of Gods is his name; he proclaimed his name over us from the days of our ancestors and sent us, saying, Go to Pharaoh and say to him, Send my people away that they may serve me.

48 Now therefore send us, that we may take a journey for three days in the wilderness and there may sacrifice to him, for from the days of our going down to Egypt, he has not taken from our hands either burnt offering, oblation or sacrifice; if you will not send us, his anger will be set ablaze against you and he will strike Egypt either with the plague or with the sword.

49 And Pharaoh said to them, Tell me now his power and his might. They said to him, He created the heaven and the earth, the seas and all their fish; he formed the light, created the darkness, caused rain on the earth and watered it, and made the herbage and grass to sprout; he created man and beast and the animals of the forest, the birds of the air and the fish of the sea, and by his mouth they live and die.

50 Certainly he created you in your mother's womb and put into you the breath of life, and reared you and placed you on the royal throne of Egypt, and he will take your breath and soul from you and return you to the ground from where you were taken.

51 And the anger of the king was set ablaze at their words and he said to them, But who among all the Gods of nations can do this? My river is my own, and I have made it for myself.

52 And he drove them from him; he ordered the labor on Israel to be more severe than it was yesterday and before.

53 Moses and Aaron went out from the king's presence, and they saw the children of Israel in an evil condition for the taskmasters had made their labor extremely heavy.

54 Moses returned to the Lord and said, Why have you ill-treated your people? For since I came to speak to Pharaoh what you sent me for, he has greatly ill-used the children of Israel.

55 The Lord said to Moses, Look and you will see that with an outstretched hand and heavy plagues, Pharaoh will send the children of Israel from his land.

56 And Moses and Aaron lived among their brothers the children of Israel in Egypt.

57 As for the children of Israel the Egyptians embittered their lives with the heavy work which they imposed on them.

CHAPTER 80

1 And at the end of two years, the Lord again sent Moses to Pharaoh to bring forth the children of Israel, and to send them out of the land of Egypt.

2 Moses went and came to the house of Pharaoh, and he spoke to him the words of the Lord who had sent him, but Pharaoh would not listen to the voice of the Lord; God roused his might in Egypt on Pharaoh and his subjects, and God struck Pharaoh and his people with very great and severe plagues.

3 The Lord sent by the hand of Aaron and turned all the waters of Egypt into blood, with all their streams and rivers.

4 And when an Egyptian came to drink and draw water, he looked into his pitcher, and behold all the water was turned into blood; when he came to drink from his cup the water in the cup became blood.

5 And when a woman kneaded her dough and cooked her food, their appearance was turned to that of blood.

6 The Lord sent again and caused all their waters to bring forth frogs and all the frogs came into the houses of the Egyptians.

7 And when the Egyptians drank, their bellies were filled with frogs and they danced in their bellies as they dance when in the river.

8 All their drinking water and cooking water turned to frogs, also when they lay in their beds their perspiration bred frogs.

9 In spite of all this the anger of the Lord did not turn from them, and his hand was stretched out against all the Egyptians to strike them with every heavy plague.

10 He sent and changed their dust to lice, and the lice became in Egypt to the height of two cubits on the earth.

11 The lice were also very numerous in the flesh of man and beast, in all the inhabitants of Egypt; also on the king and queen the Lord sent the lice, and it grieved Egypt greatly on account of the lice.

12 Still the anger of the Lord did not turn away, and his hand was still stretched out over Egypt.

13 And the Lord sent all kinds of beasts of the field into Egypt, and they came and destroyed all Egypt, man and beast, and trees and all things that were in Egypt.

14 And the Lord sent fiery serpents, scorpions, mice, weasels, toads, together with others creeping in dust.

15 Flies, hornets, fleas, bugs and gnats, each swarm according to its kind.

16 And all reptiles and winged animals according to their kind came to Egypt and upset the Egyptians greatly.

17 The fleas and flies came into the eyes and ears of the Egyptians.

18 The hornet came on them and drove them away, and they removed from it into their inner rooms, and it pursued them.

19 When the Egyptians hid themselves on account of the swarm of animals, they locked their doors after them, and God ordered the Sulanuth which was in the sea to come up and go into Egypt.

20 She had long arms, ten cubits in length of the cubit of a man.

21 And she went on the roofs and uncovered the raftering and flooring and cut them, and stretched forth her arm into the house and removed the lock and the bolt, and opened the houses of Egypt.

22 Afterward came the swarm of animals into the houses of Egypt, and the swarm of animals destroyed the Egyptians, and it upset them greatly.

23 Still the anger of the Lord did not turn away from the Egyptians, and his hand was yet stretched forth against them.

24 God sent the pestilence and the pestilence pervaded Egypt, in the horses and asses and in the camels, in herds of oxen and sheep and in man.

25 When the Egyptians rose up early in the morning to take their cattle to pasture they found all their cattle dead.

26 There remained of the cattle of the Egyptians only one in ten, and of the cattle belonging to Israel in Goshen not one died.

27 And God sent a burning inflammation in the flesh of the Egyptians, which burst their skins; it became a severe itch in all the Egyptians from the soles of their feet to the crowns of their heads.

28 And many boils were in their flesh, that their flesh wasted away until they became rotten and putrid.

29 Still the anger of the Lord did not turn away, and his hand was still stretched out over all Egypt.

30 And the Lord sent a very heavy hail, which struck their vines and broke their fruit trees and dried them up that they fell on them.

31 Also every green herb became dry and perished, for a mingling fire descended with the hail, therefore the hail and the fire consumed all things.

32 Also men and beasts that were found abroad perished of the flames of fire and of the hail, and all the young lions were exhausted.

33 And the Lord sent and brought numerous locusts into Egypt, the Chasel, Salom, Chargol, and Chagole, locusts each of its kind, which devoured all that the hail had left remaining.

34 Then the Egyptians rejoiced at the locusts, although they consumed the produce of the field, and they caught them in abundance and salted them for food.

35 And the Lord turned a mighty wind of the sea which took away all the locusts, even those that were salted, and thrust them into the Red Sea; not

one locust remained within the boundaries of Egypt.

36 God sent darkness on Egypt, that the whole land of Egypt and Pathros became dark for three days so that a man could not see his hand when he lifted it to his mouth.

37 At that time many of the people of Israel died who had rebelled against the Lord and who would not listen to Moses and Aaron, and believed not in them that God had sent them.

38 And who had said, We will not go forth from Egypt because we'll perish with hunger in a desolate wilderness. They were those who would not listen to the voice of Moses.

39 The Lord plagued them in the three days of darkness, and the Israelites buried them in those days without the Egyptians knowing of them or rejoicing over them.

40 The darkness was very great in Egypt for three days, and any person who was standing when the darkness came remained standing in his place; he that was sitting remained sitting, and he that was lying continued lying in the same state; he that was walking remained sitting on the ground in the same spot; and this thing happened to all the Egyptians until the darkness had passed away.

41 The days of darkness passed away and the Lord sent Moses and Aaron to the children of Israel saying, Celebrate your feast and make your Passover, for behold I come in the middle of the night among all the Egyptians; I will strike all their firstborn, from the firstborn of a man to the first born of a beast, and when I see your Passover, I will pass over you.

42 And the children of Israel did according to all that the Lord had commanded Moses and Aaron, thus did they in that night.

43 It came to pass in the middle of the night that the Lord went forth in the midst of Egypt and struck all the firstborn of the Egyptians, from the firstborn of man to the firstborn of beast.

44 And Pharaoh rose up in the night, he and all his servants and all the Egyptians, and there was a great cry throughout Egypt in that night for there was not a house in which there was not a corpse.

45 Also the likenesses of the firstborn of Egypt which were carved in the walls at their houses were destroyed and fell to the ground.

46 Even the bones of their firstborn who had died before this and whom they had buried in their houses were raked up by the dogs of Egypt on that night and dragged before the Egyptians and cast before them.

47 And all the Egyptians saw this evil which had suddenly come on them,

and all the Egyptians cried out with a loud voice.

48 And all the families of Egypt wept on that night, each man for his son and each man for his daughter, being the firstborn, and the tumult of Egypt was heard at a distance on that night.

49 Bathia the daughter of Pharaoh went forth with the king on that night to seek Moses and Aaron in their houses; they found them in their houses eating and drinking and rejoicing with all Israel.

50 And Bathia said to Moses, Is this the reward for the good which I have done to you, who have reared you and made you grow and prosper and you have brought this evil on me and my father's house?

51 And Moses said to her, Certainly ten plagues did the Lord bring on Egypt; did any evil accrue to you from any of them? Did one of them affect you? And she said, No.

52 And Moses said to her, Although you are the firstborn to your mother, you shall not die and no evil shall reach you in the midst of Egypt.

53 And she said, What advantage is it to me when I see the king, my brother, and all his household and subjects in this evil, whose firstborn perish with all the firstborn of Egypt?

54 And Moses said to her, Certainly your brother and his household and subjects, the families of Egypt, would not listen to the words of the Lord, therefore did this evil come on them.

55 Pharaoh king of Egypt approached Moses and Aaron and some of the children of Israel who were with them in that place, and he prayed to them saying,

56 Rise up and take your brothers, all the children of Israel who are in the land with their sheep and oxen, and all belonging to them; they shall leave nothing remaining, only pray for me to the Lord your God.

57 And Moses said to Pharaoh, Behold you are your mother's firstborn, yet fear not for you will not die, for the Lord has commanded that you shall live in order to show you his great might and strong stretched out arm.

58 Pharaoh ordered the children of Israel to be sent away, and all the Egyptians strengthened themselves to send them, for they said, We are all perishing.

59 And all the Egyptians sent the Israelites forth with great riches, sheep and oxen and precious things according to the oath of the Lord between him and our Father Abraham.

60 And the children of Israel delayed going away until night, and when the Egyptians came to them to bring them out, they said to them, Are we thieves, that we should go forth at night?

61 And the children of Israel asked of the Egyptians, vessels of silver and vessels of gold, and garments, and the children of Israel stripped the Egyptians.

62 Moses hurried and rose up and went to the river of Egypt and brought up from there the coffin of Joseph and took it with him.

63 The children of Israel also brought up each man his father's coffin with him, and each man the coffins of his tribe.

CHAPTER 81

1 The children of Israel journeyed from Rameses to Succoth, about six hundred thousand men on foot besides the little ones and their wives.

2 Also a mixed multitude went up with them, flocks and herds, even much cattle.

3 The temporary time of the children of Israel who lived in the land of Egypt in hard labor was two hundred and ten years.

4 And at the end of two hundred and ten years, the Lord brought forth the children of Israel from Egypt with a strong hand.

5 The children of Israel traveled from Egypt and from Goshen and from Rameses, and encamped in Succoth on the fifteenth day of the first month.

6 The Egyptians buried all their firstborn whom the Lord had smitten, and all the Egyptians buried their slain for three days.

7 The children of Israel traveled from Succoth and encamped in Ethom, at the end of the wilderness.

8 On the third day after the Egyptians had buried their firstborn, many men rose up from Egypt and went after Israel to make them return to Egypt, for they regretted that they had sent the Israelites away from serving them.

9 One man said to his neighbor, Certainly Moses and Aaron spoke to

Pharaoh saying, We will go a three days' journey in the wilderness and sacrifice to the Lord our God.

10 So now let us rise up early in the morning and make them return; it shall be that if they return with us to Egypt to their masters, then we will know that there is faith in them, but if they will not return then will we fight with them, and make them come back with great power and a strong hand.

11 All the nobles of Pharaoh rose up in the morning, and with them about seven hundred thousand men; they went forth from Egypt on that day and came to the place where the children of Israel were.

12 And all the Egyptians looked and saw Moses and Aaron and all the children of Israel were sitting before Pi-hahiroth, eating and drinking and celebrating the feast of the Lord.

13 All the Egyptians said to the children of Israel, Certainly you said, We will go a journey for three days in the wilderness and sacrifice to our God and return.

14 So now this day makes five days since you went; why do you not return to your masters?

15 Moses and Aaron answered them, saying, Because the Lord our God has testified in us saying, You shall no more return to Egypt, but take yourselves to a land flowing with milk and honey; as the Lord our God had sworn to our ancestors to give to us.

16 And when the nobles of Egypt saw that the children of Israel did not listen to them to return to Egypt, they prepared themselves to fight with Israel.

17 The Lord strengthened the hearts of the children of Israel over the Egyptians so that they gave them a severe beating; the battle was severe on the Egyptians and all the Egyptians fled from before the children of Israel; many of them perished by the hand of Israel.

18 And the nobles of Pharaoh went to Egypt and told Pharaoh, saying, The children of Israel have fled and will no more return to Egypt, and in this manner did Moses and Aaron speak to us.

19 Pharaoh heard this thing, and his heart and the hearts of all his subjects were turned against Israel; they repented that they had sent Israel, and all the Egyptians advised Pharaoh to pursue the children of Israel to make them come back to their burdens.

20 They said each man to his brother, What is this which we have done,

that we have sent Israel from our service?

21 The Lord strengthened the hearts of all the Egyptians to pursue the Israelites, for the Lord desired to overthrow the Egyptians in the Red Sea.

22 Pharaoh rose up and harnessed his chariot; he ordered all the Egyptians to assemble, not one man was left excepting the little ones and the women.

23 And all the Egyptians went forth with Pharaoh to pursue the children of Israel, and the camp of Egypt was a very large and strong camp, about ten hundred thousand men.

24 All of this camp went and pursued the children of Israel to bring them back to Egypt, and they reached them encamping by the Red Sea.

25 The children of Israel lifted up their eyes, and saw all the Egyptians pursuing them; the children of Israel were greatly terrified at them and the children of Israel cried to the Lord.

26 On account of the Egyptians, the children of Israel divided themselves into four divisions and they were divided in their opinions for they were afraid of the Egyptians, and Moses spoke to each of them.

27 The first division was of the children of Reuben, Simeon, and Issachar, and they decided to cast themselves into the sea, for they were greatly afraid of the Egyptians.

28 And Moses said to them, Fear not, stand still and see the salvation of the Lord which He will effect this day for you.

29 The second division was of the children of Zebulun, Benjamin and Naphtali, and they resolved to go back to Egypt with the Egyptians.

30 And Moses said to them, Fear not, for as you have seen the Egyptians this day, so shall you see them no more for ever.

31 The third division was of the children of Judah and Joseph, and they resolved to go to meet the Egyptians to fight with them.

32 And Moses said to them, Stand in your places for the Lord will fight for you, and you shall remain silent.

33 And the fourth division was of the children of Levi, Gad, and Asher, and they resolved to go into the midst of the Egyptians to confound them. Moses said to them, Remain in your stations and fear not, only call to the Lord that he may save you out of their hands.

34 After this Moses rose up from among the people and prayed to the Lord and said,

35 O Lord God of the whole earth, save now your people whom you brought forth from Egypt, and let not the Egyptians boast that power and might are theirs.

36 So the Lord said to Moses, Why do you cry to me? Speak to the children of Israel that they shall proceed, and stretch out your rod on the sea and divide it and the children of Israel shall pass through it.

37 And Moses did so; he lifted up his rod on the sea and divided it.

38 And the waters of the sea were divided into twelve parts, and the children of Israel passed through on foot with shoes, as a man would pass through a prepared road.

39 The Lord displayed to the children of Israel his wonders in Egypt and in the sea by the hand of Moses and Aaron.

40 When the children of Israel had entered the sea the Egyptians came after them, and the waters of the sea covered them and they all sank in the water; not one man was left except Pharaoh, who gave thanks to the Lord and believed in him, therefore the Lord did not cause him to perish at that time with the Egyptians.

41 The Lord ordered an angel to take him from among the Egyptians, who cast him on the land of Ninevah and he reigned over it for a long time.

42 On that day the Lord saved Israel from the hand of Egypt, and all the children of Israel saw that the Egyptians had perished; they beheld the great hand of the Lord in what he had performed in Egypt and in the sea.

43 Then sang Moses and the children of Israel this song to the Lord, on the day when the Lord caused the Egyptians to fall before them.

44 And all Israel sang in concert saying, I will sing to the Lord for He is greatly exalted, the horse and his rider has he cast into the sea, consider that it is written in the book of the law of God.

45 After this the children of Israel proceeded on their journey and encamped in Marah; the Lord gave to the children of Israel statutes and judgments in that place in Marah, and the Lord commanded the children of Israel to walk in all his ways and to serve him.

46 They journeyed from Marah and came to Elim; in Elim were twelve springs of water and seventy date trees and the children encamped there by the waters.

47 They journeyed from Elim and came to the wilderness of Sin, on the fifteenth day of the second month after their departure from Egypt.

48 At that time the Lord gave manna to the children of Israel to eat, and the Lord caused food to rain from heaven for the children of Israel day by day.

49 And the children of Israel ate the manna for forty years, all the days that they were in the wilderness, until they came to the land of Canaan to possess it.

50 They proceeded from the wilderness of Sin and encamped in Alush.

51 And they proceeded from Alush and encamped in Rephidim.

52 When the children of Israel were in Rephidim, Amalek the son of Eliphaz, the son of Esau, the brother of Zepho, came to fight with Israel.

53 And he brought with him eight hundred and one thousand men, magicians and conjurers, and he prepared for battle with Israel in Rephidim.

54 They carried on a great and severe battle against Israel, and the Lord delivered Amalek and his people into the hands of Moses and the children of Israel, and into the hand of Joshua, the son of Nun, the Ephrathite, the servant of Moses.

55 The children of Israel struck Amalek and his people at the edge of the sword, but the battle was very severe on the children of Israel.

56 And the Lord said to Moses, Write this thing as a memorial for you in a book, and place it in the hand of Joshua, the son of Nun your servant; you shall command the children of Israel, saying, When you come to the land of Canaan, you shall utterly wipe out the remembrance of Amalek from under heaven.

57 And Moses did so, and he took the book and wrote on it these words, saying,

58 Remember what Amalek has done to you in the road when you went forth from Egypt.

59 He met you in the road and struck your rear, even those that were feeble behind you when you were faint and weary.

60 Therefore it shall be when the Lord your God shall have given you rest from all your enemies round about in the land which the Lord your God gives you for an inheritance, to possess it, that you shall blot out the remembrance of Amalek from under heaven, you shall not forget it.

61 The king who shall have pity on Amalek or on his memory or on his offspring, behold I will blame him, and I will cut him off from among his people.

62 And Moses wrote all these things in a book, and he advised the children of Israel respecting all these matters.

CHAPTER 82

1 The children of Israel proceeded from Rephidim and camped in the wilderness of Sinai, in the third month from their going forth from Egypt.

2 At that time Reuel the Midianite, the father-in-law of Moses, came with Zipporah his daughter and her two sons for he had heard of the wonders of the Lord which he had done to Israel, that he had delivered them from the hand of Egypt.

3 Reuel came to Moses in the wilderness where he was camped, where the mountain of God was.

4 And Moses went forth to meet his father-in-law with great honor, and all Israel was with him.

5 Reuel and his children remained among the Israelites for many days, and Reuel knew the Lord from that day forward.

6 In the third month from the children of Israel's departure from Egypt, on the sixth day, the Lord gave to Israel the ten commandments on Mount Sinai.

7 All Israel heard all these commandments, and all Israel rejoiced greatly in the Lord on that day.

8 And the glory of the Lord rested on Mount Sinai; he called to Moses and Moses came in the midst of a cloud and ascended the mountain.

9 Moses was on the mount forty days and forty nights; he ate no bread and drank no water, and the Lord instructed him in the standards and judgments in order to teach the children of Israel.

10 And the Lord wrote the ten commandments which he had commanded the children of Israel on two tablets of stone, which he gave to Moses to command the children of Israel.

11 At the end of forty days and forty nights, when the Lord had finished speaking to Moses on Mount Sinai, the Lord gave to Moses the tablets of stone written with the finger of God.

12 When the children of Israel saw that Moses delayed coming down

from the mount, they gathered round Aaron and said, As for this man Moses, we know not what has become of him.

13 Now therefore rise up, make to us a god who shall go before us, so that you shall not die.

14 Aaron was greatly afraid of the people, and he ordered them to bring him gold and he made it into a molten calf for the people.

15 The Lord said to Moses, before he had come down from the mount, Go down, for your people whom you brought forth from Egypt have corrupted themselves.

16 They have made to themselves a molten calf and have bowed down to it; now therefore leave me, that I may consume them from off the earth for they are a stubborn people.

17 And Moses sought the countenance of the Lord, and he prayed to the Lord for the people on account of the calf which they had made; afterward he descended from the mount and in his hands were the two tablets of stone which God had given him to command the Israelites.

18 When Moses approached the camp and saw the calf which the people had made, the anger of Moses was set ablaze and he broke the tablets under the mount.

19 Moses came to the camp; he took the calf and burned it with fire, and ground it till it became fine dust and scattered it on the water, and gave it to the Israelites to drink.

20 There died of the people by the swords of each other about three thousand men who had made the calf.

21 The next morning Moses said to the people, I will go up to the Lord, perhaps I may make atonement for your sins which you have sinned to the Lord.

22 And Moses again went up to the Lord, and he remained with the Lord forty days and forty nights.

23 And during the forty days Moses entreaed the Lord on behalf of the children of Israel, and the Lord listened to the prayer of Moses, and the Lord was begged of him on behalf of Israel.

24 Then spoke the Lord to Moses to cut out two stone tablets and to bring them up to the Lord, who would write on them the ten commandments.

25 Moses did so, and he came down and fashioned the two tablets and went up to Mount Sinai to the Lord, and the Lord wrote the ten commandments on the tablets.

26 Moses remained yet with the Lord forty days and forty nights, and the Lord instructed him in standards and judgments to give to Israel.

27 The Lord commanded him respecting the children of Israel that they should make a sanctuary for the Lord that his name might rest therein, and the Lord showed him the likeness of the sanctuary and the likeness of all its vessels.

28 And at the end of the forty days, Moses came down from the mount and the two tablets were in his hand.

29 And Moses came to the children of Israel and spoke to them all the words of the Lord, and he taught them laws, rules and judgments which the Lord had taught him.

30 Moses told the children of Israel the word of the Lord, that a sanctuary should be made for him to dwell among the children of Israel.

31 And the people rejoiced greatly at all the good which the Lord had spoken to them through Moses, and they said, We will do all that the Lord has spoken to you.

32 And the people rose up like one man and they made generous offerings to the sanctuary of the Lord; each man brought the offering of the Lord for the work of the sanctuary and for all its service.

33 All the children of Israel brought each man of all that was found in his possession for the work of the sanctuary of the Lord, gold, silver and brass, and every thing that was serviceable for the sanctuary.

34 All the wise men who were practiced in work came and made the sanctuary of the Lord, according to all that the Lord had commanded, every man in the work in which he had skill; all the wise men in heart made the sanctuary and its furniture and all the vessels for the holy service as the Lord had commanded Moses.

35 And the work of the sanctuary of the tabernacle was completed at the end of five months; the children of Israel did all that the Lord had commanded Moses.

36 And they brought the sanctuary and all its furniture to Moses; like to the representation which the Lord had shown to Moses, so did the children of Israel.

37 And Moses saw the work, and behold they did it as the Lord had commanded him, so Moses blessed them.

CHAPTER 83

1 In the twelfth month, in the twenty-third day of the month, Moses took Aaron and his sons and dressed them in their garments and anointed them, and did to them as the Lord had commanded him, and Moses brought up all the offerings which the Lord had on that day commanded him.

2 Moses afterward took Aaron and his sons and said to them, For seven days you shall remain at the door of the tabernacle, for thus am I commanded.

3 And Aaron and his sons did all that the Lord had commanded them through Moses, and they remained for seven days at the door of the tabernacle.

4 On the eighth day, being the first day of the first month, in the second year from the Israelites' departure from Egypt, Moses erected the sanctuary and put in all the furniture of the tabernacle and all the furniture of the sanctuary, and he did all that the Lord had commanded him.

5 Moses called to Aaron and his sons, and they brought the burnt offering and the sin offering for themselves and the children of Israel, as the Lord had commanded Moses.

6 On that day the two sons of Aaron, Nadab and Abihu, took strange fire and brought it before the Lord who had not commanded them to do it, and a fire went forth from before the Lord and consumed them, and they died before the Lord on that day.

7 Then on the day when Moses had completed erecting the sanctuary, the princes of the children of Israel began to bring their offerings before the Lord for the dedication of the altar.

8 And they brought up their offerings each prince for one day, a prince each day for twelve days.

9 And all the offerings which they brought, each man in his day, one silver charger weighing one hundred and thirty shekels, one silver bowl of seventy shekels after the shekel of the sanctuary, both of them full of fine

flour mingled with oil for a meat offering;

10 One spoon, weighing ten shekels of gold, full of incense;

11 One young bullock, one ram, one lamb of the first year for a burnt offering;

12 And one kid of the goats for a sin offering.

13 For a sacrifice of peace offering: two oxen, five rams, five male goats, five lambs of a year old.

14 Thus did the twelve princes of Israel day by day, each man in his day.

15 It was after this in the thirteenth day of the month, that Moses commanded the children of Israel to observe the Passover.

16 And the children of Israel kept the Passover in its season in the fourteenth day of the month; as the Lord had commanded Moses, so did the children of Israel.

17 And in the second month, on the first day thereof, the Lord spoke to Moses saying,

18 Number the heads of all the males of the children of Israel from twenty years old and upward, you and your brother Aaron and the twelve princes of Israel.

19 And Moses did so, and Aaron came with the twelve princes of Israel, and they counted the children of Israel in the wilderness of Sinai.

20 And the number of the children of Israel by the houses of their fathers, from twenty years old and upward, were six hundred and three thousand, five hundred and fifty.

21 But the children of Levi were not numbered among their brothers the children of Israel.

22 And the number of all the males of the children of Israel from one month old and upward, was twenty-two thousand, two hundred and seventy-three.

23 And the number of the children of Levi from one month old and above, was twenty-two thousand.

24 Moses placed the priests and the Levites each man to his service and to his burden to serve the sanctuary of the tabernacle, as the Lord had commanded Moses.

25 And on the twentieth day of the month, the cloud was taken away from the tabernacle of testimony.

26 At that time the children of Israel continued their journey from the wilderness of Sinai, they took a journey of three days and the cloud rested on the wilderness of Paran; there the anger of the Lord was set ablaze against Israel, for they had provoked the Lord in asking him for meat to eat.

27 And the Lord listened to their voice, and gave them meat which they ate for one month.

28 But after this the anger of the Lord was set ablaze against them, and he struck them with a great slaughter, and they were buried there in that place.

29 The children of Israel called that place Kebroth Hattaavah, because there they buried the people that lusted flesh.

30 And they departed from Kebroth Hattaavah and pitched in Hazeroth, which is in the wilderness of Paran.

31 And while the children of Israel were in Hazeroth, the anger of the Lord was set ablaze against Miriam on account of Moses, and she became leprous, white as snow.

32 She was confined outside the camp for seven days until she had been received again after her leprosy.

33 The children of Israel afterward departed from Hazeroth and camped in the end of the wilderness of Paran.

34 At that time, the Lord spoke to Moses to send twelve men from the children of Israel, one man to a tribe, to go and explore the land of Canaan.

35 Moses sent the twelve men and they came to the land of Canaan to search and examine it, and they explored the whole land from the wilderness of Sin to Rechob as you come to Chamoth.

36 At the end of forty days they came to Moses and Aaron, and they brought him word as it was in their hearts; ten of the men brought up an evil report to the children of Israel, of the land which they had explored saying, It is better for us to return to Egypt than to go to this land, a land that consumes its inhabitants.

37 But Joshua the son of Nun and Caleb the son of Jephuneh, who were of those that explored the land said, The land is very good.

38 If the Lord delights in us, then he will bring us to this land and give it to us for it is a land flowing with milk and honey.

39 But the children of Israel would not listen to them, and they listened to the words of the ten men who had brought up an evil report of the land.

40 The Lord heard the murmurings of the children of Israel and he was angry and swore, saying,

41 Certainly not one man of this wicked generation shall see the land from twenty years old and upward except Caleb the son of Jephuneh and Joshua the son of Nun.

42 But certainly this wicked generation shall perish in this wilderness, and their children shall come to the land and they shall possess it. So the anger of the Lord was set ablaze against Israel and he made them wander in the wilderness for forty years until the end of that wicked generation because they did not follow the Lord.

43 And the people lived in the wilderness of Paran a long time, and they afterward proceeded to the wilderness by the way of the Red Sea.

CHAPTER 84

1 At that time Korah the son of Jetzer the son of Kehath the son of Levi, took many men of the children of Israel and they rose up and quarreled with Moses and Aaron and the whole congregation.

2 And the Lord was angry with them and the earth opened its mouth and swallowed them up, with their houses and all belonging to them, and all the men belonging to Korah.

3 After this God made the people go round by the way of Mount Seir for a long time.

4 At that time the Lord said to Moses, Provoke not a war against the children of Esau, for I will not give to you of any thing belonging to them, as much as the sole of the foot could tread on, for I have given Mount Seir for an inheritance to Esau.

5 Therefore did the children of Esau fight against the children of Seir in former times, and the Lord had delivered the children of Seir into the hands of the children of Esau, and destroyed them from before them and the children of Esau lived in their stead to this day.

6 So the Lord said to the children of Israel, Fight not against the children of Esau your brothers for nothing in their land belongs to you, but you may buy food of them for money and eat it, and you may buy water of them for money and drink it.

7 And the children of Israel did according to the word of the Lord.

8 The children of Israel wandered in the wilderness, going round by the way of Mount Sinai for a long time, and touched not the children of Esau; they continued in that district for nineteen years.

9 At that time Latinus king of the children of Chittim died, in the forty-fifth year of his reign, which is the fourteenth year of the children of Israel's departure from Egypt.

10 They buried him in his place which he had built for himself in the land of Chittim, and Abimnas reigned in his place for thirty-eight years.

11 The children of Israel passed the boundary of the children of Esau in those days, at the end of nineteen years, and they came and passed the road of the wilderness of Moab.

12 And the Lord said to Moses, Besiege not Moab, and do not fight against them, for I will give you nothing of their land.

13 And the children of Israel passed the road of the wilderness of Moab for nineteen years, and they did not fight against them.

14 In the thirty-sixth year of the children of Israel's departing from Egypt the Lord struck the heart of Sihon, king of the Amorites; he waged war and went forth to fight against the children of Moab.

15 And Sihon sent messengers to Beor the son of Janeas, the son of Balaam, counsellor to the king of Egypt and to Balaam his son, to curse Moab in order that it might be delivered into the hand of Sihon.

16 And the messengers went and brought Beor the son of Janeas, and Balaam his son, from Pethor in Mesopotamia; so Beor and Balaam his son came to the city of Sihon and they cursed Moab and their king in the presence of Sihon king of the Amorites.

17 So Sihon went out with his whole army and he went to Moab and fought against them; he subdued them and the Lord delivered them into his hands, and Sihon killed the king of Moab.

18 Sihon took all the cities of Moab in the battle; he also took Heshbon from them, for Heshbon was one of the cities of Moab, and Sihon placed his princes and his nobles in Heshbon, and Heshbon belonged to Sihon in those days.

19 Therefore the parable speakers (wise men), Beor and Balaam his son, uttered these words, saying, Come to Heshbon, the city of Sihon will be built and established.

20 Woe to you Moab! You are lost, O people of Kemosh! Behold it is

written on the book of the law of God.

21 And when Sihon had conquered Moab, he placed guards in the cities which he had taken from Moab, and a considerable number of the children of Moab fell in battle into the hand of Sihon; he made a great capture of them, sons and daughters, and he killed their king; so Sihon turned back to his own land.

22 And Sihon gave numerous presents of silver and gold to Beor and Balaam his son, and he dismissed them, and they went to Mesopotamia to their home and country.

23 At that time all the children of Israel passed from the road of the wilderness of Moab, and returned and surrounded the wilderness of Edom.

24 So the whole congregation came to the wilderness of Sin in the first month of the fortieth year from their departure from Egypt, and the children of Israel lived there in Kadesh of the wilderness of Sin, and Miriam died there and she was buried there.

25 At that time Moses sent messengers to Hadad king of Edom, saying, Thus says your brother Israel, Let me pass I pray you through your land, we will not pass through field or vineyard, we will not drink the water of the well; we will walk in the king's road.

26 And Edom said to him, You shall not pass through my country. And Edom went forth to meet the children of Israel with a mighty people.

27 And the children of Esau refused to let the children of Israel pass through their land, so the Israelites left them and did not fight against them.

28 For before this the Lord had commanded the children of Israel, saying, You shall not fight against the children of Esau. Therefore the Israelites went away from them and did not fight against them.

29 So the children of Israel departed from Kadesh, and all the people came to Mount Hor.

30 At that time the Lord said to Moses, Tell your brother Aaron that he shall die there, for he shall not come to the land which I have given to the children of Israel.

31 And Aaron went up at the command of the Lord to Mount Hor, in the fortieth year, in the fifth month, in the first day of the month.

32 And Aaron was one hundred and twenty-three years old when he died in Mount Hor.

CHAPTER 85

1 The king Arad the Canaanite, who lived in the south, heard that the Israelites had come by the way of the spies, and he arranged his forces to fight against the Israelites.

2 And the children of Israel were greatly afraid of him, for he had a great and courageous army, so the children of Israel resolved to return to Egypt.

3 The children of Israel turned back about the distance of three days' journey to Maserath Beni Jaakon, for they were greatly afraid on account of the king Arad.

4 And the children of Israel would not get back to their places, so they remained in Beni Jaakon for thirty days.

5 When the children of Levi saw that the children of Israel would not turn back, they were zealous for the sake of the Lord; they rose up and fought against the Israelites their brothers, and killed of them a great many and forced them to turn back to their place, Mount Hor.

6 And when they returned, king Arad was still arranging his host for battle against the Israelites.

7 Israel vowed a vow saying, If you will deliver this people into my hand, then I will utterly destroy their cities.

8 The Lord listened to the voice of Israel, and he delivered the Canaanites into their hands; he utterly destroyed them and their cities, and he called the name of the place Hormah.

9 The children of Israel journeyed from Mount Hor and camped in Oboth, and they journeyed from Oboth and they camped at Ije-abarim, in the border of Moab.

10 And the children of Israel sent to Moab, saying, Let us pass now through your land into our place, but the children of Moab would not allow the children of Israel to pass through their land, for the children of Moab were greatly afraid that the children of Israel should do to them as Sihon king of the Amorites had done to them, who had taken their land and had slain many of them.

11 Therefore Moab would not permit the Israelites to pass through his land, and the Lord commanded the children of Israel, saying that they should not fight against Moab, so the Israelites removed themselves from

Moab.

12 And the children of Israel journeyed from the border of Moab; they came to the other side of Arnon, the border of Moab, between Moab and the Amorites, and they camped on the border of Sihon, king of the Amorites, in the wilderness of Kedemoth.

13 The children of Israel sent messengers to Sihon, king of the Amorites, saying,

14 Let us pass through your land; we will not turn into the fields or into the vineyards; we will go along by the king's highway until we shall have passed your border. But Sihon would not let the Israelites pass.

15 So Sihon collected all the people of the Amorites and went forth into the wilderness to meet the children of Israel, and he fought against Israel in Jahaz.

16 The Lord delivered Sihon king of the Amorites into the hands of the children of Israel, and Israel struck all the people of Sihon with the edge of the sword and avenged the cause of Moab.

17 The children of Israel took possession of the land of Sihon from Aram to Jabuk, to the children of Ammon, and they took all the booty of the cities.

18 Israel took all these cities, and Israel lived in all the cities of the Amorites.

19 All the children of Israel resolved to fight against the children of Ammon, to take their land also.

20 So the Lord said to the children of Israel, Do not besiege the children of Ammon, neither stir up battle against them, for I will give nothing to you of their land; the children of Israel listened to the word of the Lord, and did not fight against the children of Ammon.

21 The children of Israel turned and went up by the way of Bashan to the land of Og, king of Bashan, and Og the king of Bashan went out to meet the Israelites in battle; he had with him many courageous men, and a very strong force from the people of the Amorites.

22 And Og king of Bashan was a very powerful man, but Naaron his son was greatly powerful, even stronger than he was.

23 And Og said in his heart, Behold now the whole camp of Israel takes up a space of several miles. Now will I strike them at once without sword or spear.

24 Og went up Mount Jahaz and took from there one large stone, the length of which was three parsa, and he placed it on his head, and resolved to throw it on the camp of the children of Israel to strike all the Israelites with that stone.

25 And the angel of the Lord came and pierced the stone on the head of Og, and the stone fell on the neck of Og so that Og fell to the earth on account of the weight of the stone on his neck.

26 At that time the Lord said to the children of Israel, Be not afraid of him for I have given him and all his people and all his land into your hands, and you shall do to him as you did to Sihon.

27 Moses went down to him with a small number of the children of Israel, and Moses struck Og with a stick at the ankles of his feet and killed him.

28 The children of Israel afterward pursued the children of Og and all his people; they beat and destroyed them till there was no remnant left of them.

29 Moses afterward sent some of the children of Israel to spy out Jaazer, for Jaazer was a very famous city.

30 The spies went to Jaazer and explored it, and the spies trusted in the Lord; they fought against the men of Jaazer.

31 These men took Jaazer and its villages and the Lord delivered them into their hands, and they drove out the Amorites who had been there.

32 And the children of Israel took the land of the two kings of the Amorites, sixty cities which were on the other side of Jordan, from the brook of Arnon to Mount Herman.

33 The children of Israel journeyed and came into the plain of Moab which is on this side of Jordan, by Jericho.

34 And the children of Moab heard all the evil which the children of Israel had done to the two kings of the Amorites, to Sihon and Og; so all the men of Moab were greatly afraid of the Israelites.

35 The elders of Moab said, Behold the two kings of the Amorites, Sihon and Og, who were more powerful than all the kings of the earth, if they could not stand against the children of Israel how then can we stand before them?

36 Certainly they sent us a message before now to pass through our land on their way, and we would not allow them; now they will turn on us with their heavy swords and destroy us. Moab was distressed on account of the children of Israel and they were greatly afraid of them, and they counselled together what was to be done to the children of Israel.

37 The elders of Moab decided and took one of their men, Balak the son of Zippor the Moabite, and made him king over them at that time, and Balak was a very wise man.

38 And the elders of Moab rose up and sent to the children of Midian to make peace with them, for a great battle and enmity had been in those days between Moab and Midian, from the days of Hadad the son of Bedad king of Edom, who struck Midian in the field of Moab, to these days.

39 The children of Moab sent to the children of Midian and made peace with them, and the elders of Midian came to the land of Moab to make peace on behalf of the children of Midian.

40 And the elders of Moab counselled with the elders of Midian what to do in order to save their lives from Israel.

41 All the children of Moab said to the elders of Midian, The children of Israel shall lick up all that are round about us, as the ox licks up the grass of the field, for thus did they do to the two kings of the Amorites who are stronger than we are.

42 The elders of Midian said to Moab, We have heard that at the time when Sihon king of the Amorites fought against you, when he prevailed over you and took your land, he had sent to Beor the son of Janeas and to Balaam his son from Mesopotamia, and they came and cursed you; therefore did the hand of Sihon prevail over you, that he took your land.

43 Now therefore you send also to Balaam his son for he still remains in his land and give him his wage, that he may come and curse all the people of whom you are afraid; so the elders of Moab heard this thing, and it pleased them to send to Balaam the son of Beor.

44 So Balak the son of Zippor king of Moab sent messengers to Balaam, saying,

45 Behold there is a people come out from Egypt, see how they cover the face of the earth and they are against me.

46 So now come and curse this people for me for they are too mighty for me; perhaps I shall succeed to fight against them and drive them out, for I heard that he whom you bless is blessed, and whom you curse is cursed.

47 So the messengers of Balak went to Balaam and brought Balaam to curse the people to fight against Moab.

48 And Balaam came to Balak to curse Israel, and the Lord said to Balaam, Curse not this people for they are blessed.

49 And Balak urged Balaam day by day to curse Israel, but Balaam did

not listen to Balak on account of the word of the Lord which he had spoken to Balaam.

50 And when Balak saw that Balaam would not accede to his wish, he rose up and went home; Balaam also returned to his land and he went from there to Midian.

51 The children of Israel journeyed from the plain of Moab and camped by Jordan from Beth-jesimoth even to Abel-shittim, at the end of the plains of Moab.

52 When the children of Israel stayed in the plain of Shittim, they began to commit prostitution with the daughters of Moab.

53 The children of Israel approached Moab, and the children of Moab pitched their tents opposite to the camp of the children of Israel.

54 The children of Moab were afraid of the children of Israel, and the children of Moab took all their daughters and their wives of beauty and attractive appearance, and dressed them in gold and silver and costly garments.

55 The children of Moab seated those women at the door of their tents in order that the children of Israel might see them and turn to them, and not fight against Moab.

56 All the children of Moab did this thing to the children of Israel, and every man placed his wife and daughter at the door of his tent; all the children of Israel saw the act of the children of Moab, and the children of Israel turned to the daughters of Moab and coveted them, and they went to them.

57 It came to pass that when a Hebrew came to the door of the tent of Moab and saw a daughter of Moab, and desired her in his heart and spoke with her at the door of the tent that which he desired, while they were speaking together the men of the tent would come out and speak to the Hebrew like these words:

58 Certainly you know that we are brothers, we are all the descendants of Lot and the descendants of Abraham his brother, why then will you not remain with us, and why will you not eat our bread and our sacrifice?

59 When the children of Moab had thus overwhelmed him with their speeches and enticed him by their flattering words, they seated him in the tent and cooked and sacrificed for him, and he ate of their sacrifice and of their bread.

60 They then gave him wine and he drank and became intoxicated; they placed before him a beautiful damsel and he did with her as he liked, for

he knew not what he was doing, as he had drunk plentifully of wine.

61 Thus did the children of Moab to Israel in that place, in the plain of Shittim, and the anger of the Lord was set ablaze against Israel on account of this matter; he sent a pestilence among them and there of the Israelites twenty-four thousand men died.

62 Then there was a man of the children of Simeon whose name was Zimri, the son of Salu, who connected himself with the Midianite Cosbi, the daughter of Zur, king of Midian, in the sight of all the children of Israel.

63 And Phineas the son of Elazer, the son of Aaron the priest, saw this wicked thing which Zimri had done; he took a spear and rose up and went after them, pierced them both and killed them, and the pestilence ceased from the children of Israel.

CHAPTER 86

1 At that time after the pestilence, the Lord said to Moses and to Elazer the son of Aaron the priest,

2 Count the heads of the whole community of the children of Israel, from twenty years old and upward, all that went forth in the army.

3 And Moses and Elazer numbered the children of Israel after their families, and the number of all Israel was seven hundred thousand, seven hundred and thirty.

4 The number of the children of Levi, from one month old and upward, was twenty-three thousand, and among these there was not a man of those numbered by Moses and Aaron in the wilderness of Sinai.

5 For the Lord had told them that they would die in the wilderness, so they all died, and not one had been left of them excepting Caleb the son of Jephuneh, and Joshua the son of Nun.

6 And it was after this that the Lord said to Moses, Say to the children of Israel to avenge on Midian the cause of their brothers the children of Israel.

7 Moses did so, and the children of Israel chose from among them twelve thousand men, being one thousand to a tribe, and they went to Midian.

8 And the children of Israel warred against Midian, and they killed every male, also the five princes of

Midian, and Balaam the son of Beor they killed with the sword.

9 And the children of Israel took the wives of Midian captive, with their little ones and their cattle, and all belonging to them.

10 They took all the booty and all the valuables, and they brought it to Moses and to Elazer to the plains of Moab.

11 Moses and Elazer and all the princes of the congregation went forth to meet them with joy.

12 And they divided all the goods of Midian, and the children of Israel had been revenged on Midian for the cause of their brothers the children of Israel.

CHAPTER 87

1 At that time the Lord said to Moses, Behold your days are approaching to an end, take now Joshua the son of Nun your servant and place him in the tabernacle and I will command him, and Moses did so.

2 The Lord appeared in the tabernacle in a pillar of cloud, and the pillar of cloud stood at the entrance of the tabernacle.

3 The Lord commanded Joshua the son of Nun and said to him, Be strong and courageous, for you shall bring the children of Israel to the land which I swore to give them, and I will be with you.

4 And Moses said to Joshua, Be strong and courageous, for you will make the children of Israel inherit the land, and the Lord will be with you; he will not leave you nor turn away from you, be not afraid or disheartened.

5 Moses called to all the children of Israel and said to them, You have seen all the good which the Lord your God has done for you in the wilderness.

6 Now therefore observe all the words of this law and walk in the way of the Lord your God, turn not from the way which the Lord has commanded you, either to the right or to the left.

7 And Moses taught the children of Israel rules and judgments and laws to do in the land as the Lord had commanded him.

8 And he taught them the way of the Lord and his laws; behold they are written on the book of the law of God which he gave to the children of Israel by the hand of Moses.

9 And Moses finished commanding the children of Israel, and the Lord said to him, Go up to the Mount Abarim and die there, and be gathered to your people as Aaron your brother was gathered.

10 And Moses went up as the Lord had commanded him, and he died there in the land of Moab by the order of the Lord, in the fortieth year from the Israelites going forth from the land of Egypt.

11 And the children of Israel wept for Moses in the plains of Moab for thirty days, and the days of weeping and mourning for Moses were completed.

CHAPTER 88

1 It was after the death of Moses that the Lord said to Joshua the son of Nun,

2 Rise up and pass the Jordan to the land which I have given to the children of Israel, and you shall make the children of Israel inherit the land.

3 Every place on which the sole of your feet treads shall belong to you; from the wilderness of Lebanon to the great river, the river of Perath, shall be your boundary.

4 No man shall stand up against you all the days of your life; as I was with Moses, so will I be with you, only be strong and of good courage to observe all the law which Moses commanded you; turn not from the way either to the right or to the left, in order that you may prosper in all that you do.

5 And Joshua commanded the officers of Israel, saying, Pass through the camp and command the people, saying, Prepare for yourselves provisions, for in three days more you will pass the Jordan to possess the land.

6 The officers of the children of Israel did so, and they commanded the

people and they did all that Joshua had commanded.

7 Joshua sent two men to spy out the land of Jericho, and the men went and spied out Jericho.

8 And at the end of seven days they came to Joshua in the camp and said to him, The Lord has delivered the whole land into our hands; the inhabitants thereof are melted with fear because of us.

9 And it came to pass after that, that Joshua rose up in the morning and all Israel with him, and they journeyed from Shittim; Joshua and all Israel with him passed the Jordan, and Joshua was eighty-two years old when he passed the Jordan with Israel.

10 The people went up from Jordan on the tenth day of the first month, and they camped in Gilgal at the eastern corner of Jericho.

11 And the children of Israel kept the Passover in Gilgal in the plains of Jericho, on the fourteenth day of the month, as it is written in the law of Moses.

12 The manna ceased at that time on the morning of the Passover, and there was no more manna for the children of Israel and they ate of the produce of the land of Canaan.

13 Jericho was entirely closed against the children of Israel, no one came out or went in.

14 And it was in the second month, on the first day of the month, that the Lord said to Joshua, Rise up, behold I have given Jericho into your hand with all the people there; all your fighting men shall go round the city, once each day, thus shall you do for six days.

15 And the priests shall blow on trumpets; when you hear the sound of the trumpet, all the people shall give a great shouting, that the walls of the city shall fall down; all the people shall go up every man against his opponent.

16 And Joshua did so according to all that the Lord had commanded him.

17 On the seventh day they went round the city seven times, and the priests blew on trumpets.

18 At the seventh round, Joshua said to the people, Shout, for the Lord has delivered the whole city into our hands.

19 Only the city and all that it contains shall be accursed to the Lord, and keep yourselves from the accursed thing, that you make the camp of Israel accursed and trouble it.

20 But all the silver and gold and brass and iron shall be consecrated to

the Lord, they shall come into the treasury of the Lord.

21 And the people blew on trumpets and made a great shouting, and the walls of Jericho fell down; all the people went up, every man straight before him, and they took the city and utterly destroyed all that was in it, both man and woman, young and old, ox and sheep and ass, with the edge of the sword.

22 And they burned the whole city with fire; only the vessels of silver and gold, brass and iron, they put into the treasury of the Lord.

23 Joshua swore at that time, saying, Cursed be the man who builds Jericho; he shall lay the foundation thereof in his firstborn, and in his youngest son he shall set up the gates of it.

24 And Achan the son of Carmi, the son of Zabdi, the son of Zerah, son of Judah, dealt treacherously in the accursed thing, and he took of the accursed thing and hid it in the tent, and the anger of the Lord was set ablaze against Israel.

25 It was after this when the children of Israel had returned from burning Jericho, Joshua sent men to spy out also Ai, and to fight against it.

26 And the men went up and spied out Ai, and they returned and said, Let not all the people go up with you to Ai, only let about three thousand men go up and strike the city, for the men there are few.

27 And Joshua did so; there went up with him of the children of Israel about three thousand men, and they fought against the men of Ai.

28 And the battle was severe against Israel, and the men of Ai struck thirty-six men of Israel, and the children of Israel fled from before the men of Ai.

29 When Joshua saw this thing, he tore his garments and fell on his face to the ground before the Lord, he with the elders of Israel, and they put dust on their heads.

30 And Joshua said, Why O Lord did you bring this people over the Jordan? What shall I say after the Israelites have turned their backs against their enemies?

31 So now all the Canaanites, inhabitants of the land, will hear this thing and surround us and cut off our name.

32 And the Lord said to Joshua, Why do you fall on your face? Rise, get up, for the Israelites have sinned and taken of the accursed thing; I will no more be with them unless they destroy the accursed thing from among them.

33 And Joshua rose up and assembled the people, and brought the Urim by the order of the Lord, and the tribe of Judah was taken, and Achan the son of Carmi was taken.

34 Joshua said to Achan, Tell me my son, what have you done, and Achan said, I saw among the spoil a goodly garment of Shinar and two hundred shekels of silver, and a wedge of gold of fifty shekels weight; I coveted them and took them, and behold they are all hid in the earth in the middle of the tent.

35 And Joshua sent men who went and took them from the tent of Achan, and they brought them to Joshua.

36 Joshua took Achan and these utensils, and his sons and daughters and all belonging to him, and they brought them into the valley of Achor.

37 Joshua burned them there with fire, and all the Israelites stoned Achan with stones; they raised over him a heap of stones, therefore he called that place the valley of Achor. So the Lord's anger was appeased, and Joshua afterward came to the city and fought against it.

38 And the Lord said to Joshua, Fear not, neither be dismayed, behold I have given into your hand Ai, her king and her people, and you shall do to them as you did to Jericho and her king, only the goods and the cattle there you shall take for yourselves; lay an ambush for the city behind it.

39 So Joshua did according to the word of the Lord, and he chose from among the sons of war thirty thousand courageous men; he sent them and they lay in ambush for the city.

40 And he commanded them, saying, When you shall see us we will flee before them with cunning, and they will pursue us; you shall then rise out of the ambush and take the city, and they did so.

41 Joshua fought, and the men of the city went out toward Israel, not knowing that they were lying in ambush for them behind the city.

42 Joshua and all the Israelites pretended to be wearied out before them, and they fled by the way of the wilderness with cunning.

43 The men of Ai gathered all the people who were in the city to pursue the Israelites; they went out and were drawn away from the city; not one remained and they left the city open and pursued the Israelites.

44 Those who were lying in ambush rose up out of their places, hurried to come to the city and took it and set it on fire; the men of Ai turned back, and there the smoke of the city ascended to the skies, and they had no means of retreating either one way or the other.

45 All the men of Ai were in the midst of Israel, some on this side and

some on that side, and they struck them so that not one of them remained.

46 The children of Israel took Melosh king of Ai alive and they brought him to Joshua, and Joshua hanged him on a tree and he died.

47 And the children of Israel returned to the city after having burned it; they struck all those that were in it with the edge of the sword.

48 The number of those that had fallen of the men of Ai, both man and woman, was twelve thousand; only the cattle and the goods of the city they took to themselves, according to the word of the Lord to Joshua.

49 And all the kings on this side Jordan, all the kings of Canaan, heard of the evil which the children of Israel had done to Jericho and to Ai, and they gathered themselves together to fight against Israel.

50 Only the inhabitants of Gibeon were greatly afraid of fighting against the Israelites that they should perish, so they acted cunningly; they came to Joshua and to all Israel and said to them, We have come from a distant land, so now make a covenant with us.

51 And the inhabitants of Gibeon over-reached the children of Israel, and the children of Israel made a covenant with them, and they made peace with them; the princes of the congregation swore to them, but afterward the children of Israel knew that they were neighbors to them and were dwelling among them.

52 But the children of Israel killed them not; for they had sworn to them by the Lord, and they became hewers of wood and drawers of water.

53 Joshua said to them, Why did you deceive me, to do this thing to us? And they answered him, Because it was told to your servants all that you had done to all the kings of the Amorites, and we were greatly afraid of our lives, and we did this thing.

54 Joshua appointed them on that day to hew wood and to draw water, and he divided them for slaves to all the tribes of Israel.

55 And when Adonizedek king of Jerusalem heard all that the children of Israel had done to Jericho and to Ai, he sent to Hoham king of Hebron and to Piram king at Jarmuth, and to Japhia king of Lachish and to Deber king of Eglon, saying,

56 Come up to me and help me, that we may strike the children of Israel and the inhabitants of Gibeon who have made peace with the children of Israel.

57 And they gathered themselves together and the five kings of the Amorites went up with all their camps, a mighty people numerous as the

sand of the seashore.

58 All these kings came and camped before Gibeon, and they began to fight against the inhabitants of Gibeon, and all the men of Gibeon sent to Joshua, saying, Come up quickly to us and help us, for all the kings of the Amorites have gathered together to fight against us.

59 Joshua and all the fighting people went up from Gilgal, and Joshua came suddenly to them and struck these five kings with a great slaughter.

60 And the Lord confounded them before the children at Israel, who struck them with a terrible slaughter in Gibeon, and pursued them along the way that goes up to Beth Horon to Makkedah; they fled from before the children of Israel.

61 And while they were fleeing, the Lord sent on them hailstones from heaven, and more of them died by the hailstones than by the slaughter of the children of Israel.

62 The children of Israel pursued them, and they still struck them in the road, going on and smiting them.

63 And when they were smiting, the day was declining toward evening and Joshua said in the sight of all the people, Sun, stand still on Gibeon, and you moon in the valley of Ajalon, until the nation shall have revenged itself on its enemies.

64 The Lord listened to the voice of Joshua, and the sun stood still in the midst of the heavens, and it stood still six and thirty moments, and the moon also stood still and hurried not to go down a whole day.

65 And there was no day like that, before it or after it that the Lord listened to the voice of a man, for the Lord fought for Israel.

CHAPTER 89

1 Then Joshua spoke this song on the day that the Lord had given the Amorites into the hand of Joshua and the children of Israel, and he said it in the sight of all Israel,

2 You have done mighty things, O Lord, you have performed great deeds; who is like you? My lips shall sing to your name.

3 My goodness and my fortress, my high tower, I will sing a new song to you; with thanksgiving I will sing to you, you are the strength of my

salvation.

4 All the kings of the earth shall praise you, the princes of the world shall sing to you, the children of Israel shall rejoice in your salvation; they shall sing and praise your power.

5 To you, O Lord, we confided; we said you are our God, for you were our shelter and strong tower against our enemies.

6 To you we cried and were not ashamed, in you we trusted and were delivered; when we cried to you, you heard our voice, you delivered our souls from the sword, you showed to us your grace, you gave to us your salvation, you rejoiced our hearts with your strength.

7 You went forth for our salvation, with your arm you redeemed your people; you answered us from the heavens of your holiness, you saved us from ten thousands of people.

8 The sun and moon stood still in heaven, and you stood in your wrath against our oppressors and commanded your judgments over them.

9 All the princes of the earth stood up, the kings of the nations had gathered themselves together, they were not moved at your presence; they desired your battles.

10 You rose against them in your anger, and brought down your wrath on them; you destroyed them in your anger, and cut them off in your heart.

11 Nations have been consumed with your fury, kingdoms have declined because of your wrath, you wounded kings in the day of your anger.

12 You poured out your fury on them, your wrathful anger took hold of them; you turned their iniquity on them, and cut them off in their wickedness.

13 They spread a trap and fell therein; in the net they hid, their foot was caught.

14 Your hand was ready for all your enemies who said, Through their sword they possessed the land, through their arm they lived in the city; you filled their faces with shame, you brought their horns down to the ground, you terrified them in your wrath and destroyed them in your anger.

15 The earth trembled and shook at the sound of your storm over them, you did not withhold their souls from death, and brought down their lives to the grave.

16 You pursued them in your storm, you consumed them in your whirlwind, you turned their rain into hail, they fell in deep pits so that they could not rise.

17 Their carcasses were like rubbish cast out in the middle of the streets.

18 They were consumed and destroyed in your anger, you saved your people with your might.

19 Therefore our hearts rejoice in you, our souls exalt in your salvation.

20 Our tongues shall relate your might, we will sing and praise your wondrous works.

21 For you did save us from our enemies, you did deliver us from those who rose up against us, you did destroy them from before us and depress them beneath our feet.

22 Thus shall all your enemies perish O Lord, and the wicked shall be like chaff driven by the wind, and your beloved shall be like trees planted by the waters.

23 So Joshua and all Israel with him returned to the camp in Gilgal, after having smitten all the kings, so that not a remnant was left of them.

24 And the five kings fled alone on foot from battle and hid themselves in a cave, and Joshua sought for them in the field of battle and did not find them.

25 And it was afterward told to Joshua, saying, The kings are found and there, they are hidden in a cave.

26 And Joshua said, Appoint men to be at the mouth of the cave to guard them, that they not take themselves away. And the children of Israel did so.

27 And Joshua called to all Israel and said to the officers of battle, Place your feet on the necks of these kings, and Joshua said, So shall the Lord do to all your enemies.

28 Joshua commanded afterward that they should kill the kings and cast them into the cave, and put great stones at the mouth of the cave.

29 Joshua went afterward with all the people that were with him on that day to Makkedah, and he struck it with the edge of the sword.

30 He utterly destroyed the souls and all belonging to the city, and he did to the king and people there as he had done to Jericho.

31 He passed from there to Libnah and he fought against it; the Lord delivered it into his hands and Joshua struck it with the edge of the sword,

and all the souls there and he did it and to the king there as he had done to Jericho.

32 From there he passed on to Lachish to fight against it, and Horam king of Gaza went up to assist the men of Lachish, and Joshua struck him and his people until there was none left to him.

33 Joshua took Lachish and all the people there, and he did to it as he had done to Libnah.

34 Joshua passed from there to Eglon, and he took that also; he struck it and all the people there with the edge of the sword.

35 From there he passed to Hebron and fought against it and took it and utterly destroyed it; he returned from there with all Israel to Debir and fought against it and struck it with the edge of the sword.

36 And he destroyed every soul in it, he left none remaining; he did to it and the king thereof as he had done to Jericho.

37 Joshua struck all the kings of the Amorites from Kadesh-barnea to Azah; he took their country at once, for the Lord had fought for Israel.

38 And Joshua with all Israel came to the camp to Gilgal.

39 When at that time Jabin king of Chazor heard all that Joshua had done to the kings of the Amorites, Jabin sent to Jobat king of Midian, and to Laban king of Shimron, to Jephal king of Achshaph, and to all the kings of the Amorites, saying,

40 Come quickly to us and help us, that we may strike the children of Israel before they come on us and do to us as they have done to the other kings of the Amorites.

41 And all these kings listened to the words of Jabin, king of Chazor, and they went forth with all their camps, seventeen kings, and their people were as numerous as the sand on the seashore, together with horses and chariots innumerable; they came and camped together at the waters of Merom, and they were met together to fight against Israel.

42 The Lord said to Joshua, Fear them not, for tomorrow about this time I will deliver them up all slain before you, you shall cripple their horses and burn their chariots with fire.

43 And Joshua with all the men of war came suddenly on them and struck them, and they fell into their hands, for the Lord had delivered them into the hands of the children of Israel.

44 So the children of Israel pursued all these kings with their camps and

struck them until there was none left of them, and Joshua did to them as the Lord had spoken to him.

45 Joshua returned at that time to Chazor and struck it with the sword and destroyed every soul in it and burned it with fire; from Chazor, Joshua passed to Shimron and struck it and utterly destroyed it.

46 From there he passed to Achshaph and he did to it as he had done to Shimron.

47 From there he passed to Adulam and he struck all the people in it, and he did to Adulam as he had done to Achshaph and to Shimron.

48 He passed from them to all the cities of the kings which he had smitten, and he struck all the people that were left of them and he utterly destroyed them.

49 Only their booty and cattle the Israelites took to themselves as a prey, but every human being they struck; they permitted not a soul to live.

50 As the Lord had commanded Moses so did Joshua and all Israel, they failed not in anything.

51 So Joshua and all the children of Israel struck the whole land of Canaan as the Lord had commanded them, and struck all their kings, being thirty and one kings, and the children of Israel took their whole country.

52 Besides the kingdoms of Sihon and Og which are on the other side Jordan, of which Moses had smitten many cities, Moses gave them to the Reubenites and the Gadites and to half the tribe of Manasseh.

53 And Joshua struck all the kings that were on this side of Jordan to the west, and gave them for an inheritance to the nine tribes and to the half tribe of Israel.

54 For five years Joshua carried on the war with these kings, and he gave their cities to the Israelites, and the land became tranquil from battle throughout the cities of the Amorites and the Canaanites.

CHAPTER 90

1 At that time in the fifth year after the children of Israel had passed over Jordan, after the children of Israel had rested from their war with the

Canaanites, great and severe battles arose between Edom and the children of Chittim, and the children of Chittim fought against Edom.

2 Abianus king of Chittim went forth in that year, that is in the thirty-first year of his reign, and a great force with him of the mighty men of the children of Chittim, and he went to Seir to fight against the children of Esau.

3 Hadad the king of Edom heard of his report, and he went forth to meet him with many people and a strong force, and engaged in battle with him in the field of Edom.

4 And the hand of Chittim prevailed over the children of Esau, and the children of Chittim killed of the children of Esau two and twenty thousand men, and all the children of Esau fled from before them.

5 The children of Chittim pursued them and they reached Hadad king of Edom, who was running before them and they caught him alive, and brought him to Abianus king of Chittim.

6 And Abianus ordered him to be slain; Hadad king of Edom died in the forty-eighth year of his reign.

7 And the children of Chittim continued their pursuit of Edom; they struck them with a great slaughter and Edom became subject to the children of Chittim.

8 And the children of Chittim ruled over Edom, and Edom came under the hands of the children of Chittim and became one kingdom from that day.

9 From that time they could no more lift up their heads, and their kingdom became one with the children of Chittim.

10 Abianus placed officers in Edom and all the children of Edom became subject to Abianus, and Abianus turned back to his own land, Chittim.

11 When he returned he renewed his government and built for himself a spacious and fortified palace for a royal residence, and reigned securely over the children of Chittim and over Edom.

12 In those days, after the children of Israel had driven away all the Canaanites and the Amorites, Joshua was old and advanced in years.

13 And the Lord said to Joshua, You are old, advanced in life, and a great part of the land remains to be possessed.

14 Now therefore divide this land for an inheritance to the nine tribes and to the half tribe of Manasseh, and Joshua rose up and did as the Lord had

spoken to him.

15 And he divided the whole land to the tribes of Israel as an inheritance according to their divisions.

16 But to the tribe at Levi he gave no inheritance. The offerings of the Lord are their inheritance as the Lord had spoken of them by the hand of Moses.

17 Joshua gave Mount Hebron to Caleb the son of Jephuneh, one portion above his brothers, as the Lord had spoken through Moses.

18 Therefore Hebron became an inheritance to Caleb and his children to this day.

19 Joshua divided the whole land by lots to all Israel for an inheritance, as the Lord had commanded him.

20 And the children of Israel gave cities to the Levites from their own inheritance, and suburbs for their cattle, and property; as the Lord had commanded Moses so did the children of Israel, and they divided the land by lot whether great or small.

21 They went to inherit the land according to their boundaries, and the children of Israel gave to Joshua the son of Nun an inheritance among them.

22 By the word of the Lord they gave to him the city which he required, Timnath-serach in Mount Ephraim, and he built the city and lived therein.

23 These are the inheritances which Elazer the priest and Joshua the son of Nun and the heads of the fathers of the tribes portioned out to the children of Israel by lot in Shiloh, before the Lord, at the door of the tabernacle, and they left off dividing the land.

24 And the Lord gave the land to the Israelites, and they possessed it as the Lord had spoken to them, and as the Lord had sworn to their ancestors.

25 And the Lord gave to the Israelites rest from all their enemies around them, and no man stood up against them; the Lord delivered all their enemies into their hands, and not one thing failed of all the good which the Lord had spoken to the children of Israel, yes, the Lord performed everything.

26 Joshua called to all the children of Israel and he blessed them, and commanded them to serve

the Lord, and afterward sent them away; they went each man to his city, and each man to his inheritance.

27 And the children of Israel served the Lord all the days of Joshua, and the Lord gave them rest from all around them, and they lived securely in their cities.

28 It came to pass in those days, that Abianus king of Chittim died, in the thirty-eighth year of his reign, that is the seventh year of his reign over Edom; they buried him in his place which he had built for himself, and Latinus reigned in his stead fifty years.

29 During his reign he brought forth an army, and he went and fought against the inhabitants of Britannia and Kernania, the children of Elisha son of Javan, and he succeeded over them and made them subjects.

30 He then heard that Edom had revolted from under the hand of Chittim, and Latinus went to them and struck them and subdued them, and placed them under the hand of the children of Chittim; Edom became one kingdom with the children of Chittim all the days.

31 And for many years there was no king in Edom, and their government was with the children of Chittim and their king.

32 It was in the twenty-sixth year after the children of Israel had passed the Jordan, that is the sixty-sixth year after the children of Israel had departed from Egypt, that Joshua was old, advanced in years, being one hundred and eight years old in those days.

33 Joshua called to all Israel, to their elders, their judges and officers, after the Lord had given to all the Israelites rest from all their enemies round about; Joshua said to the elders of Israel and to their judges, Behold I am old, advanced in years, and you have seen what the Lord has done to all the nations whom he has driven away from before you, for it is the Lord who has fought for you.

34 Now therefore strengthen yourselves to keep and to do all the words of the law of Moses, not to deviate from it to the right or to the left, and not to come among those nations who are left in the land; neither shall you make mention of the name of their gods, but you shall cleave to the Lord your God, as you have done to this day.

35 Joshua greatly encouraged the children of Israel to serve the Lord all their days.

36 And all the Israelites said, We will serve the Lord our God all our days, we and our children, and our children's children, and our offspring forever.

37 Joshua made a covenant with the people on that day and he sent away the children of Israel, and they went each man to his inheritance and to his

city.

38 And it was in those days, when the children of Israel were dwelling securely in their cities, that they buried the coffins of the tribes of their ancestors which they had brought up from Egypt, each man in the inheritance of his children; the twelve sons of Jacob did the children of Israel bury, each man in the possession of his children.

39 And these are the names of the cities where they buried the twelve sons of Jacob, whom the children of Israel had brought up from Egypt:

40 They buried Reuben and Gad on this side of Jordan, in Romia, which Moses had given to their children.

41 And Simeon and Levi they buried in the city Mauda, which he had given to the children of Simeon, and the suburb of the city was for the children of Levi.

42 And Judah they buried in the city of Benjamin opposite Bethlehem.

43 And the bones of Issachar and Zebulun they buried in Zidon, in the portion which fell to their children.

44 Dan was buried in the city of his children in Eshtael, and Naphtali and Asher they buried in Kadesh-naphtali, each man in his place which he had given to his children.

45 And the bones of Joseph they buried in Shechem in the part of the field which Jacob had purchased from Hamor, and which became to Joseph for an inheritance.

46 And they buried Benjamin in Jerusalem opposite the Jebusite, which was given to the children of Benjamin; the children of Israel buried their fathers each man in the city of his children.

47 And at the end of two years, Joshua the son of Nun died, one hundred and ten years old, and the time which Joshua judged Israel was twenty-eight years; Israel served the Lord all the days of his life.

48 And the other affairs of Joshua and his battles and his reproofs with which he reproved Israel, and all which he had commanded them, and the names of the cities which the children of Israel possessed in his days, they are written in the book of the words of Joshua to the children of Israel and in the book of the wars of the Lord, which Moses and Joshua and the children of Israel had written.

49 And the children of Israel buried Joshua in the border of his inheritance, in Timnath-serach which was given to him in Mount Ephraim.

50 And Elazer the son of Aaron died in those days; they buried him in a

hill belonging to Phineas his son, which was given him in Mount Ephraim.

CHAPTER 91

1 At that time, after the death of Joshua, the children of the Canaanites were still in the land, and the Israelites resolved to drive them out.

2 And the children of Israel asked of the Lord, saying, Who shall first go up for us to the Canaanites to fight against them? And the Lord said, Judah shall go up.

3 And the children of Judah said to Simeon, Go up with us into our lot, and we will fight against the Canaanites and we likewise will go up with you in your lot; so the children of Simeon went with the children of Judah.

4 The children of Judah went up and fought against the Canaanites, so the Lord delivered the Canaanites into the hands of the children of Judah; they struck in Bezek ten thousand men.

5 They fought with Adonibezek in Bezek, he fled from before them, and they pursued him and caught him; they took hold of him and cut off his thumbs and great toes.

6 And Adonibezek said, Three score and ten kings having their thumbs and great toes cut off, gathered their meat under my table, as I have done, so God has rewarded me; they brought him to Jerusalem and he died there.

7 And the children of Simeon went with the children of Judah, and they struck the Canaanites with the edge of the sword.

8 The Lord was with the children of Judah, and they possessed the mountain, and the children of Joseph went up to Bethel, the same is Luz, and the Lord was with them.

9 And the children of Joseph spied out Bethel, and the watchmen saw a man going forth from the city, and they caught him and said to him, Show us now the entrance of the city and we will show kindness to you.

10 And that man showed them the entrance of the city, and the children of Joseph came and struck the city with the edge of the sword.

11 The man with his family they sent away, and he went to the Hittites and he built a city; he called the name there Luz, so all the Israelites lived

in their cities, and the children at Israel lived in their cities; the children of Israel served the Lord all the days of Joshua, and all the days of the elders, who had lengthened their days after Joshua, and saw the great work of the Lord which he had performed for Israel.

12 And the elders judged Israel after the death of Joshua for seventeen years.

13 All the elders also fought the battles of Israel against the Canaanites and the Lord drove the Canaanites from before the children of Israel in order to place the Israelites in their land.

14 And he accomplished all the words which he had spoken to Abraham, Isaac, and Jacob, and the oath which he had sworn, to give to them and to their children the land of the Canaanites.

15 The Lord gave to the children of Israel the whole land of Canaan as he had sworn to their ancestors, and the Lord gave them rest from those around them, and the children of Israel lived securely in their cities.

16 Blessed be the Lord forever, amen, and amen.

17 Strengthen yourselves, and let the hearts of all you that trust in the Lord. Be of good courage.

Joseph B. Lumpkin

Lessons and Commentary
Commentary and Study Guide by Leigh Smith

Waters

<u>1st Case - Waters of the Universe</u>

Dad, will you make me something out of wood? Yes my son, but first we need to create space!!! (Leigh)

In the beginning God created the heavens and the earth. The earth was without form, and void; and darkness was on the face of the deep. And the Spirit of God was hovering over the face of the waters. Then God said, "Let there be light"; and there was light. And God saw the light, that it was good; and God divided the light from the darkness. God called the light Day, and the darkness He called Night. So the evening and the morning were the first day. Then God said, "Let there be a firmament in the midst of the waters, and let it divide the water from the waters." Thus God made the firmament, and divided the waters which were under the firmament from the waters which were above the firmament; and it was so. And God called the firmament Heaven. So the evening and the morning were the second day. (Gen 1:1-8)

The firmament, the continuous arch (ark?) of heaven, is the atmosphere of planet earth. This is where the separation of the waters took place, the lower waters became, of the Earth, the land and seas etc. and the upper waters became, the heavenly hosts of planets, stars, sun and moon etc. Note the 'earthly waters' are separated from the 'heavenly waters'.

Then God said, "Let the waters under the heavens be gathered together into one place, and let the dry land appear"; and it was so. And God called the dry land Earth, and the gathering together of the waters He called Seas. And God saw that it was good. (Gen 1:9-10)

Then God said, "Let there be lights in the firmament of the heavens to divide the day from the night; and let them be for signs and seasons, and for days and years; And let them be for lights in the firmament of the heavens to give light on the earth"; and it was so. Then God made two great lights: the greater light to rule the day, and the lesser light to rule the night. He made the stars also. God set them in the firmament of the heavens to give light on the earth, and to rule over the day and over the night, and to divide the light from the darkness. And God saw that it was good. (Gen 1:14-18)

God creates the Sun, the Moon and Stars and establishes their orbits.

2nd Case - Waters of the planet

Then the Lord said to Noah, "Come into the ark, you and all your household, because I have seen that you are righteous before Me in this generation." (Gen 7:1)

And it came to pass after seven days that the waters of the flood were on the earth. In the six hundredth year of Noah's life, in the second month, the seventeenth day of the month, on that day all the fountains of the great deep were broken up, and the windows of heaven were opened. And the rain was on the earth forty days and forty nights. (Gen 7:11-12)

The Ark of God which Noah built from wood by God's plan in five years, separated the righteous people from the unrighteous people. (people ~ waters, separated by the waters of the flood.)

3rd Case - Waters of the Red Sea

And the Lord said to Moses, "Why do you cry to Me? Tell the children of Israel to go forward. But lift up your rod, and stretch out your hand over the sea and divide it. And the children of Israel shall go on dry ground through the midst of the sea." (Exo 14:15-16)

Then Moses stretched out his hand over the sea; and the Lord caused the sea to go back by a strong east wind all that night, and made the sea into dry land, and the waters were divided. (Exo 14:21)

Then the Lord said to Moses, "Stretch out your hand over the sea, that the waters may come back upon the Egyptians, on their chariots, and on their horsemen." And Moses stretched out his hand over the sea; and when the morning appeared, the sea returned to its full depth, while the Egyptians were fleeing into it. So the Lord overthrew the Egyptians in the midst of the sea. Then the waters returned and covered the chariots, the horsemen, and all the army of Pharaoh that came into the sea after them. Not so much as one of them remained.

(Exo 14:26-28)

The Israelites crossed through the waters of the sea, by an ark of dry land, in the sea. The righteous people were separated from the unrighteous by crossing the waters of the Red Sea.

The rod of God, held in the hand by Moses, is described in the book of Jasher.

And afterward Moses went into the garden of Reuel which was behind the house, and he there prayed to the Lord his God, who had done mighty wonders for him. It was while he prayed he looked opposite to him, and there a sapphire stick was placed in the ground, which was planted in the midst of the garden. He approached the stick and looked, and saw <u>the name of the Lord God of hosts was engraved on it</u>, written and developed on the stick. And he read it and stretched forth his hand and he plucked it like a forest tree from the thicket, and the stick was in his hand. This is the stick with which all the works of our God were performed, after he had created heaven and earth and all the host of them, seas, rivers and all their fish. (Jas 77:38-42)

This rod was the testimony of God before Moses received the two tablets of stone.

Then Moses took his wife and his sons and set them on a donkey, and he returned to the land of Egypt. And Moses took the rod of God in his hand. (Exo 4:20)

When Aaron collected the manna in a pot, which was to be stored in the Ark, the only Testimony Moses had at that time was the rod of God, by which he performed the many miracles.

And Moses said to Aaron, "Take a pot and put an omer of manna in it, and lay it up before the Lord, to be kept for your generations." As the Lord commanded Moses, so Aaron laid it up before the Testimony, to be kept. (Exo 16:33-34)

And when He had made an end of speaking with him on Mount Sinai, He gave Moses two tablets of the Testimony, tablets of stone, written with the finger of God. (Exo 31:18)

Three references to the cross, the disciples and Jesus Christ to come. Bitter waters were made sweet in Exo 15:23-27. In Exo 17:1-7, first the rock / Jesus is beaten (1st strike), then crucified (2nd strike), and then in Num 20:1-13 Moses is told to speak to the rock / Jesus to release the living water. This shows the change in the method to release the power of God; from using the rod of God, the Testimony of God's authority, the law ("It is written"); to the righteous people using the authority of the spoken name of Jesus. Now the Bible is also the Word of God, which is our Testimony.

<u>4th Case - Waters of the river Jordan</u>

And the Lord said to Joshua, "This day I will begin to exalt you in the sight of all Israel, "Behold, the ark of the covenant of the Lord of all the earth is crossing over before you into the Jordan. Now therefore, take for yourselves twelve men from the tribes of Israel, one man from every tribe. And it shall come to pass, as soon as the soles of the feet of the priests who bear the ark of the Lord, the Lord of all the earth, shall rest in the waters of the Jordan, that the waters of the Jordan shall be cut off, the waters that come down from upstream, and they shall stand as a heap." So it was, when the people set out from their camp to cross over the Jordan, with the priests bearing the ark of the covenant before the people, and as those who bore the ark came to the Jordan, and the feet of the priests who bore the ark dipped in the edge of the water (for the Jordan overflows all its banks during the whole time of harvest), that the waters which came down from upstream stood still, and rose in a heap very far away at Adam, the city that is beside Zaretan. So the waters that went down into the Sea of Arabah, the salt sea, failed, and were cut off; and the people crossed over opposite Jericho. Then the priests who bore the ark of the covenant of the Lord stood firm on dry ground in the midst of the Jordan; and all Israel crossed over on dry ground, until all the people had crossed completely over the Jordan. (Jos 3:7-17)

'for the Jordan overflows all its banks during the whole time of harvest' - this day of harvest, speaks to me of Judgement Day when all peoples of the world will be resurrected for judgement by the Lord.

These shall be punished with everlasting destruction from the presence of the Lord and from the glory of His power, when He comes, in that Day, to be glorified in His saints and to be admired among all those who believe, because our testimony among you was believed.

(2Th 1:9-10)

'the waters which came down from upstream stood still, and rose in a heap very far away at Adam' - this reminded me of the following scripture.

For until the law sin was in the world, but sin is not imputed when there is no law. Nevertheless death reigned from Adam to Moses, even over those who had not sinned according to the likeness of the transgression of Adam, who is a type of Him who was to come. But the free gift is not like the offence. For if by the one man's offence many died, much more the grace of God and the gift by the grace of the one Man, Jesus Christ, abounded to many. (Rom 5:13-14)

The circumcised Israelites refused to enter the land of Canaan, disobeying God. It was the uncircumcised that accepted the offer of God and went over the Jordan. Joshua circumcised them on the other side. The righteous people were separated from the unrighteous by crossing the waters of the Jordan river.

At that time the Lord said to Joshua, "Make flint knives for yourself, and circumcise the sons of Israel again the second time." So Joshua made flint knives for himself, and circumcised the sons of Israel at the hill of the foreskins. And this is the reason why Joshua circumcised them: All the people who came out of Egypt who were males, all the men of war, had died in the wilderness on the way, after they had come out of Egypt. For all the people who came out had been circumcised, but all the people born in the wilderness, on the way as they came out of Egypt, had not been circumcised. For the children of Israel walked forty years in the wilderness, till all the people who were men of war, who came out of Egypt, were consumed, because they did not obey the voice of the Lord - to whom the Lord swore that He would not show them the land which the Lord had sworn to their fathers that He would give us, "a land flowing with milk and honey." (Jos 5:2-6)

Moses said;

"Therefore circumcise the foreskin of your heart, and be stiff-necked no longer." (Deu 10:16)

And also;

"Rejoice, O Gentiles, with His people; for He will avenge the blood of His servants, and render vengeance to His adversaries; He will provide atonement for His land and His people."

(Deu 32:43)

Paul said;

"Circumcision is nothing and uncircumcision is nothing, but keeping the commandments of God is what matters." (1Co 7:19)

And also;

"For we through the Spirit eagerly wait for the hope of righteousness by faith. For in Christ Jesus neither circumcision nor uncircumcision avails anything, but faith working through love." (Gal 5:5-6)

<u>5th Case - Waters of Baptism</u>

In those days John the Baptist came preaching in the wilderness of Judea, and saying, "Repent, for the kingdom of heaven is at hand!" (Mat 3:1-2)

Then Jesus came from Galilee to John at the Jordan to be baptized by him. And John tried to prevent Him, saying, "I need to be baptized by You, and are You coming to me?" But Jesus answered and said to him, "Permit it to be so now, for thus it is fitting for us to fulfill all righteousness." Then he allowed Him. When He had been baptized, Jesus came up immediately from the water; and behold, the heavens were opened to Him, and He saw the Spirit of God descending like a dove and alighting upon Him. And suddenly a voice came from heaven, saying, "This is My beloved Son, in whom I am well pleased." (Mat 3:13-17)

This practice of introducing the new covenant with the old covenant procedures is maintained. Jesus is the <u>perfect sacrifice</u> <u>offered once</u> for the redemption of all people to God. His righteous blood cleanses all our sins. He entered <u>the Most Holy Place</u> and now He serves as our <u>High Priest</u>.

But Christ came as <u>High Priest</u> of the good things to come, with the greater and more perfect <u>tabernacle</u> not made with human hands, that is, not of this creation. Not with the <u>blood of goats and calves</u>, but with <u>His own blood</u> He entered <u>the Most Holy Place</u> <u>once for all</u>, having obtained <u>eternal redemption</u>. (Heb 9:11-12)

And for this reason He is the Mediator of the new covenant, by means of death, for the redemption of the transgressions <u>under the first covenant</u>, that those who are called may receive the promise of the eternal inheritance. (Heb 9:15)

Then the eleven disciples went away into Galilee, to the mountain which Jesus had appointed for them. When they saw Him, they worshipped Him; but some doubted. And Jesus came and spoke to them, saying,

"All authority has been given to Me in heaven and on earth. Go therefore and make disciples of all the nations, baptizing them in the name of the Father and of the Son and of the Holy Spirit, teaching them to observe all things that I have commanded you; and lo, I am with you always, even to the end of the age." Amen. (Mat 28:16-20)

This last separation of the righteous people from the unrighteous people by the waters of baptism, takes place on an individual, personal basis. We hereby publicly declare our belief in God the Father, the Son and Holy Spirit; and our commitment to follow Him in spirit and in truth.

-oOo-

Comfortably Numb

I have been enjoying the details of the Book of Jasher, and have been thrilled to discover many revelations of people and situations which are only lightly described in the Bible. Yesterday I came across the following in Jasher and it made me concerned, as I had remembered it differently in Genesis and Exodus. I felt numb.

The children of Israel journeyed from Rameses to Succoth, about six hundred thousand men on foot besides the little ones and their wives. Also a mixed multitude went up with them, flocks and herds, even much cattle. The temporary time of the children of Israel who lived in the land of Egypt in hard labor was two hundred and ten years. And at the end of two hundred and ten years, the Lord brought forth the children of Israel from Egypt with a strong hand.

(Jasher 81:1-4)

Yes, there it is 210 years!

Then He said to Abram: "Know certainly that your descendants will be strangers in a land that is not theirs, and will serve them, and they will afflict them four hundred years. And also the nation whom they serve I will judge; afterward they shall come out with great possessions."

(Gen 15:13-14)

Now the sojourn of the children of Israel who lived in Egypt was four hundred and thirty years. And it came to pass at the end of the four hundred and thirty years - on that very same day - it came to pass that all the armies of the Lord went out from the land of Egypt. (Exo 12:40-41)

Okay, now I was beginning to panic, I've read 80 chapters of Jasher and now I find a mistake! I went back to Genesis and started to investigate calmly.

Now these were the names of the children of Israel, Jacob and his sons, who went to Egypt: Reuben was Jacob's firstborn. The sons of Reuben were Hanoch, Pallu, Hezron, and Carmi. The sons of Simeon were Jemuel, Jamin, Ohad, Jachin, Zohar, and Shaul, the son of a Canaanite woman. The sons of Levi were Gershon, Kohath, and Merari. The sons of Judah were Er, Onan, Shelah, Perez, and Zerah (but Er and Onan died in the land of Canaan). The sons of Perez were Hezron and Hamul. The sons of Issachar were Tola, Puvah, Job, and Shimron. The sons of Zebulun were Sered, Elon, and Jahleel. These were the sons of Leah, whom she bore to Jacob in Padan Aram, with his daughter Dinah. All the persons, his sons and his daughters, were thirty-three. (Gen 46:8-15)

And the sons of Kohath were Amram, Izhar, Hebron, and Uzziel. And the years of the life of Kohath were one hundred and thirty-three. The sons of Merari were Mahli and Mushi. These are the families of Levi according to their generations. Now Amram took for himself Jochebed, his father's sister, as wife; and she bore him Aaron and Moses. And the years of the life of Amram were one hundred and thirty-seven. (Exo 6:18-20)

Then Moses and Aaron did so; just as the Lord commanded them, so they did. And Moses was eighty years old and Aaron eighty-three years old when they spoke to Pharaoh.

(Exo 7:6-7)

According to these verses :-

1)   Jacob, Levi and Kohath entered Egypt. Amram and Jochebed, Kohath's sister were born later.

2) Kohath, the father of Amram, lived a total of one hundred and thirty-three years.

3) Amram, the father of Moses and Aaron, lived a total of one hundred and thirty-seven years.

If you add up the lives of Kohath, Amram and Moses, 133 + 137 + 80 = 350 years!!!

This is very short of 430 and 400 years, and far too much for 210 years!!!

Okay that approach doesn't work!!! So I went back to the Book of Jasher.

It was the fifteenth year of Abram's dwelling in the land of Canaan, which is the seventieth year of the life of Abram, the Lord appeared to Abram in that year and said to him, I am the Lord who brought you out from Ur Casdim to give you this land for an inheritance. Now therefore walk before me and be perfect and keep my commands, for to you and to your descendants I will give this land for an inheritance, from the river Mitzraim to the great river Euphrates. (Jasher 13:17-18)

Abraham called the name of the son which Sarah gave birth to him, Isaac. And Abraham circumcised his son Isaac at eight days old, as God had commanded Abraham to do to his descendants after him; Abraham was one hundred and Sarah was ninety years old when Isaac was born to them. (Jasher 21:2-3)

It was about that time that Abraham died, in the fifteenth year of the life of Jacob and Esau, the sons of Isaac, and all the days of Abraham were one hundred and seventy-five years. He died and was gathered to his people in good old age, old and satisfied with days, and Isaac and Ishmael his sons buried him. (Jasher 26:29)

Jacob lived in the land of Egypt seventeen years, and the days of Jacob, and the years of his life were a hundred and forty seven years. (Jasher 56:1)

And the children of Levi were Gershon, Kehath and Merari, and their sister Jochebed, who was born to them in their going down to Egypt. (Jasher 59:9)

There was a man in the land of Egypt of the children of Levi, whose name was Amram, the son of Kehath, the son of Levi, the son of Israel. And this man went and took a wife, namely Jochebed the daughter of Levi his father's sister, and she was one hundred and twenty-six years old, and he came to her. And the woman conceived and gave birth to a daughter, and she called her name Miriam, because in those days the Egyptians had embittered the lives of the children of Israel. She conceived again and gave birth to a son and she called his name Aaron, for in the days of her conception, Pharaoh began to spill the blood of the male children of Israel. (Jasher 67:2-4)

In the fifty-fifth year of the reign of Pharaoh king of Egypt, that is in the hundred and fifty-seventh year of the Israelites going down into Egypt, Moses reigned in Cush. Moses was twenty-seven years old when he began to reign over Cush, and forty years he did reign.

(Jasher 73:1-2)

According to these verses :-

1)   Abram was seventy years old when the Lord blesses, and tells him of the inheritance of his descendants.

2)   Abraham was one hundred years old when Isaac was born.

3)   When Abraham dies at one hundred and seventy-five years old Jacob is 15 years old.

4)   Jacob was one hundred and thirty years old when he goes down to Egypt.

5)   Moses was born one hundred and thirty years after the Israelites entered Egypt.

6)   Moses was eighty years old when he led the Israelites out of Egypt.

When Abraham first receives the promise, he is 70 years old. One hundred and five years later, he dies, Jacob is fifteen. One hundred and fifteen years later, Jacob goes down to Egypt. One hundred and thirty years later, Moses is born. Eighty years later Moses leads the Israelites out of Egypt.

Therefore : 105 + 115 + 130 + 80 = 430 years. Bingo!

Then He said to Abram: "Know certainly that your descendants will be strangers in a land that is not theirs, and will serve them, and they will afflict them four hundred years. And also the nation whom they serve I will judge; afterward they shall come out with great possessions."
(Gen 15:13-14)

Remember Abraham, Isaac, Jacob and sons were all strangers in the land. And from when Isaac was born till the Israelites left Egypt, was 400 years, so this agrees.

Now the sojourn of the children of Israel who lived in Egypt was four hundred and thirty years. And it came to pass at the end of the four hundred and thirty years - on that very same day - it came to pass that all the armies of the Lord went out from the land of Egypt. (Exo 12:40-41)

From the first promise to Abram at 70 years of age till the Israelites left Egypt, was 430 years, so this also agrees.

The temporary time of the children of Israel who lived in the land of Egypt in hard labor was two hundred and ten years. (Jasher 81:3)

So the Israelites were in Egypt for 210 years, not exactly what I would call temporary!!!

-oOo-

Joseph B. Lumpkin

Racial Offences

Here is the account of Miriam's racial offence against Moses and his Ethiopian wife.

An important lesson to us all regarding gossip, flippant remarks and criticism of others. They actually got off lightly compared to the rebellion of Korah in Numbers 16.

It's good to see how the Book of Jasher compliments the Bible and vice versa, with additional details for the enlightenment of the reader. (leigh)

<u>1B</u>

So Moses went and returned to Jethro his father-in-law, and said to him, "Please let me go and return to my brethren who are in Egypt, and see whether they are still alive."

And Jethro said to Moses, "Go in peace." Now the Lord said to Moses in Midian,

"Go, return to Egypt; for all the men who sought your life are dead." Then Moses took his wife and his sons and set them on a donkey, and he returned to the land of Egypt. And Moses took the rod of God in his hand. And the Lord said to Moses, "When you go back to Egypt, see that you do all those wonders before Pharaoh which I have put in your hand. But I will harden his heart, so that he will not let the people go. Then you shall say to Pharaoh, 'Thus says the Lord: "Israel is My son, My firstborn. So I say to you, let My son go that he may serve Me. But if you refuse to let him go, indeed I will kill your son, your firstborn." ' " And it came to pass on the way, at the encampment, that the Lord met him and sought to kill him. (Exo 4:18-24)

<u>1J</u>

And the Lord said to Moses, Go, return to Egypt for all those men who sought your life are dead, and you shall speak to Pharaoh to send forth the children of Israel from his land. The Lord showed him to do signs and wonders in Egypt before the eyes of Pharaoh and the eyes of his subjects, in order that they might believe that the Lord had sent him. Moses listened to all that the Lord had commanded him, and he returned to his father-in-law and told him these things, and Reuel said to him, Go in peace.

Moses rose up to go to Egypt and took his wife and sons with him; he was at an inn in the road, and an angel of God came down, and sought an occasion against him. He wished to kill him on account of his firstborn son because he had not circumcised him and had gone contrary to the covenant which the Lord had made with Abraham. For Moses had listened to the words of his father-in-law which he had spoken to him, not to circumcise his first born son, so he did not circumcise him. (Jasher 79:5-10)

2B

Then Zipporah took a sharp stone and cut off the foreskin of her son and cast it at Moses' feet, and said, "Surely you are a husband of blood to me!" So He let him go. Then she said, "You are a husband of blood!" - because of the circumcision. (Exo 4:25-26)

2J

Zipporah saw the angel of the Lord seeking an occasion against Moses, and she knew that this thing was because of his not having circumcised her son Gershom. Zipporah hurried and took some of the sharp rock stones that were there, and circumcised her son, and delivered her husband and her son from the hand of the angel of the Lord.

(Jasher 79:11-12)

3B

And the Lord said to Aaron, "Go into the wilderness to meet Moses." So he went and met him on the mountain of God, and kissed him. So Moses told Aaron all the words of the Lord who had sent him, and all the signs which He had commanded him. Then Moses and Aaron went and gathered together all the elders of the children of Israel. And Aaron spoke all the words which the Lord had spoken to Moses. Then he did the signs in the sight of the people. So the people believed; and when they heard that the Lord had visited the children of Israel and that He had looked on their affliction, then they bowed their heads and worshipped. (Exo 4:27-31)

3J

Aaron the son of Amram, the brother of Moses, was in Egypt walking at the river side on that day. And the Lord appeared to him in that place; he said to him, Go now toward Moses in the wilderness. And he went and met him in the mountain of God, and he kissed him. Aaron lifted up his eyes and saw Zipporah the wife of Moses and her children, and he said to Moses, Who are these to you? And Moses said to him, They are my wife and sons which God gave to me in Midian; the thing grieved Aaron on account of the woman and her children. Aaron said to Moses, Send away the woman and her children that they may go to her father's house, and Moses listened to the words of Aaron, and did so.

Zipporah returned with her children and they went to the house of Reuel, and remained there until the time arrived when the Lord had visited his people and brought them forth from Egypt from the hand of Pharaoh. Moses and Aaron came to Egypt to the community of the children of Israel and spoke to them all the words of the Lord, and the people rejoiced a very great rejoicing. (Jasher 79:13-19)

4B

And Jethro, the priest of Midian, Moses' father-in-law, heard of all that God had done for Moses and for Israel His people - that the Lord had brought Israel out of Egypt. Then Jethro, Moses' father-in-law, took Zipporah, Moses' wife, after he had sent her back, with her two sons, of whom the name of one was Gershom (for he said, "I have been a stranger in a foreign land") and the name of the other was Eliezer (for he said, "The God of my father was my help, and delivered me from the sword of Pharaoh"); and Jethro, Moses' father-in-law, came with his sons and his wife to Moses in the wilderness, where he was encamped at the mountain of God. Now he had said to Moses, "I, your father-in-law Jethro, am coming to you with your wife and her two sons with her." So Moses went out to meet his father-in-law, bowed down, and kissed him. And they asked each other about their well-being, and they went into the tent. (Exo 18:1-7)

4J

The children of Israel proceeded from Rephidim and camped in the wilderness of Sinai, in the third month from their going forth from Egypt. At that time Reuel the Midianite, the father-in-law of Moses, came with Zipporah his daughter and her two sons for he had heard of the wonders of the Lord which he had done to Israel, that he had delivered them from the hand of Egypt. Reuel came to Moses in the wilderness where he camped, where the mountain of God was. And Moses went forth to meet his father-in-law with great honor, and all Israel was with him. Reuel and his children remained among the Israelites for many days, and Reuel knew the Lord from that day forward. (Jasher 82:1-5)

5B

Then Miriam and Aaron spoke against Moses because of the Ethiopian woman whom he had married; for he had married an Ethiopian woman. So they said, "Has the Lord indeed spoken only through Moses? Has he not spoken through us also? And the Lord heard it.

(Now the man Moses was very humble, more than all men who were on the face of the earth.) Suddenly the Lord said to Moses, Aaron and Miriam, "Come out, you three, to the tabernacle of meeting!" So the three came out.

Then the Lord came down in the pillar of cloud and stood in the door of the tabernacle, and called Aaron and Miriam. And they both went forward.

Then He said, "Hear now My words: If there is a prophet among you, I, the Lord, make Myself known to him in a vision; I speak to him in a dream. Not so with My servant Moses; he is faithful in all My house. I speak with him face to face, even plainly, and not in dark sayings; and he sees the form of the Lord. Why then were you not afraid to speak against My servant Moses?"

So the anger of the Lord was aroused against them, and He departed. And when the cloud departed from above the tabernacle, suddenly Miriam became leprous, as white as snow. Then Aaron turned toward Miriam, and there she was, a leper.

So Aaron said to Moses, "Oh, my lord! Please do not lay this sin on us, in which we have done foolishly and in which we have sinned. Please do not let her be as one dead, whose flesh is half consumed when he comes out of his mother's womb!"

So Moses cried out to the Lord, saying, "Please heal her, O God, I pray!"

Then the Lord said to Moses, "If her father had but spit in her face, would she not be shamed seven days? Let her be shut out of the camp seven days, and afterward she may be received again."

So Miriam was shut out of the camp seven days, and the people did not journey till Miriam was brought in again. And afterward the people moved from Hazeroth and camped in the wilderness of Paran. (Num 12:1-16)

5]

And they departed from Kebroth Hattaavah, and pitched in Hazeroth, which is in the wilderness of Paran. And while the children of Israel were in Hazeroth, the anger of the Lord was set ablaze against Miriam on account of Moses, and she became leprous, white as snow. She was confined outside the camp for seven days until she had been received again after her leprosy. The children of Israel afterward departed from Hazeroth and camped in the end of the wilderness of Paran. (Jasher 83:30-33)

-oOo-

North, South, East and West

The Lord's promise to Abraham

And the Lord said to Abram, after Lot had separated from him: "Lift your eyes now and look from the place where you are - northwards, southward, eastward, and westward; for all the land which you see I give to you and your descendants forever. And I will make your descendants as the dust of the earth; so that if a man could number the dust of the earth, then your descendants also could be numbered. Arise, walk in the land through its length and its width, for I give it to you." Then Abram moved his tent, and went and dwelt by the terebinth trees of Mamre, which are in Hebron, and built an altar there to the Lord. (Gen 13:14-18)

The Lord's promise to Isaac

There was a famine in the land, besides the first famine that was in the days of Abraham. And Isaac went to Abimelech king of the Philistines, in Gerar. Then the Lord appeared to him and said: "Do not go down to Egypt; live in the land of which I shall tell you. Dwell in this land, and I will be with you and bless you; for to you and your descendants I give all these lands, and I will perform the oath which I swore to Abraham your father. And I will make your descendants multiply as the stars of heaven; I will give to your descendants all these lands; and in your seed all nations of the earth shall be blessed; because Abraham obeyed My voice and kept My charge, My commandments, My statutes, and My laws." So Isaac dwelt in Gerar. (Gen 26:1-6)

The Lord's promise to Jacob

Now Jacob went out from Beersheba and went toward Haran. So he came to a certain place and stayed there all night, because the sun had set. And he took one of the stones of that place and put it at his head, and he lay down in that place to sleep. Then he dreamed, and behold, a ladder was set up on the earth, and its top reached to heaven; and there the angels of God were ascending and descending on it. And behold, the Lord stood above it and said:

"I am the Lord God of Abraham your father and the God of Isaac; the land on which you lie I will give to you and your descendants. Also your descendants shall be as the dust of the earth; you shall spread abroad to the west and the east, to the north and the south; and in you and in your seed all the families of the earth shall be blessed. Behold, I am with you and will keep you wherever you go, and will bring you back to this land; for I will not leave you until I have done what I have spoken to you." Then Jacob awoke from his sleep and said, "Surely the Lord is in this place, and I did not know it." And he was afraid and said, "How awesome is this place! This is none other than the house of God, and this is the gate of heaven!" Then Jacob rose early in the morning, and took the stone that he had put at his head, set it up as a pillar, and poured oil on top of it. And he called the name of that place Bethel; but the name of that city had been Luz previously. Then Jacob made a vow, saying, "If God will be with me, and keep me in this way that I am going, and give me bread to eat and clothing to put on, so that I come back to my father's house in peace, then the Lord shall be my God. And this stone which I have set as a pillar shall be God's house, and all that You give me I will surely give a tenth to You." (Gen 28:10-22)

The instructions of Jacob

Jacob lived in the land of Egypt seventeen years, and the days of Jacob, and the years of his life were a hundred and forty seven years. At that time Jacob was attacked with that illness of which he died and he sent and called for his son Joseph from Egypt, and Joseph his son came from Egypt and came to his father. Jacob said to Joseph and to his sons, Behold I die, and the God of your ancestors will visit you and bring you back to the land which the Lord swore to give to you and to your children after you; now therefore when I am dead, bury me in the cave which is in Machpelah in Hebron in the land of Canaan, near my ancestors. Jacob made his sons swear to bury him in Machpelah, in Hebron, and his sons swore to him concerning this thing. And he commanded them, saying, Serve the Lord your God, for He who delivered your fathers will also deliver you from all trouble. And Jacob said, Call all your children to me, and all the children of Jacob's sons came and sat before him, and Jacob blessed them, and he said to them, The Lord God of your fathers shall grant you a thousand times as much and bless you, and may He give you the blessing of your father Abraham. And all the children of Jacob's sons went forth on that day after he had blessed them. On the next day Jacob again called for his sons and they all assembled and came to him and sat before him, and Jacob on that day blessed his sons before his death; each man did he bless according to his blessing. So it is written in the book of the law of the Lord pertaining to Israel.   (! See Gen 47:27-31, Gen 48:1-22, Gen 49:1-33 and Gen 50:1-14)

And Jacob said to Judah, I know my son that you are a mighty man for your brothers; reign over them, and your sons shall reign over their sons forever. Only teach your sons the bow and all the weapons of war, (! 2Sa 1:18) in order that they may fight the battles of their brother who will rule over his enemies. (! King David) And Jacob again commanded his sons on that day, saying, Behold I shall this day be gathered to my people; carry me up from Egypt and bury me in the cave of Machpelah as I have commanded you. But take care I pray you that none of your sons carry me, only yourselves, and this is the manner you shall do to me, when you carry my body to go with it to the land of Canaan to bury me: Judah,

Issachar and Zebulun shall carry my bier at the eastern side; Reuben, Simeon and Gad at the south; Ephraim, Manasseh and Benjamin at the west; Dan, Asher and Naphtali at the north.

Let not Levi carry with you, for he and his sons will carry the ark of the covenant of the Lord with the Israelites in the camp, neither let Joseph my son carry, for as a king so let his glory be; but Ephraim and Manasseh shall be in their stead. Thus shall you do to me when you carry me away; do not neglect anything of all that I command you and it shall come to pass when you do this to me, that the Lord will remember you favorably and your children after you forever. And you my sons, honor each his brother and his relative, and command your children and your children's children after you to serve the Lord God of your ancestors always. In order that you may prolong your days in the land, you and your children and your children's children forever, when you do what is good and upright in the sight of the Lord your God, to follow in all His ways. (Jasher 56:1-16)

The Tribes and Leaders by Armies

And the Lord spoke to Moses and Aaron, saying: "Everyone of the children of Israel shall camp by his own standard, beside the emblems of his father's house; they shall camp some distance from the tabernacle of meeting. On the east side, toward the rising of the sun, those of the standard of the forces with Judah shall camp according to their armies..... Those who camp next to him shall be the tribe of Issachar..... Then comes the tribe of Zebulun..... On the south side shall be the standard of the forces with Rueben according to their armies..... Those who camp next to him shall be the tribe of Simeon..... Then comes the tribe of Gad..... And the tabernacle of meeting shall move out with the camp of the Levites in the middle of the camps; as they camp, so they shall move out, everyone in his place, by their standards. On the west side shall be the standard of the forces with Ephraim according to their armies..... Next to him comes the tribe of Manasseh..... Then comes the tribe of Benjamin..... The standard of the forces with Dan shall be on the north side according to their armies..... Those who camp next to him shall be the tribe of Asher.....

Then comes the tribe of Naphtali..... These are the ones who were numbered of the children of Israel by their fathers' houses. All who were numbered according to their armies of the forces were six hundred and three thousand five hundred and fifty. But the Levites were not numbered among the children of Israel, just as the Lord commanded Moses. Thus the children of Israel did according to all that the Lord commanded Moses; so they camped by their standards and so they broke camp, each one by his family, according to their fathers' houses. (Num 2:1-34)

Joseph B. Lumpkin

Bronze is associated with disobedience and sin

"I will set My face against you, and you shall be defeated by your enemies. Those who hate you shall reign over you, and you shall flee when no one pursues you. And after this, if you do not obey Me, then I will punish you seven times more for your sins. I will break the pride of your power; I will make your heavens like iron and your earth like bronze. And your strength shall be spent in vain; for your land shall not yield its produce, nor shall the trees of the land yield their fruit." (Lev 26:17-20)

"The Lord will make the plague cling to you until He has consumed you from the land which you are going to possess. The Lord will strike you with consumption, with fever, with inflammation, with severe burning fever, with the sword, with scorching, and with mildew; they shall pursue you until you perish. And your heavens which are over your head shall be bronze, and the earth which is under you shall be iron. The Lord will change the rain of your land to powder and dust; from the heaven it shall come down on you until you are destroyed. The Lord will cause you to be defeated before your enemies; you shall go out one way against them and flee seven ways before them; and you shall become troublesome to all the kingdoms of the earth." (Deu 28:21-25)

Now it came to pass, when Rehoboam had established the kingdom and had strengthened himself, that he forsook the law of the Lord, and all Israel along with him. So Shishak King of Egypt came up against Jerusalem, and took away the treasures of the house of the Lord and the treasures of the king's house; he took everything. He carried away the gold shields which Solomon had made. Then King Rehoboam made bronze shields in their place, and committed them to the hands of the captains of the guard, who guarded the doorway of the king's house. And whenever the king entered the house of the Lord, the guard would go and bring them out; then they would take them back into the guardroom. When he humbled himself, the wrath of the Lord turned from him, so as not to destroy him completely; and things also went well in Judah. (2Ch 12:1, 9-12)

"What strength do I have, that I should hope? And what is my end, that I should prolong my life? Is my strength the strength of stones? Or is my flesh bronze? Is my help not within me? And is success driven from me?" (Job 6:11-13)

And a champion went out from the camp of the Philistines, named Goliath, from Gath, whose height was six cubits and a span. He had a bronze helmet on his head, and he was armed with a coat of mail, and the weight of the coat was five thousand shekels of bronze. And he had bronze armor on his legs and a bronze javelin between his shoulders. Now the staff of his spear was like a weaver's beam, and his iron spearhead weighed six hundred shekels; and a shieldbearer went before him. "This day the Lord will deliver you into my hand, and I will strike you and take your head from you. ....Then all this assembly shall know that the Lord does not save with sword and spear; for the battle is the Lord's, and He will give you into our hands." Then David put his hand in his bag and took out a stone; and he slung it and struck the Philistine in his forehead, so that the stone sank into his forehead, and he fell on his face to the earth. Therefore David ran and stood over the Philistine, took his sword and drew it out of its sheath and killed him, and cut off his head with it. And when the Philistines saw that their champion was dead, they fled. (1Sa 17:4-7, 46-47, 49, 51)

The Bronze Serpent

Then they journeyed from Mount Hor by the way of the Red sea, to go around the land of Edom; and the soul of the people became very discouraged on the way. And the people spoke against God and against Moses: "Why have you brought us up out of Egypt to die in the wilderness? For there is no food and no water, and our soul loathes this worthless bread."

So the Lord sent fiery serpents among the people, and they bit the people; and many of the people of Israel died. Therefore the people came to Moses, and said, "We have sinned for we have spoken against the Lord and against you; pray to the Lord that He take away the serpents from us." So Moses prayed for the people. Then the Lord said to Moses,

"Make a fiery serpent, and set it on a pole; and it shall be that everyone who is bitten, when he looks at it, shall live." So Moses made a bronze serpent, and put it on a pole; and so it was, if a serpent had bitten anyone, when he looked at the bronze serpent, he lived.

(Num 21:4-9)

"Look to Me, and be saved, all you ends of the earth! For I am God, and there is no other."

(Isa 45:22)

"And as Moses lifted up the serpent in the wilderness, even so must the Son of Man be lifted up, that whoever believes in Him should not perish but have eternal life." (Joh 3:14-15)

The reforms of Hezekiah

And he did what was right in the sight of the Lord, according to all that his father David had done. He removed the high places and broke the sacred pillars, cut down the wooden image and broke in pieces the bronze serpent that Moses had made; for until those days the children of Israel burned incense to it, and called it Nehushtan. (! bronze thing)

He trusted in the Lord God of Israel, so that after him was none like him among the kings of Judah, nor who were before him. For he held fast to the Lord; he did not depart from following Him, but kept His commandments, which the Lord had commanded Moses. (2Ki 18:3-6)

The Bronze Laver

Then the Lord spoke to Moses, saying: "You shall also make a laver of bronze, with its base also of bronze, for washing. You shall put it between the tabernacle of meeting and the altar. And you shall put water in it, for Aaron and his sons shall wash their hands and their feet in water from it. When they go into the tabernacle of meeting, or when they come near the altar to minister, to burn an offering made by fire to the Lord, they shall wash with water, lest they die. So they shall wash their hands and their feet, lest they die. And it shall be a statute forever to them - to him and his descendants throughout their generations."

(Exo 30:17-21)

The Bronze Laver for the Temple built by Solomon

And he made the Sea of cast bronze, ten cubits from one brim to the other; it was completely round. It's height was five cubits, and a line of thirty cubits measured its circumference.

Below its brim were ornamental buds encircling it all around, ten to a cubit, all the way around the Sea. The ornamental buds were cast in two rows when it was cast.

It stood on twelve oxen: three looking toward the north, three looking toward the west, three looking toward the south, three looking toward the east; the Sea was set upon them, and all their back parts pointed inward. It was a handbreadth thick; and its brim was shaped like the brim of a cup, like a lily blossom. It contained two thousand baths.

(1Ki 7:23-26 and 2Ch 4:2-5)

What shall I render to the Lord for all His benefits toward me?

I will take up the cup of salvation, and call upon the name of the Lord. (Psa 116:12-13)

Jesus answered and said to her, "If you knew the gift of God, and who it is who says to you, 'Give Me a drink,' you would have asked Him, and He would have given you living water." Jesus answered and said to her, "Whoever drinks of this water will thirst again, but whoever drinks of the water that I shall give him will never thirst. But the water that I shall give him will become in him a fountain of water springing up into everlasting life." (Joh 4:10, 13-14)

Now it came to pass in those days that He went out to the mountain to pray, and continued all night in prayer to God. And when it was day, He called his disciples to Himself; and from them He chose twelve whom He also named apostles: Simon, whom He also named Peter, and Andrew his brother; James and John; Philip and Bartholomew; Matthew and Thomas; James the son of Alphaeus, and Simon called the Zealot; Judas the son of James, and Judas Iscariot who also became a traitor. (Luk 6:12-16)

And when He had called His twelve disciples to Him, He gave them power over unclean spirits, to cast them out, and to heal all kinds of sickness and all kinds of disease. (Mat 10:1)

And Jesus came and spoke to them, saying, "All authority has been given to Me in heaven and on earth. Go therefore and make disciples of all the nations, baptizing them in the name of the Father and of the Son and of the Holy Spirit, teaching them to observe all things that I have commanded you; and lo, I am with you always, even to the end of the age." Amen.

(Mat 28:18-20)

But when the kindness and the love of God our Savior toward man appeared, not by works of righteousness which we have done, but according to His mercy He saved us, through the washing of regeneration and renewing of the Holy Spirit, whom He poured out on us abundantly through Jesus Christ our Savior, that having been justified by His grace we should become heirs according to the hope of eternal life. (Tit 3:4-7)

-oOo-

Tongues

And the Lord said, "My Spirit shall not strive with man forever, for he is indeed flesh; yet his days shall be one hundred and twenty years." (Gen 6:3)

To Eber were born two sons: the name of one was Peleg, for in his days the earth was divided; and his brothers name was Joktan. (Gen 10:25)

These are the generations of Shem: Shem had Arpachshad and Arpachshad had Shelach, and Shelach had Eber and to Eber were born two children, the name of one was Peleg, for in his days the sons of men were divided, and in the latter days the earth was divided. And the name of the second was Yoktan, meaning that in his day the lives of the sons of men were diminished and lessened. (Jasher 7:19-20)

Now the whole earth had one language and one speech. And it came to pass, as they journeyed from the east, that they found a plain in the land of Shinar, and they dwelt there. Then they said to one another, "Come, let us make bricks and bake them thoroughly." They had brick for stone, and they had asphalt for mortar. And they said, "Come, let us build ourselves a city, and a tower whose top is in the heavens; let us make a name for ourselves, lest we be scattered abroad over the face of the whole earth." But the Lord came down to see the city and the tower which the sons of men had built. And the Lord said, "Indeed the people are one and they all have one language, and this is what they begin to do; now nothing that they propose to do will be withheld from them. "Come, let Us go down and there confuse their language, that they may not understand one another's speech." So the Lord scattered them abroad from there over the face of all the earth, and they ceased building the city. Therefore its name is called Babel, because there the Lord confused the language of all the earth; and from there the Lord scattered them abroad over the face of all the earth. (Gen 11:1-9)

And King Nimrod reigned securely, and all the earth was under his control, and all the earth was of one tongue and words of union. And all the princes of Nimrod and his great men took counsel together: Phut, Mitzraim, Cush and Canaan with their families, and they said to each other, Come let us build ourselves a city and in it a strong tower and its top reaching heaven, and we will make ourselves famed so that we may reign on the whole world, in order that the evil of our enemies may cease from us; that we may reign mightily over them, and that we may not become scattered over the earth on account of their wars. They all went before the king, and they told the king these words, and the king agreed with them in this affair, and he did so. (Jasher 9:20-22)

They built the tower and the city, and they did this thing daily until many days and years were elapsed. And God said to the seventy angels who stood foremost before Him, to those who were near to Him, saying, Come let us descend and confuse their tongues, that one man shall not understand the language of his neighbor, and they did so to them. (Jasher 9:31-32)

And they ceased building the city and the tower; therefore he called that place Babel, for there the Lord confounded the Language of the whole earth; behold it was at the east of the land of Shinar. (Jasher 9:37)

And it shall come to pass afterward that I will pour out My Spirit on all flesh; your sons and your daughters shall prophesy, your old men shall dream dreams, your young men shall see visions. And also on My menservants and on My maidservants I will pour out My Spirit in those days. (Joel 2:28-29)

John answered, saying to all, "I indeed baptize you with water; but One mightier than I is coming, whose sandal strap I am not worthy to loose. He will baptize you with the Holy Spirit and fire." (Luk 3:16)

When the Day of Pentecost had fully come, they were all with one accord in one place. And suddenly there came a sound from heaven, as of a rushing mighty wind, and it filled the whole house where they were sitting. Then there appeared to them divided tongues, as of fire, and one sat upon each of them. And they were all filled with the Holy Spirit and began to speak with other tongues, as the Spirit gave them utterance. (Act 2:1-4)

And there were dwelling in Jerusalem Jews, devout men, from every nation under heaven. And when this sound occurred, the multitude came together, and were confused, because everyone heard them speak in his own language. Then they were all amazed and marveled, saying to one another, "Look, are not all these who speak Galileans? And how is it that we hear, each in our own language in which we were born? Parthians and Medes and Elamites, those dwelling in Mesopotamia, Judea and Cappadocia, Pontus and Asia, Phrygia and Pamphylia, Egypt and the parts of Libya adjoining Cyrene, visitors from Rome, both Jews and Proselytes, Cretans and Arabs - we hear them speaking in our own tongues the wonderful works of God." So they were all amazed and perplexed, saying to one another, "Whatever could this mean?" Others mocking said, "They are full of new wine." (Act 2:5-13)

While Peter was still speaking these words, the Holy Spirit fell upon all those who heard the word. And those of the circumcision who believed were astonished, as many as came with Peter, because the gift of the Holy Spirit had been poured out on the Gentiles also. For they heard them speak with tongues and magnify God. Then Peter answered, "Can anyone forbid water, that these should not be baptized who have received the Holy Spirit just as we have?"

And he commanded them to be baptized in the name of the Lord. Then they asked him to stay a few days. (Act 10:44-48)

And it happened, while Apollos was at Corinth, that Paul, having passed through the upper regions, came to Ephesus. And finding some disciples he said to them, "Did you receive the Holy Spirit when you believed?" So they said to him, "We have not so much as heard whether there is a Holy Spirit." And he said to them, "Into what then were you baptized?" So they said, "Into John's baptism." Then Paul said, "John indeed baptized with a baptism of repentance, saying to the people that they should believe on Him who would come after him, that is, on Christ Jesus." When they heard this, they were baptized in the name of the Lord Jesus. And when Paul had laid hands on them, the Holy Spirit came upon them, and they spoke with tongues and prophesied. Now the men were about twelve in all. (Act 19:1-7)

O Lord, You have searched me and known me. You know my sitting down and my rising up; You understand my thought afar off. You comprehend my path and my lying down, and are acquainted with all my ways. For there is not a word on my tongue, but behold, O Lord, You know it altogether. (Psa 139:1-4)

The preparations of the heart belong to man, but the answer of the tongue is from the Lord. All the ways of a man are pure in his own eyes, but the Lord weighs the spirits. (Pro 16:1-2)

For with stammering lips and another tongue He will speak to this people, to whom He said, "This is the rest with which you may cause the weary to rest," and, "This is the refreshing"; yet they would not hear. (Isa 28:11-12)

The eyes of those who see will not be dim, and the ears of those who hear will listen. Also the heart of the rash will understand knowledge, and the tongue of the stammerers will be ready to speak plainly. (Isa 32:4)

You will not see a fierce people, a people of obscure speech, beyond perception, of a stammering tongue that you cannot understand. (Isa 33:19)

And He said to them, "Go into all the world and preach the gospel to every creature. He who believes and is baptized will be saved; but he who does not believe will be condemned. And these signs will follow those who believe: In My name they will cast out demons; they will speak with new tongues; they will take up serpents; and if they drink anything deadly, it will by no means hurt them; they will lay hands on the sick, and they will recover." (Mar 16:15-18)

Pursue love, and desire spiritual gifts, but especially that you may prophesy. For he who speaks in a tongue does not speak to men but to God, for no one understands him; however, in the spirit he speaks mysteries. But he who prophesies speaks edification and exhortation and comfort to men. He who speaks in a tongue edifies himself, but he who prophesies edifies the church. I wish you all spoke with tongues, but even more that you prophesied; for he who prophesies is greater then he who speaks with tongues, unless indeed he interprets, that the church may receive edification. (1Co 14:1-5)

Therefore let him who speaks in a tongue pray that he may interpret. For if I pray in a tongue, my spirit prays, but my understanding is unfruitful. What is the conclusion then? I will pray with the spirit, and I will also pray with the understanding. I will sing with the spirit, and I will also sing with the understanding. (1Co 14:13-15)

Therefore tongues are for a sign, not to those who believe but to unbelievers; but prophesying is not for unbelievers but for those who believe. (1Co 14:22)

If anyone thinks himself to be a prophet or spiritual, let him acknowledge that the things which I write to you are the commandments of the Lord. But if anyone is ignorant, let him be ignorant. Therefore, brethren, desire earnestly to prophesy, and do not forbid to speak with tongues. Let all things be done decently and in order. (1Co 14:37-40)

There are diversities of gifts, but the same Spirit. There are differences of ministries, but the same Lord. And there are diversities of activities, but it is the same God who works all in all. But the manifestation of the Spirit is given to each one for the profit of all: for to one is given the word of wisdom through the Spirit, to another the word of knowledge through the same Spirit, to another faith by the same Spirit, to another gifts of healings by the same Spirit, to another the working of miracles, to another prophecy, to another discerning of spirits, to another different kinds of tongues, to another the interpretation of tongues. But one and the same Spirit works all these things, distributing to each one individually as He wills. For as the body is one and has many members, but all the members of that one body, being many, are one body, so also is Christ. (1Co 12:4-12)

There is one body and one Spirit, just as you were called in one hope of your calling; one Lord, one faith, one baptism; one God and Father of all, who is above all, and through all, and in you all. (Eph 4:4-6)

"But you, do not be called 'Rabbi'; for One is your teacher, the Christ, and you are all brethren. Do not call anyone on earth your father; for One is your Father, He who is in heaven. And do not be called teachers; for One is your Teacher, the Christ. But he who is greatest among you shall be your servant. And whoever exalts himself will be humbled, and he who humbles himself will be exalted." (Mat 23:8-12)

To the law and to the testimony! If they do not speak according to this word, it is because there is no light in them. (Isa 8:20)

Therefore I make known to you that no one speaking by the Spirit of God calls Jesus accursed, and no one can say that Jesus is Lord except by the Holy Spirit. (1Co 12:3)

Now John answered Him, saying, "Teacher, we saw someone who does not follow us casting out demons in Your name, and we forbade him because he does not follow us."

But Jesus said, "Do not forbid him, for no one who works a miracle in My name can soon afterward speak evil of Me. For he who is not against us is on our side. For whoever gives you a cup of water to drink in My name, because you belong to Christ, assuredly, I say to you, he will by no means lose his reward. (Mar 9:38-41)

Beloved, do not believe every spirit, but test the spirits, whether they are of God; because many false prophets have gone out into the world. By this you know the Spirit of God: Every spirit that confesses that Jesus Christ has come in the flesh is of God, and every spirit that does not confess that Jesus Christ has come in the flesh is not of God. And this is the spirit of the Antichrist, which you have heard was coming, and is now already in the world. You are of God, little children, and have overcome them, because He who is in you is greater than he who is in the world. (1Jo 4:1-4)

"Beware of false prophets, who come to you in sheep's clothing, but inwardly they are ravenous wolves. You will know them by their fruits. Do men gather grapes from thornbushes or figs from thistles? Even so, every good tree bears good fruit, but a bad tree bears bad fruit. A good tree cannot bear bad fruit, nor can a bad tree bear good fruit. Every tree that does not bear good fruit is cut down and thrown into the fire. Therefore by their fruits you will know them." (Mat 7:15-20)

"A good man out of the good treasure of his heart brings forth good; and an evil man out of the evil treasure of his heart brings forth evil. For out of the abundance of the heart his mouth speaks." (Luk 6:43)

But there were also false prophets among the people, even as there will be false teachers among you, who will secretly bring in destructive heresies, even denying the Lord who brought them, and bring on themselves swift destruction. But these, like natural brute beasts made to be caught and destroyed, speak evil of the things they do not understand, and will utterly perish in their own corruption, and will receive the wages of unrighteousness, as those who count it pleasure to carouse in the daytime. They are spots and blemishes, carousing in their own deceptions while they feast with you, having eyes full of adultery and that cannot cease from sin, enticing unstable souls. They have a heart trained in covetous practices, and are accursed children. They have forsaken the right way and gone astray, following the way of Balaam the son of Beor, who loved the wages of unrighteousness; but he was rebuked for his iniquity: a dumb donkey speaking with a man's voice restrained the madness of the prophet. These are wells without water, clouds carried by a tempest, for whom is reserved the blackness of darkness forever. For when they speak great swelling words of emptiness, they allure through the lusts of the flesh, through lewdness, the ones who have actually escaped from those who live in error. While they promise them liberty, they themselves are slaves of corruption; for by whom a person is overcome, by him also he is brought into bondage. For if, after they have escaped the pollutions of the world through the knowledge of the Lord and Savior Jesus Christ, they are again entangled in them and overcome, the latter end is worse for them than the beginning. (2Pe 2:1,12-20)

-oOo-

Ephraim

And to Joseph were born two sons before the years of famine came, whom Asenath, the daughter of Poti-Pherah priest of On, bore to him. Joseph called the name of the first born Manasseh: "For God has made me forget all my toil and all my father's house." And the name of the second he called Ephraim: "For God has caused me to be fruitful in the land of affliction." (Gen 41:50-52)

Then Jacob said to Joseph: "God Almighty appeared to me at Luz in the land of Canaan and blessed me, and said to me, 'Behold, I will make you fruitful and multiply you, and I will make of you a multitude of people, and give this land to your descendants after you as an everlasting possession.' And now your two sons, Ephraim and Manasseh, who were born to you in the land of Egypt before I came to you in Egypt, are mine; as Reuben and Simeon, they shall be mine. (Gen 48:3-5)

And Joseph took them both, Ephraim with his right hand toward Israel's left hand, and Manasseh with his left hand toward Israel's right hand, and brought them near him. Then Israel stretched out his right hand and laid it on Ephraim's head, who was the younger, and his left hand on Manasseh's head, guiding his hands knowingly, for Manasseh was the firstborn. And he blessed Joseph, and said:

"God, before whom my fathers Abraham and Isaac walked, The God who has fed me all my life long to this day, The Angel who has redeemed me from all evil, Bless the lads; let my name be named upon them, and the name of my fathers Abraham and Isaac; and let them grow into a multitude in the midst of the earth."

Now when Joseph saw that his father laid his right hand on the head of Ephraim, it displeased him; so he took hold of his father's hand to remove it from Ephraim's head to Manasseh's head. And Joseph said to his father, "Not so, my father, for this one is the firstborn; put your right hand on his head." But his father refused and said, "I know, my son, I know. He also shall become a people, and he also shall be great; but truly his younger brother shall be greater than he, and his descendants shall become a multitude of nations." So he blessed them that day, saying, "'By you Israel will bless, saying, 'May God make you as Ephraim and as Manasseh!' " And thus he set Ephraim before Manasseh. (Gen 48:13-20)

At that time in the hundred and eightieth year of the Israelites going down into Egypt, there went forth from Egypt courageous men, thirty thousand on foot, from the children of Israel who were all of the tribe of Joseph, of the children of Ephraim the son of Joseph. For they said the period was completed which the Lord had appointed to the children of Israel in the times of old, which he had spoken to Abraham. And these men prepared themselves, and each man put his sword at his side, and every man his armor on him, and they trusted to their strength; they went out together from Egypt with a mighty hand. But they brought no provision for the road, only silver and gold, not even did they bring bread for that day in their hands, for they thought of getting their provision for pay from the Philistines; if not they would take it by force. These men were very mighty and bold men; one man could pursue a thousand and two could rout ten thousand, so they trusted their strength and went together as they were. They directed their course toward the land of Gath, and they went down and found the shepherds of Gath feeding the cattle of the children of Gath. They said to the shepherds, Give us some of the sheep for pay that we may eat, for we are hungry; we have eaten no bread this day.

And the shepherds said, Are they our sheep or cattle that we should give them to you even for pay? So the children of Ephraim approached to take them by force.

And the shepherds of Gath shouted over them so their cry was heard at a distance; all the children of Gath went out to them. When the children of Gath saw the evil doings of the children of Ephraim, they returned and assembled the men of Gath; they put on each man his armor and came forth to the children of Ephraim for battle. And they engaged with them in the valley of Gath, and the battle was severe; they struck from each other a great many on that day. And on the second day the children of Gath sent to all the cities of the Philistines that they should come to their help, saying, Come up to us and help us, that we may strike the children of Ephraim who have come forth from Egypt to take our cattle, and to fight against us without cause. And the souls of the children of Ephraim were exhausted with hunger and thirst, for they had eaten no bread for three days. Forty thousand men went out from the cities of the Philistines to the assistance of the men of Gath.

These men were engaged in battle with the children of Ephraim, and the Lord delivered the children of Ephraim into the hands of the Philistines. They struck all the children of Ephraim, all who had gone forth from Egypt, none were remaining but ten men who had run away from the engagement. This evil was from the Lord against the children of Ephraim for they went contrary to the word of the Lord in going forth from Egypt, before the period had arrived which the Lord in the days of old had appointed to Israel. And of the Philistines also there fell a great many, about twenty thousand men, and their brothers carried them and buried them in their cities. And the slain of the children of Ephraim remained forsaken in the valley of Gath for many days and years and were not brought to burial, and the valley was filled with men's bones. The men who had escaped from the battle came to Egypt and told all the children of Israel all that had happened to them. Their father Ephraim mourned over them for many days, and his brothers came to console him. And he came to his wife and she gave birth to a son, and he called his name Beriah, for she was unfortunate in his house. (Jasher 75:1-22)

The sons of Ephraim were Shuthelah, Bered his son, Tahath his son, Eladah his son, Tahath his son, Zabad his son, Shuthelah his son, and Ezer and Elead. The men of Gath who were born in that land killed them because they came down to take away their cattle. Then Ephraim their father mourned many days, and his brethren came to comfort him. And when he went in to his wife, she conceived and bore a son; and he called his name Beriah, because tragedy had come upon his house. Now his daughter was Sheerah, who built Lower and Upper Beth Horon and Uzzen Sheerah; and Rephah was his son, as well as Resheph, and Telah his son, Tahan his son, Elishama his son, Nun his son, and Joshua his son. (1Ch 7:20-27)

Then the runners went throughout all Israel and Judah with the letters from the king (! Hezekiah) and his leaders, and spoke according to the command of the king: "Children of Israel, return to the Lord God of Abraham, Isaac, and Israel; then He will return to the remnant of you who have escaped from the hand of the kings of Assyria. And do not be like your fathers and your brethren, who trespassed against the Lord God of their fathers, so that He gave them up to desolation, as you see. Now do not be stiff-necked, as your fathers were, but yield yourselves to the Lord; and enter His sanctuary, which He has sanctified forever, and serve the Lord your God, that the fierceness of His wrath may turn away from you. For if you return to the Lord, your brethren and your children will be treated with compassion by those who lead them captive, so that they may come back to this land; for the Lord your God is gracious and merciful, and will not turn His face from you if you return to Him." So the runners passed from city to city through the country of Ephraim and Manasseh, as far as Zebulun; but they laughed at them and mocked them. Nevertheless some from Asher, Manasseh, and Zebulun humbled themselves and came to Jerusalem. Also the hand of God was on Judah to give them singleness of heart to obey the command of the king and the leaders, at the word of the Lord. (2Ch 30:6-12)

Woe to the crown of pride, to the drunkards of Ephraim, whose glorious beauty is a fading flower which is at the head of the verdant valleys, to those who are overcome with wine! Behold, the Lord has a mighty and strong one, like a tempest of hail and a destroying storm, like a flood of mighty waters overflowing, who will bring them down to the earth with His hand. The crown of pride, the drunkards of Ephraim, will be trampled underfoot; and the glorious beauty is a fading flower which is at the head of the verdant valley, like the first fruit before the summer, which an observer sees; he eats it up while it is still in his hand. (Isa 28:1-4)

"Ephraim has encircled Me with lies, and the house of Israel with deceit; but Judah still walks with God, even with the Holy One who is faithful." (Hos 11:12)

For He established a testimony in Jacob, and appointed a law in Israel, which He commanded our fathers, that they should make them known to their children; that the generation to come might know them, the children who would be born, that they may arise and declare them to their children, that they may set their hope in God, and not forget the works of God, but keep His commandments; and may not be like their fathers, a stubborn and rebellious generation, a generation that did not set its heart aright, and whose spirit was not faithful to God. The children of Ephraim, being armed and carrying bows, turned back in the day of battle. They did not keep the covenant of God; they refused to walk in His law, and forgot His works and His wonders that He had shown them. Marvelous things He did in the sight of their fathers, in the land of Egypt, in the field of Zoan. He divided the sea and caused them to pass through; and He made the waters stand up like a heap. In the daytime also He led them with the cloud, and all the night with a light of fire. He split the rocks in the wilderness, and gave them drink in abundance like the depths. He also brought streams out of the rock, and caused waters to run like rivers. (Psa 78:5-16)

For thus says the Lord: "Sing with gladness for Jacob, and shout among the chief of the nations; proclaim, give praise, and say, 'O Lord, save Your people, the remnant of Israel!' Behold, I will bring them from the north country, and gather them from the ends of the earth, among them the blind and the lame, the woman with child and the one who labors with child, together; a great throng shall return there. They shall come with weeping, and with supplications I will lead them. I will cause them to walk by the rivers of waters, in a straight way in which they shall not stumble; for I am a Father to Israel, and Ephraim is My firstborn. Hear the word of the Lord, O nations, and declare it in the isles afar off, and say, 'He who scattered Israel will gather him, and keep him as a shepherd does his flock.' (Jer 31:7-10)

The hand of the Lord came upon me and brought me out in the Spirit of the Lord, and set me down in the midst of the valley; and it was full of bones. Then He caused me to pass by them all around, and behold, there were very many in the open valley; and indeed they were very dry. And He said to me, "Son of man, can these bones live?" So I answered,

"O Lord God, You know." Again He said to me, "Prophesy to these bones, and say to them, 'O dry bones, hear the word of the Lord! Thus says the Lord God to these bones:

"Surely I will cause breath to enter into you, and you shall live. I will put sinews on you and bring flesh upon you, cover you with skin and put breath in you; and you shall live. Then you shall know that I am the Lord." ' "

So I prophesied as I was commanded; and as I prophesied, there was a noise, and suddenly a rattling; and the bones came together, bone to bone. Indeed, as I looked, the sinews and the flesh came upon them, and the skin covered them over; but there was no breadth in them.

Also He said to me, "Prophesy to the breath, prophesy, son of man, and say to the breath, 'Thus says the Lord God: "Come from the four winds, O breath, and breathe on these slain, that they may live." ' "

So I prophesied as He commanded me, and breath came into them, and they lived, and stood upon their feet, an exceedingly great army. Then He said to me, "Son of man, these bones are the whole house of Israel. They indeed say, 'Our bones are dry, our hope is lost, and we ourselves are cut off!' "Therefore prophesy and say to them, 'Thus say the Lord God: "Behold, O My people, I will open your graves and cause you to come up from your graves, and bring you into the land of Israel. Then you shall know that I am the Lord, when I have opened your graves, O My people, and brought you up from your graves. I will put My Spirit in you, and you shall live, and I will place you in your own land. Then you shall know that I, the Lord, have spoken it and performed it," says the Lord.' " (Eze 37:1-14)

Again the word of the Lord came to me, saying, "As for you, son of man, take a stick for yourself and write on it: 'For Judah and for the children of Israel, his companions.'

Then take another stick and write on it, 'For Joseph, the stick of Ephraim, and for all the house of Israel, his companions.' Then join them one to another for yourself into one stick, and they will become one in your hand. And when the children of your people speak to you, saying, 'Will you not show us what you mean by these?' - say to them,

'Thus says the Lord God: "Surely I will take the stick of Joseph, which is in the hand of Ephraim, and the tribes of Israel, his companions; and I will join them with it, with the stick of Judah, and make them one stick, and they will be one in My hand." '

And the sticks on which you write will be in your hand before their eyes. Then say to them, 'Thus says the Lord God: "Surely I will take the children of Israel from among the nations, wherever they have gone, and will gather them from every side and bring them into their own land; and I will make them one nation in the land, on the mountains of Israel; and one king shall be king over them all; they shall no longer be two nations, nor shall they ever be divided into two kingdoms again. They shall not defile themselves anymore with their idols, nor with their detestable things, nor with any of their transgressions; but I will deliver them from all their dwelling places in which they have sinned, and will cleanse them. Then they shall be My people, and I will be their God.

David My servant shall be king over them, and they shall all have one shepherd; they shall also walk in My judgments and observe My statutes, and do them. Then they shall dwell in the land that I have given to Jacob My servant, where your fathers dwelt; and they shall dwell there, they, their children, and their children's children, forever; and My servant David shall be their prince forever. Moreover I will make a covenant of peace with them, and it shall be an everlasting covenant with them; I will establish them and multiply them, and I will set My sanctuary in their midst forevermore. My tabernacle also shall be with them; indeed I will be their God, and they shall be My people. The nations also will know that I, the Lord, sanctify Israel, when My sanctuary is in their midst forevermore." ' "   (Eze 37:15-28)

O God, You have taught me from my youth; and to this day I declare Your wondrous works. Now also when I am old and grayheaded, O God, do not forsake me, until I declare Your strength to this generation, Your power to everyone who is to come. Also Your righteousness, O God, is very high, You who have done great things; O God, who is like You? You, who have shown me great and severe troubles, shall revive me again, and bring me up again from the depths of the earth. You shall increase my greatness, and comfort me on every side. (Psa 71:17-21)

For God is my King from of old, working salvation in the midst of the earth.

Have respect to the covenant; for the dark places of the earth are full of the haunts of cruelty. (Psa 74:12, 20)

"Rejoice greatly, O daughter of Zion! Shout, O daughter of Jerusalem! Behold, your King is coming to you; He is just and having salvation, lowly and riding on a donkey, a colt, the foal of a donkey. I will cut off the chariot from Ephraim and the horse from Jerusalem; the battle bow shall be cut off. He shall speak peace to the nations; His dominion shall be 'from sea to sea, and from the River to the ends of the earth.' As for you also, because of the blood of your covenant, I will set your prisoners free from the waterless pit. Return to the stronghold, you prisoners of hope. Even today I declare that I will restore double to you. For I have bent Judah, My bow, fitted the bow with Ephraim, and raised up your sons, O Zion, against your sons, O Greece, and made you like the sword of a mighty man." Then the Lord will be seen over them, and His arrow will go forth like lightning. The Lord God will blow the trumpet, and go with whirlwinds from the south. The Lord of hosts will defend them; they shall devour and subdue with slingstones. They shall drink and roar as if with wine; they shall be filled with blood like basins, like the corners of the altar. The Lord their God will save them in that day, as the flock of His people. For they shall be like the jewels of a crown, lifted like a banner over His land - for how great is its goodness and how great its beauty! Grain shall make the young men thrive, and new wine the young women. (Zec 9:9-17)

"I will strengthen the house of Judah, and I will save the house of Joseph. I will bring them back, because I have mercy on them. They shall be as though I had not cast them aside; for I am the Lord their God, and I will hear them. Those of Ephraim shall be like a mighty man, and their heart shall rejoice as if with wine. Yes, their children shall see it and be glad; their heart shall rejoice in the Lord. I will whistle for them and gather them, for I will redeem them; and they shall increase as they once increased." (Zec 10:6-8)

-oOo-

Husband of Blood

To the woman He said: "I will greatly multiply your sorrow and your conception; in pain you shall bring forth children; your desire shall be for your husband, and he shall rule over you." (Gen 3:16)

In those days Moses, the son of Amram, in Midian, took Zipporah, the daughter of Reuel the Midianite, for a wife. And Zipporah walked in the ways of the daughters of Jacob, she was nothing short of the righteousness of Sarah, Rebecca, Rachel and Leah. And Zipporah conceived and gave birth to a son and he called his name Gershom, for he said, I was a stranger in a foreign land; but he circumcised not his foreskin, at the command of Reuel his father-in-law. And she conceived again and gave birth to a son, but circumcised his foreskin, and called his name Eliezer, for Moses said, Because the God of my fathers was my help and delivered me from the sword of Pharaoh.

(Jasher 78:7-10)

And the Lord said to Moses, Go, return to Egypt for all those men who sought your life are dead, and you shall speak to Pharaoh to send forth the children of Israel from his land. The Lord showed him to do signs and wonders in Egypt before the eyes of Pharaoh and the eyes of his subjects, in order that they might believe that the Lord had sent him. Moses listened to all that the Lord had commanded him, and he returned to his father-in-law and told him these things, and Reuel said to him, Go in peace.

Moses rose up to go to Egypt and took his wife and sons with him; he was at an inn in the road, and an angel of God came down, and sought an occasion against him. He wished to kill him on account of his firstborn son because he had not circumcised him and had gone contrary to the covenant which the Lord had made with Abraham. For Moses had listened to the words of his father-in-law which he had spoken to him, not to circumcise his first born son, so he did not circumcise him. Zipporah saw the angel of the Lord seeking an occasion against Moses, and she knew that this thing was because of his not having circumcised her son Gershom. Zipporah hurried and took some of the sharp rock stones that were there, and circumcised her son, and delivered her husband and her son from the hand of the angel of the Lord. (Jasher 79:5-12)

And it came to pass on the way, at the encampment, that the Lord met him and sought to kill him. Then Zipporah took a sharp stone and cut off the foreskin of her son and cast it at Moses' feet, and said, "Surely you are a husband of blood to me!" So He let him go.

Then she said, "You are a husband of blood!" - because of the circumcision.

(Exo 4:24-26)

"Therefore circumcise the foreskin of your heart, and be stiff-necked no longer."

(Deu 10:16)

"And the Lord your God will circumcise your heart and the heart of your descendants, to love the Lord your God with all your heart and with all your soul, that you may live."

(Deu 30:6)

For unto us a Child is born, unto us a Son is given; and the government will be upon His shoulder. And His name will be called Wonderful, Counselor, Mighty God, Everlasting Father, Prince of Peace. Of the increase of His government and peace there will be no end, upon the throne of David and over His kingdom, to order it and establish it with judgment and justice from that time forward, even forever. The zeal of the Lord of hosts will perform this. (Isa 9:6-7)

And in that day you will say: "O Lord, I will praise You; though You were angry with me, Your anger is turned away, and You comfort me. Behold, God is my salvation, I will trust and not be afraid; 'For Yah, the Lord, is my strength and song; He also has become my salvation.' " Therefore with joy you will draw water from the wells of salvation. And in that day you will say: "Praise the Lord, call upon His name; declare His deeds among the peoples, make mention that His name is exalted. Sing to the Lord, for He has done excellent things; this is known in all the earth. Cry out and shout, O inhabitant of Zion, for great is the Holy One of Israel in your midst!" (Isa 12:1-6)

Lift up your eyes, look around and see; all these gather together and come to you. "As I live," says the Lord, "You shall surely clothe yourselves with them all as an ornament, and bind them on you as a bride does." (Isa 49:18)

"Do not fear, for you will not be ashamed; neither be disgraced, for you will not be put to shame; for you will forget the shame of your youth, and will not remember the reproach of your widowhood anymore. For your Maker is your husband, The Lord of hosts is His name; and your Redeemer is the Holy One of Israel; He is called the God of the whole earth. For the Lord has called you like a woman forsaken and grieved in spirit, like a youthful wife when you were refused," says your God.

"For a mere moment I have forsaken you, but with great mercies I will gather you. With a little wrath I hid My face from you for a moment; but with everlasting kindness I will have mercy on you," says the Lord, your Redeemer. (Isa 54:4-8)

"Also the sons of the foreigner who join themselves to the Lord, to serve Him, and to love the name of the Lord, to be His servants - everyone who keeps from defiling the Sabbath, and holds fast My covenant - even them I will bring to My holy mountain, and make them joyful in My house of prayer. Their burnt offerings and their sacrifices will be accepted on My altar; for My house shall be called a house of prayer for all nations." The Lord God, who gathers the outcasts of Israel, says, "Yet I will gather to him Others besides those who are gathered to him." (Isa 56:6-8)

I will greatly rejoice in the Lord, my soul shall be joyful in my God; for He has clothed me with garments of salvation, He has covered me with the robe of righteousness, as a bridegroom decks himself with ornaments, and as a bride adorns herself with her jewels. For as the earth brings forth its bud, as the garden causes the things that are sown in it to spring forth, so the Lord God will cause righteousness and praise to spring forth before all the nations. (Isa 61:10-11)

For as a young man marries a virgin, so shall your sons marry you; and as the bridegroom rejoices over the bride, so shall your God rejoice over you. (Isa 62:5)

Can a virgin forget her ornaments, or a bride her attire? Yet My people have forgotten Me days without number. (Jer 2:32)

"They say, 'If a man divorces his wife, and she goes from him and becomes another man's, may he return to her again?' Would not that land be greatly polluted? But you have played the harlot with many lovers; yet return to Me," says the Lord. (Jer 3:1)

"Return, O backsliding children," says the Lord; "for I am married to you. I will take you, one from a city and two from a family, and I will bring you to Zion. And I will give you shepherds according to My heart, who will feed you with knowledge and understanding."

(Jer 3:14-15)

Surely, as a wife treacherously departs from her husband, so have you dealt treacherously with Me, O house of Israel," says the Lord. (Jer 3:20)

"Behold, the days are coming," says the Lord, "When I will make a new covenant with the house of Israel and with the house of Judah - not according to the covenant that I made with their fathers in the day that I took them by the hand to lead them out of the land of Egypt, My covenant which they broke, though I was a husband to them," says the Lord. "But this is the covenant that I will make with the house of Israel after those days," says the Lord: "I will put My law in their minds, and write it on their hearts; and I will be their God, and they shall be My people. No more shall every man teach his neighbor, and every man his brother, saying, 'Know the Lord,' for they all shall know Me, from the least of them to the greatest of them," says the Lord. "For I will forgive their iniquity, and their sin I will remember no more." (Jer 31:31-34)

Thus says the Lord: "Again there shall be heard in this place - of which you say, 'It is desolate, without man and without beast' - in the cities of Judah, in the streets of Jerusalem that are desolate, without man and without inhabitant and without beast, the voice of joy and the voice of gladness, the voice of the bridegroom and the voice of the bride, the voice of those who will say: 'Praise the Lord of hosts, for the Lord is good, for His mercy endures forever' - and of those who will bring the sacrifice of praise into the house of the Lord. For I will cause the captives of the land to return as at first," says the Lord. (Jer 33:10-11)

"And it shall be, in that day," says the Lord, "that you will call Me 'My Husband,' and no longer call Me 'My Master,' " (Hos 2:16)

"Thus says the Lord: 'I will return to Zion, and dwell in the midst of Jerusalem. Jerusalem shall be called the City of Truth, The Mountain of the Lord of hosts, The Holy Mountain.' " (Zec 8:3)

Then the disciples of John came to Him, saying, "Why do we and the Pharisees fast often, but Your disciples do not fast?" And Jesus said to them, "Can the friends of the bridegroom mourn as long as the bridegroom is with them? But the days will come when the bridegroom will be taken away from them, and then they will fast."

(Mat 9:14-15 also Mar 2:18-20 and Luk 5:33-35)

"Then the kingdom of heaven shall be likened to ten virgins who took their lamps and went out to meet the bridegroom. Now five of them were wise, and five were foolish. Those who were foolish took their lamps and took no oil with them, but the wise took oil in their vessels with their lamps. But while the bridegroom was delayed, they all slumbered and slept. And at midnight a cry was heard: 'Behold, the bridegroom is coming; go out to meet him!' Then all those virgins arose and trimmed their lamps.

And the foolish said to the wise, 'Give us some of your oil, for our lamps are going out.' But the wise answered, saying, 'No, lest there should not be enough for us and you; but go rather to those who sell, and buy for yourselves.' And while they went to buy, the bridegroom came, and those who were ready went in with him to the wedding; and the door was shut. Afterward the other virgins came also, saying, 'Lord, Lord, open to us!' But he answered and said, 'Assuredly, I say to you, I do not know you.'

Watch therefore, for you know neither the day nor the hour in which the Son of Man is coming." (Mat 25:1-13)

Now the Pharisees, who were lovers of money, also heard all these things, and they derided Him. And He said to them, "You are those who justify yourselves before men, but God knows your hearts. For what is highly esteemed among men is an abomination in the sight of God. The law and the prophets were until John. Since that time the kingdom of God has been preached, and everyone is pressing into it. And it is easier for heaven and earth to pass away than for one tittle of the law to fail. Whoever divorces his wife and marries another commits adultery; and whoever marries her who is divorced from her husband commits adultery. (Luk 16:14-18)

John answered and said, "A man can receive nothing unless it has been given to him from heaven. You yourselves bear me witness, that I said, 'I am not the Christ,' but, 'I have been sent before Him.' He who has the bride is the bridegroom; but the friend of the bridegroom, who stands and hears him, rejoices greatly because of the bridegroom's voice. Therefore this joy of mine is fulfilled." (Joh 3:27-29)

Or do you not know, brethren (for I speak to those who know the law), that the law has dominion over a man as long as he lives? For the woman who has a husband is bound by the law to her husband as long as he lives. But if the husband dies, she is released from the law of her husband. So then if while her husband lives, she marries another man, she will be called an adulteress; but if her husband dies, she is free from that law, so that she is no adulteress, though she has married another man. Therefore, my brethren, you also have become dead to the law through the body of Christ, that you may be married to another - to Him who was raised from the dead, that we should bear fruit to God.

For when we were in the flesh, the sinful passions which were aroused by the law were at work in our members to bear fruit to death. But now we have been delivered from the law, having died to what we were held by, so that we should serve in the newness of the Spirit and not in the oldness of the letter. (Rom 7:1-6)

Oh, that you would bear with me in a little folly - and indeed you do bear with me. For I am jealous for you with godly jealousy. For I have betrothed you to one husband, that I may present you as a chaste virgin to Christ. (2Co 11:1-2)

Wives, submit to your own husbands as to the Lord. For the husband is head of the wife, as also Christ is head of the church; and He is the Savior of the body. Therefore, just as the church is subject to Christ, so let the wives be to their own husbands in everything. Husbands, love your wives, just as Christ also loved the church and gave himself for her, that He might sanctify and cleanse her with the washing of water by the word, that He might present her to Himself a glorious church, not having spot or wrinkle or any such thing, but that she should be holy and without blemish. So husbands ought to love their own wives as their own bodies; he who loves his wife loves himself.

For no one ever hated his own flesh, but nourishes and cherishes it, just as the Lord does the church. (Eph 5:22-29)

Then a voice came from the throne, saying, "Praise our God, all you His servants and those who fear Him, both small and great!" And I heard, as it were, the voice of a great multitude, as the sound of many waters and as the sound of mighty thunderings, saying, "Alleluia! For the Lord God Omnipotent reigns! Let us be glad and rejoice and give Him glory, for the marriage of the Lamb has come, and His wife has made herself ready." And to her it was granted to be arrayed in fine linen, clean and bright, for the fine linen is the righteous acts of the saints. Then he said to me, "Write: 'Blessed are those who are called to the marriage supper of the Lamb!'" And he said to me, "These are the true sayings of God." (Rev 19:5-9)

Then I, John, saw the holy city, New Jerusalem, coming down out of heaven from God, prepared as a bride adorned for her husband. (Rev 21:2)

Then one of the seven angels who had the seven bowls filled with the seven last plagues came to me and talked with me, saying, "Come, I will show you the bride, the Lamb's wife." And he carried me away in the Spirit to a great and high mountain, and showed me the great city, the holy Jerusalem, descending out of heaven from God, having the glory of God. Her light was like a most precious stone, like a jasper stone, clear as crystal.

(Rev 21:9-11)

"I, Jesus, have sent My angel to testify to you these things in the churches.

I am the Root and the Offspring of David, the Bright and Morning Star."

And the Spirit and the bride say, "Come!" And let him who hears say, "Come!"

And let him who thirsts come. Whoever desires, let him take the water of life freely.

(Rev 22:16-17)

-oOo-

Watch What You Say!

Isaac the son of Abraham was growing up in those days, and Abraham his father taught him the way of the Lord to know the Lord, and the Lord was with him. When Isaac was thirty-seven years old, Ishmael his brother was going about with him in the tent. And Ishmael boasted of himself to Isaac, saying, I was thirteen years old when the Lord spoke to my father to circumcise us, and I did according to the word of the Lord which He spoke to my father, and I gave my soul to the Lord, and I did not go contrary to His word which He commanded my father. Isaac answered Ishmael, saying, Why do you boast to me about this, about a little bit of your flesh which you did take from your body, concerning which the Lord commanded you? As the Lord lives, the God of my father Abraham, if the Lord should say to my father, Take now your son Isaac and bring him up an offering before me, I would not refrain but I would joyfully accede to it. And the Lord heard the word that Isaac spoke to Ishmael, and it seemed good in the sight of the Lord, and he thought to try Abraham in this matter.

(Jasher 22:40-45)

At that time the word of the Lord came to Abraham, and said to him, Abraham. And Abraham said, Here I am. He said to him, Take now your son, your only son whom you love, even Isaac, and go to the land of Moriah, and offer him there for a burnt offering on one of the mountains which shall be shown to you, for there you will see a cloud and the glory of the Lord. (Jasher 23:1-2)

Sarah said to Abraham, O my lord, I pray you take care of your son, and watch over him, for I have no other son or daughter but him. Turn not away from him. If he is hungry give him bread, and if he is thirsty give him water to drink; do not let him go on foot, neither let him sit in the sun. Neither let him go by himself in the road, neither force him from whatever he may desire, but do to him as he may say to you. (Jasher 23:10-12)

And Abraham went with Isaac his son to bring him up as an offering before the Lord, as He had commanded him. Abraham took two of his young men with him, Ishmael the son of Hagar and Eliezer his servant, and they went together with them. (Jasher 23:20-21)

And on the third day Abraham lifted up his eyes and saw the place at a distance which God had told him of. A pillar of fire appeared to him that reached from the earth to heaven, and a cloud of glory on the mountain, and the glory of the Lord was seen in the cloud. And Abraham said to Isaac, My son, do you see in that mountain, which we perceive at a distance, that which I see on it? And Isaac answered and said to his father, I see and there is a pillar of fire and a cloud, and the glory of the Lord is seen on the cloud. And Abraham knew that his son Isaac was accepted before the Lord for a burnt offering.

Abraham said to Eliezer and to Ishmael his son, Do you also see that which we see on the mountain which is at a distance? And they answered and said, We see nothing more than like the other mountains of the earth. Abraham knew that they were not accepted before the Lord to go with them, and Abraham said to them, Stay here with the ass while I and Isaac my son will go to yonder mount and worship there before the Lord and then return to you. Eliezer and Ishmael remained in that place, as Abraham had commanded. (Jasher 23:41-48)

And Abraham took wood for a burnt offering and placed it on his son Isaac, and he took the fire and the knife, and they both went to that place. When they were on the way Isaac said to his father, Behold, I see here the fire and the wood, and where then is the lamb that is to be the burnt offering before the Lord? And Abraham answered his son Isaac, saying, The Lord has made choice of you my son, to be a perfect burnt offering instead of the lamb. And Isaac said to his father, I will do all that the Lord spoke to you with joy and cheerfulness of heart. Abraham again said to Isaac his son, Is there in your heart any thought or counsel concerning this, which is not proper? Tell me my son, I pray you, O my son conceal it not from me. And Isaac answered his father Abraham and said to him, O my father, as the Lord lives and as your soul lives, there is nothing in my heart to cause me to deviate either to the right or to the left from the word that He has spoken to you. Neither limb nor muscle has moved or stirred at this, nor is there in my heart any thought or evil counsel concerning this. But I am of joyful and cheerful heart in this matter, and I say, Blessed is the Lord who has this day chosen me to be a burnt offering before Him. (Jasher 23:49-56)

Abraham greatly rejoiced at the words of Isaac, and they went on and came together to that place that the Lord had spoken of. Abraham approached to build the altar in that place, and Abraham was weeping. Isaac took stones and mortar until they had finished building the altar. And Abraham took the wood and placed it in order on the altar which he had built. He took his son Isaac and bound him in order to place him on the wood which was on the altar, to kill him for a burnt offering before the Lord. Isaac said to his father, Bind me securely and then place me on the altar that I should not turn and move, and break loose from the force of the knife on my flesh and thereof profane the burnt offering; and Abraham did so. (Jasher 23:58-61)

And Abraham bound his son Isaac and placed him on the altar on the wood, and Isaac stretched forth his neck on the altar before his father. Abraham stretched forth his hand to take the knife to kill his son as a burnt offering before the Lord. (Jasher 23:65)

At that time the Lord appeared to Abraham and called to him from heaven, and said to him, Lay not your hand on the lad, neither do anything to him, for now I know that you fear God in performing this act, and in not withholding your son, your only son, from me. And Abraham lifted up his eyes and looked, and behold, a ram was caught in a thicket by his horns; that was the ram which the Lord God had created in the earth in the day that He made earth and heaven. For the Lord had prepared this ram from that day, to be a burnt offering instead of Isaac. (Jasher 23:69-71)

Abraham sprinkled some of the blood of the ram on the altar, and he exclaimed and said, This is in the place of my son, and may it be considered this day as the blood of my son before the Lord. And all that Abraham did on this occasion by the altar, he would exclaim and say, This is in place of my son, and may it this day be considered before the Lord in the place of my son; and Abraham finished the whole service by the altar, and the service was accepted before the Lord, and was accounted as if it had been Isaac; and the Lord blessed Abraham and his descendants on that day. (Jasher 23:74-75) Also read this account in Gen 22:1-18

<u>Don't babble, speak clearly!</u>

Now the whole earth had one language and one speech. And it came to pass, as they journeyed from the east, that they found a plain in the land of Shinar, and they dwelt there. Then they said to one another, "Come, let us make bricks and bake them thoroughly."

They had brick for stone, and they had asphalt for mortar. And they said, "Come, let us build ourselves a city, and a tower whose top is in the heavens; let us make a name for ourselves, <u>lest we be scattered abroad over the face of the whole earth</u>."

But the Lord came down to see the city and the tower which the sons of men had built. And the Lord said, "Indeed the people are one and they all have one language, and this is what they begin to do; now nothing that they propose to do will be withheld from them. Come, let Us go down and there confuse their language, that they may not understand one another's speech."

So the Lord scattered them abroad from there over the face of all the earth, and they ceased building the city. Therefore its name is called Babel, because there the Lord confused the language of all the earth; <u>and from there the Lord scattered them abroad over the face of all the earth</u>. (Gen 11:1-9)

<u>Well! You said it?</u>

Then Caleb quieted the people before Moses, and said, "Let us go up at once and take possession, for we are well able to overcome it." But the men who had gone up with him said, "We are not able to go up against the people, for they are stronger than we." (Num 13:30-31)

So all the congregation lifted up their voices and cried, and the people wept that night. And all the children of Israel complained against Moses and Aaron, and the whole congregation said to them, "If only we had died in the land of Egypt! <u>Or if only we had died in this wilderness!</u> Why has the Lord brought us to this land to fall by the sword, <u>that our wives and children should become victims</u>? Would it not be better for us to return to Egypt?" So they said to one another, "Let us select a leader and return to Egypt." (Num 14:1-4)

And the Lord spoke to Moses and Aaron, saying,

"How long shall I bear with this evil congregation who complain against Me?

I have heard the complaints which the children of Israel make against Me. Say to them,

'As I live,' says the Lord, 'just as you have spoken in My hearing, so I will do to you:

The carcasses of you who have complained against Me shall fall in this wilderness, all of you who were numbered, according to your entire number, from twenty years old and above. Except for Caleb the son of Jephunneh and Joshua the son of Nun, you shall by no means enter the land which I swore I would make you dwell in. But your little ones, whom you said would be victims, I will bring in, and they shall know the land which you have despised. But as for you, your carcasses shall fall in this wilderness. And your sons shall be shepherds in the wilderness forty years, and bear the brunt of your infidelity, until your carcasses are consumed in the wilderness. According to the number of the days in which you spied out the land, forty days, for each day you shall bear your guilt one year, namely forty years, and you shall know My rejection. I the Lord have spoken this.

I will surely do so to all this evil congregation who are gathered together against Me.

In this wilderness they shall be consumed, and there they shall die.' "

Now the men whom Moses sent to spy out the land, who returned and made all the congregation complain against him by bringing a bad report of the land, those very men who brought the evil report about the land, died by the plague before the Lord. But Joshua the son of Nun and Caleb the son of Jephunneh remained alive, of the men who went to spy out the land. (Num 14:26-38)

Solomon said :

These six things the Lord hates, Yes, seven are an abomination to Him: A proud look, A lying tongue, Hands that shed innocent blood, A heart that devises wicked plans, Feet that are swift in running to evil, A false witness who speaks lies, and one who sows discord among brethren. (Pro 6:16-19)

A fools mouth is his destruction, and his lips are the snare of his soul. He who answers a matter before he hears it, it is folly and shame to him. Death and life are in the power of the tongue, and those who love it will eat its fruit. (Pro 18:7, 13, 21)

To do righteousness and justice is more acceptable to the Lord than sacrifice. He who follows righteousness and mercy finds life, righteousness, and honor. Whoever guards his mouth and tongue keeps his soul from troubles. (Pro 21:3, 21, 23)

-oOo-

Noah's Ark

Noah : The Lord says we only have five years to build the Ark, boys!

Shem : What must we do first Dad?

Noah : Go-pher wood!

Jasher 5:1-36

It was in the eighty-fourth year of the life of Noah that Enoch the son of Seth died; he was nine hundred and five years old at his death. (Gen 5:11)

In the one hundred and seventy ninth year of the life of Noah, Cainan the son of Enosh died, and the age of Cainan was nine hundred and ten years, and he died. (Gen 5:14)

And in the two hundred and thirty fourth year of the life of Noah, Mahlallel the son of Cainan died, and the days of Mahlallel were eight hundred and ninety-five years, and he died. (Gen 5:17)

Jared the son of Mahlallel died in those days, in the three hundred and thirty-sixth year of the life of Noah; and all the days of Jared were nine hundred and sixty-two years, and he died. (Gen 5:20)

And all who followed the Lord died in those days, before they saw the evil which God declared to do on earth.

After the lapse of many years, in the four hundred and eightieth year of the life of Noah, when all those men who followed the Lord had died away from among the sons of men, and only Methuselah was then left, God said to Noah and Methuselah,

"Speak ye, and proclaim to the sons of men, saying,

'Thus says the Lord, return from your evil ways and turn away from your works, and the Lord will repent of the evil that he declared to do to you, so that it shall not come to pass.'

For thus says the Lord,

'Behold I give you a period of one hundred and twenty years; if you will turn to me and turn away from your evil ways, then will I also turn away from the evil which I told you, and it shall not exist,'

says the Lord." (Gen 6:3)

And Noah and Methuselah spoke all the words of the Lord to the sons of men, day after day, constantly speaking to them. But the sons of men would not listen to them, nor incline their ears to their words, and they were stubborn. And the Lord granted them a period of one hundred and twenty years, saying,

"If they will return, then will God repent of the evil, so as not to destroy the earth."

Noah the son of Lamech refrained from taking a wife in those days to beget children, for he said,

"Certainly now God will destroy the earth, wherefore then shall I beget children?"

Noah was a just man, he was perfect in his generation, and the Lord chose him to raise up offspring from his offspring, on the face of the earth. (Gen 6:9)

And the Lord said to Noah,

"Take to you a wife, and beget children, for I have seen you righteous before me in this generation. You shall raise up offspring, and your children with you, in the midst of the earth;"

and Noah went and took a wife, and he chose Naamah the daughter of Enoch, and she was five hundred and eighty years old. And Noah was four hundred and ninety-eight years old, when he took Naamah for a wife. Naamah conceived and gave birth to a son, and he called his name Japheth (H3315 = expansion), saying,

"God has enlarged me in the earth;"

and she conceived again and gave birth to a son, and he called his name Shem (H8035 = posterity), saying,

"God has made me a remnant, to raise up descendants in the midst of the earth."

And Noah was five hundred and two years old when Naamah gave birth to Shem, and the boys grew up and went in the ways of the Lord, in all that Methuselah and Noah their father taught them. (Gen 6:10)

Lamech the father of Noah, died in those days; yet verily he did not go with all his heart in the ways of his father, and he died in the hundred and ninety-fifth year of the life of Noah. And all the days of Lamech were seven hundred and seventy years, and he died.

(Gen 5:31)

All the sons of men who knew the Lord, died in that year before the Lord brought evil on them; for the Lord willed them to die, so as not to behold the evil that God would bring on their brothers and relatives, as He had declared to do.

In that time, the Lord said to Noah and Methuselah,

"Stand forth and proclaim to the sons of men all the words that I spoke to you in those days, perchance they may turn from their evil ways, and I will then repent of the evil and will not bring it."

And Noah and Methuselah stood forth, and said in the ears of the sons of men, all that God had spoken concerning them. But the sons of men would not listen, neither would they incline their ears to all their declarations.

It was after this that the Lord said to Noah,

"The end of all flesh is come before me on account of their evil deeds, and behold I will destroy the earth. (Gen 6:13)

And take with you gopher wood, and go to a certain place and make a large ark, and place it in that spot. (Gen 6:14)

Thus shall you make it; three hundred cubits in length, fifty cubits broad and thirty cubits high. (Gen 6:15)

And you shall make a door, open at its side, and to a cubit you (Gen 6:16) shall finish above, and cover it within and without with pitch. (Gen 6:14)

And behold I will bring the flood of waters on the earth, and all flesh will be destroyed; from under the heavens all that is on earth shall perish. (Gen 6:17)

You and your household shall go and gather two couples of all living things, male and female, and bring them to the ark, to raise up offspring from them on earth. (Gen 6:18-20)

Gather to you all food that is eaten by all animals, that there may be food for you and for them. (Gen 6:21)

You shall choose for your sons three maidens from the daughters of men, and they shall be wives to your sons."

And Noah rose up, and he made the ark, in the place where God had commanded him, and Noah did as God had ordered him. In his five hundred and ninety-fifth year Noah commenced to make the ark, and he made the ark in five years, as the Lord had commanded. Then Noah took the three daughters of Eliakim, son of Methuselah, for wives for his sons, as the Lord had commanded Noah. It was at that time Methuselah the son of Enoch died; he was nine hundred and sixty years old at his death. (Gen 5:27)

Jasher 6:1-42

At that time, after the death of Methuselah, the Lord said to Noah,

"Go with your household into the ark; behold I will gather to you all the animals of the earth, the beasts of the field and the fowls of the air, and they shall all come and surround the ark. You shall go and seat yourself by the doors of the ark, and all the beasts, the animals, and the fowls, shall assemble and place themselves before you, and such of them as will come and crouch before you, you shall take and deliver into the hands of your sons, who will bring them to the ark, and all that will stand before you, you shall leave." (Gen 7:1-3)

And the Lord brought this about on the next day, and animals, beasts and fowls came in great multitudes and surrounded the ark. Noah went and seated himself by the door of the ark, and of all flesh that crouched before him he brought into the ark, and all that stood before him he left on earth. A lioness came with her two whelps, male and female, and the three crouched before Noah; the two whelps rose up against the lioness and struck her, and made her flee from her place, and she went away, and they returned to their places and crouched on the earth before Noah. And the lioness ran away, and stood in the place of the lions. And Noah saw this and wondered greatly, and he rose and took the two whelps and brought them into the ark. Noah brought into the ark from all living creatures that were on earth, so that there was none left but those which Noah brought into the ark. Two and two came to Noah into the ark, but from the clean animals and clean fowls, he brought seven couples as God had commanded him. (Gen 7:5)

And all the animals, and beasts, and fowls were still there, and they surrounded the ark at every place, and the rain had not descended till seven days after.

On that day the Lord caused the whole earth to shake, and the sun darkened, and the foundations of the world raged, and the whole earth was moved violently, and the lightning flashed, and the thunder roared, and all the fountains in the earth were broken up, such as was not known to the inhabitants before; and God did this mighty act in order to terrify the sons of men, that there might be no more evil on earth. And still the sons of men would not return from their evil ways, and they increased the anger of the Lord at that time, and did not even direct their hearts to all this. At the end of seven days, in the six hundredth year of the life of Noah, the waters of the flood were on the earth. (Gen 7:4,6)

All the fountains of the deep were broken up, and the windows of heaven were opened, and the rain was on the earth forty days and forty nights. (Gen 7:11-12)

And Noah and his household, and all the living creatures that were with him, came into the ark on account of the waters of the flood, and the Lord shut him in. (Gen 7:16)

All the sons of men that were left on the earth became exhausted through evil on account of the rain, for the waters were coming more violently on the earth, and the animals and beasts were still surrounding the ark. And the sons of men assembled together, about seven hundred thousand men and women, and they came to Noah to the ark. They called to Noah, saying,

"Open for us that we may come to you in the ark -- and wherefore shall we die?"

And Noah, with a loud voice answered them from the ark, saying,

"Have you not all rebelled against the Lord, and said that He does not exist? Therefore the Lord brought on you this evil, to destroy and cut you off from the face of the earth. Is not this the thing that I spoke to you of one hundred and twenty years back, and you would not listen to the voice of the Lord, and now do you desire to live on earth?"

They said to Noah,

"We are ready to return to the Lord; only open for us that we may live and not die."

And Noah answered them, saying,

"Behold now that you see the trouble of your souls, you wish to return to the Lord; why did you not return during these hundred and twenty years, which the Lord granted you as the determined period? But now you come and tell me this on account of the troubles of your souls, now also the Lord will not listen to you, neither will He give ear to you on this day, so that you will not now succeed in your wishes."

The sons of men approached in order to break into the ark, to come in on account of the rain, for they could not bear the rain on them. And the Lord sent all the beasts and animals that stood around the ark. And the beasts overpowered them and drove them from that place, and every man went his way and they again scattered themselves on the face of the earth.

The rain was still descending on the earth, and it descended forty days and forty nights, and the waters prevailed greatly on the earth; all flesh that was on the earth or in the waters died, whether men, animals, beasts, creeping things or birds of the air, and there only remained Noah and those that were with him in the ark. (Gen 7:17-23)

The waters prevailed and they greatly increased on the earth, and they lifted up the ark and it was raised from the earth. And the ark floated on the face of the waters; it was tossed on the waters so that all the living creatures within were turned about like pottage in a cauldron. Great anxiety seized all the living creatures that were in the ark, and the ark was like to be broken. And all the living creatures that were in the ark were terrified: the lions roared, and the oxen lowed, and the wolves howled, and every living creature in the ark spoke and lamented in its own language, so that their voices reached to a great distance, and Noah and his sons cried and wept in their troubles; they were greatly afraid that they had reached the gates of death.

And Noah prayed to the Lord, and cried to Him on account of this, and he said,

"O Lord help us, for we have no strength to bear this evil that has encompassed us, for the waves of the waters have surrounded us, mischievous torrents have terrified us, the snares of death have come before us; answer us, O Lord, answer us, light up Your countenance toward us and be gracious to us, redeem us and deliver us." (Psa 18:1-24 & Psa 124)

The Lord listened to the voice of Noah, and the Lord remembered him. And a wind passed over the earth; the waters were still and the ark rested. (Gen 8:1)

The fountains of the deep and the windows of heaven were stopped, and the rain from heaven was restrained. (Gen 8:2)

And the waters decreased in those days, and the ark rested on the mountains of Ararat. (Gen 8:3-4)

Noah then opened the windows of the ark, and Noah still called out to the Lord at that time and he said,

"O Lord, who did form the earth and the heavens and all that are therein, bring forth our souls from this confinement, and from the prison wherein you have placed us, for I am much wearied with sighing."

And the Lord listened to the voice of Noah, and said to him,

"When you have completed a full year you shall then go forth."

And at the revolution of the year, when a full year was completed to Noah's dwelling in the ark, the waters were dried from off the earth, and Noah put off the covering of the ark. (Gen 8:13)

At that time, on the twenty-seventh day of the second month, the earth was dry, but Noah and his sons and those that were with him did not go out from the ark until the Lord told them. (Gen 8:14)

And the day came that the Lord told them to go out, and they all went out from the ark. (Gen 8:15)

They went and returned every one to his way and to his place, and Noah and his sons lived in the land that God had told them; they served the Lord all their days, and the Lord blessed Noah and his sons on their going out from the ark. (Gen 8:16-19)

And He said to them,

"Be prolific and fill all the earth; become strong and increase abundantly in the earth and reproduce therein." (Gen 9:1)

-oOo-

Abel's Prayer

As a child I used to love to hear stories that started with 'Long, long ago ......'. It was reassuring to think that adults were wise and knew all that happened long ago! One grows up to discover that people generally have no idea, and that each person only concentrates on their own personal sphere of life, endeavouring to learn all that they can about their own environment, and chosen professional discipline.

I am amused to hear various 'experts' expressing their opinions on the earth's past history. They throw figurers around of millions and billions of years, to the closest 10 or 100 million. Personally, I don't have any confidence in values when the people talk of measurements with a variance of 10% or greater! That just sounds like a guess to me!

I once heard an Analytical Chemist comment on his laboratory analyzers (used to measure various concentrations of elements in solution). He was laughing at the time when he said, "We like to measure in parts per million, and report in percentage!" Knowing that his analyzers could accurately determine concentrations of standard solutions to the fourth figure after the decimal point; this gave him confidence that the results he was reporting expressed in percentage, were very accurate. His knowledge, of the analyzers performance to the true standard, gave him faith and confidence in his work.

So then, how do Christian's build their faith in God?

"So then faith comes by hearing, and hearing by the word of God." (Rom 10:17)

"Yes, and all who desire to live godly in Christ Jesus will suffer persecution. But evil men and imposters will grow worse and worse, deceiving and being deceived. But you must continue in the things which you have learned and been assured of, knowing from whom you have learned them, and that from childhood you have known the Holy Scriptures, which are able to make you wise for salvation through faith which is in Christ Jesus. All scripture is given by inspiration of God, and is profitable for doctrine, for reproof, for correction, for instruction in righteousness, that the man of God may be complete, thoroughly equipped for every good work." (2Ti 3:12-17)

"Do not quench the Spirit. Do not despise prophecies.

Test all things; hold fast what is good. Abstain from every form of evil." (1Th 5:19-22)

There are many books of scripture that were not bound together with the Bible. I have found these books to build up, and not break down my faith. They testify to the same events in the Bible as being true, and provide additional information, background and detail to the accounts in the Bible. After all, if you read something you don't like, you can always research it further to discover the truth; but if you have no knowledge of the subject, you will just remain ignorant! The chances of making a mistake is greater when one performs work in a state of ignorance, than when one has knowledge and a deeper understanding of the work to be performed!

Whoever loves instruction loves knowledge (Pro 12:1)

Here follows a good example of the combining testimony of scripture.

The Book of Genesis

Cain murders Abel

Now Adam knew Eve his wife, and she conceived and bore Cain, and said,

"I have acquired a man from the Lord."

Then she bore again, this time his brother Abel. Now Abel was a keeper of sheep, but Cain was a tiller of the ground. And in the process of time it came to pass that Cain brought an offering of the fruit of the ground to the Lord. Abel also brought of the firstborn of his flock and of their fat. And the Lord respected Abel and his offering, but He did not respect Cain and his offering. And Cain was very angry, and his countenance fell. So the Lord said to Cain,

"Why are you angry? And why has your countenance fallen? If you do well, will you not be accepted? And if you do not do well, sin lies at the door. And its desire is for you, but you should rule over it."

Now Cain talked with Abel his brother; and it came to pass, when they were in the field, that Cain rose up against Abel his brother and killed him. Then the Lord said to Cain,

"Where is Abel your brother?"

He said,

"I do not know. Am I my brother's keeper?"

And He said,

"What have you done? The voice of your brother's blood cries out to Me from the ground. So now you are cursed from the earth, which has opened its mouth to receive your brother's blood from your hand. When you till the ground, it shall no longer yield its strength to you. A fugitive and a vagabond you shall be on the earth."

And Cain said to the Lord,

"My punishment is greater than I can bear! Surely You have driven me out this day from the face of the ground; I shall be hidden from Your face; I shall be a fugitive and a vagabond on the earth, and it will happen that anyone who finds me will kill me."

And the Lord said to him,

"Therefore, whoever kills Cain, vengeance shall be taken on him sevenfold."

And the Lord set a mark on Cain, lest anyone finding him should kill him.

The family of Cain

Then Cain went out from the presence of the Lord and dwelt in the land of Nod on the east of Eden. And Cain knew his wife, and she conceived and bore Enoch. And he built a city, and called the name of the city after the name of his son - Enoch. To Enoch was born Irad; and Irad begot Mehujael, and Mehujael begot Methushael, and Methushael begot Lamech. Then Lamech took for himself two wives: the name of one was Adah, and the name of the second was Zillah. And Adah bore Jabal. He was the father of those who dwell in tents and have livestock. His brother's name was Jubal. He was the father of all those who play the harp and flute. And as for Zillah, she bore Tubal-Cain (!descendant of Cain), an instructor of every craftsman in bronze and iron. And the sister of Tubal-Cain was Naamah. Then Lamech said to his wives:

"Adah and Zillah, hear my voice; Wives of Lamech, listen to my speech! For I have killed a man for wounding me, even a young man for hurting me. If Cain shall be avenged sevenfold, then Lamech seventy-sevenfold."

And Adam knew his wife again, and she bore a son and named him Seth,

"For God has appointed another seed for me instead of Abel, whom Cain killed."

And as for Seth, to him also a son was born; and he named him Enosh. Then men began to call on the name of the Lord. (Gen 4:1-26)

"Every moving thing that lives shall be food for you. I have given you all things, even as the green herbs. But you shall not eat flesh with its life, that is, its blood. Surely for your lifeblood I will demand a reckoning; from the hand of every beast I will require it, and from the hand of man. From the hand of every man's brother I will require the life of man. Whoever sheds man's blood, by man his blood shall be shed; for in the image of God He made man." (Gen 9:3-6)

'For the life of the flesh is in the blood, and I have given it to you upon the altar to make atonement for your souls; for it is the blood that makes atonement for the soul.' (Lev 17:11)

"Greater love has no one than this, than to lay down one's life for his friends."

(Joh 15:13)

The Book of Enoch

I saw the spirit of a dead man, and his voice went out to heaven and made petitions. And I asked Raphael the angel who was with me, and I said to him:

'This spirit which petitions, Whose is it, whose voice goes up and petitions heaven?'

And he answered me saying:

'This is the spirit which went out from Abel, whom his brother Cain slew, and he makes his suit against him until his offspring is destroyed from the face of the earth, and his offspring are annihilated from among the children of men.'

(Enoch 22:4-7)

The Book of Jasher

And Adam and his wife went contrary to the command of God which He commanded them, and God knew it, and His anger was set ablaze against them and He cursed them. And the Lord God drove them that day from the garden of Eden, to till the ground from which they were taken, and they went and lived at the east of the garden of Eden; and Adam had sex with his wife Eve and she bore two sons and three daughters. She called the name of the first born Cain, saying,

"I have obtained a man from the Lord,"

and the name of the other she called Abel, for she said,

"Empty we came into the earth, and empty we shall be taken from it."

And the boys grew up and their father gave them a possession in the land; and Cain was a farmer of the ground, and Abel a keeper of sheep. And it was at the expiration of a few years, that they brought a first-fruit offering to the Lord, and Cain brought from the fruit of the ground, and Abel brought from the firstlings of his flock from the fat thereof, and God turned and inclined to Abel and his offering, and a fire came down from the Lord from heaven and consumed it.

And to Cain and his offering the Lord did not turn, and He did not incline to it, for he had brought from the inferior fruit of the ground before the Lord, and Cain was jealous against his brother Abel on account of this, and he sought an opportunity to kill him.

Some time after, Cain and Abel his brother went one day into the field to do their work; and they were both in the field, Cain farming and plowing his ground, and Abel feeding his flock; and the flock passed that part which Cain had plowed in the ground, and it sorely grieved Cain on this account. And Cain approached his brother Abel in anger, and he said to him,

"What gives you the right to come and live here and bring your flock to feed in my land?"

And Abel answered his brother Cain and said to him,

"What gives you the right to eat the flesh of my flock and clothe yourself with their wool? Take off the wool of my sheep with which you have clothed yourself, and pay me for their resources you have used and flesh which you have eaten, and when you shall have done this, I will then go from your land as you have said."

Cain said to his brother Abel,

"Certainly if I kill you this day, who will require your blood from me?"

And Abel answered Cain, saying,

"Certainly God who has made us in the earth, he will avenge my cause, and He will require my blood from you should you kill me, for the Lord is the judge and arbiter, and it is He who will repay man according to his evil, and the wicked man according to the wickedness that he may do on earth. And now, if you should kill me here, certainly God knows your secret views, and will judge you for the evil which you did declare to do to me this day."

When Cain heard the words which Abel his brother had spoken, the anger of Cain was set ablaze against his brother Abel for declaring this thing. Cain hurried and rose up, and took the iron part of his plowing instrument, with which he suddenly struck his brother and he killed him, and Cain spilt the blood of his brother Abel on the earth, and the blood of Abel streamed on the earth before the flock.

And after this Cain repented having slain his brother, and he was sadly grieved, and he wept over him and it troubled him greatly. Cain rose up and dug a hole in the field, wherein he put his brother's body, and he turned the dust over it. And the Lord knew what Cain had done to his brother, and the Lord appeared to Cain and said to him,

"Where is Abel your brother that was with you?"

And Cain lied, and said,

"I do not know. Am I my brother's keeper?"

And the Lord said to him,

"What have you done? The voice of your brother's blood cries to me from the ground where you have slain him. For you have slain your brother and have lied before Me, and imagined in your heart that I saw you not, nor knew all your actions. But you did this thing and did kill your brother for naught and because he spoke rightly to you, and now, therefore, cursed be you from the ground which opened its mouth to receive your brother's blood from your hand, and wherein you did bury him. It shall be when you till it, the land will no longer give you its strength as in the beginning, for thorns and thistles shall the ground produce, and you shall be moving and wandering in the earth until the day of your death."

And at that time Cain went out from the presence of the Lord, from the place where he was, and he went moving and wandering in the land toward the east of Eden, he and all those belonging to him. Cain had sex with his wife in those days, and she conceived and gave birth to a son, and he called his name Enoch, saying,

"In that time the Lord began to give him rest and quiet in the earth."

At that time Cain also began to build a city: and he built the city and he called the name of the city Enoch, according to the name of his son; for in those days the Lord had given him rest on the earth, and he did not move about and wander as in the beginning. And Irad was born to Enoch, and Irad had Mechuyael and Mechuyael had Methusael.

It was in the hundred and thirtieth year of the life of Adam on the earth, that he again had sex with Eve his wife, and she conceived and gave birth to a son and he looked like Adam, and she called his name Seth, saying,

"Because God has appointed me another offspring in the place of Abel, for Cain has slain him."

And Seth lived one hundred and five years, and he had a son; and Seth called the name of his son Enosh, saying,

"Because in that time the sons of men began to reproduce, and to afflict their souls and hearts by disobeying and rebelling against God."

It was in the days of Enosh that the sons of men continued to rebel and go contrary to God, to increase the anger of the Lord against the sons of men. (Jasher 1:11-2:3)

When Cainan was seventy years old, he had three sons and two daughters. These are the names of the children of Cainan; the name of the first born was Mahlallel, the second was Enan, and the third was Mered, and their sisters were Adah and Zillah; these are the five children of Cainan that were born to him. Lamech, the son of Methusael, became related to Cainan by marriage, and he took his two daughters for his wives, and Adah conceived and gave birth to a son to Lamech, and she called his name Jabal. And she again conceived and gave birth to a son, and called his name Jubal; and Zillah, her sister, was unable to conceive in those days and had no offspring. (Jasher 2:15-18)

And in the end of days and years, when Zillah became old, the Lord opened her womb. She conceived and gave birth to a son and she called his name Tubal Cain, saying,

"After I had withered away I have obtained him from Almighty God."

And she conceived again and gave birth to a daughter, and she called her name Naamah, for she said,

"After I had withered away have I obtained pleasure and delight."

Lamech was old and advanced in years, and his eyes were dim that he could not see, and Tubal Cain, his son, was leading him and it was one day that Lamech went into the field and Tubal Cain his son was with him, and while they were walking in the field, Cain the son of Adam advanced towards them; for Lamech was very old and could not see much, and

Tubal Cain his son was very young. Tubal Cain told his father to draw his bow, and with the arrows he struck Cain, who was yet far off, and he killed him, because he appeared to be an animal to them. And the arrows entered Cain's body although he was at a distance from them, and he fell to the ground and died.

The Lord rewarded Cain's evil according to his wickedness, which he had done to his brother Abel, according to the word of the Lord which he had spoken. And it came to pass when Cain had died, that Lamech and Tubal went to see the animal which they had slain, and they saw, and behold Cain their grandfather was fallen dead on the earth.

Lamech was very much grieved at having done this, and in clapping his hands together (in grief) he struck his son and caused his death. And the wives of Lamech heard what Lamech had done, and they sought to kill him. The wives of Lamech hated him from that day, because he killed Cain and Tubal Cain, and the wives of Lamech separated from him, and would not listen to him in those days. And Lamech came to his wives, and he begged them to listen to him about this matter. He said to his wives Adah and Zillah,

"Hear my voice O wives of Lamech, attend to my words, for now you have imagined and said that I killed a man with my wounds, and a child with my stripes for they did no violence, but certainly know that I am old and grayheaded, and that my eyes are heavy through age, and I did this thing unknowingly."

And the wives of Lamech listened to him in this matter, and they returned to him with the advice of their father Adam, but they bore no children to him from that time, knowing that God's anger was increasing in those days against the sons of men, to destroy them with the waters of the flood for their evil acts. Mahlallel the son of Cainan lived sixty-five years and he had Jared; and Jared lived sixty-two years and he had Enoch. (Jasher 2:23-37)

Joseph B. Lumpkin

The Book of Jubilees

The angel of the presence (of the Lord) spoke to Moses according to the word of the Lord ... (Jub 2:1)

In the third week in the second jubilee she gave birth to Cain, and in the fourth jubilee she gave birth to Abel, and in the fifth jubilee she gave birth to her daughter Awan. In the first year of the third jubilee, Cain killed Abel because God accepted the sacrifice of Abel, and did not accept the offering of Cain. And he killed him in the field, and his blood cried from the ground to heaven, complaining because he had killed him. The Lord blamed Cain, because he had killed Abel, and He made him a fugitive on the earth because of the blood of his brother, and He cursed him on the earth. Because of this it is written on the heavenly tablets, "Cursed is he who kills his neighbor treacherously, and let all who have seen and heard say, 'So be it', and the man who has seen and not reported it, let him be accursed as the one committing it." For this reason we announce when we come before the Lord our God all the sin that is committed in heaven and on earth, and in light and in darkness, and everywhere.

And Adam and his wife mourned for Abel four weeks of years, and in the fourth year of the fifth week they became joyful, and Adam knew his wife again, and she gave birth to a son, and he called his name Seth, for he said,

"God has raised up a second offspring to us on the earth instead of Abel; for Cain killed him."

In the sixth week he begat his daughter Azura. And Cain took Awan his sister to be his wife and she gave birth to Enoch at the close of the fourth jubilee.

In the first year of the first week of the fifth jubilee, houses were built on the earth, and Cain built a city, and called its name after the name of his son Enoch. Adam knew Eve his wife and she gave birth to a total of nine sons. In the fifth week of the fifth jubilee Seth took Azura his sister to be his wife, and in the fourth year of the sixth week she gave birth to Enos. He began to call on the name of the Lord on the earth.

In the seventh jubilee in the third week Enos took Noam his sister to be his wife, and she gave birth to a son in the third year of the fifth week, and he called his name Kenan (!Cainan). At the close of the eighth jubilee Kenan took Mualeleth his sister to be his wife, and she gave birth to a son in the ninth jubilee, in the first week in the third year of this week, and he called his name Mahalalel.

In the second week of the tenth jubilee Mahalalel took to him to wife Dinah, the daughter of Barakiel the daughter of his father's brother, and she gave birth to a son in the third week in the sixth year, and he call his name Jared, for in his days the angels of the Lord descended on the earth, those who are named the Watchers, that they should instruct the children of men, and that they should do judgment and uprightness on the earth.

In the eleventh jubilee Jared took to himself a wife, and her name was Baraka, the daughter of Rasujal, a daughter of his father's brother, in the fourth week of this jubilee, and she gave birth to a son in the fifth week, in the fourth year of the jubilee, and he called his name Enoch.

He was the first among men that are born on earth who learned writing and knowledge and wisdom and who wrote down the signs of heaven according to the order of their months in a book, that men might know the seasons of the years according to the order of their separate months.

He was the first to write a testimony and he testified to the sons of men among the generations of the earth, and recounted the weeks of the jubilees, and made known to them the days of the years, and set in order the months and recounted the Sabbaths of the years as we made them, known to him. And what was and what will be he saw in a vision of his sleep, as it will happen to the children of men throughout their generations until the day of judgment; he saw and understood everything, and wrote his testimony, and placed the testimony on earth for all the children of men and for their generations.

In the twelfth jubilee, in the seventh week of it, he took to himself a wife, and her name was Edna, the daughter of Danel, the daughter of his father's brother, and in the sixth year in this week she gave birth to a son and he called his name Methuselah. He was with the angels of God these six jubilees of years, and they showed him everything that is on earth and in the heavens, the rule of the sun, and he wrote down everything. And he testified to the Watchers, who had sinned with the daughters of men; for these had begun to unite themselves, so as to be defiled with the daughters of men, and Enoch testified against them all. And he was taken from among the children of men, and we conducted him into the Garden of Eden in majesty and honor, and there he wrote down the condemnation and judgment of the world, and all the wickedness of the children of men. Because of it God brought the waters of the flood on all the land of Eden; for there he was set as a sign and that he should testify against all the children of men, that he should recount all the deeds of the generations until the day of condemnation. He burnt the incense of the sanctuary, even sweet spices acceptable before the Lord on the Mount. For the Lord has four places on the earth, the Garden of Eden, and the Mount of the East, and this mountain on which you are this day, Mount Sinai, and Mount Zion which will be sanctified in the new creation for a sanctification of the earth; through it will the earth be sanctified from all its guilt and its uncleanness throughout the generations of the world.

In the fourteenth jubilee Methuselah took to himself a wife, Edna the daughter of Azrial, the daughter of his father's brother, in the third week, in the first year of this week, and he begat a son and called his name Lamech.

In the fifteenth jubilee in the third week Lamech took to himself a wife, and her name was Betenos the daughter of Baraki'il, the daughter of his father's brother, and in this week she gave birth to a son and he called his name Noah, saying, "This one will comfort me for my trouble and all my work, and for the ground which the Lord has cursed."

At the close of the nineteenth jubilee, in the seventh week in the sixth year of it, Adam died, and all his sons buried him in the land of his creation, and he was the first to be buried in the earth. He lacked seventy years of one thousand years, because one thousand years are as one day in the testimony of the heavens. Therefore was it written concerning the tree of knowledge, "On the day that you eat of it you shall die." Because of this he did not complete the one thousand years but instead he died during it.

At the close of this jubilee Cain was killed after him in the same year; because his house fell on him and he died in the middle of his house, and he was killed by its stones. With a stone he had killed Abel, and by a stone he was killed in righteous judgment.

For this reason it was ordained on the heavenly tablets, with the instrument with which a man kills his neighbor with the same shall he be killed. In the same manner that he wounded him, in like manner shall they deal with him."

In the twenty-fifth jubilee Noah took to himself a wife, and her name was Emzara, the daughter of Rake'el, the daughter of his father's brother, in the first year in the fifth week, and in the third year of it she gave birth to Shem, in the fifth year of it she gave birth to Ham, and in the first year in the sixth week she gave birth to Japheth.

(Jub 4:1-32)

<u>Summary</u>

As you have seen, these books contain a wealth of information which is not in the Bible. The dates, names and events described, all add to one's understanding, supporting the Bible's text and statements. The four Gospels don't match details exactly either!

According to the Genesis 4&5 the following bloodlines are listed:

Adam - Cain - Enoch - Irad - Mehujael - Methushael - Lamech - Jabel, Jubal, Tubal-Cain.

Adam - Abel (killed by Cain).

Adam - Seth - Enosh - Cainan - Mahalalel - Jared - Enoch - Methuselah - Lamech - Noah.

Only Noah, Shem, Ham and Japheth, and their four wives survived the flood. The rest of the unrighteous descendants of Adam that were still alive when the flood came were drowned. Lamech the son of Methusael, became related to Cainan by marriage as he took his two daughters for his wives (Adah and Zillah).

Referring to the book of Jubilees we find out that Cain was killed by his house falling on him. Perhaps it meant, it was the members of his household that killed him, meaning Lamech and Tubal-Cain. If the arrow had a point made from flint-stone that would support both texts.

It's interesting that Cain and Tubal-Cain died on the same day as 'Tubal-Cain' means 'descendant of Cain'. This is an answer to Abel's prayer in the Book of Enoch!

There may be a few things which don't quite add up, but information which does not match in parts, is far better than no information at all. After all, if I wanted to believe in 'nothing', I would believe in Evolution!

Quotes from :

'The Lost Book of Enoch' by Joseph B. Lumpkin - ISBN : 0-9746336-6-6

'The Book of Jasher'   by Joseph B. Lumpkin - ISBN : 1933580143

'The Book of Jubilees'   by Joseph B. Lumpkin - ISBN : 19633580097

-oOo-

Three Doors

"If you do well, will you not be accepted? And if you do not do well, sin lies at the door. And its desire is for you, but you should rule over it." (Gen 4:7)

1) The Door of the Ark

So God looked upon the earth, and indeed it was corrupt; for all flesh had corrupted their way on the earth. And God said to Noah, "The end of all flesh has come before Me, for the earth is filled with violence through them; and behold, I will destroy them with the earth. Make yourself an ark of gopherwood; make rooms in the ark, and cover it inside and outside with pitch. And this is how you shall make it: The length of the ark shall be three hundred cubits, its width fifty cubits, and its height thirty cubits. You shall make a window for the ark, and you shall finish it to a cubit from above; and set the door of the ark in its side. You shall make it with lower, second, and third decks. And behold, I Myself am bringing floodwaters on the earth, to destroy from under heaven all flesh in which is the breath of life; everything that is on the earth shall die. But I will establish My covenant with you; and you shall go into the ark - you, your sons, your wife, and your sons' wives with you. And of every living thing of all flesh you shall bring two of every sort into the ark, to keep them alive with you; they shall be male and female."

(Gen 6:12-19)

So those that entered, male and female of all flesh, went in as God had commanded him; and the Lord shut him in. (Gen 7:16)

At that time, after the death of Methuselah, the Lord said to Noah,

"Go with your household into the ark; behold I will gather to you all the animals of the earth, the beasts of the field and the fowls of the air, and they shall all come and surround the ark. You shall go and seat yourself by the doors of the ark, and all the beasts, the animals, and the fowls, shall assemble and place themselves before you, and such of them as will come and crouch before you, you shall take and deliver into the hands of your sons, who will bring them to the ark, and all that will stand before you, you shall leave."

And the Lord brought this about on the next day, and animals, beasts and fowls came in great multitudes and surrounded the ark. Noah went and seated himself by the door of the ark, and of all flesh that crouched before him he brought into the ark, and all that stood before him he left on earth. A lioness came with her two whelps, male and female, and the three crouched before Noah; the two whelps rose up against the lioness and struck her, and made her flee from her place, and she went away, and they returned to their places and crouched on the earth before Noah. And the lioness ran away, and stood in the place of the lions. And Noah saw this and wondered greatly, and he rose and took the two whelps and brought them into the ark. Noah brought into the ark from all living creatures that were on earth, so that there was none left but those which Noah brought into the ark. Two and two came to Noah into the ark, but from the clean animals and clean fowls, he brought seven couples as God had commanded him. And all the animals, and beasts, and fowls were still there, and they surrounded the ark at every place, and the rain had not descended till seven days after. (Jas 6:1-10)

The door of the Ark, separated the living from the dead!

2) Old Covenant - The Doorway of the Presence of God

Salvation

Now the Lord spoke to Moses and Aaron in the land of Egypt, saying,

"This month shall be your beginning of months; it shall be the first month of the year to you. Speak to all the congregation of Israel, saying: 'On the tenth of this month every man shall take for himself a lamb, according to the house of his father, a lamb for a household. And if the household is too small for the lamb, let him and his neighbor next to his house take it according to the number of the persons; according to each man's need you shall make your count for the lamb. Your lamb shall be without blemish, a male of the first year. You may take it from the sheep or from the goats. Now you shall keep it until the fourteenth day of the same month. Then the whole assembly of the congregation of Israel shall kill it at twilight. And they shall take some of the blood and put it on the two doorposts and on the lintel of the houses where they eat it. Then they shall eat the flesh on that night; roasted in the fire, with unleavened bread and with bitter herbs they shall eat it. Do not eat it raw, nor boiled at all with water, but roasted in fire - its head with its legs and its entrails. You shall let none of it remain until morning, and what remains of it until morning you shall burn with fire. And thus you shall eat it: with a belt on your waist, your sandals on your feet, and your staff in your hand. So you shall eat it in haste. It is the Lord's Passover. For I will pass through the land of Egypt on that night, and will strike all the firstborn in the land of Egypt, both man and beast; and against all the gods of Egypt I will execute judgement: I am the Lord. Now the blood shall be a sign for you on the houses where you are. And when I see the blood, I will pass over you; and the plague shall not be on you to destroy you when I strike the land of Egypt.' " (Exo 12:1-13)

Then Moses called for all the elders of Israel and said to them, "Pick out and take lambs for yourselves according to your families, and kill the Passover lamb. And you shall take a bunch of hyssop, dip it in the blood that is in the basin, and strike the lintel and the two doorposts with the blood that is in the basin. And none of you shall go out of the door of his house until morning. For the Lord will pass through to strike the Egyptians; and when He sees the blood on the lintel and on the two doorposts, the Lord will pass over the door and not allow the destroyer to come into your houses to strike you." (Exo 12:21-23)

Reference to crucifixion

"But if the servant plainly says, 'I love my master, my wife, and my children; I will not go out free,' then his master shall bring him to the door, or to the doorpost, and his master shall pierce his ear with an awl; and he shall serve him forever." (Exo 21:5-6)

"You shall remember that you were a slave in the land of Egypt, and the Lord your God redeemed you; therefore I command you this thing today. And if it happens that he says to you, 'I will not go away from you,' because he loves you and your house, since he prospers with you, then you shall take an awl and thrust it through his ear to the door, and he shall be your servant forever. Also to your female servant you shall do likewise."

(Deu 15:15-17)

Reference to Baptism and washing away the blood of sins

"And Aaron and his sons you shall bring to the door of the tabernacle of meeting, and you shall wash them with water." (Exo 29:4)

"Then you shall bring Aaron and his sons to the door of the tabernacle of meeting and wash them with water." (Exo 40:12)

He hung the screen at the door of the tabernacle. And he put the altar of burnt offering before the door of the tabernacle of the tent of meeting, and offered upon it the burnt offering and the grain offering, as the Lord had commanded Moses. He set the laver between the tabernacle of meeting and the altar, and put water there for washing; and Moses, Aaron, and his sons would wash their hands and their feet with water from it. Whenever they went into the tabernacle of meeting, and when they came near the altar, they washed, as the Lord had commanded Moses. (Exo 40:28-32)

"When I passed by you again and looked upon you, indeed your time was the time of love; so I spread My wing over you and covered your nakedness. Yes, I swore an oath to you and entered into a covenant with you, and you became Mine," says the Lord God.

"Then I washed you in water; yes, I thoroughly washed off your blood, and I anointed you with oil." (Eze 16:8-9)

Reference to Communion and the Passover Lamb

"Then Aaron and his sons shall eat the flesh of the ram, and the bread that is in the basket, by the door of the tabernacle of meeting. They shall eat those things with which the atonement was made, to consecrate and to sanctify them; but an outsider shall not eat them, because they are holy. And if any of the flesh of the consecration offerings, or of the bread, remains until the morning, then you shall burn the remainder with fire. It shall not be eaten, because it is holy." (Exo 29:32-34)

And Moses said to Aaron and his sons, "Boil the flesh at the door of the tabernacle of meeting, and eat it there with the bread that is in the basket of consecration offerings, as I commanded, saying, 'Aaron and his sons shall eat it.' What remains of the flesh and of the bread you shall burn with fire." (Lev 8:31-32)

Reference to God's presence within us at the door of our hearts

So it was, whenever Moses went out to the tabernacle, that all the people rose, and each man stood at his tent door and watched Moses until he had gone into the tabernacle. And it came to pass, when Moses entered the tabernacle, that the pillar of cloud descended and stood at the door of the tabernacle, and the Lord talked with Moses. All the people saw the pillar of cloud standing at the tabernacle door, and all the people rose and worshipped, each man in his tent door. So the Lord spoke to Moses face to face, as a man speaks to his friend. And he would return to the camp, but his servant Joshua the son of Nun, a young man, did not depart from the tabernacle. (Exo 33:8-11)

So Moses and Aaron went from the presence of the assembly to the door of the tabernacle of meeting, and they fell on their faces. And the glory of the Lord appeared to them. (Num 20:6)

Reference to the blood sacrifice and fat offering (The Lord's food - Eze 44:7)

"And the priest shall sprinkle the blood on the altar of the Lord at the door of the tabernacle of meeting, and burn the fat for a sweet aroma to the Lord." (Lev 17:6)

And the Lord spoke to Moses, saying, "Speak to the children of Israel, saying: 'You shall not eat any fat, of ox or sheep or goat. And the fat of an animal that dies naturally, and the fat of what is torn by wild beasts, may be used in any other way; but you shall by no means eat it. For whoever eats the fat of the animal of which men offer an offering made by fire to the Lord, the person who eats it shall be cut off from his people. Moreover you shall not eat any blood in any of your dwellings, whether of bird or beast. Whoever eats any blood, that person shall be cut off from his people.'" (Lev 7:23-27)

Reference to the Law and the new spirit in our hearts - The call to repentance

"Hear, O Israel: The Lord our God, the Lord is one! You shall love the Lord our God with all your heart, with all your soul, and with all your strength. And these words which I command you today shall be in your heart. You shall teach them diligently to your children, and shall talk of them when you sit in your house, when you walk by the way, when you lie down, and when you rise up. You shall bind them as a sign on your hand, and they shall be as frontlets between your eyes. You shall write them on the doorposts of your house and on your gates." (Deu 6:4-9)

"Then I will give them one heart, and I will put a new spirit within them, and take the stony heart out of their flesh, and give them a heart of flesh, that they may walk in My statutes and keep My judgments and do them; and they shall be My people, and I will be their God. But as for those whose hearts follow the desire for their detestable things and their abominations, I will recompense their deeds on their own heads," says the Lord God. (Eze 11:19-21)

"Behold the days are coming," says the Lord, "when I will make a new covenant with the house of Israel and with the house of Judah - not according to the covenant that I made with their fathers in the day that I took them by the hand to lead them out of the land of Egypt, My covenant which they broke, though I was a husband to them," says the Lord. "But this is the covenant that I will make with the house of Israel after those days," says the Lord: "I will put My law in their minds, and write it on their hearts; and I will be their God, and they shall be My people. No more shall every man teach his neighbor, and every man his brother, saying, 'Know the Lord,' for they all shall know Me, from the least of them to the greatest of them," says the Lord. "For I will forgive their iniquity, and their sin I will remember no more." (Jer 31:31-34)

"Behold, all souls are Mine; the soul of the father as well as the soul of the son are Mine; the soul who sins shall die. But if a man is just and does what is lawful and right; "

"If he has walked in My statutes and kept My judgments faithfully - He is just; He shall surely live!" says the Lord God. (Eze 18:4-5,9)

"Therefore I will judge you, O house of Israel, every one according to his ways," says the Lord God. "Repent, and turn from all your transgressions, so that iniquity will not be your ruin. Cast away from you all the transgressions which you have committed, and get yourselves a new heart and a new spirit. For why should you die, O house of Israel?

For I have no pleasure in the death of one who dies," says the Lord God.

"Therefore turn and live!" (Eze 18:30-32)

3) New Covenant - The Door of Salvation

"Most assuredly, I say to you, he who does not enter the sheepfold by the door, but climbs up some other way, the same is a thief and a robber. But he who enters by the door is the shepherd of the sheep. To him the doorkeeper opens, and the sheep hear his voice; and he calls his own sheep by name and leads them out. And when he brings out his own sheep, he goes before them; and the sheep follow him, for they know his voice. Yet they will by no means follow a stranger, but will flee from him, for they do not know the voice of strangers."

Jesus used this illustration, but they did not understand the things which He spoke to them. Then Jesus said to them again,

"Most assuredly, I say to you, I am the door of the sheep. All who ever came before Me are thieves and robbers, but the sheep did not hear them. I am the door. If anyone enters by Me, he will be saved, and will go in and out and find pasture. The thief does not come except to steal, and to kill, and to destroy. I have come that they may have life, and that they may have it more abundantly. I am the good shepherd. The good shepherd gives His life for the sheep. But a hireling, he who is not the shepherd, one who does not own the sheep, sees the wolf coming and leaves the sheep and flees; and the wolf catches the sheep and scatters them. The hireling flees because he is a hireling and does not care about the sheep. I am the good shepherd; and I know My sheep, and am known by My own. As the Father knows Me, even so I know the Father; and I lay down My life for the sheep. And other sheep I have which are not of this fold; them also I must bring, and they will hear My voice; and there will be one flock and one shepherd. Therefore My Father loves Me, because I lay down My life that I may take it again. No one takes it from Me, but I lay it down of Myself. I have power to lay it down, and I have power to take it again. This command I have received from My Father."

(Joh 10:1-18)

"Let not your heart be troubled; you believe in God, believe also in Me. In My Father's house are many mansions; if it were not so, I would have told you. I go to prepare a place for you. And if I go and prepare a place for you, I will come again and receive you to Myself; that where I am, there you may be also. And where I go you know, and the way you know." Thomas said to Him, "Lord, we do not know where You are going, and how can we know the way?" Jesus said to him, "I am the way, the truth, and the life. No one comes to the Father except through Me." (Joh 14:1-6)

"Enter by the narrow gate; for wide is the gate and broad is the way that leads to destruction, and there are many who go in by it. Because narrow is the gate and difficult is the way which leads to life, and there are few who find it." (Mat 7:13-14)

"Not everyone who says to Me, 'Lord, Lord,' shall enter the kingdom of heaven, but he who does the will of My Father in heaven. Many will say to Me in that day, 'Lord, Lord, have we not prophesied in Your name, cast out demons in Your name, and done many wonders in Your name?' And then I will declare to them, 'I never knew you; depart from Me, you who practice lawlessness!' " (Mat 7:21-23)

"Then the kingdom of heaven shall be likened to ten virgins who took their lamps and went to meet the bridegroom. Now five of them were wise, and five were foolish. Those who were foolish took their lamps and took no oil with them, but the wise took oil in their vessels with their lamps. But while the bridegroom was delayed, they all slumbered and slept. And at midnight a cry was heard:

'Behold, the bridegroom is coming; go out to meet him!'

Then all those virgins arose and trimmed their lamps. And the foolish said to the wise,

'Give us some of your oil, for our lamps are going out.'

But the wise answered, saying,

'No, lest there should not be enough for us and you; but go rather to those who sell, and buy for yourselves.'

And while they went to buy, the bridegroom came, and those who were ready went in with him to the wedding; and the door was shut. Afterward the other virgins came also, saying, 'Lord, Lord, open to us!'

But he answered and said,

'Assuredly, I say to you, I do not know you.'

Watch therefore, for you know neither the day nor the hour in which the Son of Man is coming." (Mat 25:1-13)

And He went through the cities and villages, teaching, and journeying toward Jerusalem. Then one said to Him, "Lord, are there few who are saved?" And He said to them,

"Strive to enter through the narrow gate, for many, I say to you, will seek to enter and will not be able. When once the Master of the house has risen up and shut the door, and you begin to stand outside and knock at the door, saying, 'Lord, Lord, open for us,' and He will answer and say to you, 'I do not know you, where you are from,' then you will begin to say, 'We ate and drank in Your presence, and You taught in our streets.' But He will say, 'I tell you I do not know you, where you are from. Depart from Me, all you workers of iniquity.' There will be weeping and gnashing of teeth, when you see Abraham and Isaac and Jacob and all the prophets in the kingdom of God, and yourselves thrust out. They will come from the east and the west, from the north and the south, and sit down in the kingdom of God. And indeed there are last who will be first, and there are first who will be last." (Luk 13:22-30)

"Most assuredly, I say to you, he who believes in Me has everlasting life. I am the bread of life. Your fathers ate the manna in the wilderness, and are dead. This is the bread which comes down from heaven, that one may eat of it and not die. I am the living bread which came down from heaven. If anyone eats of this bread, he will live forever; and the bread that I shall give is My flesh, which I shall give for the life of the world."

The Jews therefore quarreled among themselves, saying,

"How can this Man give us His flesh to eat?"

Then Jesus said to them,

"Most assuredly, I say to you, unless you eat the flesh of the Son of Man and drink His blood, you have no life in you. Whoever eats My flesh and drinks My blood has eternal life, and I will raise him up at the last day. For My flesh is food indeed, and My blood is drink indeed. He who eats My flesh and drinks My blood abides in Me, and I in him. As the living Father sent Me, and I live because of the Father, so he who feeds on Me will live because of Me. This is the bread which came down from heaven - not as your fathers ate the manna, and are dead. He who eats this bread will live forever."

These things He said in the synagogue as He taught in Capernaum. (Joh 6:47-59)

And as they were eating, Jesus took bread, blessed and broke it, and gave it to the disciples and said,

"Take, eat; this is My body."

Then He took the cup, and gave thanks, and gave it to them, saying,

"Drink from it, all of you. For this is My blood of the new covenant, which is shed for many for the remission of sins. But I say to you, I will not drink of this fruit of the vine from now on until that day when I drink it new with you in My Father's kingdom."

And when they had sung a hymn, they went out to the Mount of Olives. (Mat 26:26-30)

But Christ came as High Priest of the good things to come, with the greater and more perfect tabernacle not made with hands, that is, not of this creation. Not with the blood of goats and calves, but with His own blood He entered the Most Holy Place once for all, having obtained eternal redemption. For if the blood of bulls and goats and the ashes of a heifer, sprinkling the unclean, sanctifies for the purifying of the flesh, how much more shall the blood of Christ, who through the eternal Spirit offered Himself without spot to God, cleanse your conscience from dead works to serve the living God? And for this reason He is the Mediator of the new covenant, by means of death, for the redemption of the transgressions under the first covenant, that those who are called may receive the promise of the eternal inheritance. (Heb 9:11-15)

And according to the law almost all things are purified with blood, and without shedding of blood there is no remission. Therefore it was necessary that the copies of the things in the heavens should be purified with these, but the heavenly things themselves with better sacrifices than these. For Christ has not entered the holy places made with hands, which are copies of the true, but into heaven itself, now to appear in the presence of God for us; not that He should offer Himself often, as the high priest enters the Most Holy Place every year with blood of another - He then would have had to suffer often since the foundation of the world; but now, once at the end of the ages, He has appeared to put away sin by the sacrifice of Himself. And as it is appointed for men to die once, but after this the judgment, so Christ was offered once to bear the sins of many. To those who eagerly wait for Him He will appear a second time, apart from sin, for salvation. (Heb 9:22-28)

Therefore, brethren, having boldness to enter the Holiest by the blood of Jesus, by a new and living way which He consecrated for us, through the veil, that is, His flesh, and having a High Priest over the house of God, let us draw near with a true heart in full assurance of faith, having our hearts sprinkled from an evil conscience and our bodies washed with pure water. Let us hold fast the confession of our hope without wavering, for He who promised is faithful. And let us consider one another in order to stir up love and good works, not forsaking the assembling of ourselves together, as is the manner of some, but exhorting one another, and so much the more as you see the Day approaching. For if we sin willfully after we have received the knowledge of the truth, there no longer remains a sacrifice for sins, but a certain fearful expectation of judgment, and fiery indignation which will devour the adversaries. Anyone who has rejected Moses' law dies without mercy on the testimony of two or three witnesses. Of how much worse punishment, do you suppose, will he be thought worthy who has trampled the Son of God underfoot, counted the blood of the covenant by which he was sanctified a common thing, and insulted the Spirit of grace? (Heb 10:19-29)

"For where two or three are gathered together in My name, I am there in the midst of them." (Mat 18:20)

Now it happened, as we went to prayer, that a certain slave girl possessed with a spirit of divination met us, who brought her masters much profit by fortune-telling. This girl followed Paul and us, and cried out, saying, "These men are the servants of the Most High God, who proclaim to us the way of salvation." And this she did for many days. But Paul, greatly annoyed, turned and said to the spirit, "I command you in the name of Jesus Christ to come out of her." And he came out that very hour. But when her masters saw that their hope of profit was gone, they seized Paul and Silas and dragged them into the marketplace to the authorities. And they brought them to the magistrates, and said, "These men, being Jews, exceedingly trouble our city; and they teach customs which are not lawful to us, being Romans, to receive or observe."

Then the multitude rose up together against them; and the magistrates tore off their clothes and commanded them to be beaten with rods. And when they had laid many stripes on them, they threw them into prison, commanding the jailer to keep them securely. Having received such a charge, he put them into the inner prison and fastened their feet in the stocks. But at midnight Paul and Silas were praying and singing hymns to God, and the prisoners were listening to them. Suddenly there was a great earthquake, so that the foundations of the prison were shaken; and immediately all the doors were opened and everyone's chains were loosed. And the keeper of the prison, awakening from sleep and seeing the prison doors open, supposing the prisoners had fled, drew his sword and was about to kill himself. But Paul called with a loud voice, saying, "Do yourself no harm, for we are all here." Then he called for a light, ran in, and fell down trembling before Paul and Silas. And he brought them out and said, "Sirs, what must I do to be saved?" So they said, "Believe on the Lord Jesus Christ, and you will be saved, you and your household." Then they spoke the word of the Lord to him and to all who were in his house. And he took them the same hour of the night and washed their stripes. And immediately he and all his family were baptized. Now when he had brought them into his house, he set food before them; and he rejoiced, having believed in God with all his household. (Act 16:16-34)

Now He who establishes us with you in Christ and has anointed us in God, who also has sealed us and given us the Spirit in our hearts as a guarantee. (2Co 1:21-22)

Let no corrupt word proceed out of your mouth, but what is good for necessary edification, that it may impart grace to the hearers. And do not grieve the Holy Spirit of God, by whom you were sealed for the day of redemption. (Eph 4:29-30)

"Behold, I stand at the door and knock. If anyone hears My voice and opens the door, I will come in to him and dine with him, and he with Me. To him who overcomes I will grant to sit with Me on My throne, as I also overcame and sat down with My Father on His throne. He who has an ear, let him hear what the Spirit says to the churches."

(Rev 3:20-22)

-oOo-

You are Gods

Abram and the idols

In the fiftieth year of the life of Abram, son of Terah, Abram came forth from the house of Noah, and went to his father's house. And Abram knew the Lord, and he followed in his ways and instructions, and the Lord his God was with him. Terah his father was in those days still captain of the host of king Nimrod, and he still followed strange gods.

And Abram came to his father's house and saw twelve gods standing there in their temples, and the anger of Abram was set ablaze when he saw these images in his father's house. And Abram said, "As the Lord lives these images shall not remain in my father's house; so shall the Lord who created me do to me if in three days' time I do not break them all." Abram went from them, and his anger burned within him.

And Abram hurried and went from the chamber to his father's outer court, and he found his father sitting in the court, and all his servants with him, and Abram came and sat before him. Abram asked his father, saying, "Father, tell me where is God who created heaven and earth, and all the sons of men on earth, and who created you and me." And Terah answered his son Abram and said, "Behold those who created us are all with us in the house." And Abram said to his father, "My lord, show them to me I pray you." And Terah brought Abram into the chamber of the inner court, and Abram saw, and behold the whole room was full of gods of wood and stone, twelve great images and others less than they without number. And Terah said to his son, "Behold, these are they which made all you see on earth, and which created me and you, and all mankind." Terah bowed down to his gods, and he then went away from them, and Abram, his son, went away with him.

When Abram had gone from them he went to his mother and sat before her, and he said to his mother, "Behold, my father has shown me those who made heaven and earth, and all the sons of men. Now, therefore, hurry and fetch a kid from the flock, and make of it savory meat, that I may bring it to my father's gods as an offering for them to eat; perhaps I may thereby become acceptable to them." And his mother did so; she fetched a kid, and made savory meat thereof, and brought it to Abram, and Abram took the savory meat from his mother and brought it before his father's gods, and he drew nigh to them that they might eat; and Terah his father, did not know of it.

Abram saw on the day when he was sitting among them, that they had no voice, no hearing, no motion, and not one of them could stretch forth his hand to eat. And Abram mocked them, and said, "Certainly the savory meat that I prepared has not pleased them, or perhaps it was too little for them, and for that reason they would not eat; therefore tomorrow I will prepare fresh savory meat, better and more plentiful than this, in order that I may see the result."

It was on the next day that Abram directed his mother concerning the savory meat, and his mother rose and fetched three fine kids from the flock; she made of them some excellent savory meat, such as her son was fond of, and she gave it to her son Abram, and Terah his father did not know of it.

Abram took the savory meat from his mother and brought it before his father's gods into the chamber; he came nigh to them that they might eat, and he placed it before them, and Abram sat before them all day thinking perhaps they might eat. Abram viewed them, and behold they had neither voice nor hearing, nor did one of them stretch forth his hand to the meat to eat. And in the evening of that day in that house Abram was clothed with the spirit of God. He called out and said, "Woe to my father and this wicked generation, whose hearts are all inclined to vanity, who serve these idols of wood and stone which can neither eat, smell, hear nor speak, who have mouths without speech, eyes without sight, ears without hearing, hands without feeling, and legs which cannot move; like them are those that made them and that trust in them."

When Abram saw all these things his anger was set ablaze against his father, and he hurried and took a hatchet in his hand, and came to the chamber of the gods; he broke all his father's gods. And when he was done breaking the images, he placed the hatchet in the hand of the great god which was there before them, and he went out; and Terah his father came home, for he had heard at the door the sound of the striking of the hatchet; so Terah came into the house to know what this was about.

Terah, having heard the noise of the hatchet in the room of images, ran to the room to the images, and he met Abram going out. And Terah entered the room and found all the idols fallen down and broken, and the hatchet in the hand of the largest, which was not broken, and the savory meat which Abram his son had made was still before them. When Terah saw this his anger was greatly set ablaze, and he hurried and went from the room to Abram.

And he found Abram his son sitting in the house; and he said to him, "What is this work you have done to my gods?" Abram answered his father and he said, "Not so my lord, for I brought savory meat before them, and when I came near to them with the meat that they might eat, they all at once stretched forth their hands to eat before the great one had put forth his hand to eat. And the large one saw their works that they did before him, and his anger was violently set ablaze against them, and he went and took the hatchet that was in the house and came to them and broke them all, and behold the hatchet is yet in his hand as you see."

And Terah's anger was set ablaze against his son Abram, when he spoke this; and Terah said to Abram his son in his anger, "What is this tale that you have told? You speak lies to me. Is there in these gods spirit, soul or power to do all you have told me? Are they not wood and stone, and have I not myself made them, and can you speak such lies, saying that the large god that was with them struck them? It is you that did place the hatchet in his hands, and then said he struck them all."

Abram answered his father and said to him, "And how can you then serve these idols in whom there is no power to do any thing? Can those idols in which you trust deliver you? Can they hear your prayers when you call on them? Can they deliver you from the hands of your enemies, or will they fight your battles for you against your enemies, that you should serve wood and stone which can neither speak nor hear? And now certainly it is not good for you nor for the sons of men that are connected with you, to do these things; are you so silly, so foolish or so short of understanding that you will serve wood and stone, and do after this manner?"

"And forget the Lord God who made heaven and earth, and who created you in the earth, and thereby bring a great evil on your souls in this matter by serving stone and wood? Did not our fathers in days of old sin in this manner, and the Lord God of the universe brought the waters of the flood on them and destroyed the whole earth? And how can you continue to do this and serve gods of wood and stone, who cannot hear, or speak, or deliver you from oppression, thereby bringing down the anger of the God of the universe on you? Now therefore my father refrain from this, and bring not evil on your soul and the souls of your household." And Abram hurried and sprang from before his father, and took the hatchet from his father's largest idol, with which Abram broke it and ran away.

Terah, seeing all that Abram had done, hurried to go from his house; he went to the king and he came before Nimrod and stood before him, and he bowed down to the king and the king said, "What do you want?" And he said, "I beseech you my lord, to hear me - Now fifty years back a child was born to me, and thus has he done to my gods and thus has he spoken; and now therefore, my lord and king, send for him that he may come before you, and judge him according to the law, that we may be delivered from his evil."

The king sent three men of his servants, and they went and brought Abram before the king. And Nimrod and all his princes and servants were that day sitting before him, and Terah also sat before them. And the king said to Abram, "What is this that you have done to your father and to his gods?" And Abram answered the king in the words that he spoke to his father, and he said, "The large god that was with them in the house did to them what you have heard."

And the king said to Abram, "Had they power to speak and eat and do as you have said?" And Abram answered the king, saying, "And if there is no power in them why do you serve them and cause the sons of men to err through your follies? Do you imagine that they can deliver you or do anything small or great, that you should serve them? And why will you not sense the God of the whole universe, who created you and in whose power it is to kill and keep alive? O foolish, simple, and ignorant king, woe to you forever."

"I thought you would teach your servants the upright way, but you have not done this; you have filled the whole earth with your sins and the sins of your people who have followed your ways. Do you not know, or have you not heard, that this evil which you do, our ancestors sinned therein in days of old, and the eternal God brought the waters of the flood on them and destroyed them all, and also destroyed the whole earth on their account? And will you and your people rise up now and do like this work, in order to bring down the anger of the Lord God of the universe, and to bring evil on you and the whole earth?"

"Now therefore put away this evil deed which you did, and serve the God of the universe, as your soul is in his hands, and then it will be well with you. And if your wicked heart will not listen to my words to cause you to turn away from your evil ways, and to serve the eternal God, then you will die in shame in the latter days, you, your people and all who are connected with you, hearing your words or walking in your evil ways." When Abram had ceased speaking before the king and princes, Abram lifted up his eyes to the heavens, and he said, "The Lord sees all the wicked, and he will judge them."

(Jasher 11:13-61)

The first two commandments of God

And God spoke all these words, saying:

"I am the Lord your God, who brought you out of the land of Egypt, out of the house of bondage. You shall have no other gods before Me. You shall not make for yourself a carved image - any likeness of anything that is in heaven above, or that is in the earth beneath, or that is in the water under the earth; you shall not bow down to them nor serve them. For I, the Lord your God, am a jealous God, visiting the iniquity of the fathers upon the children to the third and fourth generations of those who hate Me, but showing mercy to thousands, to those who love Me and keep My commandments." (Exo 20:1-6)

The Law of the Altar

Then the Lord said to Moses, "Thus you shall say to the children of Israel:

'You have seen that I have talked with you from heaven. You shall not make anything to be with Me - gods of silver or gods of gold you shall not make for yourselves. An altar of earth you shall make for Me, and you shall sacrifice on it your burnt offerings and your peace offerings, your sheep and your oxen. In every place where I record My name I will come to you, and I will bless you. And if you make Me an altar of stone, you shall not build it of hewn stone; for if you use your tool on it, you have profaned it. Nor shall you go up by steps to My altar, that your nakedness may not be exposed on it.' " (Exo 20:22-26)

Gideon and the altar of Baal

Now the Angel of the Lord came and sat under the terebinth tree which was in Ophrah, which belonged to Joash the Abiezrite, while his son Gideon threshed wheat in the winepress, in order to hide it from the Midianites.

And the Angel of the Lord appeared to him, and said to him, "The Lord is with you, you mighty man of valor!" Gideon said to Him, "O my lord, if the Lord is with us, why then has all this happened to us? And where are all His miracles which our fathers told us about, saying, 'Did not the Lord bring us up from Egypt?' But now the Lord has forsaken us and delivered us into the hands of the Midianites."

Then the Lord turned to him and said, "Go in this might of yours, and you shall save Israel from the hand of the Midianites. Have I not sent you?" So he said to Him, "O my Lord, how can I save Israel? Indeed my clan is the weakest in Manasseh, and I am the least in my father's house." And the Lord said to him, "Surely I will be with you, and you shall defeat the Midianites as one man." Then he said to Him, "If now I have found favor in Your sight, then show me a sign that it is You who talk with me. Do not depart from here, I pray, until I come to You and bring out my offering and set it before You." And He said, "I will wait until you come back."

So Gideon went in and prepared a young goat, and unleavened bread from an ephah of flour. The meat he put in a basket, and he put the broth in a pot; and he brought them out to Him under the terebinth tree and presented them. The Angel of God said to him, "Take the meat and the unleavened bread and lay them on this rock, and pour out the broth." And he did so. Then the Angel of the Lord put out the end of the staff that was in His hand, and touched the meat and the unleavened bread; and fire rose out of the rock and consumed the meat and the unleavened bread. And the Angel of the Lord departed out of his sight. Now Gideon perceived that He was the Angel of the Lord.

So Gideon said, "Alas, O Lord God! For I have seen the Angel of the Lord face to face." Then the Lord said to him, "Peace be with you; do not fear, you shall not die." So Gideon built an altar there to the Lord, and called it The-Lord-Is-Peace. To this day it is still in Ophrah of the Abiezrites.

Now it came to pass the same night that the Lord said to him, "Take your father's young bull, the second bull of seven years old, and tear down the altar of Baal that your father has, and cut down the wooden image that is beside it; and build an altar to the Lord your God on top of this rock in the proper arrangement, and take the second bull and offer a burnt sacrifice with the wood of the image which you shall cut down." So Gideon took ten men from among his servants and did as the Lord had said to him. But because he feared his father's household and the men of the city too much to do it by day, he did it by night. And when the men of the city arose early in the morning, there was the altar of Baal, torn down; and the wooden image that was beside it was cut down, and the second bull was being offered on the altar which had been built.

So they said to one another, "Who has done this thing?" And when they had inquired and asked, they said, "Gideon the son of Joash has done this thing." Then the men of the city said to Joash, "Bring out your son, that he may die, because he has torn down the altar of Baal, and because he has cut down the wooden image that was beside it." But Joash said to all who stood against him, "Would you plead for Baal? Would you save him? Let the one who would plead for him be put to death by morning! If he is a god, let him plead for himself, because his altar has been torn down!" Therefore on that day he called him Jerubbaal (! Let Baal Plead), saying, "Let Baal plead against him, because he has torn down his altar." (Jud 6:11-32)

The futility of idols

"The poor and needy seek water, but there is none, their tongues fail for thirst.

I, the Lord, will hear them;

I, the God of Israel, will not forsake them.

I will open rivers in desolate heights, and fountains in the midst of the valleys;

I will make the wilderness a pool of water, and the dry land springs of water.

I will plant in the wilderness the cedar and the acacia tree, the myrtle and the oil tree;

I will set in the desert the cypress tree and the pine and the box tree together, that they may see and know, and consider and understand together, that the hand of the Lord has done this, and the Holy One of Israel has created it."

"Present your case," says the Lord.

"Bring forth your strong reasons," says the King of Jacob.

"Let them bring forth and show us what will happen; let them show the former things, what they were, that we may consider them, and know the latter end of them; or declare to us the things to come. Show the things that are to come hereafter, that we may know that you are gods; yes, do good or do evil, that we may be dismayed and see it together. Indeed you are nothing, and your work is nothing; he who chooses you is an abomination. I have raised up one from the north, and He shall come; from the rising of the sun He shall call on My name; and He shall come against princes as though mortar, as the potter treads clay. Who has declared from the beginning, that we may know? And former times, that we may say, 'He is righteous'?"

"Surely there is no one who shows,

Surely there is no one who declares,

Surely there is no one who hears your words."

"The first time I said to Zion, 'Look, there they are!' and I will give to Jerusalem one who brings good tidings. For I looked, and there was no man; I looked among them, but there was no counselor, who, when I asked of them, could answer a word. Indeed they are all worthless; their works are nothing; their molded images are wind and confusion."

(Isa 41:17-29)

Thus says the Lord, the King of Israel, and His Redeemer, the Lord of hosts:

"I am the First and I am the Last; besides Me there is no God. And who can proclaim as I do? Then let him declare it and set it in order for Me, since I appointed the ancient people. And the things that are coming and shall come, let them show these to them. Do not fear, nor be afraid; have I not told you from that time, and declared it? You are My witnesses. Is there a God besides Me? Indeed there is no other Rock; I know not one."

"Those who make an image, all of them are useless, and their precious things shall not profit; they are their own witnesses; they neither see nor know, that they may be ashamed. Who would form a god or mold an image that profits him nothing? Surely all his companions would be ashamed; and the workmen, they are mere men. Let them all be gathered together, let them stand up; yet they shall fear, they shall be ashamed together. The blacksmith with the tongs works one in the coals, fashions it with hammers, and works it with the strength of his arms. Even so, he is hungry, and his strength fails; he drinks no water and is faint."

"The craftsman stretches out his rule, he marks one out with chalk; he fashions it with a plane, he marks it out with the compass, and makes it like the figure as a man, according to the beauty of a man, that it may remain in the house. He cuts down cedars for himself, and takes the cypress and the oak; he secures it for himself among the trees of the forest. He plants a pine, and the rain nourishes it."

"Then it shall be for a man to burn, for he will take some of it and warm himself; yes, he kindles it and bakes bread; indeed he makes a god and worships it; he makes it a carved image, and falls down to it. He burns half of it in the fire; with this half he eats meat; he roasts a roast, and is satisfied. He even warms himself and says, 'Ah! I am warm, I have seen the fire.' And the rest of it he makes into a god, his carved image. He falls down before it and worships it, prays to it and says, 'Deliver me, for you are my god!' "

"They do not know nor understand; for He has shut their eyes, so that they cannot see, and their hearts, so that they cannot understand. And no one considers in his heart, nor is there knowledge nor understanding to say, 'I have burned half of it in the fire, yes, I have also baked bread on its coals; I have roasted meat and eaten it; and shall I make the rest of it an abomination? Shall I fall down before a block of wood?'

He feeds on ashes; a deceived heart has turned him aside; and he cannot deliver his soul, nor say, 'Is there not a lie in my right hand?' "

"Remember these, O Jacob, and Israel, for you are My servant; I have formed you, you are My servant; O Israel, you will not be forgotten by Me!" (Isa 44:6-21)

God stands in the congregation of the mighty; He judges among the gods.

How long will you judge unjustly, and show partiality to the wicked? Selah.

Defend the poor and fatherless; do justice to the afflicted and needy.

Deliver the poor and needy; free them from the hand of the wicked.

They do not know, nor do they understand; they walk about in darkness; all the foundations of the earth are unstable.

I said, "You are gods, and all of you are children of the Most High.

But you shall die like men, and fall like one of the princes."

Arise, O God, judge the earth; for You shall inherit all nations. (Psa 82)

The Shepherd knows His sheep

Now it was the Feast of Dedication in Jerusalem, and it was winter. And Jesus walked in the temple, in Solomon's porch. Then the Jews surrounded Him and said to Him, "How long do You keep us in doubt? If You are the Christ, tell us plainly." Jesus answered them, "I told you, and you do not believe. The works that I do in My Father's name, they bear witness of Me. But you do not believe, because you are not of My sheep, as I said to you. My sheep hear My voice, and I know them, and they follow Me. And I give them eternal life, and they shall never perish; neither shall anyone snatch them out of My hand. My Father, who has given them to Me, is greater than all; and no one is able to snatch them out of My Father's hand. I and My Father are one."

Then the Jews took up stones again to stone Him. Jesus answered them, "Many good works I have shown you from My Father. For which of those works do you stone Me?" The Jews answered Him, saying, "For a good work we do not stone You, but for blasphemy, and because You, being a Man, make Yourself God."

Jesus answered them, "Is it not written in your law, 'I said, "You are gods"'? If He called them gods, to whom the word of God came (and the Scripture cannot be broken), do you say of Him whom the Father sanctified and sent into the world, 'You are blaspheming', because I said, 'I am the Son of God'? If I do not do the works of My Father, do not believe Me; but if I do, though you do not believe Me, believe the works, that you may know and believe that the Father is in Me, and I in Him."

Therefore they sought again to seize Him but He escaped out of their hand. And He went away again beyond the Jordan to the place where John was baptizing at first, and there He stayed. Then many came to Him and said, "John performed no sign, but all the things that John spoke about this Man were true." And many believed in Him there. (Joh 10:22-42)

"Ho! Everyone who thirsts, come to the waters; and you who have no money, come, buy and eat. Yes, come, buy wine and milk without money and without price. Why do you spend money for what is not bread, and your wages for what does not satisfy? Listen carefully to Me, and eat what is good, and let your soul delight itself in abundance."

(Isa 55:1-2)

-oOo-

Noah's Prayers

The rain was still descending on the earth, and it descended forty days and forty nights, and the waters prevailed greatly on the earth; all flesh that was on the earth or in the waters died, whether men, animals, beasts, creeping things or birds of the air, and there only remained Noah and those that were with him in the ark.

The waters prevailed and they greatly increased on the earth, and they lifted up the ark and it was raised from the earth. And the ark floated on the face of the waters; it was tossed on the waters so that all the living creatures within were turned about like pottage in a cauldron.

Great anxiety seized all the living creatures that were in the ark, and the ark was like to be broken. And all the living creatures that were in the ark were terrified: the lions roared, and the oxen lowed, and the wolves howled, and every living creature in the ark spoke and lamented in its own language, so that their voices reached to a great distance, and Noah and his sons cried and wept in their troubles; they were greatly afraid that they had reached the gates of death. And Noah prayed to the Lord, and cried to Him on account of this, and he said,

"O Lord help us, for we have no strength to bear this evil that has encompassed us, for the waves of the waters have surrounded us, mischievous torrents have terrified us, the snares of death have come before us; answer us, O Lord, answer us, light up Your countenance toward us and be gracious to us, redeem us and deliver us."

The Lord listened to the voice of Noah, and the Lord remembered him. And a wind passed over the earth; the waters were still and the ark rested. The fountains of the deep and the windows of heaven were stopped, and the rain from heaven was restrained.

And the waters decreased in those days, and the ark rested on the mountains of Ararat. Noah then opened the windows of the ark, and Noah still called out to the Lord at that time and he said,

"O Lord, who did form the earth and the heavens and all that are therein, bring forth our souls from this confinement, and from the prison wherein you have placed us, for I am much wearied with sighing."

And the Lord listened to the voice of Noah, and said to him,

"When you have completed a full year you shall go forth."

And at the revolution of the year, when a full year was completed to Noah's dwelling in the ark, the waters were dried from off the earth, and Noah put off the covering of the ark. At that time, on the twenty-seventh day of the second month, the earth was dry, but Noah and his sons and those that were with him did not go out from the ark until the Lord told them.

And the day came that the Lord told them to go out, and they all went out from the ark. They went and returned every one to his way and to his place, and Noah and his sons lived in the land that God had told them; they served the Lord all their days, and the Lord blessed Noah and his sons on their going out from the ark. And He said to them,

"Be prolific and fill all the earth; become strong and increase abundantly in the earth and reproduce therein." (Jas 6:26-42)

Psalms

Hear me when I call, O God of my righteousness! You have relieved me in my distress; have mercy on me, and hear my prayer. How long, O you sons of men, will you turn my glory to shame? How long will you love worthlessness and seek falsehood? Selah

But know that the Lord has set apart for Himself him who is godly; the Lord will hear when I call to Him. Be angry, and do not sin. Meditate within your heart on your bed, and be still. Selah

Offer the sacrifices of righteousness, and put your trust in the Lord. There are many who say, "Who will show us any good?" Lord, lift up the light of Your countenance upon us. You have put gladness in my heart, more than in the season that their grain and wine increased. I will both lie down in peace, and sleep; for You alone, O Lord, make me dwell in safety. (Psa 4:1-8)

I will bless the Lord who has given me counsel; my heart also instructs me in the night season. I have set the Lord always before me; because He is at my right hand I shall not be moved. Therefore my heart is glad, and my glory rejoices; my flesh also will rest in hope. For You will not leave my soul in Sheol, nor will You allow Your Holy One to see corruption. You will show me the path of life; in Your presence is fullness of joy; at Your right hand are pleasures forevermore. (Psa 16:7-11)

I will love You, O Lord, my strength. The Lord is my rock and my fortress and my deliverer; my God, my strength, in whom I will trust; my shield and the horn of my salvation, my stronghold. I will call upon the Lord, who is worthy to be praised; so shall I be saved from my enemies.

The pangs of death surrounded me, and the floods of ungodliness made me afraid. The sorrows of Sheol surrounded me; the snares of death confronted me. In my distress I called upon the Lord, and cried out to my God; He heard my voice from His temple, and my cry came before Him, even to His ears.

He sent from above, He took me; He drew me out of many waters. He delivered me from my strong enemy, from those who hated me, for they were too strong for me. They confronted me in the day of my calamity, but the Lord was my support. He also brought me out into a broad place; He delivered me because He delighted in me.

The Lord rewarded me according to my righteousness; according to the cleanness of my hands He has recompensed me. For I have kept the ways of the Lord, and have not wickedly departed from my God. For all His judgments were before me, and I did not put away His statutes from me. I was also blameless before Him, and I kept myself from my iniquity. Therefore the Lord has recompensed me according to my righteousness, according to the cleanness of my hands in His sight. (Psa 18:1-6, 16-24)

The voice of the Lord is over the waters; the God of glory thunders; the Lord is over many waters. The voice of the Lord is powerful; the voice of the Lord is full of majesty. The Lord sat enthroned at the flood, and the Lord sits as King forever. (Psa 29:3-4, 10)

I acknowledged my sin to You, and my iniquity I have not hidden. I said, "I will confess my transgressions to the Lord," and You forgave the iniquity of my sin. Selah

For this cause everyone who is godly shall pray to You in a time when You may be found; surely in a flood of great waters they shall not come near Him. You are my hiding place; You shall preserve me from trouble; You shall surround me with songs of deliverance. Selah (Psa 32:5-7)

O my God, my soul is cast down within me; therefore I will remember You from the land of the Jordan, and from the heights of Hermon, from the Hill Mizar. Deep calls to deep at the noise of Your waterfalls; all Your waves and billows have gone over me. The Lord will command His lovingkindness in the daytime, and in the night His song shall be with me - a prayer to the God of my life. (Psa 42:6-8)

Behold You desire truth in the inward parts, and in the hidden part You will make me to know wisdom. (Psa 51:6)

Vows made to You are binding upon me, O God; I will render praises to You, for You have delivered my soul from death. Have You not kept my feet from falling, that I may walk before God in the light of the living? (Psa 56:12-13)

By awesome deeds in righteousness You will answer us, O God of our salvation, You who are the confidence of all the ends of the earth, and of the far-off seas; Who established the mountains by His strength, being clothed with power; You who still the noise of the seas, the noise of their waves, and the tumult of the peoples. They also who dwell in the farthest parts are afraid of Your signs; You make the outgoings of the morning and evening rejoice. (Psa 65:5-8)

For God is my King from of old, working salvation in the midst of the earth. You divided the sea by Your strength; You broke the heads of the sea serpents in the waters. You broke the heads of Leviathan in pieces, and gave him as food to the people inhabiting the wilderness. You broke open the fountain and the flood; You dried up mighty rivers. The day is Yours, the night also is Yours; You have prepared the light and the sun. You have set all the borders of the earth; You have made summer and winter. (Psa 74:12-17)

You are the God who does wonders; You have declared Your strength among the peoples. You have with Your arm redeemed Your people, the sons of Jacob and Joseph. Selah

The waters saw You, O God; the waters saw You, they were afraid; the depths also trembled. The clouds poured out water; the skies sent out a sound; Your arrows also flashed about. The voice of Your thunder was in the whirlwind; the lightnings lit up the world; the earth trembled and shook. Your way was in the sea, Your path in the great waters, and Your footsteps were not known. You led Your people like a flock by the hand of Moses and Aaron. (Psa 77:14-20)

"I removed his shoulder from the burden; his hands were freed from the baskets. You called in trouble, and I delivered you; I answered you in the secret place of thunder; I tested you at the waters of Meribah. Selah" (Psa 81:6-7)

O my God, make them like the whirling dust, like the chaff before the wind! As the fire burns the woods, and as the flame sets the mountains on fire, so pursue them with Your tempest, and frighten them with Your storm. Fill their faces with shame, that they may seek Your name, O Lord. (Psa 83:13-16)

Those who go down to the sea in ships, who do business on great waters, they see the works of the Lord, and His wonders in the deep. For He commands and raises the stormy wind, which lifts up the waves of the sea. They mount up to the heavens, they go down again to the depths; their soul melts because of trouble. They reel to and fro, and stagger like a drunken man, and are at their wits' end. Then they cry out to the Lord in their trouble, and He brings them out of their distresses. He calms the storm, so that its waves are still. Then they are glad because they are quiet; so He guides them to their desired haven. (Psa 107:23-30)

"If it had not been the Lord who was on our side," Let Israel now say - "If it had not been the Lord who was on our side, when men rose up against us, then they would have swallowed us alive, when their wrath was kindled against us; then the waters would have overwhelmed us, the stream would have gone over our soul; then the swollen waters would have gone over our soul." Blessed be the Lord, who has not given us as prey to their teeth. Our soul has escaped as a bird from the snare of the fowlers; the snare is broken, and we have escaped. Our help is in the name of the Lord, who made heaven and earth. (Psa 124:1-8)

Out of the depths I have cried to You, O Lord; Lord, hear my voice! Let Your ears be attentive to the voice of my supplications. If You, Lord, should mark iniquities, O Lord, who could stand? But there is forgiveness with You, that You may be feared. I wait for the Lord, my soul waits, and in His word I do hope. (Psa 130:1-5)

Let us go into His tabernacle; let us worship at His footstool. Arise, O Lord, to Your resting place, You and the ark of your strength. Let your priests be clothed with righteousness, and let Your saints shout for joy. (Psa 132:7-9)

For I know that the Lord is great, and our Lord is above all gods. Whatever the Lord pleases He does, in heaven and in earth, in the seas and in all deep places. He causes the vapors to ascend from the ends of the earth; He makes lightning for the rain; He brings the wind out of His treasuries. (Psa 135:5-7)

To Him who alone does great wonders, for His mercy endures forever; to Him who by wisdom made the heavens, for His mercy endures forever; to Him who laid out the earth above the waters, for His mercy endures forever; to Him who made great lights, for His mercy endures forever - the sun to rule by day, for His mercy endures forever; the moon and stars to rule by night, for His mercy endures forever. (Psa 136:4-9)

-oOo-

Accuser

And the Lord God commanded the man, saying, "Of every tree of the garden you may freely eat; but of the tree of the knowledge of good and evil you shall not eat, for in the day that you eat of it you shall surely die." (Gen 2:16-17)

Now the serpent was more cunning than any beast of the field which the Lord God had made. And he said to the woman, "Has God indeed said, 'You shall not eat of every tree of the garden'?" And the woman said to the serpent, "We may eat the fruit of the trees of the garden; but of the fruit of the tree which is in the midst of the garden, God has said, 'You shall not eat it, nor shall you touch it, lest you die.' " Then the serpent said to the woman, "You will not surely die. For God knows that in the day you eat of it your eyes will be opened, and you will be like God, knowing good and evil." So when the woman saw that the tree was good for food, that it was pleasant to the eyes, and a tree desirable to make one wise, she took of its fruit and ate. She also gave to her husband with her, and he ate. Then the eyes of both of them were opened, and they knew that they were naked; and they sewed fig leaves together and made themselves coverings. (Gen 3:1-7)

And the Lord God said to the woman, "What is this you have done?" The woman said, "The serpent deceived me, and I ate." So the Lord God said to the serpent:

"Because you have done this, you are cursed more than all cattle, and more than every beast of the field; on your belly you shall go, and you shall eat dust all the days of your life. And I will put enmity between you and the woman, and between your seed and her Seed; He shall bruise your head, and you shall bruise His heel." (Gen 3:13-15)

"How you are fallen from heaven, O Lucifer, son of the morning! How you are cut down to the ground, you who weakened the nations! For you have said in your heart: 'I will ascend into heaven, I will exalt my throne above the stars of God; I will also sit on the mount of the congregation on the farthest sides of the north; I will ascend above the heights of the clouds, I will be like the Most High.' Yet you shall be brought down to Sheol, to the lowest depths of the Pit." (Isa 14:12-15)

"You were the seal of perfection, full of wisdom and perfect in beauty. You were in Eden, the garden of God; every precious stone was your covering: the sardius, topaz, and diamond, beryl, onyx, and jasper, sapphire, turquoise, and emerald with gold. The workmanship of your timbrels and pipes was prepared for you on the day you were created. You were the anointed cherub who covers; I established you; you were on the holy mountain of God; you walked back and forth in the midst of fiery stones. You were perfect in your ways from the day you were created, till iniquity was found in you. By the abundance of your trading you became filled with violence within, and you sinned; therefore I cast you as a profane thing out of the mountain of God; and I destroyed you, O covering cherub, from the midst of the fiery stones." (Eze 28:12-16)

In that day the Lord with His severe sword, great and strong, will punish Leviathan that twisted serpent; and He will slay the reptile that is in the sea. (Isa 27:1)

"The wolf and the lamb shall feed together, the lion shall eat straw like the ox, and dust shall be the serpent's food. They shall not hurt nor destroy in all My holy mountain," says the Lord. (Isa 65:25)

And in the hundred and twenty-fifth year of Israel's going down into Egypt, all the Egyptians saw that their counsel did not succeed against Israel, but that they increased and grew and the land of Egypt and the land of Goshen were filled with the children of Israel. So all the elders of Egypt and its wise men came before the king and bowed down to him and sat before him. And all the elders of Egypt and the wise men there said to the king, "May the king live forever; you did counsel us the counsel against the children of Israel, and we did to them according to the word of the king. But in proportion to the increase of the labor so do they increase and grow in the land, and look the whole country is filled with them. So now our lord and king, the eyes of all Egypt are on you to give them advice with your wisdom, by which they may rule over Israel to destroy them, or to diminish them from the land."

The king answered them saying, "Give your counsel in this matter that we may know what to do to them."

And an officer, one of the king's counselors, whose name was Job, from Mesopotamia, in the land of Uz, answered the king, saying, "If it please the king, let him hear the counsel of his servant;" the king said to him, "Speak."

And Job spoke before the king, the princes, and before all the elders of Egypt, saying, "Behold the counsel of the king which he advised formerly respecting the labor of the children of Israel is very good, and you must not remove from them that labor forever. But this is the advice counselled by which you may lessen them, if it seems good to the king to afflict them. Behold we have feared war for a long time, and we said, 'When Israel becomes prolific in the land, they will drive us from the land if a war would take place.' If it please the king, let a royal decree go forth, and let it be written in the laws of Egypt which shall not be revoked, 'That every male child born to the Israelites, his blood shall be spilled on the ground.' And by doing this, when all the male children of Israel will have died, the evil of their wars will cease; let the king do so and send for all the Hebrew midwives and order them in this matter to execute it."

So the thing pleased the king and the prince; the king did according to the word of Job. The king sent for the Hebrew midwives to be called, of which the name of one was Shephrah, and the name of the other Puah. And the midwives came before the king, and stood in his presence.

The king said to them, "When you do the office of a midwife to the Hebrew woman, and see them on the stools, if it be a son then you shall kill him, but if it be a daughter then she shall live. But if you will not do this thing, then will I burn you up and all your houses with fire." But the midwives feared God and did not listen to the king of Egypt nor to his words; when the Hebrew women brought forth to the midwife son or daughter, then did the midwife do all that was necessary to the child and let it live; thus did the midwives all the days. (Jas 66:10-27)

Now there was a day when the sons of God came to present themselves before the Lord, and Satan also came among them. And the Lord said to Satan, "From where do you come?" So Satan answered the Lord and said, "From going to and fro on the earth, and from walking back and forth on it." Then the Lord said to Satan, "Have you considered My servant Job, that there is none like him on the earth, a blameless and upright man, one who fears God and shuns evil?" So Satan answered the Lord and said, "Does Job fear God for nothing? Have You not made a hedge around him, around his household, and around all that he has on every side? You have blessed the work of his hands, and his possessions have increased in the land. But stretch out Your hand and touch all that he has, and he will surely curse You to Your face!" And the Lord said to Satan, "Behold, all that he has is in your power; only do not lay a hand on his person." So Satan went out from the presence of the Lord. (Job 1:6-12)

While he was still speaking, another also came and said, "Your sons and daughters were eating and drinking wine in their oldest brother's house, and suddenly a great wind came from across the wilderness and struck the four corners of the house, and it fell on the young people, and they are dead; and I alone have escaped to tell you!" Then Job arose, tore his robe, and shaved his head; and he fell to the ground and worshiped. And he said: "Naked I came from my mother's womb, and naked shall I return there. The Lord gave, and the Lord has taken away; Blessed be the name of the Lord." In all this Job did not sin nor charge God with wrong. (Job 1:18-22)

Again there was a day when the sons of God came to present themselves before the Lord, and Satan came also among them to present himself before the Lord. And the Lord said to Satan, "From where do you come?"

Satan answered the Lord and said, "From going to and fro on the earth, and from walking back and forth on it."

Then the Lord said to Satan, "Have you considered My servant Job, that there is none like him on the earth, a blameless and upright man, one who fears God and shuns evil? And still he holds fast to his integrity, although you incited Me against him, to destroy him without cause."

So Satan answered the Lord and said, "Skin for skin! Yes, all that a man has he will give for his life. But stretch out Your hand now, and touch his bone and his flesh, and he will surely curse You to Your face!"

And the Lord said to Satan, "Behold, he is in your hand, but spare his life."

So Satan went out from the presence of the Lord, and struck Job with painful boils from the sole of his foot to the crown of his head. And he took for himself a potsherd with which to scrape himself while he sat in the midst of the ashes.

Then his wife said to him, "Do you still hold fast to your integrity? Curse God and die!" But he said to her, "You speak as one of the foolish women speaks. Shall we indeed accept good from God, and shall we not accept adversity?" In all this Job did not sin with his lips. (Job 2:1-10)

And the Lord restored Job's losses when he prayed for his friends. Indeed the Lord gave Job twice as much as he had before. (Job 42:10)

By His Spirit He adorned the heavens; His hand pierced the fleeing serpent. (Job 26:13)

Then they journeyed from Mount Hor by the Way of the Red sea, to go around the land of Edom; and the soul of the people became very discouraged on the way. And the people spoke against God and against Moses: "Why have you brought us up out of Egypt to die in the wilderness? For there is no food and no water, and our soul loathes this worthless bread." So the Lord sent fiery serpents among the people, and they bit the people; and many of the people of Israel died. Therefore the people came to Moses, and said, "We have sinned, for we have spoken against the Lord and against you; pray to the Lord that He take away the serpents from us." So Moses prayed for the people. Then the Lord said to Moses, "Make a fiery serpent, and set it on a pole; and it shall be that everyone who is bitten, when he looks at it, shall live." So Moses made a bronze serpent, and put it on a pole; and so it was, if a serpent had bitten anyone, when he looked at the bronze serpent, he lived. (Num 21:4-9)

"For behold, I will send serpents among you, vipers which cannot be charmed, and they shall bite you," says the Lord. (Jer 8:17)

"Though they dig into hell, from there My hand shall take them; though they climb up to heaven, from there I will bring them down; and though they hide themselves on top of Carmel, from there I will search and take them; though they hide from My sight at the bottom of the sea, from there I will command the serpent and it shall bite them; though they go into captivity before their enemies, from there I will command the sword and it shall slay them. I will set My eyes on them for harm and not for good." (Amo 9:2-4)

Then he showed me Joshua the high priest standing before the Angel of the Lord, and Satan standing at his right hand to oppose him. And the Lord said to Satan, "The Lord rebuke you, Satan! The Lord who has chosen Jerusalem rebuke you! Is this not a brand plucked from the fire?" Now Joshua was clothed with filthy garments, and was standing before the Angel. Then He answered and spoke to those who stood before Him, saying, "Take away the filthy garments from him." And to him He said, "See, I have removed your iniquity from you, and I will clothe you with rich robes." And I said, "Let them put a clean turban on his head." So they put a clean turban on his head, and they put the clothes on him. And the Angel of the Lord stood by. (Zec 3:1-5)

Then Jesus was led up by the Spirit into the wilderness to be tempted by the devil. And when He had fasted forty days and forty nights, afterward He was hungry. Now when the tempter came to Him, he said,

"If you are the Son of God, command that these stones become bread."

But He answered and said, "It is written, 'Man shall not live by bread alone, but by every word that proceeds from the mouth of God.' "

Then the devil took Him up into the holy city, set Him on the pinnacle of the temple, and said to Him,

"If you are the Son of God, throw yourself down. For it is written:

'He shall give His angels charge over You,' and,

'In their hands they shall bear you up, lest you dash your foot against a stone.' "

Jesus said to him, "It is written again, 'You shall not tempt the Lord your God.' "

Again, the devil took Him up on an exceedingly high mountain, and showed Him all the kingdoms of the world and their glory. And he said to Him,

"All these things I will give You if You will fall down and worship me."

Then Jesus said to him, "Away with you, Satan! For it is written, 'You shall worship the Lord your God, and Him only you shall serve.' "

Then the devil left Him, and behold, angels came and ministered to Him.

(Mat 4:1-11 also Luk 4:1-13)

From that time Jesus began to show to His disciples that He must go to Jerusalem, and suffer many things from the elders and chief priests and scribes, and be killed, and be raised the third day. Then Peter took Him aside and began to rebuke Him, saying,

"Far be it from You, Lord; this shall not happen to You!" But He turned and said to Peter, "Get behind Me, Satan! You are an offence to Me, for you are not mindful of the things of God, but the things of men." (Mat 16:21-23 also Mar 8:31-33)

Then the eleven disciples went away into Galilee, to the mountain which Jesus had appointed for them. When they saw Him, they worshipped Him; but some doubted. And Jesus came and spoke to them, saying, "All authority has been given to Me in heaven and on earth. Go therefore and make disciples of all the nations, baptizing them in the name of the Father and of the Son and of the Holy Spirit, teaching them to observe all things that I have commanded you; and lo, I am with you always, even to the end of the age." Amen. (Mat 28:16-20)

"The kingdom of heaven is like a man who sowed good seed in his field; but while men slept, his enemy came and sowed tares among the wheat and went his way. But when the grain had sprouted and produced a crop, then the tares also appeared... He who sows the good seed is the Son of Man. The field is the world, the good seeds are the sons of the kingdom, but the tares are the sons of the wicked one. The enemy who sowed them is the devil, the harvest is the end of the age and the reapers are the angels. Therefore as the tares are gathered and burned in the fire, so it will be at the end of this age. The Son of Man will send out His angels, and they will gather out of His kingdom all things that offend, and those who practice lawlessness, and will cast them into the furnace of fire. There will be wailing and gnashing of teeth. Then the righteous will shine forth as the sun in the kingdom of their Father. He who has ears to hear, let him hear!"

(Mat 13:24-26, 37-43)

"Listen! Behold, a sower went out to sow. And it happened, as he sowed, that some seed fell by the wayside; and the birds of the air came and devoured it. And these are the ones by the wayside where the word is sown. When they hear, Satan comes immediately and takes away the word that was sown in their hearts." (Mar 4:3, 15)

Later He appeared to the eleven as they sat at the table; and He rebuked their unbelief and hardness of heart, because they did not believe those who had seen Him after He had risen. And He said to them, "Go into all the world and preach the gospel to every creature. He who believes and is baptized will be saved; but he who does not believe will be condemned. And these signs will follow those who believe: In My name they will cast out demons; they will speak with new tongues; they will take up serpents; and if they drink anything deadly, it will by no means hurt them; they will lay hands on the sick, and they will recover." (Mar 16:14-18)

Then the seventy returned with joy, saying, "Lord, even the demons are subject to us in Your name." And He said to them, "I saw Satan fall like lightning from heaven. Behold, I give you the authority to trample on serpents and scorpions, and over all the power of the enemy, and nothing shall by any means hurt you. Nevertheless do not rejoice in this, that the spirits are subject to you, but rather rejoice because your names are written in heaven." (Luk 10:17-20)

Now the Feast of Unleavened Bread drew near, which is called Passover. And the chief priests and the scribes sought how they might kill Him, for they feared the people. Then Satan entered Judas, surnamed Iscariot, who was numbered among the twelve. So he went his way and conferred with the chief priests and captains, how he might betray Him to them. And they were glad, and agreed to give him money. So he promised and sought opportunity to betray Him to them in the absence of the multitude. (Luk 22:1-6)

And having dipped the bread, He gave it to Judas Iscariot, the son of Simon. Now after the piece of bread, Satan entered him. Then Jesus said to him, "What you do, do quickly." Having received the bread, he then went out immediately. And it was night. (Joh 13:26-27, 30)

And the Lord said, "Simon, Simon! Indeed, Satan has asked for you, that he may sift you as wheat. But I have prayed for you, that your faith should not fail; and when you have returned to Me, strengthen your brethren." But he said to Him, "Lord, I am ready to go with You, both to prison and to death." Then He said, "I tell you, Peter, the rooster shall not crow this day before you will deny three times that you know Me." (Luk 22:31-34)

"No one has ascended to heaven but He who came down from heaven, that is, the Son of Man who is in heaven. And as Moses lifted up the serpent in the wilderness, even so must the Son of Man be lifted up, that whoever believes in Him should not perish but have eternal life. For God so loved the world that He gave His only begotten Son, that whoever believes in Him should not perish but have everlasting life." (Joh 3:13-16)

"Most assuredly, I say to you, he who believes in Me has everlasting life. I am the bread of life. Your fathers ate manna in the wilderness, and are dead. This is the bread which comes down from heaven, that one may eat of it and not die. I am the living bread which came down from heaven. If anyone eats of this bread, he will live forever; and the bread that I shall give is My flesh, which I shall give for the life of the world." (Joh 6:47-51)

Jesus said to Paul

"I am Jesus, whom you are persecuting. But rise and stand on your feet; for I have appeared to you for this purpose, to make you a minister and a witness both of the things which you have seen and of the things which I will yet reveal to you. I will deliver you from the Jewish people, as well as from the Gentiles, to whom I now send you, to open their eyes, in order to turn them from darkness to light, and from the power of Satan to God, that they may receive forgiveness of sins and an inheritance among those who are sanctified by faith in Me." (Act 26:15-18)

Now when they had escaped, they then found out that the island was called Malta. And the natives showed us unusual kindness; for they kindled a fire and made us all welcome, because of the rain that was falling and because of the cold. But when Paul had gathered a bundle of sticks and laid them on the fire, a viper came out because of the heat, and fastened on his hand. So when the natives saw the creature hanging from his hand, they said to one another, "No doubt this man is a murderer, whom, though he has escaped the sea, yet justice does not allow to live." But he shook off the creature into the fire and suffered no harm. However, they were expecting that he would swell up or suddenly fall down dead. But after they had looked for a long time and saw no harm come to him, they changed their minds and said that he was a god. (Act 28:1-6)

Now I urge you, brethren, note those who cause divisions and offenses, contrary to the doctrine which you learned, and avoid them. For those who are such do not serve our Lord Jesus Christ, but their own belly, and by smooth words and flattering speech deceive the hearts of the simple. For your obedience has become known to all. Therefore I am glad on your behalf; but I want you to be wise in what is good, and simple concerning evil. And the God of peace will crush Satan under your feet shortly. The grace of our Lord Jesus Christ be with you. Amen. (Rom 16:17-20)

It is actually reported that there is sexual immorality among you, and such sexual immorality as is not named among the Gentiles - that a man has his father's wife! In the name of our Lord Jesus Christ, when you are gathered together, along with my spirit, with the power of our Lord Jesus Christ, deliver such a one to Satan for the destruction of the flesh, that his spirit may be saved in the day of the Lord Jesus. (1Co 5:1, 4-5)

Now concerning the things of which you wrote to me: It is good for a man not to touch a woman. Nevertheless, because of sexual immorality, let each man have his own wife, and let each woman have her own husband. Let the husband render to his wife the affection due to her, and likewise also the wife to her husband. The wife does not have authority over her own body, but the husband does. And likewise the husband does not have authority over his own body, but the wife does. Do not deprive one another except with consent for a time, that you may give yourselves to fasting and prayer; and come together again so that Satan does not tempt you because of your lack of self-control. But I say this as a concession, not as a commandment. For I wish that all men were even as I myself. But each one has his own gift from God, one in this manner and another in that. But I say to the unmarried and to the widows: It is good for them if they remain even as I am; but if they cannot exercise self control, let them marry. For it is better to marry than to burn with passion. (1Co 7:1-9)

The Israelites (see Num 20:11)

For they drank of that spiritual Rock that followed them, and that Rock was Christ. But with most of them God was not well pleased, for their bodies were scattered in the wilderness. Now these things became our examples, to the intent that we should not lust after evil things as they also lusted. And do not become idolaters as were some of them. As it is written, "The people sat down to eat and drink, and rose up to play."

Nor let us commit sexual immorality, as some of them did, and in one day twenty-three thousand fell; nor let us tempt Christ, as some of them also tempted, and were destroyed by serpents; nor complain, as some of them also complained, and were destroyed by the destroyer. Now all these things happened to them as examples, and they were written for our admonition, upon whom the ends of the ages have come. Therefore let him who thinks he stands take heed lest he fall. No temptation has overtaken you except such as is common to man; but God is faithful, who will not allow you to be tempted beyond what you are able, but with the temptation will also make the way of escape, that you may be able to bear it. (1Co 10:4-13)

Now whom you forgive anything, I also forgive. For if indeed I have forgiven anything, I have forgiven that one for your sakes in the presence of Christ, lest Satan should take advantage of us; for we are not ignorant of his devices. (2Co 2:10-11)

For I am jealous for you with godly jealousy. For I have betrothed you to one husband, that I may present you as a chaste virgin to Christ. But I fear, lest somehow, as the serpent deceived Eve by his craftiness, so your minds may be corrupted from the simplicity that is in Christ. (2Co 11:2-3)

False doctrines

But what I do, I will also continue to do, that I may cut off the opportunity from those who desire an opportunity to be regarded just as we are in the things of which they boast. For such are false apostles, deceitful workers, transforming themselves into apostles of Christ. And no wonder! For Satan himself transforms himself into an angel of light. Therefore it is no great thing if his ministers also transform themselves into ministers of righteousness, whose end will be according to their works. (2Co 11:12-15)

For though I might desire to boast, I will not be a fool; for I will speak the truth. But I refrain, lest anyone should think of me above what he sees me to be or hears from me. And lest I should be exalted above measure by the abundance of the revelations, a thorn in the flesh was given to me, a messenger of Satan to buffet me, lest I be exalted above measure. (2Co 12:6-7)

For the mystery of lawlessness is already at work; only He who now restrains will do so until He is taken out of the way. And then the lawless one will be revealed, whom the Lord will consume with the breath of His mouth and destroy with the brightness of His coming. The coming of the lawless one is according to the working of Satan, with all power, signs, and lying wonders, and with all unrighteous deception among those who perish, because they did not receive the love of the truth, that they might be saved. And for this reason God will send them strong delusion, that they should believe the lie, that they all may be condemned who did not believe the truth but had pleasure in unrighteousness. (2Th 2:7-12)

Repent and be saved

Therefore submit to God. Resist the devil and he will flee from you. Draw near to God and He will draw near to you. Cleanse your hands, you sinners; and purify your hearts, you double-minded. Lament and mourn and weep! Let your laughter be turned to mourning and your joy to gloom. Humble yourselves in the sight of the Lord, and He will lift you up.

(Jam 4:7-10)

Beloved, do not believe every spirit, but test the spirits, whether they are of God; because many false prophets have gone out into the world. By this you know the Spirit of God: Every spirit that confesses that Jesus Christ has come in the flesh is of God, and every spirit that does not confess that Jesus Christ has come in the flesh is not of God. And this is the spirit of the Antichrist, which you have heard was coming, and is now already in the world. (1Jo 4:1-3)

Whoever believes that Jesus is the Christ is born of God, and everyone who loves Him who begot also loves him who is begotten of Him. We know that whoever is born of God does not sin; but he who has been born of God keeps himself, and the wicked one does not touch him. We know that we are of God, and the whole world lies under the sway of the wicked one. And we know that the Son of God has come and has given us an understanding, that we may know Him who is true; and we are in Him who is true, in His Son Jesus Christ. This is the true God and eternal life. Little children keep yourselves from idols. Amen. (1Jo 5:1, 18-21)

Be sober, be vigilant; because your adversary the devil walks about like a roaring lion, seeking whom he may devour. Resist him, steadfast in the faith, knowing that the same sufferings are experienced by your brotherhood in the world. But may the God of all grace, who called us to His eternal glory by Christ Jesus, after you have suffered a while, perfect, establish, strengthen, and settle you. (1Pe 5:8-10)

Yet Michael the archangel, in contending with the devil, when he disputed about the body of Moses, dared not bring against him a reviling accusation, but said, "The Lord rebuke you!" (Jude 9)

And war broke out in heaven: Michael and his angels fought with the dragon; and the dragon and his angels fought, but they did not prevail, nor was a place found for them in heaven any longer. So the great dragon was cast out, that serpent of old, called the Devil and Satan, who deceives the whole world; he was cast to the earth, and his angels were cast out with him. Then I heard a loud voice saying in heaven, "Now salvation and strength, and the kingdom of our God, and the power of His Christ have come, for the accuser of our brethren, who accused them before our God day and night, has been cast down. And they overcame him by the blood of the Lamb and by the word of their testimony, and they did not love their lives to the death. Therefore rejoice, O heavens, and you who dwell in them! Woe to the inhabitants of the earth and the sea! For the devil has come down to you, having great wrath, because he knows that he has a short time." (Rev 12:7-12)

Then I saw an angel coming down from heaven, having the key to the bottomless pit and a great chain in his hand. He laid hold of the dragon, that serpent of old, who is the Devil and Satan, and bound him for a thousand years; and he cast him into the bottomless pit, and shut him up, and set a seal on him, so that he should deceive the nations no more till the thousand years were finished. But after these things he must be released for a little while. (Rev 20:1-3)

Now when the thousand years have expired, Satan will be released from his prison and will go out to deceive the nations which are in the four corners of the earth, Gog and Magog, to gather them together to battle, whose number is as the sand of the sea. They went up on the breadth of the earth and surrounded the camp of the saints and the beloved city. And fire came down from God out of heaven and devoured them. The devil, who deceived them, was cast into the lake of fire and brimstone where the beast and the false prophet are. And they will be tormented day and night forever and ever.

Then I saw a great white throne and Him who sat on it, from whose face the earth and the heaven fled away. And there was found no place for them. And I saw the dead, small and great, standing before God, and books were opened. And another book was opened, which is the Book of Life. And the dead were judged according to their works, by the things which were written in the books. The sea gave up the dead who were in it, and Death and Hades delivered up the dead who were in them. And they were judged, each one according to his works. Then Death and Hades were cast into the lake of fire. This is the second death. And anyone not found written in the Book of Life was cast into the lake of fire. (Rev 20:7-15)

-oOo-

Once, Twice, Thrice

I have noticed that the Lord uses multiple examples in His Word to teach us His Laws and principles of righteousness. For example the defensive, 'She is my Sister excuse', is used three times in Genesis 12:13, 20:2 and 26:7 to enrich Abraham (x2) and Isaac (x1).

Preachers love to scare congregations with the future 'Antichrist' and the 'Desolation of the Temple scenario'. I believe this does pertain to the future, but these events have also occurred in the past. These past examples are there to teach us, to be able to recognise the future threats.

The Temple was first built by Solomon and desecrated later by King Manasseh around 666BC (2Ki 21:1-18). It was destroyed by King Nebuchadnezzar when he attacked and destroyed Jerusalem. After the 70 year exile in Babylon, the temple was rebuilt by Zerubbabel, Ezra and Nehemiah; and then desecrated again by King Antiochus in 167BC. It was purified and rededicated through the efforts of Mattathias, Judas Maccabaeus and his brothers in the year 164BC.

Jesus Christ made the Temple desolate at His crucifixion, when the curtain dividing the most holy place, from the rest of the Temple was torn from top to bottom. This signified the end of a building, as being the dwelling place for the Spirit of God. The Old Covenant ended, and the New Covenant began. The Temple has no role in New Covenant Christians worship, but it is still significant to the Jewish, Old Covenant worship.

As Paul said; "Do you not know that you are the temple of God and that the Spirit of God dwells in you? If anyone defiles the temple of God, God will destroy him. For the temple of God is holy, which temple you are." (1Co 3:16-17)

The Temple in Jerusalem, was completely destroyed by the Roman's siege of Jerusalem in 70AD. I believe Israel will build another 'Holy Temple' in Jerusalem in the future; which will again be desecrated by the future Antichrist; as Bible prophesies are concerned with Jerusalem and the middle east region. This Antichrist will be thrown into the lake of fire along with the beast, so he must be worse than all who came before him.

An Antichrist is a person who makes people worship something, or someone else, a substitute false-christ or false-god. John explains the 'spirit of the Antichrist';

"By this you know the Spirit of God: Every spirit that confesses that Jesus Christ has come in the flesh is of God, and every spirit that does not confess that Jesus Christ has come in the flesh is not of God. And this is the spirit of the Antichrist, which you have heard was coming, and is now already in the world." (1Jo 4:2-3)

Paul clearly had the 'spirit of the Antichrist' before his conversion. He was present at the stoning of Stephen and zealously persecuted the Christian's of Jerusalem.

Then they cried out with a loud voice, stopped their ears, and ran at him with one accord; and they cast him out of the city and stoned him. And the witnesses laid down their clothes at the feet of a young man named Saul. And they stoned Stephen as he was calling on God and saying, "Lord Jesus, receive my spirit." Then he knelt down and cried out with a loud voice, "Lord, do not charge them with this sin." And when he had said this, he fell asleep. Now Saul was consenting to his death.

At that time a great persecution arose against the church which was at Jerusalem; and they were all scattered throughout the regions of Judea and Samaria, except the apostles. And devout men carried Stephen to his burial, and made great lamentation over him. As for Saul, he made havoc of the church, entering every house, and dragging off men and women, committing them to prison. (Act 7:57-8:3)

I believe Saul is also referred to in Daniel's seventy week prophecy, regarding the Messiah. Jesus was baptised, 3½ years later He was crucified, and 3½ years later Stephen was stoned; ending the 7 year Christian outreach, to the Jews of Jerusalem.

"Then He shall confirm a covenant with many for one week; but in the middle of the week He shall bring an end to sacrifice and offering. And on the wing of abominations shall be one who makes desolate, even until the consummation, which is determined, is poured out on the desolate." (Dan 9:27)

Anybody can have the spirit of the antichrist, but to be 'The Antichrist', one has to be:

1)   Ruling or controlling the whole world.

2)   Be extremely wealthy, with all material means at their disposal.

3)   Be leading people away from God on a large scale; by worshipping idols, or by worshipping a false-christ person.

I believe we can recognise the future Antichrist, and know what to look out for, by examining the character traits of two previous Antichrists, Nimrod and Solomon. Unlike Saul who became Paul, both men started out righteous; and both ended up working against God, corrupted by their selfish pride and vain confidence in the wealth of their kingdoms.

Nimrod

And Cush the son of Ham, the son of Noah, took a wife in those days in his old age, and she gave birth to a son, and they called his name Nimrod, saying, "At that time the sons of men again began to rebel and go contrary to God;" the child grew up, and his father loved him greatly, for he was the son of his old age.

The garments of skin which God made for Adam and his wife, when they went out of the garden, were given to Cush. For after the death of Adam and his wife, the garments were given to Enoch, the son of Jared, and when Enoch was taken up to God, he gave them to Methuselah, his son. At the death of Methuselah, Noah took them and brought them to the ark, and they were with him until he went out of the ark. And in their going out, Ham stole those garments from Noah his father; he took them and hid them from his brothers. When Ham had his first born Cush, he gave him the garments in secret, and they were with Cush many days. Cush also concealed them from his sons and brothers, and when Cush had begotten

Nimrod, he gave him those garments through his love for him, and Nimrod grew up, and when he was twenty years old he put on those garments.

Nimrod became strong when he put on the garments, and God gave him might and strength, and he was a mighty hunter in the earth. He was a mighty hunter in the field, and he hunted the animals and he built altars, and he offered on them the animals before the Lord. Nimrod strengthened himself, and he rose up from among his brothers, and he fought the battles of his brothers against all their enemies round about.

The Lord delivered all the enemies of his brothers in his hands, and God prospered him from time to time in his battles, and he reigned on earth. Therefore it became current in those days, when a man ushered forth those that he had trained for battle, he would say to them, "Like God did to Nimrod who was a mighty hunter in the earth, and who succeeded in the battles that prevailed against his brothers, that he delivered them from the hands of their enemies: so may God strengthen us and deliver us this day."

And when Nimrod was forty years old, there was a war between his brothers and the children of Japheth, so that they were in the power of their enemies. Nimrod went forth at that time, and he assembled all the sons of Cush and their families, about four hundred and sixty men; he hired also from some of his friends and acquaintances about eighty men, and he gave them their hire; he went with them to battle, and when he was on the road, Nimrod strengthened the hearts of the people that went with him. And he said to them, "Do not fear, neither be alarmed, for all our enemies will be delivered into our hands, and you may do with them as you please." All the men that went were about five hundred, and they fought against their enemies; they destroyed them, and subdued them, and Nimrod placed standing officers over them in their respective places.

He took some of their children as security, and they were all servants to Nimrod and to his brothers, and Nimrod and all the people that were with him turned homeward. When Nimrod had joyfully returned from battle, after having conquered his enemies, all his brothers, together with those who knew him before, assembled to make him king over them and they placed the regal crown on his head.

He set over his subjects and people, princes, judges, and rulers, as is the custom among kings. He placed Terah the son of Nahor the prince of his host, and he dignified him and elevated him above all his princes. And while he was reigning according to his heart's desire, after having conquered all his enemies around, he advised with his counselors to build a city for his palace, and they did so.

They found a large valley opposite to the east, and they built him a large and extensive city, and Nimrod called the name of the city that he built Shinar, for the Lord had vehemently shaken his enemies and destroyed them. Nimrod lived in Shinar, and he reigned securely, and he fought with his enemies and he subdued them; he prospered in all his battles, and his kingdom became very great. All nations and tongues heard of his fame, and they gathered themselves to him, and they bowed down to the earth; they brought him offerings, and he became their lord and king, and they all lived with him in the city at Shinar; Nimrod reigned in the earth over all the sons of Noah, and they were all under his power and counsel.

And all the earth was of one tongue and words of union, but Nimrod did not go in the ways of the Lord; he was more wicked than all the men that were before him, from the days of the flood until those days. He made gods of wood and stone, he bowed down to them, he rebelled against the Lord, and taught all his subjects and the people of the earth his wicked ways; Mardon his son was more wicked than his father.

And every one that heard of the acts of Mardon the son of Nimrod would say, concerning him, "From the wicked goes forth wickedness." Therefore it became a proverb in the whole earth, saying, "From the wicked goes forth wickedness", and it was current in the words of men from that time to this. (Jas 7:23-48)

And King Nimrod reigned securely, and all the earth was under his control, and all the earth was of one tongue and words of union. And all the princes of Nimrod and his great men took counsel together: Phut, Mitzraim, Cush and Canaan with their families, and they said to each other, "Come let us build ourselves a city and in it a strong tower and its top reaching heaven, and we will make ourselves famed so that we may reign on the whole world, in order that the evil of our enemies may cease from us; that we may reign mightily over them, and that we may not become scattered over the earth on account of their wars."

They all went before the king, and they told the king these words, and the king agreed with them in this affair, and he did so. All the families assembled consisting of about six hundred thousand men, and they went to seek an extensive piece of ground to build the city and the tower, and they sought in the whole earth and they found none like one valley at the east of the land of Shinar, about two days' walk, and they journeyed there and they lived there.

And they began to make bricks and burn fires to build the city and the tower that they had imagined to complete. And the building of the tower was to them a transgression and a sin, and they began to build it. While they were building against the Lord God of heaven, they imagined in their hearts to war against Him and to ascend into heaven.

And all these people and all the families divided themselves in three parts; the first said, "We will ascend into heaven and fight against him;" the second said, "We will ascend to heaven and place our own gods there and serve them;" and the third part said, "We will ascend to heaven and strike him with bows and spears."

And God knew all their works and all their evil thoughts, and He saw the city and the tower which they were building. They built themselves a great city and a very high and strong tower; on account of its height, the mortar and bricks did not reach the builders in their ascent to it until those who went up had completed a full year, and after that, they reached the builders and gave them the mortar and the bricks; thus was it done daily. And behold these ascended and others descended the whole day; and if a brick should fall from their hands and get broken, they would all weep over it; if a man fell and died, none of them would look at him.

The Lord knew their thoughts, and it came to pass when they were building they cast the arrows toward the heavens, and all the arrows fell on them filled with blood; when they saw them they said to each other, "Certainly we have slain all those that are in heaven." For this was from the Lord in order to cause them to err, and in order to destroy them from off the face of the ground. They built the tower and the city, and they did this thing daily until after many days and years were elapsed.

And God said to the seventy angels who stood foremost before Him, to those who were near to Him, saying, "Come, let Us descend and confuse their tongues, that one man shall not understand the language of his neighbor," and they did so to them. From that day following, they forgot each man his neighbor's tongue, and they could not understand to speak in one tongue; when the builder took from the hands of his neighbor lime or stone which he did not order, the builder would cast it away and throw it on his neighbor, that he would die. And they did so many days, and they killed many of them in this manner.

The Lord struck the three divisions that were there, and He punished them according to their works and designs; those who said, "We will ascend to heaven and serve our gods," became like apes and elephants; those who said, "We will strike the heaven with arrows," the Lord killed them, one man through the hand of his neighbor; and the third division of those who said, "We will ascend to heaven and fight against him," the Lord scattered them throughout the earth. Those who were left among them, when they knew and understood the evil which was coming on them, turned away from the building, and they also became scattered on the face of the whole earth.

And they ceased building the city and the tower; therefore he called that place Babel, for there the Lord confounded the language of the whole earth; behold it was at the east of the land of Shinar. As to the tower which the sons of men built, the earth opened its mouth and swallowed up one third part thereof, and a fire also descended from heaven and burned another third, and the other third is left to this day; it is of that part which was aloft, and its circumference is three days' walk. Many of the sons of men died in that tower, a people without number. (Jas 9:20-39)

Nimrod son of Cush was still in the land of Shinar, and he reigned over it and lived there, and he built cities in the land of Shinar. These are the names of the four cities which he built, and he called their names after the occurrences that happened to them in the building of the tower: He called the first Babel, saying, "Because the Lord there confounded the language of the whole earth." The name of the second he called Erech, "Because God had dispersed them." And the third he called Eched, saying, "There was a great battle at that place;" the forth he called Calnah, "Because his princes and mighty men were consumed there, and they troubled the Lord; they rebelled and went contrary to Him."

When Nimrod had built these cities in the land of Shinar, he placed in them the remainder of his people, his princes and his mighty men that were left in his kingdom. Nimrod lived in Babel, and there he renewed his reign over the rest of his subjects, and he reigned securely, and the subjects and princes of Nimrod called his name Amraphel, saying that at the tower his princes and men fell through his means.

Notwithstanding this, Nimrod did not return to the Lord, and he continued in wickedness and teaching wickedness to the sons of men; and Mardon, his son, was worse than his father and continued to add to the abominations of his father. And he caused the sons of men to sin; therefore it is said, "From wickedness goes forth wickedness."

At that time there was a war between the families of the children of Ham, as they were dwelling in the cities which they had built. And Chedorlaomer, king of Elam, went away from the families of the children of Ham; he fought with them and he subdued them, and he went to the five cities of the plain; he fought against them, and he subdued them, and they were under his control. And they served him twelve years and gave him a yearly tax. (Jas 11:1-11)

At that time Chedorlaomer king of Elam sent to all the neighboring kings, to Nimrod, king of Shinar who was then under his power, and to Tidal, king of Goyim, and to Arioch, king of Elasar, with whom he made a covenant, saying, "Come up to me and assist me, that we may strike all the towns of Sodom and its inhabitants, for they have rebelled against me these thirteen years."

These four kings went up with all their camps, about eight-hundred thousand men, and they went as they were, and struck every man they found in their road. And the five kings of Sodom and Gomorrah, Shinab king of Admah, Shemeber king of Zeboyim, Bera king of Sodom, Bersha king of Gomorrah, and Bela king of Zoar, went out to meet them, and they all joined together in the valley of Siddim. These nine kings made war in the valley of Siddim; and the kings of Sodom and Gomorrah were smitten before the kings of Elam. The valley of Siddim was full of lime pits and the kings of Elam pursued the kings of Sodom, and the kings of Sodom with their camps fell into the lime pits; all that remained went to the mountain for safety.

The five kings of Elam came after them and pursued them to the gates of Sodom, and they took all that there was in Sodom. They plundered all the cities of Sodom and Gomorrah, and they also took Lot, Abram's brother's son, and his property; they seized all the goods of the cities of Sodom, and they went away.

Unic, Abram's servant, who was in the battle, saw this, and told Abram all that the kings had done to the cities of Sodom, and that Lot was taken captive by them. Abram heard this, and he rose up with about three hundred and eighteen men that were with him, and that night he pursued these kings and struck them; they all fell before Abram and his men, and there was none remaining but the four kings who fled, and they each went his own road. Abram recovered all the property of Sodom, and he also recovered Lot and his property, his wives and little ones and all belonging to him, so that Lot lacked nothing. (Jas 16:1-8)

Solomon

And it came to pass, when Solomon had finished building the house of the Lord and the king's house, and all Solomon's desire which he wanted to do, that the Lord appeared to Solomon the second time, as He had appeared to him at Gibeon. And the Lord said to him: "I have heard your prayer and your supplication that you have made before Me; I have consecrated this house which you have built to put My name there forever, and My eyes and My heart will be there perpetually. Now if you walk before Me as your father David walked, in integrity of heart and in uprightness, to do according to all that I have commanded you, and if you keep My statutes and My judgements, then I will establish the throne of your kingdom over Israel forever, as I promised David your father, saying, 'You shall not fail to have a man on the throne of Israel.'

But if you or your sons at all turn from following Me, and do not keep My commandments and My statutes which I have set before you, but go and serve other gods and worship them, then I will cut off Israel from the land which I have given them; and this house which I have consecrated for My name I will cast out of My sight. Israel will be a proverb and a byword among the peoples. And as for this house, which is exalted, everyone who passes by it will be astonished and will hiss, and say, 'Why has the Lord done thus to this land and to this house?' Then they will answer, 'Because they forsook the Lord their God, who brought their fathers out of the land of Egypt, and have embraced other gods, and worshipped them and served them; therefore the Lord has brought all this calamity on them.' " (1Ki 9:1-9)

The weight of gold that came to Solomon yearly was six hundred and sixty-six talents (22644kg) of gold, besides that from the traveling merchants, from the income of traders, from all the kings of Arabia, and from the governors of the country. And King Solomon made two hundred large shields of hammered gold; six hundred shekels (7,2kg) of gold went into each shield. He also made three hundred shields of hammered gold; three minas of gold (1,8kg) went into each shield. The king put them in the House of the Forest of Lebanon. Moreover the king made a great throne of ivory, and overlaid it with pure gold. The throne had six steps, and the top of the throne was round at the back; there were armrests on either side of the place of the seat, and two lions stood beside the armrests. Twelve lions stood there, one on each side of the six steps; nothing like this had been made for any other kingdom. All King Solomon's drinking vessels were gold, and all the vessels of the House of the Forest of Lebanon were pure gold. Not one was silver, for this was accounted as nothing in the days of Solomon.

For the king had merchant ships at sea with the fleet of Hiram. Once every three years the merchant ships came bringing gold, silver, ivory, apes, and monkeys. So King Solomon surpassed all the kings of the earth in riches and wisdom. Now all the earth sought the presence of Solomon to hear his wisdom, which God had put in his heart. Each man brought his present: articles of silver and gold, garments, armor, spices, horses, and mules, at a set rate year by year. And Solomon gathered chariots and horsemen; he had one thousand four hundred chariots and twelve thousand horsemen, whom he stationed in the chariot cities and with the king at Jerusalem.

The king made silver as common in Jerusalem as stones, and he made cedar trees as abundant as the sycamores which are in the lowland. Also Solomon had horses imported from Egypt and Keveh; the king's merchants bought them in Keveh at the current price. Now a chariot that was imported from Egypt cost six hundred shekels of silver, and a horse one hundred and fifty; and thus, through their agents, they exported them to all the kings of the Hittites and the kings of Syria. (1Ki 10:14-29)

But King Solomon loved many foreign women, as well as the daughter of Pharaoh: women of the Moabites, Ammonites, Edomites, Sidonians, and Hittites - from the nations of whom the Lord had said to the children of Israel, "You shall not intermarry with them, nor they with you. Surely they will turn away your hearts after their gods."

Solomon clung to these in love. And he had seven hundred wives, princesses, and three hundred concubines; and his wives turned away his heart. For it was so, when Solomon was old, that his wives turned his heart after other gods; and his heart was not loyal to the Lord his God, as was the heart of his father David.

For Solomon went after Ashtoreth the goddess of the Sidonians, and after Milcom the abomination of the Ammonites. Solomon did evil in the sight of the Lord, and did not fully follow the Lord, as did his father David. Then Solomon built a high place for Chemosh the abomination of Moab, on the hill that is east of Jerusalem, and for Molech the abomination of the people of Ammon. And he did likewise for all his foreign wives, who burned incense and sacrificed to their gods. So the Lord became angry with Solomon, because his heart had turned from the Lord God of Israel, who had appeared to him twice, and had commanded him concerning this thing, that he should not go after other gods; but he did not keep what the Lord had commanded.

Therefore the Lord said to Solomon, "Because you have done this, and have not kept My covenant and My statutes, which I have commanded you, I will surely tear the kingdom away from you and give it to your servant. Nevertheless I will not do it in your days, for the sake of your father David; I will tear it out of the hand of your son. However I will not tear away the whole kingdom; I will give one tribe to your son for the sake of My servant David, and for the sake of Jerusalem which I have chosen."

(1Ki 11:1-13)

Question

Now, when the World officially has a single global: leader, government, currency, language, reaction force, church, religion, etc. and 'The Antichrist' challenges me to do something that conflicts with God's Word; will my faith be strong enough, to refuse and say, "No, I'm not doing that, at any cost!"? Will I stand up to testify for my Lord and my God, as Stephen did? Or will I reply as Peter first did, and deny, deny, deny?

-oOo-

Min Dae!

'Min Dae' is a saying from my National Service days, meaning 'few days left to go'.

According to my calculations, history consists of 99.6% of the time allocated for mankind to make the correct choice!

We can construct the following table from the book of Genesis.

Gen Anno Mundi	Person	Father at age	Bible verse
1 130	Adam	130	Gen 5:3
2 235	Seth	105	Gen 5:6
3 325	Enosh	90	Gen 5:9

4 395	Cainan	70	Gen 5:12
5 460	Mahalalel	65	Gen 5:15
6 622	Jared	162	Gen 5:18
7 687	Enoch	65	Gen 5:21
8 874	Methuselah	187	Gen 5:25
9 1056	Lamech	182	Gen 5:28
10 1558	Noah (2nd son)	502	Gen 5:32
11 1658	Shem	100	Gen 11:10
12 1693	Arphaxad	35	Gen 11:12
13 1723	Salah	30	Gen 11:14
14 1757	Eber	34	Gen 11:16
15 1787	Peleg	30	Gen 11:18
16 1819	Reu	32	Gen 11:20
17 1849	Serug	30	Gen 11:22
18 1878	Nahor	29	Gen 11:24
19 1948	Terah	70	Gen 11:26
20 2048	Abraham	100	Gen 21:5

Okay, according to Genesis; Noah's flood happened when Noah was 600y, in 1656AM and Abraham was born in 1948AM.

It was the fifteenth year of Abram's dwelling in the land of Canaan, which is the seventieth year of the life of Abram, the Lord appeared to Abram in that year and said to him, I am the Lord who brought you out from Ur Casdim to give you this land for an inheritance. Now therefore walk before me and be perfect and keep my commands, for to you and to your descendants I will give this land for an inheritance, from the river Mitzraim to the great river Euphrates. (Jasher 13:17-18)

Now the sojourn of the children of Israel who lived in Egypt was four hundred and thirty years. And it came to pass at the end of the four hundred and thirty years - on that very same day - it came to pass that all the armies of the Lord went out from the land of Egypt. (Exo 12:40-41)

Abraham receives the 1st promise of the 430 year prophecy, when he was 70 years old.

Then He said to Abram: "Know certainly that your descendants will be strangers in a land that is not theirs, and will serve them, and they will afflict them four hundred years. And also the nation whom they serve I will judge; afterward they shall come out with great possessions."

(Gen 15:13-14)

Isaac was Sarah's child, and he was born when Abraham was 100 years old. Ishmael was also blessed by the Lord, but now the 400 year period, for the descendants started.

And it came to pass in the four hundred and eightieth year after the children of Israel had come out of the land of Egypt, in the fourth year of Solomon's reign over Israel, in the month of Ziv, which is the second month, that he began to build the house of the Lord. (1Ki 6:1)

Solomon begins to build the house of the Lord in the 4th year of his 40 year reign.

This was 480 years after the Exodus from the land of Egypt.

And the period that Solomon reigned in Jerusalem over all Israel was forty years. Then Solomon rested with his fathers, and was buried in the City of David his father. And Rehoboam his son reigned in his place. (1Ki 11:42-43)

There is general agreement that Rehoboam - Solomon's son reigned from 930BC and that this date is historically verifiable, but I believe it was in 1005BC.

And I saw thrones, and they sat on them, and judgment was committed to them. Then I saw the souls of those who had been beheaded for their witness to Jesus and for the word of God, who had not worshipped the beast or his image, and had not received his mark on their foreheads or on their hands. And they lived and reigned with Christ for a thousand years. But the rest of the dead did not live again until the thousand years were finished. This is the first resurrection. Blessed and holy is he who has part in the first resurrection. Over such the second death has no power, but they shall be priests of God and of Christ, and shall reign with Him a thousand years. (Rev 20:4-6)

The 1000 year Sabbath starts with the first resurrection and Judgement day begins with the second resurrection.

Event	Anno Mundi	Year
Adam created	1	3969 BC
Noah born	1056	2914 BC
Noah's flood	1656	2314 BC
Abraham born	1948	2022 BC

Abraham @ 70y BC	2018	1952
Abraham @ 100y BC	2048	1922
Exodus from Egypt BC	2448	1522
Solomon 4th year BC	2928	1042
Solomon 40th year BC	2964	1006
Rehoboam reigns BC	2965	1005
Jesus born BC	3966	4
Jesus crucified AD	4000	31
Now AD	5978	2009
1000y Sabbath begins? AD	6000	2031
Judgement day? AD	7000	3031

Heaven and earth will pass away, but My words will by no means pass away. But of that day and hour no one knows, not even the angels of heaven, but My Father only. Therefore you also be ready, for the Son of Man is coming at an hour you do not expect. (Mat 24:35-36,44)

-oOo-

Nimrod's Death

Nimrod's dream (1st Part)

At the expiration of two years from Abram's going out of the fire, that is in the fifty-second year of his life, behold king Nimrod sat in Babel on the throne, and the king fell asleep and dreamed that he was standing with his troops and hosts in a valley opposite the king's furnace. And he lifted up his eyes and saw a man in the likeness of Abram coming forth from the furnace; he came and stood before the king with his drawn sword, and then sprang to the king with his sword, when the king fled from the man, for he was afraid; while he was running, the man threw an egg on the king's head, and the egg became a great river. And the king dreamed that all his troops sank in that river and died, and the king took flight with three men who were before him and he escaped. The king looked at these men and they were clothed in princely dresses as the garments of kings, and had the appearance and majesty of kings.

Nimrod's dream (2nd Part)

And while they were running, the river again turned to an egg before the king; there came forth from the egg a young bird which came before the king, and flew at his head and plucked out the king's eye. The king was grieved at the sight, and he awoke out of his sleep and his spirit was agitated; he felt a great terror.

The interpretation of Nimrod's dream (1st Part)

In the morning the king rose from his couch in fear, and he ordered all the wise men and magicians to come before him, when the king related his dream to them. And a wise servant of the king, whose name was Anuki, answered the king, saying, "This is nothing else but the evil of Abram and his offspring which will spring up against my Lord and king in the latter days. And behold the day will come when Abram and his offspring and the children of his household will war with my king, and they will strike all the king's hosts and his troops. And as to what you have said concerning three men which you did see like yourself, and which did escape, this means that only you will escape with three kings from the kings of the earth who will be with you in battle."

The interpretation of Nimrod's dream (2nd Part)

"And that which you saw of the river which turned to an egg as at first, and the young bird plucking out your eye, this means nothing else but the offspring of Abram which will kill the king in latter days. This is my king's dream, and this is its interpretation, and the dream is true, and the interpretation which your servant has given you is right." (Jasher 12:45-56)

The fulfillment of Nimrod's dream (1st Part)

And it came to pass in the days of Amraphel (! Nimrod) king of Shinar, Arioch king of Ellasar, Chedorlaomer king of Elam, and Tidal king of nations, that they made war with Bera king of Sodom, Birsha king of Gomorrah, Shinab king of Admah, Shemeber king of Zeboiim, and the king of Bela (that is , Zoar). All these joined together in the Valley of Siddim (that is, the Salt Sea). Twelve years they served Chedorlaomer, and in the thirteenth year they rebelled. In the fourteenth year Chedorlaomer and the kings that were with him came and attacked the Rephaim in Ashteroth Karnaim, the Zuzim in Ham, the Emim in Shaveh Kiriathaim, and the Horites in their mountain of Seir, as far as El Paran, which is by the wilderness. Then they turned back and came to En Mishpat (that is Kadesh), and attacked all the country of the Amalekites, and also the Amorites who dwelt in Hazezon Tamar. And the king of Sodom, the king of Gomorrah, the king of Admah, the king of Zeboiim, and the king of Bela (that is, Zoar) went out and joined together in battle in the Valley of Siddim against Chedorlaomer king of Elam, Tidal king of nations, Amraphel (! Nimrod) king of Shinar, and Arioch king of Ellasar – four kings against five. Now the Valley of Siddim was full of asphalt pits; and the kings of Sodom and Gomorrah fled; some fell there, and the remainder fled to the mountains. Then they took all the goods of Sodom and Gomorrah, and all their provisions, and went their way. They also took Lot, Abram's brother's son who dwelt in Sodom, and his goods, and departed.

Then one who had escaped came and told Abram the Hebrew, for he dwelt by the terebinth trees of Mamre the Amorite, brother of Eshcol and brother of Aner; and they were allies with Abram. Now when Abram heard that his brother was taken captive, he armed his three hundred and eighteen trained servants who were born in his own house, and went in pursuit as far as Dan. He divided his forces against them by night, and he and his servants attacked them and pursued them as far as Hobah, which is north of Damascus. So he brought back all the goods, and also brought back his brother Lot and his goods, as well as the women and the people. And the king of Sodom went out to meet him at the Valley of Shaveh (that is, the King's Valley), after his return from the defeat of Chedorlaomer and the kings who were with him. (Gen 14:1-17)

The fulfillment of Nimrod's dream (2nd Part)

Esau at that time, after the death of Abraham, frequently went in the field to hunt. Nimrod king of Babel, the same was Amraphel, also frequently went with his mighty men to hunt in the field, and to walk about with his men in the cool of the day. Nimrod was observing Esau all those days, for jealousy was formed in the heart of Nimrod against Esau.

On a certain day Esau went in the field to hunt, and he found Nimrod walking in the wilderness with his two men. All his mighty men and his people were with him in the wilderness, but they kept at a distance; they went from him in different directions to hunt, and Esau concealed himself from Nimrod, and he lurked for him in the wilderness. And Nimrod and his men that were with him did not know him. Nimrod and his men frequently walked about in the field at the cool of the day, and to know where his men were hunting in the field. Nimrod and two of his men that were with him came to the place where they were, when Esau appeared suddenly from his lurking place, drew his sword, and hurriedly ran to Nimrod and cut off his head. Esau fought a desperate fight with the two men that were with Nimrod, and when they called out to him, Esau turned to them and struck them to death with his sword. All the mighty men of Nimrod, who had left him to go to the wilderness, heard the cry at a distance, and they knew the voices of those two men; they ran to know the cause of it and they found their king and the two men that were with him lying dead in the wilderness. When Esau saw the mighty men of Nimrod coming at a distance, he fled, and thereby escaped. Esau took the valuable garments of Nimrod which Nimrod's father had bequeathed to Nimrod, with which Nimrod prevailed over the whole land; he ran and concealed them in his house.

Esau took those garments and ran into the city on account of Nimrod's men, and he came to his father's house wearied and exhausted from fight, and he was ready to die through grief when he approached his brother Jacob and sat before him. And he said to his brother Jacob, "Behold I shall die this day; wherefore then do I want the birthright?" <u>And Jacob acted wisely with Esau in this matter,</u> and Esau sold his birthright to Jacob, <u>for it was so brought about by the Lord</u>. Esau's portion in the cave of the field of Machpelah, which Abraham had bought from the children of Heth for the possession of a burial ground, Esau also sold to Jacob, and Jacob bought all this from his brother Esau for value given. Jacob wrote all of this in a book and he testified the same with witnesses, and sealed it, and the book remained in the hands of Jacob.

When Nimrod the son of Cush died, his men lifted him up and brought him in consternation, and buried him in his city, and all the days that Nimrod lived were two hundred and fifteen years and he died. The days that Nimrod reigned on the people of the land were one hundred and eighty-five years; and Nimrod died by the sword of Esau in shame and contempt, and the descendants of Abraham caused his death as he had seen in his dream. At the death of Nimrod his kingdom became divided into many divisions, and all those parts that Nimrod reigned over were restored to the respective kings of the land, who recovered them after the death of Nimrod. All the people of the house of Nimrod were for a long time enslaved to all the other kings of the land. (Jasher 27:1-17)

Now Isaac pleaded with the Lord for his wife, because she was barren; and the Lord granted his plea, and Rebekah his wife conceived. But the children struggled together within her; and she said, "If all is well, why am I like this?" So she went to inquire of the Lord. And the Lord said to her: "Two nations are in your womb, two peoples shall be separated from your body; one people shall be stronger than the other, and the older shall serve the younger."

So when her days were fulfilled for her to give birth, indeed there were twins in her womb. And the first came out red. He was like a hairy garment all over; so they called his name Esau (! Hairy). Afterward his brother came out, and his hand took hold of Esau's heel; so his name was called Jacob (! Supplanter). Isaac was sixty years old when she bore them. So the boys grew. And Esau was a skillful hunter, a man of the field; but Jacob was a mild man, dwelling in tents. And Isaac loved Esau because he ate of his game, but Rebekah loved Jacob. Now Jacob cooked a stew; and Esau came in from the field, and he was weary. And Esau said to Jacob, "Please feed me with that same red stew, for I am weary." Therefore his name was called Edom (! Red). But Jacob said, "Sell me your birthright as of this day." And Esau said, "Look, I am about to die; so what is this birthright to me?" Then Jacob said, "Swear to me as of this day." So he swore to him, and sold his birthright to Jacob. And Jacob gave Esau bread and stew of lentils; then he ate and drank, arose, and went his way. Thus Esau despised his birthright. (Gen 25:21-34)

Pursue peace with all people, and holiness, without which no one will see the Lord: looking carefully lest anyone fall short of the grace of God; lest any root of bitterness springing up cause trouble, and by this many become defiled; lest there be any fornicator or profane person like Esau, who for one morsel of food sold his birthright. For you know that afterward, when he wanted to inherit the blessing, he was rejected, for he found no place for repentance, though he sought it diligently with tears. (Heb 12:14-17)

There is no mention of Nimrod's dream in Genesis and the account of Esau selling his birthright to Jacob for a meal is from Jacob's viewpoint. I've heard people preach that Jacob was a devious person, but with the knowledge of the account in Jasher the whole perspective changes. Clearly Nimrod was punished for abandoning God and his kingdom was taken from him and given to the surrounding kings. Abram was blessed because he walked with God and kept God's laws and commandments. After Nimrod and the other three kings conquer the five kings, Abram conquers the four kings with a much smaller force of men, because God was with him.

Esau lusted for the valuable garments of Nimrod, because he knew that they had made Nimrod successful. He killed Nimrod and two of his men. Running for his life he stole the garments and hid them in his house. Fearing for his life he ran to his father's house and found Jacob with the food he had prepared. Knowing that he could be discovered by Nimrod's men, he gave no thought to selling his birthright for what he thought was his last meal. Esau was a murderer, and this is not revealed in Genesis. Clearly this order of events was from the Lord, because of the outcome. Jacob was not the cheating schemer some people make him out to be. Isaac was also clearly mislead by his stomach, because he loved the game which Esau brought home. I think the accounts in Jasher reveal the true nature of the circumstance, and without this knowledge the reader is left with many questions. There is also no mention in Genesis of Jacob's schooling in righteousness under Shem and Eber, for thirty-two years. Esau had refused to go, and spent his time hunting instead. These facts from the Book of Jasher, gives one the balanced perspective required for a sound understanding of these Biblical accounts.

-oOo-

Millenary

So when Jesus had received the sour wine, He said, "It is finished!" And bowing His head, He gave up His spirit. (Joh 19:30)

I've noticed that the Lord often uses 'three events' in the Bible, to emphasize the more important lessons. After completing 'Min Dae', I realised I had to research what happened in the years 2000AM and 3000AM, as these would probably have reference to the crucifixion of our Lord in 4000AM. Here is the table again.

Event	Anno Mundi	Year
Adam created	1	3969 BC
Noah born	1056	2914 BC
Noah's flood	1656	2314 BC
Abraham born	1948	2022 BC
Abraham @ 70y	2018	1952 BC

Abraham @ 100y BC	2048	1922
Exodus from Egypt BC	2448	1522
Solomon 4th year BC	2928	1042
Solomon 40th year BC	2964	1006
Rehoboam reigns BC	2965	1005
Jesus born BC	3966	4
Jesus crucified AD	4000	31
Now AD	5978	2009
1000y Sabbath begins? AD	6000	2031
Judgement day? AD	7000	3031

2000AM

1998AM

When Abraham was fifty years old, 1998AM, he destroyed his father's twelve gods, and he was brought before King Nimrod, by his father Terah, to answer for his actions.

Terah, seeing all that Abram had done, hurried to go from his house; he went to the king and he came before Nimrod and stood before him, and he bowed down to the king and the king said, "What do you want?" And he said, "I beseech you my lord, to hear me - Now fifty years back a child was born to me, and thus has he done to my gods and thus has he spoken; and now therefore, my lord and king, send for him that he may come before you, and judge him according to the law, that we may be delivered from his evil."

The king sent three men of his servants, and they went and brought Abram before the king. And Nimrod and all his princes and servants were that day sitting before him, and Terah also sat before them. And the king said to Abram, "What is this that you have done to your father and to his gods?" And Abram answered the king in the words that he spoke to his father, and he said, "The large god that was with them in the house did to them what you have heard."

And the king said to Abram, "Had they power to speak and eat and do as you have said?" And Abram answered the king, saying, "And if there be no power in them why do you serve them and cause the sons of men to err through your follies? Do you imagine that they can deliver you or do anything small or great, that you should serve them? And why will you not sense the God of the whole universe, who created you and in whose power it is to kill and keep alive? O foolish, simple, and ignorant king, woe to you forever."

"I thought you would teach your servants the upright way, but you have not done this; you have filled the whole earth with your sins and the sins of your people who have followed your ways. Do you not know, or have you not heard, that this evil which you do, our ancestors sinned therein in days of old, and the eternal God brought the waters of the flood on them and destroyed them all, and also destroyed the whole earth on their account? And will you and your people rise up now and do like this work, in order to bring down the anger of the Lord God of the universe, and to bring evil on you and the whole earth?"

"Now therefore put away this evil deed which you did, and serve the God of the universe, as your soul is in His hands, and then it will be well with you. And if your wicked heart will not listen to my words to cause you to turn away from your evil ways, and to serve the eternal God, then you will die in shame in the latter days, you, your people and all who are connected with you, hearing your words or walking in your evil ways." When Abram had ceased speaking before the king and princes, Abram lifted up his eyes to the heavens, and he said, "The Lord sees all the wicked, and he will judge them." (Jasher 11:50-61)

When the king heard the words of Abram he ordered him to be put into prison; and Abram was ten days in prison. At the end of those days the king ordered that all the kings, princes and governors of different provinces and the sages should come before him, and they sat before him, and Abram was still in the house of confinement. The king said to the princes and sages, "Have you heard what Abram, the son of Terah, has done to his father? Thus has he done to him, and I ordered him to be brought before me, and thus has he spoken; his heart did not misgive him, neither did he stir in my presence, and behold now he is confined in the prison. Therefore decide what judgment is due to this man who reviled the king; who spoke and did all the things that you heard."

And they all answered the king saying, "<u>The man who reviles the king should be hanged on a tree; but having done all the things that he said and having despised our gods, he must therefore be burned to death, for this is the law in this matter.</u> If it pleases the king do this, let him order his servants to kindle a fire both night and day in your brick furnace, and then we will cast this man into it."

And the king did so, and he commanded his servants that they should prepare <u>a fire for three days and three nights</u> in the kings furnace, that is in Casdim; and the king ordered then to take Abram from prison and bring him out to be burned. And all the king's servants, princes, lords, governors, and judges, and all the inhabitants of the land, about nine hundred thousand men, stood opposite the furnace to see Abram. And all the women and little ones crowded on the roofs and towers to see what was going on with Abram, and they all stood together at a distance; and there was not a man left that did not come that day to behold the scene.

When Abram was come, the conjurors of the king and the sages saw Abram, and they cried out to the king, saying, "Our sovereign lord, certainly this is the man whom we know to have been <u>the child at whose birth the great star swallowed the four stars</u>, which we declared to the king fifty years ago. And behold now his father has also gone contrary to your commands, and mocked you by bringing you another child, which you did kill."

And when the king heard their words, he was greatly angered, and he ordered Terah to be brought before him. And the king said, "Have you heard what the conjurors have spoken? Now tell me truly, how did you? If you speak truth you shall be acquitted."

Seeing the king's anger was so much set ablaze, Terah said to the king, "My lord and king, you have heard the truth, and what the sages have spoken is right." And the king said, "How could you do this thing, to go contrary to my orders and to give me a child that you did not beget, and to take value for him?" Terah answered the king, "Because my tender feelings were excited for my son, at that time, I took a son of my handmaid, and I brought him to the king." And the king said, "Who advised you to do this? Tell me, do not hide anything from me, and them you shall not die."

And Terah was greatly terrified in the king's presence, and he said to the king, "It was Haran my eldest son who advised me to do this." Haran was in those days that Abram was born, two and thirty years old. But Haran did not advise his father to do anything, for Terah said this to the king in order to deliver his soul from the king, for he feared greatly. The king said to Terah, "Haran your son who advised you to do this shall die through fire with Abram; for the sentence of death is on him for having rebelled against the king's desire in doing this thing."

Haran at that time felt inclined to follow the ways of Abram, but he kept it within himself. And Haran said in his heart, "Behold now the king has seized Abram on account of these things which Abram did, and it shall come to pass, that if Abram prevail over the king I will follow him, but if the king prevail I will go after the king."

When Terah had spoken this to the king concerning Haran his son, the king ordered Haran to be seized with Abram. And they brought them both, Abram and Haran his brother, to cast them into the fire; and all the inhabitants of the land and the king's servants and princes and all the women and little ones were there standing over them that day.

And the king's servants took Abram and his brother, and they stripped them of all their clothes excepting their lower garments which were on them. And they bound their hands and feet with linen cords, and the servants of the king lifted them up and cast them both into the furnace.

The Lord loved Abram and he had compassion over him, and the Lord came down and delivered Abram from the fire and he was not burned. But all the cords with which they bound him were burned, while Abram remained and walked about in the fire. Haran died when they had cast him into the fire, and he was burned to ashes, for his heart was not perfect with the Lord; and those men who cast him into the fire, the flame of the fire spread over them, and they were burned, and twelve of them died.

Abram walked in the midst of the fire three days and three nights, and all the servants of the king saw him walking in the fire, and they came and told the king, saying, "Behold we have seen Abram walking about in the midst of the fire, and even the lower garments which are on him are not burned, but the cord with which he was bound is burned." When the king heard their words his heart fainted and he would not believe them; so he sent other faithful princes to see this matter, and they went and saw it and told it to the king. And the king rose to go and see it, and he saw Abram walking to and fro in the midst of the fire, and he saw Haran's body burned, and the king wondered greatly.

The king ordered Abram to be taken out from the fire; and his servants approached to take him out and they could not, for the fire was round about and the flame ascending toward them from the furnace. The king's servants fled from it, and the king rebuked them, saying, "Make haste and bring Abram out of the fire that you shall not die. The servants of the king again approached to bring Abram out, and the flames came on them and burned their faces so that eight of them died. When the king saw that his servants could not approach the fire that would burn them, the king called to Abram, "O servant of the God who is in heaven, go forth from amidst the fire and come here before me." And Abram listened to the voice of the king, and he went forth from the fire and came and stood before the king.

When Abram came out, the king and all his servants saw Abram coming before the king with his lower garments on him that were not burned, but the cord with which he was bound was burned. And the king said to Abram, "How is it that you were not burned in the fire?" Abram said to the king, "The God of heaven and earth in whom I trust and who has all in His power, He delivered me from the fire into which you did cast me."

Haran the brother of Abram was burned to ashes, and they sought for his body; they found it consumed. Haran was eighty-two years old when he died in the fire of Casdim. And the king, princes, and inhabitants of the land, seeing that Abram was delivered from the fire, came and bowed down to Abram. And Abram said to them, "<u>Do not bow to me, but bow down to the God of the world who made you, and serve Him, and go in His ways for it is He who delivered me from out of this fire; it is He who created the souls and spirits of all men, and formed man in his mother's womb, and brought him forth into the world; it is He who will deliver those who trust in Him from all pain</u>."

This thing seemed very wonderful in the eyes of the king and princes, that Abram was saved from the fire and that Haran was burned. And the king gave Abram many presents and he gave him his two head servants from the king's house; the name of one was Oni and the name of <u>the other was Eliezer</u>. All the king's, princes and servants gave Abram many gifts of silver and gold and pearl, and the king and his princes sent him away, and he went in peace. Abram went forth from the king in peace, and many of the king's servants followed him, and about three hundred men joined him. And Abram returned on that day and went to his father's house, he and the men that followed him, and Abram served the Lord his God all the days of his life; he walked in His ways and followed His law. From that day forward Abram inclined the hearts of the sons of men to serve the Lord.

At that time Nahor and Abram took to themselves wives, the daughters of their brother Haran; the wife of Nahor was Milca and the name of Abram's wife was Sarai. And Sarai, wife of Abram, was unable to conceive; she had no children in those days. (Jasher 12:1-44)

<u>2000AM</u>

At the expiration of two years from Abram's going out of the fire, that is in the fifty-second year of his life, behold king Nimrod sat in Babel on the throne, and the king fell asleep and dreamed that he was standing with his troops and hosts in a valley opposite the king's furnace. And he lifted up his eyes and <u>saw a man in the likeness of Abram coming forth from the furnace; he came and stood before the king with his drawn sword</u>, and then sprang to the king with his sword, when the king fled from the man, for he was afraid; while he was running, the man threw an egg on the king's head, and the egg became a great river. <u>And the king dreamed that all his troops sank in that river and died</u>, and <u>the king took flight with three men</u> who were before him and he escaped. <u>The king looked at these men and they were clothed in princely dresses as the garments of kings</u>, and had the appearance and majesty of kings. And while they were running, the river again turned to an egg before the king; there came forth from the egg a young bird which came before the king, and flew at his head and plucked out the king's eye. The king was grieved at the sight, and he awoke out of his sleep and his spirit was agitated; he felt a great terror.

In the morning the king rose from his couch in fear, and he ordered all the wise men and magicians to come before him, when the king related his dream to them. And a wise servant of the king, whose name was Anuki, answered the king, saying, "This is nothing else but the evil of Abram and his offspring which will spring up against my Lord and king in the latter days. And behold the day will come when Abram and his offspring and the children of his household will war with my king, and they will strike all the king's hosts and his troops. And as to what you have said concerning three men which you did see like yourself, and which did escape, this means that only you will escape with three kings from the kings of the earth who will be with you in battle. And that which you saw of the river which turned to an egg as at first, and the young bird plucking out your eye, this means nothing else but the offspring of Abram which will kill the king in latter days. This is my king's dream, and this is its interpretation, and the dream is true, and the interpretation which your servant has given you is right. Now therefore my king, certainly you know that it is now fifty-two years since your sages saw this at the birth of Abram, and if my king will suffer Abram to live in the earth it will be to the injury of my lord and king, for all the days that Abram lives neither you nor your kingdom will be established, for this was known formerly at his birth; and why will not my king kill him, that his evil may be kept from you in latter days?"

And Nimrod listened to the voice of Anuki; he sent some of his servants in secret to go and seize Abram and bring him before the king to suffer death. Eliezer, Abram's servant whom the king had given him, was at that time in the presence of the king, and he heard what Anuki had advised the king, and what the king had said to cause Abram's death. Eliezer said to Abram, "Hasten, rise up and save your soul, that you may not die through the hands of the king, for thus did he see in a dream concerning you, and thus did Anuki interpret it, and thus also did Anuki advise the king concerning you."

Abram listened to the voice of Eliezer, and Abram hurried and ran for safety to the house of Noah and his son Shem, and he concealed himself there and found a place of safety; and the king's servants came to Abram's house to seek him, but they could not find him, and they searched throughout the country and he was not to be found; they went and searched in every direction and he was not to be met with. And when the king's servants could not find Abram they returned to the king, but the king's anger against Abram was stilled, as they did not find him, and the king drove from his mind this matter concerning Abram.

Abram was concealed in Noah's house for one month, until the king had forgotten this matter, but Abram was still afraid of the king; and Terah came to see Abram his son secretly in the house of Noah, and Terah was very great in the eyes of the king. Abram said to his father, "<u>Do you not know that the king thinks to kill me</u>, and to annihilate my name from the earth by the advice of his wicked counselors? Now whom have you here and what have you in this land? Arise, let us go to the land of Canaan, that we may be delivered from his hand, that you not perish also through him in the latter days. Do you not know or have you not heard, that it is not through love that Nimrod gives you all this honor, but it is only for his benefit that he bestows all this good on you? <u>And if he does to you greater good than this</u>, certainly there are only vanities of the world, for wealth and riches cannot avail in the days of wrath and anger. Now therefore listen to my voice, and let us arise and go to the land of Canaan, out of the reach of injury from Nimrod; and serve the Lord who created you in the earth and it will be well with you; and cast away all the vain things which you pursue."

And Abram ceased to speak when Noah and his son Shem answered Terah, saying "True is the word which Abram hath said to you." And Terah listened to the voice of his son Abram, and Terah did all that Abram said, for this was from the Lord that the king should not cause Abram's death. (Jasher 12:45-70)

King Nimrod had tried to burn Abram to death. The Lord stepped in and saved Abram, but Haran was burned to death because his heart was not right with the Lord. In the year 2000AM Nimrod had a second dream, about Abram's victory over himself and three other kings in a battle. He tried for the third time to have Abram killed, but Abram fled to the righteous house of Noah and Shem. So Abram left the land of the wicked ruler, and escaped death.

<u>3000AM</u>

<u>2965AM</u>

And Rehoboam the son of Solomon reigned in Judah. <u>Rehoboam</u> was forty-one years old when he became king. He <u>reigned seventeen years in Jerusalem</u>, the city which the Lord had chosen out of all the tribes of Israel, to put His name there. His mother's name was Naamah, an Ammonitess. <u>Now Judah did evil in the sight of the Lord</u>, and they provoked Him to jealousy with their sins which they committed, more than all that their fathers had done.

(1Ki 14:21-22 and 2Ch 12:13-14)

<u>2982AM</u>

In the eighteenth year of King Jeroboam the son of Nebat, <u>Abijam</u> became king over Judah. He <u>reigned three years in Jerusalem</u>. His mother's name was Maachah the grand-daughter of Abishalom. And <u>he walked in the sins of his father</u>, which he had done before him; <u>his heart was not loyal to the Lord his God</u>, as was the heart of his father David. (1Ki 15:1-3)

In the eighteenth year of King Jeroboam, <u>Abijah</u> became king over Judah. He <u>reigned three years in Jerusalem</u>. His mother's name was Michaiah the daughter of Uriel of Gibeah. And there was war between Abijah and Jeroboam. (2Ch 13:1-2)

<u>2985AM</u>

In the twentieth year of Jeroboam king of Israel, <u>Asa</u> became king over Judah. And he <u>reigned forty-one years in Jerusalem</u>. His grand-mother's name was Maachah the grand-daughter of Abishalom. <u>Asa did what was right in the eyes of the Lord</u>, as did his father David.

(1Ki 15:9-11)

So Abijah rested with his fathers, and they buried him in the City of David. Then Asa his son reigned in his place. In his days the land was quiet for ten years. Asa did what was good and right in the eyes of the Lord his God, for he removed the altars of the foreign gods and the high places, and broke down the sacred pillars and cut down the wooden images. He commanded Judah to seek the Lord God of their fathers, and to observe the law and the commandment. He also removed the high places and the incense altars from all the cities of Judah, and the kingdom was quiet under him. (2Ch 14:1-5)

3000AM

Now the Spirit of God came upon Azariah the son of Oded. And he went out to meet Asa, and said to him: "Hear me, Asa, and all Judah and Benjamin. The Lord is with you while you are with Him. If you seek Him, He will be found by you; but if you forsake Him, He will forsake you. For a long time Israel has been without the true God, without a teaching priest, and without law; but when in their trouble they turned to the Lord God of Israel, and sought Him, He was found by them. And in those times there was no peace to the one who went out, nor to the one who came in, but great turmoil was on all the inhabitants of the lands. So nation was destroyed by nation, and city by city, for God troubled them with every adversity. But you, be strong and do not let your hands be weak, for your work shall be rewarded!"

And when Asa heard these words and the prophecy of Azariah the prophet, he took courage, and removed the abominable idols from all the land of Judah and Benjamin and from the cities which he had taken in the mountains of Ephraim; and he restored the altar of the Lord that was before the vestibule of the Lord. Then he gathered all Judah and Benjamin, and those who dwelt with them from Ephraim, Manasseh, and Simeon, for they came over to him in great numbers from Israel when they saw that the Lord his God was with him.

So they gathered together at Jerusalem in the third month, in the fifteenth year of the reign of Asa. And they offered to the Lord at that time seven hundred bulls and seven thousand sheep from the spoil they had brought. Then they entered into a covenant to seek the Lord God of their fathers with all their heart and with all their soul; and whoever would not seek the Lord God of Israel was to be put to death, whether small or great, whether man or woman. Then they took an oath before the Lord with a loud voice, with shouting and trumpets and rams' horns. And all Judah rejoiced at the oath, for they had sworn with all their heart and sought

Him with all their soul; and He was found by them, and the Lord gave them rest all around.

Also he removed Maachah, the mother of Asa the king, from being queen mother, because she had made an obscene image of Asherah; and Asa cut down her obscene image, then crushed and burned it by the Brook Kidron. But the high places were not removed from Israel. Nevertheless the heart of Asa was loyal all his days. He also brought into the house of God the things that his father had dedicated and that he himself had dedicated: silver and gold and utensils. And there was no war until the thirty-fifth year of the reign of Asa. (2Ch 15:1-19)

So in 2965AM Rehoboam starts to rule over Judah and rules seventeen years in Jerusalem. Abijam/Abijah rules for three years after him. Abijah dies and Asa his son succeeds him as king in the year 2985AM. Years later, Asa was returning from winning a battle against Zerah the Ethiopian. Zerah had been accompanied by a superior force of men, but Asa had cried out to the Lord his God for His help. The Lord and His army, had struck the Ethiopians before Asa and Judah, and the Ethiopians had fled. Asa and his men had pursued them to Gerar and plundered the cities. Then they had returned to Jerusalem with huge amounts of spoil, sheep and camels. King Asa and his people were met by the prophet Azariah on their return.

This account reminds me of when Melchizedek king of Salem (Shem) met Abraham on his return, from winning the battle against the four kings; Chedorlaomer, Amraphel (Nimrod), Arioch and Tidal. This was the event in Nimrod's dream, in 2000AM, which had driven him to attempt to kill Abram for the third time. The bread and the wine served to Abraham, also testifies of Jesus Christ's sacrifice on the cross.

Then Melchizedek king of Salem brought out bread and wine; he was the priest of God Most High. And he blessed him and said: "Blessed be Abram of God Most High, possessor of heaven and earth; and blessed be God Most High, who has delivered your enemies into your hand." And he gave him a tithe of all. (Gen 14:18-20)

King Asa had honoured the Lord, and the Lord had helped them to win the battle against Zerah the Ethiopian. Azariah reminds them of the Lord's promise, to assist those who seek Him. In the fifteenth year of his reign, King Asa arranged a huge sacrifice to the Lord, and all the people swore an oath to the Lord. "And all Judah rejoiced at the oath, for they had sworn with all their heart and sought Him with all their soul; and He was found by them, and the Lord gave them rest all around." This was the year 3000AM, 1000 years before the crucifixion of Jesus Christ.

Here are two references to the crucifixion, as being on the fourth day after selection.

Now the Lord spoke to Moses and Aaron in the land of Egypt, saying, "This month shall be your beginning of months; it shall be the first month of the year to you. Speak to all the congregation of Israel, saying: 'On the tenth of this month every man shall take for himself a lamb, according to the house of his father, a lamb for a household. And if the household is too small for the lamb, let him and his neighbor next to his house take it according to the number of the persons; according to each man's need you shall make your count for the lamb. Your lamb shall be without blemish, a male of the first year. You may take it from the sheep or from the goats. Now you shall keep it until the fourteenth day of the same month. Then the whole assembly of the congregation of Israel shall kill it at twilight. (Exo 12:1-6)

And Ezra came to Jerusalem in the fifth month, which was in the seventh year of the king. On the first day of the first month he began his journey from Babylon, and on the first day of the fifth month he came to Jerusalem, according to the good hand of his God upon him. For Ezra had prepared his heart to seek the Law of the Lord, and to do it, and to teach statutes and ordinances in Israel. (Ezr 7:8-10)

Our Father set aside His own Son, from the beginning of Creation, to redeem Mankind from Sin. Jesus was born as a man, and four thousand years after Adam was created (on the 4th day), He was sacrificed on the cross by the multitude and His blood was shed to redeem us from Sin. Remember, Adam also died (930y) in the 'day' that he sinned!

Whether the 1st resurrection will take place in 2031AD I can't say for sure, but I will say, "I believe it will take place 2000 years after the crucifixion of Jesus."

Heaven and earth will pass away, but My words will by no means pass away. But of that day and hour no one knows, not even the angels of heaven, but My Father only. Therefore you also be ready, for the Son of Man is coming at an hour you do not expect. (Mat 24:35-36,44)

-oOo-

Jochebed

If one talks about a miraculous birth, who do you think about? Mary, mother of Jesus and Sarah, mother of Isaac? I want to inform you of another woman, who easily fits into this category, but is largely unknown; because the church has ignored the wisdom of the Book of Jasher, which supplies the missing information. We know that the Israelites were in Egypt for 210 years and that Moses was 80 years old, when he and Aaron spoke to Pharaoh; but the account of the Israelites entering Egypt, reveals an amazing mother.

And Moses was eighty years old and Aaron eighty-three years old when they spoke to Pharaoh. (Exo 7:7)

Now Amram took for himself Jochebed, his father's sister, as wife; and she bore him Aaron and Moses. And the years of the life of Amram were one hundred and thirty-seven. (Exo 6:20)

And a man of the house of Levi went and took as wife a daughter of Levi. So the woman conceived and bore a son. And when she saw that he was a beautiful child, she hid him three months. But when she could no longer hide him, she took <u>an ark of bulrushes</u> for him, <u>daubed it with asphalt and pitch</u>, put the child in it, and laid it in the reeds by the river's bank. And his sister stood afar off, to know what would be done to him.

(Exo 2:1-4)

These are the families of the Levites: the family of the Libnites, the family of the Hebronites, the family of the Mahlites, the family of the Mushites, and the family of the Korathites. And Kohath begot Amram. The name of Amram's wife was <u>Jochebed the daughter of Levi, who was born to Levi in Egypt; and to Amram she bore Aaron and Moses and their sister Miriam</u>. (Num 26:58-59)

From these scriptures, Jochebed's importance does not stand out, but let's ask Jasher!

It was about that time that Abraham died, in the fifteenth year of the life of Jacob and Esau, the sons of Isaac, and all the days of Abraham were one hundred and seventy-five years. He died and was gathered to his people in good old age, old and satisfied with days, and Isaac and Ishmael his sons buried him. (Jasher 26:29)

Jacob lived in the land of Egypt seventeen years, and the days of Jacob, and the years of his life were a hundred and forty seven years. (Jasher 56:1)

And the children of Levi were Gershon, Kehath and Merari, <u>and their sister Jochebed, who was born to them in their going down to Egypt</u>. And the sons of Judah were Er, Onan, Shelah, Perez and Zarach. And Er and Onan died in the land of Canaan; and the sons of Perez were Chezron and Chamul. And the sons of Issachar were Tola, Puvah, Job and Shomron. And the sons of Zebulun were Sered, Elon and Jachleel, and the son of Dan was Chushim. (Jasher 59:9-13)

The sons of Levi were Gershon, Kohath and Merari. The sons of Judah were Er, Onan, Shelah, Perez and Zerah (but Er and Onan died in the land of Canaan). The sons of Perez were Hezron and Hamul. The sons of

Issachar were Tola, Puvah, Job and Shimron. The sons of Zebulun were Sered, Elon and Jahleel. (Gen 46:11-14)

All the souls that went forth from the loins of Jacob were <u>seventy</u> souls; these are they who came with Jacob their father to Egypt to dwell there: and Joseph and all his brothers lived securely in Egypt, and they ate of the best of Egypt all the days of the life of Joseph. And Joseph lived in the land of Egypt ninety-three years, and <u>Joseph reigned over all Egypt eighty years</u>. (Jasher 59:19-20)

All the persons who went with Jacob to Egypt, who came from his body, besides Jacob's sons' wives, were sixty-six persons in all. And the sons of Joseph who were born to him in Egypt were two persons. All the persons of the house of Jacob who went to Egypt were <u>seventy</u>. (Gen 46:26-27)

Genesis concentrates on the people who went into Egypt, seventy in all; but Jasher also mentions Jochebed, who was born on their entering into Egypt. So Jochebed's birth coincides with the event of Israel entering the land of Egypt.

There was a man in the land of Egypt of the children of Levi, whose name was Amram, the son of Kehath, the son of Levi, the son of Israel. And this man went and took a wife, namely Jochebed the daughter of Levi his father's sister, <u>and she was one hundred and twenty-six years old</u>, and he came to her. And the woman conceived and gave birth to a daughter, and she called her name <u>Miriam,</u> because in those days the Egyptians had <u>embittered the lives of the children of Israel</u>. She conceived again and gave birth to a son and she called his name <u>Aaron,</u> for in the days of her conception, <u>Pharaoh began to spill the blood of the male children of Israel</u>. (Jasher 67:2-4)

The king ordered an announcement to be issued and a law to be made throughout the land of Egypt, saying, "<u>Every male child born to the Hebrews from this day forward shall be thrown into the water</u>." Pharaoh called to all his servants, saying, "Go now and search throughout the land of Goshen where the children of Israel are, and see that every son born to the Hebrews will be cast into the river, but every daughter you shall let live." And when the children of Israel heard this thing which Pharaoh had commanded, to cast their male children into the river, some of the people separated from their wives and others adhered to them. (Jasher 67:51-53)

It was at that time the spirit of God was on Miriam the daughter of Amram the sister of Aaron, and she went forth and prophesied about the house, saying, "Behold a son will be born to us from my father and mother this time, and he will save Israel from the hands of Egypt." And when Amram heard the words of his daughter, he went and took his wife back to the house, after he had driven her away at the time when Pharaoh ordered every male child of the house of Jacob to be thrown into the water.

So Amram took Jochebed his wife, three years after he had driven her away, and he came to her and she conceived. At the end of seven months from her conception she brought forth a son, and the whole house was filled with great light as of the light of the sun and moon at the time of their shining. And when the woman saw the child that it was good and pleasing to the sight, she hid him for three months in an inner room. In those days the Egyptians conspired to destroy all the Hebrews there. And the Egyptian women went to Goshen where the children of Israel were, and they carried their young ones on their shoulders, their babes who could not yet speak.

And in those days, when the women of the children of Israel brought forth, each woman had hidden her son from the Egyptians, that the Egyptians might not know of their bringing forth, and might not destroy them from the land. And the Egyptian women came to Goshen and their children who could not speak were on their shoulders, and when an Egyptian woman came into the house of a Hebrew woman her babe began to cry. And when it cried the child that was in the inner room answered it, so the Egyptian women went and told it at the house of Pharaoh. And Pharaoh sent his officers to take the children and kill them; thus did the Egyptians to the Hebrew women all the days.

And it was at that time, about three months from Jochebed's concealment of her son, that this thing was known in Pharaoh's house. And the woman hurried to take away her son before the officers came, and she took for him an ark of bulrushes, and daubed it with slime and with pitch and put the child therein, and she laid it in the flags by the river's brink. And his sister Miriam stood afar off to learn what would be done to him, and what would become of her words. (Jasher 68:1-14)

The 210y that the Hebrews spent in Egypt, were marked by the birth of Jochebed, and the 80th birthday of Moses. Jochebed was 126y old when she married Amram and must have been about 130y old when she gave birth to Moses! 130y + 80y = 210 years, that's a clear benchmark for the period in Egypt! Jochebed gave birth to a prophetess and the two key males, who lead the Israelites out of Egypt; and her children were Levites. Israel increased from 70, to 100's of thousands of people. Egypt acquired all the wealth of the region, throughout the years of drought; thanks to the wisdom, the Lord gave Joseph. Then in turn the Egyptians gave their wealth to Israel; when they left with Moses, Aaron and Miriam, after their 210y stay. Miriam was very young when she prophesied about Moses, and we also knew she was a prophetess, due to the following Bible text:-

Then <u>Miriam the prophetess,</u> the sister of Aaron, took the timbrel in her hand; and all the women went out after her with timbrels and with dances. (Exo 15:20)

The birth of Moses, reminds me of the birth of Noah, as described in the Book of Enoch.

And after some days my son Methuselah took a wife for his son, Lamech, and she became pregnant by him and bore a son. And his body was white as snow and red as the blooming of a rose, and the hair of his head and his long curls were white as wool, and his eyes beautiful. And when he opened his eyes, <u>he lit up the whole house like the sun,</u> and the whole house was very bright. And on it he levitated (arose) in the hands of the midwife, opened his mouth, and conversed with the Lord of righteousness.

And his father, Lamech, was afraid of him and fled, and came to his father Methuselah. And he said to him: "I have begotten a strange son, different and unlike man, and resembling the sons of the God of heaven; and his nature is different and he is not like us, and his eyes are as the rays of the sun, and his face glorious. And it seems to me that he did not spring from me but from the angels, and I fear that in his days a wonder may be performed on the earth. And now, my father, I am here to ask you and beg you that you may go to Enoch, our father, and learn from him the truth, for his dwelling-place is among the angels."

And when Methuselah heard the words of his son, he came to me to the ends of the earth; for he had heard that I was there, and he cried aloud, and I heard his voice and I came to him. And I said to him: "Behold, here am I, my son, why have you come to me?"

And he answered and said: "Because of a great cause of anxiety have I come to you, and because of a disturbing vision have I approached. And now, my father, hear me. To Lamech, my son, there has been born a son, the like of whom there is none other, and his nature is not like man's nature, and the color of his body is whiter than snow and redder than the bloom of a rose, and the hair of his head is whiter than white wool, and his eyes are like the rays of the sun, and he opened his eyes and the whole house lit up. And he levitated (arose) in the hands of the midwife, and opened his mouth and blessed the Lord of heaven. And his father Lamech became afraid and fled to me, and did not believe that he sprung from him, but that he was in the likeness of the angels of heaven; and now I have come to you that you may make known to me the truth."

And I, Enoch, answered and said to him: "The Lord will do a new thing on the earth, and this I have already seen in a vision, and make known to you that in the generation of my father Jared <u>some of the angels of heaven violated the word of the Lord</u>. And they commit sin and broke the law, and have had sex (united themselves) with women and committed sin with them, and have married some of them, and have had children by them. And <u>they shall produce on the earth giants</u> not according to the spirit, but according to the flesh, and there shall be great punishment on the earth, and the earth shall be cleansed from all impurity."

"There shall come a great destruction over the whole earth, and <u>there shall be a flood (deluge) and a great destruction for one year</u>. And this son who has been born to you shall be left on the earth, and his three children shall be saved with him: when all mankind that are on the earth shall die, he and his sons shall be saved. And now make known to your son, Lamech, that he who has been born is in truth his son, and call his name Noah; for he shall be left to you, and he and his sons shall be saved from the destruction, which shall come on the earth on account of all the sin and all the unrighteousness, which shall be full (completed) on the earth in his days."

"And after that (flood) there shall be more unrighteousness than which was done before on the earth; for I know the mysteries of the holy ones; for He, the Lord, has showed me and informed me, and I have read (them) in heavenly tablets. And I saw written about them that generation after generation shall transgress, until a generation of righteousness arises, and transgression is destroyed and sin passes away from the earth, and all manner of good comes on it. And now, my son, go and make known to your son Lamech that this son, which has been born, is in truth his son, and this is no lie."

And when Methuselah had heard the words of his father Enoch, for he had shown to him everything in secret, he returned and showed those things to him and called the name of that son Noah; for he will comfort the earth after all the destruction.

Another book which Enoch wrote for his son Methuselah and for those who will come after him, and keep the law in the last days. You who have done good shall wait for those days until an end is made of those who work evil; and an end of the power of the wrongdoers. And wait until sin has passed away indeed, for their names shall be blotted out of the book of life and out of the holy books, and their (children) seed shall be destroyed for ever, and their spirits shall be killed, and they shall cry and lament in a place that is a chaotic desert, and they shall be burned in the fire; for there is no earth there.

I saw something there like an invisible cloud; because it was so deep I could not look over it, and I saw a flame of fire blazing brightly, and things like shining mountains circling and sweeping back and forth. And I asked one of the holy angels who was with me and said to him: "What is this bright thing (shining)? For it is not heaven but there was only the flame of a blazing fire, and the voice of weeping and crying and moaning, lamenting, and agony."

And he said to me: "This place which you see are where the spirits of sinners and blasphemers, and of those who work wickedness, are cast and the spirits of those who pervert everything that the Lord hath spoken through the mouth of the prophets and even the prophesies (things that shall be). For some of them are written and inscribed above in heaven, in order that the angels may read them and know that which shall befall the sinners, and the spirits of the humble, and of those who have afflicted their bodies, and been recompensed by God; and of those who have been abused (put to shame) by wicked men: Who love God and loved neither gold nor silver nor any of the good things which are in the world, but gave over their bodies to torture. Who, since they were born, longed not after earthly food, but regarded everything as a passing breath, and lived accordingly, and the Lord tried them much, and their spirits were found pure so that they should bless His name. And all the blessing destined for them I have recounted in the books. And he has assigned them their reward, because they have been found to love heaven more than their life in the world, and though they were trodden under foot by wicked men, and experienced abuse and reviling from them and were put to shame, they blessed Me."

"And now I will summon the spirits of the good who belong to the generation of light, and I will transform those who were born in darkness, who in flesh were not rewarded with such honor as their faithfulness deserved. And I will bring out in shining those who have loved My holy name, and I will seat each on the throne of his honor. And they shall shine for time without end; for righteousness is the judgment of God; because to the faithful He will give faithfulness in the habitation of upright paths. And they shall see those who in darkness led into darkness, while the righteous shall shine. And the sinners shall cry aloud and see them shining, and they indeed will go where day and seasons are written down (prescribed) for them." (Enoch 106:1 – 108:14)

"For as the new heavens and the new earth which I will make shall remain before Me," says the Lord, "So shall your descendants and your name remain. And it shall come to pass that from one New Moon to another, and from one Sabbath to another, all flesh shall come to worship before Me," says the Lord. "And they shall go forth and look upon the corpses of the men who have transgressed against Me. For their worm does not die, and their fire is not quenched. They shall be an abhorrence to all flesh." (Isa 66:22-24)

Now it came to pass, when men began to multiply on the face of the earth, and daughters were born to them, that <u>the sons of God saw the daughters of men</u>, that they were beautiful; and <u>they took wives for themselves of all whom they chose</u>. And the Lord said, "My Spirit shall not strive with man forever, for he is indeed flesh; yet his days shall be one hundred and twenty years." <u>There were giants on the earth in those days</u>, and also afterward, when the sons of God came in to the daughters of men and they bore children to them. Those were the mighty men who were of old, men of renown. Then the Lord saw that the wickedness of man was great in the earth, and that every intent of the thoughts of his heart was only evil continually.

And the Lord was sorry that He had made man on the earth, and He was grieved in His heart. So the Lord said, "I will destroy man whom I have created from the face of the earth, both man and beast, creeping thing and birds of the air, for I am sorry that I have made them." But Noah found grace in the eyes of the Lord. (Gen 6:1-8)

Beloved, while I was very diligent to write to you concerning our common salvation, I found it necessary to write to you exhorting you to contend earnestly for the faith which was once for all delivered to the saints. For certain men have crept in unnoticed, who long ago were marked out for this condemnation, ungodly men, who turn the grace of our God into lewdness and deny the only Lord God and our Lord Jesus Christ. But I want to remind you, though you once knew this, that the Lord, having saved the people out of the land of Egypt, afterward destroyed those who did not believe. <u>And the angels who did not keep their proper domain, but left their own abode, He has reserved in everlasting chains under darkness for the judgment of the great day;</u> as Sodom and Gomorrah, and the cities around them <u>in a similar manner to these, having given themselves over to sexual immorality and gone after strange flesh, are set forth as an example, suffering the vengeance of eternal fire.</u> Likewise also these dreamers defile the flesh, reject authority, and speak evil of dignitaries. Yet Michael the archangel, in contending with the devil, when he disputed about the body of Moses, dared not bring against him a reviling accusation, but said, "The Lord rebuke you!"

But these speak evil of whatever they do not know; and whatever they know naturally, like brute beasts, in these things they corrupt themselves. Woe to them! For they have gone in the way of Cain, have run greedily in the error of Balaam for profit, and perished in the rebellion of Korah. These are spots in your love feasts, while they feast with you without fear, serving only themselves. They are clouds without water, carried about by the winds; late autumn trees without fruit, twice dead, pulled up by the roots; raging waves of the sea, foaming up their own shame; <u>wandering stars for whom is reserved the blackness of darkness forever</u>. Now, Enoch, the seventh from Adam, prophesied about these men also, saying, "Behold, <u>the Lord comes with ten thousands of His saints, to execute judgment on all</u>, to convict all who are ungodly among them of all their ungodly deeds which they have committed in an ungodly way, and of all the harsh things which ungodly sinners have spoken against Him."

These are grumblers, complainers, walking according to their own lusts; and they mouth great swelling words, flattering people to gain advantage. But you, beloved, remember the words which were spoken before by the apostles of our Lord Jesus Christ: how they told you that there would be mockers in the last time who would walk according to their own ungodly lusts. These are sensual persons, who cause divisions, not having the Spirit. But you, beloved, building yourselves up on your most holy faith, praying in the Holy Spirit, keep yourselves in the love of God, looking for the mercy of our Lord Jesus Christ unto eternal life. And on some have compassion, making a distinction; <u>but others save with fear</u>, <u>pulling them out of the fire</u>, <u>hating even the garment defiled by the flesh</u>. (Jue 3-23)

-oOo-

Third Reference

Have you ever read a portion of the Bible, and wished that there was more about the topic. I have, often, and its this interest in the Bible, which drove me to search out all scripture I could find which covered the Bible topics. Some have asked me why I read these books, as they are not recognised by others. My answer is that <u>my salvation</u> depends on the strength of <u>my faith</u>, and I will read everything that increases my faith in the Word of God. There are two references to the Book of Jasher in the Bible, but I've discovered a subtle third. This study illustrates the value of the Book of Jasher.

1st Reference

And the men of Gibeon sent to Joshua at the camp at Gilgal, saying, "Do not forsake your servants; come up to us quickly, save us and help us, for all the kings of the Amorites who dwell in the mountains have gathered together against us."

So Joshua ascended from Gilgal, he and all the people of war with him, and all the mighty men of valor. And the Lord said to Joshua, "Do not fear them, for I have delivered them into your hand; not a man of them shall stand before you."

Joshua therefore came upon them suddenly, having marched all night from Gilgal. So the Lord routed them before Israel, killed them with a great slaughter at Gibeon, chased them along the road that goes to Beth Horon, and struck them down as far as Azekah and Makkedah. And it happened, as they fled before Israel and were on the descent of Beth Horon, that the Lord cast down large hailstones from heaven on them as far as Azekah, and they died. There were more who died from the hailstones than the children of Israel killed with the sword. Then Joshua spoke to the Lord <u>in the day when the Lord delivered up the Amorites before the children of Israel</u>, and he said in the sight of Israel: "Sun, stand still over Gibeon; and Moon, in the Valley of Aijalon."

So the sun stood still, and the moon stopped, till the people had revenge upon their enemies. <u>Is this not written in the Book of Jasher?</u> So the sun stood still in the midst of heaven, and did not hasten to go down for about a whole day. And there has been no day like that, before it or after it, that the Lord heeded the voice of a man; for the Lord fought for Israel. Then Joshua returned, and all Israel with him, to the camp at Gilgal. (Jos 10:6-15)

And they gathered themselves together and the five kings of the Amorites went up with all their camps, a mighty people numerous as the sand of the seashore. All these kings came and camped before Gibeon, and they began to fight against the inhabitants of Gibeon, and all the men of Gibeon sent to Joshua, saying, "Come up quickly to us and help us, for all the kings of the Amorites have gathered together to fight against us."

Joshua and all the fighting people went up from Gilgal, and Joshua came suddenly to them and struck these five kings with a great slaughter. And the Lord confounded them before the children of Israel, who struck them with a terrible slaughter in Gibeon, and pursued them along the way that goes up to Beth Horon to Makkedah; they fled from before the children of

Israel. And while they were fleeing, the Lord sent on them hailstones from heaven, and more of them died by the hailstones than by the slaughter of the children of Israel. The children of Israel pursued them, and they still struck them in the road, going on and smiting them. And when they were smiting, the day was declining toward evening and Joshua said in the sight of all the people, "Sun, stand still on Gibeon, and you moon in the valley of Ajalon, until the nation shall have revenged itself on its enemies."

The Lord listened to the voice of Joshua, and the sun stood still in the midst of the heavens, and it stood still six and thirty moments, and the moon also stood still and hurried not to go down a whole day. And there was no day like that, before it or after it that the Lord listened to the voice of a man, for the Lord fought for Israel.

(Jas 88:57-65)

2nd Reference

Then David lamented with this lamentation over Saul and over Jonathan his son, and he told them to teach the children of Judah the Song of the Bow; indeed it is written in the Book of Jasher: (2Sa 1:17-18)

And Jacob said to Judah, I know my son that you are a mighty man for your brothers; reign over them, and your sons shall reign over their sons forever. Only teach your sons the bow and all the weapons of war, in order that they may fight the battles of their brother who will rule over his enemies. And Jacob again commanded his sons on that day, saying, Behold I shall this day be gathered to my people; carry me up from Egypt and bury me in the cave of Machpelah as I have commanded you. (Jas 56:8-10)

3rd Reference

Another subtle reference to Jasher is found in 1Samuel 24, when David is talking to Saul. After he had the opportunity to kill Saul in the cave, but did not take it.

"Let the Lord judge between you and me, and let the Lord avenge me on you. But my hand shall not be against you. As the proverb of the ancients says, 'Wickedness proceeds from the wicked.' But my hand shall not be against you. After whom has the king of Israel come out? Whom do you pursue? A dead dog? A flea? Therefore let the Lord be judge, and judge between you and me, and see and plead my case, and deliver me out of your hand." (1Sa 24:12-15)

And all the earth was of one tongue and words of union, but Nimrod did not go in the ways of the Lord; he was more wicked than all the men that were before him, from the days of the flood until those days. He made gods of wood and stone, he bowed down to them, he rebelled against the Lord, and taught all his subjects and the people of the earth his wicked ways; Mardon his son was more wicked than his father. And every one that heard of the acts of Mardon the son of Nimrod would say, concerning him, "From the wicked goes forth wickedness." <u>Therefore it became a proverb in the whole earth</u>, saying, "<u>From the wicked goes forth wickedness</u>", and it was current in the words of men from that time to this. (Jas 7:46-48)

In the 1st reference; the Lord told Abraham about the day of battle with the Amorites 470 years earlier. "But in the fourth generation they shall return here, <u>for the iniquity of the Amorites is not yet complete</u>." (Gen 15:16) Israel returns to fight the Amorites forty years after, leaving Egypt and receiving the Law.

Let's look at what Paul said in Galatians, before we look at Genesis 15 in detail.

Now to Abraham and his Seed were the promises made. He does not say, "And to seeds," as of many, but as of one, "And to your Seed," who is Christ. And this I say, that the law, <u>which was four hundred and thirty years later</u>, cannot annul the covenant that was confirmed before by God in Christ, that it should make the promise of no effect.

For if the inheritance is of the law, it is no longer of promise; but God gave it to Abraham by promise. (Gal 3:16-18)

After these things the word of the Lord came to Abram in a vision, saying, "<u>Do not be afraid, Abram. I am your shield, your exceedingly great reward</u>." But Abram said, "Lord God, what will You give me, seeing I go childless, and the heir of my house is Eliezer of Damascus?" Then Abram said, "Look, You have given me no offspring; indeed one born in my house is my heir!" And behold, the word of the Lord came to him, saying,

"This one shall not be your heir, but one who will come from your own body shall be your heir."

Then He brought him outside and said, "Look now toward heaven, and count the stars if you are able to number them." And He said to him, "So shall your descendants be."

<u>And he believed in the Lord,</u> <u>and He accounted it to him for righteousness</u>. Then He said to him, "I am the Lord, who brought you out of Ur of the Chaldeans, to give you this land to inherit it." And he said, "Lord God, how shall I know that I will inherit it?"

So He said to him, "Bring Me a three-year-old heifer, a three-year-old female goat, a three-year-old ram, a turtledove, and a young pigeon." Then he brought all these to Him and cut them in two, down the middle, and placed each piece opposite the other; but he did not cut the birds in two. And when the vultures came down on the carcasses, Abram drove them away. Now when the sun was going down, a deep sleep fell upon Abram; and behold, horror and great darkness fell upon him. Then He said to Abram: "<u>Know certainly that your descendants will be strangers in a land that is not theirs, and will serve them, and they will afflict them four hundred years</u>. And also the nation whom they serve I will judge; afterward they shall come out with great possessions. Now as for you, you shall go to your fathers in peace; you shall be buried at a good old age. <u>But in the fourth generation they shall return here</u>, <u>for the iniquity of the Amorites is not yet complete</u>."

And it came to pass, when the sun went down and it was dark, that behold, there appeared a smoking oven and a burning torch that passed between those pieces. On the same day the Lord made a covenant with Abram, saying: "To your descendants I have given this land, <u>from the river of Egypt to the great river</u>, <u>the River Euphrates</u> – the Kenites, the Kenezzites, the Kadmonites, the Hittites, the Perizzites, the Rephaim, the Amorites, the Canaanites, the Girgashites, and the Jebusites." (Gen 15:1-21)

Now Abraham was one hundred years old when his son Isaac was born to him. (Gen 21:5)

Paul talks about 430 years after the Covenant, the Lord tells Abraham about the 400 years of affliction, and the fourth generation will return. We know that Abraham was 100 years old, when his first true descendant,

Isaac was born. So it looks like the Covenant was made, when Abraham was 70 years old, but wouldn't it be nice to be sure? Let's ask Jasher!

It was <u>in the fifteenth year of Abram's dwelling in the land of Canaan</u>, which is the <u>seventieth year of the life of Abram</u>, the Lord appeared to Abram in that year and said to him, "I am the Lord who brought you out from Ur Casdim to give you this land for an inheritance, <u>from the river Mitzraim to the great river Euphrates</u>. And you shall come to your fathers in peace and in good age, and <u>the fourth generation shall return here</u> in this land and shall inherit it forever. And <u>Abram built an altar</u>, and he called on the name of the Lord who appeared to him, and <u>he brought up sacrifices on the altar to the Lord</u>.

(Jas 13:17-19)

At that time Abram returned and went to Haran to see his father and mother, and his father's household, and Abram and his wife and all belonging to him returned to Haran; <u>Abram lived in Haran five years</u>. And many of the people of Haran, <u>about seventy-two men, followed Abram and Abram taught them the instruction of the Lord and his ways, and he taught them to know the Lord</u>. In those days the Lord appeared to Abram in Haran, and He said to him, "Behold, <u>I spoke to you twenty years ago saying</u>, 'Go forth from your land, from your birth-place and from your father's house, to the land which I have shown you to give it to you and to your children, for there in that land I will bless you, and make you a great nation, and make your name great, and in you shall the families of the earth be blessed.' Now therefore arise, go forth from this place, you, your wife, and all belonging to you, also every one born in your house <u>and all the souls you have made in Haran</u>, and bring them out with you from here, and rise to return to the land of Canaan." And Abram arose and took his wife Sarai and all belonging to him and all that were born to him in his house <u>and the souls which they had made in Haran</u>, and they came out to go to the land of Canaan. Abram went and returned to the land of Canaan, according to the word of the Lord. And Lot the son of his brother Haran went with him; <u>Abram was seventy-five years old when he went forth from Haran to return to the land of Canaan</u>. And he came to the land of Canaan according to the word of the Lord to Abram, and he pitched his tent and he lived in the plain of Mamre, and with him was Lot his brother's son, and all belonging to him. And the Lord again appeared to Abram and said, "To your offspring I will give this land;" there he built an altar to the Lord who appeared to him, which is still to this day in the plains of Mamre. (Jas 13:20-28)

This is the second time that Abraham leaves Haran, and he brings seventy-two converts with him. Lot also comes with him along with Abram's servants and their offspring. Abram had stayed there for another five years and he was now seventy-five years old. Note that the Lord first spoke to Abraham when he was fifty-five years old. Looking at the Book of Genesis, this is where the story of Abraham begins in Genesis 12:1.

Now <u>the Lord had said</u> to Abram: "Get out of your country, from your family and from your father's house, to a land that I will show you. I will make you a great nation; I will bless you and make your name great; and you shall be a blessing. I will bless those who bless you, and I will curse him who curses you; and in you all the families of the earth shall be blessed." So Abram departed as the Lord had spoken to him, and Lot went with him. And Abram was seventy-five years old when he departed from Haran. Then Abram took Sarai his wife and Lot his brother's son, and all their possessions that they had gathered, and <u>the people whom they had acquired in Haran</u> (! the converts), and they departed to go to the land of Canaan. So they came to the land of Canaan. Abram passed through the land to the place of Shechem, as far as the terebinth tree of Moreh. And the Canaanites were then in the land. Then the Lord appeared to Abram and said, "To your descendants I will give this land." And there he built an altar to the Lord, who had appeared to him. (Gen 12:1-7)

By referring to Jasher, we can see that the sequence in Genesis is changed around a little, and that Genesis 15 actually happened five years before Genesis 12. Abraham was seventy years old when he received the promise and made the Covenant with the Lord.

-oOo-

Jannes and Jambres

<u>According to the Book of Jasher</u>

Moses and Aaron came to Egypt to the community of the children of Israel and spoke to them all the words of the Lord, and the people rejoiced a very great rejoicing. Moses and Aaron rose up early the next day and went to the house of Pharaoh, and they took in their hands the stick of God.

When they came to the king's gate, two young lions were confined there with iron instruments; no person went out or came in from before them, unless those whom the king ordered to come, when the conjurors came and withdrew the lions by their incantations, and this brought them to the king.

Moses hurried and lifted up the stick on the lions and loosed them, and Moses and Aaron came into the king's house. The lions also came with them in joy, and they followed them and rejoiced as a dog rejoices over his master when he comes from the field. When Pharaoh saw this thing he was astonished at it and was greatly terrified at the report, for their appearance was like the appearance of the children of God. And Pharaoh said to Moses, "What do you require?" And they answered him saying, "The Lord God of the Hebrews has sent us to you, to say, 'Send forth my people that they may serve Me.' "

When Pharaoh heard their words he was greatly terrified before them, and he said to them, "Go today and come back to me tomorrow." And they did according to the word of the king.

When they had gone Pharaoh sent for Balaam the magician and to Jannes and Jambres his sons and to all the magicians and conjurors and counselors which belonged to the king, they all came and sat before the king. And the king told them all the words which Moses and his brother Aaron had spoken to him; the magicians said to the king, "But how could the men come to you, on account of the lions which were confined at the gate?" The king said, "Because they lifted up their rod against the lions and loosed them, and came to me, and the lions also rejoiced as a dog rejoices to meet his master." Balaam the son of Beor, the magician answered the king saying, "There are none other than magicians like ourselves. So now send for them and let them come and we will try them," and the king did so.

In the morning Pharaoh sent for Moses and Aaron to come before the king, and they took the rod of God and came to the king and spoke to him saying, "Thus says the Lord God of the Hebrews, 'Send away My people that they may serve me.' " And the king said to them, "But who will believe you that you are the messengers of God and that you come to me by his order? Now therefore <u>give a wonder or sign in this matter</u>, and then the words which you speak will be believed."

Aaron hurried and threw the rod out of his hand before Pharaoh and before his servants, and the rod turned into a serpent. The sorcerers saw this and each man cast his rod on the ground and they became serpents. The serpent of Aaron's rod lifted up its head and opened its mouth to swallow the rods of the magicians. Balaam the magician answered and said, "This thing has been from the days of old that a serpent should swallow its fellow, and that living things devour each other."

"So now restore it to a rod as it was at first and we will also restore our rods as they were at first; if your rod shall swallow our rods we will know that the spirit of God is in you, and if not, you are only a magician like ourselves."

Aaron hurried and stretched forth his hand and caught hold of the serpent's tail and it became a rod in his hand; the sorcerers did the same with their rod and got hold each man of the tail of his serpent, and they became rods as at first. When they were restored to rods, the rod of Aaron swallowed up their rods. And when the king saw this thing, he ordered the book of records that related to the kings of Egypt to be brought; they brought the book of records, the chronicles of the kings of Egypt in which all the idols of Egypt were inscribed, for they thought they would find there the name of Jehovah, but they found it not. And Pharaoh said to Moses and Aaron, "Behold I have not found the name of your God written in this book, and <u>His name I do not know</u>." The counselors and wise men answered the king, "We have heard that the God of the Hebrews is a son of the wise, the son of ancient kings."

Pharaoh turned to Moses and Aaron and said to them, "I know not the Lord whom you have declared, neither will I send His people away." And they answered and said to the king, "The Lord God of Gods is His name; He proclaimed His name over us from the days of our ancestors and sent us, saying, "Go to Pharaoh and say to him, 'Send My people away that they may serve Me.' Now therefore send us, that we may take a journey for three days in the wilderness and there may sacrifice to Him, for from the days of our going down to Egypt, He has not taken from our hands either burnt offering, oblation or sacrifice; if you will not send us, His anger will be set ablaze against you and He will strike Egypt either with the plague or with the sword."

And Pharaoh said to them, "Tell me now His power and His might." They said to him, "He created the heaven and the earth, the seas and all their fish; He formed the light, created the darkness, caused rain on the earth and watered it, and made the herbage and grass to sprout; He created man and beast and the animals of the forest, the birds of the air and the fish of the sea, and by His mouth they live and die. Certainly He created you in your mother's womb and put into you the breath of life, and reared you and placed you on the royal throne of Egypt, and He will take your breath and soul from you and return you to the ground from where you were taken."

And the anger of the king was set ablaze at their words and he said to them, "But who among all the gods of nations can do this? My river is my own, and I have made it for myself." And he drove them from him; he ordered the labor on Israel to be more severe than it was yesterday and before. Moses and Aaron went out from the king's presence, and they saw the children of Israel in an evil condition for the taskmasters had made their labor extremely heavy.

Moses returned to the Lord and said, "Why have You ill-treated Your people? For since I came to speak to Pharaoh what You sent me for, he has greatly ill-used the children of Israel. The Lord said to Moses, "Look and you will see that with an outstretched hand and heavy plagues, Pharaoh will send the children of Israel from his land." And Moses and Aaron lived among their brothers the children of Israel in Egypt. As for the

Joseph B. Lumpkin

children of Israel the Egyptians embittered their lives with the heavy work which they imposed on them. (Jas 79:19-57)

And <u>at the end of two years</u>, the Lord again sent Moses to Pharaoh to bring forth the children of Israel, and to send them out of the land of Egypt. Moses went and came to the house of Pharaoh, and he spoke to him the words of the Lord who had sent him, but Pharaoh would not listen to the voice of the Lord; God roused His might in Egypt on Pharaoh and his subjects, and God struck Pharaoh and his people with very great and severe plagues. The Lord sent by the hand of Aaron and turned all the waters of Egypt into blood, with all their streams and rivers. And when an Egyptian came to drink and draw water, he looked into his pitcher, and behold all the water was turned into blood; when he came to drink from his cup the water in the cup became blood. And when a woman kneaded her dough and cooked her food, their appearance was turned to that of blood.

The Lord sent again and caused all their waters to bring forth frogs and all the frogs came into the houses of the Egyptians. And when the Egyptians drank, their bellies were filled with frogs and they danced in their bellies as they danced when in the river. All their drinking water and cooking water turned to frogs, also when they lay in their beds their perspiration bred frogs.

In spite of all this the anger of the Lord did not turn from them, and His hand was stretched out against all the Egyptians to strike them with every heavy plague. He sent and changed their dust to lice, and the lice became in Egypt to the height of two cubits on the earth. They lice were also very numerous in the flesh of man and beast, in all the inhabitants of Egypt; also on the king and queen the Lord sent the lice, and it grieved Egypt greatly on account of the lice.

Still the anger of the Lord did not turn away, and His hand was still stretched out over Egypt. And the Lord sent all kinds of beasts of the field into Egypt, and they came and destroyed all Egypt, man and beast, and trees and all things that were in Egypt. And the Lord sent fiery serpents, scorpions, mice, weasels, toads, together with others creeping in dust. Flies, hornets, fleas, bugs, <u>each swarm according to its kind</u>. And all reptiles and winged animals according to their kind came to Egypt and upset the Egyptians greatly. The fleas and flies came into the eyes and ears of the Egyptians. The hornet came on them and drove them away, and they removed from it into their inner rooms, and it pursued them. When the Egyptians hid themselves on account of the swarm of animals, they locked their doors after them, and God ordered the Sulanuth which was in the sea to come up and go into Egypt. She had long arms, ten cubits in length of the cubit of a man. And she went on the roofs and uncovered the raftering and flooring and cut them, and stretched forth her arm into the house and removed the lock and the bolt, and opened the houses of Egypt. Afterward came the swarm of animals into the houses of Egypt, and the swarm of animals destroyed the Egyptians, and it upset them greatly.

Still the anger of the Lord did not turn away from the Egyptians, and His hand was yet stretched forth against them. God sent the pestilence and the pestilence pervaded Egypt, in the horses and asses and in the camels, in herds of oxen and sheep and in man. When the Egyptians rose up early in the morning to take their cattle to pasture they found all their cattle dead. There remained of the cattle of the Egyptians only one in ten, and <u>of the cattle belonging to Israel in Goshen not one died</u>.

And God sent a burning inflammation in the flesh of the Egyptians, which burst their skins; it became a severe itch in all the Egyptians from the soles of their feet to the crowns of their heads. And many boils were in their flesh, that their flesh wasted away until they became rotten and putrid.

Still the anger of the Lord did not turn away, and His hand was still stretched out over all Egypt. And the Lord sent a very heavy hail, which struck their vines and broke their fruit trees and dried them up that they fell on them. Also every green herb became dry and perished, for a mingling fire descended with the hail, therefore the hail and the fire consumed all things. Also men and beasts that were found abroad perished of the flames of fire and of the hail, and all the young lions were exhausted.

And the Lord sent and brought numerous locusts into Egypt, the Chasel, Salom, Chargol, and Chagole, locusts each of its kind, which devoured all that the hail had left remaining. Then the Egyptians rejoiced at the locusts, although they consumed the produce of the field, and they caught them in abundance and salted them for food. And the Lord turned a mighty wind of the sea which took away all the locusts, even those that were salted, and thrust them into the Red Sea; not one locust remained within the boundaries of Egypt.

God sent darkness on Egypt, that the whole land of Egypt and Pathros became dark for three days so that a man could not see his hand when he lifted it to his mouth. At that time many of the people of Israel died who had rebelled against the Lord and who would not listen to Moses and Aaron, and believed not in them that God had sent them. And who had said, "We will not go forth from Egypt because we'll perish with hunger in a desolate wilderness." They were those who would not listen to the voice of Moses. The Lord plagued them in the three days of darkness, and the Israelites buried them in those days without the Egyptians knowing of them or rejoicing over them. The darkness was very great in Egypt for three days, and any person who was standing when the darkness came remained standing in his place; he that was sitting remained sitting, and he that was lying continued lying in the same state; he that was walking remained sitting on the ground in the same spot; and this thing happened to all the Egyptians until the darkness had passed away.

The days of darkness passed away and the Lord sent Moses and Aaron to the children of Israel saying, "Celebrate your feast and make your Passover, for behold I come in the middle of the night among all the Egyptians; I will strike all their firstborn, from the firstborn of a man to the firstborn of a beast, and when I see your Passover, I will pass over you." And the children of Israel did according to all that the Lord had commanded Moses and Aaron, thus did they in that night. It came to pass in the middle of the night that the Lord went forth in the midst of Egypt and struck all the firstborn of the Egyptians, from the firstborn of man to the firstborn of beast. And Pharaoh rose up in the night, he and all his servants and all the Egyptians, and there was a great cry throughout Egypt in that night for there was not a house in which there was not a corpse.

Also the likenesses of the firstborn of Egypt which were carved in the walls at their houses were destroyed and fell to the ground. Even the bones of their firstborn who had died before this and whom they had buried in their houses were raked up by the dogs of Egypt on that night and dragged before the Egyptians and cast before them. And all the Egyptians saw this evil which had suddenly come on them, and all the Egyptians cried out with a loud voice. And all the families of Egypt wept on that night, each man for his son and each man for his daughter, being the firstborn, and the tumult of Egypt was heard at a distance on that night. Bathia the daughter of Pharaoh went forth with the king on that night to seek Moses and Aaron in their houses; they found them in their houses eating and drinking and rejoicing with all Israel.

And Bathia said to Moses, "Is this the reward for the good which I have done to you, who have reared you and made you grow and prosper and you have brought this evil on me and my father's house?" And Moses said to her, "Certainly ten plagues did the Lord bring on Egypt; did any evil accrue to you from any of them? Did one of them affect you?" And she said, "No." And Moses said to her, "Although you are the firstborn to your mother, you shall not die and no evil shall reach you in the midst of Egypt." And she said, "What advantage is it to me when I see the king, my brother, and all his household and subjects in this evil, whose firstborn perish with all the firstborn of Egypt?"

And Moses said to her, "Certainly your brother and his household and subjects, the families of Egypt, would not listen to the words of the Lord, therefore did this evil come on them."

Pharaoh king of Egypt approached Moses and Aaron and some of the children of Israel who were with them in that place, and he prayed to them saying, "Rise up and take your brothers, all the children of Israel who are in the land with their sheep and oxen, and all belonging to them; they shall leave nothing remaining, only pray for me to the Lord your God." And Moses said to Pharaoh, "Behold you are your mother's firstborn, yet fear not for you will not die, for the Lord had commanded that you shall live in order to show you His great might and strong stretched out arm. Pharaoh ordered the children of Israel to be sent away, and all the Egyptians strengthened themselves to send them, for they said, "We are all perishing."

And all the Egyptians sent the Israelites forth with great riches, sheep and oxen and precious things according to the oath of the Lord between Him and our Father Abraham. And the children of Israel delayed going away until night, and when the Egyptians came to bring them out, they said to them, "Are we thieves, that we should go forth at night?" And the children of Israel asked of the Egyptians, vessels of silver and vessels of gold, and garments, and the children of Israel stripped the Egyptians. Moses hurried and rose up and went to the river of Egypt and brought up from there the coffin of Joseph and took it with him. The children of Israel also brought up each man his father's coffin with him, and each man the coffins of his tribe. (Jas 80:1-63)

According to the Book of Exodus

Afterward Moses and Aaron went in and told Pharaoh, "Thus says the Lord God of Israel: 'Let My people go, that they may hold a feast to Me in the wilderness.' " And Pharaoh said, "Who is the Lord, that I should obey His voice to let Israel go? I do not know the Lord, nor will I let Israel go." So they said, "The God of the Hebrews has met with us. Please, let us go three days' journey into the desert and sacrifice to the Lord our God, <u>lest He fall upon us with pestilence or with the sword.</u>"

Then the king of Egypt said to them, "Moses and Aaron, why do you take the people from their work? Get back to your labor." And Pharaoh said, "Look, the people of the land are many now, and you make them rest from their labor!" So the same day Pharaoh commanded the taskmasters of the people and their officers, saying, "You shall no longer give the people straw to make brick as before. Let them go and gather straw for themselves. And you shall lay on them the quota of bricks which they made before. You shall not reduce it. For they are idle; therefore they cry out, saying, 'Let us go and sacrifice to our God.' Let more work be laid on the men, that they may labor in it, and let them not regard false words." And the taskmasters of the people and their officers went out and spoke to the people, saying, "Thus says Pharaoh: 'I will not give you straw. Go, get yourselves straw where you can find it; yet none of your work will be reduced.' "

So the people were scattered abroad throughout all the land of Egypt to gather stubble instead of straw. And the taskmasters forced them to hurry, saying, "Fulfill your work, your daily quota, as when there was straw." Also the officers of the children of Israel, whom Pharaoh's taskmasters had set over them, were beaten and were asked, "Why have you not fulfilled your task in making brick both yesterday and today, as before?"

Then the officers of the children of Israel came and cried out to Pharaoh, saying, "Why are you dealing thus with your servants? There is no straw given to your servants, and they say to us, 'Make brick!' And indeed your servants are beaten, but the fault is in your own people." But he said, "You are idle! Idle! Therefore you say, 'Let us go and sacrifice to the Lord.' Therefore go now and work; for no straw shall be given you, yet you shall deliver the quota of bricks." And the officers of the children of Israel saw that they were in trouble after it was said, "You shall not reduce any bricks from your daily quota." Then, as they came from Pharaoh, they met Moses and Aaron who stood there to meet them. And they said to them, "Let the Lord look on you and judge, because you have made us abhorrent in the sight of Pharaoh and in the sight of his servants, to put a sword in their hand to kill us."

So Moses returned to the Lord and said, "Lord, why have You brought trouble on this people? Why is it You have sent me? For since I came to Pharaoh to speak in Your name, he has done evil to this people; neither have You delivered Your people at all." Then the Lord said to Moses, "Now you shall see what I will do to Pharaoh. For with a strong hand he will let them go, and with a strong hand he will drive them out of his land." And God spoke to Moses and said to him: "I am the LORD. I appeared to Abraham, to Isaac, and to Jacob, as God Almighty, but by My name LORD I was not known to them. I have also established My covenant with them, to give them the land of Canaan, the land of their pilgrimage, in which they were strangers. And I have also heard the groaning of the children of Israel whom the Egyptians keep in bondage, and I have remembered My covenant. Therefore say to the children of Israel: 'I am the LORD; I will bring you out from under the burdens of the Egyptians, I will rescue you from their bondage, and <u>I will redeem you with an outstretched arm and with great judgments</u>. <u>I will take you as My people, and I will be your God</u>. Then you shall know that I am the LORD your God who brings you out from under the burdens of the Egyptians. And <u>I will bring you into the land which I swore to give to Abraham, Isaac, and Jacob</u>; and <u>I will give it to you as a heritage</u>: I am the LORD.' " So Moses spoke thus to the children of Israel; but they did not heed Moses, because of anguish of spirit and cruel bondage.

And the Lord spoke to Moses, saying, "Go in, tell Pharaoh king of Egypt to let the children of Israel go out of his land." And Moses spoke before the Lord, saying, "The children of Israel have not heeded me. How then shall Pharaoh heed me, for I am of uncircumcised lips?" Then the Lord spoke to Moses and Aaron, and gave them a command for the children of Israel and for Pharaoh king of Egypt, to bring the children of Israel out of the land of Egypt. (Exo 5:1-6:13)

And it came to pass, on the day the Lord spoke to Moses in the land of Egypt, that the Lord spoke to Moses, saying, "I am the LORD. Speak to Pharaoh king of Egypt all that I say to you." But Moses said before the Lord, "Behold, I am of uncircumcised lips, and how shall Pharaoh heed me?" So the Lord said to Moses: "See, I have made you as God to Pharaoh, and Aaron your brother shall be your prophet. You shall speak all that I command you. And Aaron your brother shall tell Pharaoh to send the children of Israel out of his land. And I will harden Pharaoh's heart, and multiply My signs and My wonders in the land of Egypt."

"But Pharaoh will not heed you, so that I may lay My hand on Egypt and bring My armies and My people, the children of Israel, out of the land of Egypt by great judgments. And the Egyptians shall know that I am the LORD, when I stretch out My hand on Egypt and bring out the children of Israel from among them." Then Moses and Aaron did so; just as the Lord commanded them, so they did. And Moses was eighty years old and Aaron eighty-three years old when they spoke to Pharaoh. (Exo 6:28-7:7)

Then the Lord spoke to Moses and Aaron, saying, "When Pharaoh speaks to you, saying, "Show a miracle for yourselves,' then you shall say to Aaron, 'Take your rod and cast it before Pharaoh, and let it become a serpent.' " So Moses and Aaron went into Pharaoh, and they did so, just as the Lord commanded. And Aaron cast down his rod before Pharaoh and before his servants, and it became a serpent. But Pharaoh also called the wise men and the sorcerers; so the magicians of Egypt, they also did in like manner with their enchantments. For every man threw down his rod, and they became serpents. But Aaron's rod swallowed up their rods. And Pharaoh's heart grew hard, and he did not heed them, as the Lord had said.

So the Lord said to Moses: "Pharaoh's heart is hard; he refuses to let the people go. Go to Pharaoh in the morning, when he goes out to the water, and you shall stand by the river's bank to meet him; and the rod which was turned to a serpent you shall take in your hand. And you shall say to him, 'The Lord God of the Hebrews has sent me to you, saying, "Let My people go, that they may serve Me in the wilderness"; but indeed, until now you would not hear! Thus says the Lord: "By this you shall know that I am the Lord. Behold, I will strike the waters which are in the river with the rod that is in my hand, and they shall be turned to blood. And the fish that are in the river shall die, the river shall stink, and the Egyptians will loathe to drink the water of the river." ' "

Then the Lord spoke to Moses, "Say to Aaron, 'Take your rod and stretch out your hand over the waters of Egypt, over their streams, over their rivers, over their ponds, and over all their pools of water, that they may become blood. And there shall be blood throughout all the land of Egypt, both in buckets of wood and pitchers of stone.' "

And Moses and Aaron did so, just as the Lord commanded. So he lifted up the rod and struck the waters that were in the river, in the sight of Pharaoh and in the sight of his servants. And all the waters that were in the river turned to blood. The fish that were in the river died, the river stank, and the Egyptians could not drink the water of the river. So there was blood throughout all the land of Egypt. Then the magicians of Egypt did so with their enchantments; and Pharaoh's heart grew hard, and he did not heed them, as the Lord had said. And Pharaoh turned and went into his house. Neither was his heart moved by this. So all the Egyptians dug all around the river for water to drink, because they could not drink the water of the river. And seven days passed after the Lord had struck the river. (Exo 7:8-25)

And the Lord spoke to Moses, "Go to Pharaoh and say to him, 'Thus says the Lord: "Let My people go, that they may serve Me. But if you refuse to let them go, behold, I will smite all your territory with frogs. So the river shall bring forth frogs abundantly, which shall go up and come into your house, into your bedroom, on your bed, into the houses of your servants, on your people, into your ovens, and into your kneading bowls. And the frogs shall come up on you, on your people, and on your servants." ' "

Then the Lord spoke to Moses, "Say to Aaron, 'Stretch out your hand with your rod over the streams, over the rivers, and over the ponds, and cause frogs to come up on the land of Egypt.' " So Aaron stretched out his hand over the waters of Egypt, and the frogs came up and covered the land of Egypt. And the magicians did so with their enchantments, and brought up

<u>frogs on the land of Egypt</u>. Then Pharaoh called for Moses and Aaron, and said, "Entreat the Lord that He may take away the frogs from me and from my people; and I will let the people go, that they may sacrifice to the Lord." And Moses said to Pharaoh, "Accept the honor of saying when I shall intercede for you, for your servants, and for your people, to destroy the frogs from you and your houses, that they may remain in the river only." So he said, "Tomorrow." And he said, "Let it be according to your word, that you may know that there is no one like the Lord our God. And the frogs shall depart from you, from your houses, from your servants, and from your people. They shall remain in the river only."

Then Moses and Aaron went out from Pharaoh. And Moses cried out to the Lord concerning the frogs which He had brought against Pharaoh. So the Lord did according to the word of Moses. And the frogs died out of the fields. They gathered them together in heaps, and the land stank. But when Pharaoh saw that there was relief, he hardened his heart and did not heed them, as the Lord had said. (Exo 8:1-15)

So the Lord said to Moses, "Say to Aaron, 'Stretch out your rod, and strike the dust of the land, so that it may become lice throughout all the land of Egypt.'" And they did so. For Aaron stretched out his hand with his rod and struck the dust of the earth, and it became lice on man and beast. All the dust of the land became lice throughout all the land of Egypt. Now <u>the magicians so worked with their enchantments to bring forth lice, but they could not</u>. So there were lice on man and beast. Then <u>the magicians said to Pharaoh</u>, "<u>This is the finger of God.</u>" But Pharaoh's heart grew hard, and he did not heed them, just as the Lord had said. (Exo 8:16-19)

The separation of the peoples

And the Lord said to Moses, "Rise early in the morning and stand before Pharaoh as he comes out to the water. Then say to him, 'Thus says the Lord: "Let My people go, that they may serve Me. Or else, if you will not let My people go, behold, I will send <u>swarms</u> of flies on you and your servants, on your people and into your houses. The houses of the Egyptians shall be <u>full of swarms</u> of flies, and also the ground on which they stand. And in that day I will set apart the land of Goshen, in which My people dwell, that <u>no swarms</u> of flies <u>shall be there,</u> <u>in order that you may know that I am the LORD</u> in the midst of the land. <u>I will make a</u>

difference between My people and your people. Tomorrow this sign shall be." ' "

And the Lord did so. Thick swarms of flies came into the house of Pharaoh, into his servants' houses, and into all the land of Egypt. The land was corrupted because of the swarms of flies. Then Pharaoh called for Moses and Aaron, and said, "Go, sacrifice to your God in the land." And Moses said, "It is not right to do so, for we would be sacrificing the abomination of the Egyptians to the Lord our God. If we sacrifice the abomination of the Egyptians before their eyes, then will they not stone us? We will go three days' journey into the wilderness and sacrifice to the Lord our God as He will command us."

So Pharaoh said, "I will let you go, that you may sacrifice to the Lord your God in the wilderness; only you shall not go very far away. Intercede for me." Then Moses said, "Indeed I am going out from you, and I will entreat the Lord, that the swarms of flies may depart tomorrow from Pharaoh, from his servants, and from his people. But let Pharaoh not deal deceitfully anymore in not letting the people go to sacrifice to the Lord." So Moses went out from Pharaoh and entreated the Lord. And the Lord did according to the word of Moses; He removed the swarms of flies from Pharaoh, from his servants, and from his people. Not one remained. But Pharaoh hardened his heart at this time also; neither would he let the people go. (Exo 8:20-32)

Then the Lord said to Moses, "Go in to Pharaoh and tell him, 'Thus says the Lord God of the Hebrews: "Let My people go, that they may serve Me. For if you refuse to let them go, and still hold them, behold, the hand of the Lord will be on your cattle in the field, on the horses, on the donkeys, on the camels, on the oxen, and on the sheep - a very severe pestilence. And the Lord will make a difference between the livestock of Israel and the livestock of Egypt. So nothing shall die of all that belongs to the children of Israel." ' "

Then the Lord appointed a set time, saying, "Tomorrow the Lord will do this thing in the land." So the Lord did this thing on the next day, and all the livestock of Egypt died; but of the livestock of the children of Israel, not one died. Then Pharaoh sent, and indeed, not even one of the livestock of the Israelites was dead. But the heart of Pharaoh became hard, and he did not let the people go. (Exo 9:1-7)

So the Lord said to Moses and Aaron, "Take for yourselves handfuls of ashes from a furnace, and let Moses scatter it toward the heavens in the sight of Pharaoh. And it will become fine dust in all the land of Egypt, and it will cause boils that break out in sores on man and beast throughout all the land of Egypt." Then they took ashes from the furnace and stood before Pharaoh, and Moses scattered them toward heaven. And they caused boils that break out in sores on man and beast.

And <u>the magicians could not stand before Moses because of the boils</u>, for the boils were on the magicians and on all the Egyptians. But the Lord hardened the heart of Pharaoh; and he did not heed them, just as the Lord had spoken to Moses. (Exo 9:8-12)

Then the Lord said to Moses, "Rise early in the morning and stand before Pharaoh, and say to him, 'Thus says the Lord God of the Hebrews: "Let My people go, that they may serve Me, for at this time I will send all My plagues to your very heart, and on your servants and on your people, that you may know that there is none like Me in all the earth. Now if I had stretched out My hand and struck you and your people with pestilence, then you would have been cut off from the earth. But indeed for this purpose I have raised you up, <u>that I may show My power in you, and that My name may be declared in all the earth</u>. As yet you exalt yourself against My people in that you will not let them go. Behold, tomorrow about this time I will cause very heavy hail to rain down, such as has not been in Egypt since its founding until now. Therefore send now and gather your livestock and all that you have in the field, for the hail shall come down on every man and every animal which is found in the field and is not brought home; and they shall die." ' "

He who feared the word of the Lord among the servants of Pharaoh made his servants and his livestock flee to the houses. But he who did not regard the word of the Lord left his servants and his livestock in the field. Then the Lord said to Moses, "Stretch out your hand toward heaven, that there may be hail in all the land of Egypt - on man, on beast, and on every herb of the field, throughout the land of Egypt."

And Moses stretched out his rod toward heaven; and the Lord sent thunder and hail, and fire darted to the ground. And the Lord rained hail on the land of Egypt. So there was hail, and fire mingled with the hail, so very heavy that there was none like it in all the land of Egypt since it became a nation. And the hail struck throughout the whole land of Egypt, all that was in the field, both man and beast; and the hail struck every herb of the field and broke every tree of the field.

Only in the land of Goshen, where the children of Israel were, there was no hail. And Pharaoh sent and called for Moses and Aaron, and said to them, "I have sinned this time. The Lord is righteous, and my people and I are wicked. Entreat the Lord, that there may be no more mighty thundering and hail, for it is enough. I will let you go, and you shall stay no longer." So Moses said to him, "As soon as I have gone out of the city, I will spread out my hands to the Lord; the thunder will cease, and there will be no more hail, that you may know that the earth is the Lord's. But as for you and your servants, I know that you will not yet fear the Lord God."

Now the flax and the barley were struck, for the barley was in the head and the flax was in bud. But the wheat and the spelt were not struck, for they are late crops. So Moses went out of the city from Pharaoh and spread out his hands to the Lord; then the thunder and the hail ceased, and the rain was not poured on the earth. And when Pharaoh saw that the rain, the hail, and the thunder had ceased, he sinned yet more; and he hardened his heart, he and his servants. So the heart of Pharaoh was hard; neither would he let the children of Israel go, as the Lord had spoken by Moses. (Exo 9:13-35)

Now the Lord said to Moses, "Go in to Pharaoh; for I have hardened his heart and the hearts of his servants, that I may show these signs of Mine before him, and that you may tell in the hearing of your son and your son's son the mighty things I have done in Egypt, and My signs which I have done among them, that you may know that I am the LORD." So Moses and Aaron came in to Pharaoh and said to him, "Thus says the Lord God of the Hebrews: 'How long will you refuse to humble yourself before Me? Let My people go, that they may serve Me. Or else, if you refuse to let My people go, behold, tomorrow I will bring locusts into your territory. And they shall cover the face of the earth, so that no one will be able to see the earth; and they shall eat the residue of what is left, which remains to you from the hail, and they shall eat every tree which grows up for you out of the field. They shall fill your houses, the houses of all your servants, and the houses of all the Egyptians - which neither your fathers nor your fathers' fathers have seen, since the day that they were on the earth to this day.' " And he turned and went out from Pharaoh.

Then Pharaoh's servants said to him, "How long shall this man be a snare to us? Let the men go, that they may serve the Lord their God. Do you not yet know that Egypt is destroyed?" So Moses and Aaron were brought again to Pharaoh, and he said to them, "Go, serve the Lord your God. Who are the ones that are going?" And Moses said, "We will go with our young and our old; with our sons and our daughters, with our flocks and our herds we will go, for we must hold a feast to the Lord." Then he said to them, "The Lord had better be with you when I let you and your little ones go! Beware, for evil is ahead of you. Not so! Go now, you who are men, and serve the Lord, for that is what you desired." And they were driven out from Pharaoh's presence.

Then the Lord said to Moses, "Stretch out your hand over the land of Egypt for the locusts, that they may come upon the land of Egypt, and eat every herb of the land - all that the hail has left." So Moses stretched out his rod over the land of Egypt, and the Lord brought an east wind on the land all that day and all that night. When it was morning, the east wind brought the locusts. And the locusts went up over all the land of Egypt and rested on all the territory of Egypt. They were very severe; previously there had been no such locusts as they, nor shall there be such after them. For they covered the face of the whole earth, so that the land was darkened; and they ate every herb of the land and all the fruit of the trees which the hail had left. So there remained nothing green on the trees or on the plants of the field throughout all the land of Egypt.

Then Pharaoh called for Moses and Aaron in haste, and said, "I have sinned against the Lord your God and against you. Now therefore, please forgive my sin only this once, and entreat the Lord your God, that He may take away from me this death only." So he went out from Pharaoh and entreated the Lord. And the Lord turned a very strong west wind, which took the locusts away and blew them into the Red Sea. There remained not one locust in all the territory of Egypt. But the Lord hardened Pharaoh's heart, and he did not let the children of Israel go. (Exo 10:1-20)

Then the Lord said to Moses, "Stretch out your hand toward heaven, that there may be darkness over the land of Egypt, darkness which may even be felt." So Moses stretched out his hand toward heaven, and <u>there was thick darkness in all the land of Egypt three days. They did not see one</u>

another; nor did anyone rise from his place for three days. But all the children of Israel had light in their dwellings.

Then Pharaoh called to Moses and said, "Go, serve the Lord; only let your flocks and your herds be kept back. Let your little ones also go with you." But Moses said, "You must also give us sacrifices and burnt offerings, that we may sacrifice to the Lord our God. Our livestock also shall go with us; not a hoof shall be left behind. For we must take some of them to serve the Lord our God, and even we do not know with what we must serve the Lord until we arrive there." But the Lord hardened Pharaoh's heart, and he would not let them go. Then Pharaoh said to him, "Get away from me! Take heed to yourself and see my face no more! For in the day you see my face you shall die!" So Moses said, "You have spoken well. I will never see your face again." (Exo 10:21-29)

And the Lord said to Moses, "I will bring one more plague on Pharaoh and on Egypt. Afterward he will let you go from here. When he lets you go, he will surely drive you out of here altogether. Speak now in the hearing of the people, and let every man ask from his neighbor and every woman from her neighbor, articles of silver and articles of gold." And the Lord gave the people favor in the sight of the Egyptians. Moreover the man Moses was very great in the land of Egypt, in the sight of Pharaoh's servants and in the sight of the people. Then Moses said, "Thus says the Lord: 'About midnight I will go out into the midst of Egypt; and all the firstborn in the land of Egypt shall die, from the firstborn of Pharaoh who sits on his throne, even to the firstborn of the female servant who is behind the handmill, and all the firstborn of the animals. Then there shall be a great cry throughout all the land of Egypt, such as was not like it before, nor shall be like it again. But against none of the children of Israel shall a dog move its tongue, against man or beast, that you may know that the Lord does make a difference between the Egyptians and Israel.' And all these your servants shall come down to me and bow down to me, saying, 'Get out, and all the people who follow you!' After that I will go out."

Then he went out from Pharaoh in great anger. But the Lord said to Moses, "Pharaoh will not heed you, so that My wonders may be multiplied in the land of Egypt." So Moses and Aaron did all these wonders before Pharaoh; and the Lord hardened Pharaoh's heart, and he did not let the children of Israel go out of his land. (Exo 11:1-10)

Now the Lord spoke to Moses and Aaron in the land of Egypt, saying, "This month shall be your beginning of months; it shall be the first month of the year to you. Speak to all the congregation of Israel, saying: 'On the tenth of this month every man shall take for himself a lamb, according to the house of his father, a lamb for a household. And if the household is too small for the lamb, let him and his neighbor next to his house take it according to the number of the persons; according to each man's need you shall make your count for the lamb. Your lamb shall be without blemish, a male of the first year. You may take it from the sheep or from the goats. Now you shall keep it until the fourteenth day of the same month. Then the whole assembly of the congregation of Israel shall kill it at twilight. And they shall take some of the blood and put it on the two doorposts and on the lintel of the houses where they eat it. Then they shall eat the flesh on that night; roasted in fire, with unleavened bread and with bitter herbs they shall eat it. Do not eat it raw, nor boiled at all with water, but roasted in fire – its head with its legs and its entrails. You shall let none of it remain until morning, and what remains of it until morning you shall burn with fire. And thus you shall eat it: with a belt on your waist, your sandals on your feet, and your staff in your hand. So you shall eat it in haste. It is the Lord's Passover.'

'For I will pass through the land of Egypt on that night, and will strike all the firstborn in the land of Egypt, both man and beast; and against all the gods of Egypt I will execute judgment: I am the LORD. Now the blood shall be a sign for you on the houses where you are. And when I see the blood, I will pass over you; and the plague shall not be on you to destroy you when I strike the land of Egypt. So this day shall be to you a memorial; and you shall keep it as a feast to the Lord throughout your generations. You shall keep it as a feast by an everlasting ordinance. Seven days you shall eat unleavened bread. On the first day you shall remove leaven from your houses. For whoever eats leavened bread from that first day until the seventh day, that person shall be cut off from Israel. On the first day there shall be a holy convocation for you. No manner of work shall be done on them; but that which everyone must eat – that only may be prepared by you. So you shall observe the Feast of Unleavened Bread, for on this same day I will have brought your armies out of the land of Egypt. Therefore you shall observe this day throughout your generations as an everlasting ordinance. In the first month, on the fourteenth day of the month at evening, you shall eat unleavened bread, until the twenty-first day of the month at evening. For seven days no leaven shall be found in your houses, since whoever eats what is leavened, that same person shall be cut off from the congregation of Israel, whether he is a stranger or a native of the land. You shall eat nothing leavened; in all your dwellings you shall eat unleavened bread.' "

Then Moses called for all the elders of Israel and said to them, "Pick out and take lambs for yourselves according to your families, and kill the Passover lamb. And you shall take a bunch of hyssop, dip it in the blood that is in the basin, and <u>strike the lintel and the two doorposts with the blood</u> that is in the basin. And none of you shall go out of the door of his house until morning. For the Lord will pass through to strike the Egyptians; and when He sees the blood on the lintel and on the two doorposts, <u>the Lord will pass over the door and not allow the destroyer to come into your houses to strike you</u>. And you shall observe this thing as an ordinance for you and your sons forever. It will come to pass when you come to the land which the Lord will give you, just as He promised, that you shall keep this service. And it shall be, when your children say to you, 'What do you mean by this service?' that you shall say, 'It is the Passover sacrifice of the Lord, who passed over the houses of the children of Israel in Egypt when He struck the Egyptians and delivered our households.' " So the people bowed their heads and worshiped. Then the children of Israel went away and did so; just as the Lord had commanded Moses and Aaron, so they did. (Exo 12:1-28)

And it came to pass at midnight that the Lord struck all the firstborn in the land of Egypt, from the firstborn of Pharaoh who sat on his throne to the firstborn of the captive who was in the dungeon, and all the firstborn of livestock. So Pharaoh rose in the night, he, all his servants, and all the Egyptians; and there was a great cry in Egypt, for there was not a house where there was not one dead. (Exo 12:29-30)

Then he called for Moses and Aaron by night, and said, "Rise, go out from among my people, both you and the children of Israel. And go, serve the Lord as you have said. Also take your flocks and your herds, as you have said, and be gone; and bless me also." And the Egyptians urged the people, that they might send them out of the land in haste. For they said, "We shall all be dead." So the people took their dough before it was leavened, having their kneading bowls bound up in their clothes on their shoulders.

Now the children of Israel had done according to the word of Moses, and they had asked from the Egyptians articles of silver, articles of gold, and clothing. And the Lord had given the people favor in the sight of the Egyptians, so that they granted them what they requested. Thus they plundered the Egyptians. Then the children of Israel journeyed from Rameses to Succoth, about six hundred thousand men on foot, besides children. <u>A mixed multitude went up with them also</u>, and flocks and herds – a great deal of livestock. And <u>they baked unleavened cakes of the dough which they had brought out of Egypt</u>; for it was not leavened, because they were driven out of Egypt and could not wait, <u>nor had they prepared provisions for themselves</u>. Now the sojourn of the children of Israel who lived in Egypt was four hundred and thirty years – <u>on that very same day</u> – it came to pass that all the armies of the Lord went out from the land of Egypt. <u>It is a night</u> of solemn observance to the Lord for bringing them out of the land of Egypt. This is that <u>night of the Lord</u>, a solemn observance for all the children of Israel throughout their generations. (Exo 12:31-42)

Therefore thus says the Lord God of hosts: "O My people, who dwell in Zion, do not be afraid of the Assyrian. <u>He shall strike you with a rod and lift up his staff against you, in the manner of Egypt</u>. For yet a little while and the indignation will cease, as will My anger in their destruction." And the Lord of hosts will stir up a scourge for him like the slaughter of Midian at the rock of Oreb; <u>as His rod was on the sea, so will He lift it up in the manner of Egypt</u>. It shall come to pass in that day that his burden will be taken away from your shoulder, and his yoke from your neck, and the yoke will be destroyed because of the anointing oil. (Isa 10:24-27)

There shall come forth <u>a Rod from the stem of Jesse, and a Branch shall grow out of his roots</u>. The Spirit of the Lord shall rest upon Him, the Spirit of wisdom and understanding, the Spirit of counsel and might, the Spirit of knowledge and of the fear of the Lord. His delight is in the fear of the Lord, and He shall not judge by the sight of His eyes, nor decide by the hearing of His ears; but with righteousness He shall judge the poor, and decide with equity for the meek of the earth; <u>He shall strike the earth with the rod of His mouth, and with the breath of His lips He shall slay the wicked</u>. Righteousness shall be the belt of His loins, and faithfulness the belt of His waist.

(Isa 11:1-5)

"And in that day there shall be <u>a Root of Jesse</u>, who shall stand as a banner to the people; for <u>the Gentiles shall seek Him, and His resting place shall be glorious</u>."

It shall come to pass in that day that <u>the Lord shall set His hand again the second time to recover the remnant of His people who are left</u>, from Assyria and Egypt, from Pathros and Cush, from Elam and Shinar, from Hamath and the islands of the sea.

He will set up a banner <u>for the nations</u>, and will assemble the outcasts of Israel, and gather together the dispersed of Judah <u>from the four corners of the earth</u>. Also the envy of Ephraim shall depart, and the adversaries of Judah shall be cut off; Ephraim shall not envy Judah, and Judah shall not harass Ephraim. But they shall fly down upon the shoulder of the Philistines toward the west; together they shall plunder the people of the East; they shall lay their hand on Edom and Moab; and the people of Ammon shall obey them. The Lord will utterly destroy the tongue of the Sea of Egypt; with His mighty wind He will shake His fist over the River, and strike it in the seven streams, and make men cross over dry-shod.

There will be a highway <u>for the remnant of His people</u> who will be left from Assyria, <u>as it was for Israel in the day that he came up from the land of Egypt</u>. (Isa 11:10-16)

And in that day you will say: "O Lord, I will praise You; though You were angry with me, Your anger is turned away, and You comfort me. Behold, <u>God is my salvation</u>, I will trust and not be afraid; 'For Yah, the Lord, is my strength and song; <u>He also has become my salvation</u>.' " <u>Therefore with joy you will draw water from the wells of salvation</u>. And in that day you will say: "Praise the Lord, call upon His name; <u>declare His deeds among the peoples, make mention that His name is exalted</u>. Sing to the Lord, for He has done excellent things; this is known in all the earth. Cry out and shout, O inhabitant of Zion, for great is the Holy One of Israel in your midst!" (Isa 12:1-6)

"Behold, the days are coming," says the Lord, "that <u>I will raise to David a Branch of righteousness; a King shall reign and prosper, and execute judgment and righteousness in the earth</u>. In His days Judah will be saved, and Israel will dwell safely; now this is His name by which He will be called: THE LORD OUR RIGHTEOUSNESS. Therefore, behold, the days are coming," says the Lord, "that they shall no longer say, 'As the Lord lives who brought up the children of Israel from the land of Egypt,' but,

'As the Lord lives who brought up and led the descendants of the house of Israel from the north country and from all the countries where I had driven them.' And they shall dwell in their own land." (Jer 23:5-8)

Moreover the word of the Lord came to Jeremiah a second time, while he was still shut up in the court of the prison, saying, "Thus says the Lord who made it, the Lord who formed it to establish it (the Lord is His name): 'Call to Me, and I will answer you, and show you great and mighty things, which you do not know.' For thus says the Lord, the God of Israel, concerning the houses of this city and the houses of the kings of Judah, which have been pulled down to fortify against the siege mounds and the sword: 'They come to fight the Chaldeans, but <u>only to fill their places with the dead bodies of men whom I will slay in My anger and My fury, all for whose wickedness I have hidden My face from this city</u>. Behold, I will bring it health and healing; I will heal them and reveal to them the abundance of peace and truth. And I will cause the captives of Judah and the captives of Israel to return, and <u>will rebuild those places as at the first</u>. I will cleanse them from all their iniquity by which they have sinned against Me, and I will pardon all their iniquities by which they have sinned and by which they have transgressed against Me.'

<u>'Then it shall be to Me a name of joy, a praise, and an honor before all nations of the earth</u>, who shall hear all the good that I do to them; they shall fear and tremble for all the goodness and all the prosperity that I provide for it.' Thus says the Lord: 'Again there shall be heard in this place - of which you say, "It is desolate, without man and without beast" - in the cities of Judah, in the streets of Jerusalem that are desolate, without man and without inhabitant and without beast, the voice of joy and the voice of gladness, the voice of the bridegroom and the voice of the bride, the voice of those who will say: "<u>Praise the Lord of hosts, for the Lord is good, for His mercy endures forever</u>" - and <u>of those who will bring the sacrifice of praise into the house of the Lord</u>. For I will cause the captives of the land to return as at the first,' says the Lord.

Thus says the Lord of Hosts: 'In this place which is desolate, without man and without beast, and in all its cities, there shall again be a dwelling place of shepherds causing their flocks to lie down. In the cities of the mountains, in the cities of the lowland, in the cities of the South, in the land of Benjamin, in the places around Jerusalem, and in the cities of Judah, the flocks shall again pass under the hands of him who counts them,' says the Lord. 'Behold the days are coming,' says the Lord, 'that I will perform that good thing which I have promised to the house of Israel and to the house of Judah: In those days and at that time <u>I will cause to grow up to David a Branch of righteousness; He shall execute judgment and righteousness in the earth</u>. In those days Judah will be saved, and Jerusalem will dwell safely. And this is the name by which she will be called: THE LORD OUR RIGHTEOUSNESS.' For thus says the Lord: 'David shall never lack a man to sit on the throne of the house of Israel; nor shall the priests, the Levites, lack a man to offer burnt offerings before Me, to kindle grain offerings, and to sacrifice continually.' " (Jer 33:1-16)

"I, Jesus, have sent My angel to testify to you these things in the churches. <u>I am the Root and the Offspring of David</u>, the Bright and Morning Star." And the Spirit and the bride say, "Come!" And let him who hears say, "Come!" And let him who thirsts come. Whoever desires, let him take the water of life freely. (Rev 22:16-17)

Good Advice

You therefore, my son, be strong in the grace that is in Christ Jesus. And the things that you have heard from me among many witnesses, commit these to faithful men who will be able to teach others also. You therefore must endure hardship as a good soldier of Jesus Christ. No one engaged in warfare entangles himself with the affairs of this life, that he may please him who enlisted him as a soldier. And also if anyone competes in athletics, he is not crowned unless he competes according to the rules. The hardworking farmer must be first to partake of the crops. Consider what I say, and may the Lord give you understanding in all things. Remember that <u>Jesus Christ, of the seed of David, was raised from the dead</u> according to my gospel, for which I suffer trouble as an evildoer, even to the point of chains; but the word of God is not chained. Therefore I endure all things for the sake of the elect, that they also may obtain the salvation which is in Christ Jesus with eternal glory. This is a faithful saying:

For if we died with Him, we shall also live with Him.

If we endure, we shall also reign with Him.

If we deny Him, He also will deny us.

If we are faithless, He remains faithful;

He cannot deny Himself.

Remind them of these things, charging them before the Lord not to strive about words to no profit, to the ruin of the hearers. Be diligent to present yourself approved to God, a worker who does not need to be ashamed, rightly dividing the word of truth. But shun profane and idle babblings, for they will increase to more ungodliness. And their message will spread like cancer. Hymenaeus and Philetus are of this sort, who have strayed concerning the truth, saying that the resurrection is already past; and they overthrow the faith of some. Nevertheless the solid foundation of God stands, having this seal: "<u>The Lord knows those who are His</u>," and, "<u>Let everyone who names the name of Christ depart from iniquity</u>."

<u>But in a great house there are not only vessels of gold and silver, but also of wood and clay,</u> some for honor and some for dishonor. Therefore if anyone cleanses himself from the latter, he will be a vessel for honor, sanctified and useful for the Master, prepared for every good work. Flee also youthful lusts; but pursue righteousness, faith, love, peace with those who call on the Lord out of a pure heart. But avoid foolish and ignorant disputes, knowing that they generate strife.

And a servant of the Lord must not quarrel but be gentle to all, able to teach, patient, in humility correcting those who are in opposition, if God perhaps will grant them repentance, so that they may know the truth, and that they may come to their senses and escape the snare of the devil, having been taken captive by him to do his will.

But know this, that in the last days perilous times will come: For men will be lovers of themselves, lovers of money, boasters, proud, blasphemers, disobedient to parents, unthankful, unholy, unloving, unforgiving, slanderers, without self-control, brutal, despisers of good, traitors, headstrong, haughty, lovers of pleasure rather than lovers of God, having a form of godliness but denying its power. And from such people turn away! For of this sort are those who creep into households and make captives of gullible women loaded down with sins, led away by various lusts, always learning and never able to come to the knowledge of the truth. Now <u>as Jannes and Jambres resisted Moses,</u> <u>so do these also resist the truth:</u> <u>men of corrupt minds,</u> disapproved concerning the faith; but they will progress no further, for their folly will be manifest to all, as theirs also was.

(2Ti 2:1-3:9)

Summary

"Why so many pages?" You may ask. "Well, I'm glad you asked that question!"

Firstly, congratulations on reading all these pages. It is quite a lot of scripture for one to absorb but one has to read all the scripture, to understand what I'm going to try and explain. Did you notice how the account in Jasher supports Exodus?

Paul says, "There is a natural body, and there is a spiritual body:

And so it is written, "The first man Adam became a living being." The last Adam became a life-giving spirit. However, the spiritual is not first, but the natural, and afterward the spiritual. The first man was of the earth, made of dust; the second Man is the Lord from heaven. As was the man of dust, so also are those who are made of dust; and as is the heavenly Man, so also are those who are heavenly. And as we have borne the image of the man of dust, we shall also bear the image of the heavenly Man." (1Co 15:44-49)

Also the Warning:

Therefore we must give the more earnest heed to the things we have heard, lest we drift away. For if the word spoken through angels proved steadfast, and every transgression and disobedience received a just reward, how shall we escape if we neglect so great a salvation, which at the first began to be spoken by the Lord, and was confirmed to us by those who heard Him, God also bearing witness both with signs and wonders, with various miracles, and gifts of the Holy Spirit, according to His own will? For He has not put <u>the world to come</u>, of which we speak, in subjection to angels.

(Heb 2:1-5)

God sees all of Time, from the beginning to the end, together; and the Bible is written with this same mindset. We have to realise that it is written as a whole, a testament to Jesus Christ. Who, was from the Beginning The Lamb set aside on the first day, to redeem Man from the Sin which would enter this world by his hand. Jesus was born as a man, on the fourth day. Four thousand years after Adam. He was sacrificed on the cross by the multitude, and His blood was shed to Redeem us from Sin, and Save us from the lake of fire, in the Day of Judgment to come.

Today we are living in a spiritual Egypt, our taskmasters are Umusdudis and Umusdudat. These taskmasters make us work till we drop! There are another two taskmasters; who are self appointed. They present themselves after we have trained our minds in the ways of Egypt; Imushavdis and Imushavdat. Bowing to these taskmasters keeps our minds focussed, away from the truth of God's Word.

It is only after careful reflection, meditation etc. when we realise, that the material things are only temporary. The physical and material will pass away, but the spiritual will remain forever. Provided that the spirit concerned is Righteous, by having accepted 'The Sacrifice', Who was prepared by God from the Beginning of this earth. I say, 'this earth', because 'this earth' is no longer perfect as it is contaminated by Sin and Death. It wasn't purely by accident either! God knew that Man could only learn his lesson on Sin, if he experienced it for himself. The next earth will be perfect, because there will only be the Righteous living there with God, from its creation.

Isaiah knew this when he wrote:

"For as the new heavens and the new earth which I will make shall remain before Me," says the Lord, "So shall your descendants and your name remain. And it shall come to pass that from one New Moon to another, all flesh shall come to worship before Me," says the Lord. (Isa 66:22-23)

The sentence that started this study of mine, was in Jasher, "The counselors and wise men answered the king, "We have heard that the God of the Hebrews is a son of the wise, the son of ancient kings." I suddenly realised that these men were talking about a prophecy about Jesus. I included the verses from Isaiah and Jeremiah to illustrate this point.

You will probably need to read this study a few times to see all the relevant contexts. Don't worry! The study is patient, and you should also read the rest of the Bible; to prove for yourself, that what I'm saying is true. Be quick, before its too late! I think we have till 2031, but I may be wrong! You or I may die before then and once one has died there is no second opportunity for salvation! Jannes and Jambres, opposed Moses and worked against God's will and purpose. They were also able to perform the first three signs, in front of Pharaoh. There are many of these types of people around, to discourage and distract us! Watch out for them, and be careful to avoid their influence and corrupting knowledge! Arm yourself with the knowledge and understanding of God's Word.

-oOo-

Joseph B. Lumpkin

Notes from Latter-Day Saints

One of the most learned L.D.S. scholars, Hugh Nibley, has stated:

"Of interest to Latter-day Saints is the Book of Jasher, one of the first English translations of which was published in Salt Lake City. "There can be little doubt that the book of Jasher was a national epic," according to Cyrus Gordon; but how much of this particular book goes back to the original? "The time is ripe," he says, "for a fresh investigation of such genuine sources of Scripture, particularly against the background of the Dead Sea Scrolls." Hugh Nibley, Collected Works of Hugh Nibley, Vol. 7, p. 40.

  Let us take up the challenge of this noted scholar and submit the following details as a proof to the authenticity of the Book of Jasher. There are many details in the Book of Jasher which are not found in the Bible, but which are found in modern day revelation, especially in the Doctrine and Covenants (1835) and the Book of Moses (Inspired translation of Genesis, 1831), both of which were published before the Book of Jasher became available to the Prophet Joseph Smith in 1840. Thus, if we believe that these newer revelations are inspired, we are pressed to agree that those books agreeing with them and written before them were also inspired. Here are some examples.

Cainan Becomes Wise At 40 Year of Age

Jasher 2:10 And Enosh lived ninety years and he had Cainan. 11 Cainan grew up and he was forty years old, and he became wise and had knowledge and skill in all wisdom, and he reigned over all the sons of men, and he led the sons of men to wisdom and knowledge; for Cainan was a very wise man and had understanding in all wisdom, and with his wisdom he ruled over spirits and demons.

"God called upon Cainan in the wilderness in the fortieth year of his age" (D&C 107:45)

The Book of Jasher reports that when Cainan was forty years old he became wise and wrote prophecies. Five years before Jasher became available, the Lord revealed to Joseph Smith that God had called upon Cainan in his fortieth year. Here we have two witnesses that agree on the very year in which Cainan had a revelation (D&C) and hence could suddenly prophesy the future (Jasher). Remember, Cainan lived long before the Flood, and there is no way to know anything about him except through revelation or records preserved on the ark. In all modern revelations that is the only new fact revealed about Cainan, and it explain where the new-found wisdom of Cainan mentioned in the Book of Jasher came from.

Lamech's Wives Rebel

Jasher 2: 26 Lamech was old and advanced in years, and his eyes were dim that he could not see, and Tubal Cain, his son, was leading him and it was one day that Lamech went into the field and Tubal Cain his son was with him, and while they were walking in the field, Cain the son of Adam advanced towards them; for Lamech was very old and could not see much, and Tubal Cain his son was very young.

27 Tubal Cain told his father to draw his bow, and with the arrows he struck Cain, who was yet far off, and he killed him, because he appeared be an animal to them.

28 And the arrows entered Cain's body although he was at a distance from them, and he fell to the ground and died.

29 The Lord rewarded Cain's evil according to his wickedness, which he had done to his brother Abel, according to the word of the Lord which he had spoken.

30 And it came to pass when Cain had died, that Lamech and Tubal went to see the animal which they had slain, and they saw, and behold Cain their grandfather was fallen dead on the earth.

31 Lamech was very much grieved at having done this, and in clapping his hands together (in grief) he struck his son and caused his death.

32 And the wives of Lamech heard what Lamech had done, and they sought to kill him.

33 The wives of Lamech hated him from that day, because he killed Cain

and Tubal Cain, and the wives of Lamech separated from him, and would not listen to him in those days.

34 And Lamech came to his wives, and he begged them to listen to him about this matter.

35 He said to his wives Adah and Zillah, Hear my voice O wives of Lamech, attend to my words, for now you have imagined and said that I killed a man with my wounds, and a child with my stripes for they did no violence, but certainly know that I am old and grey-headed, and that my eyes are heavy through age, and I did this thing unknowingly.

36 And the wives of Lamech listened to him in this matter, and they returned to him with the advice of their father Adam, but they bore no children to him from that time, knowing that God's anger was increasing in those days against the sons of men, to destroy them with the waters of the flood for their evil acts.

37 Mahlallel the son of Cainan lived sixty-five years and he had Jared; and Jared lived sixty-two years and he had Enoch.

Lamech told his wives about secret murder oaths and "they rebelled against him" and declared the secret abroad, so that Lamech was cast out, lest he should die. (Moses 5:53-54)

The story about Lamech, Cain's descendant, makes almost no sense at all if read only in Genesis. The Bible say only that Lamech told his two wives,

"I have slain a man to my wounding, and a young man to my hurt. If Cain shall be avenged sevenfold, truly Lamech seventy and sevenfold" (Gen. 4:23-24).

The Bible never explains was he means. It only explains that the two victims were his ancestor Cain and his own son Tubalcain (Gen. 4:22), but adds that Lamech insisted that both deaths were accidental. His defense is presented in Jasher as true, but it is difficult to believe because his alibi was that he mistook Cain to be an animal, and then when he and his son discovered his mistake, he clapped his hands together so violently that he accidentally killed Tubalcain also (Jasher 2:26-31). Upon learning of the deaths, his wives sought to kill him. The story only makes sense when it is revealed in the book og Jasher that Lamech was totally blind and was hunting with the assistance of the young and unseasoned Tubalcain. Yet, the second death seems so unlikely even the story in Jasher fails to satisfy.

The Book of Moses tells us the "rest of the story" which was not known to the author of Jasher. It clarifies that it was actually his great-grandfather Irad whom Lamech had killed (rather than Cain), and that it had been premeditated murder, done in order to keep his secret oaths hidden (Moses 5:49-50). While the accounts disagree on who was murdered, they agree on the detail that his wives rebelled against him because of it.

The Book of Jasher seems to be an authentic account from secular history as one would read a newspaper. Lamech slew someone but it was an accident and the Lord revealing the hidden part of the story that the murder was done to protect secret oaths.

Enoch Is Called By God

Jasher 3:3 It was at the expiration of many years, while he was serving the Lord, and praying before him in his house, that an angel of the Lord called to him from Heaven, and he said, Here am I. 4 And he said, Rise, go forth from your house and from the place where you hide yourself, and appear to the sons of men, in order that you may teach them the way in which they should go and the work which they must accomplish in order to enter into the ways of God

"And he heard a voice from heaven saying: Enoch, my son, prophesy unto this people and say unto them — Repent" (Moses 6:27)

Fear of Enoch

Jasher 3: 20 And he did in this manner for many years, and he afterward concealed himself for six days, and appeared to his people one day in seven; and after that once in a month, and then once in a year, until all the kings, princes and sons of men sought for him, and desired again to see the face of

Enoch, and to hear his word; but they could not, as all the sons of men were greatly afraid of Enoch, and they feared to approach him on account of the Godlike awe that was seated on his countenance; therefore no man could look at him, fearing he might be punished and die.

"And it came to pass when they heard him, no man laid hands on him; for fear came on all them that heard him; for he walked with God.... And as Enoch spake forth the words of God, the people trembled, and could not stand in his presence.... And I was clothed upon with glory" (Moses 6:39,47; 7:3)

The books of Jasher and Moses both add more than two full pages about this one prophet. Three points of agreement are listed in the table, which coincide in many details, such as people being in great fear of Enoch. The last one appears to be a secular account in Jasher, stating that Enoch's entire city was taken up to heaven with him. It only reports that facts that after Enoch ascended into heaven in a great whirlwind, that when his followers were sought, all that was found was a lot of snow and ice.

Enoch's City, Zion is Translated

Jasher 3: 38 All those kings went to the place and they found the earth there filled with snow, and on the snow were large stones of snow, and one said to the other, Come, let us break through the snow and see, perhaps the men that remained with Enoch are dead, and are now under the stones of snow, and they searched but could not find Enoch, for he had ascended into heaven.

"And Enoch and all his people walked with God, and he dwelt in the midst of Zion; and it came to pass that Zion was not, for God received it up into his own bosom; and from thence went forth the saying, Zion is fled." (Moses 7:69)

This continues the story and the agreement between the books of Moses and Jasher, expanding on the ascended city and its people.

Methuselah's Famine

Jasher 4: 5 And the Lord was greatly wroth against them, and the Lord continued to destroy the offspring in those days, so that there was neither sowing nor reaping in the earth. 6 For when they sowed the ground in order that they might obtain food for their support, behold, thorns and thistles were produced which they did not sow.

"And there came forth a great famine into the land, and the Lord cursed the earth with a sore curse" (Moses 8:4)

The two accounts agree that there was a famine in the days of Methuselah. Jasher adds details of what kind of "sore curse" the Lord put on the ground. Jasher reports that weeds grew instead of the planted crops, and the Book of Moses focuses on the heavenly side saying, the Lord cursed the ground. The two accounts together give a more complete view.

Look for other fine books by Joseph Lumpkin

The Lost Book Of Enoch: A Comprehensive Transliteration
ISBN: 0974633666

The Gospel of Thomas: A Contemporary Translation
ISBN: 0976823349

The Book of Jubilees; The Little Genesis, The Apocalypse of Moses
ISBN: 1933580097

Fallen Angels, The Watchers, and The Origins of Evil: A Problem of Choice
ISBN: 1933580100

Many other books and various translations are available through www.fifthestatepub.com.
A complete catalog may be found at www.amazon.com.

www.ingramcontent.com/pod-product-compliance
Lightning Source LLC
Chambersburg PA
CBHW060511230426
43665CB00013B/1479